MANY PASTS:

Readings in
American Social History

Volume one / 1600–1876

MANY PASTS:

Readings in
American Social History

Volume one | 1600-1876

Edited by
HERBERT G. GUTMAN
City College of the City University of New York

GREGORY S. KEALEY
University of Rochester

Prentice-Hall, Inc., Englewood Cliffs, New Jersey

Library of Congress Cataloging in Publication Data

GUTMAN, HERBERT GEORGE, COMP.
    Many pasts: readings in American social history.

    Includes bibliographies.
    CONTENTS: v. 1. 1600-1876.
    1. United States—Social conditions—
Addresses, essays, lectures. 1. Kealey, Gregory S.,
joint comp. II. Title.
HN57.G85   309.1′73   72-12861
ISBN 0-13-815936-X (v. 1)

Printed in the United States of America

10 9 8 7 6 5 4 3 2 1

PRENTICE-HALL INTERNATIONAL, INC., *London*
PRENTICE-HALL OF AUSTRALIA, PTY. LTD., *Sydney*
PRENTICE-HALL OF CANADA, LTD., *Toronto*
PRENTICE-HALL OF INDIA PRIVATE LIMITED, *New Delhi*
PRENTICE-HALL OF JAPAN, INC., *Tokyo*

Contents

MANY PASTS:

Readings in
American Social History

Volume one / 1600–1876

Introduction

"The mystery of the human condition," anthropologist Sidney W. Mintz has
written, "is not in what man has, but what he does with what he has."
This question applies both to the contemporary world and to the world of the
past. One of the important questions in the new social history, it is equally
applicable to a colonial indentured servant (or slave) and to a colonial
merchant, to an early-nineteenth-century New England mill girl and to
her Yankee employer, to a mid-nineteenth-century Irish immigrant and to an
early-twentieth-century Italian or Jewish immigrant, to an unskilled Gilded Age
factory worker and to a rural tenant farmer, to a resident of a contemporary
inner-city ghetto and to a third-generation American who has moved from
a ghetto to a suburban setting. This two-volume collection of historical
writings in United States social history explores the many dimensions of that
"mystery" over time. It spans the entire American experience, reaching
back into early-colonial society and then returning to the present day. The
readings have been selected to satisfy three objectives: first, to acquaint
readers with some of those historians whose writings in American social
history directly or indirectly focus on the critical intersections between culture

and society; second, to supplement in essential ways the traditional political emphasis in most general American history courses; and, third, to illustrate how diverse methods of historical inquiry have been (and are being) used by a range of historians to shed light on important, but often neglected, aspects of the American past.

These unusual principles of selection are meant to give a distinctive quality to these volumes. Most collections of readings often either lack a clear central focus or are organized to illuminate, nearly exclusively, powerful political processes central to our national history. By intent, the emphasis in these pages is quite different. Here we emphasize the structure of American society, how that structure changed, and especially how those changes were experienced, interpreted, and responded to by those men and women who are part of Michael Harrington's "other America." These groups, of course, have varied in composition over time and behaved in quite dissimilar ways, but all have shared unequally in both the material rewards available to them as contrasted with their better situated *contemporaries*, and in the attention devoted to them by historians. A library wall can be filled with studies of the careers of men like Abraham Lincoln, Theodore Roosevelt, or Woodrow Wilson, but a library shelf with books on either colonial indentured servants or early-twentieth century East- and South-European immigrants would remain half empty. Such groups deserve attention for many reasons. We do not study them to "expose" their conditions. Others have done that in great detail. Nor is there reason to idealize or romanticize their life-style or behavior. Put simply, they, too, have a past, and that past deserves to be fully understood. Their everyday lives and common beliefs were subtle and complex in texture, and often distinctive. It is that distinctiveness in historical experiences, and even in behavior and thought, which allows us to talk of many American pasts, not "the American past" or "the American experience." Moreover, only the study of these experiences makes possible comparisons over time and within a particular time period between persons of different social classes, sexes, and ethnic origins. But such comparisons—comparisons that explore similarities and differences— require first that we examine the interior histories of the groups and their relationships to other segments in a society. "The daily job of living did not end with enslavement," Mintz writes of the seventeenth- and eighteenth-century Afro-Americans, "and the slaves could and did create viable patterns of life, for which their pasts were pools of available symbolic and material resources." This was as true for other oppressed and dependent classes and social groups as for the slaves, and the first concern of their historian is to recreate those "viable patterns of life" and to explain how and why they changed over time.

These groups deserve attention for yet other compelling reasons. Their perceptions of the larger society cast a light on it that is often unavailable elsewhere. More than this, just as the changing structure of American society affected them in important ways, their behavior also helped to shape the larger social system. In studying such groups, we therefore gain insight into the larger society and its changing class and social structure. This is not a trivial point. The distinguished French historian Fernand Braudel said it well:

> Victorious events come about as the result of many possibilities, among which life has finally made its choices. For one possibility which actually is realized, innumerable others have been drowned. These are the ones which have left little trace for the historian. And yet it is necessary to give them their place because the losing movements are forces which have at every moment affected the final outcome.

Clearly (with concrete examples from the American experience), it is not possible to understand fully the behavior of slave owners without first studying the behavior of slaves. It is not possible to grasp the sources of middle- and upper-class reform movements in the late-nineteenth and early-twentieth centuries without first understanding the behavior of farmers and of native and immigrant urban workers. It is not possible to assess the significance of the New Deal without first examining the ways in which countless Americans expressed their discontents in the 1930s outside the settled political process. Part of the excitment of the new social history is that in retrieving the past experiences of the neglected groups, we enrich our understanding of other groups and of large, long-term historical processes.

American social history is still in its infancy as a branch of historical inquiry. As the sociologist Norman Birnbaum has written, "insofar as major aspects of its past are concerned" the United States "remains an unknown country." Birnbaum nevertheless predicts "a voyage of self-discovery that may yet revise some of our notions of social provenance." He is right. More, however, is involved in such a "voyage" than the social historian shifting the focus of attention to lower-class groups or, as is quite fashionable, to the "certitude" found in "quantitative data." The readings in these volumes should make that clear. Good social history of the lower-classes (and other classes as well) demands a conceptual clarity and rigor no less severe than, say, the study of Florentine paintings, demographic movements in medieval Europe, land tenure systems in Latin America, or business cycles in nineteenth-century America. Nothing of importance is gained by shifting the focus of historical interest and then asking of a new subject narrow or restricting questions.

The conceptual framework—that is, the ways in which historians frame questions about particular aspects of the past and go about answering them—is critical. For that reason, the conceptual apparatus used in these two volumes deserves brief attention.

The volumes have been organized and the readings chosen to focus on the interaction over time between *society and culture*. The emphasis is on how the two interacted to shape the behavior and thought of neglected social classes, but again we should note that this interaction also shaped the behavior and thought of the better-advantaged social classes. *American society* has changed greatly in the past three centuries and so has *American culture*. The two sets of changes are closely related but *not* similar, and the distinction between them is essential to studying and understanding lower-class groups. "There is no such thing," the British social historian E. P. Thompson has written, "as economic growth which is not, at the same time, growth or change of a culture." Nevertheless Thompson warns, "We should not assume any automatic or over-direct correspondence between the dynamic of economic growth and the dynamic of social or cultural life."

Broadly described, in its essential structure American society has passed through three distinctive stages of development. Until the 1830s and 1840s, nearly all Americans lived in a *preindustrial society*, that is, a society in which everyday behavior (work, family life, leisure patterns, etc.) are not yet affected by machinery and the new technological and organizational imperatives associated with the Industrial Revolution. Old America was not simply an "agrarian" society; it was a preindustrial society similar to, but also different from, the more settled and traditional pre-modern societies in other parts of the world. (Preindustrial cultures, it should be emphasized, varied greatly in their interior structure. Slaves and their owners, Indians and the pioneer farmers who helped drive them to the West, and artisans and the merchants who marketed their goods, for example, all lived in a pre-modern world but experienced it and responded to it in quite distinctive ways.) Between the 1840s and the end of the nineteenth century, preindustrial American society *became* industrial American society. Here was a profound and radical shift that took half a century, and directly or indirectly transformed work and leisure, politics and ideology, family life and associational activities. Not all social classes and distinctive groups were affected similarly by this process. All brought to the process itself distinctive historical experiences. The central tension in this rapidly changing world was between the Old and the New America. Twentieth-century American social history differs radically from either of these two earlier "stages." By the end of the nineteenth century, the United States had *become* an industrial society, and much of twentieth-century American social history has centered about the processes and problems particular to a *maturing* industrial society.

So much, in brief, for the larger structural changes in American society. But what of *American culture*? Here, the writings of the Polish sociologist Zygmunt Bauman and certain contemporary American anthropologists will help. Bauman writes:

Human behavior, whether individual or collective, is invariably the resultant
of two factors: the cognitive systems as well as the goals and patterns of
behavior as defined by culture system(s), on the one hand, and the system of
real contingencies as defined by the social structure on the other. A complete
interpretation of social processes can only be achieved when both systems,
as well as their interaction, are taken into consideration.

Bauman's distinction between *culture* and *society* is profoundly important to the
study of social history. Altogether too often, American social historians have
emphasized "society" at the expense of "culture" in describing historical
patterns of lower-class life and behavior. It is essential, of course, to define
the particular "real contingencies" in a given society and for a particular
social class, sex, or ethnic community. However, it should not be assumed, as
some habitually do, that these were the only determinants of behavior.
Scant attention is given to the ways in which accumulated past experiences
("culture") in the different strata of particular societies affected the choices
made by men and women. But it is precisely this cultural-societal interaction
that helps to begin the unravelling of the "mystery" posed by Sidney Mintz.
   Another anthropologist, Eric Wolf, sharpens our understanding of the
critical differences between culture and society:

> By culture, I mean the historically developed forms through which the members
> of a given society relate to each other. By society, I mean the element of
> action, of human manoeuver within the field provided by cultural forms,
> human manoeuver which aims either at preserving a given balance of
> life-chances and life-risks or at changing it.

Mintz himself expands on this distinction in a manner especially useful to the
student of social history:

> . . . We see culture depicted as a kind of resource, and society as a kind of
> arena—the distribution is between sets of historically available alternatives
> or forms on the one hand, and the societal circumstances or setting within which
> these forms may be employed, on the other. . . . Culture is *used;* and any
> analysis of its use immediately brings into view the arrangements of persons in
> social groups for whom cultural forms confirm, reinforce, maintain, change,
> or deny particular arrangements of status, power, and identity.

Brief concrete examples help illustrate the theoretical point. When machinery
or new technology displaced the traditional skills of an artisan, the "real
contingencies" available to him altered radically. But in dealing with them,
he was affected by the accumulated historical experiences related to his
older craft life. Emancipation radically altered the slaves' status by expanding

the "arena" (society) within which southern blacks could make choices, but their particular choices were also shaped by the patterns of work and life (culture) they had known as slaves. A similar analysis allows us to examine in new ways the behavior of migrant and immigrant groups, native and foreign-born, white and non-white.

Careful attention to the critical intersection between culture and society in the past contributes to the examination of particular patterns of human behavior and processes of social change in new ways. Not all the historians included in this collection of readings explicitly make these distinctions, but nearly all use evidence in critical or imaginative ways tending toward this view. For each period, where available, readings have been chosen that emphasize in different ways the cultural-societal interaction and thereby, at quite different times in our past, describe the determinants of such important historical "facts" as family behavior, work habits, ethnic identity and self-assertion, collective self-protection, and peaceful and violent conflict. A subtle awareness of how past (culture) and present (society) have shaped, and continue to shape, human behavior also permits us to go beyond the increasingly sterile disputes between so-called "consensus" historians and so-called "conflict" historians. "There is no more need for romances," Walt Whitman insisted nearly a century ago. "Let facts and history be properly told."

section 1

The Colonial World
1600-1763

America was born in the seventeenth century, and the dynamics of that birth and subsequent historical developments demand an analysis of the metropolitan societies that planted these tender offshoots in the new world. The culture of the metropolis that spawned colonial aims was essential to the making of America.

Men and women came to America heavily laden with an already existing perceptual framework. They carried not only preconceptions of the new society but also whole cultures—ways of life—to test the new realities against. These old world cultures clashed with the exigencies of the new world and demanded modification and adaptation.

The new world itself represented a key ingredient in the mercantile world system. Mercantilism implied a positive use of the state, governmental responsibility for the public welfare, and the belief that the world possessed limited resources for which nation-states competed. It was also deeply grounded in a traditional hierarchial social structure. America represented a colonial object of this world vision, but the colonists simultaneously began to adapt such theories to their own interests. Notions of state action and state responsibility for the general welfare were well established in colonial America. The third mercantile canon—the aggressive nation-state—came to fruition in America with the War for Independence, which established a new metropolis, the United States.

Mercantilism was both a labor system and a general political-philosophical ideology. The adaptation of both systems to America took many forms. In the realm of labor, government control was an accepted principle in England. This notion was carried to America but the specificities of new world "conditions" forced changes to be made in it. A constant labor shortage and the need for new work discipline demanded the development of different social and economic devices. In England, labor had been free except for bound apprentices; in America, a system of bond and debt servitude was devised. Simultaneously, the Americas became the chief benefactor of the African slave trade, which represented yet another method of coping with the new labor problem.

The men and women—European and African, whether free, bound, or slave—who composed this new labor force were not solely the dependent objects of mercantile manipulation, and the process of transforming a frontier wilderness into an organized society was not a simple one. In turn, the growing society developed its own social and economic structure, and it was experienced and interpreted in different ways by different social classes. Not all these differences and disagreements revealed themselves in the politics of colonial life. But much in the politics of early colonial society can be best understood in relation to the larger social, economic, and cultural context. The diverse European and African cultures, "transplanted" to the colonies, were not "transformed" by the wilderness experience, but they became adapted to it. Merchants and artisans adapted older ways to retain, but also to reshape, their lives. So did freehold English, German, and Scotch-Irish farmers and African tribesmen.

The following books are suggested for further reading:

ELI HECKSHER, *Mercantilism,* London: Allen & Unwin, Ltd., 1935.

CURTIS P. NETTELS, *The Roots of American Civilization,* New York: Appleton-Century-Crofts, 1963.

CLARENCE VER STEEG, *The Formative Years, 1607–1763,* New York: Hill & Wang, Inc., 1964.

ERIC WILLIAMS, *Capitalism and Slavery,* New York: Capricorn Books, G. P. Putnam's Sons, 1966.

WILLIAM APPLEMAN WILLIAMS, *Contours of American History,* Chicago: Quadrangle Books, 1966.

The Labor Problem at Jamestown, 1607-1618

EDMUND S. MORGAN

Edmund Morgan here returns to seventeenth-century England to unearth
neglected aspects of the Jamestown experience. He shows that in order to
understand the early colonists, it is necessary to study the old world from
which they departed and the new world they entered. The men and women
who settled Virginia were not blank ciphers; they were seventeenth-century
British artisans, laborers, farmers, and gentlemen. As Morgan argues,
contemporary metropolitan "ideas and attitudes about work" provide "clues
to habits of thinking that may have conditioned the colonists' perception of
what confronted them." Preindustrial work habits and distorted expectations
of new world riches were carried to Virginia and early threatened the
survival of the Jamestown colony. Morgan concludes provocatively that
successful colonization came only with the emergence of plantation slavery in
Virginia.

Edmund S. Morgan, "The Labor Problem at Jamestown, 1607–1618," *American Historical
Review*, 76 (June, 1971), 595–611. Copyright Edmund S. Morgan. Reprinted and footnotes omitted by permission of the author.

The following article is suggested for further reading:

E. P. THOMPSON, "Time, Work-Discipline, and Industrial Capitalism," *Past & Present*, no. 38 (1967), 56–97.

The story of Jamestown, the first permanent English settlement in America, has a familiar place in the history of the United States. We all know of the tribulations that kept the colony on the point of expiring: the shortage of supplies, the hostility of the Indians, the quarrels among the leaders, the reckless search for gold, the pathetic search for a passage to the Pacific, and the neglect of the crucial business of growing food to stay alive. Through the scene moves the figure of Captain John Smith, a little larger than life, trading for corn among the Indians and driving the feckless crew to work. His departure in October 1609 results in near disaster. The settlers fritter away their time and energy, squander their provisions, and starve. Sir Thomas Gates, arriving after the settlement's third winter, finds only sixty men out of six hundred still alive and those sixty scarcely able to walk.

In the summer of 1610 Gates and Lord La Warr get things moving again with a new supply of men and provisions, a new absolute form of government, and a new set of laws designed to keep everybody at work. But when Gates and La Warr leave for a time, the settlers fall to their old ways. Sir Thomas Dale, upon his arrival in May 1611, finds them at "their daily and usuall workes, bowling in the streetes." But Dale brings order out of chaos. By enlarging and enforcing the colony's new law code (the famous *Lawes Divine, Morall and Martiall*) he starts the settlers working again and rescues them from starvation by making them plant corn. By 1618 the colony is getting on its feet and ready to carry on without the stern regimen of a Smith or a Dale. There are still evil days ahead, as the Virginia Company sends over men more rapidly than the infant colony can absorb them. But the settlers, having found in tobacco a valuable crop for export, have at last gone to work with a will, and Virginia's future is assured.

The story probably fits the facts insofar as they can be known. But it does not quite explain them. The colony's long period of starvation and failure may well be attributed to the idleness of the first settlers, but idleness is more an accusation than an explanation. Why did men spend their time bowling in the streets when their lives depended on work? Were they lunatics, preferring to play games rather than clear and plow and plant the crops that could have kept them alive?

The mystery only deepens if we look more closely at the efforts of Smith, Gates, La Warr, and Dale to set things right. In 1612 John Smith described his work program of 1608: "the company [being] divided into tennes, fifteenes, or as the businesse required, 4 hours each day was spent in worke, the rest in pastimes and merry exercise." Twelve years later Smith rewrote this passage and changed the figure of four hours to six hours. But even so, what are we to make of a six-hour day in a colony teetering on the verge of extinction?

The program of Gates and La Warr in the summer of 1610 was no more strenuous. William Strachey described it:

> it is to be understood that such as labor are not yet so taxed but that easily they perform the same and ever by ten of the clock have done their morning's work: at what time they have their allowances [of food] set out ready for them, and until it be three of the clock again they take their own pleasure, and afterward, with the sunset, their day's labor is finished.

The Virginia Company offered much the same account of this period. According to a tract issued late in 1610, "the setled times of working (to effect all themselves, or the Adventurers neede desire) [requires] no more pains than from sixe of clocke in the morning until ten, and from two of the clocke in the afternoone till foure." The long lunch period described for 1610 was also a feature of the *Lawes Divine, Morall and Martiall* as enforced by Dale. The total working hours prescribed in the *Lawes* amounted to roughly five to eight hours a day in summer and three to six hours in winter.

It is difficult, then, to escape the conclusion that there was a great deal of unemployment or underemployment at Jamestown, whether it was the idleness of the undisciplined in the absence of strong government or the idleness of the disciplined in the presence of strong government. How are we to account for this fact? By our standards the situation at Jamestown demanded hard and continuous work. Why was the response so feeble?

One answer, given by the leaders of the colony, is that the settlers included too many ne'er-do-wells and too many gentlemen who "never did know what a dayes work was." Hard work had to wait until harder men were sent. Another answer may be that the Jamestown settlers were debilitated by hunger and disease. The victims of scurvy, malaria, typhoid, and diphtheria may have been left without the will or the energy to work. Still another answer, which has echoed through the pages of our history books, attributed the difficulty to the fact that the settlement was conducted on a communal basis: everybody worked for the Virginia Company and everybody was fed (while supplies lasted) by the company, regardless of how much he worked or failed. Once land was distributed to individuals and men were allowed to work for themselves, they gained the familiar incentives of private enterprise and bent their shoulders to the wheel. These explanations are surely all valid they are all supported by the testimony of contemporaries—and they go far toward explaining the lazy pioneers of Jamestown. But they do not reach to a dimension of the problem that contemporaries would have overlooked because they would have taken it for granted. They do not tell us what ideas and attitudes about work, carried from England, would have led the first English settlers to expect so little of themselves in a situation that demanded so much. The Jamestown settlers did not leave us the kind of private papers that would enable us to examine directly their ideas and attitudes, as we can those of the Puritans who settled New England a few years later. But in the absence of direct evidence we may discover among the ideas current in late sixteenth- and early seventeenth-century England some clues to the probable state of mind of the first Virginians, clues to the way they felt about work, whether in the Old World or the New, clues to habits of thinking that may have conditioned their perceptions of what confronted them at Jamestown, clues even to the tangled web of motives that made later Virginians masters of slaves.

Englishmen's ideas about the New World at the opening of the seventeenth century were based on a century of European exploration and settlement. The Spanish, whose exploits surpassed all others, had not attempted to keep their success a secret, and by the middle of the sixteenth century Englishmen interested in America had begun translating Spanish histories and memoirs in an effort to rouse their countrymen to emulation. The land that emerged from these writings was, except in the Arctic regions, an Eden, teeming with gentle and generous people who, before the Spanish conquest, had lived without labor, or with very little, from the fruits of a bountiful nature. There were admittedly some unfriendly exceptions who made a habit of eating their more attractive neighbors; but they were a minority, confined to a few localities, and in spite of their ferocity were scarcely a match for Europeans armed with guns. Englishmen who visited the New World confirmed the reports of natural abundance. Arthur Barlowe, for example, reconnoitering the North Carolina coast for Walter Raleigh, observed that "the earth bringeth foorth all things in aboundance, as in the first creation, without toile or labour," while the people were "most gentle, loving, and faithfull, void of all guile, and treason, and such as lived after the manner of the golden age. . . ."

English and European readers may have discounted the more extravagant reports of American abundance, for the same authors who praised the land often gave contradictory accounts of the hardships they had suffered in it. But anyone who doubted that riches were waiting to be plucked from Virginia's trees had reason to expect that a good deal might be plucked from the people of the land. Spanish experience had shown that Europeans could thrive in the New World without undue effort by exploiting the natives. With a mere handful of men the Spanish had conquered an enormous population of Indians in the Caribbean, Mexico, and Peru and had put them to work. In the chronicles of Peter Martyr Englishmen learned how it was done. Apart from the fact that the Indians were naturally gentle, their division into a multitude of kingdoms, frequently at odds with one another, made it easy to play off one against another. By aiding one group against its enemies the Spaniards had made themselves masters of both.

The story of English plans to imitate and improve on the Spanish strategy is a long one. It begins at least as early as Francis Drake's foray in Panama, in 1572–73, when he allied with a band of runaway slaves to rob a Spanish mule train carrying treasure from Peru across the isthmus to Nombre de Dios on the Caribbean. The idea of joining with dissident natives or slaves either against their Spanish masters or against their wicked cannibalistic neighbors became an important ingredient in English plans for colonizing the New World. Martin Frobisher's experiences with the Eskimos in Baffin Land and Ralph Lane's with the Indians at Roanoke should perhaps have disabused the English of their expectations; but they found it difficult to believe that any group of natives, and especially the noble savages of North America, would fail to welcome what they called with honest pride (and some myopia) the "gentle government" of the English. If the savages first encountered by a colonizing expedition proved unfriendly, the thing to do was to make contact with their milder neighbors and rescue them from the tyranny of the unfriendly tribe, who must be their enemies and were probably cannibals to boot.

The settlers at Jamestown tried to follow the strategy, locating their settlement as the plan called for, near the mouth of a navigable river, so that they would have access to the interior tribes if the coastal ones were hostile. But as luck would have it, they picked an area with a more powerful, more extensive, and more effective Indian government than existed anywhere else on the Atlantic Coast. King Powhatan had his enemies, the Monacans of the interior, but he felt no great need of English assistance against them, and he rightly suspected that the English constituted a larger threat to his hegemony than the Monacans did. He submitted with ill grace and no evident comprehension to the coronation ceremony that the Virginia Company arranged for him, and he kept his distance from Jamestown. Those of his warriors who visited the settlement showed no disposition to work for the English. The Monacans, on the other hand, lived too far inland (beyond the falls) to serve as substitute allies, and the English were thus deprived of their anticipated native labor.

They did not, however, give up their expectations of getting it eventually. In 1615 Ralph Hamor still thought the Indians would come around "as they are easily taught and may be lenitic and faire usage . . . be brought, being naturally though ingenious, yet idlely given, to be no lesse industrious, nay to exceede our English." Even after the massacre of 1622 Virginians continued to dream of an Indian labor supply, though there was no longer to be any gentleness in obtaining it. Captain John Martin thought it better to exploit than exterminate the Indians, if only because they could be made to work in the heat of the day, when Englishmen would not. And William Claiborne in 1626 invented a device (whether mechanical or political is not clear) that he claimed would make it possible to keep Indians safely in the settlements and put them to work. The governor and council gave him what looks like the first American patent or copyright, namely a three-year monopoly, to "have holde and enjoy all the benefitt use and profitt of this his project or inventione," and they also assigned him a recently captured Indian, "for his better experience and tryall of his inventione."

English expectations of the New World and its inhabitants died hard. America was supposed to be a land of abundance, peopled by natives who would not only share that abundance with the English but increase it under English direction. Englishmen simply did not envisage a need to work for the mere purpose of staying alive. The problem of survival as they saw it was at best political and at worst military.

Although Englishmen long remained under the illusion that the Indians would eventually become useful English subjects, it became apparent fairly early that Indian labor was not going to sustain the founders of Jamestown. The company in England was convinced by 1609 that the settlers would have to grow at least part of their own food. Yet the settlers themselves had to be driven to that life-saving task. To understand their ineffectiveness in coping with a situation that their pioneering descendants would take in stride, it may be helpful next to inquire into some of the attitudes toward work that these first English pioneers took for granted. How much work and what kind of work did Englishmen at the opening of the seventeenth century consider normal?

The laboring population of England, by law at least, was required to work much harder than the regimen at Jamestown might lead us to expect. The famous Statute of Artificers of 1563 (re-enacting similar provisions from the Statute of Laborers of 1495) required all laborers to work from five in the morning to seven or eight at night from mid-March to mid-September, and during the remaining months of the year from daybreak to night. Time out for eating, drinking, and rest was not to exceed two and a half hours a day. But these were injunctions not descriptions. The Statute of Laborers of 1495 is preceded by the complaint that laborers "waste much part of the day . . . in late coming unto their work, early departing therefrom, long sitting at their breakfast, at their dinner and noon-meat, and long time of sleeping after noon." Whether this statute or that of 1563 (still in effect when Jamestown was founded) corrected the situation is doubtful. The records of local courts show varying efforts to enforce other provisions of the statute of 1563, but they are almost wholly silent about this provision, in spite of the often-expressed despair of masters over their lazy and negligent laborers.

It may be said that complaints of the laziness and irresponsibility of workmen can be met with in any century. Were such complaints in fact justified in sixteenth- and early seventeenth-century England? There is some reason to believe that they were, that life during those years was characterized by a large amount of idleness or underemployment. The outstanding economic fact of the sixteenth and early seventeenth century in England was a rapid and more or less steady rise in prices, followed at some distance by a much smaller rise in wages, both in industry and in agriculture. The price of provisions used by a laborer's family rose faster than wages during the whole period from 1500 to 1640. The government made an effort to narrow the gap by requiring the justices in each county to readjust maximum wages at regular intervals. But the wages established by the justices reflected their own nostalgic notions of what a day's work ought to be worth in money, rather than a realistic estimate of what a man could buy with his wages. In those counties, at least, where records survive, the level of wages set by the justices crept upward very slowly before 1630.

Wages were so inadequate that productivity was probably impaired by malnutrition. From a quarter to a half of the population lived below the level recognized at the time to constitute poverty. Few of the poor could count on regular meals at home, and in years when the wheat crop failed, they were close to starvation. It is not surprising that men living under these conditions showed no great energy for work and that much of the population was, by modern standards, idle much of the time. The health manuals of the day recognized that people normally slept after eating, and the laws even prescribed a siesta for laborers in the summer time. If they slept longer and more often than the laws allowed or the physicians recommended, if they loafed on the job and took unauthorized holidays, if they worked slowly and ineffectively when they did work, it may have been due at least in part to undernourishment and to the variety of chronic diseases that undernourishment brings in its train.

Thus low wages may have begot low productivity that in turn justified low wages. The reaction of employers was to blame the trouble on deficiencies, not of diet or wages, but of character. A prosperous yeoman like Robert Loder, who kept close track of his expenses and profits, was always bemoaning the indolence of his servants. Men who had large amounts of land that they could either rent out or work with hired labor generally preferred to rent because labor was so inefficient and irresponsible.

Even the division of labor, which economists have customarily regarded as a means of increased productivity, could be a source of idleness. Plowing, for example, seems to have been a special skill—a plowman was paid at a higher rate than ordinary farm workers. But the ordinary laborer's work might have to be synchronized with the plowman's, and a whole crew of men might be kept idle by a plowman's failure to get his job done at the appropriate time. It is difficult to say whether this type of idleness, resulting from failure to synchronize the performance of related tasks, was rising or declining; but cheap, inefficient, irresponsible labor would be unlikely to generate pressures for the careful planning of time.

The government, while seeking to discourage idleness through laws requiring long hours of work, also passed laws that inadvertently discouraged industry. A policy that might be characterized as the conservation of employment frustrated those who wanted to do more work than others. English economic policy seems to have rested on the assumption that the total amount of work for which society could pay was strictly limited and must be rationed so that everyone could have a little, and those with family responsibilities could have a little more. It was against the law for a man to practice more than one trade or one craft. And although large numbers of farmers took up some handicraft on the side, this was to be discouraged, because "for one man to be both an husbandman and an Artificer is a gatheringe of divers mens livinges into one mans hand." So as not to take work away from his elders, a man could not independently practice most trades until he had become a master through seven years of apprenticeship. Even then, until he was thirty years old or married, he was supposed to serve some other master of the trade. A typical example is the case of John Pikeman of Barking, Essex, a tailor who was presented by the grand jury because he "being a singleman and not above 25 years of age, does take in work of tailoring and works by himself to the hindrance of other poor occupiers, contrary to the law."

These measures doubtless helped to maintain social stability in the face of a rapid population increase, from under three million in 1500 to a probable four and a half million in 1640 (an increase reflected in the gap between wages and prices). But in its efforts to spread employment so that every able-bodied person would have a means of support, the government in effect discouraged energetic labor and nurtured the workingman's low expectations of himself. By requiring masters to engage apprentices for seven-year terms and servants (in agriculture and in most trades) for the whole year rather than the day, it prevented employers from hiring labor only when there was work to be done and prevented the diligent and effective worker from replacing the ineffective. The intention to spread work is apparent in the observation of the Essex justices that labor by the day caused "the great depauperization of other labourers." But labor by the year meant that work could be strung out to occupy an unnecessary amount of time, because whether or not a master had enough work to occupy his servants they had to stay and he had to keep them. The records show many instances of masters attempting to turn away a servant or apprentice before the stipulated term was up, only to have him sent back by the courts with orders that the master "entertain" him for the full period. We even have the extraordinary spectacle of the runaway master, the man who illegally fled from his servants and thus evaded his responsibility to employ and support them.

In pursuit of its policy of full employment in the face of an expanding population, the government often had to create jobs in cases where society offered none. Sometimes men were obliged to take on a poor boy as a servant whether they needed him or not. The parish might lighten the burden by paying a fee, but it might also fine a man who refused to take a boy assigned to him. To provide for men and women who could not be foisted off on unwilling employers, the government established houses of correction in every county, where the inmates toiled at turning wool, flax, and hemp into thread or yarn, receiving nothing but their food and lodging for their efforts. By all these means the government probably did succeed in spreading employment. But in the long run its policy, insofar as it was effective, tended to depress wages and to diminish the amount of work expected from any one man.

Above and beyond the idleness and underemployment that we may blame on the lethargy and irresponsibility of underpaid labor, on the failure to synchronize the performance of related tasks, and on the policy of spreading work as thinly as possible, the very nature of the jobs to be done prevented the systematic use of time that characterizes modern industrialized economies. Men could seldom work steadily, because they could work only at the tasks that could be done at the moment; and in sixteenth- and seventeenth-century England the tasks to be done often depended on forces beyond human control: on the weather and the seasons, on the winds, on the tides, on the maturing of crops. In the countryside work from dawn to dusk with scarcely an intermission might be normal at harvest time, but there were bound to be times when there was very little to do. When it rained or snowed, most farming operations had to be stopped altogether (and so did some of the stages of cloth manufacture). As late as 1705 John Law, imagining a typical economy established on a newly discovered island, assumed that the persons engaged in agriculture would necessarily be idle, for one reason or another, half the time.

To be sure, side by side with idleness and inefficiency, England exhibited the first signs of a rationalized economy. Professor J. U. Nef has described the many large-scale industrial enterprises that were inaugurated in England in the late sixteenth and early seventeenth centuries. And if the development of systematic agricultural production was advancing less rapidly than historians once supposed, the very existence of men like Robert Loder, the very complaints of the idleness and irresponsibility of laborers, the very laws prescribing hours of work all testify to the beginnings of a rationalized economy. But these were beginnings only and not widely felt. The laborer who seemed idle or irresponsible to a Robert Loder probably did not seem so to himself or to his peers. His England was not a machine for producing wool or corn. His England included activities and pleasures and relationships that systematic-minded employers would resent and that modern economists would classify as uneconomic. At the opening of the seventeenth century, England was giving him fewer economic benefits than she had given his grandfathers so that he was often ready to pull up stakes and look for a better life in another county or another country. But a life devoted to more and harder work than he had known at home might not have been his idea of a better life.

Perhaps we may now view Jamestown with somewhat less surprise at the idle and hungry people occupying the place: idleness and hunger were the rule in much of England much of the time; they were facts of life to be taken for granted. And if we next ask what the settlers thought they had come to America to do, what they thought they were up to in Virginia, we can find several English enterprises comparable to their own that may have served as models and that would not have led them to think of hard, continuous disciplined work as a necessary ingredient in their undertaking.

If they thought of themselves as settling a wilderness, they would look for guidance to what was going on in the northern and western parts of England and in the high parts of the south and east. Here were the regions, mostly wooded, where wastelands still abounded, the goal of many in the large migrant population of England. Those who had settled down were scattered widely over the countryside in isolated hovels and hamlets and lived by pasture farming, that is, they cultivated only small plots of ground and ran a few sheep or cattle on the common land. Since the gardens required little attention and the cattle hardly any, they had most of their time to themselves. Some spent their spare hours on handicrafts. In fact, they supplied the labor for most of England's minor industries, which tended to locate in pasture-farming regions, where agriculture made fewer demands on the inhabitants, than in regions devoted to market crops. But the pasture farmers seem to have offered their labor sporadically and reluctantly. They had the reputation of being both idle and independent. They might travel to the richer arable farming regions to pick up a few shillings in field work at harvest time, but their own harvests were small. They did not even grow the wheat or rye for their own bread and made shift to live in hard times from the nuts and berries and herbs that they gathered in the woods.

Jamestown was mostly wooded, like the pasture-farming areas of England and Wales; and since Englishmen used the greater part of their own country for pasture farming, that was the obvious way to use the wasteland of the New World. If this was the Virginians' idea of what they were about, we should expect them to be idle much of the time and to get grain for bread by trading rather than planting (in this case not wheat or rye but maize from the Indians); we should even expect them to get a good deal of their food, as they did, by scouring the woods for nuts and berries.

As the colony developed, a pasture-farming population would have been quite in keeping with the company's expectation of profit from a variety of products. The Spaniards' phenomenal success with raising cattle in the West Indies was well known. And the proposed employment of the settlers of Virginia in a variety of industrial pursuits (iron works, silk works, glass works, shipbuilding) was entirely fitting for a pasture-farming community. The small gardens assigned for cultivation by Governor Dale in 1614 will also make sense: three acres would have been far too small a plot of land to occupy a farmer in the arable regions of England, where a single man could handle thirty acres without assistance. But it would be not at all inappropriate as the garden of a pasture farmer. In Virginia three acres would produce more than enough corn to sustain a man for a year and still leave him with time to make a profit for the company or himself at some other job—if he could be persuaded to work.

Apart from the movement of migrant workers into wastelands, the most obvious English analogy to the Jamestown settlement was that of a military expedition. The settlers may have had in mind not only the expeditions that subdued the Irish but also those dispatched to the European continent in England's wars. The Virginia Company itself seems at first to have envisaged the enterprise as partly military, and the *Lawes Divine, Morall and Martiall* were mostly martial. But the conception carried unfortunate implications for the company's expectations of profit. Military expeditions were staffed from top to bottom with men unlikely to work. The nucleus of sixteenth-century English armies was the nobility and the gangs of genteel ruffians they kept in their service, in wartime to accompany them into the field (or to go in their stead), in peacetime to follow them about as living insignia of their rank. Work was not for the nobility nor for those who wore their livery. According to the keenest student of the aristocracy in this period, "the rich and well-born were idle almost by definition." Moreover they kept "a huge labor force . . . absorbed in slothful and parasitic personal service." Aside from the gentlemen retainers of the nobility and their slothful servants the military expeditions that England sent abroad were filled out by misfits and thieves whom the local constables wished to be rid of. It was, in fact, government policy to keep the able-bodied and upright at home and to send the lame, the halt, the blind, and the criminal abroad.

The combination of gentlemen and ne'er-do-wells of which the leaders at Jamestown complained may well have been the result of the company's using a military model for guidance. The Virginia Company was loaded with noblemen (32 present or future earls, 4 countesses, 3 viscounts, and 19 barons). Is it possible that the large number of Jamestown settlers listed as gentlemen and captains came from among the retainers of these lordly stockholders and that the rest of the settlers included some of the gentlemen's personal servants as well as a group of hapless vagabonds or migratory farm laborers who had been either impressed or lured into the enterprise by tales of the New World's abundance? We are told, at least, that persons designated in the colony's roster as "laborers" were "for most part footmen, and such as they that were Adventurers brought to attend them, or such as they could perswade to goe with them, that never did know what a dayes work was."

If these men thought they were engaged in a military expedition, military precedent pointed to idleness, hunger, and death, not to the effective organization of labor. Soldiers on campaign were not expected to grow their own food. On the other hand they *were* expected to go hungry often and to die like flies even if they never saw an enemy. The casualty rates on European expeditions resembled those at Jamestown and probably from the same causes: disease and undernourishment.

But the highest conception of the enterprise, often expressed by the leaders, was that of a new commonwealth on the model of England itself. Yet this, too, while it touched the heart, was not likely to turn men toward hard, effective, and continuous work. The England that Englishmen were saddled with as a model for new commonwealths abroad was a highly complex society in which the governing consideration in accomplishing a particular piece of work was not how to do it efficiently but who had the right or the duty to do it, by custom, law, or privilege. We know that the labor shortage in the New World quickly diminished considerations of custom, privilege, and specialization in the organization of labor. But the English model the settlers carried with them made them think initially of a society like the one at home, in which each of them would perform his own special task and not encroach on the rights of other men to do other tasks. We may grasp some of the assumptions about labor that went into the most intelligent planning of a new commonwealth by considering Richard Hakluyt's recommendation that settlers include both carpenters and joiners, tallow chandlers and wax chandlers, bowyers and fletchers, men to roughhew pike staffs and other men to finish them.

If Jamestown was not actually troubled by this great an excess of specialization, it was not the Virginia Company's fault. The company wanted to establish at once an economy more complex than England's, an economy that would include not only all the trades that catered to ordinary domestic needs of Englishmen but also industries that were unknown or uncommon in England: a list of artisans the company wanted for the colony in 1611 included such specialists as hemp planters and hemp dressers, gun makers and gunstock makers, spinners of pack thread and upholsterers of feathers. Whatever idleness arose from the specialization of labor in English society was multiplied in the New World by the presence of unneeded skills and the absence or shortage of essential skills. Jamestown had an oversupply of glassmakers and not enough carpenters or blacksmiths, an oversupply of gentlemen and not enough plowmen. These were Englishmen temporarily baffled by missing links in the economic structure of their primitive community. The later jack-of-all-trades American frontiersman was as yet unthought of. As late as 1618 Governor Argall complained that they lacked the men "to set their Ploughs on worke." Although they had the oxen to pull them, "they wanted men to bring them to labour, and Irons for the Ploughs, and harnesse for the Cattell." And the next year John Rolfe noted that they still needed "Carpenters to build and make Carts and Ploughs, and skilfull men that know how to use them, and traine up our cattell to draw them; which though we indeavour to effect, yet our want of experience brings but little to perfection but planting Tobacco."

Tobacco, as we know, was what they kept on planting. The first shipload of it, sent to England in 1617, brought such high prices that the Virginians stopped bowling in the streets and planted tobacco in them. They did it without benefit of plows, and somehow at the same time they managed to grow corn, probably also without plows. Seventeenth-century Englishmen, it turned out, could adapt themselves to hard and varied work if there was sufficient incentive.

But we may well ask whether the habits and attitudes we have been examining had suddenly expired altogether. Did tobacco really solve the labor problem in Virginia? Did the economy that developed after 1618 represent a totally new set of social and economic attitudes? Did greater opportunities for profit completely erase the old attitudes and furnish the incentives to labor that were needed to make Virginia a success? The study of labor in modern underdeveloped countries should make us pause before we say yes. The mere opportunity to earn high wages has not always proved adequate to recruit labor in underdeveloped countries. Something more in the way of expanded needs or political authority or national consciousness or ethical imperatives has been required. Surely Virginia, in some sense, became a success. But how did it succeed? What kind of success did it have? Without attempting to answer, I should like very diffidently to offer a suggestion, a way of looking ahead at what happened in the years after the settlement of Jamestown.

The founders of Virginia, having discovered in tobacco a substitute for the sugar of the West Indies and the silver of Peru, still felt the lack of a native labor force with which to exploit the new crop. At first they turned to their own overpopulated country for labor, but English indentured servants brought with them the same haphazard habits of work as their masters. Also like their masters, they were apt to be unruly if pressed. And when their terms of servitude expired—if they themselves had not expired in the "seasoning" that carried away most immigrants to Virginia —they could be persuaded to continue working for their betters only at exorbitant rates. Instead they struck out for themselves and joined the ranks of those demanding rather than supplying labor. But there was a way out. The Spanish and Portuguese had already demonstrated what could be done in the New World when a local labor force became inadequate: they brought in the natives of Africa.

For most of the seventeenth century Virginians were unable to compete for the limited supply of slaves hauled across the ocean to man the sugar plantations of the Americas. Sugar was a more profitable way to use slaves than tobacco. Moreover, the heavy mortality of newcomers to Virginia made an investment in Africans bound for a lifetime more risky than the same amount invested in a larger number of Englishmen, bound for a term that was likely to prove longer than a Virginia lifetime.

But Virginians continued to be Englishmen: the more enterprising continued to yearn for a cheaper, more docile, more stable supply of labor, while their servants loafed on the job, ran away, and claimed the traditional long lunch hour. As the century wore on, punctuated in Virginia by depression, discontent, and rebellion, Virginia's position in the market for men gradually improved: the price of sugar fell, making it less competitive with tobacco; the heavy mortality in the colony declined, making the initial outlay of capital on slaves less risky; and American and European traders expanded their infamous activities in Africa. The world supply of slaves, which had fallen off in the second quarter of the seventeenth century, rose sharply in the third quarter and continued to rise.

With these developments the Virginians at last were able to acquire substitute natives for their colony and begin, in their own English way, to Hispanize Virginia. By the middle of the eighteenth century Africans constituted the great majority of the colony's entire labor force. This is not to say that plantation slavery in Virginia or elsewhere can be understood simply as a result of inherited attitudes toward work confronting the economic opportunities of the New World. The forces that determined the character of plantation slavery were complex. But perhaps an institution so archaic and at the same time so modern as the plantation cannot be fully understood without taking into consideration the attitudes that helped to starve the first settlers. of the colony where the southern plantation began.

Indian Cultural Adjustment to European Civilization

NANCY OESTREICH LURIE

That the encounter between the European migrants to America and the entrenched native population was often bitter and vicious is well known. Here Nancy Lurie describes the early years of such contact in Virginia, and emphasizes the strength of the Indian culture.

A complex Indian world maintained itself over time and against white onslaughts, thus demonstrating a strong cultural persistence. Although badly defeated in 1622, 1644, and again in 1675, the natives maintained much of their earlier way of life. Only after the almost complete destruction of their economic system by war were they forced to accommodate themselves to the newly prevalent Euro-American life.

Nancy Oestreich Lurie, "Indian Cultural Adjustment to European Civilization," in James Morton Smith, ed., *Seventeenth-Century America* (Chapel Hill, N.C.: University of North Carolina Press, 1959), pp. 33–60. Published for the Institute of Early American History and Culture. Reprinted and footnotes omitted by permission of the publisher.

In 1907, on the 300th anniversary of the beginning of English colonization in America, James Mooney made the brief observation that the
Jamestown settlers "landed among a people who already knew and hated
whites." In effect, this remark summed up the accepted anthropological
explanation for the Indians' unpredictable behavior; it indicated why they
alternated elaborate expressions and actions of good will with apparent
treachery. Mooney implied that the Indians' attitude and behavior were
more than justified by the demonstrated greed and aggressiveness of the
whites.

Little work was done in the succeeding years to explore the complete
significance of Mooney's remark or to probe more deeply into underlying
motivations for the Indians' actions. This neglect was inevitable, since
attention had to be devoted to a more fundamental problem. Before
achieving an understanding of Indian reaction to the effects of contact
with Europeans, it was necessary to establish a valid and cohesive picture
of aboriginal culture. * Thanks to the labors of such scholars as Mooney,
Frank G. Speck, David I. Bushnell, John R. Swanton, Maurice A.
Mook, and others, the fragmentary data relating to native life have been
gathered into comprehensive and analytical accounts concerned with such
problems as Indian demography, the cultural and linguistic identity of
given tribes, tribal locations, and the prehistoric diffusion and changes in
Indian cultures.

Likewise, in the past fifty years, general theoretical techniques of
ethnological interpretation have been refined through field research in
observable situations of culture contact. These acculturational studies,
which are an invaluable aid in the interpretation of historical data, have
investigated the reasons why some groups lose their cultural identity
in a situation of culture contact while other groups continue to preserve
ethnic integrity despite widespread alterations of purely native patterns.
With this backlog of necessary information and analysis, anthropologists
have begun a more intensive consideration of the dynamics of culture
contact in ethnohistorical terms.

Turning to Mooney's contention, there is evidence that the Virginia
Indians had several opportunities to form opinions about Europeans both
in terms of direct experience and of information communicated to them.
Direct knowledge of Europeans may have occurred as early as the first

---

* It must be noted that while the concept of culture can be and often is treated
as an abstraction with an existence almost unto itself, this is no more than a semantic
devise. Human ideas and reasoning underlie culture and cultural change. Whenever
possible, I have devoted attention to the factors of human motivation which give
overt expression to observable cultural characteristics. The terms Indian culture and
European civilization merely indicate that comparisons are made of two cultures
having distinct origins and historical traditions, differing only in the local expressions
of certain universal aspects of culture.

quarter of the sixteenth century, when Giovanni de Verrazano and Estevan Gomez are believed to have made observations in the Chesapeake Bay region. Of somewhat greater significance is the alleged founding of a Spanish Jesuit mission on the York River in 1570. According to this theory, the missionaries were killed by Indians under the leadership of a native known as Don Luis de Valasco, who had lived in Spain, where he was educated and converted to Christianity. The Spaniards had hoped that he would act as guide and model in the proselytizing of his people, but it appears that the effects of his early life negated his later training. In 1572 a punitive expedition under Pedro Menendez de Aviles attacked and defeated the Indians responsible for the destruction of the mission; in succeeding years Menendez made other forays into the region. A recent study insists that this area must have been along the Virginia coast.

Whether or not the case for a sixteenth-century mission in Virginia has been proved is problematical. Many details are uncertain: the precise location of the mission on the York River, the tribal affiliations of Don Luis, the extent of his leadership, his age at the time he lived in Spain, and his possible genealogical affiliations with the ruling hierarchy of the Virginia Indians of the seventeenth century. However, historical investigation leaves no doubt of Spanish activity at this time, and these ventures must have occurred between St. Augustine and the Potomac River. The natives of Virginia, who borrowed cultural traits from neighboring tribes along the coast and further inland, could have received news of European explorations to the south and west by the same routes that carried·purely native ideas. Generalized impressions of Europeans were doubtless prevalent in the Virginia area long before 1607.

The Spaniards came to America primarily as adventurers and fortune seekers. Although they attempted to found settlements their efforts usually met with failure. They plundered Indian villages but did not remain long in any one region; they were frequently routed by angry Indians or by their own inability to subsist in a strange terrain. After 1520, raids were conducted along the Gulf and southern Atlantic coast to obtain slaves for shipment to the West Indies. News of these incursions may have reached Virginia via the various coast tribes, and similarly Virginia natives may have heard of De Soto's hapless wanderings to the south and west. Even though the Spaniards later achieved success in colonization in Florida through the use of missionaries, the first hostile impressions had been made.

The French entered the scene to the south of Virginia in 1562. Because of lack of supplies and Spanish aggression, they failed in their attempts to establish a foothold in the region. However, the interests of France as well as of Britain were served by unknown numbers of piratical freebooters from the Caribbean area who touched along the coast of the Carolinas and intrigued with the Indians. Not until 1580 was Spain able to dislodge foreign intruders and punish recalcitrant Indians. Even then, Spanish dominion remained precarious, although the Spanish Franciscans continued to extend their missions up the coast. Finally, in 1597, a general uprising among the Carolina tribes destroyed these religious outposts and forced Spain again to concentrate most of her forces in Florida.

Thus, during much of the sixteenth century Europeans were active in regions immediately adjacent to Virginia and possibly in Virginia itself. Their activity was often associated with violence, and there was sufficient time for rumors concerning them to have reached the Virginia natives before any direct contacts were made. By the time the English attempted to found colonies on the east coast toward the close of the sixteenth century, they encountered difficulties which may have been more than the simple result of European inexperience in developing techniques for survival in the New World. Raleigh's enterprise, for example, may have been singularly ill-timed. A general unrest in Indian-white relationships marked the period from 1577 to 1597 in the Carolina region where Raleigh's followers chose to remain. Pemisipan, a Secotan chief who attempted to organize opposition to the British in 1585, could hardly have been blamed if he saw a curious similarity to accounts he may have heard concerning the Spanish when, for the trifling matter of the theft of a silver cup, the English burned the corn and destroyed the buildings at his village of Aquascogoc.

The later events at Cape Henry, the first landfall of the Jamestown colonists, suggest that the immediate hostility expressed by the Indians was inspired by fear of reprisals for the fate of Raleigh's colony. The Indians who attacked the English belonged to the Chesapeake tribe, immediately adjacent to the tribes with whom Pemisipan conspired. It is also possible, as Mooney implies, that by 1607 the Virginia Indians evaluated any sudden appearance of Europeans as evil and took immediate measures to repel them. However, this view oversimplifies several important factors. Long before any Europeans arrived at Jamestown, the Indians had been fighting over matters of principle important to them, such as possession of land and tribal leadership. If they were aware of the fate of other Indians at the hands of Europeans, there was no reason for them to assume that their fate would be similar; they were not necessarily allied with the beleaguered tribes, nor did they share a sense of racial kinship. Sharp cultural differences and even sharper linguistic differences separated the various Indian societies. While there was reason to fear and hate the Europeans as invaders who made indiscriminate war on all Indians, the fear was only that of being taken unawares and the hate could be modified if the tribes which had fallen victim thus far were strangers or even enemies. If the Indians of Virginia had any knowledge of Europeans, they must have been aware that the white men were fundamentally outnumbered, frequently unable to support themselves in an environment which the Indians found eminently satisfactory, and that European settlements were usually short lived. The appearance of the English was probably far less alarming than 350 years of hindsight indicate ought to have been the case.

This is demonstrated by the fact that the Virginia Indians under the leadership of Powhatan seem to have made their first adjustments to Europeans in terms of existing native conditions. Primary among these conditions were Powhatan's efforts to gain firmer control over his subject tribes and to fight tribes traditionally at enmity with his followers. It was expedient to help the settlers stay alive, for they could be useful allies in his established plans; but at the same time he could not allow them to gain ascendancy. The situation was complicated by factionalism in Powhatan's ranks and lack of accord among the settlers. However, recognition of the fundamental aboriginal situation makes the early events at Jamestown understandable on a rational basis. It offers a logical foundation for subsequent developments in Indian-white relationships and Indian adjustments to European civilization as the result of something more than barbaric cupidity and a thirst for the white man's blood.

Certainly a wary sensitivity to any sign of hostility or treachery characterized the behavior of both whites and Indians at the outset of settlement at Jamestown. The Europeans were still seriously concerned about the probable fate of Raleigh's colony and they had already been attacked by the Indians at Cape Henry. The Indians, in turn, may well have possessed information concerning the alarmingly retributive temperament of Europeans, at least in terms of the incident at nearby Aquascogoc, if not through generalized opinions derived from the long history of intermittent European contact along the east coast.

Nevertheless, the party of Europeans that set out on exploration of the country about Jamestown encountered a welcome at the various Indian villages different from the greetings offered at Cape Henry. Except for one cold but not overtly hostile reception in the Weanoc country, the white men were feted, fed, and flattered. At the same time a suggestion of the uncertainty of the next years occurred before the exploring party had even returned to their headquarters—at Jamestown the remaining colonists were attacked by a party of local Indians. Events of this nature as well as the general observations recorded during the first two years at Jamestown are particularly instructive in any attempt to understand Indian motivations and policy regarding the British.

The narratives are difficult to follow because of the variety of orthographies employed for Indian words. Certain features remain speculative because initial communication between whites and Indians was limited to the use of signs and the few native words that could be learned readily. However, it is possible to see native culture in terms of regularities and consistencies which were not obvious to the colonists. Likewise, the apparent inconsistencies on the part of the natives, recounted by the settlers as innate savage treachery, indicate that the aboriginal culture was in a process of growth, elaboration, and internal change. These phases of culture, which included both extensive tendencies of intertribal confederation and divisive reactions expressed by individual tribes, were interrupted and redirected but not initiated by the arrival of Europeans in 1607.

From the viewpoint of the twentieth century, it is difficult to realize that the material differences between the Indians and the European colonists, who lived before the full development of the industrial revolution, were equalled if not outweighed by the similarities of culture. This was especially true in Virginia, where a local florescence of culture and a demonstrated ability to prevail over other tribes gave the Indians a sense of strength which blinded them to the enormity of the threat posed by the presence of Europeans. There was actually little in the Europeans' imported bag of tricks which the Indians could not syncretize with their own experience. Metal was not unknown to them: they used native copper, brought in from the West, for decorative purposes. Metal weapons and domestic utensils were simply new and effective forms of familiar objects to accomplish familiar tasks. Even guns were readily mastered after the noise, which evoked astonishment at first, was understood as necessary to their operation. Likewise, fabrics and articles of personal adornment were part of Indian technology. Many utilitarian objects such as nets, weirs, and gardening implements were very similar in both Indian and European culture. European ships were simply larger and different, as was fitting for a people interested in traveling greater distances by open water than the Indians had ever cared to do.

Expansive accounts of the size and permanence of the great European cities could easily have been likened by the natives to the impressive aboriginal developments in the lower Mississippi Valley; archeological evidence suggests that knowledge of this cultural complex was widespread. Even if these Indian models of nascent urbanization are discounted, the statements made by Europeans about their country and king may well have sounded like the exaggerations of outnumbered strangers endeavoring to buttress their weaknesses with talk of powerful but distant brothers. This explanation is admittedly conjectural, although we find ample documentation of the Indians' disinclination to admit any significant superiority in white culture at a somewhat later period. During the early nineteenth century, when the industrial revolution was underway and the eastern United States was heavily populated by whites, Indian visitors were brought from the West in the hope that they would be cowed by the white man's power and cease resistance to the forces of civilization. The Indians remained singularly unimpressed. Furthermore, at the time Jamestown was founded in the seventeenth century, the only knowledge Indians possessed concerning Europeans indicated that Indians were well able to oppose white settle-ment. Raleigh's ill-fated colony was a clear reminder of the Europeans' mortality.

Although the early accounts tend to take a patronizing view of the Indians, the points on which the Europeans felt superior had little meaning for the aborigines: literacy, different sexual mores, ideas of modesty, good taste in dress and personal adornment, and Christian religious beliefs. The argument of technological superiority at that time was a weak one; despite guns and large ships the Europeans could not wrest a living from a terrain which, by Indian standards, supported an exceptionally large population. Scientific knowledge of generally predictable group reactions thus suggests that the degree of ethnocentrism was probably equal on both sides of the contact between Indians and Europeans in Virginia. Recognition of the Indians' self-appraisal is necessary for a clear understanding of their basis of motivation and consequent behavior in relation to Europeans.

Moreover, it was evident to the colonists that they were dealing with a fairly complex society, exhibiting many characteristics of leadership, social classes, occupational specialization, social control, and economic concepts that were eminently comprehensible in European terms. If the exploring parties overstated the case when they translated *weròance* as "king" and likened tribal territories to European kingdoms, they at least had a truer understanding of the nature of things than did the democratic Jefferson, who first designated the Virginia tribes as the "Powhatan Con-federacy." Since the term "Confederacy" is so firmly entrenched in the literature, it will be retained here as a matter of convenience; but, in re-ality, Powhatan was in the process of building something that approximated an empire. By 1607 it was not an accomplished fact, but the outlines were apparent and the process was sufficiently advanced to allow a geographical description of the extent of Powhatan's domain.

Powhatan's influence, if not his undisputed control, extended over some thirty Algonkian-speaking tribes along the entire length of the present Virginia coast, including the Accohannoc and Accomac of the Eastern Shore. The nucleus of this domain consisted of six tribes which were cen-trally located in the region drained by the James, Pamunkey, and Mat-taponi rivers. These tribes were the Powhatan, Arrohattoc, Pamunkey, Youghtanund, Appomattoc, and Mattaponi, with Powhatan's own tribe, the Pamunkey, consistently referred to in the early narratives as the largest and most powerful. The Confederacy was bounded to the north and south by other Algonkian tribes. Except on the basis of their declared political allegiance, the uniformity of language and culture in the region makes it difficult to differentiate between the tribes within the Confederacy and even between the Confederacy and neighboring Maryland and Carolina groups.

It is generally accepted that these Algonkian peoples moved into the lower coastal region from the north. According to their own account this had occurred about three hundred years before Jamestown was settled, although recent archeological investigations suggest a longer occupation. Once arrived, the Algonkians acquired numerous cultural traits from the Southeast culture area and developed many similarities to the interior Muskhogean-speaking groups. Some of these new elements were in turn transferred to the more northerly Algonkians, but they never existed there in the cohesive complexity found in the tidelands.

Powhatan inherited the six central tribes as an already unified inter-tribal organization and extended his domain by conquest from the south bank of the Potomac to the Norfolk region. The Chesapeake Indians are included in the Confederacy, but this southernmost group was not fully under Powhatan's control at the same time the settlers arrived. Their attack on the colonists at Cape Henry gave Powhatan the opportunity to gain favor with the English by swiftly avenging the hostile action. Although some historians have implied that Powhatan destroyed the entire tribe, it is far more likely that he simply killed the leaders and placed trusted kinsmen in these positions.

Powhatan's method of fighting and his policy of expanding political control combined a reasoned plan of action with quick ferocity and a minimum of bloodshed. Indian warfare was generally limited to surprise attacks and sniping from cover. Constant replacements of fighting men kept the enemy occupied and wore down their resistance, while actual casualties were relatively limited in number. Accounts of Powhatan's conquests and the occurrences observed after 1607 point to a carefully devised method of establishing his control over a wide territory. Entire communities might be killed if they proved exceptionally obstinate in rendering homage and paying tribute, but in most cases Powhatan simply defeated groups of questionable loyalty and upon their surrender moved them to areas where he could keep better watch over them. Trusted members of the Confederacy were then sent to occupy the vacated regions, while Powhatan's relatives were distributed throughout the tribes in positions of leadership. Mook's studies indicate that the degree of Powhatan's leadership decreased in almost direct proportion to the increase in geographical distance between the Pamunkey and the location of a given tribe. Throughout the entire region, however, the combination of ample sustenance, effective techniques of production, provident habits of food storage, and distribution of supplies through exchange offset shortcomings in the political framework connecting the tribes and helped to cement social ties and produce a commonality of culture.

Despite certain internal dissensions the Confederacy can be seen as a unified bloc, distinct from neighboring tribes. To the north were numerous small Algonkian-speaking tribes, either friendly or representing no serious danger to Powhatan. They tended to shade off in cultural characteristics toward the more northern Algonkian types to be found along the coast into New England. The best known of these tribes was the Nanticoke in eastern Maryland and Delaware. North of the Potomac lived the Conoy (Piscataway), Tocwough, Ozinie, and others, about whom little is recorded. At a later date the tribes in this region were known collectively as the "Doeg" Indians. Beyond the Conoy and up into the present state of Pennsylvania were the Susquehanna, in Captain John Smith's judgment a powerful and impressive group, distinguished from the Virginia tribes in both language and culture. However, they seem to have felt closer ties of friendship with the Algonkians than they did with their Iroquoian linguistic affiliates to the north. The Nansemond and Chesapeake tribes formed the southern terminus of the Confederacy, and beyond them in the Carolina region were a number of linguistically and culturally similar tribes extending along the coast to the Neuse River. The Roanoke narratives and particularly the illustrations of John White provide somewhat fuller documentation for the southerly neighbors of the Confederacy than is available for the northern Algonkian groups.

The western border, formed by the fall line and paralleling the coast, was characterized by greater cultural and linguistic differences than those observed to the north and south of the Confederacy; it also represented a definite danger area for Powhatan. Virtually all Indian occupation ended somewhat east of the falls, however, allowing a strip of land a mile to ten or twelve miles wide as a safe margin between the Powhatan tribes and their nearest neighbors, who were also their deadliest enemies, the tribes of the Virginia piedmont region. These peoples have long been designated as Siouan-speaking but a recent study casts doubt on this identification. It is now suggested that these groups spoke a highly divergent and extremely old dialect of the basic Algonkian language stock. Except for linguistic distinctiveness little is known about these piedmont people. This is most unfortunate, since they appear to figure as a key to much of Powhatan's policy toward the English and helped to influence the course of Indian adjustment to European settlement. A few of these tribes are known by name, but they are usually considered as having comprised two major confederacies, comparable in some measure to the groupings associated with Powhatan. These were the Manahoac on the upper Rappahannock and surrounding region, and the Monacan along the upper James and its tributary streams. Both were aggressive groups, and their incursions were a constant threat to the tidelands Indians. Powhatan's desire to subdue these westerly tribes as a matter of protection was underscored by another consideration: copper, highly prized by the Virginia Confederacy, came from the West, and the enemy tribes formed an obstacle to trade for that commodity.

Thus, at the outset of colonization in 1607 Powhatan's policies can best be understood in relation to circumstances antedating the arrival of the Jamestown settlers. Powhatan saw the whites in his territory as potential allies and as a source of new and deadly weapons to be used in furthering his own plans for maintaining control over his Confederacy and protecting the Confederacy as a whole against the threat posed by the alien tribes of the piedmont region. Likewise, existing concepts of intertribal trade in foodstuffs and other commodities were extended to include trade with the newly arrived whites. It is worth noting that European novelties, apart from weapons, were of far less interest to Powhatan than the fact that the British possessed copper, an object vested with traditional native values and heretofore obtained with great difficulty.

In the initial stages of contact between the Indians and the whites, therefore, it is hardly surprising that Powhatan and his people felt at least equal to the English. The chieftain could appreciate the foreigners as allies in the familiar business of warfare and trade, but in general there seemed little to emulate in European culture and much to dislike about the white men. However, even in the most difficult phases of their early relationship, Powhatan did not indulge in a full-scale attack against the settlers. At that time he was still engaged in strengthening his Confederacy and perhaps he could not risk extensive Indian defection to the side of the whites. But there is an equal likelihood that Powhatan's primary motivation was the desire to control and use the whites for his own purposes rather than to annihilate them.

At the time Jamestown was founded, native civilization was enjoying a period of expansion, and Powhatan had ample reason for sometimes considering the English as more an annoyance than a serious danger. The unusually rich natural environment and the security offered by the Confederacy stimulated the growth of social institutions and cultural refinements. In addition, the Virginia Indians were exceptionally powerful and, by aboriginal standards, their population was large: the entire Confederacy numbered some 8,500 to 9,000 people, or a density of approximately one person to every square mile. The Indians lived according to a well-ordered and impressively complex system of government. They dwelled in secure villages, had substantial houses and extensive gardens, and had a notable assemblage of artifacts for utilitarian, religious, and decorative purposes.

The Indians won the grudging respect of the colonists for their advanced technology, but the Europeans were contemptuous of their seemingly hopeless commitment to superstition, while their ceremonialism appeared to the whites a ridiculous presumption of dignity. A typical bias of communication between Europeans and Indians is seen in Smith's account of the Quiyoughcohannock chief who begged the settlers to pray to the Christian God for rain because their own deities had not fulfilled the

Indians' requests. Smith asserted that the Indians appealed to the whites because they believed the Europeans' God superior to their own, just as the Europeans' guns were superior to bows and arrows. Yet Smith notes with some wonder that the Quiyoughcohannock chief, despite his cordiality and interest in the Christian deity, could not be prevailed upon to "forsake his false Gods." Actually this chief of one of the lesser tribes of the Confederacy illustrated the common logic of polytheistic people who often have no objection to adding foreign deities to their pantheon if it seems to assure more efficient control of the natural universe. The chief was not interested in changing his religious customs in emulation of the Europeans; he merely wished to improve his own culture by judicious borrowing—a gun at one time, a supernatural being at another.

Nor would the chief have dared respond to a new religion in its entirety, even if such an unlikely idea had occurred to him. The whole structure of tribal life relied upon controlling the mysterious aspects of the world by a traditional body of beliefs which required the use of religious functionaries, temples, idols, and rituals. These were awesome arrangements and not to be treated lightly, although improvement by minor innovations might be permitted.

The geopolitical sophistication of the Virginia tribes is reflected in the secular hierarchy of leadership which extended in orderly and expanding fashion from the villages, through the separate tribes, up to Powhatan as head of the entire Confederacy. A gauge of the complexity of government is the fact that the Confederacy shared with the Europeans such niceties of civilization as capital punishment. In small societies having a precarious economy, indemnities in goods or services are usually preferred to taking the life of a culprit even in crimes as serious as murder. However, where the life of the offender or one of his kinsmen is exacted for the life of the victim, punishment is the concern of the particular families involved; the rest of the group merely signifies approval of the process as a means of restoring social equilibrium after an offense is committed. Powhatan's government, however, was much closer to that of the English than it was to many of the tribes of North America. Punishment was meted out by a designated executioner for an offense against the society as the society was symbolized in the person of the leader.

Nevertheless, despite its elaborate civil structure, the Confederacy exhibited a universal rule of any society: a complex theory of government does not necessarily assure complete success in application. Powhatan not only had unruly subjects to deal with, but entire tribes in his domain could not be trusted. Relations between whites and Indians therefore were always uncertain, largely because of political developments within the Confederacy. When the colonists were supported by Powhatan, they were in mortal danger from those dissatisfied tribes of the Confederacy which had the foresight to realize that the English might one day assist Powhatan to enforce his authority. When Powhatan and his closest associates turned upon the settlers, the less dependable tribes became friendly to the whites.

In view of this morass of political allegiances, it is little wonder that early accounts of the settlers are replete with material which seems to prove the innate treachery of the Indians. Yet the militant phases of Indian activity, as illustrated by the initial attack on Jamestown and Powhatan's vengeance on the offending Chesapeake tribe, must be seen as part of a larger policy involving alternative methods of settling inter-group differences. Although the settlers knew that dissatisfaction among Powhatan's followers offered a means of preventing a coordinated Indian attack, they also discovered that established mechanisms of diplomacy existed among the Indians that could be employed for their benefit. For example, the Jamestown settlement was located in the territory of the Paspehegh tribe, and relations with this tribe frequently became strained. The Powhatan forces represented by the leaders of the Pamunkey, Arrohattoc, Youghtanund, and Mattaponi offered to act as intermediaries in negotiating peace with the Paspehegh and other hostile tribes or, if necessary, to join forces with the settlers in an armed assault on mutual enemies.

If the Europeans found it difficult to live among the Indians, the Europeans seemed equally unpredictable to the Indians. Early in his relationship with the English, Powhatan was promised five hundred men and supplies for a march on the Monacan and Manahoac; but instead of finding wholehearted support among his allies for this campaign, Powhatan discovered that the whites were helpless to support themselves in the New World. As time wore on and they became increasingly desperate for food, the Europeans were less careful in the difficult business of trying to distinguish friends from enemies. They extorted supplies promiscuously, driving hard bargains by the expedient of burning villages and canoes.

It is problematical whether, as Smith implies, Powhatan was actually unable to destroy the handful of English because he could not organize his tribes for a full-scale offensive or whether he was biding his time in the hope of eventually establishing a clear-cut power structure in which the colonists would be allowed to survive but remain subservient to his designs in native warfare. At any rate, after two years of English occupation at Jamestown, Powhatan moved from his traditional home on the Pamunkey River some fifteen miles from the Europeans and settled in a more remote village upstream on the Chickahominy River. Violence flared periodically during these early years: colonists were frequently killed and often captured. Sometimes, being far from united in their allegiance, they fled to the Indian villages, where they were usually well treated. Captives and runaways were exchanged as hostages when one side or the other found it convenient. However, if Powhatan was willing to take advantage of dissident feeling among the whites, he was no fool and he finally put to death two colonists who seemed to be traitors to both sides at the same time. The execution was much to Smith's satisfaction, for it saved him from performing the task and assured a far more brutal punishment than he would have been able to inflict upon the renegades.

Throughout the period from 1607 to 1609, the chronicles include a complexity of half-told tales involving alliances and enmities and mutual suspicions, of Indians living among settlers and settlers living among Indians. Although this interaction was of an individual nature, the two groups learned something of each other; yet each side maintained its own values and traditions as a social entity. The Indians were primarily concerned with obtaining new material goods. By theft, trade, and the occupation of European artisans in their villages, they increased their supply of armaments and metal work. With the use of Indian guides and informants, the settlers became familiar with the geography of the region, and they also learned the secrets of exploiting their new environment through techniques of native gardening. For the most part, however, conscious efforts to bridge the cultural gap were unavailing. There was one amusing attempt to syncretize concepts of Indian and European monarchy and thereby bring about closer communications, when Powhatan was treated to an elaborate "coronation." The chief *weroance* was only made more vain by the ceremonies; he was by no means transformed into a loyal subject of the English sovereign, as the white settlers had intended.

An increasing number of settlers arrived in Virginia and, with the help of Indians who by this time had ample reason to let the whites perish, managed to weather the hazards of the "starving time." As the whites became more firmly established, competition between Europeans and Indians took on the familiar form of a struggle for land. Armed clashes occurred frequently, but there were no organized hostilities, and the Indians continued to trade with the English. A peace which was formally established in 1614 and lasted until 1622 is often attributed to a refinement of Powhatan's sensibilities because of the marriage of Pocahontas and John Rolfe. Although Pocahontas was indeed the favorite child of Powhatan, it is likely that the chieftain's interest in her marriage was not entirely paternal. This strengthening of the social bond between Indians and Europeans helped solidify Powhatan's power and prestige among the confederated tribes, as he was thus enduringly allied with the whites.

Continuation of harmony between Indians and whites for a period of eight years was doubtless rendered possible because enough land still remained in Virginia for both settlers and Indians to live according to their accustomed habits. The seriousness of the loss of Indian land along the James River was lessened by the existence of a strip of virtually unoccupied territory just east of the fall line which ran the length of the Confederacy's holdings. If properly armed and not disturbed by internal dissensions and skirmishes with the English, the Powhatan tribes could afford to settle at the doorstep of their piedmont neighbors and even hope to expand into enemy territory. Hostilities require weapons, and peaceful trade with the English meant easier access to arms which the Confederacy could turn against the Monacan and Manahoac. It is also possible that by this time Powhatan realized the vast strength of the English across the sea and was persuaded to keep the settlers as friends. Knowledge of Europe would have been available to the chieftain through such Indians as Machumps, described by William Strachey as having spent "somtym in England" as well as moving "to and fro amongst us as he dares and as Powhatan gives him leave."

Whatever were Powhatan's reasons for accepting the peace, it appears that he utilized the lull in hostilities to unify the Confederacy and deal with his traditional enemies. We have no direct evidence of activities against the piedmont tribes, for there is little historical data regarding the western area at this time. However, by the time the fur trade became important in the West the Monacan and Manahoac had lost the power which had once inspired fear among the tribes of the Confederacy. In view of Powhatan's years of scheming and the probable closer proximity of the Confederacy to the piedmont region after 1614, it may be conjectured that the Virginia chieftain and his people took some part in the downfall of the Monacan and Manahoac.

When Powhatan died in 1618, his brother Opechancanough succeeded him as leader of the Confederacy. Opechancanough continued to observe Powhatan's policy of peace for four years, although relations between Indians and Europeans were again degenerating. The Indians' natural resources were threatened as the increasing tobacco crops encroached on land where berries had grown in abundance and game had once been hunted. In the face of European advance, the Indians became restive and complained of the settlers' activities; but these signs went unnoticed by the colonists. Opechancanough was aware that the real danger to the Confederacy arose from neither internal dissensions nor traditional Indian enemies but from the inexorable growth of European society in Virginia. He was apparently able to convince all the member tribes of this fact, if they had not already drawn their own conclusions. The subsequent uprising of 1622 was a well-planned shock to the English; it was alarming not so much for the destruction wrought, since by that time the Europeans could sustain the loss of several hundred people, but for the fact that the Confederacy could now operate as a unified fighting organization. This was a solidarity which Powhatan either had been unable or was disinclined to achieve.

Doubtless Opechancanough expected reprisals, but he was totally unprepared for the unprecedented and utter devastation of his lands and the wholesale slaughter of his people. The tribes were scattered, some far beyond the traditional boundaries of their lands, and several of the smaller groups simply ceased to exist as definable entities. Gradually as the fury of revenge died down, the remnants of the Confederacy regrouped and began to return to their homelands. However, the settlers were no longer complacent about their Indian neighbors. In addition to campaigning against the natives, they erected a string of fortifications between Chesiac and Jamestown, and they tended to settle Virginia in the south rather than toward the north and west. In effect, therefore, Opechancanough accomplished a limited objective; a line was established between Indians and Europeans, but the line was only temporary and the Indians paid a terrible price.

Moreover, the cultural gap widened during the ensuing years. Following the period of reprisals the Indians were left to make a living and manage their affairs as best they could. Many old grievances seemed to be forgotten, and the natives gave the appearance of accepting their defeat for all time. Opechancanough, who had eluded capture immediately after the attack of 1622, remained at large, but the Europeans attempted to win tribes away from his influence rather than hunt him down at the risk of inflaming his followers. Finally, white settlement once more began to spread beyond the safety of concentrated colonial population. Tensions were re-created on the frontier, and there were minor skirmishes; the Indians complained to the English, but they also continued their trading activities. Thus matters continued for more than twenty years until large-scale hostilities again broke out.

The uprising of 1644 was surprisingly effective. It is generally known that in both the 1622 and the 1644 uprisings the percentage of Indians killed in relation to the total Indian population was far greater than the percentage of settlers killed in relation to the total white population. Yet with far fewer Indians to do the fighting, Opechancanough managed to kill at least as many Europeans in the second attack as he had in the first. The uprising is another proof that the Indians' method of adjusting to changes wrought by the Europeans continued to be an attempt to prevail over or remove the source of anxiety—the settlers—rather than to adapt themselves to the foreign culture. Certainly the Indians never felt that their difficulties would be resolved by assimilation among the whites, a solution which the colonists at times hoped to effect through the adoption of Indian children, intermarriage, and Indian servitude.

Hopeless though the uprising appears in retrospect, it was entirely logical within Opechancanough's own cultural frame of reasoning. It is impossible to determine whether the Indians were aware of the futility of their action, nor do we know enough about the psychology of these people to ascribe to them such a grim fatalism that they would prefer a quick and honorable death to the indignities of living in subjection to the whites. But there is something impressive about Opechancanough, an old and enfeebled man, being carried on a litter to the scene of battle. Whatever the outcome his days were numbered. His young warriors, however, knew of the horrible reprisals of 1622 and they understood the cost of being defeated by the white man. Yet they too were willing to risk an all-out attack.

There is little doubt that Opechancanough realized the danger inherent in rebellion. He was a shrewd strategist and a respected leader. It is entirely possible that he hoped for assistance from forces outside the Confederacy. Tension had existed between the whites of Virginia and Maryland for a number of years, and in one instance the Virginians had hoped to incite the Confederacy against their neighbors. Maryland had been settled only ten years before the second uprising, and although hostile incidents between whites and Indians had occurred, her Indian policy had been more just and humane than Virginia's. If Opechancanough did expect military assistance from whites for his uprising against whites, he had historical precedent to inspire him. Powhatan had exploited factionalism among the Jamestown settlers, and it may be that the tension between Virginia and Maryland suggested an extension of his policy to Opechancanough. Whatever the motivations behind Opechancanough's design for rebellion, the second uprising attested to the strength of the old Confederacy and indicated clearly the stubborn resistance of the Indians to cultural annihilation.

Although the usual revenge followed the attack of 1644, Virginia's Indian policy was beginning to change. The Powhatan tribes were too seriously reduced in numbers to benefit greatly by the progress, but their treatment at the hands of the colonists following the uprising marked a new development in Indian-white relations, one which eventually culminated in the modern reservation system. In 1646 a formal treaty was signed with the Powhatan Confederacy establishing a line between Indian and white lands and promising the Indians certain rights and protection in their holdings. While their movements were to be strictly regulated, the natives were guaranteed recognition for redress of wrongs before the law. There were two particularly important features of the treaty. First, the Indians were to act as scouts and allies against the possibility of outside tribes' invading the colony; this policy was in contrast to the earlier device of attempting to win the friendship of peripheral tribes to enforce order among the local Indians. Second, and consistent with the growing importance of the fur trade in colonial economics, the Indians were to pay a tribute each year in beaver skins. During the following years various legislative acts were adopted to protect the Indians in their rights and establish mutual responsibilities with the tribes.

As the treaty of 1646 symbolized the establishment of new policies in dealing with the Indians, so did the circumstances surrounding Bacon's Re-

bellion afford a glimpse of other future developments. Within the tangled
events of the Rebellion was an indication of the later effects of the frontier
on many Indian groups. The Rebellion reflected the heretofore traditional
rivalry between Indians and whites; its outcome marked the final defeat
of the Virginia Indians and the complete demise of some tribes. But in
the records of Bacon's Rebellion appears a new element which was to have
continuing influence in Indian adjustment to Europeans. By 1675 Indian-
white relations were no longer highly localized. The English began to
appreciate the need for greater unity among their scattered colonies—the
struggle of European countries to establish sovereignty over all of North
America had begun—and they recognized the value of the Indians as allies
rather than opponents in the design of empire.

The turmoil of international rivalry delayed the movement of settlement inland, and the development of the fur trade also promoted isolation
of the West. The fur traders strongly opposed pioneer settlement, in order
to protect the natural habitat of the beaver—and incidentally the status
quo of the Indians who engaged in the actual business of hunting and
trapping the animals. Thus circumstances combined to give the Indians
of the inland tribes a vital delay. From the beginning of contact, the
western natives had an opportunity to meet the white man on equal terms,
and they came to accept the presence of Europeans as a permanent and
in many ways a desirable phenomenon. They developed policies of negotiation, diplomacy, and warfare, and distinguished one European group from
another as ally or enemy as seemed most expedient to their own interests.
This was in sharp contrast to the coastal situation, where hostilities represented a more clear-cut contest between Indians and whites for supremacy.

The events of Bacon's Rebellion in Virginia contributed to the final
ruin of both the tidelands and the piedmont tribes, but the complications
of alliances of interest groups illustrate the changing situation of the frontier as it affected the Indians. Initially the Rebellion involved the border
settlers of Virginia and Maryland, and the Susquehanna, Seneca, and
"Doeg" Indians. The Susquehanna had enjoyed friendly relations with the
French as early as 1615, but, living on the Susquehanna River, they were
too far removed from French outposts to benefit by the association. To the
north were their traditional enemies, the Seneca, a member tribe of the
powerful league of the Iroquois. The Seneca, however, appeared as a threat
to the colonists of Maryland, and the settlers in that area therefore allied
themselves with the Susquehanna and supplied the tribe with arms. Later
Maryland, an English colony, arranged a pact of peace with the Seneca in
accordance with the general alliance of the Iroquois league with the English
at that time. The Susquehanna, nominally allied with the French, were left
without arms or nearby allies and were thus forced by the new alliance to
retreat from their homeland. In the face of armed action they took up

residence north of the Potomac among the Algonkian-speaking tribes, although they were themselves of Iroquoian linguistic affiliation. Shifts of tribal residence and inter-Indian campaigns involved Iroquoian tribes of the Carolina region as well as certain so-called Siouan groups such as the Tutelo and Occaneechi, who were enemies of the Seneca.

Meanwhile white settlement had penetrated west and north to the extent that skirmishes between whites and the Indians occurred. The memories of the uprisings of 1622 and 1644 had not died easily among the English, and when protection furnished by Governor Berkeley seemed inadequate, an unofficial campaign against the natives was initiated by the border settlers of the once competitive Virginia and Maryland. Although the causes of Bacon's Rebellion were also deeply rooted in internal disputes among the colonists, its results were catastrophic for the Virginia Indians. Bacon's followers showed no disposition to distinguish Indians as friends or enemies; they made indiscriminate war on all natives. After Bacon's forces had decimated the Susquehanna and Algonkians, they turned upon the Occaneechi, who had long been allied with the English as middlemen in the fur trade between the coastal settlements and the tribes located farther inland. The final action was against the Pamunkey, peacefully residing on lands secured to them by the treaty of 1646. The Pamunkey king had been killed some ten years after the treaty of 1646 while serving with the colonists against a presumed invasion of the colony by a group of strange Indians known as Richeharians. Thus his people were considered doubly wronged, for they were not only at peace with the colonists, but they had made common cause with the English against Indian enemies.

Peace was finally affirmed officially with the Virginia tribes in a treaty signed in 1677. However, the effects of the Rebellion had been devastating, and after their long history of war and defeat, the Indians of the tidelands and piedmont regions found it increasingly difficult to preserve their accustomed habits of existence. This was equally true of the Susquehanna and Algonkian tribes north of the Potomac.

Nevertheless, several tribes of the Powhatan Confederacy are represented today by groups preserving a sense of social distinctiveness, based largely on historical and racial origins rather than any cultural characteristics. These tribes are the Pamunkey, Rappahannock, Mattaponi, Chickahominy, and Nansemond. The story of their survival is uncertain in its details. Often it appeared that these tribes had been swept away by the rush of history, but each time after an interval the names reappeared on contemporary documents. For example, the signatory tribes of the Confederacy in the treaty of 1677 included the Pamunkey, Appomattoc, Weanoc, Nansemond, Nantaughtacund, and Portobacco—the last a collective term for the tribes of the Eastern Shore. Also signatory to the treaty were the Iroquoian-speaking tribes of the piedmont, the Nottaway and

Meherrin, as well as Powhatan's old enemies, the Monacan. Undoubtedly the Pamunkey, the largest tribe of the Confederacy, had temporarily subsumed the unlisted Chickahominy, Mattaponi, and Rappahannock.

In a similarly complex process of development, many of the piedmont tribes which were still extant in the latter seventeenth century regrouped permanently under different names. The Nottaway, Meherrin, and Monacan, for example, were signatory to the treaty of 1677, but only the Nottaway and Meherrin signed the Treaty of Albany in 1722. However, the Christanna were named in the 1722 treaty, and this group had come to include remnant Monacan and other piedmont tribes as well as recent migrants from the Algonkian, Iroquoian, and Siouan groups of North Carolina. Governor Spotswood of Virginia gathered these tribes together in 1715 and settled them at Fort Christanna near the Carolina border in southwestern Virginia.

The condition of the Indians toward the end of the seventeenth century is illustrated in many contemporary documents. A letter from the Reverend Mr. Clayton provides a detailed and well-organized summary. It is worth special attention for its factual data and as an illustration that both whites and Indians continued to view each other from their own culture's frame of logic, without any real understanding. Describing the populational degeneration which had resulted largely from disease, deprivation, and malnutrition, the letter states:

> This is very certain that the Indian inhabitants of Virginia are now very inconsiderable as to their numbers and seem insensibly to decay though they live under the English protection and have no violence offered them. They are undoubtedly no great breeders.

Clayton, like many white observers imbued with Christian concepts of proselytization, appeared surprised that one of the most striking retentions of native patterns was the cultural aspect of religion. He noted that special structures were still set aside for temples and that the shaman or *wichiost* enjoyed a degree of prestige which was secondary only to that accorded to their "King and to their great War-Captain." The retention of this prestige illustrates secular authority distinguished from the sacred sway of the *wichiost* and shows a continuity of concepts regarding social structure. The king remained the center of authority and continued to receive homage and tribute in the form of personal services performed by other members of the tribe. Apparently the ruling position was still hereditary within a line of descent recognized as that of the chief family. None of the records are clear on this point, for lines of chieftainship are confused in the documents by the indiscriminate use of such titles as "King" and "Queen." Hereditary leadership occasionally did devolve on women, and Archer noted such a case in 1607 when he described the Queen of Appomattoc, who held her rank by virtue of some now obscure genealogical reckoning. Leadership was inherited first by the surviving male siblings and then the female siblings, and evidently passed on to the next generation only with the death of all members of the preceding generation. In later years the Queen of Pamunkey was so designated by the whites because her husband, the hereditary Pamunkey ruler, had been killed in 1656 while fighting for the British. The settlers paid his widow the honor of the title, but it is questionable whether she exercised any traditional authority within her own group, although she was their recognized representative in dealings with the colonists.

The role of the ordinary Indian woman generally receives little notice in acculturational descriptions by untrained observers, and the Clayton letter is no exception. A brief sentence notes gardening, cooking, pottery making, and the weaving of mats. The domestic phase of Indian life was easily overlooked although it changed less than other aspects. Actually, the domesticity of the whites and Indians differed only slightly. Kingdoms might rise and fall, but housekeeping, child care, cooking, and garment making had to be regularly performed in both cultures. Like many European observers, Clayton describes hunting, a principal occupation of the Indian male, as "Exercise." This error probably contributed to an early and persistent stereotype of the Indian: the industrious, overburdened woman, the slothful, pleasure-seeking man. Like all stereotypes, it is worthy of examination and it is an especially interesting example of adjustment to change. The traditional division of labor was approximately equal, the men hunting, the women gardening. These two activities supplied the principal subsistence. The English depended on the hunt in the early stages of settlement, but as soon as it ceased to have great economic importance they reverted to the European tradition of categorizing it as sport. The Indians also had their tradition: both men and women considered agriculture to be an unmanly task. When game diminished and gardening became the primary productive activity, they found it extremely difficult to make appropriate changes in the socioeconomic role of the male.

Clayton's references to the material culture of the Indians may be augmented from many sources, as this was the most easily discerned aspect of Indian life. The natives frequently observed traditional habits of dress. They continued to use indigenous material such as deerskin for clothing, but they prized European textiles, being especially fond of linen goods and a heavy woolen cloth, called a "matchcoat," which they often used instead of fur or feather mantles. Certain changes in style, if not modesty, may be noted in the matter of dress. When the Queen of Appomattoc greeted the Europeans in 1607, she wore only a skirt and a great amount of jewelry, but "all ells was naked"; but the Queen of Pamunkey was clad in Indian finery from neck to ankles for an occasion of state in 1677.

Although the blue and white shell beads known as "wampum" probably originated as a currency through the trade with the New England tribes, they were manufactured in great quantities by Europeans for use in the fur trade and by 1687 figured as a quasi currency as far south as Virginia. The Indian shaman who also acted in the capacity of physician was paid by the natives in wampum as well as in skins and other commodities. When he treated English settlers, the *wichiost* usually received his remuneration in matchcoats or rum. Further details from Clayton's letter reveal that metal armaments, tools, and utensils were in common usage by the end of the century, although the bow and arrow and native pottery continued to be available.

From Clayton's observations and comparable data it is evident that Indian adjustment to European civilization in the late seventeenth century continued to take the form of resistance whenever there remained any possibility of retaining essential elements of the old culture. Specific items were accepted, as they fitted into existing patterns and represented elaboration or improvement of familiar features. In-group recognition of the danger posed for their traditional ways is illustrated in a fragment of folklore included in Clayton's account. There was supposedly an ancient prophecy, made long before the Europeans arrived, that "bearded men . . . should come and take away their country and that there should none of the original Indians be left within a certain number of years, I think it was an hundred and fifty." This rationalization of history is a recurrent myth found among many Indian groups. It helps to preserve a degree of dignity and pride by saying in effect, "We knew it all along, but we put up an admirable fight anyway."

The cultural disorganization noted in 1687 was to be a continuing process. The prophecy of destruction has now been fulfilled, to the extent that the Indians have ceased to exist as a culturally definable entity, although remnant groups maintain their social identities and tribal names. Throughout the seventeenth and eighteenth centuries the tribes which had temporarily resided with the Pamunkey wandered back to their original territories, leaving only the Pamunkey and part of the Mattaponi on lands secured to them by colonial treaties and guaranteed today by the state of Virginia. Traditional habits were generally abandoned as it became ever more difficult to exist in the white man's world. Eventually, the only effective economic system was that practiced by the surrounding Europeans; the Indians who were not located on reservations tended to settle in neighborhoods and acquire land on an individual basis. The destruction of the native social and religious mores, almost a predictable consequence of the disastrous wars and scattering of tribes, was virtually accomplished. A civil and religious structure which had been designed to accommodate the needs and activities of thirty tribes, almost nine thousand people, was impossibly cumbersome when the population had dwindled to one thousand people who were not in regular communication with one another and who were at any rate overwhelmingly occupied with the problem of sheer physical survival. The Indians in time found social and religious satisfaction in the traditions of their white neighbors; but they remained socially distinct from them.

Despite the loss of their own culture, many Indians remain aware of their historical origins. Beginning in 1908 with the Chickahominy, the various non-reservation natives of Virginia obtained official recognition as Indian tribes from the state government. In 1923 they formed an organization known as the "Powhatan Confederacy" and included the Nanticoke, recognized by Delaware as non-reservation Indians but otherwise not historically eligible for inclusion in the Confederacy. Showing Caucasoid and Negroid ancestry, the Nanticoke are the most racially heterogeneous of the modern confederated tribes, although a blending of racial characteristics may be seen to a lesser extent in the reservation Pamunkey and Mattaponi and the non-reservation Mattaponi, Rappahannock, Chickahominy, and Nansemond. In cultural terms the modern Virginia Indians retain little more of their heritage than tribal names and a sense of common origin. The value of Indian identity has been increased by the social isolation of dark-skinned peoples in American life, since Indians in contrast to other racial minorities have generally enjoyed a degree of prestige in the opinion of the dominant group. In the tidewater region this may well be due to the influence of socially prominent Virginians who trace their ancestry to Pocahontas; she was, after all, a "Princess."

The end result of European contact in the piedmont region presents a somewhat different picture. Along the western border of Virginia and in the adjoining regions there are well-defined groups who claim Indian descent but no longer recall any particular tribal affiliations. They are known locally as Ramps, Melungeons, Brown People, Issues, and other terms. In order to avoid the social disabilities of classification with Negroes, they cling to their unofficial classification as Indians and remain rooted in regions where their peculiar status is known. Some of these people may very well be descendants of the historic piedmont tribes of Virginia which vanished as identifiable tribal entities. Although much research remains to be done on this point, it is probable that their almost complete loss of identity, in contrast to the tidelands tribes, which at least recall their tribal origins, may be traced to the fact that they experienced disorganizing defeats at the hands of other Indians before the tidelands groups were ultimately conquered by the Europeans. The coastal Indians were in possession of European weapons at an earlier date and in all likelihood turned them against traditional enemies in the piedmont region before they found the need to use them primarily in forays against the white settlers. Thus the piedmont groups suffered a military disadvantage almost at the outset of European contact. By the time the whites penetrated to the piedmont region these tribes had already lost much of their former power. Furthermore, by the late seventeenth century they were also harassed by native enemies to the rear. Unlike the tribes further inland, the piedmont peoples did not have time to regroup effectively and take advantage of the fur trade as a means of survival by adaptation to the presence of whites. Throughout the latter part of the seventeenth century they were in the path of westward movement by the whites, northward migrations of dispossessed Carolina tribes, and southern invasions by the Seneca on warlike campaigns. Their only hope for survival was in inter-tribal mixture and intermarriage with racially alien populations, both Negro and white.

Although the Virginia Indians were utterly defeated by the close of the seventeenth century, the experience of that period laid the foundations for modern adjustment to the white man's culture. As a result of stubborn opposition to amalgamation, some tribes have survived into the mid-twentieth century as populational entities, although they have been unable to retain a distinctive culture. Their primary technique of adjustment to European civilization, at least as documented in the Virginia tidelands region, was, with few exceptions, one of rigid resistance to alien ways which held no particular attractions, except for disparate items. Their culture simply disintegrated under the strain of continued pressure placed upon it. In contrast, the tribes further inland, by their more flexible adaptation to Europeans, achieved a social and cultural continuity which is still impressive despite many material innovations from European and American civilization.

1.3

Concerted Action Among Workers

RICHARD B. MORRIS

In 1946 Richard Morris published his massive *Government and Labor in Early America*. More than twenty-five years later it remains the monumental study of free and bound labor in seventeenth- and eighteenth-century America. Drawing upon unpublished inferior court records, Morris sketched the mercantile structure of colonial America and vividly portrayed the legal and social position of artisans, laborers, and servants. A corrective to the then dominant view of the United States as a laissez-faire capitalist society from its inception, the full study showed clearly the shifting but still important role played by the state in the colonial economy. In this period, Morris argued, "both business and labor, considered government regulation the normal order." The following excerpt describes one aspect of labor's role in the mercantilist economy. Here again we see the importance of old world experience to any understanding of the new. British law governed the mercantile economy and the men who lived and worked under it could only act in ways that combined their old and new world experiences.

Richard B. Morris, *Government and Labor in Early America* (New York: Harper & Row, Publishers, 1965), pp. 136–201. Copyright Richard B. Morris. Reprinted, edited, and footnotes omitted by permission of the author.

The following books are suggested for further reading:

C. A. HERRICK, *White Servitude in Pennsylvania*, New York: Negro Universities Press, 1960.

MARCUS W. JERNEGAN, *Laboring and Dependent Classes in Colonial America*, New York: Frederick Ungar Publishing Co., Inc., 1960.

SAMUEL MCKEE, *Labor in Colonial New York*, New York: Columbia University Press, 1935.

ABBOT E. SMITH, *Colonists in Bondage*, Gloucester, Mass.: Peter Smith, 1965.

To act in concert or collectively to redress grievances both economic and political has been a deeply rooted tradition of American life. As a "nation of joiners" we have always utilized voluntary organizations, open or secret, formal or impromptu, permanent or temporary. While the resort to collective action has characterized every range of social and cultural activity, this study is confined to an analysis of instances of concerted action taken by the artisan and working classes, generally, in early American history prior to the rise of trade unions in relatively permanent form.

These economic combinations or associations of workers fall into distinct categories:

1. Combinations by master workers in certain trades to secure and maintain a monopoly of business operations and to restrain freedom of vocational choice. Against such monopoly combinations, whether of labor or of capital, those who favored freedom of trade and of occupational choice made increasing headway in the course of the eighteenth century.

2. Concerted action by workers (normally masters) in licensed trades to secure better fees or prices, customarily regulated by local authority. Such trades were regarded as invested with a public interest.

3. Concerted action by bound servants to secure a redress of grievances. Such action generally took the form of strikes, insurrectionary uprisings, or conspiracies to desert or break the contract of employment.

4. Combinations of free white workmen to resist encroachments on their trades by Negro artisans. Such action paralleled the efforts of artisan monopolists to exclude others from admission to their trades, but it was chiefly manifest in regions where Negro labor competition was especially keen.

5. Joint political action by workmen and employers in the Revolutionary years.

6. Combinations by journeymen workers to secure better working conditions —excessively rare prior to the American Revolution, but increasingly significant after that conflict had ended. . . .

COMBINATIONS TO MAINTAIN
CRAFT MONOPOLIES

Once the great emigration to Massachusetts got under way measures were adopted to preserve trade monopolies and to restrain nonresidents from entering the trades. These monopoly groups in the early colonial towns were patterned after the European craft guilds. Massachusetts for a time experimented also with the chartered company, following the English pattern. In 1644 shipbuilding was placed under the supervision of such a chartered company. Next followed the Boston shoemakers' guild, chartered in 1648. The Boston shoemakers had petitioned the court that, on account of the poor quality of shoes being sold in that town, they be formed into a company with power to regulate their calling within the town. This petition was opposed by the country shoemakers, who advanced, in a petition signed by six of their number, several reasons for their stand. Very few of the Boston shoemakers, they contended, were members "of Such a body in o'r [our] Native Country," and therefore inexperienced in guild management. According to the country shoemakers, the real trouble was not poor workmen, whom the Boston shoemakers wanted to suppress, but the poor quality of leather, which should be the subject of closer official inspection. Instead of conferring upon the Boston shoemakers exclusive jurisdiction over the industry, their opponents urged that the country shoemakers and those of Boston be given the privilege of examining the shoes made by the other group. If the shoes of either group were pronounced poor, the decision as to whether they were to be confiscated was to be put up to an impartial shoemaker. It was further urged that the Bostonians be denied the power "to hindre a free trade,"—that is, to keep country shoemakers from coming into the town. Unless that were done, either the country shoemakers would be ruined or forced to migrate to Boston to the detriment of other towns.

Notwithstanding these forceful arguments, a committee of the General Court recommended that a charter be granted to the Boston shoemakers; the General Court adopted the recommendation. The charter conferred self-government upon the guild, including the right to elect their own officers, to pass regulations for their trade subject to the approval of the Assistants or the county court, to affix penalties for breach thereof and to levy fines by distress after a trial before the masters and wardens of the guild. In addition, it gave the craftsmen a monopoly and provided that the county court, on complaint of the masters and wardens, should have the power to "suppresse" shoemakers not approved by the guild. It is most significant that the authorities included a clause prohibiting unlawful combinations to raise the price of shoes, boots, or wages and expressly denying shoemakers the right to refuse to make shoes for a customer of the leather he provided and at a reasonable rate. Finally, the charter was to be in force for three years only. At the same session the General Court granted an identical charter to the coopers of Boston and Charlestown. In neither case does it appear that the charters were renewed at the end of the three-year period. These charters set up guild constitutions based on the contemporary English pattern, in which the administrative functions were in the hands of the masters and wardens. The oligarchical type of control established in the two Massachusetts charters was actually under heavy attack in England at that time, when the cleavage between wage earners and employers was more clearly marked than in the American colonies during the period of the Puritan Revolution. These guilds did not last long enough in Massachusetts for the rank and file of the membership to resent the power of the governing body. In addition to the coopers and shoemakers, Edward Johnson in his *Wonder-Working Providence* implied that the tanners also enjoyed virtual guild powers to determine standards and prices—their products being double the prices obtaining in England at that time—and suggests that other crafts were also organized, although, in the absence of records, it is not possible to pursue his leads. A quarter century after the grant of charters to the shoemakers and coopers the hatters of Massachusetts Bay petitioned for similar privileges, but were refused until they could show that they could produce as good hats priced as cheaply as those imported.

The guild organization of master craftsmen was exceedingly rare in other colonies save for licensed trades clothed with a public interest. In the colony of New York evidence has been uncovered pointing to an organization of weavers in the Borough Town of Westchester. The mayor's court minutes of that town have the following entry for July, 1702:

> Wm Bennett Weaver makes his Application to this Court to be Admitted a freeman of the Guild of the Weavers in this Corporation. The Mayr and Alderman hauing heard a good Character of the said Wm Benet and that he is a man of Honest Life and Conversation and followes his trade of a plain Weaver do Admitt the s'd Wm Bennett to be a freeman in said Corporation and to have the Rights and Libertyes as any free man in any the like Corporations within her Majesties Realm of England.

Apart from this cryptic entry, no further record has been found of this, the only known weavers' guild in colonial America.

Somewhat more craft guild activity was found in the province of Pennsylvania. The Philadelphia Common Council granted the petitions of the cordwainers and tailors for corporate privileges to regulate their crafts, and formulated a policy of chartering other craft guilds if the artisans concerned desired "the better to serve the Publick in their Respective Capacities."

The most important of these guilds or combinations of artisans in Philadelphia was the Carpenters' Company, formed in 1724 "for the purpose of obtaining instruction in the science of architecture, and assisting such of their members as should by accident be in need of support," or the widows and minor children of the members. In order to qualify for membership one must have been a master for six years. The early members appear to have been master architects and builders like James Portius and Edmund Wooley. The admission fee was 30*s.*, and restrictions imposed upon membership led to the formation of a rival association known as "The Second Carpenters' Company," which, after a few years of separate existence, merged with the older society. When, in 1769, the admission fee was raised to £4, "The Friendship Carpenters' Company" was established which admitted members for an inconsequential fee of 5*s.* But in 1785 members of the rival association were admitted into the parent society.

The most significant activity of the company was the establishing of a "Book of Prices" for both employers and workmen with the avowed object of assuring the latter "a fair recompense for their labour and the owner . . . the worth of his money." The minutes of the company from 1724 to 1763 have unfortunately been lost, but the extant minutes beginning with the latter year indicate that the appointment of a standing committee to set prices for carpenters' work to be laid before the whole company for their approval was regularly carried out. The bylaws of the company stated the function of the committee on the book of prices to be "to fix a price on all new-fashioned Carpenter work, that may be introduced from time to time; and further to equalize such of the prices as may be requested, and to enter the same in the manuscript book to be kept by them in the Hall for that purpose for the use of the members of the Company," who were permitted to make copies. Furthermore, the committee was charged with the settlement of any differences arising in the valuation of carpenter's work, both between carpenters and their employers or between members of the company. Their decision as respects the price of such work was to be binding on the parties. Any member of the company desirous of evaluating carpenter's work who had been a member for at least five years was eligible to receive a certificate from the committee under the seal of the company provided that the applicant made oath or affirmation before an alderman or justice of the peace that he would "well and truly measure and value Carpenter work, agreeably to the standard Book of Prices of this Company, to the best of his judgment and ability, always having special regard to the quality of the work." Any member measuring work without such certificate was liable to be fined ten dollars for the first offense and to be expelled for the second. Fines were also imposed upon members for showing the book of prices to nonmembers. It is therefore apparent that the publication of these price lists was not a policy of the company in the early period.

In emulation of the Philadelphia Carpenters' Company, associations of master carpenters in other towns in the colonies began in the course of the eighteenth century to establish price scales, many of which were published. In the post-Revolutionary period it was quite customary for carpenters to issue detailed schedules of prices. In the *Rules for House-Carpenters' Work in the Town of Providence,* issued in that city in 1796, there is an introductory note to this effect:

> The Committee appointed in February, 1796, to revise the rules of carpenters' work have found upon examination that the former rules begun in the year 1750 and continued down to the present date, were calculated upon a scale of five shillings per day; and have made the following calculations upon the same principles.

In 1800 the Boston carpenters issued a book of prices which was a revision of rules adopted in that town in 1774. In an introductory statement the committee which drew up the rules discussed the principles which guided them and added:

> Upon these principles *"the Carpenters rules of work in the Town of Boston"* were formed and published in the year 1774; and several have held them up as a direction at this day, not considering that they were calculated upon a scale which bears no proportion to the price of other labor *now,* and which is by no means an equivalent compensation for the service, in reference to the raised price of the necessaries of life; and that, not only the low rate at which they were cast render them a very incompetent guide at present, but that they are besides greatly defective in not specifying one quarter part of the work now in demand. Wherefore, the Carpenters of the Town have met at sundry times to consider the propriety of forming new arrangements, and Rules, more accurate and more complete, and calculated on a scale better adjusted to the means of an honest livelihood in an equitable reward to faithful industry. They chose, accordingly, a large and respectable committee, out of their number, to form such Rules; which, being reported and unanimously approved by the whole body, they now publish for the service of the Craft,—expecting that all work will be measured by them, and executed in the best possible manner.

At a meeting of the Boston Carpenters at Mareau's Hall, August 21, 1800, it was voted that the names of the committee of twenty-one who drew up the rules be published in the book. These rules are very detailed, and lay down a schedule of prices per item rather than per diem. For example, the price schedule covers such work as framing floors of all kinds, side and ends, and roofs, laying rough boarding, putting up window frames, sashes, clapboarding, and laying shingles (per square), building stairs, wainscoting, dadoing rooms and stairs. This volume is representative of a considerable number of publications reproducing price scales agreed upon by master carpenter organizations going back as far as 1790 and continuing well down into the middle of the nineteenth century. It is apparent from the extensive schedules that were published that master house carpenters, along with cabinet- and chair-makers, had begun to organize by the eve of the Revolution, and that in some cases these organizations included journeymen or were supplemented by journeymen's organizations. . . .

The craft guilds did not take root in the South. While it is true that the incorporated trades of London were the chief subscribers to the Virginia Company venture, the guilds of mercers, grocers, fishmongers, merchant tailors, ironmongers, and clothworkers all supporting the colonization program, there is no evidence of guilds of master workmen in seventeenth-century Virginia. The merchant guilds provided for in the act of 1705 "for establishing ports and towns" appear to have been designed more as an instrument of government than as monopoly combinations.

In medieval England local craftsmen were protected from nonresidents entering the crafts in their towns. In fact, restrictions became more onerous in the course of time. As Salzman points out, the traditional attitude of the Englishman toward a stranger had always been to "heave half a brick at him." In the early colonial period the town authorities protected local workmen from interlopers. When they failed to do so, local workers took concerted action for their own protection. This medieval principle of monopolistic exclusiveness found expression in regulations of colonial towns limiting admission to the crafts to those who enjoyed the freedom of the town. Boston, for instance, made the completion of a term of apprenticeship a prerequisite to opening up a shop and limited the trades and crafts to those who had been admitted as inhabitants. During the early years the apprenticeship requirement appears to have been strictly enforced.

In 1675 a group of ship carpenters who had ridden an interloper out of Boston on a rail because he had worked in the yard without having served his full seven years' apprenticeship were fined five shillings apiece payable to the government and a like amount to the victim. John Roberts and the eight other defendants admitted the charge of having forcibly carried John Langworthy "upon a pole and by violence" from the north end of Boston to the town dock. This "occasioned a great tumult of people, meeting there with the Constable who did rescue him." The defendants justified their conduct on the ground that "hee was an interloper and had never served his time to the trade of a Ship carpenter and now came to work in theire yard and they understood such things were usuall in England."

Down through the colonial period artisans and laborers were expected to get permission from the Boston town authorities before plying their trades. Such permission was at times withheld, and violators of the town ordinance fined. In line with this policy of maintaining intact the craft and trade monopolies was the general restriction on the movements of strangers. Among those warned to depart the town were numerous laborers and artisans. In addition to the competitive motive, the authorities also wished to make reasonably certain that strangers would not be a charge upon the town. By the mid-eighteenth century the population trend which favored the growth of other colonial towns at the expense of Boston and the increase of a laissez faire spirit in that town were signalized by a noticeable decline in the number of prohibitions to exercise trades and in "warnings out."

It seems likely that in Boston as well as in other colonial towns the artisan, having served an apprenticeship and having been admitted as a freeman, could and did at times practice more than one craft or transfer to other crafts or trades if he wished. A Boston pamphlet of 1714 protested against the proposed incorporation of the town, objecting to "paying for our Freedom, that was Freeborn and in bondage to no man," and also to the possibility that shopkeepers and artisans who were undertaking several trades would have to give up the practice.

In New York the local monopoly of trades and handicrafts stemmed directly from the "burgher-right," a privilege of the inhabitants of New Amsterdam, which, after the English conquest, was carried over into the freemanship. However the cost of purchasing the freedom was nominal, and the city followed a liberal policy in admitting outsiders, both skilled and unskilled workmen. As a matter of fact, for many years prior to the Revolution the authorities admitted without cost those unable to pay the freedom dues. As the price of freemanship was low in relation to the relatively high wage scale of New York's craftsmen, it is clear that the freemanship opened the polls to all classes of citizens, including a good proportion of artisans and laborers.

Nevertheless, despite the declining legal significance of the freemanship on the eve of the Revolution, at times it was still essential for a workman who wished to secure work in New York to establish the fact that he had been an inhabitant of the city for some time prior to his application. This is the clear implication of the following advertisement in the *New-York Gazette or Weekly Post-Boy* for May 8, 1766 (Supplement):

A Large quantity of good well drest spinning Flax is wanted for the Factory in New-York: All Persons who have such to dispose of, at reasonable rate, by applying to Obadiah Wells, in Mulbery-Street, near the French Water, may have ready Money for it. N.B. None but the best sort will have the preference. Also the spinners in New-York, are hereby notified, that due Attendance will be given, every Tuesday, Thursday, and Saturday, in the Afternoon, to give out Flax and receive in Yarn; by said Wells, and to prevent Trouble, no Person who has not been an Inhabitant in this City ever since May last, will be admitted as a Spinner in the Factory. Also the said Wells, still continues receiving and selling in the Market, all sorts of Country Manufactories, such as Linens and Woollen Cloth, Stockings, etc. etc. at five per cent for Sales and Remittances.

While the principal complaints against interlopers came from the licensed trades, other groups sought protection well along into the eighteenth century, by which time laissez faire trends resulted in a greater degree of freedom of occupational choice. The General Court of Assize, sitting in New York in 1675, found Cornelius Steenwyck and six others guilty of having engaged in "divers Trades and occupations," "being aliens . . . contrary to the several Statute Lawes in such cases enacted." Their goods and chattels were accordingly forfeited to the crown.

In 1747 a large number of building-trades workers petitioned Governor George Clinton against the encroachments of interlopers from the Jerseys who came into the city "in Several numerous Companys," exercising the trades of carpenter, bricklayer, etc. "after the laying of our Taxes yearly." By offering their services at drastically lower wages (for example, at a rate per job or per specific article of workmanship of £20 or £30 less "than has been agreed for by us") and by bringing their own nails and building materials from other provinces, the outsiders constituted a serious threat to local labor. Implied in this petition is the existence of a combination of carpenters, bricklayers, and kindred workers to set a scale of wages or prices. The existence of such a combination would, aside from the concerted actions of licensed guilds such as the carmen, porters, butchers, and bakers, represent what was probably the first temporary labor union in the history of the city. Certainly the public authorities gave not the slightest encouragement to such activities, but viewed this evidence of industrial solidarity with marked suspicion. The petition was submitted to rigid scrutiny. The authorities noted that, of the ninety-nine signatures on the petition, two of the workers had "signed twice," that three names were "feigned," that one signature represented a non-existent person, another a "highlander" and accordingly suspect, that two were mere "labourers," and that one was actually a "cordwainer," and clearly out of place in the building trades. Less attention, however, was devoted to the economic issues raised by the carpenters and allied workers. The governor referred the petition to a committee, which advised the petitioners to seek their remedy under the city charter, which provided that strangers who exercised a trade in the city and failed to take up their freedom could be fined five pounds. The committee's further observation betrayed a somewhat patronizing class bias:

> Secondly, The Council observe there are about Ninety nine Names to this Petition. That the Bulk of the persons who may be supposed to have subscribed their Names are obscure people altogether unknown to us in person and name, excepting very few of them. If they are Freemen and there be at this time any real cause for such complaint, they must be ignorant and forgetful of the Obligations of the Oath of a Freeman of this City which is "The Franchise and Customs thereof to maintain and the City to keep harmless in that which in there is" and therefore the Council are of Opinion it becomes the Duty of every Freeman when the privileges of the Citizens are invaded (to use the words of the petition) and who is apprized thereof to warn the Mayor that the Remedy given by Charter may be applyed.

In 1769 Thomas Hardenbrook and other house carpenters, by petition to the common council, similarly complained against unfair competition of country carpenters coming to the city in the summer season. The council courteously referred the matter to a committee, and then let it die. But at least the applicants were spared a lecture on their civic duty.

The ship carpenters also endeavored to confine their occupation to inhabitants. Jeffrey Amherst wrote to Mayor John Cruger on August 10, 1763, that he was fitting out some transports for immediate service and that the carpenters employed on them would not venture to work without a license from the mayor. He went on to say: "I should be glad you would give them Permission, as it is of real consequence to the King's Service that those Vessels are got ready by the utmost expedition."

In 1784 a group of ship carpenters complained to the public authorities

> that George Gar shipwright lately (about sixteen or eighteen Months) from Scotland carries on his business in a manner hurtful to the Petitioners and their Brother Shipwrights: And that as the said George is not a Freeman but an Alien they conceive he is not entitled to carry on the said Busines therefore they pray that he may [be] fined and prevented for the future from carrying on the said Business, as the Charter directs.

The master workmen of Philadelphia made similar strenuous efforts to maintain the exclusive privileges to ply their trades. Shortly after the incorporation of Philadelphia the mayor and Common Council issued an ordinance forbidding nonfreemen from keeping "Open Shops, or to be master workmen." Many of the immigrants after 1716 were regarded by the town craftsmen as "not quallify'd to Exercise thear Trades." Nevertheless, the bars to the freemanship were let down early.

In general, the effect of these local regulations was to curb freedom of occupational choice until well along into the eighteenth century, by which time the authorities appeared reluctant to protect local craftsmen against transient workers and were lax in enforcing apprenticeship requirements. These laissez faire trends parallel a similar trend in contemporary England, where, despite the rise of combinations formed primarily to maintain the earlier restrictions against interlopers, the authorities encouraged the rise of a free labor market and large-scale industry.

The general restrictions against admission to the crafts were implemented by certain European guild notions about the strict separation of related trades. Edward Johnson in his *Wonder Working Providence* states that in Massachusetts Bay carpenters, joiners, glaziers, and painters "follow their trades only," implying such strict specialization had been achieved by the time he was writing. The leather industry furnished the most notable example of rigid separation of crafts. Throughout the colonies legislation was enacted time after time strictly separating the various branches of that industry. Precedent for such legislation was a series of English statutes forbidding tanners from working as shoemakers or shoemakers as tanners, keeping the crafts of tanner and currier strictly separate, and denying to both curriers and cordwainers the right to poach on the territory of the other. By the early seventeenth century these irksome restrictions were being circumvented in England, but the colonists persisted for a long time thereafter in the attempt to maintain tanning, currying, and shoemaking as separate trades. Certain towns, notable among them New Haven, restricted tanners to those who were licensed by the authorities, generally after having served a term of apprenticeship in that craft. But with the spread of laissez faire trends in eighteenth-century New England rigid craft differences were slowly eliminated. Attempts were made in Massachusetts in the years 1731 and 1732 to renew the regulations of the previous century preventing butchers, curriers, and shoemakers from pursuing the tanners' "mystery," but without success. However, as late as 1784 a Great Barrington shoemaker was prosecuted in the Berkshire court for serving as a tanner as well as a shoemaker and for tanning one hundred hides in the course of a year. . . .

CONCERTED ACTION BY WORKERS
IN LICENSED TRADES

Certain trades or occupations were in the colonial period conceived as being clothed with a public interest. They were licensed and regulated as are public utilities at the present day. The fees which they might command for their services were regulated by the town authorities and their monopolistic privileges were in some cases maintained for a considerable time after the colonial period had ended. The principal trades enjoying such monopolistic privileges were the porters, carters, butchers, and bakers, although other groups sought recognition as guilds. The monopoly trades were accustomed from earliest times to acting in concert by way of petition or even to striking to enforce their demands for higher wages or fees for services, for higher prices for their products, or to bar interlopers from working in their trades. Requirements of space have limited illustrations of such concerted action to New York City, although a few instances are also cited from other leading colonial towns, where franchised groups adopted parallel techniques of collective action.

Porters and Carmen

Going back to the Dutch period and continuing down through colonial times, the authorities of New Amsterdam and New York specifically designated the weighhouse and beer porters and laborers at the public scales, limited their number, and allowed vacancies to be filled only by express permission. In November, 1662, at the request of Joost Goderis, foreman of the porters at the weighhouse, the burgomasters decreed that the porters should each pay eight stivers weekly into a common fund established for the benefit of such of their group as were taken ill. Those "unwilling" were to be assessed double. This is probably the earliest instance of a friendly society plan in any of the colonies along the Atlantic seaboard. The carters were likewise given a franchise in this period, and those engaged in public carting were limited to the "appointed carmen."

Both groups employed concerted action to better their working conditions. In 1657 the porters refused to carry salt on the ground that they had never been required to do so in the past. In 1674 the mayor's court acted upon a petition of the corn and wine porters, and ordered that brewers, bakers, and others refrain from employing any but the corn porters or their own servants in carrying their products. In 1685 the porters petitioned that a committee be appointed as nominated by them to investigate regulations and rates prevailing in their guild. When they appeared before the common council a few months later and refused to comply with the regulations concerning the cording of wood, they were dismissed from the service. At the beginning of the following year, the council, acting upon recommendations of a committee of two, neither of whom was on the list of nominees sent up by the porters, approved a new schedule of rates, which apparently was an increase over the fees prevailing.

More than once the carters resorted to a threat to stop work and on some occasions actually did go out on strike. At the time of the Dutch reoccupation of the town they complained to the court "that there were some who intruded in that employment," and upon their departure sold their carts, horses, and privileges to cart to nonlicensed carters; in addition, they charged that certain boys were also engaged in trucking. The court decreed that these boys were not to "ride Cart any more." In 1674 they were complained of for unwillingness "to ride timber, stone and other materials for the city and public service." The court decreed that upon "their first refusal or exhibition of unwillingness, their horses" should "be immediately untackled, and they be deprived of their places as carters." What would seem to have been the first criminal prosecution for a "strike" occurred in New York City in 1677. The prosecution appears to have been founded on the idea of contempt rather than conspiracy. The common council dismissed twelve carmen, or truckmen, "for not obeying the Command and Doing their Dutyes as becomes them in their Places," and, to quote the record,

> for Such their contempt fyne either and every of them, three shillings a peece or els to carry fifteen Loads apeece to the Wharf of the Said Citty. And the said Persons being called into Cort and hearing their Discharge read unto them, They either and every of them for himself prayed to be admitted and that they would Submitt to the Judgmt of the Cort and Submitt to such Condicons as the Cort should order and direct, Upon their Admittance and for the Fees of their doeing and performing their Dutyes for the Citties buisines.

Upon submission, the court admitted them to their old places at the same rates and required them to carry the same loads on pain of losing their places and of further prosecutions for contempt.

Again in 1684 fifteen carmen went on strike and refused "to Obey, Observe and follow the Laws and Orders" of the city relating to their guild. They were "Suspended and Discharged from being any Longer Carmen" by the common council, which issued a proclamation giving "free Liberty and Lycence" to all except the discharged strikers and slaves "to Serve for Hyre or wages as Carrmen." On acknowledging their fault and paying a fine of 6s., three out of the fifteen carters were readmitted. The justification for this punishment probably rested upon their contempt of authority rather than upon their conspiracy.

In the post-Revolutionary period the carters still sought to maintain their monopoly intact. In 1785 they petitioned the council against the practice of farmers taking up temporary residence in the city during the summer season and following the carters' trade, returning to their farms later in the year. The council was stirred by the plea that the number of carters greatly exceeded the demand, "insomuch that none of them can support their Families thereby," and accordingly resolved that no addition to the number be authorized and that those who left the city with their families to reside in the country during the winter should be "deemed to have forfeited their licenses." When it appeared in 1797 that the carmen were charging extortionate fees and in many cases operating without licenses, the city authorities revoked all licenses and reorganized the carters into companies of 49, each under the supervision of a foreman.

Coopers

In 1675 the coopers of South and East Hampton requested that coopers who were not inhabitants of the Hamptons or had not served their time as apprentices be forbidden to work there. During the winter Boston coopers, who had paid neither town nor county taxes, came to the Hamptons and worked at their trade; but the Hampton coopers in turn were not accorded reciprocal privileges in Boston. The General Court of Assize ordered "that noe Cooper Shall bee admitted to make Cask without the Consent of the Magistrates and Officers of the Respective Townes."

The prosecution in 1680 of the coopers' combination was the first in the history of New York City to rest clearly on grounds of criminal combination. The coopers, twenty-two in number, "subscribed a paper of combination" not to sell casks except in accordance with rates established by themselves under penalty of 50s. to the poor. The text of the agreement reads:

> ARTICKLES OF AGREEMENT Made By and Beetwixt Wee, the Coopers in this Citty Underwritten, Doe Agree upon the Rate and Prizes of Caske that Is to Say, for euery Dry half Barll one shilling Six Pence, for euery titte Barll For Beefe or porke Three Shillings; And Wee, the Vnder Written, Doe Joyntly and Seaverally Bind ourselfes, that for Euery one that shall sell any cask Beefore mentioned under the Rate or prizes aboue Sd., that for euery Such Default Fiuety Shillinges he or they shall pay for the vse of the poore, as Wittnes our hands, this 17th Day of December, 1679.

When summoned before the governor's council they acknowledged their subscription, but denied any "ill intent." One cooper testified that the paper was written at Peter Stevenson's home, and another that a seaman, the brother of the cooper Crooke, had drafted it. The court declared the agreement null and void and fined all the subscribers 50s. "to the Church or Pious uses." Those in public employment were dismissed. Two of their number, Richard Ellyot and Andries Brestee, were in addition barred from acting as packers or cullers in the future. A combination such as this for the maintenance of prices was indubitably illegal by that time in English law. . . .

Bakers

Of all the licensed groups of master workers or producers the bakers were most consistently subjected to official regulation in colonial towns. Such regulation generally took the form of setting the assize of bread. Collective action by master bakers to adjust the assize in their own interest was a most common occurrence in the colonies. Relations between the public authorities and the bakers were frequently tense, and at times culminated in actual strikes of master workers. The bakers of Boston on numerous occasions petitioned for relief from the assize. When one of the Boston bakers attempted to undersell his competitors in 1722, the others retaliated by offering to meet his price with a better quality loaf—evidence of a price-quality combination on their part.

In New Netherland after 1656 the bakers were in many respects a licensed guild—a status which they continued to enjoy after the English occupied the town. A good deal of self-regulation was practiced in the bakers' guild, which supervised quality and recommended eligible new masters to the council.

A favorite technique of the New York bakers was to stop baking bread when the prices were not satisfactory from their point of view. Twice in 1659 the bakers went on strike, winning from the burgomasters on each occasion a favorable adjustment of the assize. In 1661 the bakers appear to have been fined for refusal to bake and to have been specifically ordered to bake good bread on pain of not being allowed to bake for one year and six weeks after it had appeared to the court that there was economic justification at that time for such a work stoppage. However, shortly thereafter the authorities were persuaded by representatives of the bakers to modify the price schedule in their favor, which they again did two years later. The bakers were equally successful in prosecuting their petitions for higher prices before the English authorities. Probably in order to forestall a strike of bakers the court of general sessions in 1696 ordered that "all Bakers within this City doe keep bread in their shops that the Inhabitants be supplyed accordingly."

Of these instances of concerted action, the combination of bakers in 1741 is the most notable. The *New-York Weekly Journal,* April 20, 1741, assigned the following item to an inconspicuous portion of the sheet: "Last Week there was a general Combination of the Bakers not to Bake, because Wheat is at a high price, which occasioned some Disturbance, and reduced some, notwithstanding their Riches, to a sudden want of Bread." The issue of law which resulted was uncovered by Golden, of counsel for the defense in *People v. Melvin* (the *New York Cordwainers' Case*), who, in 1809, described the incident to the court of general sessions:

I have had an opportunity of examining the records of the criminal proceedings of our tribunals for a great number of years back. I have found an information which was preferred in the year 1741, against certain bakers, for combining not to bake bread but on certain terms. This indictment, however, concludes contrary to the form of the statutes. And it appears that no judgment was ever rendered upon it, so that it cannot be appealed to as an authority on either side; or if it is in favour of either, it must be the defendants, because it appears that the crime there charged was laid as an offence against some statutes, and not as an offence at common law.

Emmet, special counsel for the prosecution, referred to this as

an information against journeymen bakers for a conspiracy not to bake till their wages were raised. On this they were tried and convicted before the revolution; but, as the counsel says, it does not appear that any sentence was ever passed, from which he concludes that judgment was arrested. This undoubtedly is a *non sequitur*. The criminal may have become penitent, and the object of the prosecution having been obtained, judgment may never have been moved for; besides, it is well known that those records have been in such confusion that no one can tell what has happened in almost any case. But if judgment was arrested, let me point out the fault in the information on which it may have happened. It concludes against the form of the statute, whereas it should have concluded at common law, even if there had been a colonial statute regulating that subject, which does not appear. . . . On account of this defect, perhaps, judgment was never had; but the learned counsel, by relying on this record, admits that his clients' case is similar to that of the bakers; and contends that such a combination on their part is not indictable.

The specious logic of the prosecution is of little help in determining why a conviction was not obtained. Colden's description of the information is in terms general enough to cover the strike of master bakers for higher prices recorded in the *New-York Weekly Journal*. On the other hand, there is no evidence to support Emmet's view that the case involved a strike of journeymen bakers for higher wages. The minutes of the court of general sessions contain no reference to this prosecution; those of the Supreme Court are missing for the year 1741; and the mayor's court minutes ignore the incident. No papers relating to the 1741 case are available today. The parchment information was doubtless removed from an old bundle of papers of that year by Colden in the course of his investigations and appended to the papers in the *New York Cordwainers' Case* by way of exhibit; but unfortunately the papers in the latter case are also missing. Nevertheless, the absence of the information and other papers does not preclude speculation, however idle, as to the cause for prosecuting the bakers for criminal conspiracy.

The community which received news of the bakers' combination was already in the grip of a mass hysteria which, with the possible exception of the New England witchcraft episode and the Charleston slave riots of 1739, was unrivaled in colonial history. For many weeks fires, believed to have been of incendiary origin, laid waste a good part of the lower city. Rumors of a plot of Negro slaves to burn the city gained widespread acceptance. The reckless stories of informers added to the consternation. The very same issue of the *New-York Weekly Journal* that carried the story of the bakers' combination published a proclamation by Governor George Clarke offering a reward of £100 for information leading to the conviction of anyone who set the fires which had caused destruction of property in the lower part of the island. The militia was called out. Panic-stricken souls fled with their belongings to the refuge of the Bowery or Harlem. The rest awaited the impending insurrection. During the spring months many Negroes were convicted of seditious conspiracy on highly dubious evidence and burned at the stake; and the panic was not allayed until summer.

To add to the general feeling of unrest, reports were filtering into the colony detailing the progress of the campaign against the Spaniards and vague uneasiness was felt as to the possibility of a naval attack upon the city. Wartime conditions were responsible for skyrocketing commodity prices. Wheat was at the highest level for over a generation, and the price of bread in the provision colonies was up 50 per cent over the previous year. The publication in the May 4th issue of the *Journal* of the drastic action taken a few months earlier by the court of sessions of Edinburgh to lower prices did not inspire the provincial authorities to similar action. It does show, however, that the colonies were aware of the crisis that arose in the mother country in the preceding year, when wheat prices soared to prohibitive figures and rioting broke out in the North of England and in Wales, especially in the coal fields. These incidents were fresh in the minds of the members of the common council when on April 17 they petitioned the governor and council to prohibit the exportation of wheat from the province; but the council, impressed by the point of view of the back country wheat growers, refused to take the needed action. Living in dread of arson and insurrection, strained by the stresses of war, and facing the prospect of an early famine, the population would not be expected to view with equanimity a combination in restraint of trade involving basic necessities of life, even though such combinations were not entirely unfamiliar. It is not difficult to understand, therefore, why the resolve of bakers not to bake until the city authorities raised the price of bread should, under the circumstances, have been prosecuted as a criminal conspiracy. The fact that no conviction was obtained is surprising in view of the hysterical tension which prevailed in the spring of 1741.

Precedents existed in English law for prosecuting criminally a combination of producers to raise the prices of necessities. The act of 27 Edw. III, st. 2, c. 3, against regrators, and of 37 Edw. III, c. 5, against engrossers, and more directly the act of 2 and 3 Edw. VI, c. 15, which was aimed primarily at combinations to keep up prices charged to consumers, were applicable in such a situation. There were a number of prosecutions under some one of these statutes.

Other remonstrances on the part of the New York and Albany bakers against the prevailing price schedule are on record following the short-lived strike of 1741. In the post-Revolutionary period, when collective action by handicraftsmen was of far more frequent occurrence, the bakers continued to act in concert as a group to advance their economic interests, requesting both price raises and the elimination of unlicensed competitors. They actually proposed, without success, that price regulation be entrusted to the bakers' "Society." As late as 1801 the master bakers ordered a stoppage of work in protest against the assize, an action reminiscent of the hectic crisis of 1741. In 1801 the assize was finally discontinued in New York City. The tactics adopted by the packers during the second World War in protesting against the proposals for subsidies on food products points the moral that even in our own generation food processors are prone to resort to the "strike" or to curtailment of production when they are not satisfied with the regulated price. . . .

CONCERTED ACTION BY BOUND SERVANTS

One type of collective action which had no parallel in contemporary Britain was the participation by bound servants in conspiracies to run away and entice others to join in flight, occasionally encouraging Negro slaves to participate by violent means and for illegal ends. This type of concerted action was largely confined to the Southern colonies.

Prosecutions for conspiracies to run away from service or to entice servants from their masters go back to the early history of Maryland. One instance may be cited from the Provincial Court records of 1657. Robert Chessick, who had been captured and returned home after a runaway attempt, persuaded a group of servants of several different masters to "run away with him to the Sweades." About a dozen were implicated in the plot. Chessick, their leader, had been overheard to "Swear a Great Oath" that "If they had not better Store of Victualls, he would not Stay five days with his Master." They seized a boat from a master named Osbourne and took along a goodly supply of arms. Chessick's avowed intent was to use the arms in case anyone attempted to intercept them. One of the runaways was unaccountably lost. The rest were brought back, prosecuted, and sentenced by the court, which found "that there was a Conspiracie amongst the said Examins to run away and to steale and Carry with them Gunns powder Shott and Provision and Mr. Osburne's boat." Robert Chessick was found to have been not only "one of the Chief Acters in this late designe to endeavour his and the rest their running away, but hath formerly been the Chief Instigator and Actor in a former running away and stealing and carrying with him (and the rest that then run away) Guns powder shott, a boat and Provisions." He was sentenced to receive thirty lashes on the bare back with a whip, enjoined not to depart from his master's plantation without leave, and to civil and orderly behavior "upon pain of farther Censure." Corporal punishment was also meted out to the other culprits.

When the Maryland servant chose not to run away but instead went on strike in protest against working conditions he was subject to criminal prosecution. In 1663 Richard Preston petitioned the governor and council sitting as a Provincial Court that his servants did "peremptorily and positively refuse to goe and doe their ordinary labor," and declared "that if they had not flesh they would not worke." Preston reported that he told them that he had no meat to give them. He was called away from the plantation that day and, on his return, learned that the servants had not been at work in his absence. He charged that for the most part they had not been lacking in meat since the tobacco crop was in, and were given meat two or three times a week. They continued in their "obstinate rebellious condition," even though Preston provided them with sugar, fish, oil, and vinegar. Hence, he addressed himself to the court, but agreed that if they would be content with such provisions as he could provide, he was willing that all further proceedings be dropped. He reported an offer of a note under his hand "for three or Foure of them to take my Boate to spend a weekes time or more, to see, if they could buy any provision of flesh, or any thing else, and I would pay for it, though never soe deare bought." But as they remained on strike, he asked the court to censure them "according to equity and their demeritts . . . as shall be iudged equall for such peruerse servants; Least a worse euill by their example should ensue by encouraging other servants to doe the like."

John Smith, Richard Gibbs, Samuel Copley, Samuel Styles, Henry Gorslett, and Thomas Broxam, all servants of Preston, petitioned the court by way of answer that Preston did not allow them "sufficient Provisions for the inablem't to our worke, but streightens us soe far that wee are bought soe weake, wee are not able to performe the imploym'ts hee puts us uppon. Wee desire but soe much as is sufficient, but hee will allow us nothing but Beanes and Bread." They, in turn, requested the court to see that their wants were relieved by their master.

After considering the petitions and examining the servants in person, the court chose to take a serious view of the proceedings and sentenced all six to be whipped with thirty lashes each. The two "mildest (not soe refractory as the other)" were to be pardoned on condition that they mete out the penalty to their companions. Thereupon all the servants fell on their knees and asked the forgiveness of their master as well as the court "for their misdemeanor and promising all complyance and obedience hereafter." Accordingly their penalty was suspended and they were placed on their good behavior "ever hereafter (uppon their promise of amendm't as afores'd) And Soe to bee Certifyed from Court to Court."

After the restoration of Maryland to the proprietor a serious conspiracy was nipped in the bud. In 1721 a band of convict servants conspired to seize the magazine at Annapolis in a bold stroke for freedom. The mayor's court of the provincial capital acted swiftly. Only six weeks earlier that tribunal had required "all the Convicts and other Persons of ill fame Either freemen or Servants" that had not as yet given security to post bond in the amount of £10 current money for their keeping the peace. "Upon their refusing so to be convicted." The illuminating depositions reveal that at least one of the ringleaders, a servant named Emyson, threatened his master that, if he would not accept £20 for his freedom, he would run away. The masters of the convict servants implicated in the plot were required by the court to post £30 current for each of their servant's future peaceful behavior.

The atmosphere of seventeenth-century Virginia was charged with plots and rumors of combinations of servants to run away. Discordant notes were sounded very early. All critics agreed that the early colonists were negligent and improvident. Sir Thomas Gates reported that he had seen some eat fish raw rather than fetch wood and cook it. Dissatisfied with conditions, numerous plots to desert were concocted by "mutinous loiterers," some stealing away by boat and entering upon careers of piracy, others returning to England where they proceeded to denounce conditions in Virginia. The laws drawn up by Gates in 1610 and amplified by Dale the following year to end the disorders in the colony were based to a great extent upon the military codes of the low countries. They were extremely severe, but contemporaries justified them by prevailing conditions, although in the period of dissensions at the end of the company's history Sir Thomas Smith was criticized for having sanctioned such severe laws. For mutiny against the authorities, resistance, disobedience, or neglect, the "Lawes Divine, Morall and Martiall" provided whipping for the first offense, three years in the galley for the second, and death for the third. A tradesman was required to attend to his occupation "upon perill," for the first lapse, "to have his entertainment checkt for one moneth"; for the second, for three months; the third, for one year; "and if he continue still unfaithfull and negligent therein, to be condemned to the Gally for three yeare." Overseers were to see that they executed the tasks assigned to them upon pain of such punishment as should be inflicted by a "Martiall Court." In obeying the call to work, no distinction was made by the code between soldiers and "tradesmen." Both were to be ready in the morning and the afternoon, "upon the beating of the Drum," to go to work and not return home until the drum beat again. For the first default, the culprit would be made to "lie vpon the Guard head and heeles together all night"; the second offense was to be punished by whipping, and the third by confinement to the galleys for a year. Likewise conspiracy against the public authorities was to be punished by death, and those withholding knowledge of such conspiracies were to be punished in the same manner as accessories. This Draconic code did not end conspiracies and talk of conspiracies. Early in 1612, a number of "idell men" fled to the Indians. Those taken were executed under the Dale Code. This desertion is known as "Webbes and Prices designe." The third Virginia charter of 1612 speaks of "divers lewd ill-disposed persons, both sailors and soldiers, artificers, husbandmen, labourers, and others," as having received their wages, apparel, and diet from the company in accordance with a contract to serve the company in the colony, and as having subsequently "either withdrawn, hid or concealed themselves," or "refused to go thither." Others who had gone at the expense of the company had, on arrival, "misbehaved themselves, by mutinies, sedition, or other notorious misdemeanors," or had "most treacherously" returned to England "by stealth" or without license of the authorities. Accordingly, the charter gave the Council, or any two of its members, the power to bind such recreants with good sureties for their good behavior, and, if they had already returned to England, to have them sent back to Virginia, there to be proceeded against and punished as the governor and council should think fit or in accord with the laws in force in the colony. In 1614, Coles, Kitchins, and others who had been guarding Don Diego de Molina, an important Spanish prisoner, were persuaded by that notable to flee to the Spanish settlement in Florida. They were captured after they had traveled about five days, were brought back to Jamestown, condemned, and executed. There was considerable fear in 1619 that James I's plan to send over 150 "dissolute persons" would result in mutiny. It appears likely that, included in this company, were some of the dispossessed Irish who were sent to Virginia about this time.

As far back as 1638 the servants of Captain Sibsey had "raised a mutiny" against his "agent." The Lower Norfolk court imposed a sentence of 100 lashes on each malefactor. In 1640 complaint was made to the General Court by Captain William Pierce that six of his servants and a Negro belonging to a Mr. Reginald had plotted to flee to "the Dutch plantation." Examinations of the servants revealed that they had taken Pierce's skiff and some corn, powder, shot, and guns to carry out their design and were sailing down the Elizabeth River when they were taken. The court deemed that, if unpunished, such activity set "a dangerous precedent for the future time." Therefore it sentenced a Dutch servant named Christopher Miller, "a prime agent in the business," to 30 lashes, to be branded on the cheek with the letter "R," and to work with a shackle on his leg for a whole year, "and longer if the said master shall see cause." After the expiration of his service he was to serve the colony for an additional seven years. The others were sentenced to whipping and branding and service to the colony ranging from two and one-half years to seven years. The Negro "Emanuel" was also apparently a servant, and he likewise was sentenced to be whipped and branded and to work for a whole year for his master with a shackle on his leg "or more as his master shall see cause."

However, far more serious insurrections of servants broke out in some of the Tidewater counties in the sixties. A forerunner was the trouble among Daniel Turner's servants which was litigated in the York County court in 1659. Robert Hersington, William Ives, and Edward Tomkins were boarded by their master, Jonathan Newell, at the house of Daniel Tucker and fared as Tucker's servants did, but when Newell came over, probably to check up on their complaints, Hersington told him that he had given Tucker "notice in the presence of Mr Morecroft and William Hodges that if hee would not allowe them their dyet for theire worke this Depon't would provide for them elsewhere." According to other testimony, they were supposed to get their washing, lodging, and diet, and in turn were to do some of the chores. Instead, they refused to "helpe to beat their bread but twise and one of them spooken to to helpe to beat made answeare that hee would take a bagg and goe from house to house and begg my bread before I will beat." The final outcome of this strike is not known. At the same session of court Richard Jones in the presence of others refused to "sett up his Caske" for John Roper on the ground that his pay was "not soe good as other mens."

The affair of Turner's servants was a prelude to the first extensive servant plot which broke out in York County in 1661. As in the early Maryland strike, the issue here was a controversy over diet. It appears to have been customary to allow servants meat three times a week. William Barton stated on examination that he had heard William Clutton say "he would have Meat Three times a weeke or else hee used to Keep a clash and that hee had it soe and that if that when he was at worke in the woods if they sent him bread and cheese if he thought it too little he would send it back again." In fact, Barton asserted, he would not serve as Major Beale's overseer because he could not have meat for his servants three times a week and "as many Calves for Milk as hee himself thought good, and that wheresoever hee lived the servants should have meat three times a weeke." George White confessed that the reason why "hee broake of with Mair Beale was because he could not have meat for the Servants three times a week." Friend corroborated Barton's story, but in extenuation stated that

William Clutton had told Goodwin's servant "that Servants ought to have pone and hominy and Meat twice a weeke." When Major Goodwin violated this custom by confining his servants to a diet of corn bread and water, much murmuring arose at his quarters. The ringleaders, Isaac Friend and William Clutton, proposed that they "should Joyne in a petition to send for England to the King" to have their conditions redressed. According to the examination of one Thomas Collins, Friend suggested "that they would get a matter of Forty of them together and get Gunnes and hee would be the first and lead them and cry as they went along *who would be for liberty and freed from bondage* and that there would enough come to them and they would goe through the Countrey and Kill those that made any opposition and that they would either be free or dye for it." Major Beale, when informed of the disorders, directed the servants to obey their overseer, but William Clutton arrived just at that time and demanded meat according to custom. As a result, he stirred up "a further discontent and murmuring amongst them."

In disposing of the cases, the York County court was unusually moderate. William Clutton was bound for "seditious words and speeches tending to Mutiny and tumultuous behavior of Divers Servants" who were thereby "encouraged to endeav'r and Plott to ioyne together in Companyes after a tumultuous manner by force of Armes to gaine their freedom from their Service." After several persons had declared in court that Clutton had "been accompted a very honest civill person," he was discharged by the court, on paying the sheriff's and clerk's fees. John Parker was ordered to "have a strict, diligent eye upon Isaac friend his servant, who appeares of a turbulent and unquiet spirit." Beyond that, the magistrates did not find it necessary or, perhaps, prudent to do more than to enter an order requesting "the several magistrates and masters of familyes . . . to prevent the like dangerous discourses in those parts and lawfully to look into the practice and behaviour of their severall servants." Toward the end of 1662 a law was enacted restraining unlawful meetings of servants under heavy penalties.

The unrest of the servants in York appears to have communicated itself to the adjacent county of Gloucester to the north. It was at Poplar Spring, near Purton, that some servants who had been soldiers under Cromwell plotted an insurrection in 1663. The plotters seem to have been an Oliverian faction, and included Independents, Muggletonians, Fifth Monarchy men, and other dissident elements who had been sent to the colony on long terms of indentured servitude. They planned to capitalize on the very real economic and social discontent of the servant class, but it is believed that they aimed at something more than this—a plot to overthrow Berkeley and set up an independent commonwealth in Virginia. The night before the projected uprising the conspiracy was betrayed by an informer named Berkenhead, a servant of one John Smith. Militiamen were stationed at the rendezvous and a number of the conspirators were captured, though a majority were warned in time and escaped.

Actual accounts of the scheme vary. According to one of the plotters, Thomas Collins, the plan was for the band to march upon the governor and demand release from serving one year of their terms. If the request was denied, they were to proceed to a designated island. Others, William Budell, William Poultney, and John Gunter, said nothing about seeking merely one year off, but declared that they had planned to demand their freedom, apparently unconditionally.

Indictments were returned against John Gunter, William Bell, Richard Darbishire, John Hayte, Thomas Jones, William Ball, William Poultney, William Bendell, and Thomas Collins—all styled laborers—for high treason in meeting together at Newman's Land in Gloucester County and plotting to break into the houses of Francis Willis, one of the members of the Governor's Council, and of Katherine Cooke, and to seize guns and ammunitions sufficient to arm some thirty persons who were prepared to march from house to house, seizing arms and killing any who offered resistance. Such action was deemed contrary to the statutes of 25 Edward III, c.2 and 13 Elizabeth. Of the nine indicted for high treason, four were condemned and executed. Berkenhead was given his freedom and 5,000 lbs. of tobacco, and his master was compensated for his time.

The whole episode made a profound impression on the colony. It was resolved that the thirteenth of September, the day fixed for the alleged rising, "be annually kept holy." Years later the General Court referred incidentally to the "horror yet remaining amongst us of the barbarous designs of those villaines in September 1663 who attempted at once the Subversion of our religion Lawes liberty and rights," when the colony was saved only by "God's mercy."

The York conspiracy and the Gloucester plot were responsible for several statutes. Because of the special situation in Gloucester County, and in order to prevent "servants and other idlers running away in troops by a pursuit made at the charge of the county," the county court was empowered to make such laws as should be from time to time found necessary and convenient for the prevention, pursuit, or recovery of any such runaways. A year or so later similar legislative powers were conferred on other counties in an act prohibiting servants from leaving their homes without license from their masters. Specifically, "the several respective counties (as they find cause) to take espetiall care to make such by laws within themselves, as by the act dated the third of December 1662, they are impowered as may cause a further restraint of all unlawful meetings of servants and punish the offenders."

Between the York and Gloucester episodes and Bacon's Rebellion there took place a number of combinations and conspiracies of white servants. In 1670 a group of servants led by one Thomas Miller were accused of conspiracy to steal some pipes of wine belonging to a master named Captain James Neale. Neale's servants were urged by the ring-leader to do the same and conceal their acts. In April of that year, as a result of complaints of servant trouble in the counties of York, Gloucester, and Middlesex, and with specific reference to the conspiracy of '63, the General Court issued its famous "order about Jayle birds," for-bidding any person from bringing in any convict who deserved to die in England for his offense. Again, in 1672, Katherine Newgent was sentenced to thirty lashes for complicity in a "confederacy" with other servants of Charles Scarburgh. During this same period a number of Negro riots and insurrections were reported.

Overshadowing all conspiracies and combinations of artificers and servants in Virginia was the insurrection known as Bacon's Rebellion. The details are too well known for extended comment here. It is generally recognized that not only frontiersmen figured among supporters of Bacon, but the lower classes throughout the province rendered him some measure of support. William Sherwood and Philip Ludwell depict Bacon's men as ignorant rabble. The explanation for the support of Bacon by the lower classes in Virginia is found in the economic and social history of that colony in the decade and a half prior to the rebellion. In 1650 Virginia was a flourishing province. Tobacco commanded a high figure in the European market, hired men were scarce, and wages four times as great as in England. However, the Navigation Acts depressed the tobacco plan-tations, and the lower classes seemed to have shouldered more than their proportionate share of the ensuing losses. Taxes were levied in each county for setting tannery establishments, for converting wool, flax, and hemp into cloth, and for instructing poor children in the knowledge of spinning, weaving, and other useful trades. Unfortunately, as the in-habitants of Charles City County were moved to protest, none of the plants was completed or put in operation. The administrative ineptitude and graft associated with these projects aroused the underprivileged groups, in-cluding the servant class. Berkeley stated that he had "appeased" two mutinies, "raised by some secret villains who whispered among the people that there was nothing intended by the fifty pound [levy] but the enriching of some few people." The forerunners of these outbreaks were the dis-turbances in the Tidewater counties in the sixties brought on by concerted action of servants and laboring men. When the rebellion broke out all servants did not have a free choice of action. Many of the leading planters fled to the Eastern Shore, taking their servants with them and lending Berkeley their support. Actually at one period Bacon was in command of all of Virginia except the Eastern Shore.

In February, 1677, the legislature enacted that pardon should not extend "to any servants who were ayders and assisters in the said rebellion; and by an act of this assembly were adjudged to make good the losse of tyme and damages done to their masters (or others) by leaving their masters service and imbezelling goods, or otherwise damageing their masters or others, but that they shalbe lyable to make good such damages as by the said act of assembly for that purpose shalbe provided." Another statute provided for the return of servants and other property to loyal persons and those persons concealing such servants were to be punished as felons. A statute passed in the same period "concerning servants who were out in rebellion" provided that servants who had served under Bacon, Ingram, or other rebels were punishable as runaways and were subject to prosecution at the expiration of their terms of service for whatever they plundered. The preamble to this act declares:

> Whereas many evill disposed servants in these late tymes of horrid rebellion taking advantage of the loosnes and liberty of the tyme, did depart from their service, and followed the rebells in rebellion, wholy neglecting their masters imployment whereby the said masters have suffered great damage and injury.

In order to bring about the return of the fugitive servants and sharecroppers, the legislature enacted that persons who had others, not well known, residing in their houses for less than nine months, "whether as hired servant, sharer in the crop or otherwise," were required to give a description of such persons to the justice. For neglecting to do so, they would be liable to punishment for entertaining runaway servants. The declared object of this act was "to the end servants runaway and others Fled from debt in those late rebellious tymes be the better found out and discovered, and by that meanes reduced in their service and payment and their just debts, etc." These statutes against the rebellious groups were repealed by proclamation in 1680, and in the "Act of free and general pardon, indemnity and oblivion" passed in that year there was a provision

> that noe further punishment, satisfaction or damages shal be recovered or inflicted on any christian servants that have deserted their masters or bin active in the late rebellion, then that the the time incurring betweene the said First day of May and the said sixteenth of January shal be accompted noe part of their tyme of service.

Bacon's Rebellion and its ruthless suppression did not put an end to disorders among the poorer population. In October, 1681, in answer to a query as to whether it was necessary to continue the two companies of English soldiers in Virginia, it was reported to the Lords of Trade and

Plantation that "Virginia is at present poor and more populous than ever. There is great apprehension of a rising among the servants, owing to their great necessities and want of clothes; they may plunder the store-houses and ships." The plant-cutting riots of 1682, while by no means confined to servants and laboring men, were a further fresh manifestation of discontent on the part of the lower economic groups in the colony.

The most serious insurrection of white workers in the history of the British colonies on the North American mainland actually occurred in East Florida during the British regime. Under the administration of Governor Grant, group settlements were set up by Denys Rolle at Char-lotia, on the St. Johns, and by that well-traveled Scotsman Dr. Andrew Turnbull at New Smyrna. The settlers of "Rollestown" were recruited from the English poor; discontent was rife, and ten years after its found-ing William Bartram reported that few inhabitants dwelt amid its ruins. New Smyrna was founded with the support of a friendly governor, who appointed Turnbull to the Council, and with the financial sponsorship of Sir William Duncan and Sir Richard Temple, Turnbull's partners. Because of his acquaintance with Mediterranean lands, Turnbull recruited his servants from Greece and added to their number over one hundred Italians picked up at Leghorn and a larger group of starving Minorcans to whose pleas for aid Turnbull felt he could not turn a deaf ear. In all, some 1,400 settlers sailed from Minorca for Turnbull's colony. With the notable ex-ception of the shipment of German Palatines to New York in 1710, this was perhaps the largest group of servants ever to emigrate to the British colonies in America in one expedition. The heterogeneous group overtaxed the slender resources of the colony, and, within two months after landing, a revolt broke out, led by the Greeks and Italians. The timely aid of Grant prevented the colony from being completely destroyed.

We are indebted to the governor for a graphic report to Hills-borough and the Lords of Trade of the occurrence. Turnbull had brought some planters down from the Carolinas as his guests to see the progress the settlers had made, and had set out with his party for St. Augustine on the return journey, when at midnight on the nineteenth of August, 1768, he was aroused by a messenger who reported that Carlo Forni, one of the Italian overseers, had that very morning marched into the square at New Smyrna at the head of twenty malcontents and addressed the settlers, who left their work to hear him. He declared himself com-mander-in-chief of the Italians and Greeks, whom he intended to lead to Havana, confident of Spain's protection. He held out to them freedom from a life of hard work and stern masters. The crowd grew excited, the door of the storehouse was broken down, and casks of rum were rolled into the street. When Cutter, one of the English overseers, inter-vened, he was seriously wounded and locked in one of the closets in the storeroom. About three hundred adherents of Forni—nearly all the Greeks and Italians in the colony—seized firearms and ammunition in the storehouse, plundered the dwellings of the Minorcans who refused to join the insurgents, and seized a ship loaded with provisions lying in the river.

On hearing the news, Turnbull sent an express rider at top speed to Grant at St. Augustine. Meanwhile, instead of raising sail, the insurgents caroused aboard the ship and were finally intercepted by government vessels. The rebels surrendered, and offered no further resistance, but some two score, including the leaders, escaped in an open boat. It took four months before they were overtaken on the Florida keys. When they were brought to trial at St. Augustine, the jurors were moved to compassion by their wretched condition. Three leaders were convicted of piracy. Two, including Forni, were executed, and the third pardoned on condition that he act as executioner of the other two. Three Greeks convicted of felonies were pardoned by Grant on the recommendation of Hillsborough, who insisted that amnesty be extended to all other participants. Governor Grant summed up the affair in these words:

> It was to be expected, My Lord, that so great a number of people collected together in [sic] so many parts of the world, and imported into an infant Country at the same time might get into Riots and give Trouble at times, but I did not look for their carrying things to such a Height.

He recommended that a fort be built at New Smyrna to protect the settlers from the Indians and the other planters from these very same settlers. A fort was started, but never completed, although a guard of eight men and a sergeant were stationed there permanently.

This was not the end of such disturbances at New Smyrna. The arrival of Patrick Tonyn as governor of East Florida in 1774 led to new dissension among the immigrant workers. Tonyn and Turnbull were personally antagonistic, whereas Turnbull had formerly enjoyed the complete cooperation of Governor Grant in dealing with the colony. With the outbreak of the American Revolution the Minorcans, hitherto the most pacific element in the colony, were believed to have conspired with the Spaniards at Havana. Their loyalty to the British cause was suspect when they did not join the Loyalist militia organized for the defense of the border.

Of the many issues that arose between Turnbull and Tonyn, a number concern relations with the workers in East Florida. In 1776 Turnbull memorialized the Lords of Trade to remove Governor Tonyn from office. Among the various accusations of malfeasance leveled against that official was the charge that he had obtained through chicanery receipts for wages due to certain artificers for public work. As a result, it was asserted that "the Chief Master Builder in St. Augustine refused to repair the

Platform for the Guns in the Fort on this Account." It was also charged that the "Governor brought up such Provisions as were much wanted by the Poor, that he put them into the Hands of a mean monopoliser, who sold them at double price, which was distressing to some Families." In addition, Turnbull accused the governor of treating his own servants and Negroes cruelly and of acting, himself, as executioner. Turnbull found it necessary for his own personal safety to flee to England to plead his cause in person, but during his absence conditions at New Smyrna grew serious. Charges of harsh treatment on the part of Turnbull's overseers of the servants in that colony were in some part politically inspired, but such widespread unrest resulted that it was feared that the inhabitants might join the Revolutionary cause. Tonyn encouraged the settlers to repudiate their contracts and leave New Smyrna. He offered them free-dom from indentures, land in St. Augustine, and assurances of protection if they ran away. Despite evidence of cruelty to the servants on the part of Turnbull's overseers (charges which are today believed to have been highly colored by Turnbull's political enemies), Tonyn's actions in en-couraging mass desertions and enlistments of such servants in the militia were clearly illegal and without parallel in the history of the period. He was manifestly actuated by his enmity of Turnbull and his desire to bring about the Scotsman's ruin. Furthermore, since Chief Justice Drayton was a partisan of Turnbull and refused to consider these complaints of ill usage himself but directed them to be carried before some other magis-trate, Tonyn had to intervene in his capacity of Chancellor. Turnbull memorialized Shelburne that

> the Settlement . . . was entirely abandoned by an insidious and under-hand management of Governor Tonyn who had encouraged these Settlers by specious promises to quit their labor and Plantations. He also encour-aged them not to return to fulfill their contracts with your Memorialist, as was ordered by a Sentence of the Court of Sessions after a full investi-gation of that Business on a Hearing of their Complaints which were found to be frivolous and groundless, as appears by the Sentence of that Court.

Tonyn misrepresented the action of the court, reporting to the author-ities at home that, between May and July, 1777, many of the settlers were freed by the courts and the rest set at liberty by Turnbull's at-torneys. But as a matter of fact, the only ones freed by the court were a few who had been contracted for by their parents when under age. The court of sessions declared the others legally bound to the proprietors of New Smyrna and ordered them back to the settlement. Tonyn de-liberately defied the court. When the complainants were confined by the justices and ordered to live on bread and water until "they returned to their labour in order to fulfil their contracts," Tonyn sent them provisions from his own house. Encouraged by the governor's defiance of the courts, the whole settlement moved to St. Augustine. There some sixty-five died because of inadequate food, shelter, and medical assistance. Many were soon reduced to beggary, others enlisted in the corps of Rangers, and still others built shacks on small lots assigned them north of St. Augustine. Hence, when Turnbull returned from England, he found his colony abandoned and his property and crops in serious condition. Tonyn, who had acted in a high-handed and illegal manner, wrapped himself in the mantle of patriotism and demanded Turnbull's dismissal from the Council on the ground of disloyalty. While admitting that Turnbull and his friends were "gentlemen," he charged that "in all the colonies, Georgia excepted, the principal people have been at the head of this rebellion." . . .

CONCERTED ACTION BY WHITE WORKMEN
AGAINST NEGRO ARTISANS

Local craftsmen in colonial towns sought not only to maintain their monopolistic privileges against nonresidents but also to control the labor market in general. One significant aspect of this struggle was the effort of white mechanics to keep free Negroes and Negro slaves from entering the skilled trades. While the issue of free mechanic versus slave was most sharply drawn in Charleston, center of a considerable slave population, and in the British West Indies, evidences of the conflict are found in virtually every sizable town on the Atlantic coast.

In New England servants from the British Isles were always preferred to Negro mechanics. Nevertheless, while the proportion of Negroes to whites in that area remained very small, slave labor was highly diversified and employed in many of the New England trades, both skilled and unskilled. Here as elsewhere white workers found Negro competition objectionable. According to John Adams, the resentment of white labor toward Negro slaves was an important influence in the abolition of slavery in New England.

In New York City the handicraftsmen bitterly opposed the employment of Negro slaves in the various trades. In 1686 representations were made to the common council that Negro and Indian slaves were regularly employed by their masters "to worke on the bridge Weighhouse and Markett House of this Citty about the goods of their Respective Masters." This resulted in "discouragement and Losse" to the "Sworne porters." Thereupon the council ordered that "noe Negro or Slave be suffered to work on the bridge as a Porter about any goods either imported or Exported from or into this Citty." A similar complaint was made by the sworn porters in 1691, who declared that this practice "soe much impoverisht them, that they Cannot by their Labours gett a Competency for the Maintenance of themselves and Family's." In 1737 Lieutenant Governor Clarke found it necessary to tell the legislature that "the artificers complain and with too much reason of the pernicious custom of breeding slaves to trades whereby the honest and industrious tradesmen are reduced to poverty for want of employ, and many of them forced to leave us to seek their living in other countries." As in Boston, the post-Revolutionary trend toward emancipation of the Negro slave in New York was viewed by white workers as imperiling their economic status, and the mechanics led the opposition to laws gradually emancipating the Negro.

Considerable hostility marked relations between white labor and Negroes engaged in the Philadelphia trades. It is believed that one of the motives for the Pennsylvania statute of 1712 placing a high duty on Negroes—an act passed soon after the insurrection in New York—was the opposition of white workers to slave competition. This was crystallized in an Assembly resolve of 1722.

In the Southern towns the authorities made vigorous efforts to protect white craftsmen and traders from Negro competition. The problem was especially critical in Charleston. In 1744 a number of shipwrights of that town petitioned the legislature for relief on the ground that they were reduced to poverty owing to competition from Negroes in the shipbuilding industry. The master shipwrights opposed the petition and retorted that

> Industry and a more frugal way of life [would cure the ills complained of and] that many times they have refused to work at all, or if obliged to it by necessity only on Extravagant wages, That his Majesty's Ships have been repaired and refitted only by the assistance of Our Slaves, And that without these Slaves the worst Consequences might Ensue, his Majesty's Ships may remain by the Walls at their discretion: Merchants who are bound by Charter party to load Vessels within a limitted time may be drawn into heavy demurrage, And no Mercht can have it in their power to take or refuse work upon their own terms. That there is business enough for three times the number of Carpenters, That the Complaints were with no other View than to Engross the whole Trade into their own hands and thereby to have it in their power to make their own price.

A committee of the Assembly reported it as their opinion "that the number of Negroes hired out, without a proportion of white men to do the business of ship-wrights or ship carpenters, is a discouragem't to white men of that business of ship-wrights." It further recommended that a bill be enacted for "the ascertaining of wages for Ship-wrights, as well white men as Negroes." Both recommendations for limitation of Negroes in the industry and for wage regulation were unanimously agreed to. It is thus clear that while the Assembly wished to control the craft for the benefit of the white mechanics it had, at the same time, no desire to be faced with strikes and excessive wage demands, and in the latter point it yielded to the masters. Despite a similar proposal later in the year, the interests of the employer class prevented passage of such a bill. The failure of the legislature to act left the matter up to the town, which in 1751 declared in sweeping language "that no Inhabitant of Charleston shall be permitted to keep more than two male Slaves, to work out for Hire, as Porters, Labourers, Fishermen or Handicraftsmen." The *Gazette* of October 29–November 5, 1763, reported that Negro chimney sweepers were competing with the whites and actually "had the insolence, by a combination amongst themselves, to raise the usual prices, and to refuse doing their work, unless their exorbitant demands are complied with. . . . Surely, these are evils that require some attention to suppress." In 1764 the legislature prohibited Charleston masters from employing Negroes or other slaves as mechanics or in the handicraft trades, but placed no hindrance on the teaching by mechanics and artificers of their own Negroes or other slaves in their own respective trades, "so that they have and constantly employ, one white apprentice or journeyman for every two negroes." In 1772 Charleston imposed a fine upon both master and employer, if a slave was hired out without license or badge. In the post-Revolutionary period the amount of this fine was reduced, and by 1790 the city council abolished the license system entirely because the tax had been found to be "burdensome and unequal," and Negro slaves were entrenched in virtually all the crafts.

In North Carolina the same conflict between white and Negro labor arose by the eve of the Revolution. In 1773 the pilots of Oacock Bar petitioned the Assembly that Negroes, both free and slave, be denied licenses to pilot vessels up the rivers to Bath, Edenton, and New Bern, and charged that Negroes were unlawfully competing with them and manifesting an "Insolent and Turbulent disposition." In Georgia, legislation forbidding the employment of Negroes and other slaves in the handicraft trades was enacted in 1758, and three years later a statute was passed against the hiring of Spaniards. In West Florida, despite parallel legislation which proved difficult to carry out in practice, British army officers seem to have succeeded in 1767 in reducing the rate of wages of artificers engaged for the army by employing Negroes for certain tasks.

One method adopted in most of the colonies to restrict Negro competition was to impose a duty on the importation of slaves, but such legislation was generally disallowed by the King in Council. When in 1760 South Carolina prohibited the slave trade entirely, her action was promptly disallowed. . . .

CONCERTED ACTION BY JOURNEYMEN
WORKERS FOR LABOR ENDS

Combinations by employers for purposes of trade monopoly, price fixing, and control of the labor market were more common in colonial times than combinations of journeymen and were unmolested by law. In certain fields such combinations were quite characteristic, particularly in the fisheries, the spermaceti industry, in the flour and baking trades, and among tanners. Employers combined to fix wages and control the labor market in the pre-Revolutionary period as well as during the war years that followed. For example, the *New-York Mercury* of August 7, 1758, carried the following item:

> For the encouragement of Ship-Carpenters, able Seamen, and Labourers, in the Country, and the neighbouring Provinces, to repair to the City of New-York; The Merchants of this City have agreed to give to Ship-Carpenters 8s. per Day; able Seamen 8s. and Labourers 4s. with the usual Allowance of Provisions; and no other, or greater Wages whatsoever. And all Persons liking the above Proposals, may be certain of constant employment.

One of the significant rules laid down by the "Society for the Promotion of Arts, Agriculture and Economy," organized in New York in 1764, was "That no Member do receive unto his Service any Overseer, or Gardener, or white Servant, Male or Female, who shall not be able to produce a Recommendation in Writing, from the Master, or Mistress, whom they last served, in this Colony." Agreements such as this, by no means unfamiliar to contemporary British industrialists, constituted a standing threat to labor organizers and insubordinate workers.

In 1779 the New York Chamber of Commerce was instrumental in bringing about a reduction in the town rates for carmen. In most colonial and post-colonial towns the master carpenters agreed upon a scale of prices or fees, and on at least one occasion similar action was taken by the master barbers of Boston. Such an agreement was announced in the *New England Courant* for December 7, 1724:

> On Tuesday the first of this Instant in the Evening, Thirty Two Principal Barbers of this Place, assembled at the Golden Ball, with a Trumpeter attending them, to debate some important Articles relating to their occupations; where it was proposed, that they should raise their Shaving from 8 to 10s. per Quarter, and that they should advance 5s. on the Price of making common Wiggs and 10s. on their Tye ones. It was also propos'd, that no one of their Faculty should shave or dress Wiggs on Sunday

Mornings for the future, on Penalty of forfeiting 10 pounds for every such Offense: From whence it may fairly be concluded, that in times past such a Practice has been too common among them.

Collective action by journeymen workmen in colonial towns, as distinguished from combinations by licensed trades, guild groups, or employers' trade associations, was comparatively rare, but manifestations in the form of strikes, slowdowns, and conspiracies to desert go back to the earliest days of settlement. John Winter, who was constantly struggling to keep his bound workmen and fishermen at work on Richmond Island, off the coast of Maine, in the interests of his employer, Robert Trelawny, reported in 1636 that they "fell into a mutany" against him for withholding the previous year's wages. Under the leadership of one of their number named Lander, who later successfully recovered his wages due in court, a "Consort ship" to run away was entered into and mass desertions took place. Winter issued an "order along the Cost [coast] that no man shall entertaine them," but in order to be freed from their contracts other workmen made "stryfe" to compel the overseer to "turne them away." Winter advised his employer that in the future he bind his fishermen by "a sumsion"—doubtless he meant an agreement stipulating a penalty for nonfulfillment. Again he complained that "they ar all gathered in a head togeather heare," and found it necessary to send home a brewer named Thomas Samson lest he "poyson som of men on[e] tyme or other yff he had stayed heare with vs." On a still later occasion in 1641 the workers stopped work in the afternoon in protest against inadequate food, and the carpenters engaged in one of the earliest slowdowns on record in the colonies. When rebuked, they answered: "Yf you do not like vs we will be gon, the[y] knowing our worke must be donn and no other to be gotten." The first lock out in American labor history took place in 1643 at the Gloucester yards, when a group of obstreperous shipwrights were forbidden by the authorities "to worke a stroke of worke more" upon a certain ship without further orders from the governor.

In 1741 the Boston caulkers, one of the earliest well-knit occupational groups and traditionally radical in sympathy, entered into an agreement to refuse to accept notes from their "Employer or Employers" on shops for goods or money in payment of their labor, specifying penalties for breach thereof. The newspaper, in its account of the agreement, expressed the opinion that "this good and commendable Example will soon be follow'd by Numbers of other Artificers and Tradesmen," desirous of protecting themselves against paper money inflation.

A few strikes of journeymen are recorded prior to the rise of more permanent trade unions. Because of a "late Reduction of the Wages of journeymen Taylors" in New York some twenty tailors decided in 1768 to go on strike. They offered to work in families at "three Shillings and Six Pence per Day" with "Diet." Their "House of Call" was at the "Sign of the Fox and Hounds," in Moravian (now Fulton) Street. They were careful in their public announcement to make no direct statement that they had refused to work, and merely asserted that they could no longer support themselves and their families "by working as Journeymen." This appears to have been a concert of workers to compete directly with their former masters in retaliation for a wage cut.

In 1778 the journeymen printers of New York City demanded a substantial increase in wages on the ground of the exorbitant wartime increase in the cost of living. The Tory James Rivington gave space to this important labor incident in his *Royal Gazette* of November 14, 1778.

New-York, Nov. 9, 1778.

Gentlemen,

As the necessaries of life are raised to such an enormous price, it cannot be expected that we should continue to work at the wages now given; and therefore request an addition of Three Dollars per week to our present small pittance; It may be objected that this requisition is founded upon the result of a combination to distress the Master Printers at this time, on account of the scarcity of hands; but this is far from being the case; it being really the high price of every article of life, added to the approaching dreary season. There is not one among us, we trust, that would take an ungenerous advantage of the times—we only wish barely to exist, which it is impossible to do with our present stipend.

There is scarcely a common Labourer but gets a Dollar per day and provisions, and the lowest mechanics from 12 to 16s. per Day.

We wait the result of your determination.

The Journeymen Printers

To the Master Printers, New-York.

I do consent to the above Requisition.

James Rivington

The demands of the journeymen printers were made as a group against the master printers of the city. Beginning in May of that year Rivington and other printers established a mutual daily gazette, first for five and later for six days a week, an arrangement that produced in effect the first daily in America. The protest of the printers was a threat against the continued publication of this daily, but a threat couched in courteous language. The hesitancy of the journeymen to be labeled "a combination to distress the Master Printers" is readily understandable in view of the occupation of the city at that time by the British army, which they might very well have feared would have been all too willing to introduce some of the methods used at home in dealing with labor combinations.

Strikes and slowdowns marred production in the iron industry in the middle of the eighteenth century. That indefatigable promoter, Peter Hasenclever, was harassed by labor trouble. When the artisans and laborers induced to migrate by his agents in Germany arrived at the ironworks, they demanded higher wages, despite the contracts they had made abroad, and when Hasenclever refused to accede, they proceeded to give a good colonial version of the twentieth-century "slowdown." Because of his inability to obtain competent replacements, Hasenclever was forced to yield, and their wages were raised. When their wages were not paid them promptly, the carpenters at the Hibernia Iron Works in New Jersey struck in 1774.

The only type of permanent or semipermanent organization of workers to take root in the pre-Revolutionary period was the association of craftsmen for philanthropic ends. Organized on craft lines, these "friendly societies" included masters as well as journeymen; among mariners their membership seems to have been confined to masters. The Friendly Society of Tradesmen House Carpenters, organized in New York City in 1767, was a typical mutual aid society restricted to a single trade. According to its twenty articles, membership was limited to house carpenters, "free from all bodily Distempers," and within the ages of twenty-one and forty. An initiation fee of 4s. and a monthly payment of 1s. 6d. went to a general fund which assured sick benefits for members. After the first six days of illness the member was entitled to 10s. a week during the remainder of his indisposition. Friendly societies, also known as "box clubs," had during this period spread rapidly in the mother country. Such organizations were often a mask for illegal combinations, and the boundary line between the friendly society and the trade union came to be extremely shadowy. Whether the New York society engaged in activities other than those announced at its formation cannot be determined, as no records of the organization are extant today, although its articles provided for the recording of minutes in a "Book of Transactions." However, in 1771 an organization calling itself The Society of House Carpenters announced that it was using Mr. David Philip's establishment as a house of call, where workmen could be secured "on reasonable Terms." While it is by no means clear that the two societies were by that time one and the same, it is apparent that by the eve of the Revolution the house carpenters did find it necessary to act together for certain economic ends.

A more permanent type of organization of master workmen was afforded by the marine societies which were especially strong in New England. These societies do not appear to have been formed to regulate wages or prices or to control the labor market, but rather for the relief of distressed shipmasters and their widows and children. The first of these was the "Marine Society of Boston in New England," organized in 1742. The "Fellowship Club" of Rhode Island, established in 1752, was of the same nature. Salem, New York, Philadelphia, and Newburyport soon followed suit. But combinations of mariners for higher wages were not tolerated. When, in the winter of 1779, 150 mariners went on strike for higher wages at the port of Philadelphia, the state authorities had the magistrates arrest the ringleaders and the Board of War ordered the troops out to support the officials.

With the close of the American Revolution a sharp cleavage between groups on economic or regional lines becomes apparent. Highly complex conservative-rural, radical-urban groupings were now taking on a political character, with the journeymen giving their support to the urban group, which also included the mercantile interests. In most towns, mechanics' tickets were set up and on a number of occasions craftsmen were sent to the state legislatures.

In this period employers continued to enter into trade associations to protect their economic interests, but labor for the first time turns to the more permanent type of trade-union organization. The rise of the factory, the transition from custom work to wholesale order work, and the concentration of workers in certain expanding industries served to bring about more distinct class stratifications. This period was marked by the decline of the apprenticeship system; inexpert workmen now came into direct competition with skilled journeymen, as middlemen now pitted master against master, giving their orders to the lowest cost producer and forcing masters to increase sharply the ratio of apprentices (now called "green hands") to skilled journeymen. As the vast majority of workers came to abandon hope of ever being admitted into the ranks of the employers, they turned increasingly to the strike as the best economic weapon to advance their interests and to the trade union as the most suitable form of trade organization.

Among the early strikes of the post-Revolutionary era one of the most notable was that of the New York shoemakers in 1785 for higher wages. The masters quickly retaliated by entering into an employer combination, and demanded that the workers agree to work for no one who sold English shoes, having specifically in mind a certain low-cost manufacturer named Smith. After a strike lasting three weeks, both sides withdrew their demands when Smith advertised that he needed more good workmen for his shoe factory and adroitly coupled this announcement with a low scale of prices for his shoes. More permanent manifestations of union activity did not arise until the next decade, but before the close of the century the New York typographers, carpenters, masons, and coopers had set up effective trade unions.

Labor union activity in Philadelphia in this period surpassed that in New York. In 1786 the journeymen printers went on strike to protest a reduction of wages and passed a resolution of joint support for the duration of the strike—probably the first instance on record in this country of a union strike-benefit fund. But permanent organization of this craft does not appear to have been effected in that city until 1802. Following the organization in 1789 of the Philadelphia Society of Master Cordwainers, the journeymen in the same trade formed in 1794 a union known as the "Federal Society," to protect themselves from "scab labor." On at least three occasions before the end of the century they went on strike for higher wages.

1.4

Popular Uprisings and Civil Authority in Eighteenth-Century America

PAULINE MAIER

Until recently, historians have either ignored crowd behavior or written of "mobs" as irrational and pathological. Lately important pioneering work has been written by European social historians, such as E. P. Thompson, Eric Hobsbawm, and George Rudé. Pauline Maier here begins a reexamination of the purposiveness and effect of colonial crowd behavior. Eighteenth-century crowds operated within the framework of a mercantile society that theoretically recognized a positive role for government, but often denied it in practice. Colonial crowds therefore served as extra-institutional bodies, even on occasion with quasi-legal sanction, to enforce that role. Sometimes the crowd and local authorities did not disagree but there were also bitter disputes. Writing on contemporary English bread riots, E. P. Thompson argued that the study of these crowds revealed belief in "a moral economy" that contrasted with the later "political economy." So little is known of

Pauline Maier, "Popular Uprisings and Civil Authority in Eighteenth-Century America," *William and Mary Quarterly*, 3rd ser., 27 (1970), 3–35. Reprinted by permission of the author and the publisher.

nineteenth-century crowds that we have reservations about Maier's conclusions, but none about the importance of her work. Similar forms of collective behavior as a method of expressing grievances and seeking redress for them continued, as we shall see, into the nineteenth and twentieth centuries.

The following works are suggested for further reading:

ERIC HOBSBAWM, *Primitive Rebels,* New York: W. W. Norton & Company, Inc., 1965.

GEORGE RUDÉ, *The Crowd in the French Revolution,* New York: Oxford University Press, 1959. *The Crowd in History,* New York: John Wiley & Sons, Inc., 1964.

E. P. THOMPSON, "The Moral Economy of the English Crowd in the Eighteenth Century," *Past & Present,* no. 50 (1971), 76–136.

It is only natural that the riots and civil turbulence of the past decade and a half have awakened a new interest in the history of American mobs. It should be emphasized, however, that scholarly attention to the subject has roots independent of contemporary events and founded in long-developing historiographical trends. George Rudé's studies of pre-industrial crowds in France and England, E. J. Hobsbawm's discussion of "archaic" social movements, and recent works linking eighteenth-century American thought with English revolutionary tradition have all, in different ways, inspired a new concern among historians with colonial uprisings.[1] This discovery of the early American mob promises to have a significant effect upon historical interpretation. Particularly affected are

[1] See the following by George Rudé: *The Crowd in the French Revolution* (Oxford, 1959); "The London 'Mob' of the Eighteenth Century," *The Historical Journal,* II (1959), 1–18; *Wilkes and Liberty: A Social Study of 1763 to 1774* (Oxford, 1962); *The Crowd in History: A Study of Popular Disturbances in France and England, 1730–1848* (New York, 1964). See also E. J. Hobsbawm, *Primitive Rebels: Studies in Archaic Forms of Social Movement in the 19th and 20th Centuries* (New York, 1959), esp. "The City Mob," 109–125. For recent discussions of the colonial mob see: Bernard Bailyn, *Pamphlets of the American Revolution* (Cambridge, Mass., 1965), I, 581–584; Jesse Lemisch, "Jack Tar in the Street: Merchant Seamen in the Politics of Revolutionary America," *William and Mary Quarterly,* 3d Ser., XXV (1968), 371–407; Gordon S. Wood, "A Note on Mobs in the American Revolution," *Wm. and Mary Qtly.,* 3d Ser., XXIII (1966), 635–642, and more recently Wood's *Creation of the American Republic, 1776–1787* (Chapel Hill, 1969), *passim,* but esp. 319–328. Wood offers an excellent analysis of the place of mobs and

the Revolutionary struggle and the early decades of the new nation, when events often turned upon well-known popular insurrections.

Eighteenth-century uprisings were in some important ways different than those of today—different in themselves, but even more in the political context within which they occurred. As a result they carried different connotations for the American Revolutionaries than they do today. Not all eighteenth-century mobs simply defied the law: some used extralegal means to implement official demands or to enforce laws not otherwise enforceable, others in effect extended the law in urgent situations beyond its technical limits. Since leading eighteenth-century Americans had known many occasions on which mobs took on the defense of the public welfare, which was, after all, the stated purpose of government, they were less likely to deny popular upheavals all legitimacy than are modern leaders. While not advocating popular uprisings, they could still grant such incidents an established and necessary role in free societies, one that made them an integral and even respected element of the political order. These attitudes, and the tradition of colonial insurrections on which they drew, not only shaped political events of the Revolutionary era, but also lay behind many laws and civil procedures that were framed during the 1780's and 1790's, some of which still have a place in the American legal system.

I

Not all colonial uprisings were identical in character or significance. Some involved no more than disorderly vandalism or traditional brawls such as those that annually marked Pope's Day on November 5, particularly in New England. Occasional insurrections defied established laws and authorities in the name of isolated private interests alone—a set of Hartford County, Connecticut, landowners arose in 1722, for example, after a court decision imperiled their particular land titles. Still others —which are of interest here—took on a broader purpose, and defended the interests of their community in general where established authorities failed to act.[2] This common characteristic linked otherwise diverse rural

---

extralegal assemblies in the development of American constitutionalism. Hugh D. Graham and Ted R. Gurr, *Violence in America: Historical and Comparative Perspectives* (New York, 1969), primarily discusses uprisings of the 19th and 20th centuries, but see the chapters by Richard M. Brown, "Historical Patterns of Violence in America," 45–84, and "The American Vigilante Tradition," 154–226.

[2] Carl Bridenbaugh, *Cities in the Wilderness: The First Century of Urban Life in America, 1625–1742* (New York, 1964), 70–71, 223–224, 382–384; and Carl Bridenbaugh, *Cities in Revolt: Urban Life in America, 1743–1776* (New York, 1964), 113–118; Charles J. Hoadly, ed., *The Public Records of the Colony of Connecticut . . .* (Hartford, 1872), VI, 332–333, 341–348.

uprisings in New Jersey and the Carolinas. The insurrectionists' punishment of outlaws, their interposition to secure land titles or prevent abuses at the hands of legal officials followed a frustration with established institutions and a belief that justice and even security had to be imposed by the people directly.[3] The earlier Virginia tobacco insurrection also illustrates this common pattern well: Virginians began tearing up young tobacco plants in 1682 only after Governor Thomas Culpeper forced the quick adjournment of their assembly, which had been called to curtail tobacco planting during an economic crisis. The insurrections in Massachusetts a little over a century later represent a variation on this theme. The insurgents in Worcester, Berkshire, Hampshire, Middlesex, and Bristol counties—often linked together as members of "Shays's Rebellion"—forced the closing of civil courts, which threatened to send a major portion of the local population to debtors' prison, only until a new legislature could remedy their pressing needs.[4]

This role of the mob as extralegal arm of the community's interest emerged, too, in repeated uprisings that occurred within the more densely settled coastal areas. The history of Boston, where by the mid-eighteenth century "public order . . . prevailed to a greater degree than anywhere else in England or America," is full of such incidents. During the food shortage of 1710, after the governor rejected a petition from the Boston selectmen calling for a temporary embargo on the exportation of foodstuffs one heavily laden ship found its rudder cut away, and fifty men sought to haul another outward bound vessel back to shore. Under similar circumstances Boston mobs again intervened to keep foodstuffs in the colony in 1713 and 1729. When there was some doubt a few years later whether or not the selectmen had the authority to seize a barn lying in the path of a proposed street, a group of townsmen, their faces blackened, levelled the structure and the road went through. Houses of ill fame were attacked by Boston mobs in 1734, 1737, 1771; and in the late 1760's the *New York*

---

[3] See particularly Richard M. Brown, *The South Carolina Regulators* (Cambridge, Mass., 1963). There is no published study of the New Jersey land riots, which lasted over a decade and were due above all to the protracted inability of the royal government to settle land disputes stemming from conflicting proprietary grants made in the late 17th century. See, however, "A State of Facts concerning the Riots and Insurrections in New Jersey, and the Remedies Attempted to Restore the Peace of the Province," William A. Whitehead *et al.*, eds., *Archives of the State of New Jersey* (Newark, 1883), VII, 207–226. On other rural insurrections see Irving Mark, *Agrarian Conflicts in Colonial New York, 1711–1775* (New York, 1940), Chap. IV, V; Staughton Lynd, "The Tenant Rising at Livingston Manor," *New-York Historical Society Quarterly,* XLVIII (1964), 163–177; Matt Bushnell Jones, *Vermont in the Making, 1750–1777* (Cambridge, Mass., 1939), Chap. XII, XIII; John R. Dunbar, ed., *The Paxton Papers* (The Hague, 1957), esp. 3–51.

[4] Richard L. Morton, *Colonial Virginia* (Chapel Hill, 1960), I, 303–304; Jonathan Smith, "The Depression of 1785 and Daniel Shays' Rebellion," *Wm. and Mary Qtly.,* 3d Ser., V (1948), 86–87, 91.

Gazette claimed that mobs in Providence and Newport had taken on responsibility for "disciplining" unfaithful husbands. Meanwhile in New London, Connecticut, another mob prevented a radical religious sect, the Rogerenes, from disturbing normal Sunday services, "a practice they . . . [had] followed more or less for many years past; and which all the laws made in that government, and executed in the most judicious manner could not put a stop to."[5]

Threats of epidemic inspired particularly dramatic instances of this community oriented role of the mob. One revealing episode occurred in Massachusetts in 1773–1774. A smallpox hospital had been built on Essex Island near Marblehead "much against the will of the multitude" according to John Adams. "The patients were careless, some of them wantonly so; and others were suspected of designing to spread the smallpox in the town, which was full of people who had not passed through the distemper." In January 1774 patients from the hospital who tried to enter the town from unauthorized landing places were forcefully prevented from doing so; a hospital boat was burned; and four men suspected of stealing infected clothes from the hospital were tarred and feathered, then carted from Marblehead to Salem in a long cortege. The Marblehead town meeting finally won the proprietors' agreement to shut down the hospital; but after some twenty-two new cases of smallpox broke out in the town within a few days "apprehension became general," and some "Ruffians" in disguise hastened the hospital's demise by burning the nearly evacuated building. A military watch of forty men were needed for several nights to keep the peace in Marblehead.[6]

A similar episode occurred in Norfolk, Virginia, when a group of wealthy residents decided to have their families inoculated for smallpox. Fears arose that the lesser disease brought on by the inoculations would spread and necessitate a general inoculation, which would cost "more money than is circulating in Norfolk" and ruin trade and commerce such that "the whole colony would feel the effects." Local magistrates said they could not interefere because "the law was silent in the matter." Public and private meetings then sought to negotiate the issue. Despite a hard-won

---

[5] Bridenbaugh, *Cities in Revolt,* 114; Bridenbaugh, *Cities in the Wilderness,* 196, 383, 388–389; Edmund S. and Helen M. Morgan, *The Stamp Act Crisis,* rev. ed. (New York, 1963), 159; Anne Rowe Cunningham, ed., *Letters and Diary of John Rowe, Boston Merchant, 1759–1762, 1764–1779* (Boston, 1903), 218. On the marriage riots, see *New-York Gazette* (New York City), July 11, 1765—and note, that when the reporter speaks of persons "concern'd in such unlawful Enterprises" he clearly is referring to the husbands, not their "Disciplinarians." On the Rogerenes, see item in *Connecticut Gazette* (New Haven), Apr. 5, 1766, reprinted in Lawrence H. Gipson, *Jared Ingersoll* (New Haven, 1920), 195, n. 1.

[6] John Adams, "Novanglus," in Charles F. Adams, ed., *The Works of John Adams* (Boston, 1850–1856), IV, 76–77; Salem news of Jan. 25 and Feb. 1, 1774, in *Providence Gazette* (Rhode Island), Feb. 5, and Feb. 12, 1774.

agreement, however, the pro-inoculation faction peristed in its original plan. Then finally a mob drove the newly inoculated women and children on a five-mile forced march in darkness and rain to the common Pest House, a three-year old institution designed to isolate seamen and others, particularly Negroes, infected with smallpox.[7]

These local incidents indicate a willingness among many Americans to act outside the bounds of law, but they cannot be described as anti-authoritarian in any general sense. Sometimes in fact—as in the Boston bawdy house riot of 1734, or the Norfolk smallpox incident—local magistrates openly countenanced or participated in the mob's activities. Far from opposing established institutions, many supporters of Shays's Rebellion honored their leaders "by no less decisive marks of popular favor than elections to local offices of trust and authority." [8] It was above all the existence of such elections that forced local magistrates to reflect community feelings and so prevented their becoming the targets of insurrections. Certainly in New England, where the town meeting ruled, and to some extent in New York, where aldermen and councilmen were annually elected, this was true; yet even in Philadelphia, with its lethargic closed corporation, or Charleston, which lacked municipal institutions, authority was normally exerted by residents who had an immediate sense of local sentiment. Provincial governments were also for the most part kept alert to local feelings by their elected assemblies. Sometimes, of course, uprisings turned against domestic American institutions—as in Pennsylvania in 1764, when the "Paxton Boys" complained that the colony's Quaker assembly had failed to provide adequately for their defense against the Indians. But uprisings over local issues proved *extra-institutional* in character more than they were anti-institutional; they served the community where no law existed, or intervened beyond what magistrates thought they could do officially to cope with a local problem.

The case was different when imperial authority was involved. There legal authority emanated from a capital an ocean away, where the colonists had no integral voice in the formation of policy, where governmental decisions were based largely upon the reports of "king's men" and sought

[7] Letter from "Friend to the Borough and county of Norfolk," in Purdie and Dixon's *Virginia Gazette Postscript* (Williamsburg), Sept. 8, 1768, which gives the fullest account. This letter answered an earlier letter from Norfolk, Aug. 6, 1768, available in Rind's *Va. Gaz. Supplement* (Wmsbg.), Aug. 25, 1768. See also letter of Cornelius Calvert in Purdie and Dixon's *Va. Gaz.* (Wmsbg.), Jan. 9, 1772. Divisions over the inoculation seemed to follow more general political lines. See Patrick Henderson, 'Smallpox and Patriotism, The Norfolk Riots, 1768–1769," *Virginia Magazine of History and Biography,* LXXIII (1965), 413–424.

[8] James Madison to Thomas Jefferson, Mar. 19, 1787, in Julian P. Boyd, ed., *The Papers of Thomas Jefferson* (Princeton, 1950–), XI, 223.

above all to promote the king's interests. When London's legal authority and local interest conflicted, efforts to implement the edicts of royal officials were often answered by uprisings, and it was not unusual in these cases for local magistrates to participate or openly sympathize with the insurgents. The colonial response to the White Pines Acts of 1722 and 1729 is one example. Enforcement of the acts was difficult in general because "the various elements of colonial society . . . seemed inclined to violate the pine laws—legislatures, lumbermen, and merchants were against them, and even the royal governors were divided." At Exeter, New Hampshire, in 1734 about thirty men prevented royal officials from putting the king's broad arrow on some seized boards; efforts to enforce the acts in Connecticut during the 1750's ended after a deputy of the surveyor-general was thrown in a pond and nearly drowned; five years later logs seized in Massachusetts and New Hampshire were either "rescued" or destroyed.[9] Two other imperial issues that provoked local American uprisings long before 1765 and continued to do so during the Revolutionary period were impressment and customs enforcement.

As early as 1743 the colonists' violent opposition to impressment was said to indicate a "Contempt of Government." Some captains had been mobbed, the Admiralty complained, "others emprisoned, and afterwards held to exorbitant Bail, and are now under Prosecutions carried on by Combination, and by joint Subscription towards the expense." Colonial governors, despite their offers, furnished captains with little real aid either to procure seamen or "even to protect them from the Rage and Insults of the People." Two days of severe rioting answered Commodore Charles Knowles's efforts to sweep Boston harbor for able-bodied men in November 1747. Again in 1764 when Rear Admiral Lord Alexander Colville sent out orders to "procure" men in principal harbors between Casco Bay and Cape Henlopen, mobs met the ships at every turn. When the *St. John* sent out a boat to seize a recently impressed deserter from a Newport wharf, a mob protected him, captured the boat's officer, and hurled stones at the crew; later fifty Newporters joined the colony's gunner at Fort George in opening fire on the king's ship itself. Under threat to her master the *Chaleur* was forced to release four fishermen seized off Long Island, and when that ship's captain went ashore at New York a mob seized his boat and burned it in the Fields. In the spring of 1765 after the *Maidstone* capped a six-month siege of Newport harbor by seizing "all the Men" out of a brigantine

---

[9] Bernhard Knollenberg, *Origin of the American Revolution: 1759–1776* (New York, 1965), 126, 129. See also, Robert G. Albion, *Forests and Sea Power* (Cambridge, Mass., 1926), 262–263, 265. Joseph J. Malone, *Pine Trees and Politics* (Seattle, 1964), includes less detail on the forceful resistance to the acts.

from Africa, a mob of about five hundred men similarly seized a ship's officer and burned one of her boats on the Common. Impressment also met mass resistance at Norfolk in 1767 and was a major cause of the famous *Liberty* riot at Boston in 1768.[10]

Like the impressment uprisings, which in most instances sought to protect or rescue men from the "press," customs incidents were aimed at impeding the customs service in enforcing British laws. Tactics varied, and although incidents occurred long before 1764—in 1719, for example, Caleb Heathcote reported a "riotous and tumultuous" rescue of seized claret by Newporters—their frequency, like those of the impressment "riots," apparently increased after the Sugar Act was passed and customs enforcement efforts were tightened. The 1764 rescue of the *Rhoda* in Rhode Island preceded a theft in Dighton, Massachusetts, of the cargo from a newly seized vessel, the *Polly*, by a mob of some forty men with blackened faces. In 1766 again a mob stoned a customs official's home in Falmouth (Portland), Maine, while "Persons unknown and disguised" stole sugar and rum that had been impounded that morning. The intimidation of customs officials and of the particularly despised customs informers also enjoyed a long history. In 1701 the South Carolina attorney general publicly attacked an informer "and struck him several times, crying out, this is the Informer, this is he that will ruin the country." Similar assaults occurred decades later, in New Haven in 1766 and 1769, and New London in 1769, and were then often distinguished by their brutality. In 1771 a Providence tidesman, Jesse Saville, was seized, stripped, bound hand and foot, tarred and feathered, had dirt thrown in his face, then was beaten and "almost strangled." Even more thorough assaults upon two other Rhode Island tidesmen followed in July 1770 and upon Collector Charles Dudley in April 1771. Finally, customs vessels came under attack: the *St. John* was shelled at Newport in 1764 where the customs ship *Liberty* was sunk in 1769—both episodes

[10] Admiralty to Gov. George Thomas, Sept. 26, 1743, in Samuel Hazard *et al.*, eds., *Pennsylvania Archives* (Philadelphia, 1852–1949), I, 639. For accounts of the Knowles riot, see Gov. William Shirley to Josiah Willard, Nov. 19, 1747, Shirley's Proclamation of Nov. 21, 1747, and his letter to the Board of Trade, Dec. 1, 1747, in Charles H. Lincoln, ed., *The Correspondence of William Shirley . . . 1731–1760* (New York, 1912), I, 406–419; see also Thomas Hutchinson, *History of the Province of Massachusetts Bay*, ed. Lawrence S. Mayo (Cambridge, Mass., 1936), II, 330–333; and *Reports of the Record Commissioners of Boston* (Boston, 1885), XIV, 127–130. David Lovejoy, *Rhode Island Politics and the American Revolution, 1760–1776* (Providence, 1958), 36–39, and on the *Maidstone* in particular see "O. G." in *Newport Mercury* (Rhode Island), June 10, 1765. Bridenbaugh, *Cities in Revolt*, 309–311; documents on the *St. John* episode in *Records of the Colony of Rhode Island and Providence Plantations* (Providence, 1856–1865), VI, 427–430. George G. Wolkins, "The Seizure of John Hancock's Sloop 'Liberty,'" *Massachusetts Historical Society, Proceedings* (1921–1923), LV, 239–284. See also Lemisch, "Jack Tar," *Wm. and Mary Qtly.*, 3d Ser., XXV (1968), 391–393; and Neil R. Stout, "Manning the Royal Navy in North America, 1763–1775," *American Neptune*, XXIII (1963), 179–181.

that served as prelude to the destruction of the *Gaspée* outside Providence in 1772.[11]

Such incidents were not confined to New England. Philadelphia witnessed some of the most savage attacks, and even the surveyor of Sassafras and Bohemia in Maryland—an office long a sinecure, since no ships entered or cleared in Sassafras or Bohemia—met with violence when he tried to execute his office in March 1775. After seizing two wagons of goods being carried overland from Maryland toward Duck Creek, Delaware, the officer was overpowered by a "licentious mob" that kept shouting "Liberty and Duck Creek forever" as it went through the hours-long rituals of tarring and feathering him and threatening his life. And at Norfolk, Virginia, in the spring of 1766 an accused customs informer was tarred and feathered, pelted with stones and rotten eggs, and finally thrown in the sea where he nearly drowned. Even Georgia saw customs violence before independence, and one of the rare deaths resulting from a colonial riot occurred there in 1775.[12]

[11] Heathcote letter from Newport, Sept. 7, 1719, *Records of the Colony of Rhode Island*, IV, 259–260; Lovejoy, *Rhode Island Politics*, 35–39. There is an excellent summary of the *Polly* incident in Morgan, *Stamp Act Crisis*, 59, 64–67; and see also *Providence Gaz.* (R.I.), Apr. 27, 1765. On the Falmouth incident see the letter from the collector and comptroller of Falmouth, Aug. 19, 1766, Treasury Group 1, Class 453, Piece 182, Public Records Office. Hereafter cited as T. 1/453, 182. See also the account in Appendix I of Josiah Quincy, Jr., *Reports of the Cases Argued and Adjudged in the Superior Court of Judicature of the Province of Massachusetts Bay, between 1761 and 1772* (Boston, 1865), 446–447. W. Noel Sainsbury et al., eds., *Calendar of State Papers, Colonial Series, America and the West Indies* (London, 1910), *1701*, no. 1042, xi, a. A summary of one of the New Haven informer attacks is in Willard M. Wallace, *Traitorous Hero: The Life and Fortunes of Benedict Arnold* (New York: 1954), 20–23. Arnold's statement on the affair which he led is in Malcolm Decker, *Benedict Arnold, Son of the Havens* (Tarrytown, N.Y., 1932), 27–29. Gipson, in *Jared Ingersoll*, 277–278, relates the later incidents. For the New London informer attacks, see documents of July 1769 in T. 1/471. On the Saville affair see Saville to collector and comptroller of customs in Newport, May 18, 1769, T. 1/471, and *New York Journal* (New York City), July 6, 1769. On later Rhode Island incidents see Dudley and John Nicoll to governor of Rhode Island, Aug. 1, 1770, T. 1/471. Dudley to commissioners of customs at Boston, Newport, Apr. 11, 1771, T. 1/482. On the destruction of the *Liberty* see documents in T. 1/471, esp. comptroller and collector to the governor, July 21, 1769.

[12] On Philadelphia violence see William Sheppard to commissioners of customs, Apr. 21, 1769, T. 1/471; Deputy Collector at Philadelphia John Swift to commissioners of customs at Boston, Oct. 13, 1769, *ibid.;* and on a particularly brutal attack on the son of customsman John Hatton, see Deputy Collector John Swift to Boston customs commissioners, Nov. 15, 1770, and related documents in T. 1/476. See also Alfred S. Martin, "The King's Customs: Philadelphia, 1763–1774," *Wm. and Mary Qtly.*, 3d Ser., V (1948), 201–216. Documents on the Maryland episode are in T. 1/513, including the following: Richard Reeve to Grey Cooper, Apr. 19, 1775; extracts from a Council meeting, Mar. 16, 1775; deposition of Robert Stratford Byrne, surveyor of His Majesty's Customs at Sassafras and Bohemia, and Byrne to customs commissioners, Mar. 17, 1775. On the Virginia incident see William Smith to Jeremiah Morgan, Apr. 3, 1776, Colonial Office Group, Class 5, Piece 1331, 80, Public Record Office. Hereafter cited at C. O. 5/1331, 80. W. W. Abbot, *The Royal Governors of Georgia, 1754–1775* (Chapel Hill, 1959), 174–175.

White Pines, impressment, and customs uprisings have attracted historians' attention because they opposed British authority and so seemed to presage the Revolution. In fact, however, they had much in common with many exclusively local uprisings. In each of the incidents violence was directed not so much against the "rich and powerful" [18] as against men who—as it was said after the Norfolk smallpox incident—"in every part of their conduct . . . acted very inconsistently as good neighbors or citizens." The effort remained one of safeguarding not the interests of isolated groups alone, but the community's safety and welfare. The White Pines Acts need not have provoked this opposition had they applied only to trees of potential use to the Navy, and had they been framed and executed with concern for colonial rights. But instead the acts reserved to the Crown all white pine trees including those "utterly unfit for masts, yards, or bowsprits," and prevented colonists from using them for building materials or lumber exportation even in regions where white pine constituted the principal forest growth. As a result the acts "operated so much against the convenience and even necessities of the inhabitants," Surveyor John Wentworth explained, that "it became almost a general interest of the country" to frustrate the acts' execution. Impressment offered a more immediate effect, since the "press" could quickly cripple whole towns. Merchants and masters were affected as immediately as seamen: the targeted port, as Massachusetts' Governor William Shirley explained in 1747, was drained of mariners by both impressment itself and the flight of navigation to safer provinces, driving the wages for any remaining seamen upward. When the press was of long duration, moreover, or when it took place during a normally busy season, it could mean serious shortages of food or firewood for winter, and a general attrition of the commercial life that sustained all strata of society in trading towns. Commerce seemed even more directly attacked by British trade regulations, particularly by the proliferation of customs procedures in the mid-1760's that seemed to be in no American's interest, and by the Sugar Act with its virtual prohibition of the trade with the foreign West Indies that sustained the economies of colonies like Rhode Island. As a result even when only a limited contingent of sailors participated in a customs incident officials could suspect—as did

---

These customs riots remained generally separate from the more central intercolonial opposition to Britain that emerged in 1765. Isolated individuals like John Brown of Providence and Maximilian Calvert of Norfolk were involved in both the organized intercolonial Sons of Liberty and in leading mobs against customs functionaries or informers. These roles, however, for the most part were unconnected, that is, there was no radical program of customs obstruction *per se.* Outbreaks were above all local responses to random provocation and, at least before the Townshend duties, usually devoid of explicit ideological justifications.

[13] Hobsbawm, *Primitive Rebels,* 111. For a different effort to see class division as relevant in 18th century uprisings, see Lemisch, "Jack Tar," *Wm. and Mary Qtly.,* 3d Ser., XXV (1968), 387.

the deputy collector at Philadelphia in 1770—that the mass of citizens "in their Hearts" approved of it.[14]

Because the various uprisings discussed here grew out of concerns essential to wide sections of the community, the "rioters" were not necessarily confined to the seamen, servants, Negroes, and boys generally described as the staple components of the colonial mob. The uprising of Exeter, New Hampshire, townsmen against the king's surveyor of the woods in 1754 was organized by a member of the prominent Gillman family who was a mill owner and a militia officer. Members of the upper classes participated in Norfolk's smallpox uprising, and Cornelius Calvert, who was later attacked in a related incident, protested that leading members of the community, doctors and magistrates, had posted securities for the good behavior of the "Villains" convicted of mobbing him. Captain Jeremiah Morgan complained about the virtually universal participation of Norfolkers in an impressment incident of 1767, and "all the principal Gentlemen in Town" were supposedly present when a customs informer was tarred and feathered there in 1766. Merchant Benedict Arnold admitted leading a New Haven mob against an informer in 1766; New London merchants Joseph Packwood and Nathaniel Shaw commanded the mob that first accosted Captain William Reid the night the *Liberty* was destroyed at Newport in 1769, just as John Brown, a leading Providence merchant, led that against the *Gaspée.* Charles Dudley reported in April 1771 that the men who beat him in Newport "did not come from the . . . lowest class of Men," but were "stiled Merchants and the Masters of their Vessels"; and again in 1775 Robert Stratford Byrne said many of his Maryland and Pennsylvania attackers were "from Appearance . . . Men of Property." It is interesting, too, that during Shays's Rebellion—so often considered a class uprising—"men who were of good property and owed not a shilling" were said to be "involved in the train of desperado's to suppress the courts." [15]

[14] "Friends to the borough and county of Norfolk," Purdie and Dixon's *Va. Gaz. Postscript.* (Wmsbg.), Sept. 8, 1768. Wentworth quoted in Knollenberg, *Origin of American Revolution,* 124–125. Lemisch, "Jack Tar," *Wm. and Mary Qtly.,* 3d Ser., XXV (1968), 383–385. Shirley to Duke of Newcastle, Dec. 31, 1747, in Lincoln, ed., *Shirley Correspondence,* I, 420–423. Dora Mae Clark, "The Impressment of Seamen in the American Colonies," *Essays in Colonial History Presented to Charles McLean Andrews* (New Haven, 1931), 199–200. John Swift to Boston customs commissioners, Nov. 15, 1770, T. 1/476.

[15] Malone, *White Pines,* 112. "Friends to the borough and county of Norfolk," Purdie and Dixon's *Va. Gaz. Postscript.* (Wmsbg.), Sept. 8, 1768; Calvert letter, *ibid.,* Jan. 9, 1772. Capt. Jeremiah Morgan, quoted in Lemisch, "Jack Tar," *Wm. and Mary Qtly.,* 3d Ser., XXV (1968), 391; and William Smith to Morgan, Apr. 3, 1766, C. O. 5/1331, 80. Decker, *Benedict Arnold,* 27–29; deposition of Capt. William Reid on the *Liberty* affair, July 21, 1769, T. 1/471; Ephraim Bowen's narrative on the *Gaspée* affair, *Records of the Colony of Rhode Island,* VII, 68–73; Charles Dudley to Boston customs commissioners, Apr. 11, 1771, T. 1/482, and deposition by

Opposition to impressment and customs enforcement in itself was not, moreover, the only cause of the so-called impressment or customs "riots." The complete narratives of these incidents indicate again not only that the crowd acted to support local interests, but that it sometimes enforced the will of local magistrates by extralegal means. Although British officials blamed the *St. John* incident upon that ship's customs and impressment activities, colonists insisted that the confrontation began when some sailors stole a few pigs and chickens from a local miller and the ship's crew refused to surrender the thieves to Newport officials. Two members of the Rhode Island council then ordered the gunner of Fort George to detain the schooner until the accused seamen were delivered to the sheriff, and "many People went over the Fort to assist the Gunner in the Discharge of his Duty." Only after this uprising did the ship's officers surrender the accused men.[16] Similarly, the 1747 Knowles impressment riot in Boston and the 1765 *Maidstone* impressment riot in Newport broke out after governors' request for the release of impressed seamen had gone unanswered, and only after the outbreaks of violence were the governors' requests honored. The crowd that first assembled on the night the *Liberty* was destroyed in Newport also began by demanding the allegedly drunken sailors who that afternoon had abused and shot at a colonial captain, Joseph Packwood, so they could be bound over to local magistrates for prosecution.[17]

In circumstances such as these, the "mob" often appeared only after the legal channels of redress had proven inadequate. The main thrust of the colonists' resistance to the White Pines Acts had always been made in their courts and legislatures. Violence broke out only in local situations

---

Byrne, T. 1/513. Edward Carrington to Jefferson, June 9, 1787, Boyd, ed., *Jefferson Papers,* XI, 408; and see also Smith, "Depression of 1785," *Wm. and Mary Qtly.,* 3d Ser., V (1948), 88—of the 21 men indicted for treason in Worcester during the court's April term 1787, 15 were "gentlemen" and only 6 "yeamen."

[16] Gov. Samuel Ward's report to the Treasury lords, Oct. 23, 1765, Ward Manuscripts, Box 1, fol. 58, Rhode Island Historical Society, Providence. See also deposition of Daniel Vaughn of Newport—Vaughn was the gunner at Fort George —July 8, 1764, Chalmers Papers, Rhode Island, fol. 41, New York Public Library, New York City. For British official accounts of the affair, see Lieut. Hill's version in James Munro, ed., *Acts of the Privy Council of England, Colonial Series* (London, 1912), VI, 374–376, and the report of John Robinson and John Nicoll to the customs commissioners, Aug. 30, 1765, Privy Council Group, Class 1, Piece 51, Bundle 1 (53a), Public Record Office. Hill, whose report was drawn up soon after the incident, does not contradict Ward's narrative, but seems oblivious of any warrant-granting process on shore; Robinson and Nicoll—whose report was drawn up over a year later, and in the midst of the Stamp Act turmoil—claimed that a recent customs seizure had precipitated the attack upon the *St. John*.

[17] On the Knowles and *Maidstone* incidents see above, n. 10. On the *Liberty* affair see documents in T. 1/471, esp. the deposition of Capt. William Reid, July 21, 1769, and that of John Carr, the second mate, who indicates that the mob soon forgot its scheme of delivering the crew members to the magistrates.

where no alternative was available. Even the burning of the *Gaspée* in June 1771 was a last resort. Three months before the incident a group of prominent Providence citizens complained about the ship's wanton severity with all vessels along the coast and the colony's governor pressed their case with the fleet's admiral. The admiral, however, supported the *Gaspée*'s commander, Lieutenant William Dudingston; and thereafter, the *Providence Gazette* reported, Dudingston became "more haughty, insolent and intolerable, . . . personally ill treating every master and merchant of the vessels he boarded, stealing sheep, hogs, poultry, etc. from farmers round the bay, and cutting down their fruit and other trees for firewood." Redress from London was possible but time-consuming, and in the meantime Rhode Island was approaching what its governor called "the deepest calamity" as supplies of food and fuel were curtailed and prices, especially in Newport, rose steeply. It was significant that merchant John Brown finally led the Providence "mob" that seized the moment in June when the *Gaspée* ran aground near Warwick, for it was he who had spearheaded the effort in March 1772 to win redress through the normal channels of government.[18]

II

There was little that was distinctively American about the colonial insurrections. The uprisings over grain exportations during times of dearth, the attacks on brothels, press gangs, royal forest officials, and customsmen, all had their counterparts in seventeenth- and eighteenth-century England. Even the Americans' hatred of the customs establishment mirrored the Englishman's traditional loathing of excisemen. Like the customsmen in the colonies, they seemed to descend into localities armed with extraordinary prerogative powers. Often, too, English excisemen were "thugs and brutes who beat up their victims without compunction or stole or wrecked their property" and against whose extravagances little redress was possible through the law.[19] Charges of an identical character were made in the colonies against customsmen and naval officers as well, particularly after 1763 when officers of the Royal Navy were commissioned as deputy members

---

[18] Malone, *White Pines,* 8–9, and *passim. Records of the Colony of Rhode Island,* VII, 60, 62–63, 174–175, including the deposition of Dep. Gov. Darins Sessions, June 12, 1772, and Adm. Montagu to Gov. Wanton, Apr. 8, 1772. Also, Wanton to Hillsborough, June 16, 1772, and Ephraim Bowen's narrative *ibid.,* 63–73, 90–92. *Providence Gaz.* (R.I.), Jan. 9, 1773.

[19] Max Beloff, *Public Order and Popular Disturbances, 1660–1714* (London, 1938), *passim;* Albion, *Forests and Sea Power,* 263; J. H. Plumb, *England in the Eighteenth Century* (Baltimore, 1961 [orig. publ., Oxford, 1950]), 66.

of the customs service,[20] and a history of such accusations lay behind many of the best-known waterfront insurrections. The Americans' complaints took on particular significance only because in the colonies those officials embodied the authority of a "foreign" power. Their arrogance and arbitrariness helped effect "an estrangement of the Affections of the People from the Authority under which they act," and eventually added an emotional element of anger against the Crown to a revolutionary conflict otherwise carried on in the language of law and right.[21]

The focused character of colonial uprisings also resembled those in England and even France where, Rudé has pointed out, crowds were remarkably single-minded and discriminating.[22] Targets were characteristically related to grievances: the Knowles rioters sought only the release of the impressed men; they set free a captured officer when assured he had nothing to do with the press, and refrained from burning a boat near Province House for fear the fire would spread. The Norfolk rioters, driven by fear of smallpox, forcefully isolated the inoculated persons where they would be least dangerous. Even the customs rioters vented their brutality on customs officers and informers alone, and the Shaysite "mobs" dispersed after closing the courts which promised most immediately to effect their ruin. So domesticated and controlled was the Boston mob that it refused to riot on Saturday and Sunday nights, which were considered holy by New Englanders.[23]

When colonists compared their mobs with those in the Mother Country they were struck only with the greater degree of restraint among Americans. "These People bear no Resemblance to an English Mob," John Jay wrote of the Shaysites in December 1786, "they are more temperate, cool

[20] See, for example, "A Pumkin" in the *New London Gazette* (Connecticut), May 14, 18, 1773; "O. G." in *Newport Merc.* (R.I.), June 10, 1765; *New London Gaz.* (Conn.), Sept. 22, 1769, complaints of Marylander David Bevan reprinted in Rind's *Va. Gaz.* (Wmsbg.), July 27, 1769, and *New London Gaz.* (Conn.), July 21, 1769. Stout, "Manning the Royal Navy," *American Neptune,* XXIII (1963), 174. For a similar accusation against a surveyor-general of the king's woods, see Albion, *Forests and Sea Power,* 262.

[21] Joseph Reed to the president of Congress, Oct. 21, 1779, in Hazard *et al.,* eds., *Pennsylvania Archives,* VII, 762. Five years earlier Reed had tried to impress upon Lord Dartmouth the importance of constraining Crown agents in the colonies if any reconciliation were to be made between Britain and the colonies. See his letter to Earl of Dartmouth, Apr. 4, 1774, in William B. Reed, *Life and Correspondence of Joseph Reed* (Philadelphia, 1847), I, 56–57. For a similar plea, again from a man close to the American Revolutionary leadership, see Stephen Sayre to Lord Dartmouth, Dec. 13, 1766, Dartmouth Papers, D 1778/2/258, William Salt Library, Stafford, England.

[22] Rudé, *Crowd in History,* 60, 253–254. The restraint exercised by 18th century mobs has often been commented upon. See, for example, Wood "A Note on Mobs," *Wm. and Mary Qtly.,* 3d Ser., XXIII (1966), 636–637.

[23] Joseph Harrison's testimony in Wolkins, "Seizure of Handcock's Sloop 'Liberty,' " Mass. Hist. Soc., *Proceedings,* LV, 254.

and regular in their Conduct—they have hitherto abstained from Plunder, nor have they that I know of committed any outrages but such as the accomplishment of their Purpose made necessary." Similar comparisons were often repeated during the Revolutionary conflict, and were at least partially grounded in fact. When Londoners set out to "pull down" houses of ill fame in 1688, for example, the affair spread, prisons were opened, and disorder ended only when troops were called out. But when eighteenth-century Bostonians set out on the same task, there is no record that their destruction extended beyond the bordellos themselves. Even the violence of the customs riots—which contrast in that regard from other American incidents—can sometimes be explained by the presence of volatile foreign seamen. The attack on the son of customsman John Hatton, who was nearly killed in a Philadelphia riot, occurred, for example, when the city was crowded by over a thousand seamen. His attackers were apparently Irish crew members of a vessel he and his father had tried to seize off Cape May, and they were "set on," the Philadelphia collector speculated, by an Irish merchant in Philadelphia to whom the vessel was consigned. One of the most lethal riots in the history of colonial America, in which rioters killed five people, occurred in a small town near Norfolk, Virginia, and was significantly perpetrated entirely by British seamen who resisted the local inhabitants' efforts to reinstitute peace.[24] During and immediately after the Revolutionary War some incidents occurred in which deaths are recorded; but contemporaries felt these were historical aberrations, caused by the "brutalizing" effect of the war itself. "Our citizens, from a habit of putting . . . [the British] to death, have reconciled their minds to the killing of each other," South Carolina Judge Aedanus Burke explained.[25]

To a large extent the pervasive restraint and virtual absence of bloodshed in American incidents can be be understood in terms of social and

[24] Jay to Jefferson, Dec. 14, 1786, Boyd, ed., *Jefferson Papers,* X, 597. Beloff, *Public Order,* 30. John Swift to Boston customs commissioners, Nov. 15, 1770, Gov. William Franklin's Proclamation, Nov. 17, 1770, and John Hatton to Boston custom commissioners, Nov. 20, 1770, T. 1/476. The last mentioned riot occurred in November 1762. A cartel ship from Havana had stopped for repairs in October. On Nov. 21 a rumor spread that the Spaniards were murdering the inhabitants, which drew seamen from His Majesty's ship, *Arundel,* also in the harbor, into town, where the seamen drove the Spaniards into a house, set fire to it, and apparently intended to blow it up. A dignitary of the Spanish colonial service, who had been a passenger on the cartel ship, was beaten and some money and valuables were stolen from him. Local men tried to quell the riot without success. It was eventually put down by militiamen from Norfolk. See "A Narrative of a Riot in Virginia in November 1762," T. 1/476.

[25] Burke and others to the same effect, quoted in Jerome J. Nadelhaft, The Revolutionary Era in South Carolina, 1775–1788 (unpubl. Ph.D. diss., University of Wisconsin, 1965), 151–152. See also account of the "Fort Wilson" riot of October 1779 in J. Thomas Scharf and Thompson Westcott, *History of Philadelphia, 1609–1884* (Philadelphia, 1884), I, 401–403.

military circumstance. There was no large amorphous city in America comparable to London, where England's worst incidents occurred. More important, the casualties even in eighteenth-century British riots were rarely the work of rioters. No deaths were inflicted by the Wilkes, Anti-Irish, or "No Popery" mobs, and only single fatalities resulted from other upheavals such as the Porteous riots of 1736. "It was authority rather than the crowd that was conspicuous for its violence to life and limb": all 285 casualties of the Gordon riots, for example, were rioters.[26] Since a regular army was less at the ready for use against colonial mobs, casualty figures for American uprisings were naturally much reduced.

To some extent the general tendency toward a discriminating purposefulness was shared by mobs throughout western Europe, but within the British Empire the focused character of popular uprisings and also their persistence can be explained in part by the character of law enforcement procedures. There were no professional police forces in the eighteenth century. Instead the power of government depended traditionally upon institutions like the "hue and cry," by which the community in general rose to apprehend felons. In its original medieval form the "hue and cry" was a form of summary justice that resembled modern lynch law. More commonly by the eighteenth century magistrates turned to the *posse commitatus,* literally the "power of the country," and in practice all able-bodied men a sheriff might call upon to assist him. Where greater and more organized support was needed, magistrates could call out the militia.[27] Both the *posse* and the militia drew upon local men, including many of the same persons who made up the mob. This was particularly clear where these traditional mechanisms failed to function effectively. At Boston in September 1766 when customsmen contemplated breaking into the house of merchant Daniel Malcom to search for contraband goods, Sheriff Stephen Greenleaf threatened to call for support from members of the very crowd suspected of an intent to riot; and when someone suggested during the Stamp Act riots that the militia be raised Greenleaf was told it had already risen. This situation meant that mobs could naturally assume the manner of a lawful institution, acting by habit with relative restraint and responsibility. On the other hand, the militia institutionalized the practice of forcible popular coercion and so made the formation of extralegal mobs more natural that J. R. Western has called the militia "a relic of the bad old days,"

---

[26] Rudé, *Crowd in History,* 255–257.

[27] On the "hue and cry" see Frederick Pollock and Frederic W. Maitland, *The History of English Law before the Time of Edward I* (Cambridge, Eng., 1968 [orig. publ., Cambridge, Eng., 1895]), II, 578–580, and William Blackstone, *Commentaries on the Laws of England* (Philadelphia, 1771), IV, 290–291. John Shy, *Toward Lexington: The Role of the British Army in the Coming of the American Revolution* (Princeton, 1965), 40. The English militia underwent a period of decay after 1670 but was revived in 1757. See J. R. Western, *The English Militia in the Eighteenth Century* (London, 1965).

and hailed its passing as "a step towards . . . bringing civilization and humanity into our [English] political life." [28]

These law enforcement mechanisms left magistrates virtually helpless whenever a large segment of the population was immediately involved in the disorder, or when the community had a strong sympathy for the rioters. The Boston militia's failure to act in the Stamp Act riots, which was repeated in nearly all the North American colonies, recapitulated a similar refusal during the Knowles riot of 1747.[29] If the mob's sympathizers were confined to a single locality, the governor could try to call out the militias of surrounding areas, as Massachusetts Governor William Shirley began to do in 1747, and as, to some extent, Governor Francis Bernard attempted after the rescue of the *Polly* in 1765.[30] In the case of sudden uprisings, however, these peace-keeping mechanisms were at best partially effective since they required time to assemble strength, which often made the effort wholly pointless.

When the disorder continued and the militia either failed to appear or proved insufficient, there was, of course, the army, which was used periodically in the eighteenth century against rioters in England and Scotland. Even in America peacetime garrisons tended to be placed where they might serve to maintain law and order. But since all Englishmen shared a fear of standing armies the deployment of troops had always to be a sensitive and carefully limited recourse. Military and civil spheres of authority were rigidly separated, as was clear to Lord Jeffery Amherst, who refused to use soldiers against antimilitary rioters during the Seven Years' War because that function was "entirely foreign to their command and belongs of right to none but the civil power." In fact troops could be used against British subjects, as in the suppression of civil disorder, only upon the request of local magistrates. This institutional inhibition carried, if anything, more weight in the colonies. There royal governors had quickly lost their right to declare martial law without the consent of the provincial councils that were, again, usually filled with local men.[31]

[28] Greenleaf's deposition, T. 1/446; *Providence Gaz.* (R.I.), Aug. 24, 1765; Western, *English Militia,* 74.

[29] Gov. William Shirley explained the militia's failure to appear during the opening stages of the Knowles riot by citing the militiamen's opposition to impressment and consequent sympathy for the rioters. See his letter to the Lords of Trade, Dec. 1, 1747, in Lincoln, ed., *Shirley Correspondence,* I, 417–418. The English militia was also unreliable. It worked well against invasions and unpopular rebellions, but was less likely to support the government when official orders "clashed with the desires of the citizens" or when ordered to protect unpopular minorities. Sir Robert Wolpole believed "that if called on to suppress smuggling, protect the turnpikes, or enforce the gin act, the militia would take the wrong side." Western, *English Militia,* 72–73.

[30] Shirley to Josiah Willard, Nov. 19, 1747, Lincoln, ed., *Shirley Correspondence,* I, 407; Bernard's orders in *Providence Gaz.* (R.I.), Apr. 27, 1765.

[31] Shy, *Toward Lexington,* 39–40, 44, 47, 74. Amherst, quoted in J. C. Long, *Lord Jeffery Amherst* (New York, 1933), 124.

For all practical purposes, then, when a large political unit such as an entire town or colony condoned an act of mass force, problems were raised "almost insoluble without rending the whole fabric of English law." Nor was the situation confined to the colonies. After describing England's institutions for keeping the peace under the later Stuarts, Max Beloff suggested that no technique for maintaining order was found until nineteenth-century reformers took on the task of reshaping urban government. Certainly by the 1770's no acceptable solution had been found—neither by any colonists, nor "anyone in London, Paris, or Rome, either," as Carl Bridenbaugh has put it. To even farsighted contemporaries like John Adams the weakness of authority was a fact of the social order that necessarily conditioned the way rulers could act. "It is vain to expect or hope to carry on government against the universal bent and genius of the people," he wrote, "we may whimper and whine as much as we will, but nature made it impossible when she made man." [32]

The mechanisms of enforcing public order were rendered even more fragile since the difference between legal and illegal applications of mass force was distinct in theory, but sometimes indistinguishable in practice. The English common law prohibited riot, defined as an uprising of three or more persons who performed what Blackstone called an "unlawful act of violence" for a private purpose. If the act was never carried out or attempted the offense became unlawful assembly; if some effort was made toward its execution, rout; and if the purpose of the uprising was public rather than private—tearing down whore houses, for example, or destroying all enclosures rather than just those personally affecting the insurgents—the offense became treason since it constituted a usurpation of the king's function, a "levying war against the King." The precise legal offence lay not so much in the purpose of the uprising as in its use of force and violence "wherein the Law does not allow the Use of such Force." Such unlawful assumptions of force were carefully distinguished by commentators upon the common law from other occasions on which the law authorized a use of force. It was, for example, legal for force to be used by a sheriff, constable, "or perhaps even . . . a private Person" who assembled "a competent Number of People, in Order with Force to suppress Rebels, or Enemies, or Rioters"; for a justice of the peace to raise the *posse* when opposed in detaining lands, or for Crown officers to raise "a Power as may effectually enable them to over-power any . . . Resistance" in the execution of the King's writs.[33]

[32] Shy, *Toward Lexington,* 44; Beloff, *Public Order,* 157–158; Bridenbaugh, *Cities in Revolt,* 297; C. F. Adams, ed., *Works of Adams,* IV, 74–75, V, 209.

[33] The definition of the common law of riot most commonly cited—for example, by John Adams in the Massacre trials—was from William Hawkins, *A Treatise of the Pleas of the Crown* (London, 1716), 1, 155–159. See also, Blackstone, *Commentaries,* IV, 146–147, and Edward Coke, *The Third Part of the Institutes of the Laws of England* (London, 1797), 176.

In certain situations these distinctions offered at best a very uncertain guide as to who did or did not exert force lawfully. Should a *posse* employ more force than was necessary to overcome overt resistance, for example, its members acted illegally and were indictable for riot. And where established officials supported both sides in a confrontation, or where the legality of an act that officials were attempting to enforce was itself disputed, the decision as to who were or were not rioters seemed to depend upon the observer's point of view. Impressment is a good example. The colonists claimed that impressment was unlawful in North America under an act of 1708, while British authorities and some—but not all—spokesmen for the government held that the law had lapsed in 1713. The question was settled only in 1775, when Parliament finally repealed the "Sixth of Anne." Moreover, supposing impressment could indeed be carried on, were press warrants from provincial authorities still necessary? Royal instructions of 1697 had given royal governors the "sole power of impressing seamen in any of our plantations in America or in sight of them." Admittedly that clause was dropped in 1708, and a subsequent parliamentary act of 1746, which required the full consent of the governor and council before impressment could be carried on within their province, applied only to the West Indies. Nonetheless, it seems that in 1764 the Lords of the Admiralty thought the requirement held throughout North America.[34] With the legality of impressment efforts so uncertain, especially when opposed by local authorities, it was possible to see the press gangs as "rioters" for trying *en masse* to perpetrate an unlawful act of violence. In that case the local townsmen who opposed them might be considered lawful defenders of the public welfare, acting much as they would in a *posse*. In 1770 John Adams cited opposition to press gangs who acted without warrants as an example of the lawful use of force; and when the sloop of war *Hornet* swept into Norfolk, Virginia, in September 1767 with a "bloody riotous plan . . . to impress seamen, without consulting the Mayor, or any other magistrate," the offense was charged to the pressmen. Roused by the watchman, who called out *"a riot by man of war's men,"* the inhabitants rose to back the magistrates, and not only secured the release of the impressed men but also imprisoned ten members of the press gang. The ship's captain, on the other hand, condemned the townsmen as "Rioters." Ambiguity was present, too, in Newport's *St. John* clash, which involved both impressment and criminal action on the part of royal seamen and culminated with Newporters firing on the king's ship. The Privy Council in England promptly classified the incident as a riot, but the Rhode Island governor's report boldly maintained that "the people meant nothing but to assist [the mag-

[34] Clark, "Impressment of Seamen," *Essays in Honor of Andrews,* 198–224; Stout, "Manning the Royal Navy," *American Neptune,* XXIII (1963), 178–179; and Leonard W. Labaree, ed., *Royal Instructions to British Colonial Governors, 1670–1776* (New York, 1935), I, 442–443.

istrates] in apprehending the Offenders" on the vessel, and even suggested that "their Conduct be honored with his Majesty's royal Approbation." [35]

The enforcement of the White Pines Acts was similarly open to legal dispute. The acts seemed to violate both the Massachusetts and Connecticut charters; the meaning of provisions exempting trees growing within townships (act of 1722) and those which were "the property of private persons" (act of 1729) was contested, and royal officials tended to work on the basis of interpretations of the laws that Bernhard Knollenberg has called farfetched and, in one case, "utterly untenable." The Exeter, New Hampshire, "riot" of 1734, for example, answered an attempt of the surveyor to seize boards on the argument that the authorization to seize logs from allegedly illegally felled white pine trees in the act of 1722 included an authorization to seize processed lumber. As a result, Knollenberg concluded, although the surveyors' reports "give the impression that the New Englanders were an utterly lawless lot, . . . in many if not most cases they were standing for what they believed, with reason, were their legal and equitable rights in trees growing on their own lands." [36]

Occasions open to such conflicting interpretations were rare. Most often even those who sympathized with the mobs' motives condemned its use of force as illegal and unjustifiable. That ambiguous cases did arise, however, indicates that legitimacy and illegitimacy, *posses* and rioters, represented but poles of the same spectrum. And where a mob took upon itself the defense of the community, it benefited from a certain popular legitimacy even when the strict legality of its action was in doubt, particularly among a people taught that the legitimacy of law itself depended upon its defense of the public welfare.

Whatever quasi-legal status mobs were accorded by local communities was reinforced, moreover, by formal political thought. "Riots and rebellions" were often calmly accepted as a constant and even necessary element of free government. This acceptance depended, however, upon certain essential assumptions about popular uprisings. With words that could be drawn almost verbatim from John Locke or any other English author of similar convictions, colonial writers posited a continuing moderation and purposefulness on the part of the mob. "Tho' innocent Persons may sometimes suffer in popular Tumults," observed a 1768 writer in the

[35] L. Kinvin Wroth and Hiller B. Zobel, eds., *Legal Papers of John Adams* (Cambridge, Mass., 1965), III, 253. Account of the Norfolk incident by George Abyvon, Sept. 5, 1767, in Purdie and Dixon's *Va. Gaz.* (Wmsbg.), Oct. 1, 1767. Capt. Morgan quoted in Lemisch, "Jack Tar," *Wm. and Mary Qtly.*, 3d Ser., XXV (1968), 391. Munro, ed., *Acts of the Privy Council, Colonial Series,* VI, 374; Gov. Samuel Ward to Treasury lords, Oct. 23, 1765, Ward MSS, Box 1, fol. 58.

[36] Knollenberg, *Origin of the Revolution,* 122–130; Albion, *Forests and Sea Power,* 255–258.

New York Journal, "yet the general Resentment of the People is principally directed according to Justice, and the greatest Delinquent feels it most." Moreover, upheavals constituted only occasional interruptions in well-governed societies. "Good Laws and good Rulers will always be obey'd and respected"; "the Experience of all Ages proves, that Mankind are much more likely to submit to bad Laws and wicked Rulers, than to resist good ones." "Mobs and Tumults," it was often said, "never happen but thro' Oppression and a scandalous Abuse of Power." [37]

In the hands of Locke such remarks constituted relatively inert statements of fact. Colonial writers, however, often turned these pronouncements on their heads such that observed instances of popular disorder became *prima facie* indictments of authority. In 1747, for example, New Jersey land rioters argued that "from their Numbers, Violences, and unlawful Actions" it was to be "inferred that . . . they are wronged and oppressed, or else they would never *rebell agt. the Laws.*" Always, a New York writer said in 1770, when "the People of any Government" become "turbulent and uneasy," it was above all "a certain Sign of Maladministration." Even when disorders were not directly levelled against government they provided "strong proofs that something is much amiss in the state" as William Samuel Johnson put it; that—in Samuel Adams's words—the "wheels of good government" were "somewhat clogged." Americans who used this argument against Britain in the 1760's continued to depend upon it two decades later when they reacted to Shays's Rebellion by seeking out the public "Disease" in their own independent governments that was indicated by the "Spirit of Licentiousness" in Massachusetts.[38]

Popular turbulence seemed to follow so naturally from inadequacies of government that uprisings were often described with similes from the

[37] *N.Y. Jour.* (N.Y.C.), Aug. 18, 1768 (the writer was allegedly drawing together arguments that had recently appeared in the British press); and *N.Y. Jour. Supplement* (N.Y.C.), Jan. 4, 1770. Note also that Jefferson accepted Shays's rebellion as a sign of health in American institutions only after he had been assured by men like Jay that the insurgents had acted purposely and moderately, and after he had concluded that the uprising represented no continuous threat to established government. "An insurrection in one of the 13 states in the course of 11 years that they have subsisted amounts to one in any particular state in 143 years, say a century and a half," he calculated. "This would not be near as many as has happened in every other government that has ever existed," and clearly posed no threat to the constitutional order as a whole. To David Hartley, July 2, 1787, Boyd, ed., *Jefferson Papers,* XI, 526.

[38] John Locke, *The Second Treatise of Government,* paragraphs 223–225. "A State of Facts Concerning the Riots . . . in New Jersey," *New Jersey Archives,* VII, 217. *N.Y. Jour., Supp.* (N.Y.C.), Jan. 4, 1770. Johnson to Wm. Pitkin, Apr. 29, 1768, Massachusetts Historical Society, *Collections,* 5th Ser., IX (1885), 275. Adams as "Determinus" in *Boston Gazette,* Aug. 8, 1768; and Harry A. Cushing, ed., *The Writings of Samuel Adams* (New York, 1904–1908), I, 237. Jay to Jefferson, Oct. 27, 1786, Boyd, ed., *Jefferson Papers,* X, 488.

physical world. In 1770 John Adams said that there were "Church-quakes and state-quakes in the moral and political world, as well as earthquakes, storms and tempests in the physical." Two years earlier a writer in the *New York Journal* likened popular tumults to "Thunder Gusts" which "commonly do more Good than Harm." Thomas Jefferson continued the imagery in the 1780's, particularly with his famous statement that he liked "a little rebellion now and then" for it was "like a storm in the atmosphere." It was, moreover, because of the "imperfection of all things in this world," including government, that Adams found it "vain to seek a government in all points free from a possibility of civil wars, tumults and seditions." That was "a blessing denied to this life and preserved to complete the felicity of the next." [39]

If popular uprisings occurred "in all governments at all times," they were nonetheless most able to break out in free governments. Tyrants imposed order and submission upon their subjects by force, thus dividing society, as Jefferson said, into wolves and sheep. Only under free governments were the people "nervous," spirited, jealous of their rights, ready to react against unjust provocations; and this being the case, popular disorders could be interpreted as "Symptoms of a strong and healthy Constitution" even while they indicated some lesser shortcoming in administration. It would be futile, Josiah Quincy, Jr., said in 1770, to expect "that pacific, timid, obsequious, and servile temper, so predominant in more despotic governments" from those who lived under free British institutions. From "our happy constitution," he claimed, there resulted as "very natural Effects" an "impatience of injuries, and a strong resentment of insults." [40]

This popular impatience constituted an essential force in the maintenance of free institutions. "What country can preserve it's [sic] liberties if their rulers are not warned from time to time that their people preserve the spirit of resistance?" Jefferson asked in 1787. Occasional insurrections were thus "an evil . . . productive of good": even those founded on popular error tended to hold rulers "to the true principles of their institu-

[39] Wroth and Zobel, eds., *Adams Legal Papers,* III, 249–250; *N.Y. Jour. Supp.* (N.Y.C.), Aug. 18, 1768; Jefferson to Abigail Adams, Feb. 22, 1787, Boyd, ed., *Jefferson Papers,* XI, 174. C. F. Adams, ed., *Works of Adams,* IV, 77, 80 (quoting Algernon Sydney).

[40] Jefferson to Edward Carrington, Jan. 16, 1787, Boyd, ed., *Jefferson Papers,* XI, 49, and Rev. James Madison to Jefferson, Mar. 28, 1787, *ibid.,* 252. Wroth and Zobel, eds., *Adams Legal Papers,* III, 250. Quincy's address to the jury in the soldiers' trial after the Boston Massacre in Josiah Quincy, *Memoir of the Life of Josiah Quincy, Junior, of Massachusetts Bay, 1744–1775,* ed. Eliza Susan Quincy, 3d ed. (Boston, 1875), 46. See also Massachusetts Assembly's similar statement in its address to Gov. Hutchinson, Apr. 24, 1770, Hutchinson, *History of Massachusetts Bay,* ed. Mayo, III, 365–366. This 18th century devotion to political "jealousy" resembles the doctrine of "vigilance" that was defended by 19th century vigilante groups. See Graham and Gurr, *Violence in America,* 179–183.

tion" and generally provided "a medecine necessary for the sound health of government." This meant that an aroused people had a role not only in extreme situations, where revolution was requisite, but in the normal course of free government. For that reason members of the House of Lords could seriously argue—as A. J. P. Taylor has pointed out—that "rioting is an essential part of our constitution"; and for that reason, too, even Massachusett's conservative Lieutenant Governor Thomas Hutchinson could remark in 1768 that "mobs a sort of them at least are constitutional." [41]

III

It was, finally, the interaction of this constitutional role of the mob with the written law that makes the story of eighteenth-century popular uprisings complexity itself.[42] If mobs were appreciated because they provided a check on power, it was always understood that, insofar as upheavals threatened "running to such excesses, as will overturn the whole system of government," "strong discouragements" had to be provided against them. For eighteenth-century Americans, like the English writers they admired, liberty demanded the rule of law. In extreme situations where the rulers had clearly chosen arbitrary power over the limits of law, men like John Adams could prefer the risk of anarchy to continued submission because "anarchy can never last long, and tyranny may be perpetual," but only when "there was any hope that the fair order of liberty and a free constitution would arise out of it." This desire to maintain the orderly rule of law led legislatures in England and the colonies to pass antiriot statutes and to make strong efforts—in the words of a 1753 Massachusetts law—

[41] Jefferson to William Stephen Smith, Nov. 13, 1787, Boyd, ed., *Jefferson Papers,* XII, 356, Jefferson to Carrington, Jan. 16, 1787, *ibid.,* XI, 49, Jefferson to James Madison, Jan. 30, 1787, *ibid.,* 92–93. Taylor's remarks in "History of Violence," *The Listener,* CXXIX (1968), 701. ("Members of the House of Lords . . . said . . . if the people really don't like something, then they work our carriages and tear off our wigs and throw stones through the windows of our town-houses. And this is an essential thing to have if you are going to have a free country.") Hutchinson to [John or Robert] Grant, July 27, 1768, Massachusetts Archives, XXVI, 317, State House, Boston. See also the related story about John Selden, the famous 17th century lawyer, told to the House of Commons in Jan. 1775 by Lord Camden and recorded by Josiah Quincy, Jr., in the "Journal of Josiah Quincy, Jun., During his Voyage and Residence in England from September 28th, 1774, to March 3d, 1775," Massachusetts Historical Society, *Proceedings,* L (1916–1917), 462–463. Selden was asked what lawbook contained the laws for resisting tyranny. He replied he did not know, "but I'll tell [you] what is most certain, that it has always been the custom of England—and the Custom of England is the *Law* of the *Land.*"

[42] On the developing distinction Americans drew between what was legal and constitutional, see Wood, *Creation of the American Republic,* 261–268.

to discountenance "a mobbish temper and spirit in . . . the inhabitants" that would oppose "all government and order." [43]

The problem of limiting mass violence was dealt with most intensely over a sustained period by the American Revolutionary leadership, which has perhaps suffered most from historians' earlier inattention to the history of colonial uprisings. So long as it could be maintained—as it was only fifteen years ago—that political mobs were "rare or unknown in America" before the 1760's, the Revolutionaries were implicitly credited with their creation. American patriots, Charles McLean Andrews wrote, were often "lawless men who were nothing more than agitators and demagogues" and who attracted a following from the riffraff of colonial society. It now seems clear that the mob drew on all elements of the population. More important, the Revolutionary leaders had no need to create mob support. Instead they were forced to work with a "permanent entity," a traditional crowd that exerted itself before, after, and even during the Revolutionary struggle over issues unrelated to the conflict with Britain, and that, as Hobsbawm has noted, characteristically aided the Revolutionary cause in the opening phases of conflict but was hard to discipline thereafter.[44]

In focusing popular exuberance the American leaders could work with long-established tendencies in the mob toward purposefulness and responsibility. In doing so they could, moreover, draw heavily upon the guidelines for direct action that had been defined by English radical writers since the seventeenth century. Extralegal action was justified only when all established avenues to redress had failed. It could not answer casual errors or private failings on the part of the magistrates, but had to await fundamental public abuses so egregious that the "whole people" turned against their rulers. Even then, it was held, opposition had to be measured so that no more force was exerted than was necessary for the public good. Fol-

[43] *N.Y. Jour. Supp.* (N.Y.C.), Jan. 4, 1770; Wroth and Zobel, eds., *Adams Legal Papers,* III, 250, and C. F. Adams, ed., *Works of Adams,* VI, 151. Adams's views were altered in 1815, *ibid.,* X, 181. It is noteworthy that the Boston town meeting condemned the Knowles rioters not simply for their method of opposing impressment but because they insulted the governor and the legislature, and the Massachusetts Assembly acted against the uprising only after Gov. Shirley had left Boston and events seemed to be "tending to the destruction of all government and order." Hutchinson, *History of Massachusetts Bay,* ed. Mayo, II, 332–333. *Acts and Resolves of the Province of Massachusetts Bay,* III, 647. (Chap. 18 of the Province laws, 1752–1753, "An Act for Further Preventing all Riotous, Tumultuous and Disorderly Assemblies or Companies or Persons. . . .") This act, which was inspired particularly by Pope's Day violence, was renewed after the Boston Massacre in 1770 even though the legislature refused to renew its main Riot Act of 1751. *Ibid.,* IV, 87.

[44] Arthur M. Schlesinger, "Political Mobs and the American Revolution, 1765–1776," *Proceedings of the American Philosophical Society,* XCIX (1955), 246; Charles M. Andrews, *The Colonial Background of the American Revolution,* rev. ed. (New Haven, 1939), 176; Charles M. Andrews, "The Boston Merchants and the Non-Importation Movement," Colonial Society of Massachusetts, *Transactions,* XIX (1916–1917), 241; Hobsbawm, *Primitive Rebels,* 111, 123–124.

lowing these principles colonial leaders sought by careful organization to avoid the excesses that first greeted the Stamp Act. Hutchinson's query after a crowd in Connecticut had forced the resignation of stampman Jared Ingersoll—whether "such a public regular assembly can be called a mob"— could with equal appropriateness have been repeated during the tea resistance, or in 1774 when Massachusetts *mandamus* councillors were forced to resign.[45]

From the first appearance of an organized resistance movement in 1765, moreover, efforts were made to support the legal magistrates such that, as John Adams said in 1774, government would have "as much vigor then as ever" except where its authority was specifically under dispute. This concern for the maintenance of order and the general framework of law explains why the American Revolution was largely free from the "universal tumults and all the irregularities and violence of mobbish factions [that] naturally arise when legal authority ceases." It explains, too, why old revolutionaries like Samuel Adams or Christopher Gadsden disapproved of those popular conventions and committees that persisted after regular independent state governments were established in the 1770's. "Decency and Respect [are] due to Constitutional Authority," Samuel Adams said in 1784, "and those Men, who under any Pretence or by any Means whatever, would lessen the Weight of Government lawfully exercised must be Enemies to our happy Revolution and the Common Liberty." [46]

In normal circumstances the "strong discouragements" to dangerous disorder were provided by established legislatures. The measures enacted by them to deal with insurrections were shaped by the eighteenth-century understanding of civil uprisings. Since turbulence indicated above all some shortcoming in government, it was never to be met by increasing the authorities' power of suppression. The "weakness of authority" that was a function of its dependence upon popular support appeared to contemporary Americans as a continuing virtue of British institutions, as one reason why rulers could not simply dictate to their subjects and why Britain had for so long been hailed as one of the freest nations in Europe. It was "far less dangerous to the Freedom of a State" to allow "the laws to be trampeled upon, by the licence among the rabble . . . than to dispence with their force by an act of power." Insurrections were to be answered by reform,

[45] Hutchinson to Thomas Pownall, [Sept. or Oct. 1765], Mass. Archives, XXVI, 157. Pauline Maier, From Resistance to Revolution: American Radicals and the Development of Intercolonial Opposition to Britain, 1765–1776 (unpubl. Ph.D. diss., Harvard University, 1968), I, 37–45, 72–215.

[46] C. F. Adams, ed., *Works of Adams,* IV, 51; Rev. Samuel Langdon's election sermon to third Massachusetts Provincial Congress, May 31, 1775, quoted in Richard Frothingham, *Life and Times of Joseph Warren* (Boston, 1865), 499; Samuel Adams to Noah Webster, Apr. 30, 1784, Cushing, ed., *Writings of Samuel Adams,* IV, 305–306. On Gadsden see Richard Walsh, *Charleston's Sons of Liberty* (Columbia, 1959), 87.

by attacking the "Disease"—to use John Jay's term of 1786—that lay behind them rather than by suppressing its "Symptoms." And ultimately, as William Samuel Johnson observed in 1768, "the only effectual way to prevent them is to govern with wisdom, justice, and moderation." [47]

In immediate crises, however, legislatures in both England and America resorted to special legislation that supplemented the common law prohibition of riot. The English Riot Act of 1714 was passed when disorder threatened to disrupt the accession of George I; a Connecticut act of 1722 followed a rash of incidents over land title in Hartford County; the Massachusetts act of 1751 answered "several tumultuous assemblies" over the currency issue and another of 1786 was enacted at the time of Shays's Rebellion. The New Jersey legislature passed an act in 1747 during that colony's protracted land riots; Pennsylvania's Riot Act of 1764 was inspired by the Paxton Boys; North Carolina's of 1771 by the Regulators; New York's of 1774 by the "land wars" in Charlotte and Albany County.[48] Always the acts specified that the magistrates were to depend upon the *posse* in enforcing their provisions, and in North Carolina on the militia as well. They differed over the number of people who had to remain "unlawfully, riotously, and tumultuously assembled together, to the Disturbance of the Publick Peace" for one hour after the reading of a prescribed riot proclamation before becoming judicable under the act. Some colonies specified lesser punishments than the death penalty provided for in the English act, but the American statutes were not in general more "liberal" than the British. Two of them so violated elementary judicial rights that they were subsequently condemned—North Carolina's by Britain, and New York's act of 1774 by a later, Revolutionary state legislature.[49]

In one important respect, however, the English Riot Act was reformed. Each colonial riot law, except that of Connecticut, was enacted for only one to three years, whereas the British law was perpetual. By

[47] *N.Y. Jour. Supp.* (N.Y.C.), Jan. 4, 1770; Jay to Jefferson, Oct. 27, 1786, Boyd, ed., *Jefferson Papers,* X, 488; Johnson to William Pitkin, July 23, 1768, Massachusetts Historical Society, *Collections,* 5th Ser., IX, 294–295.

[48] *The Statutes at Large* [of Great Britain] (London, 1786), V, 4–6; Hoadly, ed., *Public Records of Connecticut,* VI, 346–348 for the law, and see also 322–333, 341–348; Acts and Resolves of Massachusetts Bay, III, 544–546, for the Riot Act of 1751, and see also Hutchinson, *History of Massachusetts Bay,* ed. Mayo, III, 6–7; and *Acts and Laws of the Commonwealth of Massachusetts* (Boston, 1893), 87–88, for Act of 1786; "A State of Facts Concerning the Riots . . . in New Jersey," *N.J. Archives,* VII, 211–212, 221–222; *The Statutes at Large of Pennsylvania* . . . (n.p., 1899), VI, 325–328; William A. Saunders, ed., *The Colonial Records of North Carolina* (Raleigh, 1890), VIII, 481–486; *Laws of the Colony of New York in the Years 1774 and 1775* (Albany, 1888), 38–43.

[49] See additional instruction to Gov. Josiah Martin, Saunders, ed., *Colonial Records of North Carolina,* VIII, 515–516; and *Laws of the State of New York* (Albany, 1886), I, 20.

this provision colonial legislators avoided the shortcoming which, it was said, was "more likely to introduce *arbitrary Power* than even an *Army* itself," because a perpetual riot act meant that "in all future time" by "reading a Proclamation" the Crown had the power "of hanging up their Subjects wholesale, or of picking out Those, to whom they have the greatest Dislike." If the death penalty was removed, the danger was less. When, therefore, riot acts without limit of time were finally enacted— as Connecticut had done in 1722, Massachusetts in 1786, New Jersey in 1797—the punishments were considerably milder, providing, for example, for imprisonment not exceeding six months in Connecticut, one year in Massachusetts, and three years in New Jersey.[50]

Riot legislation, it is true, was not the only recourse against insurgents, who throughout the eighteenth century could also be prosecuted for treason. The colonial and state riot acts suggest, nonetheless, that American legislators recognized the participants in civil insurrections as guilty of a crime peculiarly complicated because it had social benefits as well as damages. To some degree, it appears, they shared the idea expressed well by Jefferson in 1787: that "honest republican governors" should be "so mild in their punishments of rebellions, as not to discourage them too much."[51] Even in countering riots the legislators seemed as intent upon preventing any perversion of the forces of law and order by established authorities as with chastising the insurgents. Reform of the English Riot Act thus paralleled the abolition of constituent treasons—a traditional recourse against enemies of the Crown—in American state treason acts of the Revolutionary period and finally in Article III of the Federal Constitution.[52] From the same preoccupation, too, sprang the limitations placed upon the regular army provided for in the Constitution in part to assure the continuation of republican government guaranteed to the states by Article IV, Section IV. Just as the riot acts were for so long limited in duration, appropriations for the army were never to extend beyond two years (Article I, Section viii, 12); and the army could be used within a state against domestic violence only after application by the legislature or governor, if the legislature could not be convened (Article IV, Section iv).

A continuing desire to control authority through popular action also underlay the declaration in the Second Amendment that "a well regulated Militia being necessary to the security of a free State," citizens were assured the "right . . . to keep and bear Arms." The militia was meant

[50] *The Craftsman* (London, 1731), VI, 263–264. Connecticut and Massachusetts laws cited in n. 45; and *Laws of the State of New Jersey* (Trenton, 1821), 279–281.

[51] Jefferson to Madison, Jan. 30, 1787, Boyd, ed., *Jefferson Papers*, XI, 93.

[52] See Bradley Chapin, "Colonial and Revolutionary Origins of the American Law of Treason," *Wm. and Mary Qtly.*, 3d Ser., XVII (1960), 3–21.

above all "to prevent the establishment of a standing army, the bane of liberty"; and the right to bear arms—taken in part from the English Bill of Rights of 1689—was considered a standing threat to would-be tyrants. It embodied "a public allowance, under due restrictions, of the *natural right of resistance and self preservation,* when the sanctions of society and laws are found *insufficient* to restrain the *violence of oppression.*" And on the basis of their eighteenth-century experience, Americans could consider that right to be "perfectly harmless. . . . If the government be equitable; if it be reasonable in its exactions; if proper attention be paid to the education of children in knowledge, and religion," Timothy Dwight declared, "few men will be disposed to use arms, unless for their amusement, and for the defence of themselves and their country." [53]

The need felt to continue the eighteenth-century militia as a counterweight to government along with the efforts to outlaw rioting and to provide for the use of a standing army against domestic insurrections under carefully defined circumstances together illustrate the complex attitude toward peacekeeping that prevailed among the nation's founders. The rule of law had to be maintained, yet complete order was neither expected nor even desired when it could be purchased, it seemed, only at the cost of forcefully suppressing the spirit of a free people. The constant possibility of insurrection—as institutionalized in the militia—was to remain an element of the United States Constitution, just as it had played an essential role in Great Britain's.

This readiness to accept some degree of tumultuousness depended to a large degree upon the lawmakers' own experience with insurrections in the eighteenth century, when "disorder' was seldom anarchic and "rioters" often acted to defend law and justice rather than to oppose them. In the years after independence this toleration declined, in part because mass action took on new dimensions. Nineteenth-century mobs often resembled in outward form those of the previous century, but a new violence was added. Moreover, the literal assumption of popular rule in the years after Lexington taught many thoughtful Revolutionary partisans what was for them an unexpected lesson—that the people were "as capable of despotism as any prince," that "public liberty was no guarantee after all of private liberty." [54] With home rule secured, attention focused more exclusively upon minority rights, which mob action had always to some extent imperiled. And the danger that uprisings carried for individual freedom became ever more egregious as mobs shed their former

[53] Elbridge Gerry in Congressional debates, quoted in Irving Brant, *The Bill of Rights, Its Origin and Meaning* (Indianapolis, 1965), 486; Samuel Adams, quoting Blackstone, as "E. A." in *Boston Gaz.,* Feb. 27, 1769, and Cushing, ed., *Writings of Samuel Adams,* I, 317. Timothy Dwight, quoted in Daniel J. Boorstin, *The Americans: The Colonial Experience* (New York, 1958), 353.

[54] Wood, *Creation of the American Republic,* 410.

restraint and burned Catholic convents, attacked nativist speakers, lynched Mormons, or destroyed the presses and threatened the lives of abolitionists.

Ultimately, however, changing attitudes toward popular uprisings turned upon fundamental transformations in the political perspective of Americans after 1776. Throughout the eighteenth century political institutions had been viewed as in a constant evolution: the colonies' relationship with Britain and with each other, even the balance of power within the governments of various colonies, remained unsettled. Under such circumstances the imputations of governmental shortcoming that uprisings carried could easily be accepted and absorbed. But after Independence, when the form and conduct of the Americans' governments were under their exclusive control, and when those governments represented, moreover, an experiment in republicanism on which depended their own happiness and "that of generations unborn," Americans became less ready to endure domestic turbulence or accept its disturbing implications. Some continued to argue that "distrust and dissatisfaction" on the part of the multitude were "always the consequence of tyranny or corruption." Others, however, began to see domestic turbulence not as indictments but as insults to government that were likely to discredit American republicanism in the eyes of European observers. "Mobs are a reproach to Free Governments," where all grievances could be legally redressed through the courts or the ballot box, it was argued in 1783. They originated there "not in Oppression, but in Licentiousness," an "ungovernable spirit" among the people. Under republican governments even that distrust of power colonists had found so necessary for liberty, and which uprisings seemed to manifest, could appear outmoded. "There is some consistency in being jealous of power in the hands of those who assume it by birth . . . and over whom we have no controul . . . as was the case with the Crown of England over America," another writer suggested. "But to be jealous of those whom we chuse, the instant we have chosen them" was absurd: perhaps in the transition from monarchy to republic Americans had "bastardized" their ideas by placing jealousy where confidence was more appropriate.[55] In short, the assumptions behind the Americans' earlier toleration of the mob were corroded in republican America. Old and new attitudes coexisted in the 1780's and even later. But the appropriateness of popular uprisings in the United States became increasingly in doubt after the Federal Constitution came to be seen as the final product of long-term institutional experimentation, "a momentous

[55] Judge Aedanus Burke's Charge to the Grand Jury at Charleston, June 9, 1783, in *South Carolina Gazette and General Advertiser* (Charleston), June 10, 1783; "A Patriot," *ibid.,* July 15, 1783; and "Another Patriot," *ibid.,* July 29, 1783; and on the relevance of jealousy of power, see a letter to Virginia in *ibid.,* Aug. 9, 1793. "Democratic Gentle-Touch," *Gazette of the State of South Carolina* (Charleston), May 13, 1784.

contribution to the history of politics" that rendered even that most glorious exertion of popular force, revolution itself, an obsolete resort for Americans.[56]

Yet this change must not be viewed exclusively as a product of America's distinctive Revolutionary achievement. J. H. Plumb has pointed out, that a century earlier, when England passed beyond her revolutionary era and progressed toward political "stability," radical ideology with its talk of resistance and revolution was gradually left behind. A commitment to peace and permanence emerged from decades of fundamental change. In America as in England this stability demanded that operative sovereignty, including the right finally to decide what was and was not in the community's interest, and which laws were and were not constitutional, be entrusted to established governmental institutions. The result was to minimize the role of the people at large, who had been the ultimate arbiters of those questions in English and American Revolutionary thought. Even law enforcement was to become the task primarily of professional agencies. As a result in time all popular upheavals alike became menacing efforts to "pluck up law and justice by the roots," and riot itself gradually became defined as a purposeless act of anarchy, "a blind and misguided outburst of popular fury," of "undirected violence with no articulated goals." [57]

[56] Wood, *Creation of the American Republic*, 612–614.
[57] J. H. Plumb, *The Origins of Political Stability, England 1675–1725* (Boston, 1967), xc, 187; John Adams on the leaders of Shays's Rebellion in a letter to Benjamin Hitchborn, Jan. 27, 1787, in C. F. Adams, ed., *Works of Adams,* IX, 551; modern definitions of riot in "Riot Control and the Use of Federal Troops," *Harvard Law Review,* LXXXI (1968), 643.

1.5

Toward an Afro-American History

SIDNEY W. MINTZ

Sidney Mintz's essay demonstrates that any history of the Americas that examines just European "antecedents" will be irrevocably flawed. The Afro-American experience requires at its start an analysis similar to the type Edmund Morgan suggested in his study of the early British colonists. African cultures interacted with other New World cultures, a process profoundly shaped by the development of chattel slavery. Nevertheless viable Afro-American slave communities developed, and in his brief discussion of resistance, communications, and self-defense, Mintz suggests some of the larger processes involved. Mintz, an anthropologist, focuses on how cultures adapt to new circumstances, even forced migration and slavery. Knowledge of these changing cultures is therefore essential to understanding the thought and behavior of slaves in quite diverse circumstances—and of their masters, too.

Sidney W. Mintz, "Toward an Afro-American History," *Journal of World History*, 13 (1971), 317–31. Reprinted and footnotes omitted by permission of the author and UNESCO.

115

The following books are suggested for further reading:

C. L. R. JAMES, *Black Jacobins,* New York: Vintage Books, Random House, Inc., 1963.

———, "The Atlantic Slave Trade and Slavery" in John A. Williams and Charles F. Harris (eds.), *Amistad* I, New York: Vintage Books, Random House, Inc., 1971, pp. 119–64.

I. INTRODUCTION

In a recent monograph, the North American historian Philip Curtin has provided substantial scholarly grounds for a drastic downward revision of prior estimates for the importations of African slaves to the New World. His total figure, from the start of the trade in the beginning of the sixteenth century until the final abolition of slavery in the Hemisphere (Brazil, 1888), is slightly below nine and one-half millions. Though this estimate halves—or reduces even more—earlier guesses about the total volume of the slave trade, we are still left with numbers that stagger the imagination. It needs to be remembered that the trade was spread over nearly four centuries; that it involved the forcible transportation of its victims; and that much of this commerce in human beings occurred long before the development of modern forms of transatlantic transportation. We need also to remember, of course, that many more Africans were involved, and were the victims of violence in slaving wars, than ever reached the Western Hemisphere. Taken as a unitary phenomenon, the African slave trade may well have been one of the single most important events in modern world history.

Enslavement, however, merely began the Afro-American saga. African slaves were distributed throughout most of the New World. Though the majority of the slaves were brought to labor on tropical plantations, particularly in that region stretching from what is today the United States south to Brazil, along the Atlantic coast and in the Caribbean islands, large numbers of slaves also reached southern portions of the Hemisphere, while many others were spread through North America, and into Canada. Thus the patterns of encounter between Africans and non-Africans, and between slaves and freemen, were highly variant and complex, even though there is an understandable tendency to think of them as occurring primarily in terms of the plantation regimen.

The end of slavery came principally in the nineteenth century (Britain: 1838; France: 1848; Netherlands: 1863; United States: 1865; Puerto Rico: 1873; Cuba: 1886; Brazil: 1888). By the end of slavery, however, the demographic and cultural character of the slave population of the Americas had changed enormously, and these changes followed no single course. In certain countries, such as independent Haiti and colonial Jamaica, persons of African ancestry predominated; in others, such persons formed minorities, sometimes quite small, within massive Amerind or European populations.

Throughout the Hemisphere, of course, there had been considerable genetic intermixture. In countries such as Argentina and Chile, the surprisingly numerous African slaves of an earlier era seem to have "disappeared" into the population at large. In other parts of the Hemisphere, on the other hand, as in Jamaica or Haiti, it is the Europeans who seem to have "disappeared". The processes of genetic intermixture must be seen as separate from the codes of social and "race" relations in various New World countries, of course; how many "Negroes" there are in any such country does not depend on genetics, as such, so much as on the criteria of classification that form part of local cultural values and attitudes. In the United States, for instance, the code of "race" relations has attempted to wall off into the category of "Negroes" all those who have any physical characteristics perceived as negroid. The code, and its attached criteria, differs for each New World country, since learned patterns of perception are culturally variable; and the categories of classification are social, not biological, in nature. The "reality" of race is thus as much a social as a biological reality, the inheritance of physical traits serving as the raw material for social sorting devices, by which both stigmata and privileges may be systematically allocated. In any case, the genetic contribution of African peoples to the populations of the New World has been massive and diffuse.

The situation is different—and in some ways far more complex—in the case of culture. Traits and elements of culture bear no pedigrees, and the social prejudices which operate in the case of physically inherited characteristics are not the same as those which function in the sphere of culture. Culture diffuses by borrowing and interchange, by learning and imitation—not genetically, but socially. As a result, the immense contribution of African cultures to the contemporary civilizations of the Americas is less noticed, and sometimes underestimated. Thus, for instance, the cultural life of such countries as Brazil and the United States is heavily "africanized", no matter what the physical appearance of those who reveal this culture-stream in their behavior. Such manifestations include linguistic forms, cuisine, folklore, religious expression, music and dance, and much else. Though it could be argued that African cultural origins are clearest in the behavior of those whose physical origins are likewise African, these two continuities are phenomenologically very different— as a moment's reflection on the diffusion of the popular music of the United States will demonstrate. Throughout the Hemisphere, African cultural influences are subtly interwoven with those emanating from other traditions (including American Indian civilizations), helping to give to the Americas their very special and distinctive flavor.

Viewed both in terms of the history of peoples and the history of cultures, then, the focus of Afro-Americana is upon a single (but highly differentiated and very massive) process of mutual acculturation and culture change, experienced by millions of persons, by no means all of whom were African in origin, spread over an entire Hemisphere, and possessing a time-depth of nearly five centuries since its beginnings. To specify this as the focus of Afro-Americana is in no way to slight previous claims. But unless the Americas are to be viewed purely in terms of their European past—a perspective that seems more and more ludicrous today— then one man's Amerindian Studies or American Studies may well be another man's Afro-American Studies.

Moreover, while Afro-American Studies are directly concerned with the historical experiences of peoples in the New World, those experiences expressed—and in even larger measure, perhaps, still express—the tangled web of relationships between the Old World and the New. The slave trade and slavery profoundly altered the character of African societies; nor was this impact, felt most intensely in West Africa, limited to that region alone. What is more, the slave trade and slavery exercised an immense influence upon Europe itself—an influence too often ignored or underemphasized. The conquests of Asia, Africa and the Americas by Europe contributed significantly to the accumulation of the wealth which underlay the Industrial Revolution (Williams, 1944), speeding the final decline of European feudalism and the emergence of strong national states, and eventually widening not only the gap between Northern Europe and Southern Europe, but also that between the "developed" and "underdeveloped" worlds.

The slave trade and slavery were of paramount importance in this process. Economically, demographically and culturally, they helped to effect the transformation of much of the New World and of large portions of Africa as well. They also contributed to the emergence of the United States from its status as a colonial dependency and, in so doing, sharply tilted the balance against European mercantilism in the growth of world trade. More—for it was and is in the history of slavery that we find the roots of the major (and still unresolved) economic and social contradiction in North American life.

Thus Afro-American Studies are related intimately to the international relationships and internal struggles of many world powers, during a time-span stretching from the Spanish Reconquest to the present day. It need hardly be mentioned that British Jamaica and French Saint Domingue were probably the most profitable overseas colonies in the history of European colonialism; that every major European naval battle for two centuries was fought over the Caribbean plantation cockpit; and that the world's first two modern revolutions—the North American and the Haitian—both found a goodly measure of their origins (albeit in very different fashion) in slavery and the slave trade. We know now that it would be short-sighted at best to study such subjects as the Louisiana Purchase, the cession of Canada to Britain, the Atlantic trade, *Négritude,* Black Power, or the political philosophy of the Third World—to name but a few random themes—without attending the slavery past. Yet it bears careful note that any of these themes can, indeed, be studied as if the slave trade and slavery had never existed—and such has been the tenor of a substantial portion of past historical scholarship.

It would be impossible—not to say pretentious—to deal here with more than a few of the many historical problems brought into view by an Afro-American perspective. The present paper is limited to a consideration of only three such problems, and none is of a scale comparable to the themes noted above. The selection purports instead to take into account certain historical processes that were internal to slavery and the slave trade—what the ethnologist might call "culture-history," rather than history in a grander sense. The slave trade and slavery gave rise to special conditions of culture change, under which the slaves were compelled to fashion new life-styles in the face of tremendous repression. Far too much of the history of these phenomena has been written from the vantage-point of the European powers, and far too little from the inside of the slave experience. Hence the intent is to call attention to some of the interior processes that typified the encounters of the slaves with their new physical and social environments, and to the positive contributions of these New World migrants in remaking the cultures of the Americas.

II. RESISTANCE

The first such problem is that of slave resistance. Slavery signified, of course, involuntary migration and coerced labor. From Argentina to Canada, slave populations gave ample evidence that New World slavery was intolerable, and they did so by resisting their condition. But the forms and frequencies of such resistance were highly variable in time and in space. There has been a wholly understandable tendency recently to equate resistance with violence, and to seek to pinpoint violent resistance, whenever possible. Such a tendency, however, runs the risk of distorting the very diverse processes by which slave populations actually dealt with the daily realities of slavery. More, to equate resistance with violence is to impose on slave consciousness a rigidity and unresourcefulness that misrepresents both the nature of the institution of slavery and the capacities of the slaves themselves. If one were to generalize about the total span of the slavery experience, it would surely be nearer the truth to contend that the masters were far more dependably violent than the slaves—hardly a daring contention when one remembers that slavery itself was rooted in acts of violence, and that the institution consistently armed itself against even the most trivial show of contrary force. The sharpest evidence of slave resistance, then, is not the historical record of armed revolts, important though these were, so much as the codes that legalized branding, flogging, burning, the amputation of limbs, hamstringing and murder to keep the slaves "non-violent". One may thus ask of codes of modern times—and there should be neither surprise nor disappointment in the discovery that considerable resistance involved as its precondition some processes of culture change, of adaptation, on the part of the slaves themselves. This is not an idle issue. The house slave who poisoned her master's family by putting ground glass in the food had first to become the family cook. The runaway slaves who created viable communities in the hinterlands of so many slave societies needed to learn techniques of cultivation in an alien environment. And the slaves who plotted armed revolts in the marketplaces had first to produce for market, and to gain permission to carry their produce there.

Thus the whole concept of resistance cries out for new interpretation, even after every armed revolt, every instance of poisoning and canefield burning, every act of abortion and self-mutilation has been fully documented. Indeed, this reinterpretation has already begun, in recent studies of *marronage,* slave life on the plantations, and the analysis of revolts, successful and unsuccessful. From such studies we are beginning to get models of resistance, each involving different levels or degrees of adaptation by the slaves—from immediate, open and unplanned violence by newly-arrived Africans to the myriad techniques of covert resistance, some employed by individuals and others by organized groups—to the daily demands of slavery. Such models will reveal, on the part of the slaves, their genuine capacities to learn and interpret, to mimic, deceive and flatter— and above all, to assess, to plan and to organize. The belated recognition of these capacities will accordingly enhance our understanding of particular modes of repression, and more—of the highly complex relationship between insight and act under extremely repressive conditions. The emphasis on instances of direct violent resistance has originated in part in a reasoning backward from contemporary conditions, without sufficient recognition that contemporary racism, vicious though it is, often offers to its victims wider ranges of response than were available to the slaves. That Toussaint l'Ouverture was a faithful coachman who helped his master to escape from Saint Domingue, for example, is no less a part of history than was his glorious leadership of the Haitian Revolution. The recognition of Toussaint as a whole man, a complex and intricate personality, does not violate our understanding of his historical role. Any acknowledgment that he, too, may have been beset by doubts and ambivalence can only increase our admiration for the man, while deepening our awareness of the historical processes of which he was a part. Again, Dallas asserts that the Jamaican Maroon (runaway slave) leader, Cudjoe, in accepting the peace bid of the planters in 1739, threw himself at the feet of Colonel Guthrie and begged his forgiveness. The assertion may be a simple canard. But if it is true, it must be balanced against the remarkable war that Cudjoe had waged against tremendous odds, and the treaty won by force of arms by him and his men.

The history of resistance is enmeshed within the wider dimensions of slavery and the slave trade, since each local situation in which the slaves found themselves had its own distinctive significance. The rate at which fresh captives from Africa were introduced into local settings; the relative proportions of African-born and "creole" slaves; the ratios of men to women; and the presence or absence of black freedmen, as well as the condition of those freedmen, all played a part in shaping the specific contexts within which the slaves defined themselves and the tenor and intensity of their resistance.

The historian of slave resistance must note from the outset that the slaves, like all human beings everywhere, were beset by all of the ordinary demands of living—to sleep, to love, to eat, to understand and to explain, to survive. The tyrannies of daily existence may have been intensified by the cruelty and capriciousness of New World slavery, but in no sense could they have been removed from consciousness. Thus, for instance, Debbasch believes that simple hunger was one of the principal motives to escape, among the slaves in the French New World colonies in the eighteenth century. In enough cases to justify his use of the label, such runaways lived off those slaves who did not run away, in a sort of direct "parasitism". It is very difficult to weigh the overall effects of this kind of resistance. Indeed, the runaways imposed a genuine and important burden on the planters, by challenging their authority, reducing their work force, and by holding out a kind of hope to those who stayed behind. Beyond this, escape often led to the actual creation of runaway communities, outside the system of slavery, and sometimes to a direct armed challenge to the system, of a heroically inspiring kind. Runaway communities were created by the slaves in the jungles of Brazil, Surinam and French Guiana, in Jamaica, Cuba, Santo Domingo and elsewhere, and such communities lasted several lifetimes in certain cases, before being destroyed or, after revolution (as in Haiti) or emancipation (as in Jamaica), becoming more assimilated to national life.

But the inspiration provided by these thrilling chronicles should not reduce the significance of other modes of resistance, some of which were built into the plantation system in subtle fashion. We know too little about the slaves' perceptions of their condition, but serious historical scholarship has begun to unravel the complex motivational substructure of the slaves, employing personal documents of ex-slaves, and general historical works dating from the slavery period. It seems essential to insist that the panorama of New World slavery was complex and highly variable; not only were there important differences—ecological, economic, social—among different slaveholding societies, and at different periods, but no community of slaves could be expected to be homogeneous in terms of personality, emotional stability, or affective commitment to or against slavery itself. It is, in fact, surprising that anyone might seriously expect such homogeneity, to judge by what is known otherwise of human communities.

Before this problem is adequately exposed—even in terms of the right questions to be asked—much more hard historical research will be necessary. Its future as a serious scholarly concern belongs to those young historians who have gone back to the archives, to start anew what was only done incompletely or uncomprehendingly before.

III. COMMUNICATION

But the problems faced by the slaves were not only those of sheer survival. Each slaving expedition brought together by force captives drawn from one or more linguistic and cultural community; by the time such captives were transported and sold, they normally entered slave groups in the New World that were very heterogeneous in ancestral culture and in language. Thus, New World slavery created, among other things, a kind of Babel, within which the slaves had to discover how to understand, and how to be understood—in short, how to communicate symbolically, in the distinctive fashion of the human species and no other. The problem of discovering how to communicate, as expressed in the development of new linguistic forms, was also a problem in rediscovering oneself.

In a magnificent personal account, *The Pleasures of Exile,* by the Barbadian poet George Lamming, the imagery of Prospero and Caliban is invoked to discuss the problems of Caribbean—here, one may read "black"—identity:

"Prospero fears that change itself will become a contagion. Caliban is sympathetic; for he knows the pain it has cost him to realise the change within himself. He is a child of the backward glance with recollection of a time when he was not even accorded the right to be angry. He has known what it means to have one's past appropriated, then languageless as his aboriginal neighbours. What, someone has asked, could the first exported slave-mother say to her child? But Caliban accepts this predicament as part of his historic acre of ground. He has been precipitated into his change. He has made it, and it has made him. Now it is Prospero's turn to submit to the remorseless logic of his own past."

The problems that faced the first exported slave-mothers were not only those of *what* to communicate, but also of *how* to communicate. For African slaves in the New World faced the immense tasks of reconstituting themselves into viable communities under slavery, and also those of forging systems of communication with which to build their new lives. In the region commonly referred to as "Afro-America", between Brazil and North America, one finds a wide dispersion of languages that are associated with the history of the slave trade and slavery. The region itself may be defined either in terms of the physical origins of the populations within it, or of the distinctive cultural characteristics of those populations. Again, the striking difference between physical type and culture must be remarked, since the languages associated with Afro-Americans are sometimes thought to be related to the physical types of those who speak them. Yet if we know anything at all about language, we know that it is—other than in terms of the universal human capacity for symbolic communication—a learned, social phenomenon.

These languages, known as *patois* or *petit-nègre* in French, "dialect" or "jargon" in English, *Sklavensprache* in German, and by a variety of other pejorative terms in other languages, either arose or matured during slavery and the slave trade, and continue to exist as standard speech in many New World societies. Their precise origins are in doubt, and the subject of considerable controversy, some authorities deriving them from a simplified trade-language variety of Portuguese, others from modified African languages, and still others from the culture-contact situation involving enslaved Africans coming from many different language-groups, and Europeans speaking such languages as English, French, Spanish, Dutch, and Portuguese. If we exclude those cases which are doubtful for linguistic reasons (such as Jamaican rural speech), we are still left with perhaps five million speakers of at least four mutually unintelligible languages, all lexically related to European languages, but none clearly attributable syntactically or morphologically to the same sources. Among these languages are Haitian Creole and its congeners, spoken in many of the French and formerly French Antilles; English-based Creoles spoken in Surinam (Dutch Guiana), and the Sea Islands of the United States; Spanish- and Portuguese-based Creoles spoken in the Dutch Antilles and perhaps in Colombia; and possibly a Dutch-based Creole as well.

The term "Creole" to describe these languages has been used here without explanation; its use is intended to distinguish them in their present form from the first media of communication employed between masters and slaves in the original contact situations. The distinction has both linguistic and social relevance. Linguistically, the systems of communication employed solely for messages between the slave group and the master group must have been specialized languages of the sort called "pidgins" in English and *langues de traite* in French. Whether all New World pidgins originated in a Portuguese-based pidgin spoken on the West African coast, as some linguists assert, or whether they arose more or less independently in different New World plantation settings, they need to be distinguished from the languages which soon became the speech of the slaves among themselves. Whatever language the first exported slave-mothers spoke to their children, the languages which became the common speech media of slave communities were no longer specialized *langues de traite,* but generalized languages suitable for everyday communication. Once a generation of children had been born, for whom one of these languages was a native tongue, the languages themselves had become *creole* languages, and were no longer pidgins.

We know far too little about the processes by which such creole languages emerged, but there is no doubt that these processes involved an expansion of each such language, and an enrichment of its sphere of expression, to make it adequate to everyday needs. It matters little, from one point of view, whether the origins of the lexicon, the morphology, the phonology and the syntax were European or African; for the processes involved were set in motion by the slaves themselves, and the languages were distinctively their own, though they sometimes came to be important media of communication, even for the master classes. Thus, for instance, the Papiamento of the Dutch Antilles, and the Creole of Haiti and Martinique are spoken today by many persons whose origins are not African, culturally or physically; yet those who originally transformed what were once very restricted pidgins into wholly generalized creoles were slaves. Precisely because it was quite clearly recognized that the African contribution to these languages was massive, it has been customary to view the languages themselves as mere corruptions of a European tongue. But such a view has nothing to recommend it, from a linguistic point of view. Haitian Creole is no more "corrupted" French than French is "corrupted" Latin, for example. Where creole languages became stabilized within whole speech communities, as in Surinam and Haiti, they were no longer simplified or reduced or deviant varieties of the languages of the masters, but wholly separate communication media, with which the European languages of the masters were mutually unintelligible. In some cases, the stabilization of such creole languages did not occur, apparently; it is not at all clear whether the speech of Jamaican country people is a creole, or whether—as is more likely—it is a significantly different dialect of English. In both kinds of cases, however, it has been fashionable to derogate the speakers of these languages and dialects—to this day, white North Americans will sometimes contend that English has been "corrupted" or "deformed" by supposed African linguistic incompetence. Yet creole languages are surely one of the most significant cultural achievements of transplanted Africans, attesting both to the resourcefulness and creative genius of the slaves, and to the capacity of language systems to expand as necessary.

Nor is this simply a matter of systems of communication as such. In related areas—folklore, myth, proverbs, and in literature generally—the creative genius of African peoples has contributed significantly to New World richness of oral and written literary forms. The argument that creole languages do not lend themselves to abstract expression—put forth most commonly by uneducated French visitors to the New World, but also subscribed to by others—is richly contradicted in fact. When a Haitian peasant comments on certain events in world affairs by suggesting that "the stick that beats the black dog can beat the white dog, too" one is hard put to contend that his language is unsuited to imagery. There is now a growing literature in creole languages, even while American Indian literature remains paltry, and European languages continue to displace African languages in Africa itself. In such New World societies as Haiti and Curaçao, and even in Martinique and Guadeloupe—where French primary education has been energetically pushed for over a century—creole languages continue to display their vitality and importance. A recent (but still unpublished) collection of poetry in the creole of Surinam—"Takitaki" or "Sranan tongo" —(assembled by the Dutch linguist Jan Voorhoeve) displays the remarkable breadth of dramatic expression of this language; while the Haitian poet Morisseau-Leroy has demonstrated what happens when Greek tragedy is transformed into a Haitian setting, in his remarkable Creole-language version of *Antigone*.

But the role of Creole languages in the modern world is not dependent solely on establishing their lexical and semantic possibilities. Since such languages commonly co-occur with other, standard European languages such as French or Dutch, it seems almost inevitable that the societies in question will be divided along language lines as well as along other dimensions, such as social class, ethnic group, and so on. It also follows that, in all such cases, the Creole language, commonly associated with the poorer and less educated segments of the society, is regarded as an inferior language (if it is conceded to be a language at all), and its use as a badge of inferiority. The wider implications of invidious distinctions of this kind have to do with problems of national education; and it is in this connection, of course, that the problems of the Creole language-speakers of the Caribbean region are united with those of non-standard English speakers in the United States, particularly (but by no means only) Afro-Americans. There is a growing controversy about the status of the non-standard English dialects spoken by Afro-Americans in the United States, and it is clearly linked to the question of African linguistic retentions or reinterpretations in the New World. In the view of some, the speech of Afro-Americans in the United States is no more than a somewhat simplified and reduced version of standard English, reflecting the inferior education provided Afro-American children, and the social isolation of their parents, in North American society. In the view of others, the speech of Afro-Americans in the United States shows clear-cut African linguistic features that have nothing at all to do with deprivation, but represent instead a positive retention of ancestral language forms. Each such view carries very serious policy implications for North American education; whatever the outcome, it seems perfectly clear that here, too, the drama of Afro-America is still being acted out, nearly five centuries after it began.

IV. ECONOMIC SELF-DEFENSE

In discussing both the nature of slave resistance and the development of new systems of communication, we have had reason to try to view the slaves on their own terms: as members of the most disadvantaged segments of profoundly divided societies, they were compelled to define themselves and to work out new patterns of life under extremely repressive conditions. The nature of repression in slave societies, however, repeatedly exposed weaknesses in the system. The fundamental contradiction of such systems lies in their need to deal with men as non-men—that is, to deny the humanity of the slaves themselves. But the slaves are human, and on one level at least, both slaves and masters know it. Since men are not machines, since they possess will, they can will to live or die—and no slavery system, no matter how humanitarian nor how cruel, has ever solved the problem. The second such contradiction is closely linked: to be most efficient, slaves had to be taught—but teaching slaves meant acknowledging their humanity, and running the risk that they would learn things they ought not to learn. This problem, too, was never solved by New World slavery. Ideally, the institution of slavery ought to have perpetuated an unbridgeable gap between slaves and free men, a gap defined in terms of political power, economic wealth, civil rights, and much else. But the gap was repeatedly bridged, and by various means, during the history of New World slavery, most often because of the contradictions built into the system. Hence one of the most interesting problems in Afro-American history is that of the ways the internal contradictions of slavery afforded the slaves their opportunities, however slight, to frustrate the institution whose victims they were. It is in examining the operation of such systems in practice that the capacities of the slaves, as reasoning human beings engaged in their own defense, are richly revealed.

The plantation system, which absorbed the majority of slaves in the New World, was based on European overseas investment in large-scale agricultural enterprise in large parts of the American sub-tropics. Wherever it flourished, its internal "logic" tended to eliminate free men from the economic process, except in certain privileged and special roles as planters, politicians, bookkeepers, militiamen and merchants. Plantations often expanded to the limits of their effectiveness, in such societies as the United States South, Brazil, and the Caribbean islands, commonly dis[en]franchising or driving out small-scale yeoman farmers and converting their holdings into parts of large estates. In general, free men could neither work within the slave plantation sphere nor compete with it for credit, markets or labor.

But the elimination of free men from the labor market in plantation regions meant in turn that the slaves would often have to fill roles and to carry out activities requiring skills of the very kind which slavery sought to enjoin. Thus, for instance, smithing, barrel- and wheel-making, artisans' jobs in the sugar mills and many other tasks devolved upon the slaves, thus further hampering the growth of socially and economically differentiated communities of free men, and increasing the internal differentiation of the slave group. Such processes of recruitment and differentiation widened the complexity of slave societies, the dependence of the master class upon the slaves and, no doubt, the ambivalence of many slaves as well toward the system of which they were a part. But these same processes gave the slaves a firmer indication of their own capacities, even in the face of continuous verbal insistence by the masters upon their inherent inferiority; they allowed the slaves to see further into the distribution of power by which the system maintained and defended itself; and they enabled the slaves to master skills that could stand them in good stead at a later time.

Clearly, none of these insights should really have occurred at all, if the system were working ideally. But such contradictions are revealed in other aspects of the system as well. Thus, for example, the definition of the slaves as property implied in turn that the slaves should not be property-holders themselves. The history of Caribbean slavery, for instance, is replete with laws aimed at limiting the rights of slaves to hold, to inherit, or to pass on wealth. Concomitantly, slaves were often forbidden to engage in gainful activities, even though they might be skilled artisans, for the notion of the slave as an earner of income was in its nature subversive in some New World slave societies. But these postulations repeatedly clashed with the demands for special skills typical of the plantation context. Accordingly, slave codes sometimes prohibited certain activities which were, in fact, commonly carried out by slaves with the full knowledge of their masters. A classic example of the contradictoriness of the system is revealed in slave-based subsistence cultivation and marketing. The seasonal character of plantation argiculture often left the slaves idle for periods of varying length; but the slaves' subsistence needs represented a constant claim upon the capital of their owners. In order to reduce this claim, it was characteristic of the planter class to seek means to keep their slave labor force productive. A major solution was to permit or compel the slaves to produce their own food, and subsistence cultivation by the slaves was typical of such classic plantation societies as Jamaica, French Saint Domingue, and Brazil. Typically, the slaves worked small plots on the plantation grounds, and acquired some customary rights to dispose of their products. In many instances, such slave production came to be integrated with the needs of the society at large, such that slave producers were furnishing a major part of the subsistence of the free sector, rather than merely supplying themselves with food. Such activities often were carried on in spite of specific prohibitions in the slave codes, and even under conditions where the slave system itself was cruel and rigid. Slave producers and marketers were often able to accumulate substantial sums of liquid wealth, to change their own standards of living, and even to pass on accumulated wealth to their descendants. Most important, in many instances such practices gave the slaves their best opportunities to acquire skills they would later be able to employ profitably as free men. In post-emancipation Jamaica, there seems little doubt that the agricultural skills the people had acquired as slaves guaranteed their successful transition to freedom in the face of desperate and vindictive attempts by the planters to tie them to the plantations after 1838.

Much the same may be demonstrated in the case of such skills as fishing, hunting, potting, veterinary medicine, and the like. It is significant that these talents, wielded by slaves, were able to develop in curious opposition to the system that actually made them possible; often, it was only after emancipation that racist societies such as the United States were able to undermine the earning power of black freemen that was based on the very skills they had acquired as slaves at an earlier time.

The significance of such processes cannot be overemphasized. The slaves represented populations that had been wrenched from their ancestral contexts, and reintegrated into pioneer societies as the most defenseless segment of the labor force. In effect, they were compelled to live a proletarian existence without the right to keep any part of the fruits of their own labor. They constituted at once the essential work force of a capitalist industrial system, bearing all of the negative consequences of that system, while being deprived of any opportunity to bargain for its rewards. Stripped thus of the traditional guarantees of tribal membership on the one hand, and denied the protections of feudal reciprocities on the other, they were individualized by slavery without being permitted to organize against it. The critical feature of their exploitation was hence to deprive them of two major accesses which European capitalism would eventually concede to its proletarian populations, as North American capitalism did for its white citizenry: political liberty and the right to accumulate individual wealth. Under such circumstances, any means by which the slaves could attach their individuality to skill, and hence to earning-power, was of great significance.

Economic self-defense, as described here, has yet another dimension, to which only transient attention can be paid: the relationship of skill (and hence, earning-power) to domestic organization. The acquisition of particular skills through which liquid wealth could be earned, accumulated, and possibly even transmitted to one's children was especially important in enabling individual slaves to define their paternity by acquiring a patrimony —in societies in which individual wealth was often a principal measure of individual worth. The significance of this rather obvious linkage has apparently been missed by some contemporary experts, who seem to believe that black North Americans can acquire a patrimony by asserting their paternity. Yet the historical record suggests that the critical capacity of racist societies to keep their victims oppressed depends on their success in interdicting their access to earning-power, not their access to one or another model of kinship organization.

V. CONCLUSIONS

In this paper, three problems associated with the struggle of African slaves against their condition in the New World setting have been briefly set forth. Each such problem was chosen for discussion because it concerned in some measure the internal organization of slave communities, and the way such communities related themselves to the society at large. We see the slaves as members of fragile human groupings, fragile because of the enormous external pressure to which they are subject. Within such groupings, people love, hate, plan and plot, join in unions, bear children, grow old— some resisting their condition at every turn, others working out complex adaptations that allow them to retain their human capacities, still others bending before the system, more or less unresistingly.

Within the framework of daily life in such communities, the slaves developed modes of communication and of economic survival that gave many of them a sense of individual worth and of self-respect, in spite of the unjust and inhuman system they labored under. Throughout, their capacity to function with skill—and, at times, even with joy—is a testament to the human spirit. One can only find it remarkable that this saga, which gripped European and North American consciousness in the period preceding abolition in the colonies and in the United States, should then have been so successfully covered up for a century, until the civil rights struggle in North America reawakened an interest in the slavery past.

The narrow compass of these problems, however, should not be permitted to conceal the wider problem-areas with which Afro-Americana is quite properly concerned. It only bears noting once more that Afro-American History is not a substitute for other kinds of history, but represents instead a "new" way—new only in its having been so thoroughly forgotten, once before—of looking at the New World and African past.

Independence and
The New Nation
1763-1815

The years 1765–1815 saw a Revolution, political independence, and the beginnings of national consolidation. It represented the maturation of an old mercantile world, but was simultaneously the seedbed of a newer laissez-faire capitalist enterprise. The necessity of breaking with England came as America strived to transform herself from colony to nation, from British subject to metropolitan power. Mercantilist ideology had always held that nations were in competition, but it had failed to predict that the colonial objects of those national wars would ever enter those battles themselves. America did.

Much of the pamphleteering of the Revolution had another effect however. The appeal to rights that the British had transgressed came from the old corporate tradition, but a new tone of egalitarianism and republicanism crept in that conflicted with older, hierarchical community norms. Thomas Paine, for example, combined a contempt for monarchy and heredity with a commitment to Jacobin democracy. Yet he never countenanced economic levelling. E. P. Thompson notes that Paine's *"Rights of Man* and Adam Smith's

Wealth of Nations supplement and nourish each other." Indeed they do, and together they represent the ideological underpinnings of the new laissez-faire world, a society of small-scale enterprise. Government attacks on old forms of privilege were possible, government supplements and aids to economic development were possible, but enterprise itself was secured.

The struggle between these two worlds was never clear-cut, and artisans fought the revolution to gain new democratic rights to augment their newly threatened, but traditional position as "free-born Americans." The incursions of a new industrialism and the development of laissez-faire were far from the world in which they resisted British tyranny abroad and native forestallers and engrossers at home. The role of artisans in the revolution was of great import and they moved in and out of alliances with other classes throughout the revolutionary and early Federal period.

The post-revolutionary society, after a number of difficult economic and diplomatic experiences, slowly established itself as a commercial trading nation engaged in complex trade ties with Europe and the West Indies. Manufacturing showed some signs of vibrancy, but domestic markets remained small due to grave transportation problems. Nevertheless, the society remained predominantly agricultural. In the south, cotton production based on slave labor was becoming increasingly profitable. Western expansion continued to play an important social role. American pre-modern class structure was based on trade, commerce, and land. The transition to industrialism would not be easy.

The following book is suggested for further reading:

E. P. THOMPSON, *The Making of the English Working Class,* London: Victor Gollancz Ltd., 1963, esp. Part One, "The Liberty Tree."

2.1

The Progress of Inequality
in Revolutionary Boston

Skillful quantitative analysis allows Allan Kulikoff to recreate vividly the
social structure of Revolutionary Boston and to describe this rigidly stratified
"consumer city." At the essay's conclusion, the author asks what social forces
kept these groups quiet after the Revolution? That is a significant question,
but even the admittedly speculative answers offered leave much to be desired.
"The possession of moderate economic success and the safety-value of
short distance migration," he says, mitigated against "class conflict." Kulikoff
thus assumes that the absence of "conflict" can be explained by moderate
success and geographic mobility. To infer behavior and thought from structure

Allan Kulikoff, "The Progress of Inequality in Revolutionary Boston," *William and Mary
Quarterly*, 3rd ser., 28 (1971), 375–81, 383–411. Reprinted and edited by permission
of the author and the publisher.

[1] Mr. Kulikoff is [at the time of this writing] a graduate student at Brandeis
University. He would like to thank Stuart Blumin, M. I. T.; John Demos, Marvin
Meyers, and members of the graduate seminar, Brandeis University; Kenneth Lock-
ridge, University of Michigan; and Paul Kleppner and Alfred Young, Northern
Illinois University, for their advice and criticism. David Fischer, Brandeis University,
who directed the paper, made numerous helpful criticisms.

is dangerous. One must study far more than census data and assessment rolls. As Sidney Mintz suggested earlier, an analysis of the behavior of disadvantaged groups must rest on an intimate acquaintance with their total life.

The following works are suggested for further reading:

NORMAN BIRNBAUM, "Afterword" in Stephen Thernstrom and Richard Sennett (eds.) *Nineteenth Century Cities*, New Haven: Yale University Press, 1971.

JAMES HENRETTA, "Economic Development and Social Structure in Colonial Boston," *William and Mary Quarterly*, 3rd ser. XXII (1965), 75–92.

STEPHEN THERNSTROM, *Poverty & Progress*, New York: Atheneum Publishers, 1970.

On February 2, 1785, the *Massachusetts Centinel* in Boston complained that "We daily see men speculating, with impunity, on the most essential articles of life, and grinding the faces of the poor and laborious as if there was no God," yet five months later to the day, Sam Adams wrote to his cousin John, "You would be surprizd to see the Equipage, the Furniture and expensive Living of too many, the Pride and Vanity of Dress which pervades thro every Class, confounding every Distinction between the Poor and the Rich." As these quotations suggest, opinion divided sharply in post-Revolutionary Boston on the direction of major social change, and impressionistic evidence can be found to sustain a broad range of interpretation. Relying on this material, historians have perpetuated the contemporary diversity of opinion. Scholars of the Progressive era, like J. Franklin Jameson, tended to agree with Adams that the Revolution had a leveling effect, while more recent studies have found some change as whigs replace tories and a new propertied class emerged, but less democratization than had been supposed.

This essay attempts to discover the magnitude of change in Boston from 1771 to 1790 by testing controllable, quantitative materials to answer the following questions: How did the town's occupational structure change? Did the distribution of wealth become more or less equal? How closely related were wealth and status? Did political power become more democratically shared? By how much did population increase? What social and economic patterns of residence could be found? What changes occurred in the rate of geographic and economic mobility?

Before the Revolution, Boston had been an intensely unequal society. Wealthy men of high status dominated government and social life. The top 10 per cent of the taxpayers in 1771 owned nearly two-thirds of the wealth and held most of the important town offices. While demanding respect from the poor, many of the wealthy lived in the center of town, segregated from the impoverished. Poorer men possessed no significant political power, but held numerous minor town offices. And largely because many poor men and women were migrating from nearby towns, the poor in Boston were becoming more numerous. These trends continued and accelerated during the war and the Confederation period. Not a less stratified, but an even more unequal society developed in Boston after the Revolution.

Late eighteenth-century Boston was a typical "consumer city" in Max Weber's phrase. It was a town of under 20,000 inhabitants in which "the purchasing power of its larger consumers rests on the retail for profit of foreign products on the local market . . . the foreign sale for profit of local products or goods obtained by native producers . . . or the purchase of foreign products and their sale . . . outside.[2]

The economy of Boston still rested squarely on foreign trade. Close to a quarter of her workers—merchants, mariners, captains, chandlers, and wharfingers—earned their livelihood from commerce. Another 15 per cent were indirectly concerned with trade. Retailers sold and distributed foreign goods; coopers made barrels bound for the sea; laborers supplied the manpower necessary to unload ships; and distillers used foreign sugar in their product.

Unlike Weber's "producer city," Boston was not an exporter of the goods she produced.[3] Most of those not engaged in commerce produced goods and services for the local market. No industrial group included large numbers of workers. About 7 per cent worked with cloth, 5 per cent with leather, and 5 per cent with metals. Construction workers were under a tenth of all those employed. The small proportion of innkeepers (3 per cent) and men in the food trades (7 per cent) showed that Boston was not a major food market; nor had a large bureaucracy developed, since only

[2] Max Weber, *The City*, trans. and ed. Don Martindale and Gertrud Neuwirth (New York, 1958), 69.
[3] *Ibid.* Philadelphia closely resembled a "producer city." See James T. Lemon, "Urbanization and the Development of Eighteenth-Century Southeastern Pennsylvania and Adjacent Delaware," *Wm. and Mary Qtly.*, 3d Ser., XXIV (1967), 504–510.

TABLE I. *Boston's occupational structure, 1790* [a]

Occupational Group	Number In Group	Number of Trades in Group	Percentage of Work Force
Government Officials	67	4	2.6
Professionals [b]	105	8	4.1
Merchants-Traders	224	3	8.7
Retailers	184	7	7.1
Sea Captains	114	1	4.4
Other Business [c]	66	6	2.6
Clerks and Scribes	66	2	2.6
Building Crafts	245	7	9.3
Cloth Trades	182	8	7.1
Leather Crafts	113	5	5.1
Food Trades	175	11	6.8
Marine Crafts	219	13	8.5
Metal Crafts	132	11	5.1
Woodworkers	106	7	4.1
Other Artisans	105	35	4.1
Transportation	80	6	3.2
Service	103	4	4.0
Mariners	117	4	4.5
Unskilled	188	4	7.4
Total Artisans	1,271	96	49.1
Total Other	1,314	49	50.9
Total Employed	2,585	145	100.0
Servants (white)	63		
Unemployed and Retired [d]	106		
Total	2,754		

Notes: [a] Boston Tax Taking and Rate Books, 1790, City Hall, Boston, Mass. Hereafter cited as Tax and Rate Books, 1790. These records were checked with the Boston city directories for 1789 and 1796, *Report of the Record Commissioners of the City of Boston* (Boston, 1876–1909), X, 171–296. Hereafter as *Record Commissioners' Report*. A total accounting of each trade is found in the [original article].

[b] Includes 20 untaxed clergymen counted in Thomas Pemberton, "A Topographical and Historical Description of Boston, 1794," Massachusetts Historical Society, *Collections*, 1st Ser., III (1794), 256–264.

[c] Includes groups such as wharfingers, chandlers, brokers, and auctioneers.

[d] Includes 23 gentlemen, 27 poor, 28 sick and poor, and 28 little or no business.

3 per cent of the labor force was employed in government—and many of these worked only part-time.

Large enterprises were uncommon: the median number of workers in ninety-six artisan crafts was only three, and the mean number thirteen. The typical middling artisan employed his sons and several other workers.

These young apprentices and journeymen lived with the families of master craftsmen, not alone in rented rooms.[4]

There was an excess population in the working ages, composed mostly of women and including many widows, who were outside the occupational structure. Between 1765 and 1800, the proportion of people in the productive ages above fifteen years increased by 17 per cent, thereby providing workers for any factories that might open. There were 19 per cent more women than men of working age in 1765, and 14 per cent more in 1800. About a tenth of these women were widows, and three-quarters of them supported dependents.[5]

Two small factories were operating in 1790, but they were not part of a general industrialization, and only one of them utilized this surplus laboring population. At a "duck cloth manufactory" employing four hundred workers in 1792, there were only seventeen male employees two years before. A few of the others were young girls; the rest were women. The factory had been established to promote American manufactures and at the same time to aid the poor. According to the *Massachusetts Centinel* in 1788, it and a small glass works "promise soon to be completed and to give employment to a great number of persons, especially females who now eat the bread of idleness, whereby they may gain an honest livelihood." By 1800, the duckcloth factory was out of business.

---

[4] Tax and Rate Books, 1790, compared with *Heads of Families At the First Census, 1790, Massachusetts* (Washington, 1906), 188–195; and "Names of the Inhabitants of the Town of Boston in 1790," *Record Commissioners' Report*, XXII, 443–511. Numerous dependent males over 16 years of age are found in the census, but not in the tax lists. Almost all of them were in homes of artisans of middling wealth. This suggests that many of them were transient journeymen and apprentices and not older sons hidden from the assessor. Tax and census records are the source for any uncited comments.

[5] Lemuel Shattuck, *Report to the Committee of the City Council Appointed to Obtain the Census of Boston for the Year 1845, . . .* (Boston, 1846), 4, 45. A sample of every sixth column of the Washington edition of the census was checked for widows; three-quarters had dependents. Joseph J. Spengler, "Demographic Factors and Early Modern Economic Development," *Daedalus*, XCVII (1968), 440–443, defines productive ages as from 15 to 65 years. Data in Shattuck does not allow such fine distinctions, but the percentage of people over 65 is probably too small to materially change the following statistics:

Age Ratios	Percentage over 15 yrs. old			Sex Ratios	Number of Men/100 Women		
	1765	1790	1800		1765	1790	1800
Total	44.30	. . .	61.93	All ages	95.48	82.07	90.27
Male	41.71	56.13	60.42	Over 15	81.42	. . .	86.14
Female	47.26	. . .	63.31				

About three-quarters of the one thousand workers in the other large enterprise, a cotton and wool card factory, were children. About a fifth of all the children in Boston from eight to sixteen years of age were probably employed there. The owners chose to hire them rather than women, since children could easily run the machinery and were paid less.

At least until 1820, Boston's occupational structure remained close to the "consumer city" model. Less than one-tenth of 1 per cent of men listed in the 1820 directory were manufacturers, and the proportion of merchants, retailers, and building tradesmen remained almost the same. Domestic commerce was becoming more important as foreign trade declined. A reduction in the percentage of mariners, captains, and marine tradesmen from 17.4 per cent in 1790 to 10.6 per cent in 1820 illustrates the trend. Meanwhile, the town had become more important as a food market, with the proportion of men in the food trades climbing from 6.8 per cent to 10.7 per cent.

Most of Boston's taxable wealth—real estate, stock in trade, and income from trade—rested in fewer and fewer hands as time passed. Boston followed a pattern similar to both American towns and rural areas. Although in the seventeenth century wealth in American towns was typically less concentrated than in sixteenth-century English towns, where the poorer half of the population owned less than a tenth of the wealth and the richest tenth owned between half and seven-tenths, the English pattern soon reappeared in America and intensified.

From 1687 to 1790, Boston's wealth became progressively more concentrated. . . .* Though the proportion of wealth held by the richest tenth of the taxpayers had almost reached its peak by 1771 and 29 per cent were without taxable property both before and after the Revolution, the wealth of the lower middle group, where assessments ranged from £25 to £100, was cut in half. Three-quarters of this decline was gained by the upper middle group, assessed between £100 and £500. . . .

Were the relatively poor becoming poorer? Brissot de Warville discovered full employment in Boston in 1788 and "saw none of those livid, ragged wretches that one sees in Europe, who, soliciting our compassion at the foot of the altar, seem to bear witness . . . against our inhumanity." Brissot's European standard of comparison allowed him to underestimate the extent of poverty in Boston. At this time, a fifth to a third of those living in English and French towns were beggars, paupers, and others who could not make a living for themselves. Another third were the near poor

---

* A Lorenz curve can be found in the original article.

TABLE II.

A. DISTRIBUTION OF TAXABLE WEALTH IN BOSTON, 1790 [a]

Assessment in Pounds	Number in Category	Percentage of Taxpayers in Category	Wealth in Category in Pounds	Percentage of Wealth in Category
0	892	29.8	0	0.0
25	388	12.9	9,700	1.0
26–50	240	8.0	11,162	1.2
51–75	148	4.9	11,012	1.2
76–100	167	5.6	16,662	1.8
101–150	186	6.2	24,938	2.7
151–200	147	4.9	27,887	3.0
201–300	186	6.2	49,113	5.3
301–400	128	4.3	46,713	5.0
401–500	116	3.9	54,300	5.9
501–700	124	4.1	75,775	8.3
701–999	71	2.4	58,775	6.1
1,000–1,999	122	4.1	159,875	17.2
2,000–4,999	58	1.9	165,250	17.8
5,000+	22	0.8	217,775	23.5
Totals	2,995	100.0	928,937	100.0

B. DISTRIBUTION OF WEALTH IN BOSTON, 1687 to 1830 [b]

Percentage of Taxpayers	Percentage of Wealth Held			
	1687	1771	1790	1830
Bottom 30	2.48	0.10	0.03	0.00
Low-Mid 30	11.29	9.43	4.80	7.92
Upper-Mid 30	39.63	27.01	30.47	26.94
Top 10	46.60	63.46	64.70	65.14
Total	100.00	100.00	100.00	100.00
Top 1%	9.51	25.98	27.14	26.15
Schutz Coefficient	.4896	.5541	.6276	.6370

Notes: [a] Tax and Rate Books, 1790. Group at 0 paid only poll tax; £25 was the first assessment. Untaxed widows found on the census are not included.

[b] See Table II A for 1790 figures; 1687 and 1771 figures from Henretta, "Economic Development and Social Structure," *Wm. and Mary Qtly.*, 3d Ser., XXII (1965), 80, 82, with those paying only poll tax added; 1830 figures were estimated from imprecise, grouped data in Shattuck, *Report,* 95. The Schutz coefficient of inequality measures income concentration—0 equals total equality, 1 total inequality. Robert R. Schutz, "On the Measurement of Income Inequality," *American Economic Review*, XLI (1951), 107–122; Blumin, "Mobility and Change," in Thernstrom and Sennett, eds., *Nineteenth-Century Cities*, 204.

of the English towns and the *sans-culottes* and *menu peuple* in French towns—persons who could become destitute in times of crisis.[6]

The poor and near poor were growing more numerous in Boston. The percentage of poor can be roughly estimated at 7 per cent of the population in 1771 and 10 per cent in 1790. The change is illustrated by the slow increase in the numbers of destitute, old, and sick men and women, and dependent children in the poorhouse at a time of relatively little population increase (see Table V): 146 in 1742, never over 180 before the Revolution, and 250 in August 1790, with 300 to 400 expected the following winter. Because personal property was not taxed, it is difficult to determine the percentage of near poor, but an estimate can be made.[7] Composed of widows, blacks, seamen, laborers, and poorer artisans who might dip below the minimum level of subsistence when unemployment increased, this group probably ranged from 30 to 40 per cent in 1771 and from 37 to 47 per cent in 1790.

Unemployed, old, or sick, most of the poor and their families lived outside the poorhouse. Alexander Lord, a poor laborer, had "gone broke, wife as broke"; they had a son under sixteen to share their misery. Jacob Bull, an old shoemaker, and his wife were both ill, but two other women lived in their household. And Samuel Goddard, "shoemaker, no business, poor and supported by charity," could provide his family of five with few comforts.[8] Only the very old, the totally destitute, and the terminally ill entered the poorhouse, for the social conditions there steadily declined. In 1790, the poorhouse was filthy, dark, crowded, and odoriferous. "Persons of every description and disease are lodged under the same roof and in some instances in the same or Contiguous Apartments, by which means

---

[6] In this paper, "poor" refers to the destitute, "near poor" to those living at or near the minimum level of subsistence. For Europe see Hoskins, *Provincial England*, 90–93; Hoskins, *Industry, Trade and People in Exeter, 1688–1800*, . . . (Manchester, Eng., 1935), 119; Pound, "Structure of Norwich," *Past and Present*, No. 34 (July 1966), 50–51; George Rudé, "La population ouvrière de Paris de 1789 à 1791," *Annales Historiques de la Révolution Française*, XXXIX (1967), 21–27; Jeffry Kaplow, "Sur la population flottante de Paris, à la fin de l'Ancien Régime," *ibid.*, 7–8; Pierre Deyon, *Amiens, Capitale Provinciale. Etude sur la Société Urbaine au 17° Siècle* (Paris, 1967), 349–357. I am indebted to Gerald Soliday, Brandeis University, for the French materials.

[7] Since the total amount of property remains unknown, any "poverty line" chosen from Table II would be arbitrary. Instead, estimates of poor have been calculated by adding poorhouse and unemployed figures from Table I and of near poor by adding the number of widows from the census to the number of persons without taxable property and of those in the lowest category of taxpayers. A fifth of the propertyless and 15% of the lowest category have been subtracted from the near poor figure to account for upward mobility. The figures, especially for 1771, are very rough, but the direction of change they indicate is accurate, and the estimates are minimal figures of the extent of poverty.

[8] "Gone broke, wife as broke," and all similar short comments are marginalia from the Tax and Rate Books, 1790.

the sick are disturbed, by the Noise of the healthy, and the infirm rendered liable to the Vices and diseases of the diseased, and profligate."

The lives of the near poor were only somewhat better than those of the poor. While the number of people per dwelling declined from 9.53 in 1742 to 7.58 in 1790 (see Table V), many of the near poor lived in grossly inferior housing. The tax assessors found 90 families living in single rooms. Sixty-five of the same families were also counted by the census taker; three-quarters of this group had families of fewer than five members. Joseph Blayner, carpenter, lived with his wife and two children in a kitchen chamber while John Cartwright, cooper, his eight children, wife, and a boarder, crowded into the back of a house. Elijah Tolams, a "very poor carpenter," lived in one room with his three children, and Ebenezer Pilsbury, shoemaker, slept and worked with his six children in only two rooms.

There was a close relationship between wealth and status. Although status was not legally defined as in England, and the reputations of various trades were unstable, the order of precedence in a parade honoring President Washington in 1789 gives some indication of the prestige of various groups. The military, town and state officers, professional men, merchants and traders, and sea captains led the parade. They were followed by forty-six different artisan crafts, "alphabetically disposed, in order to give general satisfaction." No mechanical art was deemed better than the next. Sailors brought up the rear, and laborers were not included in the line of march.

As Table III shows, the eleven wealthiest occupations included professional men of high status, merchants, retailers, along with several artisan trades. Most of those in the economic elite—men assessed over £1,000 —were in these groups. Sea captains, with a mean wealth of £240, were lower on the list than their status might indicate. Most others whose wealth fell between £100 and £260 were artisans. Immediately below a mean of £100 were the building trades, schoolmasters, and shipwrights. Other sea artisans, and such traditionally poorer trades as tailor, shoemaker, and barber, fell between £40 and £75. Bringing up the rear were the industrial trades of ropemaker and duckcloth maker, and mariners and laborers.

An analysis of variance showed a highly significant relationship between occupation and wealth, but the magnitude of this relationship was small. Only about 19.4 per cent of the variations in the wealth of all the individuals included in Table III was accounted for by differences between occupation. The rest of the variation was within each occupation.[9] In most

[9] An F test was significant at less than the .01 level. This means there is less than a 1% chance that the differences shown in Table III are random. The test is a comparison of two quantities: 1. the sum of the squared variations of each case in each occupation subtracted from the group mean; and 2. the sum of the squared

trades, a few men had wealth far above the group mean; a number of hatters, printers, and bakers, for example, owned large establishments. As a result, in all but three trades below chaisemaker on the table, the median wealth was fifty pounds or less. Most fishermen, sailors, and laborers had no taxable wealth at all.

Those who possessed the highest status, reputation, and wealth expected visible differences of "Equipage, Furniture, . . . and Dress" between themselves and the rest of society. They socialized mostly with each other and separated themselves from the masses by forming exclusive organizations. One of these, a dinner club that encouraged members to relax and enjoy good conversation, was open to only sixteen men, each admitted by a unanimous vote. Another, the Massachusetts Historical Society, was incorporated in 1794 by ministers, doctors, lawyers, and a scientist to diffuse historical learning. This group limited its membership to thirty.

Wealthy artisans were granted substantial respect. In the parade honoring President Washington, each trade was led by a member whose wealth averaged 225 per cent more than the mean wealth of his group: the leader of the tailors, Samuel Ballard, was assessed £500; goldsmith Benjamin Bert, £400; shoemaker Samuel Bangs, £500; and carpenter William Crafts, £400. Nathaniel Balch, who was assessed £925, not only led his fellows hatters in the parade, but his shop was described as "the principle lounge even of the finest people in the town. Governor Hancock himself would happen into this popular resort, ready for a joke or a political discussion with Balch."

While poorer groups were expected to defer to the elite, they in turn were accorded little respect. Not only did poorer artisans have less status than those who were richer, the elite tolerated insults and attacks on black men and old black women by lower-class whites. Prince Hall, leader of the black masonic lodge, nevertheless urged Boston's Negroes to ignore their white attackers and trust "men born and bred in Boston," because we "had rather suffer wrong than to do wrong, to the disturbance of the community and the disgrace of our reputation."

Did the elite demonstrate any sense of social responsibility toward the poor? Noblesse oblige was practically nonexistent. The Massachusetts Humane Society, founded mainly to save people from drowning, chose to

---

variations of each group subtracted from the grand mean. Eta^2, calculated from the same data, tests the strength or degree of relationship. In this case, Eta^2 was .194, which means that about 19.4% of the difference between the means in Table III is accounted for by the differences between occupational groups. See Herbert M. Blalock, Jr., *Social Statistics* (New York, 1960), 242–252, 255–257. Stuart Blumin's calculations of Eta^2 on Philadelphia data from 1860 were almost identical (.17). "The Historical Study of Vertical Mobility," *Historical Methods Newsletter*, I, No. 4 (Sept. 1968), 8–10.

TABLE III.   *Mean assessed wealth of selected occupations in Boston, 1790* [a]

Rank	Occupation	Mean Assessment in Pounds	Number of Persons in Category
1	Merchant	1,707	206
2	Lawyer	846	21
3	Doctor	795	26
4	Apothecary	657	17
5	Distiller	642	47
6	Broker	622	16
7	Retailer	601	133
8	Taverner	522	26
9	Grocer	472	33
10	Chandler	347	17
11	Wharfinger	335	24
12	Tobacconist	260	17
13	Boarder-keeper	258	24
14	Printer	247	17
15	Sea Captain	240	114
16	Hatter	233	29
17	Clerk	232	28
18	Chaisemaker	188	16
19	Baker	170	64
20	Goldsmith	166	23
21	Painter	154	34
22	Cabinetmaker	131	15
23	Cooper	130	70
24	Founder	120	15
25	Sailmaker	112	30
26	Mason	95	44
27	Carpenter	92	140
28	Schoolmaster	89	16
29	Truckman	84	50
30	Blacksmith	83	59
31	Shipwright	78	65
32	Scribe	77	38
33	Barber	65	42
34	Blockmaker	63	16
35	Tailor	61	100
36	Caulker	53	14
37	Sea Cooper	46	16
38	Shoemaker	45	78
39	Mate	41	20
40	Ropemaker [b]	35	37
41	Duckcloth maker	25	16
42	Fisherman	15	37
43	Sailor	9	58
44	Laborer	6	157

Notes: [a] Computed from Tax and Rate Books, 1790.
  [b] Excludes 5 ropewalk owners with a mean wealth of £760.

build three small huts on islands where shipwrecks were common, rather than aid the poor sailors who populated Boston's North End. Men often complained to the assessors that they were poor, sick, lame, or had "little or no business." The only relief granted them was tax abatement; seventy men found on both the 1790 census and 1790 tax lists paid no taxes.

However, benevolence to widows was considered a community responsibility. A husband's death, commented one minister, "deprives a weak and helpless woman . . . of the sole instrument of her support, the guide of her children's youth, and their only earthly dependance." Any charity granted by town or church went to them. The overseers of the poor distributed minimal aid from bequests. In 1787, for example, they gave money to sixty-six different widows, most receiving nine or twelve shillings, and only fifteen women were helped more than once. The First Church, perhaps typical, collected donations for the poor quarterly and on the Sunday before Thanksgiving. Several dozen women received a pittance of two or three shillings each month from this money.

Who held political office in Boston after the Revolution? In pre-Revolutionary Boston, wealthy men of high social status monopolized important positions. Minor offices went to those of less wealth and status and gave their holders a sense of belonging in the community. After the Revolution, recent research indicates, the Massachusetts legislature included more moderately wealthy men than before the war. Did Boston officeholding become more widely distributed?

As Table IV shows (p. 146), the economic elite still dominated the most important town offices. All the state legislators from Boston were assessed over a thousand pounds and were among the wealthiest 6.8 per cent of the population. Four were merchants, two were wealthy gentlemen, one was a doctor, one a lawyer, and one a hardware store owner. Only a quarter of the firewards, who protected valuable property in case of fire, dipped below a thousand pounds; most of them were merchants, wharfingers, and wealthy shipwrights. The school committee, a newly created agency of the government, included three clergymen, three lawyers, three doctors, and two businessmen.

Probably the two most important town offices were the selectmen and the overseers of the poor. In 1790, only one of the overseers was assessed below a thousand pounds. From 1785 to 1795, eight merchants, three hardware store owners, one auctioneer, two distillers, one apothecary, one ropewalk owner, and a wealthy baker served as overseers. During the same period, selectmen included five merchants, two lawyers, the county treasurer, a captain, a retailer, an apothecary, a wharfinger, and a wealthy hatter. Five others were probably retired businessmen, whose low assessments reduced the selectmen's mean wealth.

Remarkably little turnover occurred in these two time-consuming, nonpaying positions. From 1760 to 1770, the average selectman served between three and four years; there was a small rise in tenure between 1785 and 1795. Overseers served even longer terms. In the decade 1760 to 1770, the average overseer served four or five years; after the war tenures increased to from six to eight years. At annual elections, both before and after the Revolution, typically only one or two selectmen or overseers were replaced. Bostonians served longer and replaced their officials less frequently than did the citizens of many other Massachusetts towns before the Revolution.[10]

The middling artisans, assessed between £100 and £500, were a group far larger than the economic elite, yet after the war they still held only a small percentage of major offices. Assessors and tax collectors, full-time paid officials who determined and collected taxes, were the only powerful officers of middle-class wealth. Other positions gave artisans some recognition of their special talents, but no political power. Carpenters, joiners, and cabinetmakers dominated the position of surveyor of boards; shoemakers were sealers of leather, and coopers were cullers of hoops and staves. Marine artisans formed a majority in the fire companies, the only agencies dominated by the poor and near poor. These jobs, dirty and unpaid, gave the economic elite an opportunity to share civic participation while keeping political power in its own hands.

The elite was suspicious of any attempt to organize the laboring force politically, however deferential the organizers initially were. Artisans of middle wealth, whose share of the town's taxable property had increased

[10] See n. 30; Robert Francis Seybold, *The Town Officials of Colonial Boston, 1634–1775* (Cambridge, Mass., 1939), 289–305. For other Massachusetts towns before the Revolution, see Michael Zuckerman, *Peaceable Kingdoms: New England Towns in the Eighteenth Century* (New York, 1970), 274–276. Boston turnover and service rates were as follows:

Years	Number of Offices	Number of Officeholders	Years of Service		Rate of Turnover/Year	
			mean	median	mean	median
SELECTMEN						
1760–70	7	19	4.0	3.0	1.7	1.5
1785–95	9	23	4.3	4.0	2.2	1.0
OVERSEERS OF THE POOR						
1760–70	12	28	4.7	4.0	1.6	1.0
1785–95	12	23	6.3	8.0	1.2	0.5

TABLE IV. *Assessed wealth of Boston officeholders, 1790* [a]

Office	Mean Wealth	Median Wealth	Number in Group
State Legislators	4,044	1,750	9
Overseers of Poor	3,398	1,610	12
Fire Wards	2,850	1,350	15
School Committee	1,633	1,000	9
Clerks of Market	954	875	12
Selectmen	642	500	9
Cullers of Hoops and Staves	208	175	21
Assessors, Collectors	207	200	9
Fire Companies	125	50	138
Constables	115	75	12
Surveyors of Boards	78	50	15

Note: [a] Tax and Rate Books, 1790; *Record Commissioners' Report,* XXXI, 217–224; X, 207–211. Information for a few officers could not be determined. These included 14 members of the fire companies, 4 cullers of hoops, 3 surveyors of boards, and 3 untaxed ministers who were members of the school committee. Four legislators are missing from the table: 3 were Suffolk County senators, probably residents of other parts of the county, and the other was a representative whose name was too common to identify. All other officers are included.

since 1771, founded the Mechanics Association in 1795. Only two members of the group had belonged to the economic elite in 1790, at which time the assessments of 63 per cent of those who became members fell between £100 and £500. In 1796 the group petitioned the General Court for incorporation because "the disconnected state of the mechanics of the town of Boston . . . retarded the mechanic arts of the state" whose "situation as a manufacturing country promised the greatest extension." Twenty leading merchants were personally urged to support the petition, "to patronize an institution formed for the reciprocal benefits of the merchant and mechanic." But despite the Association's broadly conceived purpose, the legislature feared the group's potential political power and three times refused to grant incorporation. The Association finally succeeded in obtaining a charter in 1806.

The poorer sort commanded no political resource other than ineffective deferential appeals to the wealthy. The accumulated grievances of poor mechanics were partially relieved by harassing the black population; only the middling artisans were able to organize successfully. Pressure from below on the elite was nonexistent after the Revolution, and criminal activity was rare. Betwen 1787 and 1790, nine men were hanged, all for robbery, while twenty-six were punished for other crimes.

Boston's population steadily increased from 1630 to 1740 as the townsmen settled the entire Shawmut Peninsula, but after 1740 people migrated from eastern New England in large numbers, so that from 1742 to 1790 Boston's population grew only 8.4 per cent, a gain of 1.68 per cent per decade. (See Table V) During the same period, the American population overall expanded at the Malthusian rate of 34.7 per cent per decade. Migration patterns bypassed eastern New England; people generally traveled up the Connecticut Valley into western Massachusetts, New Hampshire, and Maine. The results may be seen in the differential population growth of areas of Massachusetts between 1765 and 1790: Massachusetts's total population increased 54.1 per cent; Boston's (based on the smaller population of 1765) 16.2 per cent; the surrounding towns of Brookline, Cambridge, Charlestown, Chelsea, and Roxbury, 18.3 per cent; and the eastern Massachusetts counties of Suffolk, Essex, Plymouth, and Middlesex, 28.5 per cent. Boston's population fell after 1742 but recovered by 1771 until the British occupied the city in 1776, when people left en masse for the countryside and only slowly returned. The exodus postponed major population growth until after recovery from the effects of the war. Between 1790 and 1820 the town's population increased at the rate of 31.3 per cent per decade.

Although the population remained nearly stationary until 1790, Bos-

TABLE V.   *Population and density in Boston, 1742 to 1810* [a]

Year	Population	Number of Houses	Number of People Per House
1742	16,528	1,719	9.53
1752	15,731	. . .	. . .
1760	15,631	. . .	. . .
1765	15,520	1,676	9.26
1771	16,540	1,803	9.12
1776	2,719	. . .	. . .
1780	10,000	. . .	. . .
1784	14,000	2,178	6.43
1790	18,038	2,376	7.58
1800	24,937	3,000	8.31
1810	33,788	3,970	8.51

Note: [a] Shattuck, *Report,* 5, 54; Greene and Harrington, *American Population,* 31; Worthington C. Ford, ed., *Writings of John Quincy Adams,* I (New York, 1913), 62; Valuation of Towns, 1768–1771: Boston, 1771, Massachusetts Archives, Statehouse, Boston, CXXXII. The 1771 figure was derived by multiplying the number of polls by 5.75, a figure suggested by the larger number of houses that year, and the large immigration between 1765 and 1771.

tonians began to live in less settled areas. Most, however, still crowded onto about two-thirds of the peninsula. Streets in the North End and the center of town were filled with houses; yet many areas remained uninhabited, and the empty common was almost as large as the entire North End. In 1794, Boston was still "capable of great increase as many large spots of land remain vacant." Without the pressure of large population growth, there was no need to build on inaccessible areas like Beacon Hill. The relatively high population density that resulted allowed people to conduct their business with ease by walking.[11]

Boston expanded slowly, gradually consuming her open spaces. The mean number of people per dwelling decreased from 9.53 in 1742 to 7.58 in 1790. From 1740 to 1760 few houses were built, and many were destroyed in the 1760 fire, but from 1765 to 1790 a net total of 700 new houses were constructed. A small housing boom took place between 1771 and 1790 when an average of 28.7 houses per year were built.

The new housing was probably built mostly in the open West and South Ends. As Table VI shows, these areas were gaining population. In 1742 61 per cent of the people lived in the small, crowded North End and the center of town; the remaining 39 per cent resided in the West and South Ends, about two-thirds of the town's area. Population slowly moved west and south. Ward twelve, closest to the Roxbury Neck, gained 73 per cent from 1742 to 1790; the West End gained 21 per cent; and the center of town lost population. As a result, only 43 per cent of the population lived in the North End and the center by 1790. In 1802, William Bentley, a minister from Salem, while on a walking tour, "saw the increasing wealth of the south end, so called, but the growth of West Boston by the new Bridge from Cambridge is very great. Where the population was thin . . . and there were fields and marshes, are now splendid houses and crowded Streets."

Boston's social geography was similar to other preindustrial towns. In those towns, wealthy merchants, lawyers, retailers, and noblemen lived on or near the main business streets. Residents of middling wealth generally lived next to them. On the outskirts, farthest away from the economic center of town, resided poor artisans and laborers. In Boston, both before and after the Revolution, the farther one walked from State Street, the lower the ward's mean and median wealth became.

---

[11] Pemberton, "Description of Boston," Mass. Hist. Soc., *Collections,* 1st Ser., III (1794), 249–250. The North End (wards 1–5) and the West End (ward 7) were contemporary geographical areas (*ibid.,* 267). To allow analysis the South End of the 1790s was divided into the center of town (wards 6, 8, and 9) and the South End (wards 10–12). Houses are drawn on Price's 1769 map reprinted as frontispiece to *Bostonian Society Publications,* 1st Ser., IX (1912).

TABLE VI.   *Population of Boston's neighborhoods, 1742 to 1790* [a]

	1742	1771	1790	Percentage of Change, 1742–1790
North End	6,229	6,165	6,331	+ 2
West End	1,204	1,386	1,456	+ 21
Center	3,843	3,796	3,304	− 14
South End	5,106	5,193	6,625	+ 30
Other [b]	146	. . .	322	+120
Total	16,528	16,540	18,038	+ 8

Notes: [a] Shattuck, *Report,* 3–5; Valuation of Towns, Mass. Archives, CXXXII; Tax and Rate Books, 1790; *1790 Census.* For 1771, total polls in ward were multiplied by 5.75; the 1790 figure is based on name-by-name comparison of tax and census records, with interpolations where necessary.
[b] Poorhouse in 1742; poorhouse and jail in 1790.

The center of town, with a median wealth of £125 in 1790, was the richest section. The Massachusetts Bank, the Statehouse, the market, and various retail shops were located there, mostly along State and Cornhill Streets. Families of retailers lived over their shops. Unlike those in the rest of the town, the buildings were predominantly brick. Ward nine, on the south side of State Street, was the wealthiest in town, with a fifth of its residents assessed over a thousand pounds each, but it was closely followed by surrounding wards. The richest merchants and professional men and almost half the retailers lived in these wards, but in proportion to their numbers in the total population, fewer artisans made their homes there.

Part of the South End was far from the center of town and quite poor, but a number of retailers and merchants, mostly of middling wealth, lived in wards ten and eleven. The area's median wealth in 1790 was only fifty pounds; but over half the people in ward twelve were assessed twenty-five pounds or less. This ward, almost as populous as the two others together, contained large numbers of laborers, truckmen, and leather workers. In 1790, the ward must still have seen intense building activity, because a third of the town's masons, carpenters, and painters resided there.

The undersettled West End, with a median wealth of twenty-five pounds, was poorer than the South End. Most of the town's ropemakers lived there, close to the ropewalks. This was the only part of town not to lose black population between 1742 and 1790; in 1790 blacks were most concentrated there. As the area became more densely settled, merchants

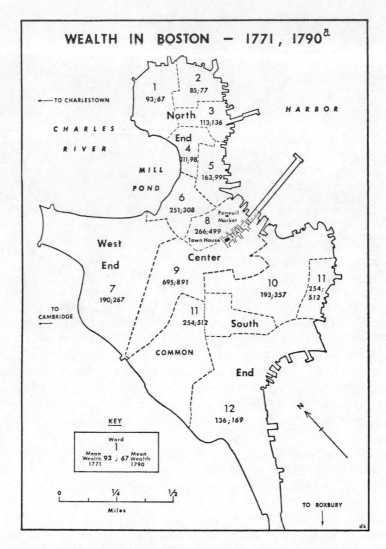

WEALTH IN BOSTON — 1771, 1790[a]

TO CHARLESTOWN

CHARLES
RIVER

HARBOR

1
93;67

2
85;77

North

3
113;136

End

4
011;98

5
163;99

MILL

POND

6
251;308

Faneuil
Market

8
266;499

Town House

West

End

7
190;267

Center

9
695;891

10
193;357

11
254;
512

11
254;512

TO
CAMBRIDGE

South

COMMON

End

12
136;169

N

KEY

Ward

1

Mean
Wealth 93 ; 67 Mean
1771   Wealth
              1790

0   ¼   ½

Miles

TO ROXBURY

dk

[a] Mass. Archives, CXXXII; Tax and Rate Books, 1790; *1790 Census*. The 1771 means were calculated by dividing the wealth of the ward by the number of polls; the 1790 means by dividing the ward's wealth by the number of people taxed with the addition of widows from the census. Untaxed widows were not included in the 1771 list, but the two sources are comparable because all polls (including each poll in multiple poll households and "polls not rateable") were included in the 1771 figure, but not in the 1790 figure. This seems to have underestimated the 1771 wealth.

TABLE VII. *Residential patterns of economic and occupational groups, Boston, 1790* [a]

A. ECONOMIC GROUPS

Percentage by Area

1790 Assessment in Pounds	North End	West End	Center	South End	Number in Group
0	46	6	14	34	1,364
1–75	41	10	13	36	776
76–275	33	8	21	38	627
276–999	20	7	35	38	498
1,000+	6	9	40	45	202
Total of All Groups	37	8	18	37	3,467

B. OCCUPATIONAL GROUPS

Percentage by Area

Occupation	North End	West End	Center	South End	Number in Group
Bakers	38	18	5	39	66
Blacksmiths	46	3	8	43	59
Building Trades	31	10	11	48	245
Coopers	70	0	3	27	70
Laborers	47	7	8	38	157
Leather Workers	33	5	10	52	108
Mariners	68	5	8	19	117
Marine Crafts [b]	72	2	6	20	193
Merchants [c]	9	12	28	51	206
Professionals	15	13	38	34	68
Retailers [d]	28	4	46	22	144
Sea Captains	46	10	16	28	114
Tailors	41	11	16	32	100
Transportation	32	4	14	50	80
Total of All Groups	40	7	16	37	1,727

Notes: [a] Tax and Rate Books, 1790. Variations in residential patterns can be seen by comparing the percentage of the total of all groups in each area with the percentage of each subgroup in the area. In Table VII A, widows from the census are included; Table VII B includes about two-thirds of all employed. A Chi Square test run on the raw data of Table VII A yielded a result that was significant at less than the .01 level. This means the probability that the distribution occurred by chance is less than 1%.

[b] Excludes ropemakers, concentrated in the West End.

[c] Includes only merchants, not other groups included under "Merchants-Traders" in Table I.

[d] Retailers and hardware store owners only.

and professional men also moved into the area; by 1790 both groups were settled there in greater proportion than throughout the town generally.

The North End was the poorest section of town in 1771, and by 1790 the wealth of its inhabitants seems to have declined. The median wealth of the area in the latter year was twenty-five pounds, but over half the people in the remote wards one and two were without taxable wealth. Most of the town's transient sailors, shipwrights, sailmakers, and other marine artisans lived there. An area dominated by marine interests, it also housed proportionately higher percentages of coopers, sea captains, laborers, tailors, and poor widows than there were in the population as a whole.

How strong was this pattern? Even though the town was small, and a few members of every economic and occupational group lived in every section, substantial economic segregation could have existed. As Table VIII shows, no group was as segregated as blacks are today. There was no necessary relationship between occupation and degree of segregation. Professional men were more integrated than merchants; blacks, laborers, and tailors clustered far less than their lower-class status might indicate. Marine artisans, with their special ship-related functions, were the most segregated trade. Wealth rather than occupation determined residence. Boston's propertyless residents—nearly 40 per cent of the population— were the most segregated group and mostly lived in economic ghettos at either end of town. Wealthier, and thus smaller, economic groups were less concentrated and spread more evenly across the city.

In late eighteenth-century Boston, individuals were becoming increasingly more mobile, moving from place to place and from one economic position to another, while society itself was becoming more stratified.

TABLE VIII. *Index of dissimilarity of economic and occupational groups, Boston, 1790* [a]

Unpropertied	56.8	Marine Crafts [b]	35.5	Transportation	11.6
Assessed £1–75	26.4	Merchants	25.9	Professionals [c]	9.8
Assessed £76–275	16.7	Building Crafts	18.6	Sea Captains	8.8
Assessed £276–999	41.7	Mariners	17.3	Tailors	8.8
Assessed £1,000+	28.5	Retailers	16.7	Leather Crafts	8.3
Blacks	10.4	Laborers	15.2	Bakers	6.7
Widows	19.1	Coopers	11.8	Blacksmiths	6.4

Notes: [a] Tax and Rate Books, 1790. For details on the construction of the index, which measures the average deviation within wards of the percentage of each group from its mean percentage in the total population and runs from 0 (perfect integration) to 100 (total segregation), see Taeuber and Taeuber, *Negroes in Cities*, 235–237.

[b] Excludes ropemakers, concentrated in the West End.

[c] Lawyers, doctors, an accountant, an apothecary, and an architect.

Almost all newcomers to Boston were "warned out," officially informed that the town would not care for them if they ever needed charity. Since there is no indication that warnings out were limited to the poor, they are rough measures of migration into Boston. While the scrutiny of the overseers may have increased over the period, the pattern found in Table IX

TABLE IX. *Warnings out in Boston, 1745 to 1792* [a]

Year	Number Warned	Number Warned/ 1000 Population
1745–1749	363	23.1
1750–1754	528	33.6
1755–1759	1,160	74.2
1760–1764	765	49.3
1765–1769	2,499	151.1
1770–1773	1,587	95.9
1791–1792	2,405	133.9

Note: [a] Warnings Out in Boston, 1745–1792, Records of the Overseers of the Poor of Boston, Mass., Mass. Hist. Soc. From 1745 to 1773, children and wives were listed with husbands; the 1791–1792 lists often include many entries under a single family name, but the relationships are not indicated. The 1791–1792 number/1000 population is comparable with the others; at that time a resident could be warned until he resided in the town four years. Robert W. Kelso, *The History of Public Poor Relief in Massachusetts, 1620–1920* (Boston, 1922), 59. This table represents minimum migration into Boston.

is too strong to be discounted. The number of migrants remained small until 1755, then in terms both of numbers and rates, rapidly increased. After 1765, at least a tenth of Boston's residents had been in town five years or less.[12]

What would explain this dramatic change in the intensity of migration? Migrants in most modern societies tend to travel short distances, going from remote villages to nearby towns and from towns to more distant cities. They stop and settle at the first place where a job is offered, and travel farther only if the opportunity disappears. These generalizations apply to post-Revolutionary Boston. Almost three-quarters of the migrants entering Boston in 1791 came from Massachusetts, and a third traveled ten miles or less. In point of origin, the other quarter principally divided

[12] Rates for 1765–1790 were almost as great as in early modern London, but less than those in antebellum Boston. E. A. Wrigley, "A Simple Model of London's Importance in Changing English Society and Economy 1650–1750," *Past and Present*, No. 37 (July 1967), 45–49; Peter R. Knights, "Population Turnover, Persistence and Residential Mobility in Boston, 1830–1860," in Thernstrom and Sennett, eds., *Nineteenth-Century Cities*, 258–274.

TABLE X.   Birth places of those warned out of Boston, 1791 [a]

Foreign	237	Other States	62	Massachusetts	740
England	84	Philadelphia	28	Within 10 miles of Boston	341
Ireland	52	New York City	19	Southeast of Boston	181
Scotland	31	Carolina	4	North of Boston	143
Africa	29	Maryland	3	West of Boston	75
Germany	16	New Hampshire	3		
France	14	Albany	3		
Nova Scotia	3	Hartford	2		
West Indies	8				

Total: 1,039

Note: [a] Warnings Out in Boston, Overseers of the Poor Records, Mass. Hist. Soc.

between foreign lands and more distant American cities like New York and Philadelphia.

The migrants formed three distinct streams. Twenty-three per cent arrived from foreign ports. The other two groups, totaling 71.2 per cent of all migrants, traveled from Massachusetts towns. Most of them, 39.8 per cent of the total, migrated from nearby coastal areas such as Charlestown, Plymouth, Cape Cod, Ipswich, Salem, and Newburyport. This seaport-to-seaport stream probably brought numerous marine artisans and mariners into Boston. If the mobility of this group was as great in the 1760s, it may help to explain the number and volatility of the crowds in pre-Revolutionary Boston. The final group, constituting 31.4 per cent of all migrants, came from neighboring agricultural areas that were experiencing population pressure on land. In these areas during the late eighteenth century, poverty and geographical mobility increased as the average size of landholdings fell. Forced off the land and unaccustomed to urban life, these men at least temporarily joined and augmented the number of poor and near poor.

Though Boston drew many people from smaller ports, declining agricultural areas, and foreign lands, her own opportunities were limited. By 1790, 45 per cent of the taxpayers in town in 1780 had disappeared from tax lists. Some had died; the rest left town. The figure is higher than that found in stable, rural communities where land is plentiful, but is low compared to nineteenth-century American cities or frontier areas.[13] Those

13 Other rates, all expressed in terms of per cent per decade: 51% in the 17th-century English towns; 22% in Dedham, Mass., 1670–1700; 56% in Boston, 1830–1860; 73% in Trempealeau Co., Wis., 1860–1880. Peter Laslett and John Harrison, "Clayworth and Cogenhoe," in H. E. Bell and R. L. Ollard, eds., *Historical Essays*

who moved out of Boston were the poorest and least successful members of the community. As Table XI shows, only 42 per cent of those without real estate (rents) in 1780 remained in town in 1790. In Newburyport between 1850 and 1880, 41 per cent of the laborers persisted during each decade, a rate almost identical to that of the unpropertied in Boston seventy years earlier. As the amount of rent reported increased, the rate of persistence rose; only one-quarter of the upper 10 per cent of those listed in 1780 had moved or died by 1790. Even if the death rates of the poor were higher, and their slippage from one list to another greater, this table suggests that a larger proportion of the poor than the rich were mobile.

TABLE XI.   *Geographic mobility in Boston, 1780 to 1790* [a]

Rent in Pounds in 1780	Number Reported in 1780	Number Missing in 1790	Persistence Rate
0	546	318	42
1–20	448	215	52
21–40	360	169	53
41–60	217	83	62
61–80	219	83	62
100–199	226	78	66
200+	209	54	74
Total	2,225	1,000	56

Note: [a] Assessors' Books, 1780, compared with Tax and Rate Books, 1790. The persistence rate is the percentage of the number reported in 1780 found on the 1790 list.

Inward and outward mobility suggests a small, but significant, floating population of men and women at the bottom of society who moved from seaport to seaport and town to town in search of work. Many of the 278 men who were assessed for only the poll tax in 1790, but who disappeared before the census was taken, were probably among them.[14] The nature of this floating population was very similar to that in nineteenth-century Newburyport. Impoverished, unemployable men dominated the wanderers in both places. The fifteen men whipped for various offenses in Boston in

1600–1750, Presented to David Ogg (London, 1963), 173–177; Kenneth Lockridge, "The Population of Dedham, Massachusetts, 1636–1736," *Economic History Review,* 2d Ser., XIX (1966), 322–324; Knights, "Population Turnover," in Thernstrom and Sennett, eds., *Nineteenth-Century Cities,* 262; Curti, *American Community,* 68.

[14] The census was taken between Aug. 2 and 22 (*Record Commissioners' Report* edition of census); when assessments were made is unknown, but assessors were elected in March and some widows of men who were taxed appear in the census.

September 1790 were transients who had not been listed by the assessors a few months earlier. Other migrants from Boston landed in the poorhouses of neighboring towns, triggering angry correspondence between their overseers and those of Boston.

Uprooted, unwanted, unhealthy migrants could call no town their home. The potent identity given an individual by his community was not theirs. Thomas Seymore, an old man living off poor relief in Abington in 1805, was born and attended school in Boston, and later moved to Barnstable, Sandwich, Weymouth, and Abington, but never "gained a settlement" by paying taxes for five successive years. In his whole life, he never found a home. Similarly, Braintree demanded in 1804 that Boston "remove Stephen Randal belonging to your town." Since his arrival there in 1802, he had received relief from the town. "He has been wandering about from place to place. . . . Some part of the time chargeable. About four weeks ago he froze himself very bad in the feet and is att the Expense of two Dollars and 50 cents per week, Besides a Dollar attendance, there is no prospect of his being better very soon."

After the Revolution, the old laws used to deal with migrants fell apart. Even though the state accepted responsibility for transients without legal residence anywhere in the commonwealth, the time limit for towns to present migrants with warnings out was extended from two years to three, four, and ultimately five years between 1790 and 1793. In 1794, when the state became responsible for all migrants, warnings out were finally eliminated. Instead, legal residency required payment of taxes on an assessed estate of sixty pounds for five successive years. A former apprentice who practiced his trade for five years or anyone over twenty-one years of age who lived in town for ten years and paid taxes for five became a resident. The law discouraged transients, but encouraged artisans with capital to remain.

But did "expensive Living . . . [pervade] thro every Class, confounding every Distinction between the Poor and the Rich," as Samuel Adams insisted? Enough examples could be found to keep him worried. Thomas Lewis was a shoemaker assessed for £40 rent in 1780 and a wharfinger taxed on £700 in 1790; Josiah Elliot was an agent for a merchant in 1780 and owned no real estate, but in 1790 he operated a hardware store and was assessed for property worth £450; Robert Davis was a leather dresser with £30 rent in 1780, and a merchant assessed £600 in 1790.

Adams failed to see more modest gains. "Mechanics of sober character, and skilled in their trades, of almost every kind, may find employment, and wages equal to their support," wrote the Boston Immigrant Society. The society was partially right. When the Mechanics Association, open only to master craftsmen, was founded in 1795, a fifth of its original members were not on the 1790 tax list; they had either been apprentices in 1790 or had entered town since that time.

A comparison of 1780 and 1790 tax lists shows that occupational mobility was very moderate and that opportunity may well have been declining. Since only those who remained in town for ten years are considered, the results are biased toward success. Only 28 per cent changed jobs, while merely 14 per cent made even minor changes in status. Changes from one artisan job to another and changes among merchants, grocers, retailers, and captains were typical—and rather trivial. Other changes resulted in new status; and about the same number rose as declined. Seventeen artisans became small shopkeepers, wharfingers, and merchants, and four advanced to professional status, while thirteen declined to laborer status. Twenty-eight tradesmen and professionals declined to artisan status, and one became a laborer.

Some new men from outlying areas probably migrated to Boston, bought tory estates, and joined the elite classes immediately after the Revolution, but opportunity soon diminished and the situation became critical. As population grew, more men competed for fewer jobs; many, according to Samuel Breck, became unemployed, "so much so that several gentlemen who associated for the purpose of building three ships had solely in view the occupation of the carpenters and tradespeople." Breck may not have

TABLE XII. *Occupational mobility in Boston, 1780 to 1790* [a]

Occupation in 1790	Occupation in 1780				Total in 1790
	Professional	Tradesman	Artisan	Marine-Laborer	
Professional	42	15	4	0	61
Tradesman [b]	0	162	17	0	179
Artisan	5	23	311	9	348
Marine-Laborer	0	1	13	24	38
Total in 1780	47	201	345	33	626

Notes: [a] Assessors' Books, 1780; Tax and Rate Books, 1790. Table XII represents only about half the people who remained in Boston during the decade. Wards 5, 6, and 10 do not have occupations listed for 1780, and Negroes and widows were rarely listed. The columns are 1780, the rows 1790 (e.g., 61 professionals in 1790, 47 in 1780, 311 artisans remained artisans over the decade, 23 tradesmen became artisans). Lateral changes within the groups, which included no change in status, involved 4 professionals, 37 tradesmen, 42 artisans, 4 marine-laborers. Total changes of status: 87. Total lateral changes: 87. Total changes: 174.

[b] Retailers, merchants, businessmen.

greatly exaggerated. The percentage of laborers and other unskilled men more than doubled: between 2 and 3 per cent were in the group in 1780; the number had grown to 7.4 per cent in 1790.[15] Within the groups staying in town for the ten years, opportunities seem to have been slightly closing at the top and opening at the bottom. While ten merchants and traders became government functionaries (all but one in a full-time position), the total number of tradesmen declined by 11 per cent. On the other hand, the number of men in the marine-laborer category declined 12 per cent.[16]

Upward mobility among sons of artisans was somewhat greater. Jackson Main discovered that the fathers of about a quarter of the merchants sampled from the 1789 directory had been artisans such as brewers, coopers, hatters, carpenters, and tailors. Since each of these trades included a few wealthy members whose sons should have risen in the normal course of events, and Main discovered none from his sample among the wealthiest merchants, his findings, like mine, point to very modest upward mobility.

While a small minority changed their status, almost two-thirds of the group changed their relative economic position in the community. Table XIII shows that 30 per cent lost and 31 per cent gained wealth. However, these figures are deceptive; probably most of those who moved during the decade feared economic decline. When geographic mobility is considered, more men lost than gained wealth. In each of the three middle categories of Table XIII, the number who fell slightly approximated the number who gained slightly. Unpropertied men who left town were probably those who could not gain a foothold in Boston, for 71 per cent of those who remained became property owners. Most made minor gains; the twenty-eight men who entered the top categories were mostly merchants who had not yet bought property in Boston in 1780. The very top category—as Sam Adams asserted—was in a state of flux; less than half the men in that group in 1780 managed to remain there in 1790, but men from the next lower category rushed to fill their places.

What all these changes meant to most workers was buying—or losing —a small piece of real estate, finding a new, somewhat different job, or receiving a small profit from one's trade. Joseph Snelling, an unpropertied

[15] Laborers constitute 6.1% of the people whose occupations in 1780 are known. However, the three wards from which there is no occupational data housed only 11% of the laborers in 1790. The figure of 6.1% is therefore far too high. A number of others in other wards have no occupations listed, and some of them may have been laborers. For a conservative estimate of the proportion of laborers, I added 3% to the number listed (38), and divided that number (50) by 2,225, the total number of males on the 1780 list. The result was 2.3%.

[16] These percentages, based on a small number of cases, must be taken as indicative only of the direction of change, not of the extent of change. It is probable that some of the difference is random. However, the figures may be minimums; Table XII probably underestimates the extent of downward mobility. See note to Table XIV.

TABLE XIII.   Property mobility in Boston, 1780 to 1790 [a]

1790 Income Groups	High 1	2	3	4	Low 5	Total in 1790
	1780 Income Groups					
High 1	55	39	15	3	7	119
2	43	85	63	7	21	219
3	12	46	107	59	39	263
4	4	17	51	87	55	214
Low 5	7	14	32	71	51	175
Total in 1780	121	201	268	227	173	990

Note: [a] Assessors' Books, 1780; Tax and Rate Books, 1790. Some persons could not be ranked. Columns are 1780, rows 1790. The income groups were determined by comparing 1780 rents (hypothetically 1/6 of the real estate assessment) with total assessments in 1790. In the table, 1 is the highest and 5 the lowest group. The real figures for each group in 1780 and 1790 respectively are: 1, £200+ and £1000+; 2, £75–£199 and £276–£999; 3, £30–£74 and £76–£275; 4, £1–£29 and £1–£75; 5, £0 for both years.

joiner in 1780, gained £25 of real estate by 1790; John Scutter, a propertyless fisherman in 1780, was a journeyman goldsmith with £25 of real estate in 1790. Tailor Samuel Beales owned £12 10s. of real estate in 1780; by 1790, he owned property assessed at £125 and had six children and four apprentices or journeymen in his house. Small losses were equally common. John Douglass, a cooper with real estate worth £12 10s. in 1780, was a combmaker without taxable property in 1790. Samuel Clark, tailor, lost real estate worth £20 over the decade, and Richard Salter, a merchant with a rent of £180 in 1780, was a small shopkeeper with property worth only £25 in 1790.

What pattern explains these small changes? Men in some trades—merchants, professional men, builders, coopers—tended to gain wealth, while others—bakers, shoemakers, tailors—tended to lose it. Whole classes, however, neither rose nor fell; some individuals in most groups became prosperous and some poor. As Table XIV illustrates, over 70 per cent of Boston's workers assumed different occupations or economic conditions over the decade. While this is a significant (and expected) tendency for some to rise or fall both in wealth and occupation, 74 per cent of those changing in one variable did not change the other.

Though occupational mobility had little relationship to economic mobility, age in most occupational groups was probably related to wealth.

TABLE XIV.   *Occupational and property mobility in Boston, 1780 to 1790* [a]

	Occupation Up	Occupation Same	Occupation Down	Total
Wealth Up	32	164	14	210
Wealth Same	26	186	33	245
Wealth Down	12	84	52	148
Total	70	434	99	603

Note: [a] Assessors' Books, 1780; Tax and Rate Books, 1790. Occupations in Table XIV are ranked as in Table III, and ranks for other occupations have been interpolated to determine direction of mobility. The occupational mobility figures are not identical to those of Table XII because of the differences in the categories of Table III; the method used here allowed inclusion of cases of lateral mobility mentioned in n. *a* to Table XII. Some cases have been lost, and several cases of men employed in 1780 and unemployed in 1790 added. Ratios of downward/downward and upward mobility in Tables XII–XIV show that Table XIV may be biased toward upward property mobility (51.7% downward/downward and upward mobility in Table XIII and only 41.3% downward in Table XIV). Since Table XIII has the larger number of cases, it should be more accurate. But with its more exact methodology, Table XIV points to a bias toward upward occupational mobility in Table XII (48.2% downward mobility in Table XII, 58% in Table XIV). Chi Square was significant at less than .01.

A young man might begin working with little money, gain wealth, and perhaps change occupations as he grew older, lose wealth when he became an old man, and leave his widow with few worldly goods. Some impressionistic evidence supports this thesis. John Hooton followed his father's trade of oarmaker in 1780 and lived at home, but by 1790 he was a wharfinger taxed for £275. In 1780 Benjamin Jervis was a propertyless journeyman working for merchant Pascol Smith; by 1790 Jervis had set up as a merchant himself and was assessed £450. Aged Joseph Morton, propertyless in 1790, had been a taverner with a rent of £200 in 1780; John Maud, an old tailor, had a £30 rent in 1780 but was propertyless in 1790.

The social condition of the town's widows also supports this thesis. In 1790, only 76 of Boston's 575 widows owned any taxable property. Widows of very successful men managed to hold on to some property: of the widows taxed, 17 were assessed under £125, 23 from £125 to £200, 21 from £201 to £500, 10 from £500 to £1,000, and 5 over £1,000. Probably some husbands lost wealth before they died; widows quickly lost the rest. Their decline in wealth and status was steeper than almost any experienced by their husbands; the resulting loneliness and unhappiness appear in the assessor's marginal comments. Widow Gray was a "dogmatic lady," and Widow Turrell was a "talking woman." A number of widows followed callings that allowed contact with the public. Twenty-eight of them combated poverty and isolation by operating boarding houses; five others owned taverns; three managed millinery shops; and eight owned other types of retail establishments.

Inequality rapidly advanced in Boston during the Revolutionary period. Wealth was less evenly distributed than before the war, and the proportion of wealth held by the poor and middling classes declined. The growth of poverty was a major problem. As continued migration increased the numbers of poor, a surplus female population of working age was only temporarily helped by the duckcloth factory. Many citizens were able to gain economic security, but unsuccessful families lived in crowded housing or wandered from place to place in search of employment.

Rich and poor were divided by wealth, ascribed status, and segregated living patterns. Individuals could rarely breach a status barrier in fewer than two generations. While social mobility may have been relatively easy for a few immediately after the Revolution, these extraordinary opportunities tended to disappear as population returned to its pre-Revolutionary size. Since political power was monopolized by the wealthy, the poor could only deferentially appeal for aid. The economic elite socialized only among themselves, never showed visitors the semi-ghetto of the North End, and rode through the South End without seeing the poor. But increased segregation could eventually undermine deference by eliminating opportunities for the lowly to defer to their superiors.

A class system based primarily on economic divisions slowly developed. Occupation and wealth determined a man's position in the community; the few titles that survived became functional descriptions of groups, not indicators of a special status. Tax records show that "gentleman" ceased to be a social distinction, but was instead a term reserved for retired tradesmen; "esquire" was a title generally limited to lawyers and public officials. Increased wealth alone could bring higher status to tradesmen and artisans —a fact probably behind Samuel Adams's complaints.

At the same time Boston was becoming more stratified, a new political philosophy emerged. Whig theory divided society and government into three orders, democracy, aristocracy, and monarchy, and demanded that each be perpetually a check and balance on the others. After the Revolution this theory slowly gave way to a model that put the people above the entire government. They held "constituent power," enabling them to call conventions to write constitutions restraining the powers of government. Sovereignty was transferred from the king (or a branch of the legislature) to the people, and political equality was enshrined in the country's legal documents.

Yet the city of Boston, increasingly democratic in theory, and increasingly stratified and divided economically and socially, managed to avoid major civil disturbances after the Revolution. Not only did social and political trends seem to run in opposite directions, but the groups of near poor who manned preindustrial crowds in Europe—apprentices, journeymen, and artisans—lived in greater profusion in Boston than in contemporary European towns. What social forces kept these groups quiet after the Revolution?

Definitive answers to this question await further research, but at least some speculation is in order. Before the Revolution, crowd action was considered a legitimate means for producing social change and protecting the community. When the monarchial order seemed to deny the people their liberties, the people took to the streets. The resulting disturbances were not class conflicts, for pre-Revolutionary crowds in America were supported by the upper classes and peopled by the near poor.

After the Revolution, the ideological props for violence slowly disintegrated. If the people were sovereign, if they held "constituent power," crowd action was a revolt against the people, not a conflict to restrain one branch of government. This change did not eliminate violence, but it altered its nature. Crowds would no longer be the weapons of one order, composed of elements from many economic classes, to be directed against another, but would be revolutionary instruments of class conflict.

Post-Revolutionary Boston, however, provided several structural restraints against this development. The possibility of moderate economic success and the safety valve of short-distance migrations probably limited the chance for confrontation. Unless economic disaster strikes a large number of men (and there is no evidence of this in Boston at this time), group conflict can be generated only when two organized interests compete for the same goods or power. But Boston's only organized society of workers—whose members were of firm middle-class standing—willingly deferred to their social superiors.

2.2

Philadelphia
in the Era of the Revolution

SAM BASS WARNER

Sam Bass Warner first discusses Philadelphia's social structure and then
analyzes major events that occurred there during the American Revolution.
He discusses bread riots, price controls, and collective actions against
monopolizers and forestallers. The radical Whigs led attacks on profiteers
"sucking the blood of their country" and appealed to the mercantile "natural
right" of the people to destroy "combinations" harmful to the "community
interest." In the polarized community, the artisans and the poor played
an important role in revolutionary events. Warner's brief discussion of
neighborhood life and of the importance of taverns grants us a glimpse
into the artisan's world in the late eighteenth century.

Sam Bass Warner, *The Private City* (Philadelphia: University of Pennsylvania Press, 1968),
pp. 2–45. Reprinted and footnotes omitted by permission of the author and the publisher.

The following article is suggested for further reading:

JESSE LEMISCH, "Jack Tar in the Streets: Merchant Seamen in the Politics of
    the American Revolution," *William and Mary Quarterly*, 3rd ser., XXV
    (1968) 371–407.

American cities have grown with the general culture of the nation, not
apart from it. Late eighteenth-century Philadelphia was no exception. Its
citizens, formerly the first wave of a Holy Experiment, had been swept up
in the tides of secularization and borne on by steady prosperity to a
modern view of the world. Like the Puritans of Massachusetts and Connecticut, the Quakers of Pennsylvania had proved unable to sustain the
primacy of religion against the solvents of cheap land and private opportunity. Quaker, Anglican, Presbyterian, Methodist, Pietist—each label had
its social and political implications—but all congregations shared in the
general American secular culture of privatism.

Already by the time of the Revolution privatism had become the
American tradition. Its essence lay in its concentration upon the individual
and the individual's search for wealth. Psychologically, privatism meant
that the individual should seek happiness in personal independence and in
the search for wealth; socially, privatism meant that the individual should
see his first loyalty as his immediate family, and that a community should
be a union of such money-making, accumulating families; politically, privatism meant that the community should keep the peace among individual
money-makers, and, if possible, help to create an open and thriving setting
where each citizen would have some substantial opportunity to prosper.

To describe the American tradition of privatism is not to summarize
the entire American cultural tradition. Privatism lies at the core of many
modern cultures; privatism alone will not distinguish the experience of
America from that of other nations. The tradition of privatism is, however,
the most important element of our culture for understanding the development of cities. The tradition of privatism has always meant that the cities
of the United States depended for their wages, employment, and general
prosperity upon the aggregate successes and failures of thousands of individual enterprises, not upon community action. It has also meant that the

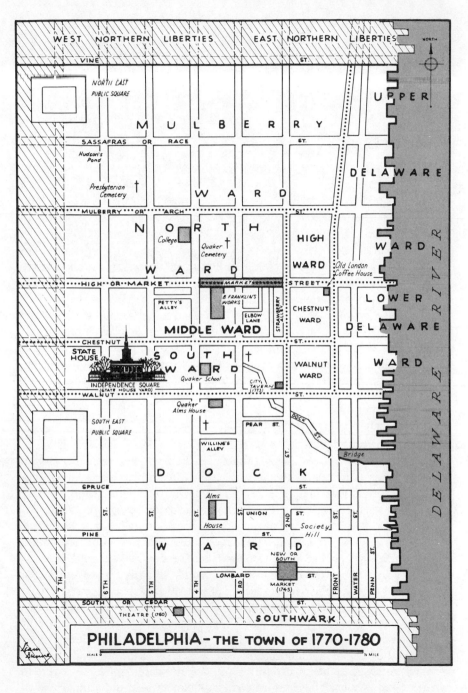

WEST NORTHERN LIBERTIES   EAST NORTHERN LIBERTIES   NORTH

VINE ST.

NORTH EAST PUBLIC SQUARE

UPPER

M U L B E R R Y

SASSAFRAS OR RACE ST.

Hudson's Pond

DELAWARE

Presbyterian Cemetery †

W A R D

MULBERRY OR ARCH ST.

N O R T H

College †

Quaker Cemetery †

HIGH

WARD

W A R D

Old London Coffee House

WARD

HIGH OR MARKET STREET

MARKET

PETTY'S ALLEY

B. FRANKLIN'S WORKS

ELBOW LANE

STRAWBERRY ALLEY

CHESTNUT WARD

LOWER

DELAWARE

MIDDLE WARD

CHESTNUT ST.

STATE HOUSE

S O U T H

W A R D

Quaker School †

CITY TAVERN (1773)

WALNUT WARD

WARD

INDEPENDENCE SQUARE (STATE HOUSE YARD)

WALNUT ST.

Quaker Alms House

SOUTH EAST PUBLIC SQUARE

† PEAR ST.

DOCK

WILLING'S ALLEY

Bridge

D O C K

6TH ST.

SPRUCE

Alms House

UNION

2ND ST.

Society Hill

FRONT ST.

WATER ST.

PENN ST.

PINE

W A R D

NEW OR SOUTH

LOMBARD ST.

MARKET (1745)

7TH ST.

6TH ST.

5TH ST.

4TH ST.

3RD ST.

SOUTH OR CEDAR ST.

THEATRE (1760)

SOUTHWARK

DELAWARE RIVER

PHILADELPHIA—THE TOWN OF 1770-1780

SCALE 0   ½ MILE

physical forms of American cities, their lots, houses, factories, and streets have been the outcome of a real estate market of profit-seeking builders, land speculators, and large investors. Finally, the tradition of privatism has meant that the local politics of American cities have depended for their actors, and for a good deal of their subject matter, on the changing focus of men's private economic activities.

In the eighteenth century the tradition of privatism and the social and economic environment of colonial towns nicely complemented each other. Later as towns grew to big cities, and big cities grew to metropolises, the tradition became more and more ill-suited to the realities of urban life. The tradition assumed that there would be no major conflict between private interest, honestly and liberally viewed, and the public welfare. The modes of eighteenth-century town life encouraged this expectation that if each man would look to his own prosperity the entire town would prosper. And so it had. . . .

Within the town three conditions confirmed its privatism—its individualized structure of work, its general prosperity, and its open society and economy. When eighteenth-century Philadelphians spoke of the individual and his search for wealth as the goal of government they were simply basing their political arguments on the common place facts of town life. The core element of the town economy was the one-man shop. Most Philadelphians labored alone, some with a helper or two. A storekeeper tended his shop by himself or with the aid of his family or a servant. Craftsmen often worked with an apprentice, or more rarely with another skilled man.

More than at later times, this Philadelphia was a town of entrepreneurs. Artisans sewed shoes, made wagons, boiled soap, or laid bricks for customers who had already placed an order. Workers did not labor under the close price and time disciplines of manufacture for large-scale inventories or big speculative wholesale markets. Most Philadelphians were either independent contractors hiring out on a job-by-job basis, or they were artisan shopkeepers retailing the products of their work. Even the establishment of a large merchant more resembled a small store than a modern wholesale house. Such a merchant frequently had a partner and the two partners carried on the business with the aid of a full-time clerk and an apprentice or servant to help with errands. When a cargo arrived at the pier the partners would hire some laborers to unload the goods and move them to the storehouse. Thus, a very large proportion of the town's men—artisans, shopkeepers, and merchants—shared the common experience of the individual entrepreneur.

In later years the work groups of factories, offices, stores, and construction crews would have enormous significance for the discipline, acculturation, and education of Philadelphia's residents. Such groups were almost entirely absent from the eighteenth-century town. Shipyard, rope-walk, and distillery workers labored in groups of five and even ten, but theirs were exceptionally large urban production units. In the colonial era the plantation, whether for agriculture or manufacture, was the character-istic place of large work gangs. In 1775, associated with Philadelphia's general run of family enterprises were only about 900 indentured servants, 600 slaves, and perhaps 200 hired servants who lived with their employers. These helpers shared the discipline of family life and work; they did not live by the modes of the work gang. Taken all together the eighteenth-century exceptions to the entrepreneurial role had but little significance for the functioning of the town's society.

A German visitor of 1750 wrote: "Pennsylvania is heaven for farm-ers, paradise for artisans, and hell for officials and preachers." By the same token, Philadelphia on the eve of the Revolution was a town of freedom and abundance for the common man. For young persons there was a great demand for apprentices in all lines of work. An unskilled laborer without connections could find work with board and wages to begin accumulating a little money for tools. An artisan who wanted to carry a few shopkeeping goods in his shop, or a storekeeper with a good reputation, could get his stock from the merchant and settle for his advance a year later.

The ordinary artisan or shopkeeper, if his health was good, could be assured of a comfortable, if frugal, living. To be sure, houses were small and rents high, and furnishings were spare compared to later levels of living: no carpets, no upholstered furniture, a sand-scrubbed floor, and whitewashed walls. Stoves and fireplaces only partially heated drafty rooms, and in severe winters the cost of firewood or imported coal was a major item of family expense. Nevertheless, at the city's markets food was cheap and plentiful. The earnings of the ordinary artisan and shopkeeper could support a wife and children without their having to take outside employ-ment. The rapid growth of the town and its trade meant regular work and good earnings for artisans and easy business, if not wealth, for shopkeepers.

Although the customary hours of work were long, sunrise to sunset, the pace of work was often easy and varied with the season. Those who worked outside their homes, like men in the building trades, took an hour for breakfast, a break in the middle of the day, and an hour for dinner in the afternoon. Coopers, shoemakers, smiths, and men who practiced their craft in their own houses and yards must have stopped work as cus-tomers and friends came in, and a trip or two to the local tavern must also have been usual. Although there were no formal vacations, the tradi-tional English holidays and frequent *ad hoc* town celebrations provided about twenty days off each year.

Franklin's *Autobiography* abounds with injunctions for regular habits, and the reputation for diligence he established by staying at his bench for the entire formal working day suggests that his was an extraordinary pace. For most workers rush seasons of hard work and long hours alternated with slack times. These variations meant days for fishing or spare moments for gossip on the streets and visits to the tavern.

Such a commonplace prosperity, generous at least by eighteenth-century standards, confirmed the privatism of the town and its age. As important a confirmation came from the openness of its economy and society. The failure of the craft guilds to control the trades of the town gave newcomers and resident artisans alike an occupational freedom unknown in Europe. Shopkeepers and artisans—and often one man was both—could take up any craft or open any line of business they wished. Although Philadelphia had inherited English regulations favoring the "freemen" of the town, established artisans could not maintain their control of the town's businesses against newcomers. The carpenters and cordwainers managed to form associations to set prices for their work, but failed when they attempted to close the membership of their trades. In Philadelphia men added trades and lines of goods as they thought demand justified. Although this freedom undoubtedly produced a great deal of incompetent craftsmanship, the importance to the individual artisan or shopkeeper of open trades and plentiful work cannot be overestimated. It meant for the common man that there was always a chance for a fresh start. This chance for a new beginning was the urban equivalent of the contemporary farmer's chance to pick up and try again in the West.

Already in these years the American pattern of social mobility by property obtained. No invidious distinction between land and trade favored some occupations over others. As eighteenth-century Philadelphians grew rich they kept their original occupations, whether they were carpenters, distillers, printers, or lawyers. Whatever a man's occupation, there were only a few channels for investment open to the rising man. Since there were no banks, private money lending was the most important investment opportunity in the town. Houses and land were also a favorite way of using savings both among the rich and those with a little capital. Only 19 percent of the families of Philadelphia owned their houses and therefore home rentals offered a safe investment. Other opportunities were shares in voyages, marine insurances, and, of course, land and farms outside the town.

The prosperity and abundant opportunity of the town should not be confused with an even distribution of wealth. According to the published tax list for 1774 the upper tenth of the taxpaying households owned 89 per cent of the taxable property. In this respect late eighteenth-century Philadelphia resembled the later Philadelphias—it was a pyramid of wealth in which about five hundred men guided the town's economic life. Its unique quality lay in the general prosperity of the common artisan and shopkeeper and the widely shared entrepreneurial experience and goals of the artisan, shopkeeper, and merchant.

The wealthy presided over a municipal regime of little government. Both in form and function the town's government advertised the lack of concern for public management of the community. The municipal corporation of Philadelphia, copied from the forms of an old English borough, counted for little. Its only important functions in the late eighteenth-century were the management of the markets and the holding of the Recorder's Court. A closed corporation, choosing its members by co-option, it had become a club of wealthy merchants, without much purse, power, or popularity.

By modern standards the town was hardly governed at all. The constable in each ward and a few watchmen provided an ineffective police, the safety of the house and shop being secured by citizens' helping each other to drive away intruders or pursue thieves. Most streets went unpaved, the public wharves little repaired. There were no public schools, no public water, and at best thin charity. . . .

The real secret of the peace and order of the eighteenth-century town lay not in its government but in the informal structure of its community. Unlike later and larger Philadelphias, the eighteenth-century town was a community. Graded by wealth and divided by distinctions of class though it was, it functioned as a single community. The community had been created out of a remarkably inclusive network of business and economic relationships and it was maintained by the daily interactions of trade and sociability. Because it was small and because every rank and occupation lived jumbled together in a narrow compass the town suffered none of the communications problems of later Philadelphias.

At most, 23,700 people lived in Philadelphia on the eve of the Revolution, 16,500 in the city proper, 7,000 in the adjacent districts of Northern Liberties and Southwark. The town crowded next to its shore. Its wharves and warehouses stretched a mile and a half along the Delaware river, but the built-up blocks of houses at their deepest point, along Market street, reached back from the river at most half a mile to about Seventh Street.

The settlement pattern of the town combined two opposing social tendencies. The clustering of marine trades and merchants next to the Delaware suggested the beginnings of the specialized industrial quarters then characteristic of European cities. On the other hand, the rummage of classes and occupations found in many Philadelphia blocks continued the old tradition of mixed work and residence characteristic of American and English country towns.

Ship carpenters, ship joiners, ship smiths, and sail makers lived and worked along the Delaware river shore. Sailors and stevedores dwelt among the yards and wharves along the entire shore, but they gathered especially on the south side of town (Dock Ward and Southwark). Mixed among them were many of the houses and shops of the merchants which were concentrated one block back from the riverfront. Together the shipbuilders, the marine trades, and the merchants pre-empted the narrow strip of frontage between the river and Second street.

The crowding of marine trades and commerce next to the port also influenced the location of other Philadelphias. Tailors, hatters, tinsmiths, and silversmiths clustered in the central wards of town (Walnut, Lower Delaware, and Middle Wards) to be near, if not in, the portside concentration of customers. Conversely, those who needed large lots, or those who could not afford expensive land, drifted toward the edge of town. Here on the fringes the building trades, weavers, dyers, tanners, distillers, and laborers dwelt in more than normal proportions.

The differential pricing of land seems to have affected the laborers more than any other occupational group in the colonial town. Surprisingly enough, they were more segregated in this period than in the mid-nineteenth century, when the immigrant laborer was such a prominent element of the city. In 1774 the special locations of the laborers were the northern and southern edges of town—the Northern Liberties and adjacent parts of the Mulberry Ward, and Southwark.

A slight ethnic clustering also existed in eighteenth-century Philadelphia, but by no means of the same intensity as later twentieth-century ethnic and racial ghettos. German immigrants and their descendants had concentrated north of Market Street, over half of them living in the North, High, and Mulberry wards of Philadelphia and in the adjacent Northern Liberties Districts. This was also the Quaker side of town. Such ethnic and religious clusters, however, did not seem to have important effects upon the functioning of the town.

One can get some idea of the quality of urban life imposed by this settlement pattern by looking at one ward in a little detail. The Constable in making his enumeration of the residents of the Middle Ward left notes on his list showing when he turned the corner of a street. This record, plus some material from tax ledgers make it possible to reconstruct the settlement pattern of this ward in 1774.

As its name suggests, the Middle Ward lay in the center of town, bounded on the north by Market Street, then the highway connecting Philadelphia to Chester and the south and to Lancaster and the west. The ward also was next to the market traffic. The sheds of the farmers' market in these years stretched up Market Street from the Delaware River only as far as Fourth Street. The Middle Ward was not a crowded dockside ward, but began just behind the dockside wards at Second Street. Its well-filled section covered five blocks to Seventh Street, Market to Chestnut. Beyond these blocks of houses the farms of the ward extended all the way west to the Schuylkill River.

Many famous Philadelphians lived within the ward. The old-fashioned Quaker radical, Anthony Benezet, the Proprietors John and Richard Penn, two opponents of the British who later turned Tory, Joseph Galloway, and James Allen, and the steadfast revolutionaries Benjamin Franklin and Daniel Clymer all lived in the center of the ward. The State House Yard (now Independence Square) stood across Chestnut Street between Fifth and Sixth streets. Such distinction, however, did not create the solid blocks of *haut bourgeois* fashion that they would today; rather it embroidered the commonplace fabric which was the revolutionary town. In 1774 the Middle Ward was the home of at least 1,401 men, women, and children of every degree and condition from Proprietor to slave.

The physical arrangements of the ward reflected the high cost of eighteenth-century housing and the crowding of Philadelphians near their port. Each of the Middle Ward's five settled blocks contained slightly less than five acres of land. On the first block of the ward (between Second and Third streets, the area nearest the Delaware River) there stood 137 dwellings, on the next 65, on the next 67, on the next 29, and on westernmost 39. To accommodate so many families in so little space some of the blocks of the ward had been cut by alleys so that little houses might be crowded onto the back lots of the houses facing the main streets. Strawberry Alley and Elbow Lane cut through the first block, Petty's Alley divided the third block, and Benjamin Franklin had begun the alley process with his house lot off Market Street in the second block of the ward. He had built a row of three houses on Market Street, thereby turning his home yard into an interior lot. His son-in-law Richard Bache, a merchant, rented one of the new row houses, Eden Haydock, a plumber, rented another, and Frederick Stonemetz, a cooper, took the third. In the early nineteenth century Franklin's home parcel became Franklin Court, an alley lot which opened up the interior of the block.

Such density of housing and such methods of land division had by 1774 destroyed the hopes of Penn and his surveyor for a "Green Town." The practice of subdividing blocks with alleys and jamming tiny houses on vacant rear yards continued strongly for the next ninety years. By 1860 the density of population in Philadelphia's inner wards reached its all-time peak. Then, in the second half of the nineteenth century the street railway opened up vast tracts of cheap suburban land and thereby destroyed the market for new alley construction. The old alleys with their dark and cramped houses, however, did not disappear at once. Rather they remained standing for years, giving discomfort to Philadelphia's poor for many generations, and the history of some alleys is not yet closed.

Already in the 1770's the crowding of the land exceeded the sanitary capabilities of the town. The streets and alleys reeked of garbage, manure, and night soil, and some private and public wells must have been dangerously polluted. Every few years an epidemic swept through the town. In the 1790's the city would pay a terrible price in deaths from recurring yellow fever.

Though dangerous to health the eighteenth-century pattern of settlement guaranteed every citizen a knowledge of town life. At such density and small scale no generation could be raised ignorant of the other side of town, of the ways of life of the working class, or of the manners of the *haut bourgeois*. Within the Middle Ward at least 346 families with 469 children, 17 hired servants, 65 indentured servants, 78 Negro slaves, and 80 tenants share the settled 25 acres. Those who left a record carried on seventy different occupations.

Although merchants and shopkeepers, hatters, innkeepers, and tavernkeepers concentrated more heavily in this ward than in most others, variety best characterizes the occupational structure of the ward as it did all the other wards of the first Philadelphia. The Proprietors, the merchants, and the doctors shared the narrow compass of the Middle Ward with such ungenteel occupations as laborer, porter, carter, skinner, watchman, crier, paver, grazier, and even goatkeeper. The outer three blocks of the ward also housed several breweries and a distillery, and every one of the five blocks contained one or more of those notorious enemies of sweet residential air—the stable.

One cannot, at this late date, reconstruct in detail the communications patterns of eighteenth-century Philadelphia, but the crowded living of the age encouraged a street and tavern life which more resembled the social habits of the later nineteenth and early twentieth-century immigrant ghettos than the isolated private family life of today's working class and middle class.

The high cost of building kept houses small, cramped, and in short supply. The common artisan's or shopkeeper's house was a narrow structure, about seventeen feet wide and twenty-five feet deep. A story-and-a-half high, it offered about eight hundred square feet of floor space on its ground floor and attic. Most often the owner plied his trade in the largest front room. The Middle Ward records show that although some families had five to seven children, most had few. The average number of children per household was 1.3, and counting servants and slaves the average household was four persons. The small houses, thus, were cramped but not severely crowded. If the artisan or shopkeeper prospered he would add a kitchen ell or more likely move to a house of similar proportion with a kitchen ell at the rear. The house of an ordinary merchant or even a craftsman who had grown rich, would be like the artisan's house with the ell, but would be two and one-half stories instead of one and one-half. Such houses of the prosperous also possessed deep lots for gardens, a shed for a cow and some chickens, and perhaps a horse.

A town of small houses, where most houses also served as stores, offices and workshops, encouraged people to live out upon the streets. Moreover, the pace of work, most of it governed by the seasons or advance orders from customers, was irregular, what one would call today a rural pace. Both the physical structure of the town and the pace of its work thus encouraged a more public, gossipy style of life than could later be sustained when a steady pace of work and larger interiors drove people into sharply defined spaces for work and residence.

The ordinary housewife shopped daily, going to the baker's for her bread, and taking her meat and pies to the baker's oven to be cooked. Street peddlers called her out for fish, eggs, and produce, and twice a week the farmers of Philadelphia County held a full market at the public stalls. As in the nineteenth century with its dark tenements and crowded row houses, sunlight must have been a great source of pleasure for women sewing and spinning and many must have worked at these and other household chores out on their doorsteps, as their tenement sisters did years later.

For the husband the eighteenth-century custom of men's gossip at the tavern provided the first Philadelphia's basic cells of community life. Every ward in the city had its inns and taverns. The 1774 tax list recorded 93 tavernkeepers and 72 innkeepers in the city of Philadelphia, Southwark, and the Northern Liberties, approximately one neighborhood drinking place for every 140 persons in the city (23,000/165). The Middle Ward, alone, held 18 inns and taverns. Some must have served purely a neighborhood custom; others, like the London Coffee House or the City Tavern served as central communications nodes for the entire city.

Then, as now, each one had its own crowd of regulars and thus each constituted an informal community cell of the city. Out of the meetings of the regulars at the neighborhood tavern or inn came much of the commonplace community development which preceded the Revolution and proved later to be essential to the governance of the city and the managment of the ward. Regular meetings of friends, or men of common occupations, led to clubs of all kinds and of every degree of formality from regular billiard sessions to fire companies and political juntos. Benjamin Franklin and the many community innovations of his junto showed the potential of these informal tavern groups. They provided the underlying social fabric of the town and when the Revolution began made it possible to quickly gather militia companies, to form effective committees of correspondence and of inspection, and to organize and to manage mass town meetings.

At the center of the town's communications system stood the merchants' coffee houses. On the eve of the Revolution Philadelphia had two such major meeting places—the old London Coffee House (established

1754), run by William Bradford, the newspaper publisher, and the new City Tavern (established 1773), just founded by a syndicate of merchants. The London Coffee House, located at Front and Market streets, adjacent to the town's principal market stalls and overlooking the Delaware, had been for many years the place where merchants gathered every noon to read incoming newspapers, to discuss prices, and to arrange for cargoes and marine insurance. These noon meetings in time ripened into the specialized institutions of exchanges, banks, and insurance companies. As yet, Philadelphia had but one insurance company and its merchants' business depended on the variety of functions of these daily tavern gatherings. For many years ship captains and travelers first stopped at the London Coffee House when they arrived in town, messages were left, auction notices posted and auctions held. Frequently on market days, after a parade through the streets, horses were auctioned in front of the tavern doors. Slaves and indentured servants stood before the same block.

As the town grew the importing merchants no longer had a need to be near the market dealers. The merchant community split into at least two parts. The new City Tavern surpassed the old London Coffee House as a place of fashion with the importing merchants, though its function remained that of its competitor. On May 19, 1774, Paul Revere brought his news of the closing of the Port of Boston to the City Tavern, and here numerous Revolutionary committees gathered. The still extant Philadelphia Assemblies were held at this new tavern, as was the endless series of banquets and balls which served the town with high entertainment.

Because the merchants' tavern was a public place in a small town it escaped the limitations of later Philadelphia merchant centers—the exchanges, the Chamber of Commerce, and the gentlemen's clubs. These later gatherings were either meeting places of specialists and thereby encouraged only the brokers' or downtown merchants' view of the city, or they were closed organizations which directed their members' attention inward toward the sociability of the group. The eighteenth-century tavern, however, opened out to all the life of the street and it did not shield the leaders of the town from contact with the life that surrounded them.

It was the unity of everyday life, from tavern, to street, to workplace, to housing, which held the town and its leaders together in the eighteenth century. This unity made it possible for the minority of Revolutionary merchants, artisans, and shopkeepers to hold together, run the town, and manage a share of the war against England, even in the face of Quaker neutrality and Tory opposition. When remonstrance turned to rebellion and political disagreement turned to war the exigencies of the conflict broke Philadelphia society apart. Thanks to the town's commonplace ideology of privatism and its inclusive patterns of social and economic intercourse, Philadelphia did not fracture along the lines of class or occupation. As befitted a seaport, merchants predominated in all the political groups of the town: among the moderate Whigs, among the radical Whigs, among the Tories, and among the Quakers. Fighting Quakers and revolutionary Episcopalians crossed boundaries of religious loyalties. With the exception of pacifist Quakers, the groupings of Philadelphia during the Revolution were first and foremost political. The divisions among Philadelphia's citizens reflected personal attitudes toward the revolutionary governments established in Pennsylvania and toward the Continental Congress. The Congress strongly influenced local politics since it then sat in Philadelphia, capital city of the thirteen colonies.

To a modern observer, half-blinded by the scenes of uncontrolled butchery in his own era, the moderation of the conflict among the political and military groups of the American Revolution appears almost incomprehensible. Within Philadelphia, at least, that moderation was sustained against all the temptations and passions of war and revolution by the lines of control which remained intact throughout the war years. The town may have split into four political groups, but each group, being a rough cross section of the community, shared much in common with the others, in experience, in expectations of human behavior, even in ideology. Through the five years of conflict in Pennsylvania (1774–1779), except for the few banished Quakers and colonial officials and the Tories who left when the British troops abandoned the city, Philadelphians of all persuasions continued to do business together and to share the everyday activities of town life. The town's network of personal communications was never severed by the Revolution to the degree that the network of personal communications was later fragmented by the changed structure and scale of the American big city. In the twentieth century we start our riots and wars with less community than the Revolutionary town had even in its most strained moments.

The inflation, food shortage, and political crisis of 1778–1779 demonstrated the interaction of conflict and control in eighteenth-century Philadelphia. During these crises the Pennsylvania and Continental governments which ruled the town struggled against chaos and bankruptcy. The temper of the leaders had been heated by accumulated frustrations. High prices and food shortages at the market set poor against rich. Yet when the crises of a year reached a violent culmination the leaders of the opposed camps turned to pacify the town rather than to seek political victory in an armed witch hunt.

This same series of crises during 1778 to 1779 also demonstrated the limits of the American tradition of privatism in the face of important urban problems. The crises foretold those conditions under which future American cities would repeatedly fail. As in the case of the modern city where the most pressing problems are those of allocating scarce land, tax, and human resources among conflicting public and private purposes, so too, eighteenth-century Philadelphia confronted the problems of allocating scarce resources among the competing demands of the army, of the city, and of trade. The ideology of privatism offered no guide to such allocation problems. It had no rule for parceling out flour to the citizens of the town save letting the buyers compete. Modern, too, was the scale of the inflation and shortages of 1778–1779. As in today's urban employment, housing, segregation, and financial disorders, the area of suffering was the city, while the area of the remedy for that suffering far exceeded the municipal boundaries. It reached beyond Philadelphia into the hinterland of the three middle colonies and beyond to national and international trade and finance.

The course of the Revolution in Philadelphia had been such that by the summer of 1778, when the town began to face its severe inflation and supply crisis, only two groups remained politically active, the radical Whigs and the moderate Whigs. Pacifist Quakers had been discredited by their inaction and had been excluded from government by test oaths. The Tory cause collapsed as an effective movement in Pennsylvania with the withdrawal of royal troops from Philadelphia on June 18, 1778. Some 3,000 Tories fled with the retreating army. . . .

The Whigs had divided into radical and moderate camps back in 1776 when the colonial Assembly's wavering opposition to independence forced the radical remedy of a declaration of independence and seizure of the government. Evidence from old tax lists suggests that the split among the Whigs was political and social, not economic. It was a division of a single class, not a war between classes. With few exceptions the leaders of the moderates were merchants. Among the radicals, too, the merchants were the largest group and the radicals could boast of several followers with heavier assessments than their rivals. However, the larger proportion of "new" money as opposed to "old" money, of professionals, of intellectuals, and of persons marginal to the established merchant group of Philadelphia seems to have distinguished the radicals from the moderates.

The moderates had been leading the opposition to England up until the spring of 1776. Then they hesitated. They hoped for compromise with London. They feared violence and destruction. They wanted to move slowly. The old Pennsylvania colonial Assembly did not have enough radical members for it to establish a new government free from any allegiance to the Crown. The radicals called a town meeting for May 20, the day of the Assembly's opening. Four thousand persons stood in the rain in the State House yard listening to militia officers and cheering for independence. The officers called for a constitutional convention to frame a new government. The Assembly, divided, harassed, and confused, succumbed and the radicals seized power, first in Philadelphia, then in all Pennsylvania. Test oaths and armed militia guaranteed the outcome of the subsequent election of delegates to the constitutional convention.

The convention first established a temporary government and then wrote a constitution for the state. The radicals, however, were too uncertain of their support in the fall of 1776 to risk submitting their constitution to the voters. Instead, pleading wartime emergency they proclaimed it. This irregularly established constitution became, and remained for the next fourteen years, the major issue of contention between radicals and moderates in Pennsylvania. Within two years the radicals had adopted the name of the Constitutional Society, the moderates the Republican Society.

While the struggle between radicals and moderates for control of the government of Pennsylvania tended to drive the two wings of the Whigs apart, the events of the early years of the war forced them to work together for their mutual defense. Pennsylvania Whigs of every opinion served in the New York, New Jersey, and Pennsylvania campaigns of 1776–1778. In the summer of 1776, after his retreat from Boston, General Howe moved his troops to New York where he won a series of victories and almost destroyed Washington's army that first fall. The following summer, in August 1777, Howe moved into Pennsylvania. He defeated Washington again at the Brandywine River and occupied Philadelphia at the close of September. The victory of the Continentals that same fall in Saratoga, New York, however, encouraged the French, who signed an alliance with the Americans in February 1778.

In the expectation that the French fleet would attack New York the British evacuated Philadelphia in June 1778. This retreat removed the restraining hand of fear of the enemy from the Whig political conflict in Pennsylvania. By the same event, politics in Philadelphia—capital of the state and the nation, and center of the middle states supply region —became suffused with the issues of wartime supply, finance, and trade.

No sooner had the British evacuated the region than provisions ran short. The wheat crop was poor. Such as it was, the Maryland and Pennsylvania harvest faced the demand of Continental and British forces as well as the needs of Philadelphia and the export trade. Prices of wheat, flour, and bread began to rise, and they rose ever higher under the spur of repeated issues of Pennsylvania and Continental loans, paper money, and quartermaster's receipts.

As always, inflation laid its heaviest tax upon those least able to pay, the poor and the common citizen. Its political direction was to array poor against rich. Moreover, since this 1778–1779 economic dislocation affected the prices and availability of staple items, it created daily grievances.

No state or local government could ignore the clamor. In August 1778 the radical-controlled Pennsylvania Council of Safety, foreseeing shortages, forbade the export of all provisions from the state. There is no way to tell whether farmers and merchants respected this order, but to the extent that it was followed it bottled up Pennsylvania supplies and thereby further deranged the northeast-middle states grain trade. In November, by a similar ruling, the Council forbade the export of flour.

Prices did not figure directly in the October state elections, although they had been rising steadily since July. The moderates charged extravagance and inefficiency and repeated their demand for a new constitutional convention. The radicals pointed with pride to their role as leaders at the moment of independence, and tried to label their opponents "Tory." The moderates gained a few seats, but their delegation to the Assembly amounted to less than one-third of the total seats. After the election, in the maneuvering over the choice of President of the Supreme Executive Council of Pennsylvania, the moderates did score a temporary victory. Joseph Reed (1741–1785), a radical lawyer, and former military secretary to General Washington, wishing to strengthen his administration, struck a bargain with the moderates. If they would support his election he agreed to call the constitutional convention which they had repeatedly demanded. On December 1, 1778, the Assembly voted him President, the highest office in the state. The manner of his election, of course, rekindled the debate on the merits of the Pennsylvania constitution of 1776.

Philadelphia radicals asked Thomas Paine (1737–1809), a member of their Philadelphia Whig Committee of Correspondence, and the author of the immensely successful *Common Sense* and *The American Crisis* pamphlets, to write a newspaper series in defense of the Constitution. Paine's essay appeared serially in the *Pennsylvania Packet* from December 1 to 12, 1778.

Paine's essay provided two important pieces of evidence about eighteenth-century Philadelphia. First, it showed that the assumption of privatism ran as strongly among radicals as it did among moderates. Second, it revealed the radicals' extremely small-scale, local vision of the city, its business and its government. Both sets of attitudes would prove in 1779, as in all later years, costly blinders upon the vision of city dwellers. . . .

Such a view of politics, presented in this essay as a contrast between an over-governed Europe and a free America, left no room for international affairs, or big projects. Indeed, it even misled its contemporary readers about the way the war was being won—through foreign credit, foreign supplies, and since April 1778, an open alliance with the French royal bureaucracy, army, and navy. For the future of Philadelphia and Pennsylvania the popular radical view not only caused the disorders of parochialism, but it also proved unable to accommodate changes in the structure of the society. In time, as industrialization and urbanization progressed, the average, middle-class citizen would no longer present himself for election, nor would voters choose him. Indeed even common-sense knowledge would fail as in modern times few men would comprehend the city as a whole, or even know several of its wards.

Even as Paine wrote his defense of the Pennsylvania Constitution, the war and the economic dislocations of the war, mocked his picture of the world. The very subjects on the colonial landscape which he had neglected now controlled daily life in Philadelphia—the movement of large armies, the inadequacies of the merchant supply network, the provisioning of the French fleet, the financing of the Continental cause.

On December 5, 1778, while Paine's essay was appearing in the *Packet,* angry Congressional conflicts intruded upon the political life of the capital town. That day Silas Deane (1737–1789) published in the same newspaper his attack on Congress and some of its radical leaders. He charged them with delaying the review of his supply dealings with France in order to foster their own political ends. This charge exposed a new side of the war to public view. Since 1776 the Philadelphia scene had been dominated by militia officers and their volunteer companies, by conventions, by town meetings and by *ad hoc* committees of every kind. Citizen volunteer government manifested itself everywhere. Now the other side of the Revolution, secret diplomacy, dealings with a foreign bureaucracy, and the methods of international merchants, came to the foreground. All were subjects beyond the experience of most Philadelphians; all lent themselves to rumor of intrigue and corruption.

The radicals in Congress and in Philadelphia saw the Deane affair as a chance to discomfort their opponents by showing their leaders to be greedy profiteers. Paine, out of personal friendship for some of the Congressional radicals, began on December 15, 1778, a series of attacks on Silas Deane and his Philadelphia associate, the moderate leader, and merchant Robert Morris (1734–1806). The ensuing exchanges, which lasted in the newspapers for about a month, raised tempers but did not settle anything. Paine disgraced himself by revealing secret information he possessed as Secretary to the Congressional Committee for Foreign Affairs. Robert Morris justified his actions by saying that his service on Congressional committees did not prevent him from engaging in private business, but such a defense could not dispel the popular impression that somehow he and Silas Deane had been profiteering. . . .

As early as the fall of 1776 complaints began in Congress that

Willing and Morris were making exorbitant profits on Continental orders. Later examination of Morris' transactions by the Continental Congress and a careful review of Morris' papers by a modern scholar has failed to show that he profiteered at public expense. Morris was as much a patriot as any of his contemporaries, and he worked long and hard for the cause. He grew very rich, as politically connected businessmen have always grown rich in wartime. Government contracts gave him the credit, capital, and connections needed to do a large-scale business. His volume of trade exceeded by far anything any merchant had handled in pre-Revolutionary times. Inflation, shortages, and the breaking of established paths of commerce guaranteed huge profits to any who could command large quantities of capital and supplies. Morris entered the Revolution as a well-trained, ambitious, and skillful merchant; he saw his opportunity, he took big risks, and he made an enormous fortune.

In January, 1779, while the Deane, Paine, and Morris controversy boiled on, the Supreme Executive Council of Pennsylvania issued a proclamation against monopolizers and forestallers who cornered provisions to raise the price of "bread and other necessaries of life" . . . until "they became ruinous to the industrious poor. . . ." The Council also appointed a committee of radicals to inquire into rumors of monopolization, but nothing came of the investigation. Flour, sugar, rum, and molasses were all selling that month at 100 percent of their prewar prices on a specie basis. Because of the enormous issues of paper money, wheat sold then in Continental currency at 465 percent and flour 936 percent of its prewar price.

When addressing the Assembly in February, President Joseph Reed spoke out strongly against "forestallers of flour and other provisions" but noted that despite diligent inquiries few prosecutions had been undertaken or were successful. He said a stronger public opinion against the price-fixers would be necessary to control such evil practices. In a city of merchants, shopkeepers, and artisans perhaps it seemed extraordinary to many to condemn a man for selling goods for the most he could get.

Throughout the winter and spring, prices of food rose month by month; shoes and clothing became dear. The newspapers published long letters complaining that society had become deranged by the inflation of currency since an ordinary man could no longer benefit by honest industry and saving. "Our people have become indolent and depraved. . . ." New men of immense wealth and extravagance were rising on the fraud and waste of wartime spending. During these early months of 1779 Army purchasing agents exacerbated the crisis by overbuying.

On April 5 the Pennsylvania Assembly passed additional laws aimed at attacking some of the current abuses in food marketing. No vendor was to refuse to accept Continental currency, and no dealer, except butchers and innkeepers, was to drive out to meet the farmers coming into the public markets with provisions. Finally, any three Justices of the Peace could sit as a committee to set an assize of bread; that is, the Justices could fix the price and weight of bakers' loaves in their town.

Early in May a mob seized a merchant and accused him of exporting flour just brought into the city for the prison. The accusation was entirely false. He was saved only by an alert city official who put the merchant temporarily in jail, secure from the mob. In the same month the militia petitioned the Council against merchants and others who grew rich instead of serving their country.

As the month of May wore on, rumors against merchants grew more insistent. A French ship, the "Victorious," had been lying at anchor for several weeks past, and a public guard had been posted on it. It was said about town that a number of merchants had tried to purchase her cargo, and that the Commerce Committee of Congress, seeking to purchase supplies for the army, had even been refused. For some reason the ship stood full loaded. Robert Morris was the agent for the ship; maybe he was trying to drive prices up.

Radical leaders could no longer ignore the drift of popular thinking and the unrest among their followers in the town. Perhaps a revival of the voluntary committees of inspection, successfully used in the 1774 embargo against England, would answer the public clamor against shortages and increasing inflation. The prices of commodities could be fixed and a few speculating merchants made public examples. Best of all, if Robert Morris could be exposed the moderate opposition would be routed. The politics of price control made a dangerous game for the town. The game meant that one group of merchants (the radical leaders) played upon popular frustration and unrest to defeat the political opposition of another group of merchants (the moderate leaders).

The radicals announced a town meeting for Monday, May 24, 1779. For several days prior to the meeting small bands of men cruised the streets cursing monopolizers and looking for trouble. Some observers feared storehouses would be broken into.

A large crowd assembled in the State House yard on the appointed afternoon. General Daniel Roberdeau (1727–1795), a merchant, radical, and popular militia leader was elected chairman and addressed the meeting.

> The dangers we are now exposed to arise from evils amongst ourselves. I scorn, and I hope every citizen here scorns, the thought of getting rich by sucking the blood of his country; yet alas! this unnatural, this cruel, this destructive practice, is the greatest cause of our present calamities. The way to make our money good is to reduce the prices of goods and provisions.

I have no doubt but combinations have been formed for raising the prices of goods and provisions, and therefore the community, in their own defense, have a natural right to counteract such combinations, and to set limits to evils which affect themselves.

The General next suggested that prices be lowered in monthly stages, as he observed they had been raised. After concluding his short speech Roberdeau read the radical's program for price control to the crowd a paragraph at a time. Item after item carried by acclamation.

The very first resolution following a preamble deploring the high prices of provisions attacked Robert Morris for creating a new inflation —in dry goods. "Since the late importation of a cargo of goods . . . the prices of all kinds of dry goods have been greatly advanced, to the injury of the public and to the detriment of trade." A committee of leading radicals, including Thomas Paine, was appointed by the meeting to wait on Mr. Morris for his explanation.

The meeting also appointed two committees to control prices. One, the Committee on Prices, was to set the monthly price schedule for all Philadelphia transactions in listed commodities; the other, the Committee of Complaints, was to sit at the courthouse from nine to noon every day to hear complaints of infractions. Offenders were to be punished by publication of their names and by referral of their cases to later town meetings for possible further punishment. The meeting adjourned with a resolution that all Tories should be banished from the town.

On June 2 prices were announced for tea, sugar, and molasses, rum, whiskey, rice, flour, coffee, and salt.

The investigation of Robert Morris became a total fiasco. The cargo of the "Victorious" had been consigned to him by a Baltimore merchant. Thereupon Morris had given the Congressional Committee on Commerce the first choice of goods aboard and "very moderate" prices for their selections. The public guard, the delay, and mystery of the ship grew out of confusion over Morris's contract with the Baltimore merchant and the ensuing necessity to renegotiate the prices of goods he had offered for sale.

On June 17 the Philadelphia Committee of Complaints tried to renew the attack when it learned of a purchase of flour for Morris's account in Lancaster County. The price had exceeded that set for Philadelphia and the Committee feared that such purchases in the country would inevitably advance prices in Philadelphia. This purchase, Morris replied, had been made for the French Navy.

The French Minister in Philadelphia angrily protested such investigation by a Philadelphia town committee and demanded that Congress put a stop to the proceedings. Congress debated the issue without resolution; it feared offending the French, and it feared offending its radical supporters in Philadelphia. As the month of June wore on inflation did not abate. Throughout the colonies the wholesale prices of all major commodities, except sugar, rose sharply all summer. The Philadelphia Committee on Prices responded by adding to its list. By July iron, leather, candles, soap, cotton, and shoes, joined the first items. Altogether the radicals were attempting to control the Philadelphia wholesale and retail prices of thirty-two different goods and commodities. In normal times the prices of these items would have been set by the interactions of trading at Philadelphia for local, regional, and international buyers and sellers.

In an attempt to strengthen support for price control, the radicals returned once again to the militia tactics of 1776. The First Artillery Company of Philadelphia, using as an excuse its absence on garrison duty during the May town meeting, published its resolutions of support in the July 1 newspaper. The formal excuses for the letter concluded with a statement that the company's men had now returned to the city. "We have arms in our hands and know the use of them." After receiving with approval the monthly roll-back scheme the letter concluded with an ominous bit of bravado ". . . we will see the virtuous, innocent and suffering part of the community redressed, and endeavor to divest this city of the disaffected, inimical, and preyers on the vitals of the inhabitants, be their rank or station what it may."

On the same day a committee of tanners, curriers and cordwainers announced that they would not be bound by the prices for leather and shoes set by the Committee on Prices because controls had failed to protect the men's living costs. They would set the prices for their work as they saw fit.

The following Saturday the Committee on Prices renewed its attack on Robert Morris. It had learned from another citizens committee in Wilmington, Delaware, that Morris's agent had purchased 182 barrels of flour in that town and "the price given exceeds the regulated market price." The citizens had again seized flour bound for the French fleet. This time the Philadelphia committee found itself in the untenable position of trying to regulate sales of flour in Wilmington, Delaware, which had been negotiated by an agent for a Philadelphia merchant, and was bound for shipment to an allied fleet then heading toward Savannah, Georgia. The inappropriateness of the Philadelphia committee's action made Morris's defense easy. Nevertheless, neither the rightness or wrongness of Morris or the committee would make inflation go away. Prices continued to rise and the controversy dragged on in the Philadelphia press and in Congress all summer.

The following week the Philadelphia Committee on Prices proposed a fiscal attack on high prices. In July, monetary control seemed a more important problem than the direct physical regulation of goods in short supply. The summer crops were good, but farmers would not sell except when they wished to purchase for themselves. They lacked any confidence in the Continental paper money. Judging the situation correctly, then, the radicals proposed a cessation of all further paper issues by Congress. Next the supply of money was to be reduced and Continental needs met by a massive door-to-door subscription of the citizens. Each citizen would be asked to contribute Continental currency to support the war. In return, he would be allowed to apply the amount of his subscription against the next three years' taxes. Unfortunately for the hopes of the scheme, those Philadelphians and Pennsylvanians who were active politically still favored the radicals over the moderates, but no longer trusted their government with credit. The rest of the public was tired of appeals to patriotism, calls for sacrifice, voluntary committees, and the war itself.

Prices remained high all summer and the normal expectation of Philadelphia citizens of cheap and plentiful food could not be satisfied. Merchants became restive under the stagnation of regulated local trade. There were signs that the radical policy was dividing the town between merchants on one side and artisans and poor citizens on the other. The radicals sought to counteract the summer's failures by a further infusion of voluntarism. They called for a Town Meeting to consider the election of a committee of 120 members from Philadelphia, Northern Liberties, and Southwark to represent all opinions and interests. On the Saturday before the town meeting, a mob led by two radicals unsuccessfully attacked a merchant's house. The merchant had given offense by publishing an unpopular article in an unpopular newspaper.

A large group of opponents of the radical regime are supposed to have attended the town meeting on Monday afternoon, July 26. The radical, General Roberdeau, was again chairman of the meeting. He reported subsequently in the newspapers that the "plan for stopping emissions and raising a revenue by subscription was unanimously approved" and the "association for regulating prices" was renewed until the end of the year "with only a few, it is thought not more than four, dissenting voices." Rain broke off the meeting until 9:00 the next morning.

After re-opening, and settling the business of the method of electing the committee of 120, the meeting proceeded to the consideration of offenders of price regulations. Robert Morris defended himself in person by denying that he or the French consul had violated any rule of the Congress or the Philadelphia committee. Next, General John Cadwalader (1742–1786) a moderate and leader of the city's "Silk Stocking Company," began to address the crowd from the speaker's platform on the subject of price controls. As often as he began he was hooted down by a "body of about 100 men, armed with clubs, who had marched in array, under their officers, with fife and drum, and placed themselves near the stage . . ." General Roberdeau could not quiet the militia, even though a voice vote for the meeting called for Cadwalader to speak.

The angry moderates then left the meeting and formed again two blocks away in the college yard on Fourth Street, between Market and Mulberry. This rump group chose Robert Morris chairman, and proceeded to pass resolutions protesting the denial of free speech, voting to acquit Morris of all charges made against him, and agreeing to participate in the forthcoming election of the committee of 120. Simultaneously, the radicals remaining in the State House yard resolved unanimously that Thomas Paine, then under attack from the moderates for his part in the Deane-Morris controversy, was "a friend of the American cause."

On Saturday, July 31, just before the election, Cadwalader published his appeal for the abolition of all price controls in the *Packet*. He began in a characteristic eighteenth-century way, identifying himself by his economic interest. "I am not, directly or indirectly, engaged in any kind of trade; I am a private citizen, and live upon the income of my estate." He correctly observed that regulation had so far worked to strangle the Philadelphia market. Price controls "must inevitably produce immediate ruin to the merchants and mechanics; and a scarcity, if not a want of every necessary of life, to the whole city."

He then noted that the tanners and cordwainers had refused to be bound by the committee's prices. A complete breakdown surely threatened as other trades would soon form committees and announce noncompliance just as the leather and shoe workers had. The state-by-state regulations were a further disruption of the market in keeping the natural surpluses of one state from reaching others. If there were to be regulations then they must "be undertaken by the united Councils of the states . . .", in short, control must be national.

Cadwalader concluded by asking his fellow Philadelphians to disband their price association and to petition Congress for the end of all restrictions on interstate trade. "A plentiful harvest has filled the country with an abundance . . . and a market would bring such quantities to the city, that there would be no want of these necessaries in the future."

Although Cadwalader's letter accurately stated the supply conditions in Pennsylvania and the effects of the regulatory associations, few Philadelphians were yet ready to abandon controls. The harvest did promise well but farmers were selling very cautiously and prices continued to rise. The merchants, though restive under the stagnation of local trade, could continue their regional and export trade on a barter basis. In August the danger of political disorders which might attend an abolition of price control must have appeared to moderate merchants to outweigh the advantages of unfettered trading. The new committee of 120, which contained some moderates, therefore carried easily 2,115 to 281 votes.

The new giant committee enjoyed no more success than its small predecessor. Philadelphia trade was dead; the merchants sold only very small quantities of goods at the regulated prices; throughout the colonies wholesale prices continued to rise steeply. Major trading in army supplies went on at free market prices beyond the city.

Congress itself pursued a conflicting and disruptive economic policy. In August it rescinded all restrictions on interstate trade. Then, in response to continued radical pressure for price control, especially from Massachusetts and Pennsylvania, it resolved that the individual states set up price control committees of their own—as if thirteen lists of state prices and thirteen different investigating committees could have brought order to Congress's supply and financial confusions. In September a group of Philadelphia merchants proposed as an alternative that taxes be levied monthly so that government finances could keep up with the onward rush of current prices.

Altogether, the summer's price-control attempts served only to heighten tensions in the town and to open a cleavage between rich and poor. The charges and counter charges in the press and the town meetings aroused the public against the merchants; yet the price-control committees created by the public clamor failed to bring the price relief the public wanted and needed. Nor could the committee have been effective, given the absence of a public granary system, of arsenals, and of an effective bureaucracy in the colonies. Repeated radical attacks on Quakers and Tories, perhaps conceived to distract public attention from the inevitable failures of the radical program, only increased the popular appetite for direct action. Moreover, the use of militia companies for threats of political reprisal strained the town's capacity for common-sense control of violence.

On the eve of the October general election of state, county, and local officials the temptations that had lurked in the conflicts of the summer broke forth. At a militia meeting to consider still another drive to rid the city of Tories and "political Quakers" the group clamored to include some moderate leaders in the sweep. James Wilson (1742–1798), a lawyer, prominent moderate leader, and defender of Robert Morris, was singled out.

Late in the morning of Monday, October 4, just eight days before the election, a band of militiamen began rounding up Quakers. In the early afternoon, after allowing their prisoners to go home for dinner, they paraded their captives through the streets of the town picking up a crowd as they went. James Wilson, meanwhile, somehow learning of the danger to himself called for protection upon the Pennsylvania Assembly, then sitting in Philadelphia. General Cadwalader's "Silk Stocking" brigade patrolled in front of Wilson's house in the morning and then, thinking all was safe, went home to dinner. As additional protection Wilson had also gathered an armed group of fellow moderates at his own home. Soon the militia band, swelled by the curious, drew up before Wilson's door. Shots were fired from the house and three militiamen killed. The angry crowd stormed the door and would have murdered everyone in the house had not Joseph Reed, President of the Pennsylvania Supreme Executive Council, arrived just at this moment with a troop of cavalry and a brigade of foot soldiers. The President's troops dispersed the militia and crowd and succeeded in quieting the city.

The incident frightened both radical and moderate leaders. Both sides attempted to prevent further confrontation of mobs and merchants; both sides rushed to use the town's traditional voluntary social controls. Francis Hopkinson, a moderate, published a "Plan for the Relief and Support of the Poor and Distressed Families of . . . Philadelphia," and began a ward-by-ward canvas for funds. The radicals announced a subscription for the families of three dead militiamen. A person believed to be Thomas Paine wrote a highly distorted and pacifying account of the incident in which he closed by saying this ". . . was not the quarrel of enemies or of parties, but the unfortunate blunder of friends."

The Wilson riot marked the climax of a year's frustration. In the anger of the moment the radicals swept the October elections, but when tempers cooled the riot proved the terminal event in a year of failure of a town's attempts to regulate its own economy. Even in Paine's and Morris's day the business scale of the town had become so large that it had exceeded the political abilities of its local citizens.

In the terms of the moment, the 1778–1779 Philadelphia inflation and provision crisis had been a serious political failure. The confrontation of the popular radical party with the moderate merchant party did not produce any successful institution which could have eased the scarcity and high prices of food. Paine and the radicals had quite properly seen that the free market was not fairly allocating flour and "necessaries" among the citizens of the town. In times of scarcity, just as in normal times, the rich outbid the poor. Morris and the moderates had as properly responded that in their ill-articulated society free, open-market trading by the merchants would in the long run bring relief from shortages and high prices. Both sides spoke half-truths. The radicals failed to recognize the need for the merchants to manage their own private network of traders, and the merchants failed to recognize the immediate needs of the city for a fair, publicly supervised allocation of food.

The poliitcal failure of 1778–1779 lay in the inability of the radicals and moderates to work out some limited supply mechanism, perhaps just for bread and flour, which could have taken advantage of the merchant network. One year later Morris and his group organized a supply bank for the Continental Army which suggested how Philadelphia's needs might have been met by a union of merchants back in 1779. Some measure of relief from the inflation and provision crisis of 1778–1779 was not a task beyond the economic capabilities of the society, but it was a task beyond the political capabilities of the society.

Such political failures would be repeated over and over again in Philadelphia's later history. The Revolution left the city a tradition of democratic forms and democratic goals grafted upon a society of private economic aspirations. Later political conflict between popular equalitarian goals and the goals of business profit would give rise to the modern municipal corporation and encourage its active participation in transportation, public safety, education, and health. These municipal functions would be the public dimensions of a city of private aspirations. Urban problems that required direct and substantial reallocation of scarce resources, problems like the 1778–1779 crisis, brought failure after failure to the future city. No urban, economic democracy emerged with time because the popular goal of Philadelphia was the individual race for wealth. This was to be the essence of the American, urban experience.

The Mechanics and the Jeffersonians:
New York, 1789-1801

ALFRED YOUNG

The new Republic was not an egalitarian society. In this essay, Alfred F. Young analyzes the politics of a new inegalitarian society by using the example of the mechanics of New York. The masters' and journeymen's switch from Federalist to Democratic-Republican loyalties in the 1790s is shown to have had its origins in bitter disputes. Although not discussed in detail, the role of the mechanics' societies, the use of town meetings, and the resurgence of revolutionary rhetoric and identification all resemble the artisan's active role in the earlier War for Independence. Here again we see ample suggestions of the vibrancy of artisan life.

The following book is suggested for further reading:

ALFRED YOUNG, *The Democratic Republicans of New York*, Chapel Hill: University of North Carolina Press, 1967.

Alfred Young, "The Mechanics and the Jeffersonians: New York, 1789–1801," *Labor History*, 5 (1964), 247–76. Reprinted and footnotes and tables omitted by permission of the author and the publisher.

In 1789, on the eve of George Washington's inaugural, New York was a solidly Federalist town. In the Congressional election of 1789, the city chose a Federalist by a vote of 2,342 to 373; in the gubernatorial poll it voted against George Clinton, anti-Federalist Governor, 833 to 385. And the mechanics of all ranks were overwhelmingly Federalist. They poured forth to celebrate Washington's inauguration just as they had marched in 1788 to celebrate ratification of the Constitution. They were active in nominating Federalists and they voted Federalist. "Almost all the gentlemen as well as all the merchants and mechanics," Virginia's Senator Grayson observed in 1789 "combined together to turn [George Clinton] out" while the "honest yeomanry" alone supported him. In 1790 anti-Federalists did not even go through the motions of nominating Assembly or Congressional candidates.

From 1789 to 1801 the major thrust of New York City politics was the effort of the anti-Federalists, then the Republicans, to win back the following they enjoyed in the immediate post-war years and establish a new one among the rapidly expanding electorate. Of necessity this was an effort to win support among the mechanics.

For the old anti-Federalist leaders this was a formidable task. George Clinton, the party chieftain and governor since 1777, was an Ulster county lawyer and landholder whose reputation was built on his services in the Revolution as a staunch Whig, wartime governor and foe of Tories. Anti-Federalist political support came primarily from the independent small farmers of Long Island, the west bank of · the Hudson and the upper Hudson valley. In New York City the small circle of Clintonian leaders, while men of lowly origins, were all successful merchants, as their homes in the fashionable part of lower Manhattan attested. John Lamb, for example, was Collector of the Port, a lucrative position; Marinus Willett was the county sheriff; Melancton Smith was busy with various speculations, some of them in William Duer's group. Henry Rutgers was born to wealth which made him one of the city's largest landlords. Only one officer of the General Society of Mechanics and Tradesmen, John Stagg, their old radical Whig compatriot, acted with the Clintonians; while the only artisan in their circle, Ezekial Robbins, a wealthy hatter, was not even a member of the Mechanics Society. They had, in fact, better connections among merchants than mechanics.

In 1791–92 when the Livingston family defected from the Federalists to form a coalition with the old anti-Federalists, they brought with them no special strength among the mechanics. They were city merchants and lawyers, and owners of tenanted estates in the upper Hudson valley. Indeed before the Revolution, in 1768–69, the Delancey faction had been able to win over mechanics against William Livingston of the famed "whig triumvirate," and in 1774–76 the radical mechanic factions usually were at loggerheads with conservatives led by Robert R. Livingston (senior and then junior), Philip Livingston and John Jay and William Duane, related to the Livingstons by marriage. The memory of Chancellor Robert R. Livingston's veto of the charter for the General Society of Mechanics in 1785 was even fresher. Moreover Aaron Burr, the young lawyer sent to the United States Senate in 1791 by the Livingstons and Clinton, in 1785 was the only city Assemblyman who had voted against the charter. Thus the loose coalition that became the "republican interest" as far as New York City politics went—the Clintons, the Livingstons and Burr—were in reality three factions in search of a following.

They found this following in stages in a long uphill battle. Their first victory did not come until the end of 1794 when they won the Congressional seat by a vote of about 1,850 to 1,650. They did not win an Assembly election until 1797, and in the closing years of the decade all the elections were nip and tuck. In the famous "battle of 1800"—the election that determined that the state's electoral votes would be cast for the Jefferson-Burr ticket—the Republicans took the assembly by 3,050 to 2,600 and squeaked through the congressional race 2,180 to 2,090 votes. Not until 1801 did they win a majority of the £100 free-holder electorate privileged to vote for Governor. Thus even at the end of the Federalist era, New York was not quite a safe Republican town; Federalists in defeat retained a sizable following. Analysis of the election returns leads ot the conclusion that the mechanics who in 1789 were overwhelmingly Federalist, by 1800–01 were divided: most were Republican; a good number stayed Federalist. The task, then, that confronts the historian is to explain how various segments of the mechanic population left the house of Federalism in response to the successive issues of the 1790s.

I

Through most of Washington's first administration, from 1789 through 1792, the honeymoon of mechanic Federalist and merchant Federalist continued. The sources of Federalist popularity among mechanics were several. Federalists were the party of the Constitution; they also appeared as the party of the Revolution. The Tories in their camp took a back seat; Colonel Alexander Hamilton ran the party and it was not missed that John Laurence, their first Congressman, had married the daughter of the famed "Liberty Boy," Alexander McDougall. Federalists were also the party of George Washington, an object of universal veneration while the city was the nation's capital in 1789–90. "Poor men love him as their own," said a character in a play by the New York dramatist, William Dunlap. The fact that the city was the capital also helped; anti-Federalists complained that the Federalist "electioneering corps" included "the masons, stone cutters, the carpenters and the mortar carriers" employed in refurbishing city hall as Federal Hall.

In drawing up slates at election time Federalists accommodated mechanics. In the 1789 election when mechanics and merchants each nominated an assembly ticket, Hamilton presided over a meeting of delegates from both groups which drew up a satisfactory coalition ticket. Hamilton claimed, with apparent impunity, in *Federalist* Essay Number 35 that "Mechanics and manufacturers will always be inclined with few exceptions, to give their votes to merchants, in preference to persons of their own professions and trades. Those discerning citizens are well aware that the mechanic and manufacturing arts furnish the materials of mercantile enterprise and industry." But just to make sure, for years Federalists ran one or more leading mechanics, including leaders of the General Society, on their annual assembly ticket.

In their policies in the first Congress, Federalists made good on some of their promises during the ratification controversy. The city's mechanics petitioned for tariff protection at once, pointing out to their brethren that "foreign importations were highly unfavorable to mechanic improvement, nourishing a spirit of dependence, defeating in a degree the purpose of our revolution and tarnishing the luster of our character." Congressman Laurence neatly balanced the interests of his constituency, pleading for higher duties on beer, candles, hemp, and cordage, (manufactured by the city's artisans), for lower duties on rum, madeira, and molasses, (imported by the West Indies merchants), couching the latter plea on behalf of the poor—"that part of the community who are least able to bear it." Early in 1792 Congress passed another mildly protective tariff bill while the anti-Federalist position was sufficiently blurred for Hamilton to be able to claim that "this faction has never ceased to resist every protection or encouragement to arts and manufactures."

Hamiltonian finance was generally supported in the city as in the state as a whole. Funding drew only a few whimpers of protest in the city; in fact it was John Stagg, the Clintonian mechanic, who helped squelch a petition that appeared among veterans on behalf of Madison's proposals for discrimination. Assumption struck sparks only among the old anti-Federalist foes of "consolidation." While Hamilton's "Report on Manufactures" does not seem to have drawn any special accolades from mechanics, his overall performance as Secretary of the Treasury gave him a prestige that outlasted his party's. On his retirement in 1795 a group of building craftsmen offered to build him a house at their own expense, and after his death in 1804 the General Society went into mourning for six weeks.

The first sign of a serious mechanic alienation from the merchants came in 1791, when the General Society's new petition for incorporation was "treated with contemptuous neglect" by the state assembly which in the same session granted a charter to the Bank of New York, the merchants' favorite. Some of the old mechanic consciousness, last apparent in 1785–86 when the charter was first rejected, now revived. "Mechanics," said a writer in Greenleaf's anti-Federalist organ, "those who assume the airs of 'the well born' should be made to know that the mechanics of this city have equal rights with the merchants, and that they are as important a set of men as any in the community." Another man pushed the issue further:

> Who will deny that a republican government is founded on democratic principles? . . . That the manufacturing interest, from its nature is, and ever will remain of the democratic denomination, none can deny. Why then incorporate large monied interests, and no democratic ones? Should we not have a wholesome check to the baneful growth of aristocratic weeds among us?

In the Spring elections of 1791 the mechanics refused to go along with the merchants ticket, nominating instead a slate that included one of their officers and two leaders of the burgeoning Tammany Society. Four of their candidates won—"our motley city representatives," Robert Troup called them in his alarmed report to Hamilton. And the following year the mechanics charter sailed through the legislature.

Once chartered, the Society grew from about 200 members in 1792 to about 600 in 1798, most of them master craftsmen. Chartered "only for charitable purposes" as the society regretfully explained, it occasionally made small loans to its members besides acting as a benefit society. And while it eschewed partisan politics, it nonetheless had the effect it anticipated of "uniting us as brethren in common interests."

Mechanics expressed some of this same spirit by flocking into the Tammany Society, described confidentially by its organizer as "a political institution founded on a strong republican basis whose democratic principles will serve in some measure to correct the aristocracy of the city." Founded in 1789, it had 300 members by the Fall of '91; and perhaps 200 more by 1795, among whom mechanics were the most numerous. Its first chief Sachem was William Mooney, an upholsterer and paper hanger. Its leaders stressed its democratic rather than its class character. Tammany "united in one patriotic band," William Pitt Smith of the Columbia faculty exclaimed, "the opulent and the industrious—the learned and the unlearned, the dignified servant of the people and the respectable plebeian, however distinguished by sentiment or by occupation." The organization was not political, and its leadership at first was predominantly Federalist. But the fact that anti-Federalists were active in Tammany and the Assemblymen elected in 1791 were Tammany figures were both omens of its political potential.

The little appreciated "bank war" and "panic" of 1792 brought to a boil such disillusionment with the Federalist honeymoon as then existed. After the Bank of the United States was chartered and a threat of a coalition of its New York branch with the Bank of New York loomed in 1791, there was a movement to charter a third bank led by "the disappointed in the direction of the existing banks," foremost among whom were the Livingstons. While the origins of the venture were speculative, "men of all classes flocked" to subscribe to its stock, as Edward Livingston claimed in extolling its advantages to "persons of small capital" and victims of the lending "favoritism" of the Bank of New York. Hamilton fought the new venture desperately; by March he knew that the "bank mania" was "made an engine to help the governor's [Clinton's] reelection." In April the "prince of speculators," William Duer, Hamilton's recently resigned Assistant Secretary, collapsed, and the bubble inflated by speculation in bank stock, securities, and land burst. Duer brought down with him not only leading merchants like the Livingstons but a host of common folk from whom he had borrowed to the hilt: "shopkeepers, widows, orphans, butchers, carmen, gardeners, market women," a businessman recorded "even the noted bawd Mrs. McCarty." All business, including that of construction, halted; and "the mechanics began to feel the effect of the failures." Small wonder, then, that a mob of about 400-500 threatened Duer's life at the debtor's jail, or that Republicans "made bitter use" of Hamilton's "attachment to Colonel Duer" in the elections. In the gubernatorial poll of 1792 Clinton ran better than he ever had in the city, receiving 603 votes, to 729 for John Jay, or 44 percent of the total.

In the Congressional election late in 1792 William Livingston— elected previously as a Federalist Assemblyman—offered the Federalists their first national challenge. "That whore in politics," as a Hamilton's informant called him, Livingston made a special appeal to the Mechanics Society for support, claiming to be responsible for their charter. He was also identified with an unsuccessful appeal to make New York City's appointive mayor elective. In a cloudy campaign in which party lines were not clearly drawn, Livingston received 700 votes to 1,900 for the successful Federalist, John Watts.

Through these minor political crises, the leaders of the Mechanics Society did not break with the Federalists. They turned down Livingston's plea for support; it was not only "repugnant to their objects to participate in elections," but he was "an improper person." Similarly they refused to endorse Governor Clinton in 1792 or Melancton Smith when he successfully sneaked into the Assembly in 1791. In the Spring of 1793 several officers of the Mechanics Society, including Robert Boyd, the radical Whig blacksmith, were still on the Federalist assembly ticket giving the party an easy victory. In short, at the end of the first Washington administration, despite a smouldering discontent with Federalism in the city, mechanics of the substantial sort and mechanics as a whole had not left the house of Federalism.

II

The parting of the ways came in Washington's second term, and the precipitant was Federalist foreign policy. The French Revolution was an initial stimulus in 1793. When the French frigate *L'Embuscade,* did battle with the English man of war *Boston* off Sandy Hook some nine boatloads of New Yorkers went out to cheer the French victory while on the shore fistfights broke out between "Whig" and "Tory" cartmen. The arrival of Citizen Edmund Genêt prompted the first open mass meeting of the decade and a welcoming committee was formed whose secretary was White Matlack, a well-to-do brewer and iron manufacturer. As a young doctor walked through the poor east side section, he heard "a dram shop full of Frenchmen singing 'Carmagnole.' The next shop I came upon some person was singing 'God Bless Great George' and which immediately procured a parcel of hearty curses upon his majesty from the rest of the company."

Actually it was Britain and not Franch that proved the real catalyst. By early 1794, because the thin wall of Federalist tariff protection was not holding the line against the competition of British manufactures, craft groups once again dispatched petitions to Congress. Then news of massive British depredations against American ships and of a British threat to renew Indian war electrified all classes; it brought the possibility of war to the state's unprotected frontier and the city's unprotected harbor. Thus Republican proposals—in Congress, Madison's old bill for discrimination against British shipping; in New York, Governor Clinton's demand to fortify the harbor and the Livingstons' strident cry for war—caught full sail the most violent wave of Anglophobia since the Revolution. At a meeting sponsored by Republicans, White Matlack was the principal speaker and mechanics were so prominent that a Federalist satirist derided the "greasy

caps" in a mock epic poem. At each good point made by a speaker, he
jibed:

> Hats, caps and leathern aprons flew
> And puffs of wondrous size and jerkins blue

In the same flurry of patriotism the city's Democratic Society came into
being: its leaders were merchants and lawyers; its members, according to
one of them, "are composed of and mingle with every class of citizens";
its meetings, according to a Federalist critic, were attended by "the lowest
order of mechanics, laborers, and draymen."

A dramatic change in city opinion was apparent in the Spring of 1794
when the Commissioners of Fortifications, headed by Governor Clinton,
called for volunteer labor to erect a fort on Governor's Island. For weeks,
the Republican paper reported, "hardly a day has passed . . . without a
volunteer party of fifty to one hundred" putting in a day's labor. A British
visitor described it vividly:

> Marching two and two towards the water side . . . a procession of young
> tradesmen going in boats to Governor's Island to give the state a day's
> work . . . drums beating and fifes playing . . . with flags flying. Today
> the whole trade of carpenters and joiners, yesterday the body of masons;
> before this the grocers, school masters, coopers and barbers; next Monday
> all the attorneys and men concerned in the law, handle the mattock and
> shovel the whole day, and carry their provisions with them.

And of course he could have added more: The Democratic Society, Tammany, the General Society of Mechanics, "all the true Republican carpenters," "the patriotic Republican sawyers," "the patriotic sailmakers"
—so they called themselves in the papers—the journeymen hatters, cordwainers, peruke makers, hairdressers, tallow chandlers, tanners and curriers; in short, it was the Constitutional parade of 1788 all over again but
under different leadership. And there was also something new: the most
recent immigrants to the city styling themselves "Irish laborers," "English
Republicans," and the "patriotic natives of Great Britain and Ireland."

The Republicans reaped a political harvest quickly. Early in April
1794, Chancellor Robert R. Livingston advised his younger brother, Edward, not to run again for the Assembly. "The mechanics and cartmen"
were Federalist; "I find no class of people on which you can depend."
A few weeks later in elections held after the work on the fort had just
begun, Federalists won but the Republican vote unexpectedly zoomed from
a high of 500 in 1793 to a range of 1,200 to 1,400. Then in the Congressional poll of December 1794–January 1795 Edward Livingston risked a
race against John Watts, the Federalist incumbent. A lawyer and city resi-

dent, a member of the aristocratic Hudson Valley family known as "Beau Ned" (the young dandy), he was presented to the voters as "the poor man's friend," a "good Whig," and "a good Republican and true friend of the French." Watts was described as a "Tory," "a paper man," "an opulent merchant" and "a friend to British measures." The year before, when Livingston ran for the Assembly, he received 214 votes; he now won 1,843 to 1,638.

In this changing climate the General Society of Mechanics and Tradesmen shifted perceptibly. John Stagg, the Clintonian and radical Whig, was returned as President; later he presided at the public meeting at which Livingston was nominated. At its Fourth of July dinner in 1794, the Society toasted "the republican societies of the City of New York"; the following year it accepted an invitation from the Democratic Society for a joint celebration of Independence Day with them, Tammany and the Coopers Society. A committee worked out the details of an observance that was repeated every year thereafter: a parade to a church (militia officers seated in front of the pulpit, the mechanics to the right of the center aisle, the Democrats to the left, Tammany and the Coopers off to either side aisle), a ceremony consisting of the reading of the Declaration of Independence followed by a patriotic oration by a Republican leader. The typical mechanic could now be portrayed in Republican hues: he was, according to a writer in the Republican paper, a hard working man who eschewed high living, opposed the "haughty well born," saved to buy a lot in the suburbs for his old age, and enjoyed a family gathering at home where his children beat time to "Yankee Doodle" and "Carmagnole."

Thus, the first Republican breakthrough came in a revival of "The Spirit of '76." Over the next few years Republicans had great difficulty transferring this new strength, which came on a national issue, to state elections. They were also unable to sustain mechanic Republicanism on national questions, as the vicissitudes of the Jay Treaty fight of 1795–96 illustrated. A "town meeting" protesting the treaty was attended by from 5,000 to 7,000 people. It was held at the noon lunch hour when, according to an irate Federalist, "our demogogues always fix their meetings in order to take in all mechanics and laborers—over whom they alone have influence." The poorer workers were especially noticeable: cartmen with their horses, "the hodmen, and the ash men and the clam men," as were recent immigrants—Scotsmen, Irish, English and French. When the vote was taken to damn the Treaty, according to one contemporary, "there was not a whole coat" among them. The Livingstons were "supported by a few of the principal citizens, the rest being made up of men of the lower class." Others claimed, however, that the leaders did not have "a majority of the lower class," or that several hundred sided with Hamilton. By the Spring of 1796, after Washington signed the treaty and Republicans in the House threatened to hold up its enforcement, anti-treaty sentiment faded. Playing on the fear of war and threatening economic coercion, Federalists were able to collect some 3,200 signatures on a pro-Treaty petition. Republicans by contrast turned out less than half of the previous year's opponents at a public rally, one-third of whom, a Federalist charged, "as is usually the case were ne-groes, sweeps, boys, Frenchmen, and curious people." The "merchants and traders," he insisted, and "the substantial mechanics" backed the Treaty.

The claim was probably justified. In the Congressional election at the end of 1796 James Watson, a wealthy merchant, received the Federalist nomination after four others had turned it down because, in Hamilton's words, "he had gotten a strong hold of most of the leading mechanics who act with us." Edward Livingston recovered his lost ground to win a second term by a safe margin of 2,362 to 1,812 votes. But his vote, a contemporary accurately put it, came from wards "chiefly inhabited by the middling and poorer classes of the people." Thus at the end of the second Washington administration the city's working population was split: the Federalists re-tained a good section of the "substantial mechanics" while the Republicans had the "middling and poorer classes" in an unstable constituency.

III

Republicans did not consolidate this foothold until they mastered the art of exploiting the class antagonisms of the poor, threats to the economic interests of particular crafts, and the aspirations of new immigrants.

Poverty in New York went hand in hand with population growth and economic progress. The city, the worldly-wise LaRochefoucauld observed in 1796, "like all great towns contains at once more riches and more wretchedness than towns less populous and commercial." A petition from one group of workers pointed out that "house rent, fuel, provisions and prices of everything necessary for the support of a family have been rising." In the winter of 1796–97 some 600 unemployed journeymen petitioned for public assistance because many "by reasons of large families" were "in want of sufficient fire and wood." For newcomers housing was the worst problem. The upper-east side near the shore—the seventh ward—was the city's worst slum. As a doctor described it, it had "narrow, crooked, flat, unpaved, muddy alleys" filled with swamps, stagnant water, "little decayed wooden huts," some inhabited by several families; all was wafted by an intolerable stench from garbage piled in the streets, putrefying excrement at the docks and a tan yard in their midst. Understandably, when a yellow-fever epidemic claimed 700 lives in the summer of 1795, it was here that the toll was heaviest.

Discontent bred of such conditions was ready for political exploitation. By 1795 there were 900 more voters in the £100 electorate for a total of 2,100 but there were 2,300 more 40 shilling renters, or a total of 5,000. Moreover, the poorer voters were concentrated in the newly-built parts of town, the fifth and especially the seventh wards along the East River, and the fourth and especially the sixth to the west along the North (or Hudson) River. In the seventh, known as the "cartman's ward," there were 870 40-shilling voters to 311 £100 voters; in the sixth the proportion was 1,298 to 223. Here was the Republican potential.

The pent-up class feeling erupted in the election of the Spring of '96 which, as Hamilton put it, "in view of the common people . . . was a question between the rich and the poor because of the 'vile affair of whipping Burke and McCredy'." Thomas Burk and Timothy Crady—Federalists could not get their names straight—were ferrymen, recent Irish immigrants who got into an altercation with Gabriel Furman, an arrogant Federalist alderman of the wealthy first ward. Accused of the crime of "insulting an alderman" they were tried without due process before a court of three aldermen and a Federalist Mayor intent upon making an example of the "impudent rascals," and were sentenced to two months in jail (Burk got twenty lashes as well).

William Keteltas, a young Republican lawyer, took this case of the "oppression of the innocent poor" to the State Assembly, demanding impeachment of the city official. After a Federalist committee exonerated them and Keteltas turned his guns on the Assembly, he was called before the Bar of the House and asked to apologize. He refused and was found guilty of contempt, whereupon the tumultuous crowd that had jammed the Assembly carried him off to jail in a handsome arm chair midst cries of "The Spirit of '76." An issue of class justice had been transformed into one of free speech. After a month of agitation from "the iron gate," Keteltas was released and escorted home by a cheering crowd. That was a Tuesday; on Friday Republicans nominated him as one of their twelve Assembly candidates. When Federalists mocked the "ragamuffins" who paraded for Keteltas, Republicans claimed them as "the men by whose mechanical labours the necessaries and conveniences of life are produced in abundance"; it was "such men as these [who] were the triumphant victors at Breed's Hill, at Saratoga, at Yorktown." The Federalists won, but the Republican slate hit its highest peak thus far.

In the September 1796 municipal elections Republicans for the first time capitalized on local issues. The Common Council was in the hands of conservative Federalist merchants elected by a tiny handful of voters. Republicans railed at the Mayor and Council for dispensing arbitrary justice, failing to curb forestalling in the markets, neglecting to keep the streets clean, and increasing expenditures and taxes. They elected two men, both of whom were disqualified on technicalities, then re-elected one of them, Jacob Delamontagnie, a secretary of the Democratic Society, by an even wider margin.

Early in 1797 Republicans took up the cause of a single craft, the seventy-five members of the Association of Tallow Chandlers and Soap Makers, whose factories the state legislature ordered removed from the city proper to the outskirts of towns—on the grounds that their fumes were a cause of epidemic. The chandlers petitioned the Assembly. The Republican Brockholst Livingston became their counsel, and at their request Dr. Samuel Latham Mitchill, the Columbia scientist and Tammany orator, prepared a pamphlet-length treatise exonerating the chandlers' "pestilential vapors," blaming the fever on "septic acid vapors," his favorite theory. The chandler issue boiled through March; in April the Republicans nominated Mitchill for the Assembly on a slate that included a tanner, a hatter, a sailmaker, and the two aldermen elected in the wake of the Keteltas affair. Federalists capitulated, endorsing half the Republican ticket, an unheard of event, and Republicans won their first Assembly election of the decade, their vote ranging between 1,600 and 2,100 to a scant 600 to 700 for the Federalists. In 1800 Dr. Mitchill, the tallow chandlers' hero, was the successful Republican candidate to replace Edward Livingston in Congress.

Republicans also won over another group, the cartmen. Numbering more than 1,000 by 1800, they were known for their "quick tempers" and "mistreating their horses." Normally they chafed under the regulations of the city fathers. In the ferryman affair a doggerel verse on broadside reminded the cartmen of their own trouble with Major Richard Varick:

> He often sits upon a bench
> Much like unto a judge, sir.
> And makes the wretches bosom wrench
> To whom he owes a grudge sir.
>
> But now he does a great offense
> It is no thing to mock at
> He takes away the cartmen's pence
> And puts them in his pocket.

By 1798 the cartmen were Republican enough for the Federalists to gerrymander the outlying seventh ward ("the cartmen's ward") out of the city into the Westchester congressional district. In the 1799 Assembly elections Federalist merchants stood at the polls and "used all their influence with the cartmen" with some success. The next year "Independent Cartman" appealed to his brethren not to submit again to such merchant pressure:

who will do the work if not us? "Will their puny clerks carry the burdens which we do?" The cartmen resisted and as a result there were only eighteen cartmen in the crowd when Hamilton, in 1801, appeared at a meeting of cartmen and appealed to "my dear fellow citizens."

From the mid–'90s on, Republicans also spoke in clear tones to the city's new immigrants. Federalists were not without experience in dealing with nationality groups politically. But to the French, Scots, English, and especially the Irish recent arrivals who ran up the cost of charity at the alms house, hated England and allegedly brought in yellow fever, Federalists were cool or hostile. Republicans, by contrast, formed the "Society for the Assistance of Persons Emigrating from Foreign Countries." They turned out en masse to welcome Joseph Priestly and in their press, Irish and Scots could read reports of struggles for liberty in their native lands. Congressman Livingston, during the xenophobia of 1798 to 1800, eloquently opposed the Alien Law, even introducing a petition from Irish aliens of New York, and in the Assembly Aaron Burr fought the proposed constitutional amendment to bar Federal office to naturalized citizens. The political fruits fell accordingly. "The poor Irish and French," one Federalist was convinced, were enough to carry the sixth and seventh wards for Jefferson in 1800.

IV

In the closing years of the decade Republicans also picked up some of the issues that from the 1780s on had been of concern to master mechanics. For one, they committed themselves to tariff protection. In the General Society a committee headed by the Republican sailmaker, George Warner, drafted a letter lamenting the growth of foreign importations; they were "an influence highly unfavorable to mechanical improvement, nourishing a spirit of dependence, defeating in a degree the purpose of our Revolution, and tarnishing the luster of our national character"—the very language was that used by Federalist mechanics in 1789. In 1801 a mass meeting of "the mechanics and manufacturers of New York City" sent a memorial to Congress beseeching the "protecting hand of government." As the reign of Jefferson approached, "A Song for Hatters" expressed the expectations of other artisans:

> Before the bad English Treaty,
> Which Jay with that nation has made
> For work we need make no entreaty
> All Jours were employed at their trade.

> Philadelphia she then had a hundred
> New York she had fifty and more
> In the first scarce the half can be numbered
> In the last there is hardly a score. . . .
>
> And what has occasion'd this falling,
> And caus'd us to fall at this rate
> 'Tis the English, whose arts are prevailing
> With our Great rulers of state. . . .
>
> When shortly in our constitution
> A Republican party will sway
> Let us all then throw in a petition
> Our grievance to do away. . . .
>
> That our party in Congress may now rule
> Let each voter for liberty stir
> And not be to England a base tool
> When Jefferson aids us and Burr.

Republicans again took up the cause of freer banking facilities. But where the Livingstons' frontal assault of 1792 failed, Aaron Burr in 1799 managed the camouflaged Bank of Manhattan through the legislature with finesse. While the new bank was primarily of concern to aspiring merchants, it is symptomatic of the mechanic interest in credit that some two dozen members of the Mechanics Society were among the charter stock subscribers. The new bank, Republicans boasted, broke the "banking monopoly" and struck a blow at usury, an object of special contempt to many working class patrons of the city's money lenders.

From 1797 on, Republicans also committed themselves clearly to direct representation of master mechanics on their assembly tickets. In 1798 they repeated their success of the previous year by running four artisans on their ticket; in 1799 they ran six new ones. Even the famous all-star slate Aaron Burr assembled for the battle of 1800 had a place on it for George Warner, sailmaker, Ezekial Robbins, hatter, and Phillip Arcularius, tanner.

The inroads Republicans made among mechanics of all types was confirmed by Federalist tactics from 1798-1801. For a while during the "half war" with France and the "reign of terror," Federalists basked in a glow of X.Y.Z. patriotism as some mechanics turned against the Republicans—now the so-called "French party"—just as they had deserted the Federalists in 1794–95 as the British party. It was almost a second honeymoon of mechanic and merchant as the Mechanics Society toasted "Millions for defense, not one cent for tribute," Tammany substituted "Yankee Doodle" for "The Marseillaise," and mechanics paraded en masse in Washington's funeral cortege. But the Federalist attitude to Republican mechanics was by this time fatally ambivalent. Besides threatening mechanics with the loss of their jobs, they beat the nativist drums, challenging naturalized aliens at the polls and attempted to suppress the city's two Republican papers. At election time when they sought to woo mechanics, Republicans warned about "the avowed despisers of mechanics who may for a few days intermingle with honest men in order to deceive them." Federalists also voted the poor from the alms house and courted free Negroes with promises of office holding and "enormous supplies of home crackers and cheese." And in the election of 1800 when Hamilton was unable to induce men of "weight and influence" to run, he arranged an Assembly slate filled with unknown artisans: a ship chandler, a baker, a bookseller, a potter, a shoemaker, a leather inspector, and spoiled the image only by including Gabriel Furman "the man who whipped the ferrymen." Federalist tactics thus can only be described as desperate and to no avail. Mechanic interest was unsurpassed in the voting in the Spring of 1800: "all business was suspended, even the workmen deserted the houses they were building"; yet Federalists lost the city.

The election returns for 1800 and 1801 indicate that the mechanics were preponderantly Republican yet were divided in their allegiances. The fact that there were two categories of voters—the £100 freeholders alone qualified to vote for senators and Governor, and the 40 shilling renters allowed to vote only for Assemblymen—enables us to differentiate roughly the voting patterns of the various strata of mechanics. First, about two thirds of the Republican vote—in 1800, about 2,200 of 3,100 votes; in 1801, 2,400 of 3,600 votes—came from the Assembly voters, the 40 shillings renters who in effect were the poorer mechanics, the cartmen, petty tradesmen and journeymen. Secondly, about one half of the total Federalist vote came from this same group—in 1800, 1,300 of their 2,600 votes; in 1801, 1,100 of 2,150 votes. Thirdly, Republicans also had significant support among the £100 freeholders who included the master craftsmen—43 per cent or 876 voters in 1800, 54 per cent or 1,266 voters in 1801. As a Republican editor proudly pointed out, this refuted the Federalist contention that Jefferson and Burr were supported only by "persons of no property."

Analysis of the returns by wards confirms this political division among both prosperous and poorer mechanics. In the sixth and seventh wards with the greatest proportion of poor voters and recent immigrants, where Republicans made their greatest effort to get out the vote, they received more than half of their total city vote in 1800 and 1801. Yet Federalists also had a following here, 800 voters in 1800, reduced to 600 the following year. By contrast, the second and third wards at the bottom of Manhattan, the centers of the fashionable wealthy merchant residences, through the entire decade gave the Federalists almost a two to one margin. The fourth and fifth wards, the midtown on both the west and east side, which were probably the most "middling" in the city, divided about evenly between the two parties. In 1802 Republicans confirmed the class basis of their support in the poorer wards when they divided the city into two congressional districts. They created their own safe district by placing the sixth and seventh wards in together with the fourth, giving the first, second, third and fifth wards to the Federalists in a district which also included Brooklyn and Richmond. Federalists did not even run a candidate in the Republican district, while Republicans ran one in the Federalist area with "no hopes of success."

By 1800–01 Republican support among mechanics, it is reasonable to hypothesize came from: 1.) master craftsmen and journeymen in many trades, especially the less prosperous ones; 2.) craftsmen as a whole in trades whose interests Republicans espoused, such as tallow chandlers and shoemakers; 3.) craftsmen in those trades most in need of protection from British manufacturers such as hatters and tanners; 4.) cartmen as a whole; 5.) newer immigrants, especially the Irish, French and to a lesser extent the Scots, and English; 6.) mechanics who had been patriots in the Revolution and responded to the revival of the "Spirit of '76."

The numerically smaller following of the Federalists may well have come from 1.) the more "substantial mechanics" in many trades to whom Hamilton's appeal for the Federalists—as the party that brought "unexampled prosperity"—was meaningful; 2.) craftsmen least in need of protection, such as the building trades; 3.) poorer tradesmen most closely dependent on and most easily influenced by merchants, such as the service trades; 4.) American-born mechanics and New England migrants who felt their status threatened by the influx of "foreigners"; 5.) new immigrants, anxious to differentiate themselves from their radical countrymen, especially the English; and 6.) mechanics of a loyalist or neutralist background who were made uneasy by the revival of anti-Toryism.

V

The New York Republicans, it should be clear, did not become a labor party. The Clintons, Livingstons and Burrites, and other merchants, landholders, lawyers and office holders ruled the party. Moreover, they had the support of a substantial segment of the merchant community, although not the men at the apex of economic power in the city. Nor did the mechanics become even an organized wing of the party, bargaining for nominations as they had with the Federalists early in the decade. Republicans always found a place for a few mechanics on their twelve-man Assembly slate and for many others on their electioneering committees. Mechanics were members, though not leaders, of the Democratic Society and leaders as well as members of the Tammany Society. George Warner, sailmaker, or Matthew Davis, printer, were speakers at the annual Republican celebration of Independence Day; James Cheetham, a former hatter, was influential as an editor and pamphleteer; and early in the 1800s a number of tanners were active enough to win a reputation as the "tannery yard clique" and "the swamp clique." But there was no assertive workingmen's faction among the Republicans as there would be in the Jacksonian era. And mechanic support was as much the product of the courting by Republican politicians as it was of the demands of the labor movement.

Nor were Republicans put to the severe test of choosing between wage workers and master craftsmen in labor disputes. Republicans, it is apparent, were sympathetic to the craft organizations. They celebrated the Fourth with the Mechanics and Coopers Societies, pleaded the cause of the Association of Tallow Chandlers, and opposed the use of prison labor to manufacture shoes, an issue close to the hearts of cordwainers. While there were a few strikes late in the decade, there was no trial of "a combination of labor" as "a criminal conspiracy" until 1809–10.

Nonetheless Republican thought was unmistakably shaped by the party's mechanic constituency. There was, to be sure, a tinge of agrarianism to some Republicans: a glorification of the yeomanry among the upstate anti-Federalist leaders; an idealization of the rural virtues in the aristocratic landholder Robert R. Livingston (who signed his newspaper articles "Cato"); a contempt for the hateful city in the poet-editor, Philip Freneau. But, understandably, Chancellor Livingston, who fearfully vetoed the Mechanics Society charter in 1785, praised the aggressive tallow chandlers in 1797 as "those respectable and useful citizens." By the late 1790s, when Republican writers analyzed the political alignment of social classes, they found a place for mechanics in the Republican coalition. The concept might be that "farmers and mechanics & co" were the "laborers, men who produce by their industry something to the common stock of commodity" opposed by the unproductive classes, or it might be that "farmers, merchants, mechanics and common laboring men" have a "common interest" against "the great landholders and monied men." The General Society of Mechanics and Tradesmen, for its part, found a place for a picture of a plowman on its membership certificate side by side with a house carpenter and a shipwright, all beneath a slogan "By Hammer and Hand All Arts Do Stand."

Perhaps the New York Republican leaders, who were neither agrarian-minded nor commercial-minded in the strict sense, will be best understood as spokesmen for productive capital. Three of the four merchant presidents of the Democratic Society, for example, invested in such productive ventures as a linen factory, a thread factory, a mine and spermaceti candle works. Chancellor Livingston, who is well known for promoting the steamboat, also experimented with manufacturing paper and reducing friction in millstones. "Mechanicks is my hobby horse," he told Joseph Priestley. He was the President and Samuel L. Mitchill the Secretary of the Society for the Promotion of Agriculture Arts and Manufactures. Mitchill was also a pioneer in industrial chemistry, and sympathized with the goal of protection for American manufactures. He congratulated Hamilton on his "Report on Manufactures" in 1792; as Republican chairman of the House Committee on Commerce and Manufactures, in 1804 he sponsored a tariff program.

New York Republicans also took up the social reforms favored by their mechanic constituents. Tammany, for example, at one dinner toasted in succession "the speedy abolition" of slavery, "a happy melioration of our penal laws" and "the establishment of public schools." William Keteltas, the hero of the ferrymen's *cause célèbre*—when incarcerated in the debtor's prison—edited a paper, *Prisoner of Hope,* which pleaded the debtor's plight. Edward Livingston, in his first term in Congress, began the reform of the criminal code, a subject that would become a life-long concern. Contrary to the contention of some historians, Republicans also lent active support to abolition. Reform was bi-partisan and several measures came to fruition when John Hay was governor, but the urban Republicans imparted a warm humanitarianism to a frosty anti-Federalism and a crusading egalitarian flavor to the genteel philanthropic humanitarianism of the city's merchants and ministers. Equally important Republican orators instilled the environmentalist concepts of the enlightenment that justified a permanent program of reform.

Neither mechanics nor Republicans made much of an issue of political reform, especially during George Clinton's long tenure as governor from 1777–95. The restrictive suffrage provisions in the state constitution and its unique Council of Appointment and Council of Revision were occasionally discussed but not widely protested. Typically, when Tunis Wortman examined the question of abolishing the property qualification to vote, in his political treatise of 1800, the city's leading democratic theorist contented himself with summarizing the pros and cons and ended by saying the question was "not decided." In 1801, when Republicans sponsored the first constitutional revision convention, they permitted universal male suffrage in the election of delegates, but restricted the convention itself to reforming the Council of Appointment.

After 1801, their mechanic constituency cautiously beckoned the Republicans towards reform on the municipal level where only freeholders of £20 or more were permitted to vote for Aldermen and the Mayor was appointed. For a while Republicans were content to broaden suffrage in their own way. Wortman as county clerk was observed "running to the poll with the books of the Mayor's court under his arm, and with a troop of ragged aliens at his tail." He was also one of the organizers of "faggot voting," a process by which a group of propertyless Republicans were qualified to vote by the joint temporary purchase of a piece of real estate. When the courts ruled out faggot voting, Republicans demanded that the voting qualifications be lowered at least to the 40 shilling leasehold requirement in Assembly elections; they also asked for the elimination of plural voting and voice voting and for the popular election of the Mayor. By 1804 they won all but the last of these demands.

It might be argued that Republicans did more within the framework of the existing political institutions to provide a greater place for mechanics. Like the old anti-Federalists, Republicans were generally distrustful of the wealthy. Unlike the anti-Federalists, who had confidence only in the yeomanry, Republicans included a role for mechanics among the *Means for the Preservation of Political Liberty,* as George Warner entitled his oration. The trouble, as this sailmaker put it, was that "tradesmen, mechanics, and the industrious classes of society consider themselves of too little consequence to the body politic." Republicans defended the right of mechanics to scrutinize political affairs in "self-created" societies and to instruct their representatives at "town meetings." When Federalists mocked such pretensions, Republicans delighted in taunting them with their own epithets, signing their newspaper articles "one of the swinish multitude" or "only a mechanic and one of the rabble." Republicans also upheld the election of mechanics to public office against Federalist scoffers who "despise mechanics because they have not snored through four years at Princeton."

The mechanic vote and viewpoint guaranteed that Republicans, in their political philosophy, would abandon the old anti-Federalist suspicion of the Constitution. For converts from Federalism like the Livingstons there was never any problem. Other Republicans straddled the constitutional question: Keteltas said he was "neither a Federal nor anti-Federal." Wortman, however, was tempted to revert to the old anti-Federalist view, and to indict the Federalists of '98. He began to collect materials for a book that would expose "the secret convention of 1787 and its members . . . , [and the] intrigues and artifices made use of, for the purpose of compelling the adoption of the constitution." But the book that appeared in 1800—Wortman's *Treatise Concerning Political Inquiry and the Liberty of the Press*—was a libertarian disquisition devoted to the Constitution and Bill of Rights. Republicans could hardly have done otherwise, for their mechanic supporters were men who had paraded for the Constitution in 1788 or had since migrated to the new democracy in order to seek its blessings. To George Warner,· the sailmaker and soldier, "the same American spirit which animated to the contest the heroes of the Revolution" prevailed in directing the national convention of '87 to the constitutional establishment of the liberty we at this day enjoy." Thus the city's Republicans, like the mechanics, were both nationalistic and democratic in their outlook.

And now to return to the question posed in the introduction as to the character and continuity of the political conflict between the years 1774 and 1801. Beyond any question, in the 1790s the mechanics were important in New York City politics. Charles Beard's observation that "neither the Republicans nor the Federalists seem to have paid much attention to capturing the vote of the mechanics" was based on inadequate evidence. In the effort to construct the party conflict as one of "agrarianism" vs "capitalism," Beard did not allow a sufficient place for the mechanics to whom even Jefferson referred sympathetically as "the yeomanry of the city." Carl Becker's projection of the conflict of the 1760s into the 1790s was misleading in another way. The implication of the continuity of mechanic allegiances—radical Whig to anti-Federalist to Jeffersonian— is insupportable. Mechanics who clearly were Federalist in 1788 remained safely Federalist until 1794 and the substantial mechanics a good deal longer, many of them through 1801 and beyond. Mechanics did not always behave as one unified class in politics. Nor can the Republicans be understood as a mechanics party if that was Becker's implication.

And yet Becker's thesis remains attractive. There was an intense struggle in New York City in the 1790s for "who shall rule at home," and if not strictly a class conflict, within it were the elements of a clash between "the privileged and the unprivileged" involving the mechanics as Becker suggested. The plot, dialogue and even character types of the 1790s bear a striking resemblance to the drama of the pre-Revolutionary era. Once again the battle cry that stirred the mechanics was British policy, the cause was American Independence, and the ideology was patriotism or "the spirit of '76." Other insistent mechanic demands thread through the last three decades of the century: for democratic participation, for social recognition, for protection for American manufactures. The new leaders of the 1790s, the Livingstons, resumed something of their pre-war position as aristocratic republicans at the head of the "popular party." The new mechanics' hero of the late 1790s, William Keteltas, was Alexander McDougall of 1769 all over again, a second "John Wilkes of America." The methods, too, were similar: the town meetings, the popular political societies, the churning printing presses. The symbolism of the July Fourth celebration perhaps completes the picture. Thus Jeffersonian Republicans of New York City, with due allowance for the rhetoric of politics, could claim that they were heirs to the "spirit of '76" and that the "revolution of 1800" was indeed the consummation of the Revolution of 1776.

2.4

Religion, Acculturation, and American Negro Slave Rebellions: Gabriel's Insurrection

GERALD MULLIN

Here, Gerald Mullin studies Gabriel's Revolt in Virginia, 1800. Slaves with artisanal skills, much exposure to the non-plantation world, and lacking well-defined relationships with their owners, provided the leadership and inspiration for the insurrection. Consciously manipulating the increasing confusion and laxity of the master class, the Virginia slaves acted to gain their freedom. Their actions were inspired, in part, by the new revolutionary ideology of equality and natural rights espoused by both the American and French Revolutions. The effect of this ideology is only one example of their extensive knowledge of the larger world. References to the French and Haitian Revolutions, to the crisis in American-French foreign relations, and their willingness to spare Frenchmen, Quakers, Methodists, and poor non-slaveholding whites are three further evidences of their political acumen. The sophistication of the slaves' communication network was shown throughout the extensive planning and recruiting for the revolt.

Gerald W. Mullin, "Religion, Acculturation, and American Negro Slave Rebellions," in *Flight and Rebellion: Slave Resistance in Eighteenth-Century Virginia* (New York: Oxford University Press, 1972). Reprinted and all footnotes except fn. 1 omitted by permission of the author and the publisher.

The following article is suggested for further reading:

MARION DE B. KILSON, "Towards Freedom: An Analysis of Slave Revolts in the U.S.," *Phylon* (1964) 175–87.

In the summer of 1800 a group of slave-artisans organized an attack on Richmond.[1] Because their plan was essentially an expression of their class and its understanding of the values and norms of the American Revolutionary era, Gabriel's Rebellion was exceptionally political in character. It never took place; and the following chapter is divided into a narrative conveying the significance of the conspiracy for its participants, and an examination of its preconditions and setting, in order to illuminate the sources of its failure.

"A SOCIETY TO FIGHT THE WHITE PEOPLE FOR [OUR] FREEDOM"

At the gallows in Richmond, Friday noon, 12 September 1800, Colonel Mayo questioned the slaves who were awaiting execution for their part in Gabriel's Rebellion. Mayo asked about his own slave, George, a fugitive and a waitingman, who was implicated in the conspiracy. George was a special slave, an assimilated, a type we have previously encountered in runaway notices. His read:

One Hundred and Fifty Doll[ar]s
REWARD
For stopping the Villain ! ! !
RAN-AWAY on the 25th of July last from the subscriber, near this city

GEORGE

A likely stout made mulatto man, 24 or 25 years of age, five feet eight or nine inches, with a conspicuous [sc]ar under his left jaw, occasioned b[y] a defective tooth, a large scar on the back of his right hand from the

[1] A version of this chapter was presented to the Wayne State University Convocation (May, 1969), "The Black Man in America: 350 Years, 1619–1969" and has been published in Peter I. Rose, ed., *Americans from Africa* (2 vols., New York, 1970), II, 53–74; and in August Meier, Elliot Rudwick, John H. Bracey, Jr., eds., *American Slavery: The Question of Resistance* (Belmont, Calif., 1971), 160–178.

cut of a knife—and a small one inclining obliquely downwards, in the middle of his forehead, occasioned by some accident when a child—stutters a little when about to speak, a bushy head of hair—legs rather small from the constant use of boots, and of sulky looks and temper, except when he chooses to force a deceitful smile—He has served an apprenticeship to the barber's trade—knows a little of shoemaking, and is, when he pleases, a very complete domestic servant.

    . . . As he has several times travelle[d] with me into the Northern states, it is possible he may obtain a forged certificate of freedom, and endeavour to go that way.

As a fugitive and insurrectionist, Mayo's George typifies the men who participated in Gabriel's Rebellion: born in Virginia (not Africa), highly assimilated, well traveled, and versatile in a variety of skilled tasks.

Mayo also asked about his friend and neighbor William Young, whose slaves instigated the rebellion. Although Young was merely negligent (it was necessary for him to publicly defend himself in the Richmond newspapers), his actions called in question the practices of other slaveowners, who on this count were as guilty as he was. This carelessness was indicative of the permissive, confused, and disordered state of slavery in the final years of the eighteenth century: careless and permissive because whites usually ignored such critical features of the slave code as the system of written passes for slaves who traveled, prohibitions against selling slaves, and the supervision of their gatherings. Slavery was also in a confused and indecisive state, because in this period of revolutionary and religious idealism reform ameliorated the slave's condition but seldom made him a free man. Such examples of "humanitarianism" as the liberalized manumission procedure, a restricted slave trade, and the encouragement of the sale of slaves in families (mothers and their children only) did not placate some slaves. Governor James Monroe's remarks to the Governor of South Carolina were representative of the slaveowners misconceptions about the effects of liberalizing slavery without abolishing it outright. "It seemed strange that the slaves should embark in this novel and unexampled enterprise," Monroe reported, "for their treatment has been more favorable since the revolution." Indeed the most puzzling and ominous development for whites was that the conspirators were the same type of relatively highly advantaged men who in the past had seen slavery as an individual problem and typically resisted as solitary fugitives passing as free men. With this avenue of escape and freedom as accessible as ever before, why, they asked, did this class of slaves turn, organize, and fight for their freedom in 1800? As John Mayo rode slowly back into Richmond pondering this "strange" and "novel enterprise" of a few very unusual slaves, we can imagine that he was preoccupied with questions such as these.

Six miles northeast of the city, two months earlier, late on the evening of the tenth of July, one of these slaves stood before a woodpile, axe in hand. He was Ben Woolfolk, a shrewdly intelligent man, hired out to William Young. George Smith, one of the most active recruiters, stepped from the scrubby, pine woods and asked Woolfolk: "would you join a free Mason society?"

"All free Masons would go to hell."
"It [is] not a free mason society I have in mind [but] a society to fight the white people for [our] freedom."

Woolfolk hedged, he would give the idea some thought; but Smith persisted, inviting him to a meeting at a neighboring plantation.

Within the next few weeks, Woolfolk, who was to become the State's principal witness, met several conspirators, including Jack Bowler, a proud and physically overpowering man, who ultimately was one of the few insurrectionists to place the rebellion above his own personal ambitions. Bowler, who was also hired out (his owner, a widow, lived in Urbanna, a small, decaying tobacco port on the lower Rappahannock River), was 28 years old, 6 feet 5 inches tall, scarred above one eye, with long hair worn in a queue and twisted at the sides. He was described by one official as "stra[i]ght made and perhaps as Strong a man as any in the State."

The process of enlisting slaves like Woolfolk intensified the confusion at the beginning of the conspiracy, and underscored the search for form and direction. Leadership positions presumably were open to anyone. But only those who were sufficiently resourceful and persuasive to obtain men and arms came to be leaders, and for a while, no one was in charge. No plans were made, few arms were obtained, and organizers and recruitment were uncoordinated. Gabriel, for example, who operated independently of Smith and Bowler, once mentioned to his brother that he first heard about the conspiracy from Bowler, who, another slave testified, was "determined to raise and Enlist Men and Contend for Command with Gabriel." To this end Bowler engaged in a bit of psychological warfare; he frequently visited the blacksmith shop where Gabriel and his brothers worked, and "repeatedly" challenged them with stories of his accomplishments: the acquisition of seven pounds of gunpowder, and the names of two Frenchmen who were allegedly his contacts. The issue of overall command for a time was unresolved because several conspirators, including Bowler, Smith, and Gabriel, were adept at enlisting slaves into the conspiracy by temporarily overcoming their caution and conservatism.

Opportunities for recruiting men were numerous. Slaves late in the century had a rich fraternal and religious life; and recruiters were sufficiently free of any kind of meaningful supervision to travel extensively to meet slaves at barbecues, Sunday afternoon drinking sessions beneath well-known bridges, at meeting-houses, and outdoor "preachings."

Since the conspirators, like the fugitive slaves before them, depended upon the rivers and watermen, they often depended upon the watermen to recruit for them. Stepney, a waterman whose master lived in Goochland, for example, was arrested for recruiting in Carterville, Cumberland County. An official there was so impressed by his effectiveness with other "batteau men," that he organized a patrol, following the discovery of the plot, which surveyed the upper waters of the James River from Powhatan to Buckingham counties. The insurrection also reached in the opposite direction seventy miles down the peninsula into Gloucester County, where it was effectively organized by another waterman and a preacher. A note left by a third conspirator indicates how religious and social gatherings were used by the organizers: "all you in gloster must keep still yet-brother X will come and prech a sermont to you soon, and then you may no more about the bissiness." Jacob, the waterman, was a skipper of a small vessel that operated off Ware Neck. In the weeks following the collapse of the conspiracy he was charged with taking refugees from that tidewater county into the southside.

Additional organizers worked among the slaves at the canal project at the falls of the James River, and at the coal pits at Tuckahoe (a few miles above Westham on the upper James). A black post rider, who rode the route between Richmond and Amherst counties, carried information into the Albemarle piedmont. He contacted slaves at Ross's Iron Works in Goochland and also brought back intelligence from slaves in the neighborhood of Point of Fork. The Fork, about forty-five miles west of Richmond, was the site of the state arsenal. According to Governor Monroe, here at the junction of the Rivanna and James rivers was the "only place of tolerable security [for whites] in the Commonwealth." Slaves in this vicinity instructed the postman to inform Gabriel that he should delay his attack until they had taken the arsenal and were then proceeding down the river to join him.

In addition to Gabriel and Bowler, three other important recruiters were George Smith, Sam Byrd, Jr., and Woolfolk himself. Byrd—like Smith, one of the first organizers—was the son of a free Negro and the slave of a man who allowed him "to hire his own time." Byrd enlisted 37 men at the Hungary Meetinghouse at Deep Run, Henrico County and "50 odd" in the town of Manchester, across the river from Richmond. At the Young's Spring meeting, he talked of several hundred recruits from Louisa, Petersburg, and "adjacent counties," and about additional trips he made to such faraway places as Hanovertown and Charlottesville; the latter is more than one hundred miles due west of Richmond.

Ben Woolfolk coordinated the Henrico and Caroline County contingents. His contact in Caroline was a blacksmith and another highly assimilated recruiter who usually did not work on his home quarter. Thornton, owned by Paul Thilman of Caroline, worked at the Hanover County courthouse. Two weeks before the attack, Thornton, with Woolfolk, left the blacksmith shop, purchased liquor at Ellis's Tavern—"to treat their men that day"—with money from a "subscription" Gabriel conducted, and moved on to recruit at a "preaching" at Littlepage's Bridge. Following the sermon, they assembled with the men on the creek, drank grog, and discussed "the War." Afterwards back in his shop, Thornton told Woolfolk that he had "about 20 to 30 men" from four plantations. Gabriel would make him a "Captain of Company," Woolfolk said; but Thornton replied, "he was a General and was to go under the name of Colo. Taylor on this occasion & would make his men obey him." Asked if he needed swords, Thornton stated he would arm his own men. Woolfolk observed that the organizers were "at a loss how to make Cartridges"; and immediately, the blacksmith made one and "gave it to him as a Sample." Thornton, a proud and competent man, was the one recruiter who did not find it necessary to exaggerate his resources in men and materials. But as was so often the case with enlistees, including some of the leading recruiters, he appeared once in the documents and the chronology of events and never again. Woolfolk summarized his Caroline County trip for the trial judges by observing: "he left the shop & knows nothing more of Thornton."

"I COULD KILL A WHITE MAN AS FREE AS EAT"

The accounts of the recruitment procedure reveal what the conspiracy meant for most slaves, and indicate how the first group lost the initiative to Gabriel and his brothers, Martin, a preacher, and Solomon, a blacksmith. Recruitment usually followed a pattern. The organizer contacted one man in a small group of blacks, and in words such as these, asked: "was he willing to fight the white people for his freedom?" The enlistee often responded by declaring his hatred for whites and his willingness to kill them without compassion, by sharing his views of the insurrection's goals, and by requesting a command position. Sometimes the leader's questions were put in the context of the slave's manhood or toughness. Patrick was asked "if he was a Man?" Woolfolk told Jacob that he "looked so poor and weakly that he could not kill a man." The response was perhaps predictable, Jacob shot back: "do not take me by my looks, I could kill a white man as free as eat." Following a Sunday barbecue, Gabriel revealed his plans to his two brothers, who locked hands and exclaimed "here are our hands & hearts. We will Wade to our Knees in blood sooner than fail in the attempt." But the leaders were seldom so effusive; and some in the face of certain death were quietly eloquent: "my name is Solomon, and [I] am good, what is of me, for fighting."

Challenges were often made before other men. In one trial, a State witness said that when he recruited the defendant, he asked if he was one of George Smith's men:

> He said yes, by God I am—He asked him if he thought he could kill White people stoutly; Yes says he by God I can; and I will fight for my freedom as long as I have breath, and that is as much as any man can do.

This enlistee's little boy, standing nearby while "minding" one of their master's children, gave his father offence, for which he was whipped. When the master's son also cried, the black man turned and said "if you were big enough you would have my shirt off, but I hope you never will be big enough."

Two members of the rank and file have left full accounts of their transformation from fugitives to insurrectionists. Gilbert, a sensitive and intense man, held deep and positive feelings for his master; while King, a waitingman, was a deeply embittered person, whose hatred for whites was unadulterated.

King's life changed dramatically one July market day in Richmond. While lounging with a group of black men before Francis Vanne's Shop, Woolfolk mentioned that he was "encouraged [by King's] language and deportment." The slave replied, he "never intended, or suffered white people to have much their way with him," and the ritual proceeded in this manner:

	Are you a true man?
PRIS[ONE]R:	I am true hearted man.
WITN[ESS]:	Can you keep a *proper,* or *important* secret?
PRIS[ONE]R:	Yes.
WITN[ESS]:	The Negroes are about to rise and fight the White people for their freedom.

"They ought to have taken the rebellion into consideration a long time ago," King said. "Yes, [he] was ready to join them at any moment," and he would "slay the white people like sheep."

After the conspiracy was discovered, King and another slave entered Mary Martin's Grog Shop "as the Guards were going out." "In a surly & abrupt style," he demanded a drink on credit. Mary refused, "I trust nobody." So King paid and turning to his friend who was journeying to visit his wife, he said he wished he could do the same. Mary joined in: "why didn't he visit his wife?" "It was too far," King said, "and the white people ha[ve] turned so comical a man can't go out of his house now but he's taken up to be hanged." He then asked his companion to tell a mutual friend: "We are all alive as yet, looking hard at the bacon, but can't get at it, as we are doing what we can. What we can't do with our Guns, we will do with Bayonets." Placing his finger to his forehead, King concluded, "nobody knows what is here yet." Mary indulged the court further: "she had no bacon in her shop—nor had they any that she saw." Even though his master petitioned for a pardon, King was condemned and executed on October 3.

Few conspirators outside the small leadership clique were as active in promoting the rebellion as William Young's Gilbert. But in his eagerness to get at whites, he encountered a number of petty, frustrating situations. At the Young's Spring meeting, he replied to Martin's vow—"to turn out & fight with his stick"—that: "he was ready with his pistol, but it was in need of Repair." When approached by Gabriel and asked if he had a sword, Gilbert said his master had one hanging up in the house, which he would get and make himself a belt for it. He also depended on the use of his master's horse, but on the day before the rebellion, he expressed "regret . . . that their master was up the Country," he would "take the Bald." There were larger disappointments compounded by the slave's feelings about himself and his owner. During the conversation about the sword, he "asked to be made a Captain," but Gabriel refused, "saying he stuttered too much to give the word of Command." Later Gilbert also said that his "Master and Mistress should be put to death, but by the men under him (as he could not do it himself) because they raised him."

"THE MAIN SPRING AND CHIEF MOVER"

Gilbert first enlisted with George Smith, who seemed unable to distinguish between a plan and its execution. In fact Smith's recruitment in itself indicated that his group was moving too slowly, indecisively, and ceremoniously. So Gilbert joined Gabriel, because, as he later testified, he realized that Gabriel "would carry the business into execution."

This explanation focuses sharply on the style of Gabriel's leadership. More than any other organizer he sensed the narcotic and self-justifying effects of revolutionary rhetoric and organization. Because he was able to make decisions, delegate responsibilities, and pursue routine tasks to their completion in order to avert the strong possibility of disaster, the rebellion came to be his. And it bore his own quietly methodical, businesslike character. But Gabriel cannot be characterized like Woolfolk and Bowler, because his most essential qualities remain hidden and are not revealed in the manuscripts. Although he is referred to in many depositions, he refused

to confess when captured. Gabriel was a powerful force pushing the conspiracy toward fruition—a man imbued not so much with messianic fervor
as with a grim sense of what had to be done. The whites also recognized
his unusual abilities; a county justice, using an especially appropriate mechanical metaphor, noted that Gabriel was "the Main Spring and Chief
Mover."

Thus the center of the rebellion shifted to Prosser's blacksmith shop,
where Gabriel and his brothers gave form and substance to the notion of
revolution. During the early summer months the conspiracy matured under
their direction. In the second week of August, when William Young left
his plantation for a fortnight, the insurrectionists returned there, ostensibly
to bury a Negro child.

"I CAN NO LONGER BEAR
WHAT [I HAVE] BORNE"

Saturday afternoon, August 10, the mourners drifted back from the black
infant's grave. Gabriel, who often used religious gatherings for his own
political purposes, invited the slaves to drink grog with him on the banks
of the spring. Understanding that he must build a following among the
country people, he ignored secrecy. He asked those assembled who wished
to join him to stand, and those who did not to sit. He and Bowler moved
among the men, promoting the war and enlisting fighters. Unsatisfied with
this cooperative arrangement, Bowler asked rhetorically what Gabriel
would do for war material, and before Gabriel replied, Bowler rushed on
and asked that those "who have agreed to engage in the Insurrection to
give him their Voice for General." "The Votes [were] taken," and "Gabriel
[had] by far the greater number." Although he had miscalculated Gabriel's
hold on the slaves, Bowler was made second in command, a "Captain of
Lighthorse."

Following the election, they debated the critical issue of when to
attack. Although the vernacular was religious, the deliberations were practical and realistic. Some, including a few leaders, were apprehensive. While
recruiting in the countryside, George Smith came to understand the plantation slave's dual nature: his bitter hatred for whites and his inability to do
much about it. So Smith argued that they defer "the business some time
longer." But Gabriel replied, "the Summer was About over, & he wished
them to enter upon the business before the winter got too cold." At this
crucial moment, with the decision in the balance, he suggested that "the
Subject should be referred" to his brother Martin, the preacher, who
stepped forward and intoned: "there was this expression in the Bible that
delays breed danger." But Martin quickly turned from scriptural sanction

to more rational, secular considerations and argued that the time for revolution was very near: the country was at peace, the soldiers were discharged, their arms "all put away," and "there were no patrols in the Country." He paused, then crossing what for many was an insurmountable barrier, Martin spoke from within. "I can no longer bear what [I have] borne." The proceedings were open, and the silence was broken by "others who spoke to the company" and said that Woolfolk had "something to say." Woolfolk also used the Bible, but to loosen the spectre of defeat. "He had heard in the days of old, when the Israelites were in Servitude to King Pharaoh, they were taken from him by the power of God—& were carried away by Moses. . . . But I can see nothing of that kind in these days." Martin quickly replied, "their cause was similar to [the] Israelites' "; but that he had read in his Bible "where God Says, if we worship him, we should have peace in all our land," and "five of you shall conquer an hundred & a hundred a thousand of our enemies." At this point Martin held the floor and made the most important decision: "after this they went into consultation upon the time they should execute the plan. [He] spoke & appointed for them to meet in three weeks which was to be a Saturday night (August 30)." With this achieved, Bowler and Gabriel withdrew into "secret conversations," which were interrupted by the appearance of Young's overseer. The conspirators dispersed after agreeing to meet in front of Moore's schoolhouse the following Sunday (while their masters met within the schoolhouse), "where a final Conclusion on the business would take place."

The conspiracy had peaked at the Young's Spring meeting. In the few weeks before the attack a certain indefinable but no less real revolutionary élan was dissipated—if sustained it might have carried the rank and file from words to deeds. During the meeting itself there were clear signs of a potentially disastrous disunity: Woolfolk's comment about the unfulfilled search for a Moses, George Smith's desire to postpone the rebellion, and the recruiters' deceptive responses to questions about the numbers they had actually enlisted.

The recruiters' exaggerated reports conveyed the enlistee's fervent promise, while in company with his friends, and the recruiters' belief that the command he received would be proportionate to the numbers of enlistees he claimed. When asked to produce their lists, moreover, the organizers often couched their response in vague allusions to the "warehouse boys," the "boys across the river" or the "boys in town." Sam Byrd was asked for his record at the Young's Spring meeting, and he said, while he did not have his list "about him," he "supposed he had about five hundred, who were to be assembled by him and given up to Gabriel on the Night [of] the Attack." Some sensed what was going on. Gilbert asked a Richmond free Negro, Matt Scott, who said he had a hundred men, for his list.

"Some other time," Scott answered; but Gilbert testified, he "never did see the list."

The recruiters' dangerously misleading estimates of men and material were further distorted by the leaders—but only on those occasions when they addressed groups of slaves in the countryside. In one instance, Gabriel himself (while displaying two bullet molds which he said he had worn out producing several pecks of shot) proclaimed that he had nearly 10,000 men: 1000 in Richmond, about 600 in Caroline County and nearly 500 at the Tuckahoe Coal Pits, "besides others at different places." Significantly, estimates of the number prepared to fight diminished as the point of departure approached. Gabriel's statement was made three weeks before the attack, while addressing the gathering at Young's Spring. A week later, August 20, a slave asked Solomon how many would follow them: the answer was 3,000; and nine days later, Gabriel's wife, Nanny, told a black man "that 1000 Men were to meet her husband near Prosser's Tavern the ensuing Night."

But Gabriel understood what was and was not happening with regard to recruitment in the countryside. He only talked of 10,000 men before gatherings of slaves of all kinds; in the privacy of Prosser's blacksmith shop, he carefully assessed his limited resources and planned accordingly. In its tactical dimensions his rebellion was a coup that would hopefully inspire an insurrection: a small guerrilla force of about two hundred men would enter Richmond at midnight, thoroughly terrorize the city by burning its warehouse district and (initially) killing indiscriminately, capturing stores of arms, and taking the governor as a hostage.

The governor, James Monroe, also understood the real nature of the rebellion. When he addressed the State Legislature in December he referred to it as an "experiment," a "project," undertaken by "bold adventurers," who relied on a "successful . . . first effort," rather than a "very extensive preconcerted combination." Against this background, the nature of the slaves' prolific discussions and recruitment is more understandable. The organizers, the "bold adventurers," sought to build a viable following among the country people who, they hoped, would follow up their initial attack. Thus Gabriel's strategy: he recognized that unless he struck suddenly, sensationally, and decisively—presenting slaves as well as free men with a *fait accompli*—there would be no mass uprising.

Gabriel's tactics, which were needlessly complicated, were not as astute as his strategy. Even though the city was the key to his plan, it was decided that the conspirators would gather six miles out in the countryside. They would then enter Richmond in three wings (two would be unarmed), from the north and south. One group would fire the wooden buildings in Rockett's, the warehouse district, in order to draw off the townsmen from the residential areas; the others, commanded by Gabriel, would capture the capitol buildings, the store of arms in the penitentiary, and kidnap the governor. When the whites returned from the fires, tired and confused, the insurgents would close with them. If successful, if the "White people agreed to their freedom," Gabriel would raise a white flag in order to notify "their brothers" outside the city, who would presumably rise up and join the fortified insurrectionists.

There were back-up plans based on the slaves' knowledge that the whites were especially vulnerable in their towns. Gabriel said that if they "sustained any considerable loss," they would "bend their course" for either of two small towns, Hanovertown or Yorktown. At this point their plans trailed off into a vague notion of attempting to "form a junction" with some slaves who "they understood from Mr. Gregory's overseer were in rebellion in some quarter of the country."

The question of who was to direct the initial military operations was also a portent of disaster. Slaves knew little of arms and less of tactical leadership. When asked by his brother whether or not Jack Bowler knew "anything about carrying on war," Gabriel replied negatively. Whom would he employ? Solomon continued. A Frenchman from Caroline County, "who was at the Siege of Yorktown," Gabriel said, "was to meet him at the Brook." The Frenchman was to be "Commander & manager the first day, after exercising the Soldiers"; following the attack, "the command was to be resigned to Gabriel."

This Frenchman was allegedly Charles Quersey who, three or four years prior to the conspiracy, had lived at Francis Corbin's in Caroline. William Young's Gilbert credited Quersey with initiating the rebellion: he "frequently advised the negroes to rise & kill the White people, and said he would help them & shew them how to fight." Gilbert had not seen him "since, but is inform'd by several Negroes, that he has been active in encouraging the Negroes in this late Business." Nineteenth-century folk, fighting desperate anti-colonial battles against overwhelmingly powerful Europeans, often had a similar view: the nationals of a European power hostile to the mother-country would miraculously appear and fight on their side. "They had understood," Woolfolk testified, "that the French were at war with this Country—for the money which was due them & that an army was landed at South Key which they hoped would assist them."

Sound in strategy but bogged down by confusing tactics, imperiled by a lack of men and military leadership, the conspiracy moved into its final days. On the day of the attack, Saturday August 30, at noon, it began to rain. By mid-evening the thunderstorm had swelled streams and washed out roads and bridges. Communication, movement, and morale collapsed. The whites later repeatedly referred to this great storm as "providential."

Although it is a moot point how many men would have met at Prosser's the midnight of August 30, no one came either Saturday or Sunday night when the attack was rescheduled. In the meantime, security was suddenly broken. For months hundreds of slaves, including women and children, had maintained secrecy while listening to the discussions and pondering their places in the new scheme of things. By Saturday morning, however, at least three slaves had informed their masters that this conspiracy was going to become reality. Monroe dispatched two cavalry troops which swept back and forth through the area of the rendezvous. But this was unnecessary because the leaders postponed the attack; one man who came to the Prosser plantation that stormy night was told by Gabriel to return the next evening. But another slave informed (her report: three or four hundred, "some from Town & some from the Country" would meet) and again, the troop commanders' reports were negative. Thus Monroe noted: "I was on the point of concluding there was no foundation for the alarm." And even when he came to a partial understanding of what he was confronting, his deployment of men in the capital indicated the governor's serious misgivings regarding the extent of the conspiracy's penetration among the plantation Negroes.

In the aftermath, the State proceeded cautiously and confidently while making arrests, using informers, and conducting the trials. Within a few days twenty slaves had been captured in Henrico and Caroline counties. Thereafter arrests continued more slowly. On September 15, Monroe wrote Jefferson that ten slaves had been executed and "at least" twenty would be condemned and "perhaps forty." The former estimate is closer to the total number executed; but the exact number of convictions is unknown because the record of payments to the slaveowners is incomplete. At least twelve slaves were acquitted, one of whom was Sam Byrd's free father, who was accused of recruiting in Hanovertown. Another seven conspirators were pardoned.

"THE BUSINESS ONLY REQUIRED A BEGINNING"

For Gabriel the final scene comprised many of the elements that so often made slavery a tragic and crazy reality for even the most talented and resourceful slaves. In his last moments of real freedom, he was aided by a white and betrayed by a black.

Richardson Taylor, who tried to carry Gabriel to safety, was the master of the schooner *Mary* and an embodiment of the fiercely contradictory values of his post-war society. Taylor was a "family man," an ex-overseer, a ship captain with a crew of slaves, and an anti-slavery Methodist. Although he later feigned innocence by virtue of his ignorance of the matter, Taylor knew about Gabriel. Before he weighed anchor in Richmond and dropped down the James toward Norfolk, several insurrectionists were tried and executed. Late Saturday night, September 17, the *Mary* conveniently ran onto Ward's Reach, four miles below the capital. The following morning Gabriel ran from a patch of woods, crossed the sand bar, and after tossing his bayonet into the water, was taken aboard. Taylor later claimed that he was "unwell" during this episode; when he awoke the ship was underway. Coming on deck he questioned his strange passenger, who said he was a free Negro, Daniel, but unfortunately, he had left his manumission papers ashore. While Taylor let the matter drop, his slave crewmen, Isham and Billy, insisted that the man was Gabriel, and "it was their opinion that he was the person (for whom) the reward was offer[e]d."

The *Mary* was eleven days in passage. Taylor overlooked numerous opportunities to put ashore and either inquire about or dispose of his strange passenger. When he was finally boarded by an official in Norfolk, he said nothing about Gabriel. But Isham, who later testified that he was to be freed if he converted to Methodism, brought the officials back to the ship. They were amazed: "Capt. Taylor is an old inhabitant been an overseer & must have known that neither free blacks nor slaves could travel in this Country without papers." This time Gabriel left in chains; and although he once mentioned he would talk about the rebellion—but only to Monroe—he remained silent while he awaited execution.

In the weeks following the trials, there were a series of small insurrectionary actions throughout the state. In November Paul Thilman, the owner of the Caroline County blacksmith, Thornton, reported that the Negroes "in the neighbourhood" of the Hanover County courthouse had been "very riotous & ungovernable" on a Thursday and Friday. On Saturday they broke into a jail and set free two insurrectionists who were handcuffed and chained to the floor. Once free, the prisoners assaulted the guard, "knocked him down stamped [on] him" and ran off. "A great number of Negroes were present & pretended" to pursue them. Thilman felt that the jail-break was well planned in that "a great number" of slaves had visited the prisoners throughout the week "under the pretence of a preaching." He reported an additional "incident" in Hanover which further indicated that the "concert" between that county's slaves and those in Caroline was still intact. Mr. Paul Woolfolk, "going down his plantation," fell in with two slaves armed with "bayonets." Woolfolk, who was armed with an axe, "threaten[ed] them with an assault" if they did not surrender. The slaves, equal to the occasion, told him "to come on, they were ready for him—that they would go where they pleased." They did, and were last reported crossing Charles Carter's plantation.

But the slaves' unusually open and violent activities were uncoordinated. In the grim days following the discovery of the conspiracy, it became clearly evident that rebellion waited on Gabriel and his few "bold adventurers." In court the following testimony was typical: "all the negroes in Petersburg were to join him [Gabriel] after he had commenced the insurrection"; "as soon as the boys on this side made a *brake,* the boys from Manchester would come over and join them." On the weekend following the storm, about a hundred and fifty slaves actually gathered at Whitlock's Mill outside Norfolk. "They never left this neighborhood until the Tuesday after it was known that the Richmond plan had failed," reported one planter. When a number of "mulattoes, negroes, & some whites, whose connections were with the negroes," were examined, they said that the people at the mill were "to do what those of Richmond were about to do." Nor did the slaves' expectations readily subside. Three months later one Benjamin DuVal wrote Monroe that he had overheard a "parcel" of Richmond Negroes talking about the "Norfolk Cowards." "Cowards & Liberty" was "several times expressed conjoined with other words that I could not distinctly hear." And one Negro said "that there never was or would be a better time than the present," and observed "that the business only required a beginning."

Three weeks after the conspiracy was discovered one of Gabriel's recruiters in Gloucester County hurriedly shoved a note into the neck of a bottle, which he dropped alongside the old road that runs past the court house to Ware's Neck. The letter concerned Jacob, the black skipper who carried refugees from Gloucester into the southside:

> September 20: 1800
> dear frind
> Tel jacob at john Williams johny is taken up and wil be hanged i is afraide so all you in gloster must keep still yet brother X will come and prech a sermont to you soon, and then you may no more about the bissiness. i must be killed if the white peple catch me and carry me to richmon
> i am your tru frind
> A.W.

In the bitter aftermath of the rebellion that did not happen, running away was once again the only alternative for slaves who refused to accept slavery. Even though insurrection was in the air, and "only required a beginning," the slaves "looked at the bacon" but "couldn't get at it."

"It is always the individual that really thinks and acts and dreams and revolts," wrote Edward Sapir many years ago. Although the significance of Gabriel's Insurrection lies in its narration, in its tragic, personal dimension, a discussion of its most strategic preconditions completes a view of the revolutionary situation of 1775 and 1800. There are essentially four ways of examining the insurrection's setting and what accounted for its failure. These categories are: the nature of the conspirators' tasks; their understanding of the values of the Revolutionary era; their views of religious revivalism; and the relationship between acculturation levels and patterns of slave behavior in the late eighteenth century.

Depositions and lists supplied by informers offer a fairly complete picture of the conspirators' place and function in society. The insurrectionists were unified by common work experiences. Several were from coal mines, iron foundries, and ropewalks—industries whose growth in scale and number was quickened by the war—or, from such new industries as the Public Canal Works. Privileged domestics, who have not fared too well in studies of American Negro slavery, were as well represented as any other group: Robin and Charles, waiters at the Eagle Tavern and Priddy's Ordinary, janitors and custodians who worked in the Capitol buildings and the penitentiary, as well as the waitingmen, King, and John Mayo's George. Blacksmiths from Goochland, Caroline, and Henrico counties, the only type of highly esteemed craftsmen represented, played a crucial role as recruiters. Several warehousemen were also implicated. Others worked at assignments which required extensive travel; they included several boatmen (from the upper waters of the James between Powhatan and Buckingham counties), and the postman who rode the route between Richmond and Charlottesville. These men were more independent than all the other conspirators, for they only rarely worked in the company of whites. While the insurrectionists' backgrounds cut across several categories—semi-skilled and skilled, routine and artistic—they all thoroughly understood society outside the plantation, in which they traveled so freely.

The conspirators, in fact, were more autonomous than the slaves they would lead. They had a life of their own—masters are conspicuously absent from their lengthy and detailed depositions—and the only whites who participated in any meaningful way in their activities were those whom the slaves could use—Methodists, petty merchants, and tavernkeepers. Several were owned by women; at least three came from estates in probate. Several who were hired out or allowed to hire their own time were also at least a step or two removed from their masters. In this period of economic readjustment and diversification, allowing a slave to hire his own time was an illegal but highly popular and profitable practice. And some were so far removed from their masters that their provenance was difficult to determine. One confused official described William Young's Gilbert in the following manner: "at the time the Fire took place at Mr. Percells, he was then living with John Young in Caroline County." And Brutus, "alias Julius," who belonged to William Anderson, had been hired out to a prominent Richmond physician, Dr. William Foushee, at which time he ran off and joined the rebellion.

These outwardly rebellious men are by now familiar. They were the same type of slave who had previously possessed the requisite skills to run off and pass as free men. But by the end of the century a significant change had taken place in the revolutionary awareness of men who had previously viewed slavery as an individual problem and resisted it as fugitives. These men and this change, in fact, are the key to the relationship between the social and personal dimensions of the conspiracy. Writing in 1801 about fugitives who became insurrectionists, St. George Tucker, aristocrat and lawyer, analyzed the conspiracy's preconditions for the state legislature. Comparing the slaves' reactions to Dunmore and Gabriel, he discussed their exceptionally rapid material and spiritual development in the "few short years" following the war. He attributed their new outlook to the growth of towns, trades, and a complementary increase in the extent of literacy among slaves. More opportunities for work in commercial areas brought about a "prodigious change" in the skilled slaves' outlook, a change Tucker characterized as the "love of freedom," and that "evolving spirit we fear." While only a few runaways, a "few solitary individuals," joined the British in 1775, the insurrectionists of 1800 organized extensively in order to "assert their claims, while rest[ing] their safety on success alone." The difference between the two rebellions, Tucker argued, was basically ideological: whereas in 1775 slaves "fought [for] freedom merely as a good; now they also claim it as a right."

Thus in the closing years of the century, revolutionary conflict and ideology were resolved for most free men, but not for black men, especially if they were artisans. Between 1775 and 1800, a type of slave who was literate, skilled, mobile, and working in a commercial environment accepted the fact that regardless of his comparatively privileged position, and the whites' efforts to ameliorate slavery, the institution would survive and grow. Skilled slaves had become sufficiently marginal to believe that the values and "rights" of the Revolutionary era were theirs also and that they were sufficiently resourceful and strategically placed to do something about their situation with the aid of other men. Nonetheless, their expanded revolutionary consciousness was still focused by their traditional and relatively advantaged positions. So, to the extent that they were motivated by ideas, these ideas established definite boundaries of their revolutionary action.

The insurrectionists' goals were essentially political. While using the rhetoric of their generation to clearly distinguish between oppressors and victims, white as well as black, they displayed a keen sense of their own time and place. One man testified that he wanted "to fight for his Country," and another said they were to "subdue the whole of the Country where Slavery was permitted but no further." "As far as I understand all the whites were to be massacred, except the Quakers, the Methodists & Frenchmen," Woolfolk testified, and "they were to be spared on account as they conceived of their being friendly to liberty." Prosser's Ben, an 18-year-old who worked beside Gabriel in the blacksmith shop, mentioned that "whites were to [be] murdered & killed indiscriminately excepting French Men, none of whome were to be touched." And another said simply, they "intended to spare all poor white women who had no slaves." The continual discussions of who was to be spared or killed, as well as the occasionally cathartic posturing that characterized the recruitment process, seldom impaired the participant's expression of his clear understanding of the leading principles of the day.

The organizers' discussions regarding Richmond are even more informative of both the origin and political character of their revolutionary style. These rational and calculating men were neither self-indulgent nor self-destructive; for at times, it seemed, they wanted a political settlement, not a reformation. Gabriel once said that all townsmen excepting those who agreed to fight with them would be killed. His brother remarked in passing that they were to possess themselves of the whites' property; and George Smith asked that they preserve the brick storehouses in Rockett's "for their own use." Recall their strategy: the insurgents would fortify the city, take the governor hostage and then—it is assumed—they would negotiate. At this point, Gabriel again set the tone. When the capital was secured, "on the day it should be agreed to," he "would dine and drink with the merchants of the City."

The occupational and ideological values which separated organizers from those they had to recruit were basically a function of their comparatively more thorough acculturation. The slaves' awareness of their profound cultural differences was sharpened by the dramatic quality of religious life at the end of the century. The country people, reluctant and suspicious, came off the quarters and gathered at the large and exciting revival meetings of the Great Awakening. Seeking spiritual assistance, they were confronted by Gabriel and his men, who used the meetings to disguise both their real intentions and the structure of their organization, and to recruit men and discuss tactics. The high point of the revival was the exhortation which, if it had been used by Gabriel, could have been the catalyst for changing religious fervor and concern for the hereafter into revolutionary action in the here-and-now. But this never happened. The leaders and their potential followers were faithful in different ways. The conspiracy was composed of autonomous men confronting religious men. Because of the nature of its leader and the rational, political character of its goals, Gabriel's Rebellion never became a viable part of the great religious revivals.

Because religious and eschatological elements often generate the large-scale rebellions of pre-industrial folk, perhaps it was not merely coincidental that one leader looked beyond the country people's fundamentalism to an even more ancient heritage which leavened their Christianity. For some, like the leader George Smith, Africa was still a very meaningful part of their lives. Smith, who was closer to the soil and the harvest cycles than any other organizer, once proposed that he hire his own time, travel down-country to what he called the "pipeing tree," and enlist the "Outlandish people." For they were "supposed to deal with Witches and Wizards, and thus [would be] useful in Armies to tell when any calamity was about to befall them." Whether or not Smith later talked about bullets turning to water is an intriguing conjecture, but he did announce to the gathering at Young's Spring that when he finished plowing his master's corn field, he would make as many crossbows "as he could," an equally fantastic proposition. Although there was no more said about wizards, crossbows, and Africa, Smith, in his own way, called attention to the one means—charisma—by which the slaves could have transcended their significant cultural and occupational differences. But his proposal (as well as Woolfolk's unfulfilled search for a Moses) calls attention to the relationship between acculturation levels and religious beliefs and practices, on the one hand, and styles of resistance, on the other. Here is the source of Gabriel's failure: at a time when revivalism was a vital force among plantation slaves, those who would lead couched their appeal in political and secular terms. Unlike Nat Turner's magnificent Old Testament visions, which transfigured him and sustained his movement, Gabriel's Rebellion, lacking a sacred dimension, was without a Moses, and thus without a following.

Preliminary research indicates that an understanding of the acculturative experience, as a hitherto neglected dimension of slavery, may also enrich our studies of the other major insurrections about which the slaves have provided ample testimony. The cultural differences among slaves—so evident and divisive in the 1800 rebellion—were also manifested in the religious contexts of the insurrections of Denmark Vesey (Charleston, South Carolina, 1822) and Nat Turner (Southampton County, Virginia, 1831).

Religion and magic sustained Nat Turner's Rebellion. Executed by plantation slaves in an economically backward area, this insurrection was not as politically coherent and extensive as Gabriel's. Turner, who was not a preacher in the conventional sense but a seer and a holy man, also politicized his men by means of dream interpretations and feats of fortune-telling and numerology. In this instance too, a celestial event (an eclipse of the sun) made a tremendous impact on the black country folk; but they were prepared to see it as a favorable sign. Denmark Vesey, the third great insurrectionist, stands midway between Gabriel and Turner. While he normally based his appeal on political grounds, he recognized the connection between religious sanctions and rebellion from below. On a few special occasions he used sermons based on the Bible; and he also delegated to Gullah Jack, a native African and "doctor," the responsibility of forming the rural blacks of the low country's sea islands into "African legions." But, like Gabriel, he failed, because his rebellion was urban-based and restricted to artisans, shopkeepers, and free Negroes. Only Nat Turner, who charged his plan with supernatural signs, and sacred, poetic language that inspired action, was able to transcend the worlds of the plantation and the city. Only Turner led a "sustained" insurrection.

But Gabriel's men were ensnared in an earlier and a different era. Although these artisans, by 1800, had become so much more numerous, strategically placed, and imbued with an ideology supporting collective action, they were still isolated—cut off not only from their own people, but from the new economic realities of the ante-bellum period. There was in this conspiracy, then, a note of cultural despair. Since the South after the introduction of Eli Whitney's gin was again moving away from manufactures and economic diversification, the occupational strata and milieu productive of this type of slave was rapidly becoming anachronistic. Hence from this threat to their way of life came this group's despair. Isaac declared "if the [insurrection] was not soon he would run off, as he was determined not to serve a white man [for] another year," and Martin said "he could no longer bear what he had borne." To a third, the transformation from slave to free man was forthrightly expressed: "I will kill or be killed." And Solomon, one of the few mulattoes in the conspiracy, joined and died even though he was to be legally free at age thirty-one.

But where were the other slaves? The reality of slavery in post-war Virginia was radically different for leaders and followers. An elite initiated, planned, and dominated Gabriel's Rebellion. In the four months before the insurrection they lived and were sustained by it; they knew one another well. Living with death, they accepted it. Slowly and profoundly freedom, revolution, and death came to be a large part of their lives. Meanwhile, the rank and file simply raised their hands at meetings; a few personalized their commitment by volunteering for specific responsibilities and acquiring weapons. Enlisting in the most inauthentic manner, they did not share the leaders' distinctive revolutionary awareness. Thus their commitment was fragile at best; and in the end, Gabriel and his men stood alone.

Slavery in eighteenth-century Virginia was remarkably flexible and unstructured, in part because the society itself was unsettled, rapidly growing, and insecure. Central to this openness was the planters' overwhelming need for self-sufficiency. Although they were politically and economically subservient to Great Britain, and absolutely dependent on African slaves, patriarchs wished to be "independent on every one but Providence."

In their quest for this goal, slaveowners esteemed highly those Africans who began to change their ways and were then capable, in their masters' eyes, of becoming skilled and of forming the very basis for the planters' vaunted autonomy. Paradoxically, acculturation—the changes by which the African's customs fell away as he acquired English and occupational specialization—ultimately created slaves who were able to challenge the security of the society itself.

Viewing acculturation as another dimension of slave behavior in the colonial period not only clarifies our understanding of adjustments to slavery, but calls attention to the most important ways in which slavery changed as it developed from the colonial to the ante-bellum period. Acculturation and work were the most important variables determining a slave's adjustment. As a new arrival, the African initially reacted to the strange and hostile society on the basis of his communal upbringing. For him, procurement was a brutal but not a brutalizing experience; the "outlandish" African remained a man, and for a time, a highly distinctive slave. In fact, until his prior cultural sanctions proved unworkable, such measurable evidence of acculturation as speaking English did not occur.

Nearly all Africans soon became "new Negroes"—field hands on the up-country quarters. For these men, as well as the field laborers and house servants on the home plantation, resistance was an inward-directed endeavor. Plantation slaves turned their limited rebelliousness back toward the plantation setting itself; their reactions were usually easily contained; they brought a direct, punitive response, and seldom improved the slave's status. But some of this resistance was cooperative, and it was especially effective because the plantation was so vulnerable to acts of sabotage.

A few Africans and many of their American-born children learned proficient English, acquired an intelligent demeanor, advanced in the work hierarchy, and so became relatively assimilated. These men were self-reliant, individualistic, and less cooperative. This is what the colonists desired; slaves who were more like themselves were slaves they could better understand. But these men, in jobs where they learned to function resourcefully in the colonial society outside the plantation, came to understand that they still had little control over their lives. When they resisted, then, it was, for three-quarters of the century, directed away from the plantations; as resourceful fugitives, the skilled slaves went to towns, passed as free men, and found work. They were still unable to escape slavery completely, however; they still contributed their labor to the society, although more on their own terms than previously.

As the assimilateds replaced the Africans in the slave population, traditional arrangements between slaves and free men, in the last quarter of the century, became dangerously outmoded. More slaves were able to resist in ways which challenged their masters' (and the society's) traditional sense of security. These developments, coupled with the changes in the economic and political realities of the revolutionary era, brought about Gabriel's Rebellion. Slavery in the nineteenth century would be based on a heritage more American than African.

The Beginnings
of a New Society
1815-1843

Between 1815 and 1843 the factory system came to America. The development of a complex transportation network of roads, river improvements, canals, and railroads opened the American hinterland to metropolitan wares. These transport improvements were developed at heavy expense to the public as first local, state, and finally the federal government spent huge sums. Many of these systems were built in direct competition with each other as east coast entrepôt cities engaged in an orgy of spending to acquire the expanding western markets.

These rapid changes affected the lives of most Americans. Agriculture was transformed in many areas from subsistence farming to production for markets, and some farmers' wives were freed from home manufacturing. Artisans in the cities began to face the denigration of their trades as various industries began the transition to machine and factory production. These changes happened over long periods of time and the development was uneven both geographically and temporally. Artisans no longer needed in cities might retreat to outlying areas to ply their trade. Equally, certain crafts resisted industrial incursions far longer periods than others.

Change of such a magnitude carried with it extreme dislocations. Overt rhetorical resistance greeted the optimistic harbingers of a better world, and movements developed in opposition to the growth of factory production. The development of an articulate labor movement in the 1830s, the Owenite and Fourierist communities, the various social reform movements, and the widespread outbreak of evangelical and perfectionist Christianity should all be seen, in part, as responses to a society undergoing profound change.

In the south, the slave system became more deeply entrenched as it spread to the southwest. As cotton profits soared and as a radical abolition movement arose in the north, sectional politics began to play a more pronounced role in the life of the country. Frequent and bitter congressional tariff debates demonstrated these new tensions. The north sought protection for its nascent industry, the south sought free trade for its commercial crops. The role of banks and the allocation of land in western expansion also aroused heated debate during this period.

The following works are suggested for further reading:

CARTER GOODRICH (ed.), *Canals and American Economic Development,* New York: Columbia University Press, 1961.

CARTER GOODRICH, *Government Promotion of American Canals & Railroads, 1800–1890,* New York: Columbia University Press, 1960.

ROBERT LIVELY, "The American Business System, A Review Article," *Business History Review* (1955) 81–96.

GEORGE ROGERS TAYLOR, *The Transportation Revolution,* New York: Harper Torchbooks, Harper & Row, Publishers, 1951.

3.1

Assault on the Artisan Life Style:
The Case of New England Shoemakers

NORMAN WARE

In this short section from *The Industrial Worker 1840–1860,* Norman Ware describes the transition from artisanal to factory production in the shoe industry. Ware begins with an analysis of the whole life of the artisan shoemakers and describes his almost complete control over the work process. He then turns to the shoemaker in his community. Finally, we see how the incursions of industrialism began to change this world and how the artisan reacted to these enforced changes.

The following book is suggested for further reading:

GEORGE TAYLOR, *The Transportation Revolution,* New York: Harper Torchbooks, Harper & Row, Publishers, 1951, Chs. 10–13.

Norman Ware, *The Industrial Worker, 1840–1860* (Chicago: Quadrangle Books, Inc., 1964), pp. 38–48. Copyright © 1964 by Quadrangle Books, Inc. Reprinted and footnotes omitted by permission of the publisher.

The changes in the boot and shoe industry in the forties and fifties were of two sorts: those that were simply a continuation and accentuation of changes found in the preceding period, and those arising from the introduction of machinery. In the preceding decades the wholesale manufacture of shoes was increasingly supplanting the custom and retail shop work and the rewards of labor had fallen correspondingly. Custom work had paid from $1.40 to $2.75 per pair from 1800 to 1810. In 1835, wholesale work paid only $1.12½ per pair. The important changes in the position of the shoemaker in our period were effected by the displacement of the merchant capitalist by the factory owner as the chief organizer of production. This change was facilitated by the failure of many of the older New England firms in the depression of 1837–39.

Thus we find three stages in the social revolution in the shoe trade up to 1860: the stage of the master workman and his journeymen, up to 1830; the merchant capitalist stage, to 1840; and the stage of the factory owner, with or without machinery, until 1860. The character of the merchant capitalist stage, from the standpoint of the master and journeyman, is seen in the protest of the journeymen cordwainers of Philadelphia in 1835:

> If we take a retrospective view of our trade we will find that a few years ago the slowest of our profession could earn at least seven or eight dollars per week and that by no greater exertion than it now requires to make four or five. . . . From that time to the present the trade has been gradually sinking, at least so far as the interests of the journeymen are concerned. The cunning men from the East have come to our city, and having capital themselves, or joining with those who had, have embarked in our business and realized large fortunes by reduction of our wages. . . .

The transition to the factory system was not far advanced in the beginning of our period. Lynn, Massachusetts, was the center of the women's shoe trade and was only emerging at this time from the domestic system. The domestic worker at Lynn had been part farmer, part artisan, part fisherman. If one of his three props failed him, he could fall back on another. He felt that he could work in the fields or in the shop as he chose, and when disinclined for either he could lock up his "ten-footer" [1] and go fishing. When it was too cold for work indoors or out, he sat in his kitchen reading. Both the men and women who worked on shoes in the earlier days did so irregularly and at their own request.

[1] The "ten-footer" was the small shoe shop beside the shoemaker's home. In size it varied from 10′ × 10′ to 14′ × 14′, and averaged about 12′ × 12′. The numbers working in these shops varied from four to eight. The shops contained benches and tools, fireplaces, and, later, stoves.

The change of status involved in the transfer to the factory system is best seen in the character of unemployment. In domestic production, unemployment meant leisure and a change of work—a change that was often pleasant and sometimes profitable. But as trade specialization and urban conditions developed, unemployment spelled increasingly want and discontent.

In 1830 nearly all the shoemakers of Lynn had owned their homes with some land about them. Even those who rented had usually large gardens where they were able to raise sufficient vegetables for their winter supply. Almost every family kept a pig and many had their own cow. Discipline in the little shop was slack. When an apprentice left his work at night, "he might be expected back in the morning, but there were no special grounds for the expectation. He might drop in the next morning or the next week."

The panic of 1837 was less distressing in its results for the Lynn shoemakers than it would have been at a later period because of the still primitive nature of the industrial situation. With a garden, a pig, and some fishing tackle the shoemaker "could bid defiance to financial tempests." In the winter he could go clam and eel hunting, and if he had two or three cords of wool split and piled in the shed he considered himself in easy circumstances.

> When the spring opened, the horizon of his hopes expanded. Less clothing and fuel were needed. The clam banks discounted more readily; haddock could be got at Swampscott so cheap that the price wasn't worth quoting. The boys could dig dandelions. . . . Then if the poor man had his little "spring pig" that he had kept through the winter, "pork and dandelions" were no small items in the bill of fare while "greens" lasted.

It is well no doubt to be skeptical of a Golden Age either past or future, and well, too, to discount reminiscences, but the evidence is considerable of the reality of the freedom and security of these people.

The shoemaker had always been regarded as a thoughtful and intelligent artistan. Every shoeshop was a lyceum. It was a common thing for the journeymen to hire a boy to read the paper to them while they worked. No villages stood higher than the shoe villages of New England, according to Amasa Walker, in the moral, social, and intellectual condition of their inhabitants. The shoemakers were distinguished for general intelligence. It was a social business, conversation was not drowned by the noise of machinery, and there were many opportunities for reading and mutual improvement.

But the days of independence, culture, and security were fast passing for the shoemakers of Lynn at the beginning of the forties. Increasingly they were being drawn into the new order of things, their standards of living declining, and their dependence upon the masters increasing. The depression of 1837–39 had done much to reduce them, but seven lean years intervened before they gave voice to their discontent. From 1831 to 1837, cash had been substituted for store orders in the payment of wages. But in the years of the depression, the process was reversed and store orders were again substituted for cash. It was claimed by the manufacturers that they were forced to accept truck in payment for shoes and that during the bad years the journeymen were glad enough to get what payment they could. But with the improvement of business conditions in 1843, the old wages and old methods of payment were continued, though prices were beginning to advance.

The store-order system of payment was the immediate cause of the protest of the shoemakers in 1844. At this date there was formed at Lynn a Journeyman Cordwainers' Society which began the publication of a workers' paper, "The Awl." The journeymen claimed that the shoe manufacturers, while pretending to pay a living wage, "did by other means reduce them to degradation and the loss of that self-respect which had made the mechanics and laborers the pride of the world"; that they had suffered much privation for several years because of the low price paid for their work; and that they were "cursed with the order system" which was known to rob the families of their support, their children of the benefit of "the higher branches of education," and themselves of many of the comforts of life, while it enriched employers and tradesmen, created distinctions "antirepublican in character, which assimilate very nearly to those that exist between the aristocracy and the laboring classes of Europe." The system was characterized as a "willful and deliberate attempt by the moneyed aristocracy to degrade, freeze, and starve the poor. . . ."

The Lynn shoemakers, after they had completed their own organization, sent a circular to the shoemakers throughout New England asking their coöperation in an attempt to get better prices. "Let us prove," they wrote, "that we are not menials or the humble subjects of a foreign despot, but free, American citizens." At the same time they admitted, "We are slaves in the strictest sense of the word. For do we not have to toil from the rising of the sun to the going down of the same for our masters—aye, masters, and for our daily bread?" Strangers, like Miss Martineau, said of them, "How happy these shoemakers must be! Look at the beautiful dwellings! How neat and comfortable they look!" But that was the bright side of the picture. "Who owns," they ask, "these neat and pretty houses which are a delight to look upon? Why, those who have grown fat upon the earnings of the toil-worn laborer. . . ."

The shoemakers signed a "declaration of independence":

Whereas, our employers have robbed us of certain rights which they will, in our opinion, never voluntarily restore . . . we feel bound to rise unitedly in our strength and burst asunder as freemen ought the shackles and fetters with which they have long been chaining and binding us, by an unjust and unchristian use of power and a host of advantages which the possession of capital and superior knowledge furnishes. . . .

Alongside this language of agitation that tends frequently to class consciousness, there is found as well the older attitude of community of interest between journeyman and boss. The shoemakers were still far from having extricated themselves from the older tradition, and much of the language in which their protests are couched must be discounted. They frequently stop themselves in their tirades against the bosses to distinguish between "good" bosses and those that were not so good. "The Awl" started out with a statement that its purpose was to benefit everyone connected with the trade. "We do not advocate the claims of the jour in opposition to those of the employer, nor seek to benefit the one at the expense of the other." But this did not involve the dependence upon the philanthropy of the employers that is to be found in the pitiful appeal of the needlewomen "To the Humane." It was as far removed from subservience as from ideas of class war. "This society," said the cordwainers, "intends . . . to respect our employers, but no more than any other man—ourselves likewise." "We hold it our duty to maintain the value of labor that it may itself be respectable . . . and respected."

As compared with other mechanics, the wages of the Lynn shoemakers were low. Some could earn from $8 to $10 a week at certain seasons of the year, and some might earn $300 to $400 a year. But as a class, they did not average more than $4 or $5 a week, while carpenters, painters and masons were receiving $1.25 to $2 a day. Taking $5 a week as the average, a journeyman would earn $260 a year. This was not paid in cash except by special agreement, but in orders on the Lynn Mechanics' Union and other stores. The journeyman had to take these orders or nothing, and the goods at these stores were marked up at exorbitant prices. In dull times it was often impossible to get adequate quantities. The loss to the worker as a result of the order system was about 33 per cent, so that his income of $260 shrank to $175, supposing he received $5 a week. If he averaged only $4 a week, his annual wage was reduced to $139.

A committee was sent out by the Lynn Society to help organize all the shoe towns in New England and arrange to have them send delegates to a New England Convention of Cordwainers to be held on August 1st. One object of this convention was to prepare for the New England Convention of Mechanics and Laborers that had been called by the Fall River mechanics and laborers. A further purpose was the fixing of a scale of prices for the shoe industry over the whole country as far south as Philadelphia, and setting a day when every journeyman should "march up to his boss and demand a just and fair compensation for his labor." They hoped, too, to do away with the practice of the employers of taking apprentices for a few weeks and "learning them to make one kind of shoe, or what is called a shoe, and thereby multiplying poor workmen and filling our market with miserable goods." Finally they proposed to raise the reputation of the town by doing their work more faithfully.

A strike call was sent to all the shoemakers' societies of New England, New York and Philadelphia. Some of the outside societies signified their intention of taking the matter up, but nothing was done and no strike took place. Several "Associated Labor Societies" were formed to make shoes from their own stock and secure to themselves the profits of their labors. Twenty-five or fifty journeymen would invest fifty to one hundred dollars each, select one of their own number as agent, and go to work.

A meeting of the New York cordwainers was held on June 26, 1844, at which the call for a New England convention was approved and it was decided to send delegates. The New York meeting asserted that labor not only "does not receive its just reward in this Republic, but that its compensation is growing less . . ." and resolved to have a union of trades, "to render labor independent of, if not master over, machines, and get a fair average of fruits for a fair average of work."

> There is no class of mechanics in New York [it was claimed by the "Tribune"] who average so great an amount of work for so little money as the journeymen shoemakers. The number of journeymen out of employment is also large. . . . There are hundreds of them in the city constantly wandering from shop to shop in search of work, while many of them have families in a state of absolute want. . . . We have been in more than fifty cellars in different parts of the city, each inhabited by a shoemaker and his family. The floor is made of rough plank laid loosely down, the ceiling is not quite so high as a tall man. The walls are dark and damp, and a wide, desolate fireplace yawns in the center to the right of the entrance. There is no outlet back and of course no yard privileges of any kind. The miserable room is lighted only by a shallow sash, partly projecting above the surface of the ground and by the little light that struggles down the steep and rotting stairs. In this . . . often live the man with his work-bench, his wife and five or six children of all ages, and perhaps a palsied grandfather or grandmother and often both. In one corner is a squalid bed and the room elsewhere is occupied by the work-bench, a cradle made from a dry-goods box, two or three broken, seatless chairs, a stew-pan and a kettle.

There were at this time 5000 to 6000 shoemakers in New York City and, as a result of recent immigration, "competition had been carried to such a degree as almost to drive the American mechanic from his work-bench." The greater part of the new journeymen were Germans, Irish and French. The shoemakers in the "men's branch" had had a society, "The United Benefit Society of Cordwainers in the Men's Branch of the City of New York," since the close of the Revolutionary War. This society had always been in a flourishing condition, and in 1845 had three hundred members, most of whom were Irish. Its objects were the regulation of hours and prices and the maintenance of sickness and death benefits.

A New York shoemaker at this time could make three pairs of bottoms a week, working ten hours a day, and was paid $1.75 to $2.25 a pair. His average wage was between $4 and $6 a week, but many could earn $7, $8, and even $9. Paid by the month, the journeyman would get from $4 to $12 and board, lodging, and washing. This was on the coarser sort of boots.

The New York cordwainers in the ladies' branch had no permanent organization, but a meeting was called in April, 1846, to protest against reduced prices. They claimed that a reduction of 29 cents had been made in prices since the spring of 1843, and that the advance gained by the strike of 1845 was lost again in the winter of 1845–46. In 1853 it was said that the New York cordwainers could average $7 to $8 a week, an increase of about $1 a week over the wages of 1842–43, "yet in consequence of the much enhanced price of provisions and rent . . . it is certain that the condition of the boot and shoe makers in this city has retrograded." There were many shops where even money wages had declined.

From 1855, or a little later, the workmen began to leave the little shops to work in the factories, and in a few years vacant "ten-footers" were seen all over Lynn. These were transformed into hen-houses or coal-pens, and some of the larger ones were sold to the poor to be fitted up as dwellings, probably improved by an addition.

Wage reductions in the shoe trade in 1858 and 1859 resulted in numerous and prolonged strikes. One of the largest of these was at Natick in 1859, when eight hundred men were successful after being out for fourteen weeks for an advance of wages to cover the reductions of the panic year. A compromise resulted from a similar strike at Marlboro, where one hundred men were out for three weeks. At Lynn, the journeymen struck against a reduction of wages in February, 1860. They had no organization at this time, but held processions and meetings and there was some rioting. Troops were called out and the Boston police were sent in. The strike spread through the shoe towns of Massachusetts and a general labor demonstration was projected for March 7th at Lynn. On March 5th, the women stitchers, binders, and machine operatives joined the strikers, and meetings were held at Liberty Hall where delegations were received from Salem, Beverly, Danvers, Woburn, Marblehead, etc. Over five thousand men and one thousand women marched in procession carrying one hundred banners and twenty-six American flags, and accompanied by five bands, and military and fire companies. It was said to have been the largest labor demonstration Massachusetts experienced up to 1880. But "the vacant places in the shops were being filled" and by April 1st the strike was over, having been utterly lost.

In 1862 the McKay machine completely revolutionized the work of the journeymen as the stitching machine had done that of the binders.

Before 1852 the binding of the upper had been done by hand by women. The price was from seventeen to twenty-five cents a pair, and a clever woman could make four pairs or even more a day for which she would receive from sixty-eight cents to one dollar. By competition and the introduction of the machine this remuneration was reduced by one half to two thirds. In 1853 binding children's shoes paid three cents for two pairs or eighteen cents a dozen, and full-sized shoes brought five cents a pair, or sixty cents a dozen. A first-rate binder, by the closest application for fourteen to seventeen hours a day, "if uninterrupted by domestic cares," could make four dozen pairs a week, for which, "after delivery and approval," she was paid $2.40. This was a maximum and represented eighty hours of labor. If the cost of light and fire were deducted the average would be nearer $1.60 a week.

3.2

The Working Men's
Party Revisited

EDWARD PESSEN

A subject of dispute among historians, the Jacksonian Workingmen's Parties are here reexamined by Edward Pessen who argues that these parties were indeed a political expression of particular working-class groups and needs. These short-lived but important parties were "multi-class" in composition. An examination of party policies suggests clearly that this fact in no way challenges their distinctive authenticity. A broadly defined concept of the "producing classes," parallel in some ways to European Jacobin movements, typified these parties. Many of the issues these parties advanced had roots in older notions of community and justice, but all also applied to the changing society.

Edward Pessen, "The Workingmen's Party Revisited," *Labor History*, 4 (1963), 203–26. Reprinted and footnotes omitted by permission of the author and the publisher.

The following works are suggested for further reading:

WALTER HUGINS, *Jacksonian Democracy and the Working Class,* Stanford: Stanford University Press, 1960.

MILTON J. NADWORNY, "New Jersey Workingmen and the Jacksonians," *Proceedings of the New Jersey Historical Society,* LXVII (July, 1945), 185–98.

EDWARD PESSEN, *Most Uncommon Jacksonians,* Albany: State University of New York, 1967.

ARTHUR M. SCHLESINGER, JR., *The Age of Jackson,* Boston: Little, Brown and Company, 1945.

WILLIAM A. SULLIVAN, *The Industrial Worker in Pennsylvania,* Harrisburg: Pennsylvania Historical & Museum Commission, 1955.

The unique feature of the American labor movement during the Jacksonian era was the establishment of Working Men's parties. Beginning in Philadelphia in 1828, a Working Men's movement spread throughout the country, reaching its climax in the 1830s. For the only time in American history, workers formed separate political organizations, largely independent of the major parties. Since one of the classic features of the modern American labor movement is precisely the extent to which it has eschewed politics, the appearance of this movement is of obvious significance. This essay will examine aspects of the movement as well as some of the issues still in controversy concerning it.

If no attempt will be made here to give a blow-by-blow account of the rise and fall of the Working Men's parties, it is because it is by now a much-told tale. A substantial literature has appeared since George Henry Evans and his contemporaries in ante-bellum America first chronicled the activities of the New York Working Men. The Working Men's movements of particular cities have been studied recently by Walter Hugins, William Sullivan, Louis Arky, Seymour Savetsky, Milton Nadworny and myself, among others, to supplement the modern accounts of the broader movement by Joseph Dorfman, Arthur M. Schlesinger, Jr. and Alden Whitman. In addition, of course, such modern authors of volumes on the history of labor as Joseph Rayback, Foster Rhea Dulles, Herbert Harris and Philip Foner also have dealt with the labor parties. To date, though, the most comprehensive and probably still the most valuable study remains the pioneering effort of Helen Sumner in John

R. Commons' *History* in 1918. In many respects it remains the basic structure on which all later works have built.

The modern discussion, focussing at it has on a few major cities, has perhaps obscured what Miss Sumner's researches long ago uncovered: the ubiquitousness of the Working Men's party. Operating under a variety of names—"Working Men's Parties," "Working Men's Republican Associations," "People's Parties," "Working Men's Societies," "Farmer's and Mechanic's Societies," "Mechanics and Other Working Men," and just plain "Working Men"—they appeared in most of the states of the union. Pennsylvania was the home of the first known group, the Philadephia party of 1828, which developed out of an earlier organization, the Mechanics' Union of Trade Associations. Other groups in Pennsylvania, some of them unknown to Miss Sumner, were organized in Phillipsburg, Lancaster, Carlisle, Pike Township in Clearfield County, Pottsville, Harrisburg, Erie, Allegheny and Mifflin Counties.

In New York State the leading, and certainly the most interesting, group was organized by Thomas Skidmore and others in New York City. Brooklyn had its own organization in which the later trade unionist John Commerford played a leading role. Parties also appeared in Troy, Albany, Rochester, Buffalo, Genesee, Utica, Syracuse (Salina), Schenectady, Geneva, Ithaca, Auburn, Batavia, Brockport, Hartford in Washington County, Canandaigua Village, Kingsbury, Lansingburgh, Glens' Falls, Palmyra, and Saratoga. A Working Men's convention in 1830 was attended by delegates from the counties of New York, Albany, Rensselaer, Cayuga, Oneida, Washington, Onondaga, Tioga, Tompkins, Montgomery, Kings, Cortland and Ontario, while it was reported that a number of other counties also had chosen delegates who for some unknown reason did not attend.

In New Jersey, groups formed not only in Newark and Trenton, as Miss Sumner noted, but in Hanover (Morris County), Orange County, Centerville, Caldwell, Paterson and Essex County as well. Organizations—albeit questionable ones which may have been "Working Men" in name only—were started in Washington, D.C. and Canton, Ohio. Working Men also formed in Zanesville and Columbiana County. In Delaware there were branches in Wilmington, New Castle County, Brandywine and Red Clay Creek.

New England had a lively movement whose Association of Farmers, Mechanics and Other Working Men has been heralded by some writers as the country's first true farmer-labor party, and by others as the first trace of industrial unionism. In addition to this group, whose members came from a number of states, Working Men organized in Boston, Dedham, Northampton, Dorchester, Hampshire and Franklin Counties in Massachusetts; New London and Lyme in Connecticut; Dover, New

Hampshire, Portland and Brunswick in Maine; and Woodstock, Burlington, Middlebury, and Calais in Vermont.

Most of our information concerning these parties comes from the pages of the dozens of journals which sprang up in this period in support of the Working Men. According to the *Delaware Free Press,* one of these journals, at least twenty newspapers in a number of states had appeared by August, 1830, which might be classified as pro-labor. Miss Sumner found evidence of "some fifty newspapers in at least fifteen states" for the period 1829–32. Naturally, these papers varied in the degree of support or attention they gave to the Working Men's cause but a substantial number of them can properly be described as organs of the political movement, so completely were they dedicated to the Working Men's issues both in their coverage and in their news slant.

In the case of several of the movement's leaders, their identification with labor consisted precisely in the fact that they edited these journals. George Henry Evans was such a figure. Another was William Heighton, an Englishman who came to this country as a youth, became a cordwainer, the founder of the Philadelphia Mechanics' Union of Trade Associations and, early in 1828, the chief editor of the *Mechanic's Free Press,* the official journal of the Philadelphia movement. This weekly has been described as the "first of the mechanics' newspapers in this country edited by journeymen and directed to them." In Philadelphia, Heighton's journal prodded workers "along the path of reform and into politics," thus helping to *initiate* the political movement. More typical was Evans' *Working Man's Advocate* in New York City, which appeared shortly *after* the Working Men organized there. In many cases the journal followed so soon after the party that the two were practically simultaneous, as in Newark, where a Newark *Village Chronicle and Farmers, Mechanics and Working Men's Advocate* came out immediately after the political movement started.

Louis Arky's description of the *Mechanic's Free Press* could apply to numerous other papers as well: "its pages presented a spectrum of reform, from Pestalozzian educational ideas and cooperative store suggestions to the views of free thinkers and reprints from works like [John] Gray's Lecture [*Lecture on Human Happiness,* London 1825, a socialistic tract]." In addition the journals carried accounts of the Working Men's acitvities in other cities as well as their own, announcements of future activities, romances, advertisements, literary excerpts and a potpourri of other material. From the point of view of the student of American labor, however, most rewarding were their editorials, the letters of contributors—often polemical and therefore piquant as well as informative—and the listings of the demands and the programs of the Working Men. Students of the history of American journalism and those who are interested in our social history also will find a treasure of material in the *New England Artisan and Farmer's, Mechanic's and Laboring Man's Repository,* the New York *Daily Sentinel,* the Indianapolis *Union and Meohanics' and Working Men's Advocate,* and the other labor journals of the period.

If the worth of Miss Sumner's contribution endures, it is also true that the recent discussion, certainly that of the past two decades—based on new evidence and reflecting new scholarly interests and frames of reference—has not only added to our knowledge but in many cases severely modified and brought into serious question her conclusions concerning some rather important matters. In this respect, the trend is perhaps similar to that in American historical writing in general: an iconoclastic revisionism which accepts no previous interpretations as sacred, inspired as it is by a relativism to which all old judgments are merely the ephemeral reflections of a forever bygone time.

It would be understatement to describe the main questions raised by the recent literature as a challenge to the traditional thesis. For these questions concern nothing less than the fundamental nature of the Working Men's movement. They simply ask: Was the movement authentic? Was it composed of bona-fide wage earners battling in the interests of wage earners? Or was it spurious, consisting instead of wily politicians who wrapped themselves in the Working Men's mantle only to hide their real identity?

According to Miss Sumner, the issue that divided the true Working Men's parties from the fraudulent was the tariff. For although her study expressed few doubts about the authenticity of most of the organizations which carried the title, she did believe that in some cases "advocates of a protective tariff assumed without warrant the popular name—'mechanics and workingmen.'" She also suspected that these "associations of so-called workingmen which favored protection generally avoided committing themselves to the usual demands of the Working Men's party." But if the organization were for free trade and in addition raised the "usual demands," her study accepts it at face value.

In challenging the authenticity of these parties, critics have focussed on a number of issues. One point of contention has been the party's origins, since the way in which the organization was started, the nature of the men involved, and the issues propelling them into action obviously tell us whether the organization was of and for workingmen or whether it was something else again—at least in its infancy.

The political movement in Philadelphia grew out of a decision by the city's Mechanics' Union of Trade Associations to enter into politics in order to promote "the interests and enlightenment of the working classes." This organization, the "first union of all the organized workmen of any city," had been organized largely through the energetic activity of William Heighton. It included the individual unions—or societies, as they were then called—of journeymen bricklayers, painters, glaziers, typographers and other groups, as well as the journeymen house carpenters whose strike for the ten-hour day in the summer of 1827 spurred the formation of the broader union. There can be little doubt as to the authenticity of the Mechanics' Union, whose appeal to its constituent societies rested primarily on its down-to-earth promise of financial support to journeymen on strike against their masters. A few months after it was organized, the bylaws of the Union were amended to provide that three months prior to general elections the membership should "nominate as candidates for public office such individuals as shall pledge themselves . . . to support and advance . . . the interests and enlightenment of the working classes." The new bylaws took immediate effect. Several months later the *Mechanic's Free Press* reported that "at a very large and respectable meeting of Journeymen House Carpenters held on Tuesday evening, July 1st [1828] . . . the Mechanics' Union of Trade Associations is entering into measures for procuring a nomination of candidates for legislative and other public offices, who will support the interest of the working classes." Thus, in the promise made by some journeymen workers to support at the polls individuals sympathetic to the working class, was born the Working Men's party of Philadelphia. The most skeptical observer can hardly deny the true workingmen's character of the party, at least at the time of its birth.

In New York City a Working Men's party appeared for the first time in 1829, when in the elections for the State Assembly held early in November eleven candidates nominated by the new party made a remarkable showing. The decision to run Working Men's candidates on a separate ticket was made at a general meeting of mechanics on October 19, 1829. In addition to approving a number of other resolutions presented by the executive body—called the Committee of Fifty—the meeting resolved "that past experience teaches that we have nothing to hope from the aristocratic orders of society; and that our only course to pursue is, to send men of our own description, if we can, to the Legislature at Albany; . . . [and] we will make the attempt at the ensuing election; and that as a proper step thereto we will invite all those of our fellow citizens who live on their own labor and none other, to meet us . . . ."

This Committee of Fifty had been elected at the second of two meetings of journeymen mechanics held earlier that year (in the last week of April). They were to give leadership in the struggle to protect the ten-hour day against an alleged employers' plot to lengthen it. The first meeting of the mechanics, which was in fact to lead directly to the nomination of candidates, and which can therefore properly be described as constituting the first meeting of the New York Working Men's party, had been called in order to combat "all attempts to compel them to work more than ten hours a day." It would appear, then, that in its origins the political movement of the New York Working Men was clearly a response of bona-fide workers to an attack on their working conditions.

Seymour Savetsky, however, after a close study of this movement which appeared to establish an intimate relationship with the Republican (or Jackson) party, concluded that "the explanation for the origin of the . . . party is to be found in the bitter internal dissensions and schisms that were wrecking the Republican party of New York. In the fractionalization of the Republican party . . . resides the explanation for the appearance of the New York Working Men's Party." While there is evidence that the emergence of the New York movement owed something to the disenchantment of some Republican (or Democratic) voters with the Tammany machine, it seems to me impossible to disagree with Walter Hugins that the party's "initial impetus was economic, a protest against unemployment and a defense of the ten-hour day." Even Jabez Hammond's contemporary account, while stressing the complexity and heterogeneity of the State movement, saw the beginnings of the New York City party as essentially due to the concern of mechanics in the building trade with onerous economic conditions. Of three leaders of the New York Working Men—Robert Dale Owen, George Henry Evans and Thomas Skidmore—it is true that only the last might be classified a worker. These men were to steer the movement in directions determined largely by doctrinaire philosophies. But this fact in no way contradicts another: that the New York Working Men's party originated in a movement of journeymen mechanics to defend their position against an anticipated attack by masters and employers.

For Boston, as for Newark and other towns in New Jersey, the evidence is not clear. The program adopted by the Boston Working Men's party, as well as the methods advocated to attain it and the candidates nominated to represent the organization politically, all raise doubts as to the nature of the movement. But according to the correspondents who reported on its first meetings in the summer of 1830, these early meetings were attended by large numbers of men who "from appearance, were warm from their workshops and from other places of daily toil, but who bore on their countenances convictions of their wrongs, and a determination to use every proper means to have them redressed."

There is considerably fuller information on the origins of the much more significant New England Association of Farmers, Mechanics and Other Working Men. Described by Miss Sumner as a "new type of labour organization, in part economic and in part political," this association was formed when delegates from the New England states, convening in Providence in December 1831, agreed to hold the first convention in Boston the following spring. The advertisement for the first convention emphasized that "the object of that convention is to mature measures to concentrate the efforts of the laboring classes, to regulate the hours of labor by one uniform standard." In short, this was a call for the ten-hour day. It is no coincidence that the date set by the first convention for the establishment of the ten-hour system—March 20, 1832—happened to be precisely the date that Boston's shipyard workers also began their strike for the ten-hour day. Certainly the workers went on strike not because the Association's Constitution directed them to do so. Rather, the Association incorporated the idea of a ten-hour system, a strike to achieve it, a war chest to finance it, and expulsion of all those who would work more than ten hours per day after March 20, because of the great influence that Boston's shipyard workers and their allies had in its councils. It was the defeat of the ten-hour strike that led the delegates to the second convention held at Boston in September to modify the clause calling for the expulsion from the Association of those who worked more than the ten-hour day. It appears incontestable that New England's most important Working Men's party was organized by workingmen to achieve —in contrast to its New York City counterpart, which sought to maintain—the ten-hour day.

The sharpest questions as to the authenticity of the Working Men's parties have been provoked by the accumulating evidence on the social and economic backgrounds of their members and leaders. The organ of the Philadelphia Working Men liked to think that in contrast to the two major parties of the time—the "Federalists," made up of lawyers and aristocrats, and the Jackson party, composed of bank speculators and office hunters—"on the Working Men's ticket . . . the candidates from first to last have been taken from the ranks of the people." But William Sullivan has shown that during its four years of existence the Philadelphia party nominated and supported very few workers as candidates for office. According to his tabulation, of the party's one hundred candidates only ten were workingmen. Twenty-three were professional men, fifty-three were merchants and manufacturers, eleven were "gentlemen" and three had no occupations recorded. Among these were some of the wealthiest men in the city, including Charles Alexander, publisher of the conservative *Daily Chronicle*. These facts lead Sullivan to doubt that the Philadelphia organization was a true workingmen's party. Louis Arky, on the other hand, found a high percentage of its early leaders—better than seventy-five per cent, in fact—workers or artisans.

The leading student of the New Jersey movement, Milton Nadworny, found little solid information about the occupations or incomes of the leaders and candidates there, although for Newark he ventures the understatement that "undoubtedly, not all of the men in the group were pure, unadulterated workingmen." Despite his findings that small businessmen and merchants often played leading parts in the movement, Nadworny nonetheless accepts it as essentially authentic.

The New York City Working Men split into at least three factions shortly after their striking political success in the fall of 1829, and there is no doubt that the largest faction had little in common with true workmen. But prior to the infiltration of the party by opportunistic elements, culminating in their ascendancy by the time of the 1830 elections, the evidence indicates that bona-fide workers were active in its ranks. Of the eleven candidates put up for the State Assembly in 1829, ten were workers; the other, a physician, got significantly fewer votes than all the rest of his colleagues in the election. In its early stages, according to George Henry Evans, the party sought not only to confine leadership to workingmen but to see that the leaders were journeymen rather than masters. That it was not successful, however, is shown by the fact that the following year even Evans' faction was supporting manufacturers as candidates for political office.

For that matter, Evans' definition of working man was a rather broad one. According to him, only one member of the seventy-man General Executive Committee of the New York party of 1830—a broker— was not a working man. Evidently, he considered the five grocers, the two merchant tailors, the oil merchant, the teacher and the farmer to be workers. The complete occupational breakdown for this committee unfortunately does not distinguish between masters and journeymen, but it does range over a broad category of occupations including carpenters, smiths, masons, painters, pianoforte makers, sash makers and porter housekeepers. Savetsky, who is not inclined to take this organization's claims at face value, nonetheless concedes that on this committee "a majority . . . belong to the laboring element in the community." His close study of the property owned by this group established that just under fifty per cent were propertyless, another ten per cent had only personal property, while only three individuals owned property assessed at more than $10,000. For the years after 1831 it has been rather conclusively shown, both by the contemporary, Jabez Hammond, and by Walter Hugins, writing in 1960, that the New York Working Men included a wide variety of social and economic types.

The Boston Working Men's party did not last long, though while it lasted it showed no animus towards men of wealth. Years ago I did a study of the social position of the candidates it supported in the municipal election of 1830 and in the congressional contest of 1831. Their mayoralty candidate, Theodore Lyman, Jr., was a wealthy ship owner, while four of their seven aldermanic candidates were among the wealthiest men in Boston. Thirty-five of their sixty choices for the State Assembly belonged to that elite group whose property was valued in excess of $2,600. Since less than two thousand persons in a population of seventy-eight thousand had this amount of property, it would appear that forty of the party's sixty-eight nominees belonged to the wealthiest segment of the community. I must admit, however, that I am not so sure of what I wrote then, that these figures "do not imply anything fraudulent," and that they reflect "middle-class aspirations and a certain naiveté" more than they raise doubts "as to the true workingmen's character" of the Boston Working Men's party. Doubts as to the actual nature of the party are indeed raised by such figures.

Doubts have also been raised by the programs of the Working Men's parties. Joseph Dorfman has not been alone in noting that some of the measures they advocated bore no relation to the economic needs of workingmen. But it is true, of course, that workingmen had needs that ranged beyond the economic. That Working Men's parties raised aloft a standard which included a wide variety of political, social, intellectual, occasionally even religious, as well as economic issues, does not necessarily testify to anything but their breadth of interests and hopes.

The programs of the parties were amazingly similar. For, as Miss Sumner observed, "substantially the same measures were advocated by the workingmen in most of the western and southern cities, as well as in New Jersey, Delaware and New England, as were advocated by their comrades in Philadelphia and New York." The program of the Philadelphia Working Men was to become the nucleus of all other programs. It included, above all, a call for a free, tax-supported school system to replace the stigmatized "pauper schools" which, according to Sullivan, provided a "highly partial and totally inadequate system of education for their children." The final copies of the *Mechanic's Free Press* contained on the masthead the following additional reforms: abolition of imprisonment for debt; abolition of all licensed monopolies; an entire revision or abolition of the prevailing militia system; a less expensive legal system; equal taxation on property; no legislation on religion; a district system of election. In addition, the Philadelphians intermittently protested against the unsanitary and overcrowded housing conditions of workingmen; the high cost of living; the long hours, low wages and poor conditions of labor, as well as the low esteem in which manual work was held; the hostility of the major parties towards labor; the mistreatment of labor unions; the lottery system—"the fruitful parent of misery and want to numberless heart-broken wives and helpless children, who have beheld the means of their subsistence lavished in the purchase of lottery tickets"; the "pernicious operating of paper money"; and such down-to-earth grievances as insufficient "hydrant water for the accommodation of the poor" and "the failure of the city to clean the streets in the remote sections of the city where the workingmen reside."

And earlier they had pressed successfully for the passage of a mechanics' lien law to assure workingmen first claim on their employers' payrolls. Nor does this exhaust a list which from time to time carried criticisms of banks and banking, charitable institutions, the sale of liquor, conspiracy laws—and, when invoked against unions, the use of prison labor, and the complexity of the laws and of the legal system.

The Working Men of New York and of other cities did not of course slavishly follow the Philadelphia program, even though they put forward grievances and demands which concentrated on the same essentials. In New York City, for example, Thomas Skidmore early won the Working Men over to the approval of an "agrarian" program calling for "equal property to all adults," a plank in the platform which was supported until the expulsion of Skidmore from the party at the end of 1829. Later, Robert Dale Owen, George Henry Evans and their supporters, championed a unique educational system known as "State Guardianship," under which working class children not only were to receive an improved education under a tax-supported program but were to board out in the new public schools as well. At one time or another, the party also stressed anti-clericalism, compensation for jurors and witnesses, direct election of the mayor, smaller electoral districts, the payment of certain political officials (for the classic reason, later emphasized by the English Chartists, that otherwise only wealthy property holders could afford to hold office), the reduction of the salaries of others, civil service reform, abolition of capital punishment, pensions for Revolutionary War veterans, a single municipal legislative chamber, and free trade. As to the half-dozen or so issues which were most emphasized, the mastheads of the labor journals which proclaimed them could have been interchanged without notable difference. On many occasions the New York *Working Man's Advocate* and the Philadelphia *Mechanic's Free Press* carried precisely the same slogans.

As has been indicated, some programs were related to local problems and issues. The New England Association reflected its rural composition by calling for a reform in land tenure laws, and its sympathy with factory operatives by insistence on factory legislation. The Working Men of Boston advocated a reduction of the fees charged by professionals as well as a reduction in what were considered to be the exorbitant expenditures of the State government. And in Cincinnati the Working Men added "improvements in the arts and sciences" to the classic appeal for equal universal education and for the abolition of licensed monopolies, capital punishment, unequal taxation on property, the prevalent militia system, and imprisonment for debt.

There is no question but that this was a broad program, substantial portions of which were supported by men and groups having nothing to do with labor. Imprisonment for debt, for example, was opposed by many people outside of the Working Men's movement—on broad humanitarian grounds in some cases, and on grounds of economic inefficiency in others. Its victims were not always the "laboring poor." The same is true for other of the reforms, including education. Yet it would be economic determinism of a very rigid sort, indeed, to insist that authentic labor organizations confine their programs to economic issues advantageous only to workers.

Much of the Working Men's program *was* in fact concerned with the economic interests of labor. Naturally, workers sought larger wages and better working conditions. But they also sought improved status in society, and some of them organized in order to support the perfectionist demands put forward by their idealistic leaders as the means of achieving this status. The program of the Working Men's parties reveals them to have been champions of social justice and a more perfect democracy, as well as critics of every kind of social abuse.

Still other questions as to the authenticity of the Working Men have been raised over the alleged closeness of their relationship with the Jacksonian party. While Arthur M. Schlesinger, Jr. sees a coalition between the two movements, critics of his thesis have interpreted the same evidence as indicating the essential fraudulence of the Working Men's parties, seeing them as being no more than front organizations for the Democrats. It is perhaps a source of comfort to these critics that their charges are similar to those made 130 years ago by some National Republican leaders and publishers.

With regard to this issue, as with others, the evidence is either inconclusive or too complex to permit black and white generalizations. Assuredly, from time to time on certain issues the two movements behaved as one. The organ of the Newark Working Men, the Newark *Village Chronicle and Farmers, Mechanics, and Workingmen's Advocate,* admitted in April of 1830 to its sympathy with the Jacksonians. And there seemed to be more than coincidence in the decision by the two parties in New Jersey that year to hold their nominating conventions for the State legislature in the same small town on the same date. Nor is it surprising that after the fall elections the Whig press denounced what it felt to be the collusion between the two parties. Five years later, the Newark Democrats still evidently depended to a large extent on the political support of the Working Men, while in 1836 the two groups jointly supported a number of legislative candidates. The leading student of the New Jersey Working Men concludes that they consistently supported the Democrats and their candidates.

In New York City the striking political success achieved by the Working Men in 1829 seems to have been the result largely of a shift in the voting habits of people who ordinarily voted for the "Republican" or Jackson party. The New York party broke into several splinter groups shortly after the 1829 election. The so-called *Sentinel* or *Advocate* wing, named after the journals published by the younger Owen and Evans, supported much of the Democratic program, especially its anti-monopoly features. In fact, according to Savetsky, this faction was simply absorbed or assimiliated into the New York Jacksonian organization after its defeat in the elections of 1830.

In New England the decision in 1833 of the New England Association to support as their gubernatorial candidate, Samuel Clesson Allen, the erstwhile champion of Andrew Jackson and opponent of the Bank of the United States, led more than one Whig journal to denounce the unholy alliance of Working Men and Jackson men. This same fact serves as the basis for Schlesinger's conclusion that at this time the Massachusetts Working Men increasingly threw themselves behind Jackson's monetary program. Yet this same New England Association Convention urged the formation of a pro-labor national political organization. When the Association again nominated Allen for Governor at its last convention in September 1834, at Northampton, it simultaneously urged rejection of the candidates of the major parties for State office. A close study of its programs, conventions, resolutions and actions indicates that from its birth in Providence in December 1831, until its demise not three years later, this organization was little concerned with, let alone sympathetic to, the Democratic Party. As for the Boston Working Men's Party, not only did it show no support whatever for the Jacksonian party, but its slate of candidates for the Board of Aldermen and the State House of Representatives included a good number of National Republicans. Although its mayoralty candidate, Theodore Lyman, Jr., had worked for Jackson's victory in 1828, he had broken with Old Hickory's party well before the 1830 municipal elections. The non-support of the Democrats by the poorer wards in the 1831 elections provoked David Henshaw, Jackson's appointee to the strategic collectorship of the port of Boston, to charge that Boston Workingmen were the enemies of the Democratic Party. (The evidence indicates that workmen were no great friends to the Working Men, either.)

In New York City not only Skidmore, but Evans and Owen and their supporters as well, regularly voiced their opposition to both major parties. Despite their occasional agreement with the Democrats on a particular issue, their press warned that Jackson had no interest in important reform. If the mid-century commentator, Jabez Hammond, can be believed, the men who "flocked to the standard of the Workingmen" in New York State were "opposed to the Albany Regency and the Jackson party."

The Philadelphia Working Men had no objections to supporting candidates of whatever social background or political persuasion. Yet their journal saw no contradiction in denying any connection with either of the major parties; in fact, it stressed the danger represented by the Democrats, "for as most of us are deserters from their ranks they view us with the same sensation as the mighty lord would the revolt of his vassals: there cannot be so much danger from the Federalists as, generally speaking, we were never inclined to trust them." In the elections of 1829, the one year in which the Philadelphia Working Men achieved an outstanding success, they combined with the anti-Jacksonians in support of eight local candidates, while endorsing only one Jackson supporter. Sullivan has concluded that "an analysis of the [Philadelphia] Working Men's Party reveals that both in its composition and its predilections, it was amazingly regular in its support of the anti-Jackson forces."

Even for New Jersey the situation was more complex than the allegations of some National Republicans would make it appear. The original platform of the New Jersey Working Men refused to align the group in support of Jackson. As the Working Men of Morris showed in 1834, they had no compunctions about nominating a Whig to office. His success goaded the Democrats into charging that the Whigs used the Working Men as tools! The following year an election rally of Newark's Working Men's party expressly stated that it preferred neither of the major parties. And although in 1836 there was a degree of cooperation between the two groups, there was evidently a falling out (before the end of the year) that may have been due to the Working Men's resentment at being used by the Jackson party.

Two points should be stressed. The program of the Working Men's Parties called for reforms that in most cases went unmentioned by the Democrats, whether on a local, state or national level. This would indicate that the movement's organizers were motivated precisely by the failure of the Democrats—not to mention the National Republicans—to work towards goals these organizers deemed of the highest importance. In addition, despite the attempt by some historians to treat the political issues and the major parties of the era in striking ideological terms, as though they represented diametrically opposed social and class viewpoints, the facts are otherwise. As Charles Sellers, Glynden Van Deusen, Bray Hammond, Richard Hofstadter and others have shown, the major parties had similar views on many important issues, differing more in tactics than in fundamental objectives, with neither party dedicated to a drastic alteration of the fabric of society. Of course there were Democrats and Democrats. But Jackson himself, and the leaders of the Democratic party in most of the states, were practical men. All of which is to say that it is to misinterpret the nature of the Democratic state machines or the national Democratic party of Andrew Jackson's day to believe that so loose, opportunistic, all-inclusive and eclectic a coalition would devote itself to the kinds of reform urged by the Working Men.

What conclusions can be drawn about the relationship between the Working Men, led by radicals who often sharply criticized the Democratic party, and Jacksonian democracy? To the extent that it, too, opposed aristocratic privilege and monopoly, the Working Men's movement may perhaps be interpreted as part of a broadly defined "Jacksonian Revolution." But neither organized nor unorganized workingmen became a fixed part of a Democratic political coalition. And if the Jacksonian movement was in fact a movement primarily devoted to achieving a freer competitive capitalism, the Working Men clearly had demands which went far beyond that objective. Yet in the large view which seeks to impose a pattern on the era, reforms of varied character, championed by diverse groups—each seeking the achievement of its own objectives—somehow merge together in a broad, all-embracing reform movement. It is only in this general sense that the Working Men of the Jacksonian era can be said to have been a part of the large, sweeping movement towards whose political expression— the Democratic party—they often displayed indifference if not actual hostility.

If it does nothing else, the discussion of the various controversies concerning the authenticity of the Working Men's parties should clearly establish one thing: it is impossible to generalize about the movement as a whole, as though all of its constituent parts were alike in all important particulars. There were Working Men and Working Men. The origin of some was obscure; of others, dubious. Some arose out of economic struggles, others out of concern for status. Some came to be dominated by opportunists, others by zealots. Thus, the only safe generalization perhaps would be that no two parties experienced precisely similar careers.

Yet it is also clear that despite inevitable differences in their circumstances and behavior these organizations, arising more or less simultaneously and calling for like reforms, had much in common. Common to the Working Men's parties in the major cities, in my opinion, was their authenticity—at least for part of their history. By authenticity I mean that they were formed by workers or men devoted to the interests of workers, sought to attract workers to membership in or at least to support of the new organizations, worked for programs designed to promote the cause and welfare of workers, and entered politics because of the failure of the major parties to concern themselves with important reforms and in the hope that these parties could be goaded or influenced into showing such concern. The authenticity of a party that conforms to this standard is not lessened by the fact that in supporting candidates to office, it asked only that they support the program, or important elements of it, while it evinced no interest in the size of their bank accounts or their social status. Nor is there anything suspect in the fact that parts of the program might also be supported by non-workers.

The origins of the Working Men in Philadelphia, New York City, Newark, and the cities of New England, stressing as they did either the working class backgrounds or the aims of their founders, strengthen the belief that the parties were not misnomers. It is true that the parties contained many men who by present definitions would not qualify as workers. But the definition of that earlier day was much more flexible. The prevailing concept was that all who performed "honest toil" were working men. Even to such a radical as George Henry Evans in 1830, only lawyers, bankers, and brokers could be designated as persons not engaged in the kind of useful occupation qualifying them for membership either in the Working Men's party or the working class. (It is interesting testimony to the growing conservatism of the New York City Working Men that a resolution incorporating Evans' sentiments was defeated as too restrictive. In the fall of 1829, on the other hand, there was strong support for the principle of confining leadership in the party to journeymen and, in Evans' words, denying a vote to any "boss who employed a large number of hands.") Additional light on this issue is thrown by the similar discussion that arose among the Philadelphia Working Men. According to the *Mechanic's Free Press,* early in the party's history (in the summer of 1828) it was decided that while employers might be present at meetings, they could not hold office. Yet one year later its Ricardian Socialist editor, William Heighton, could write: "If an employer superintends his own business (still more if he works with his own hands) he is a working man. . . . If this view of things be correct, shall we look with a jealous eye on those employers who prefer being considered working men? Who are willing to join us in obtaining our objects?" Not only for political candidates but also for mere membership in the party, the important issue evidently had become simply whether the man would join in "obtaining our objects."

It is also true that at a certain point in its career the New York party, for example, seemed to be in the hands of men who had little sympathy with its expressed program. But contemporary participants and later scholars alike are unanimous in agreeing that these elements infiltrated the party only after the dramatic success it achieved in the 1829 elections and succeeded in taking it over only by the use of money, inner party intrigue, extra-legal tactics, and newspaper excoriation, all the while continuing to pay lip service to reform. The New York Working Men underwent a *transition* that powerfully testifies to the fact that in its heyday it was not only an authentic but also an impressive organization, even frightening to some politicians. Perhaps nothing more dramatically suggests that the New York and other Working Men's parties were bona fide than the opposition, to put it mildly, they inspired in Democratic and National Republican politicians alike, and above all in most of the press. The Boston *Courier* was not alone in arguing that "the very pretension to the necessity of such a party is a libel on the community." The underlying thought of its editors, the Buckinghams, was that rich and poor, publishers and typesetters, skilled and unskilled—all are workingmen and therefore there was no need for a separate Working Men's party.

In the nation's cities, however, not only did a Working Men's party appear; it would be more accurate to say that it burst forth on the political community like a meteor, either electing its candidates, or obtaining the balance of power on its second attempt, as in the City of Brotherly Love or, in other cities, immediately after putting forward its original slate. Less than two weeks before the election, in New York City, for example, a ticket nominated for the State Assembly elected one and came near to electing several other of its candidates, amassing better than 6,000 out of 21,000 votes cast. And yet in this as in other cases the political success was decidedly ephemeral. Decline set in almost immediately, culminating a brief few years later in the party's demise and disappearance.

What accounted for the almost immediate downfall of the Working Men's party? From that time to this, attempted explanations have not been lacking. Some Philadelphia leaders bitterly blamed the workers themselves, both for their blindness to their own true interests and for their lack of courage. Other sympathizers attributed the failure to the party's mistaken policy of supporting wealthy candidates, themselves personally sympathetic to monopolies. Thomas Skidmore, himself cashiered out of the New York party for his radical views and his uncompromising fight for them, charged that the party's doom was sealed by its permitting rich men to take over, men who had no business in the party in the first place. Evans, his one-time opponent, later came to agree with him. Hammond also noted that the New York State party had within its ranks men who made their living at jobs they professed to criticize, not excluding banking. By his view, "this party, if it deserves the name of a political party, was too disjointed and composed of materials too heterogeneous to continue long in existence." New York friends of the Boston Working Men, on the other hand, explained the pathetic political showing of the New England party by its preoccupation with issues, such as religious infidelity, that were not properly the concern of a workingmen's political organization.

In her summary of the causes of the failure of the Working Men's parties, Miss Sumner listed, in addition to some of the factors mentioned by contemporaries of the movement, the onset of a general prosperity which turned the attention of workers from "politics to trade unionism"; dissension—"legitimate" when resulting from heterogeneity, "illegitimate" when started and nurtured by "professional politicians of the old parties, who worm themselves into the new problems in managing a political party; the hostile activities of the party"; the inexperience of leadership with regard to the practical parties' open enemies; and, "last but not least, the taking up of some of its most popular demands by one of the old parties." Most recent literature on the subject tends to confirm many of her judgments. For New York, both Hugins, and Savetsky before him, stress the way in which Tammany and the Democrats absorbed the program, above all its anti-monopoly features; Savetsky also calls attention to the lack of dynamic and energetic leadership such as might have been provided by a person like Frances Wright—erroneously designated by contemporary opponents of the party as its high priestess, with an eye toward tarring it with the same infidelity brush that was applied to her. Arky emphasizes the Philadelphia party's inept machinery: "for political purposes the movement was clumsily organized." Sullivan, on the other hand, stresses the lack of class consciousness of its members, threats made by employers against those who supported it, and, above all, the very nature of the party and its candidates. It is Arthur Schlesinger, Jr.'s provocative conclusion that the Working Men disappeared because "their parties [were] engaged in kind-hearted activity on the periphery of the problem"—on such issues as education, imprisonment for debt, or clericalism, whereas the Democrats stressed the core issues that really counted. Thus, "during the Bank War, laboring men began slowly to turn to Jackson as their leader, and his party as their party." Not the least questionable feature of his interpretation is its assumption that the Working Men's parties and "laboring men" were one and the same thing also is questionable. If it appears to be true, rather, that most laboring men did not vote for Jackson, it is equally true that a few exceptional cases notwithstanding, at no time did they vote even as a significant minority for the parties organized in their name.

Their own political ineptitude and inexperience, internal bickering, heterogeneous membership, lack of funds, and the infiltration of their ranks by men interested only in using them, all played an important part in bringing about the downfall of the Working Men; so did the opposition of the press, and the shrewdness and adaptability of the Democrats. Several related points also might be mentioned. Better then the major parties then or now, the Working Men's party represented the Burkean definition of a political party as a group of men united in behalf of certain political, social, and economic principles. Its membership may have been broad but the party's program was not all things to all men; it was certainly not a grab bag aimed primarily at winning office for those who professed to support it. In the American society of Tocqueville's day a distinctly class-oriented program could not expect success at the polls.

On the other hand, for a party that presumes to speak out in behalf of labor to open its lists to individuals who embody the opposite of everything it stands for is perhaps fatally to blur its image—at least in the minds of workingmen—while failing to shake the loyalties of other citizens for the traditional parties who were so much better at practical politics. Speak out the Working Men did, in a message that was idealistic and radical; and as the message became clearer, an American public seeking the main chance and increasingly optimistic about its possibilities, lost interest in the nay-saying of the radical dissenters who formulated the Working Men's program. It may well be, then, that a reform party was doomed to failure in the American society-in-flux (bemoaned by a James Fenimore Cooper), whose characteristic members quivered in anticipation of the material fortunes to be made. Such optimism, when shared by workers, is the stuff that kills off ideological politics.

Notwithstanding their failings and their ephemeral vogue, a final assessment of the Working Men's parties cannot fail to note their significance. Immediately after the results of the striking Working Men's showing in New York became known, the Democrats promised to pass the lien law for which the new party had been agitating. Nor was it a matter of a lien law alone. Even in the short run, the Democrats in New York and elsewhere hastily showed greater concern than ever before for the various reform provisions of the Working Men's program. Thus one of the factors that helped bring about their disappearance as a separate political entity was also an indication of their strength. If it is the function of radical parties in America to act as gadflies, to goad and influence rather than win elections, then the Working Men succeeded admirably.

Of course the degree of success they enjoyed is hard to measure. The Working Men were not alone in championing public education, abolition of imprisonment for debt, banking reform, reform of the militia system, factory laws, general incorporation laws, recognition of labor's right to organize unions, shorter hours of work for labor—to name some of the leading issues. It is impossible to fix with precision their contribution in comparison with that of other individuals and groups who supported one or another of these measures. But there would seem to be no queston that the role of the Working Men's parties was an important one, in some cases even greater than is usually believed. In the struggle for the creation of a public school system free from the stigma of charity or pauperism, for example, it has long been the fashion (certainly since Frank Carlton pointed it out) to accord considerable credit to the Working Men. Yet, as Sidney Jackson has shown, not only did the Working Men agitate for the establishment of such a system; they also advocated sophisticated qualitative measures that seem remarkably prescient. Among the changes they sought were an improved curriculum, less concerned with pure memory and "superannuated histories," less emphasis on strict discipline, better physical conditions for children, better trained and better paid teachers, and better equipped schools, free of clerical influences. In sum, Helen Sumner's generous estimate does not seem overdrawn: "The Working Men's party, in short, was a distinct factor in pushing forward measures which even conservative people now recognize to have been in the line of progress toward real democracy."

It has been suggested that one of the factors working against the long-run popularity of the Working Men's party was a radicalism uncongenial to opportunistic Americans. But on the other hand the party's relative popularity, brief though it was, suggests that some contemporaries were receptive to the voice of protest. The fact that a Thomas Skidmore, who favored a redistribution of property, could win acceptance as a leader of the New York party; that in removing the slogan, "all adults (are entitled to) equal property," from the third issue of the *Working Man's Advocate*, George Henry Evans went to great lengths to explain that he continued to believe essentially in the same goals; that the program of the "conservative" Cook-Guyon faction, which came to dominate the party, continued to pay lip service to radical reform—all of this indicates not only that an important minority in the Jacksonian era were disenchanted with their society and its institutions, but that it was considered politic by some astute men to cater or defer to this mood. A final significance, then, of the Working Men's party lay in the testimony its career afforded that the United States of the Jackson era was not altogether devoid of that sense of alienation that in England and on the Continent provided fertile ground for the spread of Owenite, Chartist, Fourierist and other socialist doctrines.

3.3

Women in Cotton Manufacturing

CAROLINE WARE

Factory production first came to America importantly in the cotton industry.
Initially developed in New England, the manufacturers faced a whole
realm of new problems. Not the least of these was the recruitment and
disciplining of a new labor force for the mills. As Ware outlines, two systems,
the Waltham and Rhode Island, were developed. Both depended on the
labor of women and children. Cloth production had always been part of the
colonial woman's routine, but only the coming of the factory drew women
from the home. One significant question that awaits detailed work is how this
process affected the self-image and status of the mill girls and women
and, in turn, what effect such changes had on the overall status and
role of women.

Caroline Ware, *Early New England Cotton Manufacturing* (New York: Russell & Russell,
Publishers, 1931, 1966), pp. 198–235. Reprinted by courtesy of the publisher.

The following works are suggested for further reading:

EDITH ABBOTT, *Women in Industry*. New York: Appleton-Century-Crofts, 1915.

RAY GINGER, "Labor in a Massachusetts Cotton Mill 1853–1860," *Business History Review*, XXVIII (1954), 67–81.

H. GITELMAN, "Waltham System and the Coming of the Irish," *Labor History*, VIII (1967), 227–63.

HANNAH JOSEPHSON, *Golden Threads: Mill Girls & Magnates*, New York: Duell, Sloan & Pearce, Inc., Little Brown and Company, 1949.

LUCY LARCOM, *Memories of a New England Childhood*. New York: Corinth Books, 1961 (reprint).

HARRIET ROBINSON, *Loom & Spindle*. New York: Thomas Y. Crowell Company, 1898.

VERA SHLAKMAN, *Economic History of a Factory Town*. Baltimore: Johns Hopkins University Press, 1936.

The owners of the early cotton mills were faced with a very difficult problem when they sought to secure their labor force. In the first place, the population was so small and the natural resources so great in the United States that labor for any purpose was not readily available. Women and children, as Hamilton pointed out, were the only numerous group of workers who could be spared from the farms. Even these, however, were not easy to secure for mill work because they were not accustomed to industrial labor. There was no body of pauper children in America as in England nor large numbers of cottage workers. Some few women took in a little custom work and a few children were apprenticed, but labor in America before the introduction of the factory system was almost entirely agricultural and carried on in the family unit.

In the region of New England there was a certain degree of what Hamilton called 'maturity' for manufactures by reason of the poor farms that had ceased to repay cultivation but workers drawn from such sources were not enough to build a large industry. The mills, moreover, faced always the competition of western land and the resistance of prejudice against factory labor. American labor was thus expensive and hard to get and American manufacturers were forced to devise schemes for securing their workers which would overcome the obstacles of scarcity and prejudice. As late as 1834 the French traveler, Chevalier, made the significant observation that in America, as elsewhere, competition between employers to cut down manufacturing costs tended to reduce wages, but that here it was not aided, as in Europe, by competition between laborers for the chance to work.

In discussing the labor supply of the cotton mills, we may designate the two distinct sorts of labor introduced by Slater and the Waltham company respectively as the 'family' type and the 'boarding house' type. The latter prevailed at Chicopee and Lancaster, Massachusetts, as well as in the Waltham-Lowell-Lawrence group of mills. It was characteristic of most of the large factories of New Hampshire, notably Dover, Manchester, Exeter, and Portsmouth, and several mills in Maine. In these mills, practically all the workers except the overseers and mechanics were girls who lived in company boarding houses. The 'family' type of employment was universal in Rhode Island and Connecticut and very general in southern Massachusetts. Instead of a fairly uniform group of workers, the help there was varied. Whole families moved to the mill villages where they occupied single houses or tenements, often owned by the company. Every member of the family above the age of seven or eight worked in the factory. Slater's labor force in 1816 was typical of a 'family' mill. It was made up of:

1 family with 8 members working
1 family with 7 members working
2 families each with 5 members working
4 families each with 4 members working
5 families each with 3 members working
8 single men
4 single women

The family system was the most obvious method of employment, especially to the Englishman, Slater, and to those of his employees and associates who were introduced to the industry by him and who subsequently started mills themselves. In 1832 about half of the New England factory workers were of this sort working in many small mills in the southern part of the state. Between 1816 and 1836 the *Massachusetts Spy* published advertisements for help from the cotton mills of seventeen of the towns near Worcester, almost every one of which wanted 'families of five or six children each.' The families who answered such advertisements were described by one employer as 'poor families, and generally those having the greatest number of children, those who have lived in retired situations on small and poor farms, or in hired houses. . . . These families are often very ignorant, and too often vicious.'

The boarding house arrangement, in accordance with the design of its inventors, procured labor of a very different sort. As the biographer of one of the founders of the system explained, 'those wise and patriotic men, the founders of Waltham, foresaw and guarded against the evil' of social degradation which had come with the English system, 'by the erection of boarding houses at the expense and under the control of the factory; putting at the head of them matrons of tried character, and allowing no boarders to be received except the female operatives of the mill; by stringent regulations for the government of these houses; by all these precautions they gained the confidence of the rural population, who were now no longer afraid to trust their daughters in a manufacturing town. A supply was thus obtained of respectable girls; and these, from pride of character, as well as principle, have taken especial care to exclude all others.

'It was soon found that an apprenticeship in a factory entailed no degradation of character, and was no impediment to a reputable connection in marriage. A factory-girl was no longer condemned to pursue that vocation for her life; . . . and it soon came to be considered that a few years in a mill was an honorable mode of securing a dower. The business could thus be conducted without any permanent manufacturing population. The operatives no longer form a separate caste, pursuing a sedentary employment, from parent to child, in the heated rooms of a factory; but are recruited, in a circulating current, from the healthy and virtuous population of the country.'

These 'wise and patriotic men' succeeded so well in attracting the sort of help they wanted that at Waltham there were, in 1820, often as many as forty more hands on the list than could be employed and the company was 'more puzzled to get rid of hands than to get them.' The manufacturers who adopted this system believed that it not only secured a great moral good for the community but, for themselves, a class of operatives 'as superior in intelligence and efficiency to the degraded population elsewhere employed in manufactures, as they are in morals. They are selected from a more educated class—from among persons in more easy circumstances, where the mental and physical powers have met with fuller development. This connection between morals and intellectual efficiency has never been sufficiently studied. The result is certain, and may be destined, in its consequences, to decide the question of our rivalry with England, in the manufacture of cotton.' One manufacturer who undertook to measure the relation between the type of labor and quality of output found 'that, on substituting in one of his cotton mills a better for a poorer educated class of operatives, he was enabled to add twelve or fifteen per cent to the speed of his machinery, without any increase of damage or danger from the acceleration.'

The merits of the boarding house system early attracted public attention. The editor of the *New Hampshire Sentinel* was interested in reproducing for his readers an enthusiastic account of the Waltham mills which had appeared in the *Boston Gazette*. The conclusion that 'this extensive establishment may be styled the pride of America' was confirmed by glowing descriptions of similar conditions in Lowell. What a contrast to the poor families of the other mills, 'often very ignorant and too often vicious'! Yet the boarding house system did not prove to be an unqualified success in every instance where it was tried. In Newmarket, New Hampshire, a factory employing two hundred and fifty girls, five boys and twenty men abandoned the arrangement after three years, concluding that it was necessary 'in cases of newly formed villages' but subject to 'powerful objections.' Examples of such failure are, however, rare.

Although mills of the boarding house type were few in number compared with at least a hundred and eighty-four mills in Massachusetts, many in Rhode Island and a number in Connecticut and New Hampshire which used 'family' help, they were more important to the community. Their aggregate labor force at any one time amounted to somewhat less than half the total number of mill workers but more passed through their employ than through the family mills because of the transient character of their force and they reached more parts of the country and more classes in society through the girls who went back to their country homes after a few years in the mills. Moreover, the large accumulations of capital invested in this group of mills and the social position of their owners gave them prestige which the smaller concerns lacked.

The founders of the boarding house system were very proud of the social advantages which it brought. Citizens of Lowell laid repeated stress on the high moral tone which the company regulations and the class of operatives gave to the town. The French traveler, Chevalier, was strong in commendation, concluding his description of the town with a note on the failure of the only attempt at a theater and the comment. 'Lowell is not amusing, but Lowell is clean, decent, peaceful, and wise.'

At the same time, the lesser mills sought to demonstrate that they too had the standards of the community at heart. Advertisements for workers in family mills stated that applicants must be of good moral character and industrious and must come well recommended. 'Those who are in the habit of profanity and Sabbath breaking, and intend to continue these practices, are invited not to make application.' 'Families wishing a situation near to places of public worship, will find this most delightful.' '*Active and industrious* girls. . . . To those of *fair* character, and *only* those, good encouragement and constant employment will be given.'

The effort of manufacturers to secure and retain the respect of the community by keeping up the character of their help and maintaining attractive conditions of work and life explains much that is characteristic of the labor situation in the early American mills. England had been confronted with much the same problem, a prejudice against factory work, but the solution there had been exactly the opposite. When respectable workers would not enter the mills, the English manufacturers went to the poorhouses and secured labor that had no standards, while the Americans undertook to raise the standards of work to the level of the workers and to make mill labor a respectable calling.

The problems presented by the need for skilled and for unskilled workers were essentially different. The former involved the search for quality which had to be imported or trained. The latter was solely a matter of available numbers.

Much of the skilled labor in the early mills was quite naturally English and Scotch. In spite of the strict English laws against the emigration of artisans and mechanics, a very considerable number made their way to this country. Some disguised their identity by engaging temporarily in commerce and emigrating with their savings invested in goods to sell in America. Skilled weavers, machine makers, mule spinners, dyers and calico printers were the principal emigrants. The many English and Scotch mechanics who became independent manufacturers testify to the presence of this class, while the records of nearly every company reveal the important rôle of the skilled foreigner.

The assumption of the earlier experimenters was, very reasonably, that technical skill must come from abroad. The unfortunate Beverly company sunk most of its original capital along lines pointed out by foreigners professing to know the trade. 'Destitute of the necessary information' themselves, they had been 'subject to be misled by every pretender to knowledge,' and employed 'a number of Europeans chiefly Irish,' no one of whom was 'master of any branch of the business,' while 'most of them proved deficient in some quality essential to usefulness.' After four years of such experience, the company became 'satisfied from experience that we must at last depend on the people of the country *alone* for a solid and permanent establishment.'

The few Almy and Brown letters that make any specific references to their labor force nearly always refer to foreigners. Their original 'find' had, of course, been Slater. In 1803 Obadiah Brown discovered an English stocking weaver near Philadelphia who, he thought, might be induced to come to Providence. The firm sent to Boston in 1807 to engage an English dyer on very generous terms, offering to 'accommodate' him with employment whenever he chose if he could not 'conveniently employ' himself elsewhere during the two months before they would be ready for him. They took particular interest in supplying good yarn for English and Scotch weavers in as widely separated places as Roxbury, Massachusetts, and Norfolk, Virginia. Their first yarn had been sold to a Scot, McKerries, who was using one of the first American fly-shuttles on looms in Providence. The fact that a man was an Englishman was in itself a recommendation of skill and judgment. Almy and Brown made a point of the fact that they were 'connected in business with Englishmen who have thorough knowledge of the same' and presumed that they were therefore 'able to furnish any article in this line better and consequently cheaper than any other now in the business.' They told an English wool manufacturer with whom they were planning to exchange some goods that since he was an Englishman they could trust him to give good quality.

Skilled Englishmen were similarly employed elsewhere. In 1803 James Beaumont employed an English weaver to make fine cloth from some of the first American mule-spun yarn. The Poignand and Plant Company made agreements with Philip Gallie, 'late of Jersey, now of Lancaster,' who came in 1814 and engaged to work for them for three years and with William Chadwick, 'late of Great Britain but now of Lancaster,' a mule spinner, who contracted in 1818 for two years. At Seth Bemis's factory in Watertown, six English weavers were employed in 1809 to weave cotton duck. In New Ipswich, New Hampshire, there was a settlement of Scotch weavers who made fancy checks, plaids, and twills with the yarn from Samuel Batchelder's little mill. When Batchelder became the first agent of the Hamilton Company, he took one of these Scotchmen with him to Lowell to work as a dyer for the company. Prior to 1831, block printing was done almost entirely by emigrants from Manchester.

In 1817, when unemployment was so prevalent in England, English papers described American factories as havens for distressed workmen. Some English travelers confirmed this report, others denied it. An *Emigrant's Guide* published in 1816, apparently with the purpose of persuading emigrants to go to Canada rather than to the United States, discouraged all English emigrants from seeking employment in 'the imperfect and declining manufactories of America.' On the other hand, Henry B. Fearon, traveling in 1818, assured his readers that 'in all my enquiries of farmers, innkeepers, store-keepers, manufacturers, their servants and others, I understand that employment is not difficult of obtainment by industrious and honest men.' Those who came were sometimes disappointed with the opportunities which they found here. According to the testimony of a Delaware wool manufacturer in 1828, many cotton and woolen weavers came to the United States, especially from Great Britain, but 'some of them, who are the best and most ingenious workmen, return, because they do not find employment suited to their capacity.'

Enterprising companies sent abroad for skilled workmen, if they had the means to do so, whenever they wished to undertake a new phase of the business. The Waltham company secured a machinist in 1816 and paid $448.22 for 'his passage and expenses from England.' While the Hamilton Company was getting under way, one of the directors made a trip to England to observe processes there and incidentally to engage some workmen. He took advice as to whom to engage from the agent, who wrote that there was a possibility of getting some one in America to do the finishing and packing so that 'it may not be absolutely necessary for you to engage one. Still as there are so few here who are skilful in this business and as we might be disappointed if we placed entire dependence on Mr. Prince's man, I should think it would be well, if one can be obtained at moderate wages to engage him, especially as there would be no difficulty in such an one finding employment here if we should happen not to want him. He should be well acquainted with the use and best construction of the callender and dying machine. Our fancy dyers I find are not much to be depended on. One was sent out by Mr. Duxbury at two dollars per day, the other came with him, to whom I gave a dollar ten. They are good workmen and nothing more, and about as regular in their habits as the block printers. If one can be found capable of superintending a few workmen and who understands the business practically I think it would be well to engage one.' This and other comments on irregularity in the habits of the immigrant workmen suggest that, in spite of their skill, imported hands were not always dependable.

This important group of English and Scotch workmen did not furnish all the skill in the early mills. Their labor was supplemented by that of native craftsmen from other fields, especially those ordinarily engaged in ship-building, who were eager to take advantage of a new opportunity to ply their trades during the embargo and war. With the coming of peace these skilled workers tried to return to their old employ and mechanics for the mills became very scarce. Poignand and Plant's agent recommended that the managers employ a certain workman in spite of the high wage which he demanded, for, 'to get people to go into a factory at present is almost out of the question. Peace has raised their expectations too high.'

By the twenties there were a number of men who had grown up in the industry, men whose experience in different departments of the business qualified them both as skilled hands and as overseers and superintendents. Some applied to well established factories for temporary employment in order to learn the techniques but these were not apt to be cordially received. To one application Almy and Brown replied, 'We are informed that thou art wishing to procure some information in the line of our business, through the means of the admission of a brother for a few months into one of our mills. As we have had repeated applications of the kind, that we have not seen fit to grant, being interested with those at our several mills, who have a perfect knowledge of the business and they have not been willing thus to communicate their knowledge.' One of the Waltham company's applicants was turned over to the Lancaster company but got no satisfaction there. The young man wrote, 'My wish is to obtain a practical knowledge of the art of manufacturing cotton goods and of the best mode of managing establishments for this purpose. It appears that this can only be obtained by personal attention at a well conducted factory for a length of time, say one or two years.' To this the Lancaster manager replied, 'Situated as we are, it would not be possible for us to pay you that attention you can hope to require nor could you find it easy, in so small an establishment as ours, to employ your time agreeably; neither is there here a possibility of your acquiring that range of information which a larger establishment can furnish and which you are desirous to obtain.'

It is not surprising that Almy and Brown should have wished to guard their secrets, that a small manufacturer should not have wished to be bothered with such men, and that the deliberate training of men to go out and run rival factories elsewhere might easily have become a burden to the Waltham company. In the ordinary course of business, however, a great many skilled workers were trained. A Scotch mechanic who had been employed by the Waltham company found some of the men who had worked in the Waltham shop with him running a little mill in the south and others operating a small factory at Medway, Massachusetts. By such a process, the industry became well equipped with native skilled workers.

The branches of the manufacture requiring skill were chiefly mule spinning, dyeing and finishing, and the making and repairing of machines. The latter process was of general importance since nearly every mill constructed its own machinery in addition to keeping it in working order. Mule spinning was a difficult operation while it was a hand process and even after the introduction of the self acting mule in 1840. In 1804 Almy and Brown asked several of their correspondents to advertise in their local papers for a man who knew how to spin on 'a machine called a mule' and received applications from such spinners in Philadelphia. All through the twenties, the *Manufacturers' and Farmers' Journal* carried advertisements of factories wanting mule spinners and of spinners wanting jobs. 'Blue dyers,' that is, men who had mastered the difficult art of dyeing with natural indigo, were also in great demand, as well as all classes of overseers.

The only girls who were regarded as skilled or semi-skilled workers were the first of the power loom weavers. When power looms were being introduced widely, advertisements called for girls who could tend them, but as their use became general, entirely inexperienced hands were trained as operators. Age was the only qualification that Poignand and Plant demanded of their loom tenders and they employed women who assured them that they knew nothing of the work for which they were being engaged. Until the importation of girls from Glasgow to do fancy weaving for the Amoskeag in 1867, girls came to the mills as unskilled workers.

In securing their unskilled labor force, the two types of mills employed different methods to overcome the difficulties of labor scarcity and prejudice. These methods were adapted to the situations of the mills and to the sort of labor employed.

In the family mills a very large proportion of the workers were children. The incomplete 'Digest of Manufactures' compiled by the Secretary of State from the 1820 census showed that children made up forty-five per cent of the total number employed in cotton mills in Massachusetts, fifty-five per cent in Rhode Island, and fifty-four per cent in Connecticut. By 1832, the proportion in each state had fallen to approximately twenty-two per cent in Massachusetts and forty-one per cent in Rhode Island, according to estimates based upon McLane's report. In the same year a committee of the New England Association of Farmers, Mechanics and other Workingmen estimated the mill workers under sixteen in Rhode Island, Fall River, and two New Hampshire towns as forty per cent of the working population.

The commissioners appointed in 1853 'to ascertain the number, ages, hours of labor, and opportunities for education of children employed in the manufacturing establishments of Rhode Island' found eighteen hundred and fifty-seven children under fifteen still at work in that state, twelve to twelve and a half hours a day and eleven to twelve months out of the year. The comment on this situation was that 'the above return is in one respect more favorable . . . than your honorable body, or the public generally would expect to receive,' in that the number of very young was small, only fifty-nine under nine years old and six hundred and twenty-one between nine and twelve.

For the children thus used as mill workers, employers assumed no responsibility. Only in the rarest cases was the status of apprenticeship, with its attendant obligations upon the master, carried into the mill. In one factory a group of pauper children were apprenticed and in another a boy spinner was hired 'to work a year for fifty dollars or serve three months for nothing.' Far more commonly, in fact almost universally, mill work brought to children the change in status reflected in Almy and Brown's account book before and after the introduction of machine spinning. The children who were working in the company's handicraft shops at knitting stockings, spinning cotton and wool by hand and weaving cloth received no wages but were furnished articles of clothing as 'apprentices.' In the spinning mill, on the other hand, the account for the first year shows the wages paid 'for the labor of Moses Jenckes's children' and the rest of the child labor force.

One result of the employment of so many children was to place boys in positions of responsibility at a very early age. A thirteen year old boy who had already worked in a mill for seven years was employed by the Globe Company in Tiverton, Rhode Island, to repair and set in operation its machinery which had been standing idle for some time. Another, at the age of fifteen, was sent by his father to Burrillville, Rhode Island, to superintend the equipping of a mill there and to put it in operation. He had been a mill worker since he was nine. The superintendent of the Pawtucket Thread Company in 1826, aged nineteen, had already had eleven years' experience. These cases seem less surprising if one remembers the Salem ships which circled the globe officered, sometimes entirely, by seventeen to twenty-one year old boys.

The small early mills could rely on the families of neighboring farmers for most of their child workers and, in the early twenties, some mills were still advertised as situated in a neighborhood which would furnish a sufficient labor force to operate the mills. Most, however, had already been forced to send away for extra hands.

The common recourse was to advertise in the newspapers in the nearest large center, in the hope of reaching the more remote villages and towns in the county. The *Massachusetts Spy* was seldom without an advertisement for several large families to work in one of the many small mills of Worcester county. The *Manufacturers' and Farmers' Journal* carried continually similar advertisements for the same sort of mills around Providence, its 'help wanted' column usually containing some such demands as those of February 28, 1828, when a factory in Valley Falls wanted a family to work in a cotton factory; one at Warwick desired a carder and spinner; at North Providence, there was a call for four or five families and eight or ten power loom weavers; at Smithfield, for an overseer of a spinning room and four families; at Scituate, for twenty power loom weavers and two or three families. Places for an agent and for a dresser and tender were also offered. Some advertisements called for 'two or three families with help,' expecting workers to bring into the mill not only their own family but additional workers. This arrangement was common. One of Slater's overseers agreed to furnish two weavers in addition to his three daughters and one son, another to furnish one girl and another three extra weavers.

The use of advertising to secure help does not appear to have been wholly successful or necessary, to judge from the experience of the only mill whose advertisements could be compared with additions to the labor force. Between 1818 and 1825 only one of Slater's six advertisements appears to have brought the desired response while another secured a quarter of the help which it called for. Twenty-three of the twenty-six new families who entered his employ during this period seem to have come unsolicited. When he opened a new thread mill in 1828, however, he was successful in using this means for securing additional hands. Except when a sudden increase in labor force was needed, most workers probably drifted in with the growth of towns around the mills or came through chance knowledge that there might be employment available.

Mills of the boarding house type did not resort to advertising to secure their help. A diligent search through a number of newspapers of Massachusetts and New Hampshire between 1816 and 1836 has shown not a single advertisement of any of the Lowell cotton mills, only one of a Lowell woolen mill and only two from any other mills of the boarding house type.

Their reason for not using a method commonly employed by the family mills was probably the difference in the sort of worker they were trying to attract and the situation of their establishments. Advertising was used by the small factories partly to let workers know that there were jobs available and partly to persuade them to come into the mills. As these companies did not have wide reputations and often had the only plants in their village, it was necessary to assure potential workers that they would receive employment before they could be expected to uproot their whole family, give up their homes and move to the factory town. Although farmers' children occasionally came to the family mills leaving the rest of the family on the farm, and though farmers themselves sometimes spent the winter months in mill machine shops to supplement their summer's earnings, entrance into such a factory usually meant a complete change in a family's way of life and the finding of jobs simultaneously for five or six people.

The boarding house mills, on the other hand, did not have to let people know that work was available. If we are to believe the tales in the *Lowell Offering,* there never was any lack of employment in Lowell. Girls came from long distances unheralded, selected a boarding house, perhaps where a friend from the same village lived, and the next morning found work in the mill, usually in the same room with her friend.

These mills, however, had a more difficult task than the others when it came to persuading workers to leave their good homes for the mills and they had to rely on personal contact rather than on advertising for this persuasion. They counted to some extent on girls going home for vacations and bringing friends back with them on their return. A Lancaster employee who went home sick wrote to the factory that she had found two spinners who would come back with her and several others who would like to join them because the company had such good regulations. 'Where is the mill girl,' asked a writer in the *Lowell Offering,* 'who does not know of others from the same town?'

They could not rely wholly on workers brought in by other employees, however, especially as mills became more numerous and the demand for labor greater. In addition, they sent agents into the country to represent the advantages of mill labor to the girls whom they found on the farms.

As early as 1821 Poignand and Plant were sending up into New Hampshire and Vermont to collect girls for their mill. 'I feel much uneasiness on account of the standing still of the looms for want of weavers,' wrote the agent. 'One of our friends in Brattleboro, Vermont, thinks that there would be no difficulty in getting a number of girls in that place and in the neighborhood . . . he would give every information in his power to any person you might send to effect this object.' The manager himself then went hunting for workers. 'You mention that Mr. Poignand is going beyond Keene [N.H.] for girls,' commented the agent. 'We think that this should have been done before,' and he urged them to hire a man to go hunting for help. The *Dedham Patriot* in 1831 reported that 'a valuable cargo, consisting of fifty females, was recently imported into this state from "Down East" by one of the Boston packets. Twenty of this number were consigned to Mann's factory at Franklin and the remaining thirty were sent to Lowell and Nashua.'

The agents who were sent about the country to collect girls received a commission of so much per head. The *Voice of Industry,* a labor journal, commented bitterly on the 'long, low, black wagon,' which 'makes regular trips to the north of the state, cruising around in Vermont and New Hampshire, with a "commander" whose heart must be as black as his craft, who is paid a dollar a head, for all he brings to market, and more in proportion to the distance, if they bring them from such a distance that they cannot easily get back. This is done by "hoisting false colors," and representing to the girls, that they can tend more machinery than is possible, and that the work is so very neat, and the wages such, that they can dress in silks and spend half their time in reading.'

How was it that these agents and others were able to persuade girls to come to the mills? Some people thought that they were 'seduced from their quiet and healthful homes among the mountains of New Hampshire and Vermont by the deceitful inveiglements of heartless corporations,' but the Lowell girls replied indignantly, 'with regard to their being *seduced* from their homes, . . . who and what seduces them here?' They regarded their mill experiences as an adventure and made every effort, in part through their own magazine, the *Lowell Offering,* to impress upon the public that they were free agents pursuing the dignified occupation of their choice.

They entered the mills, however, in the face of a good deal of opposition and contempt for mill work. In spite of the boarding house system, the enthusiastic accounts of travelers, and the publicity given to President Jackson's visit to Lowell where he walked for a mile between rows of beautiful girls all with silk stockings and parasols, factory work was looked upon with disfavor in many quarters. 'The ambition of woman should be to beautify and adorn the domestic circle,' wrote a New Hampshire editor in 1840, expressing a widely held view. He considered domestic service the only suitable training for the vocation of the home, 'yet how often do we see them declining to labor in a family, and preferring the quasi-slavery of a cotton factory, the last place in the world, a fashionable female academy excepted, to fit a woman for domestic society and usefulness.'

To be sure, the person who condemned factory work usually turned out to be a farmer whose real grievance was that the factories had drawn off the supply of dairy-maids, but the idea that such work was degrading seems to have been widespread. When a philanthropic lady, interested in supplying reading matter to the inmates of the Middlesex County prison, discovered that the majority of the prisoners were from Lowell, she did not stop to consider that Lowell was much the largest town in the county but concluded, 'Perhaps in a population of operatives gathered of all sorts, from all places in New England, nothing better, even under careful regulation, could be expected.'

A few champions, however, came to the rescue of the mill girls' reputations. The editor of the *State Herald* of Portsmouth, New Hampshire, condemned those who discouraged factory girls saying, 'Instead of speaking reproachfully of young women for leaving their homes to learn an honest trade, and who patiently submit to factory discipline, you ought rather to praise them. For respectability and intelligence, we do know that at many of the factories, the best of females are employed—even the daughters of judges, ministers, and representatives; . . . Seeing these facts, do you suppose we can look on with indifference, and wink at the evils to which they are subjected by facory managers, and the slanders of others?'

All evidence agrees that need was not the chief motive which brought girls to the boarding house mills. Some girls came because they were bored with their lonely, dull country life and wanted the sociability of a city full of girls, some because there were opportunities for education there and some because they wanted to feel independent. Many came for selfish, others for unselfish motives; some because their friends came home from the factory with new silk dresses, others in order to help pay off a mortgage on the family farm.

According to the agent of one of the Lowell mills in 1845, 'Their sole object in leaving home and coming here from places so remote, and entering upon an entirely new course of life, is to make more money by their exertions than they can in any other employment. They are not paupers. . . . Few intend to make this their permanent residence, or to devote their lives, or even a great portion of it, to the business of manufacturing. Their schemes are laid before the wages are earned. Gain, and not bread, is the object of their pursuit.' Mrs. Robinson explained that when she was a mill worker 'indeed, the most prevailing incentive was to secure the means of education for some *male* member of the family. To make a *gentleman* of a brother or a son, to give him a college education, was the dominant thought in the minds of a great many of these provident mill girls.' The author of a history of women published in 1835 ventured the statement that of the women gainfully employed, 'by far the largest proportion . . . do not work for support, but to gain additional luxuries, which their parents cannot afford to furnish.'

The following account from the *Offering* probably describes a representative group. 'There are girls here for every reason, and for no reason at all. I will speak to you of my acquaintances in the family here. One, who sits at my right hand at table, is in the factory because she hates her mother-in-law. She has a kind father, and an otherwise excellent home, but, as she and her mama agree about as well as cat and mouse, she has come to the factory. The one next her has a wealthy father, but, like many of our country farmers, he is very penurious, and he wishes his daughters to maintain themselves. The next is here because there is no better place for her, unless it is a Shaker Settlement. The next has a "well-off" mother, but she is a very pious woman, and will not buy her daughter so many pretty gowns and collars and ribbons and other etceteras of "Vanity Fair" as she likes; so she concluded to "help herself."

'The next is here because her parents and family are wicked infidels, and she cannot be allowed to enjoy the privileges of religion at home. The next is here because she must labor somewhere, and she has been ill treated in so many families that she has a horror of domestic service. The next has left a good home because her lover, who has gone on a whaling voyage, wishes to be married when he returns, and she would like more money than her father will give her. The next is here because her home is in a lonesome country village, and she cannot bear to remain where it is so dull. The next is here because her parents are poor, and she wishes to acquire means to educate herself. The next is here because her "beau" came, and she did not like to trust him alone among so many pretty girls.'

This writer had various sorts of advice to offer to her friends who were uncertain whether or not to come to Lowell. To the one who merely wanted to see a new city and be with her friends she said that she should stay two years because it was not advisable to learn a new occupation unless to stay as long as that, but she warned her that at the end of two years she might have acquired a distaste for the routine of a good home and quiet village and be discontent either to stay or to go back. To a girl who took care of an old lady, she said that she would find quarters in the boarding houses cramped but would earn enough to dress properly and had therefore better come to the mills unless the old lady would raise her pay. She told another girl that, in spite of her uncomfortable home, she was an important personage in her family and would be nobody in Lowell, however much greater the comforts there would be; she could dress better in Lowell but not better compared with others. She urged a girl whose relatives had made a slave of her and another who was losing her health by sedentary employment to come to the mills directly.

These comments give a picture of part, at least, of the Lowell mill population. Doubtless there were many others, less energetic and less articulate, who came to make a living and found mill work more of a burden and less of a lark.

The girls came mostly from farms in New Hampshire, Vermont, Massachusetts, and Maine. In 1841 the agent of the Boott mills examined the first seventy names on his mill registry and discovered that the average distance from which the girls had come was seventy miles. Of the eight hundred and sixteen employed by that company less than nine per cent had their homes permanently in Lowell. The girls thought that the manufacturers definitely preferred girls from out of town, 'because, in the fluctuations to which manufacturers are liable, there would be much less distress among a population who could resort to other homes, than if their entire interest was in the city.' In 1845, statistics from eight mills employing fifteen hundred and twenty girls showed thirty-three per cent to be from New Hampshire, twenty-five per cent from Maine, twenty per cent from Vermont, and twelve per cent from Massachusetts. They went home for visits in the summer and, when they left the mill for good, they went about the country as walking advertisements, far more effective than any number of printed ones.

The *Lowell Offering* itself must have done much during the forties to call people's attention to the good features of the mills, to break down prejudice, and to draw labor there. Looking back on those years, Miss Larcom comments, 'With the report of the taste for reading and study among the mill girls, and particularly after the publication of the *Offering,* the mistaken impression went abroad that a paradise of work had at last been found. Romantic young women came from a distance, with rose-colored pictures in their minds of labor turned to pastime, which were doomed to be sadly blurred by disappointment.' In 1842 the *Offering* had selling agents, doubtless girls who had gone home from the mills, in the state of Massachusetts at Boston, Saxonville, Worcester, Beverly, Chicopee, Newburyport, and Haverhill; in New Hampshire at Nashua, Dover, and Manchester; at Providence, Rhode Island; at New Haven, Hartford and Willimantic in Connecticut; in New York City and Troy, New York; at Windsor and at Middlebury College in Vermont. By 1844 agents had been added at Cabotville, Massachusetts; Concord, Boscawen, Lake Village, Meredith, Sanborton Bridge and Portsmouth, New Hampshire; and Portland, Bangor, Gorham, Saccarappa, Orono, Bath, Hallowell, and Gardiner, Maine, besides Albany, Buffalo, and Philadelphia.

Labor papers, which condemned the corporations, accused the *Offering* of being the tool of the employers, encouraged by them to paint a false picture of factory life in order to attract to the mills such an oversupply of help that 'they may be enabled to control the prices and rights of labor.' The *New Era of Industry* pointed out that members of the corporations had subscribed to the magazine to the amount of twenty-five copies each; that they had paid the editors large sums for back numbers and that the editors themselves sent copies regularly to overseers with the request that they read the magazine and recommend it to the girls under their supervision. 'If the mill authorities wish to publish such a magazine, or hire it published, they have an undoubted right to do so; but let them be honest, and not palm it off as the operatives' organ.'

There is no doubt that the magazine was written by the girls themselves and that it was a genuine expression of their life and thoughts. The integrity of its editors and the school girl tone of the material are guarantees of that fact. There was unquestionably a group of intelligent girls who read magazines, played the piano, formed an improvement circle and wrote stories. To them the mill was more like a boarding school than like a factory and in pride and self defense they undertook to vindicate themselves and to destroy adverse public opinion. Nearly every issue of the *Offering* contained such comments as, 'I will take leave of the reader, hoping that if he has hitherto had any undue prejudice against labor, or laboring people, he will overcome it, and excuse my freedom and plainness of speech.' When some one objected that the *Offering* pictured all the girls as paragons of perfection the editress replied, 'Factory girls have their faults as well as their virtues. The latter we shall point out to the community, the former to themselves.' She closed the fifth volume with the comment, 'We do think that we have effected something, if we have placed factory employment, in the eyes of the community, upon a level with other kinds of labor.'

While this assertion of self respect was surely genuine and honestly meant, it played directly into the employers' hands and the editors were not sufficiently class conscious or opposed to the employers to object. Harriet Farley, the editor, wrote Amos Lawrence thanking him for his support of the *Offering* and asking him to give the managing editor a letter of introduction for her tour of the west. The mill owners themselves were quick to see how aptly their purposes were served by this publication and to lend it their support. They realized, too, that the prime efficacy of this particular kind of publicity came from the fact that it was the girls' spontaneous work and that the corporations must not appear to be even financially back of the venture. The Hamilton Company agent wrote to the treasurer in 1845, 'I should have mentioned to you yesterday that the proprietors of the *Lowell Offering* have recently made a request to the agents of the mills here for some aid to relieve them from the embarrassment they find themselves in . . . It has been thought advisable to aid them by purchasing a lot of the back numbers to the amount of a thousand dollars . . . It was thought best that assistance should be rendered to them in the way proposed, . . . so that it might not be said that the concern is at present supported by the corporations or under their influence.'

The *Offering* thus became both the organ of a group of the girls and a tremendous aid to the employers, supplementing their own efforts to make the mills sufficiently attractive to draw a growing stream of fresh labor in from the farms.

In employing various devices for securing their help, mills took great care not to steal one another's workers. Perhaps they were so careful because they were afraid that if they once started competing for the limited labor supply they would place themselves at a disadvantage in bargaining with their workers or perhaps because of professional ethics. In any case, this attitude had been characteristic of the factory owners from the beginning of the industry.

In 1790 the Beverly Company complained that Worcester people had bribed one of the spinners whom they had taught 'to desert us as soon as she could be useful to us.' Rhode Island 'undertakers,' also, were said to have 'treated us in the same manner.' Almy and Brown were very solicitous that they should not offend one of their correspondents, a dyer, or cut into his business by employing his son. In the Lancaster company the attitude was the same. When two girls from the Chesterfield factory applied for positions in his mill, Mr. Plant stated plainly that they were not to come until they had fulfilled all their obligations at the factory where they worked. Even this did not satisfy the Chesterfield manager who protested angrily that his employees had been invited away.

P. T. Jackson wrote very apologetically to Lancaster when two of the latter factory's workers had been brought to Waltham by one of the overseers of his mill. He said that he had told the overseer, *most explicitly,* that if he ever knew of his attempting to obtain help from another factory for Waltham he should quit immediately. 'You judged rightly that we would not in the most indirect manner countenance the principle of one factory attempting to supply itself with help by enticing hands from another.' Samuel Batchelder wrote to a skilled weaver whom he thought he had hired for the Hamilton Company, 'You must be aware that the late offers you have received have been in consequence of your engagement here and that you would not have received such offers if you had returned without having engaged a place. I have always declined making any proposals to induce anyone to leave the employment of other manufacturers but I think after the arrangements I have made I could not with propriety give up the engagement.'

Slater had great difficulty with this problem. Although he tried to be careful not to take any one else's help, specifying in his advertisements that none need apply if under engagements at another mill, he and his son twice became involved in law suits over workers who had come to their factories from elsewhere. In Lowell, all the mills required that any girl who had worked in another factory in the city should bring with her a regular discharge from her former employer. By a rigid adherence to this policy the manufacturers sought to make the most of such labor as they could secure, giving as much stability as possible to what was at best a very impermanent working group.

Just how impermanent that labor force was cannot be determined with any degree of accuracy. Within individual mills there appears to have been a somewhat lower rate of turnover than has been common in more recent times, but the movement in and out of the industry must have been distinctly greater.

In comparison with the average replacement rate of sixty-three per cent in American textile mills in 1913 and 1914 and of one hundred and twenty-six per cent from 1914 to 1918, an estimated rate of from twenty-five to fifty per cent in the early years seems very low. Such estimates are, however, exceedingly inaccurate. Statistics compiled from eight Lowell mills in 1845 showed that twenty-five per cent of the girls had been in the mills for less than one year, fifty per cent less than three years. At Waltham the replacement rate seems to have been twenty-five per cent or less during the late twenties and from forty to seventy per cent during the forties, but wide variation in the total number employed largely accounts for the higher percentage in the latter period. In the Hamilton Company in 1826 and 1827 there were one hundred and seven discharges for an average employment of about three hundred, or a turnover of approximately thirty-five per cent. The agent of the Boott corporation found in 1841 that the girls in his mill had been employed for an average of four years. Doubtless the small group of girls who had been there for a number of years raised the average for the whole mill. The six girls, presumably old hands, called to testify before the Massachusetts House Committee in 1845 had been employed from one and a third to eight and a half years. There were even cases of such girls as Lucy Larcom who had been in the mills as children in the twenties and were still there in the forties.

In mills of the family type the rate of turnover was probably lower than at Waltham and Lowell, but it is practically impossible to check up this fact. No estimates were made for this type of mill and the records of the mills themselves do not yield the information accurately. Many more names were always carried on the books than were actively and continually employed, children came in and out of the mill without making a change in those who were dependent upon the factory for their livelihood, workers were shifted from one department to another and names appeared in all sorts of spellings and in unexpected places on the untidily kept rolls after temporary absence or when the clerk altered his method of listing. A close scrutiny of the Slater Company's time books reveals that in this typical mill the yearly turnover was roughly twenty per cent while a large group stayed for a long time. Many workers moved from one mill to another, judging from the frequency with which advertisements called for families experienced in mill work. Some came back into the Slater mill after a year or two. When the hard times of 1816 made that mill cut down its labor force to less than a third, in nearly every case one or two members of each family were retained on the books, and when the number of hands was again increased the following year the rest of the family was in most cases taken back.

All these estimates have little value because of the scantiness of the material, the fact that rates are not computed on a comparable basis and that they do not all take account of those who came and went within a year or of changes in total volume of employment. In the family mills, the fact that wages were paid only quarterly or semi-annually must have limited the number coming to the mill for only a few weeks, and most workers in both types of factory contracted to work for a year. The greater replacement rate in modern times is perhaps chiefly due to the numbers who work in a factory for fractions of a year. The great number who left the industry after a year or two, on the other hand, made the mill population before 1860 what Samuel Batchelder described as 'only a succession of learners.' The most characteristic feature of this labor supply was not the rate of turnover within an individual factory but the shift of workers in and out of the whole industry.

The relative abundance of workers varied, of course, with good times and with bad, labor shortages being most keenly felt in the years when the industry was expanding most rapidly. Since mill labor was so largely composed of women and children who were otherwise unemployed, it did not depend upon the competition of other trades for its volume. As the Friends of Domestic Industry pointed out, mill girls' earnings were a 'clear gain to the country. Before the establishment of these and other domestic manufactures this labor was almost without employment. Daughters are now emphatically a blessing to the farmer.' The supply depended, therefore, on the extension of the area from which workers were drawn, on the rate at which that area was depleted by westward migration and on activity within the industry itself.

By 1793, mills were already being established further back in the country in order more easily to secure workers. In the rapid expansion during the war, hands became very scarce. They were plentiful in the bad years of 1818 and 1819. When business revived two years later, the Lancaster company's looms stood still for lack of workers. Those who were thrown out of work by the failure of mills in the slump of 1829 were all employed again in the expansion of 1831. In that year an editor could advise girls to ignore threats of discharge. 'Only do the work well and behave well,' he counseled, 'and maintain your rights, and if discharged there are enough places for you to resort. There is over a dozen new factories now building, and help is scarce and will be, and must be scarcer unless some who now conduct factories pursue a different course than now practiced, and give a greater degree of freedom and respect to those employed.'

When the popularity of the boarding house mills reached a height in 1836 and 1837, reports from Lowell gave 'girls abundant' and an English competitor was worried because in America 'females may be had in any number, and their wages are reasonable.' In 1845 the agents of two Lowell mills reported that in that city there were never enough jobs for the men who applied, especially in the winter, and as for girls, 'in the cool season, female help is also most abundant. For several years past the supply has exceeded the demand from October to May; the demand has exceeded the supply during the months of July, August, and September, and for the rest of the year they have been about equal.' In the boom of 1846 the strain on the labor supply was so great that the agent of the Hamilton Company refused to make an alteration suggested by the selling house because it would require additional workers and 'hands are becoming scarce.' This was at the time when the New England girls were leaving the mills and their places had not yet been taken by the Irish. With the coming of the immigrants into the mills after 1848, labor became once more abundant.

Emigrants had begun coming to America in large numbers in the thirties but, except for the skilled workers mentioned above, few entered the mills until after 1848. By this time the depression brought upon New England agriculture by the opening up of more and better lands in the west was driving enterprising families from New Hampshire, Vermont, and Connecticut out on to the new soil beyond the frontier. As these families migrated, taking with them the daughters who had been adventuring into the mills, the corporations found their problem of securing help becoming more and more difficult. In these circumstances they turned first to the needier of the New England girls who might make mill work a permanent occupation and then to the wives and sisters of those Irish laborers who had come to the mill centers as ditch diggers and brick layers to dig canals, build mills, and construct railroads.

The growth of the Irish population in Lowell and the entrance of Irish workers into the mills appears to have been typical of the various industrial centers of New England. Their presence in that city dates from the earliest days of the town when a group of 'Paddies' were employed to build the first mill. The part of the city known for many years as the 'Paddy Camp' lands bears witness to their presence. As the number of Irish in the town increased, a priest began coming regularly once a month from Salem to celebrate mass and in 1831 the first Catholic church was dedicated. In that same year there was a spirited riot in town between the Yankees and a section of the Irish population, for reasons not given in the newspaper report. In 1835 the Irish in the town, roughly estimated at about six hundred, were distributed among the following occupations:

145 laborers.
 65 mechanics or other skilled workmen.
 50 factory workers, including all factory employments.
 24 dyers.
 17 carpet workers.
 15 workers in the bleachery.
  7 machinists.
  4 print workers.
  4 clerks.
    and widows keeping boarding-houses, merchants, and others whose employment was not listed in the city directory.

By 1837 there were so many Irish in the town that the city of Lowell opened a second school for Irish children in the basement of the Catholic Church. These schools were strongly commended by Amos Lawrence on the ground that they were 'doing for three or four hundred children there what nothing else could do.' He thought that in twenty years 'these children would be mingled with our mass of population, an active, enlightened and fine spirited body.' In 1840 the temperance movement in Lowell counted an enrolled membership of sixteen hundred Irish. The Irish Benevolent Society of Lowell was incorporated by the State Legislature in 1843.

Prior to 1840, an Irish woman in the mills was a rare sight. Miss Larcom remembers the delight with which she and the other children listened to the 'funny brogue stories of old Erin' which the 'merry gray-haired wastepicker' used to tell. Most of the Irish women went into domestic service where they dominated the trade so completely that housewives who preferred native servants and American girls looking for domestic places both had to stress nationality in their advertisements.

After 1840, however, the women began to drift into the mills. In 1842 the Merrimack Corporation was employing fifty foreigners, of whom thirty-seven were Irish (including fifteen sweepers) ten English and three Scotch. The Boott mills in 1844 contained among their eight hundred and sixteen girls forty-three illiterates, forty 'supposed to be' Irish, two English, and one Yankee. In 1845, seven per cent of the help in eight of the Lowell mills was Irish. Thereafter the proportion increased rapidly until by the early fifties half the Lowell operatives were of that nationality.

Other mill communities shared the experience of Lowell. Irish operatives first entered the Amoskeag mills in Manchester in 1840. Fall River citizens were complaining of the influx of foreigners into their mills in 1842.

In Lowell and the other boarding house mills, the Irish do not appear to have been introduced for their cheapness or to have driven the old type of worker out. Rather, conditions within the community and within the industry forced the change. Competition brought lowering of wages and the placing of pressure upon the workers until factory labor ceased to be attractive to the New England girls. At the same time the failure of agriculture in New England destroyed the class in the community which had furnished that type of mill girl. In a series of articles written for the *New England Offering* in 1849 on the crisis that mill workers were facing, one of the girls of the old type declared that the wage reductions would inevitably drive the high class New England girls out of the factories completely, for they could not work under English factory conditions in America. She trusted to the patriotism of the corporation owners to raise wages again in order to attract once more the sort of girl who had made the industry what it was.

Her attitude toward the Irish certainly did not indicate that the Irish were driving out the native girl, but rather that they were taking places already left empty. 'Many of the vacancies left by these substantial, well-educated, upright-minded girls, will be filled by the Irish; and much as I admire some traits of their national character, sincerely as I pity them and beseech for them kind treatment and room in our country, I should regret their coming into this branch of labor.'

This writer thought that the lowered wage was the principal reason for the old girls leaving since they would rather go home than submit, while the new type of worker would permit still further wage reductions, she thought. 'If the Irish and low class New England girls only remain, wages may come down. They will, on account of their comparative un-profitableness to their employers, and they will submit, since they have little energy, few aspirations . . . they will stay and the wages may be reduced again and again.'

The editor of the *Offering,* however, did not think that the whole change could be attributed to wage cuts. She felt that the old times would not return even if the old wages were restored, chiefly because the mills had lost the respect of the community. 'We everywhere meet the complaint that our Lowell girls are degenerating.' She thought the only hope was to try to restore the standards of morality which had earlier been maintained, 'the old spirit of mutual surveillance must be revived.'

Once the Irish girls had come into the mill in large numbers, they probably hastened the exodus of the old workers because of prejudice rather than because of competition. There seems to have been a good deal of feeling against the new comers on the part of the old girls, for 'pride, or self-respect, or both makes the latter step back from the field that the former enter, and leave it entirely to them.' 'Are not many of them avoided, not because they are ignorant, untidy, and passionate, but *because they are foreigners*?' queried the editor of the *Offering.* 'We have seen the emigrant shunned by those more ignorant than herself, because she was a foreigner.'

Actually the Irish workers do not appear to have been cheaper for the employers when they were first employed. When the Boston Manufacturing Company took on a group of Irish hands after a walk-out in 1848, the productivity per worker, which had been growing steadily, fell off and the company went back to making a coarser type of cloth than it had for many years.

Although the foreigners probably did not drive the Yankee girls out of the boarding house mills, their competition may have been directly felt in mills of the other sort. A petition from Fall River in 1842 declared that the influx of foreign labor had caused such reductions in wages in many departments of manufacturing establishments that American workmen could not support themselves and their families.

In mills of both types, the foreigners came in whenever there was a crisis or break in the industry's development. The Fall River fire of 1843 destroyed a number of mills and marked a turning point in the industry of that city. When the mills were reconstructed with new equipment, they were manned very largely by Irish labor. They came in as strikebreakers in the Waltham walk-out of 1848 and the Amesbury and Salisbury strikes of 1853. In the space of a decade they became the dominant element in the labor force of the cotton mills and both the companies and the communities found themselves with a labor situation radically different from that of the industry's beginning.

As the volume of immigration grew, the foreigners were regarded as a political far more than as an economic menace. With the exception of a few isolated labor champions who denounced the foreign workers, the people of New England were wholly concerned over the foreign voter.

The objection to foreigners was only a small part of the programs of labor organizations and the whole labor movement was weak, whereas political opposition formed the basis of the Native American Party which captured the legislature of Massachusetts in 1855. Samuel Morse, in a series of pamphlets in 1834 and 1835, was one of the first to sound the danger note. He urged laws to prevent immigrants from voting lest the priests should get control of the polls. He declared that if immigrants were allowed to go on voting, the native working class would soon be driven from politics but he never so much as hinted that the native workers might be driven from their jobs.

The appeals of labor agitators fell upon deaf ears. Seth Luther, in 1832, attacked the corporations for sending agents abroad to induce foreigners to come and work in their mills and for setting foreign overseers over American women and children whom they abused. 'We insist that if Congress have power to protect the owners against foreign competition in the shape of goods, they have the same right to protect the operative from foreign competition in the shape of foreign mechanics and laborers' who 'cut down wages of our own citizens.' The *Workingmen's Advocate* in the following year protested that the 'American system' protected the manufacturer while allowing him to import workmen free of duty and that 'there may be temporary advantage to workmen from "protection" to the owners of factories, but where there is a surplus of workmen, (and there is and must be a surplus of workmen in this country under our present laws respecting emigration and public lands,) the competition among the owners of factories will continually prompt them to reduce the price of wages, and they will be able and willing to obey the prompting.' These attacks were against the importation chiefly of skilled workers. A decade later, on the eve of the real 'immigrant invasion,' the *Voice of Industry* practically reiterated Seth Luther's words. 'No tariff on these! No, no, it won't do to protect the capital of American working men and women, their labor . . . for this would be anti-republican. But the rich capitalist must be protected and he will take care of the laborer.'

Who except these writers was there to regard the multiplication of foreign mill hands as disturbing? The 'good old type' of mill girl had never cared for her job as a job and when she had left the mill to go west she was much more concerned over preëmption rights, the extension of the railroads, the fate of the gold rush and even the condition of the slaves than over the future of the mill worker. Citizens of Lowell, to be sure, found the change hard on their civic pride. Foreign travelers were interested in the predominance of immigrant workers which they observed but the city historian in 1868 admitted ruefully that the 'motley crowd of Americans, English, Scotch, Irish, Dutch, and French Canadians' whom Prince

Jerome Napoleon found in the city in 1861 'were hardly likely to arouse that exquisite poetic sentiment which Chevalier felt for the factory girls of 1834.'

As for the employers, they were glad enough of a new source of supply which came to their rescue when their old was failing. Necessity had forced them to gain and hold the respect of the community in order to attract the requisite workers and they were only too eager to be relieved of that necessity by the advent of a class of labor which had no standing in the community and no prejudice against mill work. As the manufacturers were strong in their influence everywhere in New England, including the legislatures, as the various reform movements of the forties collapsed or became merged into the attack on negro slavery, and as the attention of the nation was focused on the spectacular California gold rush, it is not surprising that the foreigner entered the mills, to a large extent unnoticed and unopposed. By 1860, twenty-one per cent of the population of both Massachusetts and Rhode Island was of foreign birth.

Beauty, the Beast and the Militant Woman: A Case Study in Sex Roles and Social Stress in Jacksonian America

CARROLL SMITH-ROSENBERG

Some women found themselves in factories early in the nineteenth century but most did not. Nevertheless, the rapidly changing society that surrounded them led to a beginning reexamination of women's roles independent of the work place. One expression of this was manifested in reform movements such as the New York Moral Reform Society. Attacking the exploitation of women through prostitution, they also began to question the double standard and some at least began to examine the domestic ideal. Asserting the superiority of women, they called for the creation of a National Union of Women. As Smith-Rosenberg suggests, these groups "began to create a broader, less constricted sense of female identity."

Carroll Smith-Rosenberg, "Beauty, the Beast, and the Militant Woman: A Case Study in Sex Roles and Social Stress in Jacksonian America," *American Quarterly*, 23, No. 4, 562–84. Published by the University of Pennsylvania. Copyright 1972, Trustees of the University of Pennsylvania. Reprinted and footnotes omitted by permission of the author and the publisher.

On a spring evening in May 1834, a small group of women met at the revivalist Third Presbyterian Church in New York City to found the New York Female Moral Reform Society. The Society's goals were ambitious indeed; it hoped to convert New York's prostitutes to evangelical Protestantism and close forever the city's numerous brothels. This bold attack on prostitution was only one part of the Society's program. These self-assertive women hoped as well to confront that larger and more fundamental abuse, the double standard, and the male sexual license it condoned. Too many men, the Society defiantly asserted in its statement of goals, were aggressive destroyers of female innocence and happiness. No man was above suspicion. Women's only safety lay in a militant effort to reform American sexual mores—and, as we shall see, to reform sexual mores meant in practice to control man's sexual values and autonomy. The rhetoric of the Society's spokesmen consistently betrayed an unmistakable and deeply felt resentment toward a male-dominated society.

Few if any members of the Society were reformed prostitutes or the victims of rape or seduction. Most came from middle-class native American backgrounds and lived quietly respectable lives as pious wives and mothers. What needs explaining is the emotional logic which underlay the Society's militant and controversial program of sexual reform. I would like to suggest that both its reform program and the anti-male sentiments it served to express reflect a neglected area of stress in mid-19th century America— that is, the nature of the role to be assumed by the middle-class American woman.

American society from the 1830s to the 1860s was marked by advances in political democracy, by a rapid increase in economic, social and geographic mobility, and by uncompromising and morally relentless reform movements. Though many aspects of Jacksonianism have been subjected to historical investigation, the possibly stressful effects of such structural change upon family and sex roles have not. The following pages constitute an attempt to glean some understanding of women and women's role in antebellum America through an analysis of a self-consciously female voluntary association dedicated to the eradication of sexual immorality.

Women in Jacksonian America had few rights and little power. Their role in society was passive and sharply limited. Women were, in general, denied formal education above the minimum required by a literate early industrial society. The female brain and nervous system, male physicians and educators agreed, were inadequate to sustained intellectual effort. They were denied the vote in a society which placed a high value upon political participation; political activity might corrupt their pure feminine nature. All professional roles (with the exception of primary school education) were closed to women. Even so traditional a female role as midwife was undermined as male physicians began to establish professional control over obstetrics. Most economic alternatives to marriage (except such burdensome and menial tasks as those of seamstress or domestic) were closed to women. Their property rights were still restricted and females were generally considered to be the legal wards either of the state or of their nearest male relative. In the event of divorce, the mother lost custody of her children—even when the husband was conceded to be the erring party. Women's universe was bounded by their homes and the career of father or husband; within the home it was woman's duty to be submissive and patient.

Yet this was a period when change was considered a self-evident good, and when nothing was believed impossible to a determined free will, be it the conquest of a continent, the reform of society or the eternal salvation of all mankind. The contrast between these generally accepted ideals and expectations and the real possibilities available to American women could not have been more sharply drawn. It is not implausible to assume that at least a minority of American women would find ways to manifest a discontent with their comparatively passive and constricted social role.

Only a few women in antebellum America were able, however, to openly criticize their socially defined sexual identity. A handful, like Fanny Wright, devoted themselves to overtly subversive criticism of the social order. A scarcely more numerous group became pioneers in women's education. Others such as Elizabeth Cady Stanton, Lucretia Mott and Susan B. Anthony founded the women's rights movement. But most respectable women—even those with a sense of ill-defined grievance—were unable to explicitly defy traditional sex-role prescriptions.

I would like to suggest that many such women channeled frustration, anger and a compensatory sense of superior righteousness into the reform movements of the first half of the 19th century; and in the controversial moral reform crusade such motivations seem particularly apparent. While unassailable within the absolute categories of a pervasive evangelical world-view, the Female Moral Reform Society's crusade against illicit sexuality permitted an expression of anti-male sentiments. And the Society's "final solution"—the right to control the mores of men—provided a logical emotional redress for those feelings of passivity which we have suggested. It should not be surprising that between 1830 and 1860 a significant number of militant women joined a crusade to establish their right to define—and limit—man's sexual behavior.

Yet adultery and prostitution were unaccustomed objects of reform even in the enthusiastic and millennial America of the 1830s. The mere discussion of these taboo subjects shocked most Americans; to undertake such a crusade implied no ordinary degree of commitment. The founders of the Female Moral Reform Society, however, were able to find both legitimization for the expression of grievance normally unspoken and an impulse to activism in the moral categories of evangelical piety. Both pious activism and sex-role anxieties shaped the early years of the Female Moral Reform Society. This conjunction of motives was hardly accidental.

The lady founders of the Moral Reform Society and their new organization represented an extreme wing of that movement within American Protestantism known as the Second Great Awakening. These women were intensely pious Christians, convinced that an era of millennial perfection awaited human effort. In this fervent generation, such deeply felt millennial possibilities made social action a moral imperative. Like many of the abolitionists, Jacksonian crusaders against sexual transgression were dedicated activists, compelled to attack sin wherever it existed and in whatever form it assumed—even the unmentionable sin of illicit sexuality.

New Yorkers' first awareness of the moral reform crusade came in the spring of 1832 when the New York Magdalen Society (an organization which sought to reform prostitutes) issued its first annual report. Written by John McDowall, their missionary and agent, the report stated unhesitatingly that 10,000 prostitutes lived and worked in New York City. Not only sailors and other transients, but men from the city's most respected families, were regular brothel patrons. Lewdness and impurity tainted all sectors of New York society. True Christians, the report concluded, must wage a thoroughgoing crusade against violators of the Seventh Commandment.

The report shocked and irritated respectable New Yorkers—not only by its tone of righteous indignation and implied criticism of the city's old and established families. The report, it seemed clear to many New Yorkers, was obscene, its author a mere seeker after notoriety. Hostility quickly spread from McDowall to the Society itself; its members were verbally abused and threatened with ostracism. The society disbanded.

A few of the women, however, would not retreat. Working quietly, they began to found church-affiliated female moral reform societies. Within a year, they had created a number of such groups, connected for the most part with the city's more evangelical congregations. These pious women hoped to reform prostitutes, but more immediately to warn other God-fearing Christians of the pervasiveness of sexual sin and the need to oppose it. Prostitution was after all only one of many offenses against the Seventh Commandment; adultery, lewd thoughts and language, and bawdy literature were equally sinful in the eyes of God. These women at the same time continued unofficially to support their former missionary, John McDowall, using his newly established moral reform newspaper to advance their cause not only in the city, but throughout New York State.

After more than a year of such discreet crusading, the women active in the moral reform cause felt sufficiently numerous and confident to organize a second city-wide moral reform society, and renew their efforts to reform the city's prostitutes. On the evening of May 12, 1834, they met at the Third Presbyterian Church to found the New York Female Moral Reform Society.

Nearly four years of opposition and controversy had hardened the women's ardor into a militant determination. They proposed through their organization to extirpate sexual license and the double standard from American society. A forthright list of resolves announced their organization:

> Resolved, That immediate and vigorous efforts should be made to create a public sentiment in respect to this sin; and also in respect to the duty of parents, church members and ministers on the subject, which shall be in stricter accordance with . . . the word of God.
>
> . . . .
>
> Resolved, That the licentious man is no less guilty than his victim, and ought, therefore, to be excluded from all virtuous female society.
>
> Resolved, That it is the imperious duty of ladies everywhere, and of every religious denomination, to co-operate in the great work of moral reform.

A sense of urgency and spiritual absolutism marked this organizational meeting, and indeed all of the Society's official statements for years to come. "It is the duty of the virtuous to use every consistent moral means to save our country from utter destruction," the women warned. "The sin of licentiousness has made fearful havoc . . . drowning souls in perdition and exposing us to the vengeance of a holy God." Americans hopeful of witnessing the promised millennium could delay no longer.

The motivating zeal which allowed the rejection of age-old proprieties and defied the criticism of pulpit and press was no casual and fashionable enthusiasm. Only an extraordinary set of legitimating values could have justified such commitment. And this was indeed the case. The women moral reformers acted in the conscious conviction that God imperiously commanded their work. As they explained soon after organizing their society: "As Christians we must view it in the light of God's word—we must enter into His feelings on the subject—engage in its overthrow just in the manner he would have us. . . . We must look away from all worldly opinions or influences, for they are perverted and wrong; and individually act only as in the presence of God." Though the Society's pious activism had deep roots in the evangelicalism of the Second Great Awakening, the immediate impetus for the founding of the Moral Reform Society came from the revivals Charles G. Finney conducted in New York City between the summer of 1829 and the spring of 1834.

Charles Finney, reformer, revivalist and perfectionist theologian from western New York State, remains a pivotal figure in the history of American Protestantism. The four years Finney spent in New York had a profound influence on the city's churches and reform movements, and upon the consciences generally of the thousands of New Yorkers who crowded his revival meetings and flocked to his churches. Finney insisted that his disciples end any compromise with sin or human injustice. Souls were lost and sin prevailed, Finney urged, because men chose to sin— because they chose not to work in God's vineyard converting souls and reforming sinners. Inspired by Finney's sermons, thousands of New Yorkers turned to missionary work; they distributed Bibles and tracts to the irreligious, established Sunday schools and sent ministers to the frontier. A smaller, more zealous number espoused abolition as well, determined, like Garrison, never to be silent and to be heard. An even smaller number of the most zealous and determined turned—as we have seen—to moral reform.

The program adopted by the Female Moral Reform Society in the spring of 1834 embraced two quite different, though to the Society's founders quite consistent, modes of attack. One was absolutist and millennial, an attempt to convert all of America to perfect moral purity. Concretely the New York women hoped to create a militant nationwide women's organization to fight the double standard and indeed any form of licentiousness—beginning of course in their own homes and neighborhoods. Only an organization of women, they contended, could be trusted with so sensitive and yet monumental a task. At the same time, the Society sponsored a parallel and somewhat more pragmatic attempt to convert and reform New York City's prostitutes. Though strikingly dissimilar in method and geographic scope, both efforts were unified by an uncompromising millennial zeal and by a strident hostility to the licentious and predatory male.

The Society began its renewed drive against prostitution in the fall of 1834 when the executive committee appointed John McDowall their missionary to New York's prostitutes and hired two young men to assist him. The Society's three missionaries visited the female wards of the almshouse, the city hospital and jails, leading prayer meetings, distributing Bibles and tracts. A greater proportion of their time, however, was spent in a more controversial manner, systematically visiting—or, to be more accurate, descending upon—brothels, praying with and exhorting both the inmates and their patrons. The missionaries were specially fond of arriving early Sunday morning—catching women and customers as they awoke on the traditionally sacred day. The missionaries would announce their arrival by a vigorous reading of Bible passages, followed by prayer and hymns. At other times they would station themselves across the street from known brothels to observe and note the identity of customers. They soon found their simple presence had an important deterring effect, many men, with doggedly innocent expressions, pausing momentarily and then hastily walking past. Closed coaches, they also reported, were observed to circle suspiciously for upwards of an hour until, the missionary remaining, they drove away.

The Female Moral Reform Society did not depend completely on paid missionaries for the success of such pious harassment. The Society's executive committee, accompanied by like-thinking male volunteers, regularly visited the city's hapless brothels. (The executive committee minutes for January 1835, for example, contain a lengthy discussion of the properly discreet makeup of groups for such "active visiting.") The members went primarily to pray and to exert moral influence. They were not unaware, however, of the financially disruptive effect that frequent visits of large groups of praying Christians would have. The executive committee also aided the concerned parents (usually rural) of runaway daughters who, they feared, might have drifted to the city and been forced into prostitution. Members visited brothels asking for information about such girls; one pious volunteer even pretended to be delivering laundry in order to gain admittance to a brothel suspected of hiding such a runaway.

In conjunction with their visiting, the Moral Reform Society opened a House of Reception, a would-be refuge for prostitutes seeking to reform. The Society's managers and missionaries felt that if the prostitute could be convinced of her sin, and then offered both a place of retreat and an economic alternative to prostitution, reform would surely follow. Thus they envisioned their home as a "house of industry" where the errant ones would be taught new trades and prepared for useful jobs—while being instructed in morality and religion. When the managers felt their repentant charges prepared to return to society, they attempted to find them jobs with Christian families—and, so far as possible, away from the city's temptations.

Despite their efforts, however, few prostitutes reformed; fewer still appeared, to their benefactresses, to have experienced the saving grace of conversion. Indeed, the number of inmates at the Society's House of Reception was always small. In March 1835, for instance, the executive committee reported only fourteen women at the House. A year later, total admissions had reached but thirty—only four of whom were considered saved. The final debacle came that summer when the regular manager of the House left the city because of poor health. In his absence, the executive committee reported unhappily, the inmates seized control, and discipline and morality deteriorated precipitously. The managers reassembled in the fall to find their home in chaos. Bitterly discouraged, they dismissed the few remaining unruly inmates and closed the building.

The moral rehabilitation of New York's streetwalkers was but one aspect of the Society's attack upon immorality. The founders of the Female Moral Reform Society saw as their principal objective the creation of a woman's crusade to combat sexual license generally and the double standard particularly. American women would no longer willingly tolerate that traditional—and role-defining—masculine ethos which allotted respect to the hearty drinker and the sexual athlete. This age-old code of masculinity was as obviously related to man's social preeminence as it was contrary to society's explicitly avowed norms of purity and domesticity. The subterranean mores of the American male must be confronted, exposed and rooted out.

The principal weapon of the Society in this crusade was its weekly, *The Advocate of Moral Reform*. In the fall of 1834, when the Society hired John McDowall as its agent, it voted as well to purchase his journal and transform it into a national women's paper with an exclusively female staff. Within three years, the *Advocate* grew into one of the nation's most widely read evangelical papers, boasting 16,500 subscribers. By the late 1830s the Society's managers pointed to this publication as their most important activity.

Two themes dominated virtually every issue of the *Advocate* from its founding in January 1835, until the early 1850s. The first was an angry and emphatic insistence upon the lascivious and predatory nature of the American male. Men were the initiators in virtually every case of adultery or fornication—and the source, therefore, of that widespread immorality which endangered America's spiritual life and delayed the promised millennium. A second major theme in the *Advocate's* editorials and letters was a call for the creation of a national union of women. Through their collective action such a united group of women might ultimately control the behavior of adult males and of the members' own children, particularly their sons.

The founders and supporters of the Female Moral Reform Society entertained several primary assumptions concerning the nature of human sexuality. Perhaps most central was the conviction that women felt little sexual desire; they were in almost every instance induced to violate the Seventh Commandment by lascivious men who craftily manipulated not their sensuality, but rather the female's trusting and affectionate nature. A woman acted out of romantic love, not carnal desire; she was innocent and defenseless, gentle and passive. "The worst crime alleged against [the fallen woman] in the outset," the *Advocate's* editors explained, "is . . . 'She is without discretion.' She is open-hearted, sincere, and affectionate. . . . She trusts the vows of the faithless. She commits her all into the hands of the deceiver."

The male lecher, on the other hand, was a creature controlled by base sexual drives which he neither could nor would control. He was, the *Advocate's* editors bitterly complained, powerful and decisive; unwilling (possibly unable) to curb his own willfulness, he callously used it to coerce the more passive and submissive female. This was an age of rhetorical expansiveness, and the *Advocate's* editors and correspondents felt little constraint in their delineation of the dominant and aggressive male. "Reckless," "bold," "mad," "drenched in sin" were terms used commonly to describe erring males; they "robbed," "ruined" and "rioted." But one term above all others seemed most fit to describe the lecher— "The Destroyer."

A deep sense of anger and frustration characterized the *Advocate's* discussion of such all-conquering males, a theme reiterated again and again in the letters sent to the paper by rural sympathizers. Women saw themselves with few defenses against the determined male; his will was far stronger than that of woman. Such letters often expressed a bitterness which seems directed not only against the specific seducer, but toward all American men. One representative rural subscriber complained, for example: "Honorable men; they would not plunder; . . . an imputation on their honour might cost a man his life's blood. And yet they are so passingly mean, so utterly contemptible, as basely and treacherously to contrive . . . the destruction of happiness, peace, morality, and all that is endearing in social life; they plunge into degradation, misery, and ruin, those whom they profess to love. O let them not be trusted. Their 'tender mercies are cruel.' "

The double standard seemed thus particularly unjust; it came to symbolize and embody for the Society and its rural sympathizers the callous indifference—indeed at times almost sadistic pleasure—a male-dominated society took in the misfortune of a passive and defenseless woman. The respectable harshly denied her their friendship; even parents might reject her. Often only the brothel offered food and shelter. But what of her seducer? Conventional wisdom found it easy to condone his greater sin: men will be men and right-thinking women must not inquire into such questionable matters.

But it was just such matters, the Society contended, to which women must address themselves. They must enforce God's commandments despite hostility and censure. "Public opinion must be operated upon," the executive committee decided in the winter of 1835, "by endeavoring to bring the virtuous to treat the guilty of both sexes alike, and exercise toward them the same feeling." "Why should a female be trodden under foot," the executive committee's minutes questioned plaintively, "and spurned from society and driven from a parent's roof, if she but fall into sin—while common consent allows the male to habituate himself to this vice, and treats him as not guilty. Has God made a distinction in regard to the two sexes in this respect?" The guilty woman too should be condemned, the Moral Reform Society's quarterly meeting resolved in 1838: "But let not the most guilty of the two—the deliberate destroyer of innocence—be afforded even an 'apron of fig leaves' to conceal the blackness of his crimes."

Women must unite in a holy crusade against such sinners. The Society called upon pious women throughout the country to shun all social contact with men suspected of improper behavior—even if that behavior consisted only of reading improper books or singing indelicate songs. Churchgoing women of every village and town must organize local campaigns to outlaw such men from society and hold them up to public judgment. "Admit him not to your house," the executive committee urged, "hold no converse with him, warn others of him, permit not your friends to have fellowship with him, mark as an evildoer, stamp him as a villain and exclaim, 'Behold the Seducer.'" The power of ostracism could become an effective weapon in the defense of morality.

A key tactic in this campaign of public exposure was the Society's willingness to publish the names of men suspected of sexual immorality. The *Advocate's* editors announced in their first issue that they intended to pursue this policy, first begun by John McDowall in his *Journal.* "We think it proper," they stated defiantly, "even to expose names, for the same reason that the names of thieves and robbers are published, that the public may know them and govern themselves accordingly. We mean to let the licentious know, that if they are not ashamed of their debasing vice, we will not be ashamed to expose them. . . . It is a justice which we owe each other." Their readers responded enthusiastically to this invitation. Letters from rural subscribers poured into the *Advocate,* recounting specific instances of seduction in their towns and warning readers to avoid the men described. The editors dutifully set them in type and printed them.

Within New York City itself the executive committee of the Society actively investigated charges of seduction and immorality. A particular target of their watchfulness was the city's employment agencies—or information offices as they were then called; these were frequently fronts for the white-slave trade. The *Advocate* printed the names and addresses of suspicious agencies, warning women seeking employment to avoid them at all costs. Prostitutes whom the Society's missionaries visited in brothels, in prison or in the city hospital were urged to report the names of men who had first seduced them and also of their later customers; they could then be published in the *Advocate.* The executive committee undertook as well a lobbying campaign in Albany to secure the passage of a statute making seduction a crime for the male participant. While awaiting the passage of this measure, the executive committee encouraged and aided victims of seduction (or where appropriate their parents or employers) to sue their seducers on the grounds of loss of services.

Ostracism, exposure and statutory enactment offered immediate, if unfortunately partial, solutions to the problem of male licentiousness. But for the seduced and ruined victim such vengeance came too late. The tactic of preference, women moral reformers agreed, was to educate children, especially young male children, to a literal adherence to the Seventh Commandment. This was a mother's task. American mothers, the *Advocate's* editors repeated endlessly, must educate their sons to reject the double standard. No child was too young, no efforts too diligent in this crucial aspect of socialization. The true foundations of such a success- ful effort lay in an early and highly pietistic religious education and in the inculcation of a related imperative—the son's absolute and unques- tioned obedience to his mother's will. "Obedience, entire and unques- tioned, must be secured, or all is lost." The mother must devote herself whole-heartedly to this task for self-will in a child was an ever-recurring evil. "Let us watch over them continually. . . . Let us . . . teach them when they go out and when they come in—when they lie down, and when they rise up. . . ." A son must learn to confide in his mother instinctively; no thought should be hidden from her.

Explicit education in the Seventh Commandment itself should begin quite early for bitter experience had shown that no child was too young for such sensual temptation. As her son grew older, his mother was urged to instill in him a love for the quiet of domesticity, a repugnance for the unnatural excitements of the theater and tavern. He should be taught to prefer home and the companionship of pious women to the temptations of bachelor life. The final step in a young man's moral edu- cation would come one evening shortly before he was to leave home for the first time. That night, the *Advocate* advised its readers, the mother must spend a long earnest time at his bedside (ordinarily in the dark to hide her natural blushes) discussing the importance of maintaining his sexual purity and the temptations he would inevitably face in attempt- ing to remain true to his mother's religious principles.

Mothers, not fathers, were urged to supervise the sexual education of sons. Mothers, the Society argued, spent most time with their children; fathers were usually occupied with business concerns and found little time for their children. Sons were naturally close to their mothers and devoted maternal supervision would cement these natural ties. A mother devoted to the moral reform cause could be trusted to teach her son to reject the traditional ethos of masculinity and accept the higher—more feminine—code of Christianity. A son thus educated would be inevitably a recruit in the women's crusade against sexual license.

The Society's general program of exposure and ostracism, lobbying and education depended for effectiveness upon the creation of a national association of militant and pious women. In the fall of 1834, but a few months after they had organized their Society, its New York officers began to create such a woman's organization. At first they worked through the *Advocate* and the small network of sympathizers John McDowall's efforts had created. By the spring of 1835, however, they were able to hire a minister to travel through western New York State "in behalf of Moral Reform causes." The following year the committee sent two female missionaries, the editor of the Society's newspaper and a paid female agent, on a thousand-mile tour of the New England states. Visiting women's groups and churches in Brattleboro, Deerfield, Northampton, Pittsfield, the Stockbridges and many other towns, the ladies rallied their sisters to the moral reform cause and helped organize some forty-one new auxiliaries. Each succeeding summer saw similar trips by paid agents and managers of the Society throughout New York State and New England. By 1839, the New York Female Moral Reform Society boasted some 445 female auxiliaries, principally in greater New England. So successful were these efforts that within a few years the bulk of the Society's membership and financial support came from its auxiliaries. In February 1838, the executive committee voted to invite representatives of these auxiliaries to attend the Society's annual meeting. The following year the New York Society voted at its annual convention to reorganize as a national society—the American Female Moral Reform Society; the New York group would be simply one of its many constituent societies.

This rural support was an indispensable part of the moral reform movement. The local auxiliaries held regular meetings in churches, persuaded hesitant ministers to preach on the Seventh Commandment, urged Sunday school teachers to confront this embarrassing but vital question. They raised money for the executive committee's ambitious projects, convinced at least some men to form male moral reform societies, and did their utmost to ostracize suspected lechers. When the American Female Moral Reform Society decided to mount a campaign to induce the New York State legislature to pass a law making seduction a criminal offense, the Society's hundreds of rural auxiliaries wrote regularly to their legislators, circulated petitions and joined their New York City sisters in Albany to lobby for the bill (which was finally passed in 1848).

In addition to such financial and practical aid, members of the moral reform society's rural branches contributed another crucial, if less tangible, element to the reform movement. This was their commitment to the creation of a feeling of sisterhood among all morally dedicated women. Letters from individuals to the *Advocate* and reports from auxiliaries make clear, sometimes even in the most explicit terms, that many American women experienced a depressing sense of isolation. In part, this feeling merely reflected a physical reality for women living in rural communities. But since city- and town-dwelling women voiced similar complaints, I would like to suggest that this consciousness of isolation also reflected a sense of status inferiority. Confined by their non-maleness, antebellum American women lived within the concentric structure of a family organized around the needs and status of husbands or fathers. And such social isolation within the family—or perhaps more accurately a lack of autonomy both embodied in and symbolized by such isolation—not only dramatized, but partially constituted, a differentiation in status. The fact that social values and attitudes were established by men and oriented to male experiences only exacerbated women's feelings of inferiority and irrelevance. Again and again the Society's members were to express their desire for a feminine-sororial community which might help break down this isolation, lighten the monotony and harshness of life, and establish a countersystem of female values and priorities.

The New York Female Moral Reform Society quite consciously sought to inspire in its members a sense of solidarity in a cause peculiar to their sex, and demanding total commitment, to give them a sense of worthiness and autonomy outside woman's traditionally confining role. Its members, their officers forcefully declared, formed a united phalanx twenty thousand strong, "A UNION OF SENTIMENT AND EFFORT AMONG . . . VIRTUOUS FEMALES FROM MAINE TO ALABAMA." The officers of the New York Society were particularly conscious of the emotional importance of female solidarity within their movement—and the significant role that they as leaders played in the lives of their rural supporters. "Thousands are looking to us," the executive committee recorded in their minutes with mingled pride and responsibility, "with the expectation that the principles we have adopted, and the example we have set before the world will continue to be held up & they reasonably expect to witness our *united onward* movements till the conflict shall end in Victory."

For many of the Society's scattered members, the moral reform cause was their only contact with the world outside farm or village—the *Advocate* perhaps the only newspaper received by the family. A sense of solidarity and of emotional affiliation permeated the correspondence between rural members and the executive committee. Letters and even official reports inevitably began with the salutation, "Sisters," "Dear Sisters" or "Beloved Sisters." Almost every letter and report expressed the deep affection Society members felt for their like-thinking sisters in the cause of moral reform—even if their contact came only through letters and the *Advocate*. "I now pray and will not cease to pray," a woman in Syracuse, New York, wrote, "that your hearts may be encouraged and your hands strengthened." Letters to the Society's executive committee often promised unfailing loyalty and friendship; members and leaders pledged themselves ever ready to aid either local societies or an individual sister in need. Many letters from geographically isolated women reported that the Society made it possible for them for the first time to communicate with like-minded women. A few, in agitated terms, wrote about painful experiences with the double standard which only their correspondence with the *Advocate* allowed them to express and share.

Most significantly, the letters expressed a new consciousness of power. The moral reform society was based on the assertion of female moral superiority and the right and ability of women to reshape male behavior. No longer did women have to remain passive and isolated within the structuring presence of husband or father. The moral reform movement was, perhaps for the first time, a movement within which women could forge a sense of their own identity.

And its founders had no intention of relinquishing their new-found feeling of solidarity and autonomy. A few years after the Society was founded, for example, a group of male evangelicals established a Seventh Commandment Society. They promptly wrote to the Female Moral Reform Society suggesting helpfully that since men had organized, the ladies could now disband; moral reform was clearly an area of questionable propriety. The New York executive committee responded quickly, firmly —and negatively. Women throughout America, they wrote, had placed their trust in a female moral reform society and in female officers. Women, they informed the men, believed in both their own right and ability to combat the problem; it was decidedly a woman's, not a man's issue. "The paper is now in the right hands," one rural subscriber wrote: "This is the appropriate work for *women*. . . . Go on Ladies, go on, in the strength of the Lord."

In some ways, indeed, the New York Female Moral Reform Society could be considered a militant woman's organization. Although it was not overtly part of the woman's rights movement, it did concern itself with a number of feminist issues, especially those relating to woman's economic role. Society, the *Advocate's* editors argued, had unjustly confined women to domestic tasks. There were many jobs in society that women could and should be trained to fill. They could perform any light indoor work as well as men. In such positions—as clerks and artisans—they would receive decent wages and consequent self-respect. And this economic emphasis was no arbitrary or inappropriate one, the Society contended. Thousands of women simply had to work; widows, orphaned young women, wives and mothers whose husbands could not work because of illness or intemperance had to support themselves and their children. Unfortunately, they had now to exercise these responsibilities on the pathetically inadequate salaries they received as domestics, washerwomen or seamstresses—crowded, underpaid and physically unpleasant occupations. By the end of the 1840s, the Society had adopted the cause of the working woman and made it one of their principal concerns—in the 1850s even urging women to join unions and, when mechanization came to the garment industry, helping underpaid seamstresses rent sewing machines at low rates.

The Society sought consciously, moreover, to demonstrate woman's ability to perform successfully in fields traditionally reserved for men. Quite early in their history they adopted the policy of hiring only women employees. From the first, of course, only women had been officers and managers of the Society. And after a few years, these officers began to hire women in preference to men as agents and to urge other charitable societies and government agencies to do likewise. (They did this although the only salaried charitable positions held by women in this period tended to be those of teachers in girls' schools or supervisors of women's wings in hospitals and homes for juvenile delinquents.) In February 1835, for instance, the executive committee hired a woman agent to solicit subscriptions to the *Advocate*. That summer they hired another woman to travel through New England and New York State organizing auxiliaries and giving speeches to women on moral reform. In October of 1836, the executive officers appointed two women as editors of their journal— undoubtedly among the first of their sex in this country to hold such positions. In 1841, the executive committee decided to replace their male financial agent with a woman bookkeeper. By 1843 women even set type and did the folding for the Society's journal. All these jobs, the ladies proudly, indeed aggressively stressed, were appropriate tasks for women.

The broad feminist implications of such statements and actions must have been apparent to the officers of the New York Society. And indeed the Society's executive committee maintained discreet but active ties with the broader woman's rights movement of the 1830s, 40s and 50s; at one point at least, they flirted with official endorsement of a bold woman's rights position. Evidence of this flirtation can be seen in the minutes of the executive committee and occasionally came to light in articles and editorials appearing in the *Advocate*. As early as the mid-1830s, for instance, the executive committee began to correspond with a number of women who were then or were later to become active in the woman's rights movment. Lucretia Mott, abolitionist and pioneer feminist, was a founder and secretary of the Philadelphia Female Moral Reform Society; as such she was in frequent communication with the New York executive committee. Emma Willard, a militant advocate of women's education and founder of the Troy Female Seminary, was another of the executive committee's regular correspondents. Significantly, when Elizabeth Blackwell, the first woman doctor in either the United States or Great Britain, received her medical degree, Emma Willard wrote to the New York executive committee asking its members to use their influence to find her a job. The Society did more than that. The *Advocate* featured a story dramatizing Dr. Blackwell's struggles. The door was now open for other women, the editors urged; medicine was a peculiarly appropriate profession for sensitive and sympathetic womankind. The Society offered to help interested women in securing admission to medical school.

One of the most controversial aspects of the early woman's rights movement was its criticism of the subservient role of women within the American family, and of the American man's imperious and domineering behavior toward women. Much of the Society's rhetorical onslaught upon the male's lack of sexual accountability served as a screen for a more general—and less socially acceptable—resentment of masculine social preeminence. Occasionally, however, the *Advocate* expressed such resentment overtly. An editorial in 1838, for example, revealed a deeply felt antagonism toward the power asserted by husbands over their wives and children. "A portion of the inhabitants of this favored land," the Society admonished, "are groaning under a despotism, which seems to be modeled precisely after that of the Autocrat of Russia. . . . We allude to the tyranny exercised in the HOME department, where lordly man, 'clothed with a little brief authority,' rules his trembling subjects with a rod of iron, conscious of entire impunity, and exalting in his fancied superiority." The Society's editorialist continued, perhaps even more bitterly: "Instead of regarding his wife as a help-mate for him, an equal sharer in his joys and sorrows, he looks upon her as a useful article of furniture, which is valuable only for the benefit derived from it, but which may be thrown aside at pleasure." Such behavior, the editorial carefully emphasized, was not only commonplace, experienced by many of the Society's own members—even the wives of "Christians" and of ministers —but was accepted and even justified by society; was it not sanctioned by the Bible?

At about the same time, indeed, the editors of the *Advocate* went so far as to print an attack upon "masculine" translations and interpretations of the Bible, and especially of Paul's epistles. This appeared in a lengthy article written by Sarah Grimké, a "notorious" feminist and abolitionist. The executive committee clearly sought to associate their organization more closely with the nascent woman's rights movement. Calling upon American women to read and interpret the Bible for themselves, Sarah Grimké asserted that God had created woman the absolute equal of man. But throughout history, man, being stronger, had usurped woman's natural rights. He had subjected wives and daughters to his physical control and had evolved religious and scientific rationalizations to justify this domination. "Men have endeavored to entice, or to drive women from almost every sphere of moral action." Miss Grimké charged: " 'Go home and spin' is the . . . advice of the domestic tyrant. . . . The first duty, I believe, which devolves on our sex now is to think for themselves. . . . Until we take our stand side by side with our brother; until we read all the precepts of the Bible as addressed to woman as well as to man, and lose . . . the consciousness of sex, we shall never fulfil the end of our existence." "Those who do undertake to labor," Miss Grimké wrote from her own and her sister's bitter experiences, "are the scorn and ridicule of their own and the other sex." "We are so little accustomed *to think for ourselves,*" she continued,

> that we submit to the dictum of prejudice, and of usurped authority, almost without an effort to redeem ourselves from the unhallowed shackles which have so long bound us; almost without a desire to rise from that degradation and bondage to which we have been consigned by man, and by which the faculties of our minds, and the powers of our spiritual nature, have been prevented from expanding to their full growth, and are sometimes wholly crushed.

Each woman must re-evaluate her role in society; no longer could she depend on husband or father to assume her responsibilities as a free individual. No longer, Sarah Grimké argued, could she be satisfied with simply caring for her family or setting a handsome table. The officers of the Society, in an editorial comment following this article, admitted that she had written a radical critique of woman's traditional role. But they urged their members, "It is of immense importance to our sex to possess clear and *correct* ideas of our rights and duties."

Sarah Grimké's overt criticism of woman's traditional role, containing as it did an attack upon the Protestant ministry and orthodox interpretations of the Bible, went far far beyond the consensus of the *Advocate's* rural subscribers. The following issue contained several letters sharply critical of her and of the managers, for printing her editorial. And indeed the *Advocate* never again published the work of an overt feminist. Their membership, the officers concluded, would not tolerate explicit attacks upon traditional family structure and orthodox Christianity. Anti-male resentment and anger had to be expressed covertly. It was perhaps too threatening or—realistically—too dangerous for respectable matrons in relatively close-knit semi-rural communities in New York,

New England, Ohio or Wisconsin so openly to question the traditional relations of the sexes and demand a new and ominously forceful role for women.

The compromise the membership and the officers of the Society seemed to find most comfortable was one that kept the American woman within the home—but which greatly expanded her powers as pious wife and mother. In rejecting Sarah Grimké's feminist manifesto, the Society's members implicitly agreed to accept the role traditionally assigned woman: the self-sacrificing, supportive, determinedly chaste wife and mother who limited her "sphere" to domesticity and religion. But in these areas her power should be paramount. The mother, not the father, should have final control of the home and family—especially of the religious and moral education of her children. If the world of economics and public affairs was his, the home must be hers.

And even outside the home, woman's peculiar moral endowment and responsibilities justified her in playing an increasingly expansive role, one which might well ultimately impair aspects of man's traditional autonomy. When man transgressed God's commandments, through licentiouness, religious apathy, the defense of slavery, or the sin of intemperance—woman had both the right and duty of leaving the confines of the home and working to purify the male world.

The membership of the New York Female Moral Reform Society chose not to openly espouse the woman's rights movement. Yet many interesting emotional parallels remain to link the moral reform crusade and the suffrage movement of Elizabeth Cady Stanton, the Grimké sisters and Susan B. Anthony. In its own way, indeed, the war for purification of sexual mores was far more fundamental in its implications for woman's traditional role than the demand for woman's education—or even the vote.

Many of the needs and attitudes, moreover, expressed by suffragette leaders at the Seneca Falls Convention and in their efforts in the generation following are found decades earlier in the letters of rural women in the *Advocate of Moral Reform*. Both groups found woman's traditionally passive role intolerable. Both wished to assert female worth and values in a heretofore entirely male world. Both welcomed the creation of a sense of feminine loyalty and sisterhood that could give emotional strength and comfort to women isolated within their homes—whether in a remote farmstead or a Gramercy Park mansion. And it can hardly be assumed that the demand for votes for women was appreciably more radical than a moral absolutism which encouraged women to invade bordellos, befriend harlots and publicly discuss rape, seduction and prostitution.

It is important as well to re-emphasize a more general historical perspective. When the pious women founders of the Moral Reform Society gathered at the Third Free Presbyterian Church, it was fourteen years before the Seneca Falls Convention—which has traditionally been accepted as the beginning of the woman's rights movement in the United States. There simply was no woman's movement in the 1830s. The future leaders were either still adolescents or just becoming dissatisfied with aspects of their role. Women advocates of moral reform were among the very first American women to challenge their completely passive, home-oriented image. They were among the first to travel throughout the country without male chaperones. They published, financed, even set type for their own paper and defied a bitter and long-standing male opposition to their cause. They began, in short, to create a broader, less constricted sense of female identity. Naturally enough, they were dependent upon the activist impulse and legitimating imperatives of evangelical religion. This was indeed a complex symbiosis, the energies of pietism and the grievances of role discontent creating the new and activist female consciousness which characterized the history of the American Female Moral Reform Society in antebellum America. Their experience, moreover, was probably shared, though less overtly, by the thousands of women who devoted time and money to the great number of reform causes which multiplied in Jacksonian America. Women in the abolition and the temperance movements (and to a less extent in more narrowly evangelical and religious causes) also developed a sense of their ability to judge for themselves and of their right to publicly criticize the values of the larger society. The lives and self-image of all these women had changed—if only so little—because of their new reforming interests.

The Owenite Socialist Movement
in Britain and the United States:
A Comparative Study

JOHN F. C. HARRISON

In a fine example of the possibilities in comparative history, J. F. C. Harrison here compares the American and British followers of the communitarian reformer Robert Owen. The emergence of industrialism and the attempt to replace older collective values with new laissez-faire capitalist mores met resistance in both societies. Owenism expressed basically anti-capitalist sentiments.

The importance of evangelical religion in reform movements, even one so secular as Owenism, cannot be ignored. Perfectionist Christianity provided at least one model for the communication of egalitarian and even collectivist ideas. Harrison also differentiates Owenism in its different environs. He suggests that British philanthropy played a significant role, whereas in America it was evangelical religion that took a predominant place.

Perhaps most important for American history is the suggestion that

John F. C. Harrison, "The Owenite Socialist Movement in Britain and the United States: A Comparative Study," Labor History, 9 (1968), 324–37. Reprinted and all footnotes except footnote 1 omitted by permission of the author and the publisher.

Owenism and other forms of communitarianism must be seen in the context of working class and reform movements, and not as peculiar early-nineteenth-century anachronisms.

The following books are suggested for further reading:

A. E. BESTOR, *Backwoods Utopias,* Philadelphia: University of Pennsylvania Press, 1950.

J. F. C. HARRISON, *Quest for the New Moral World,* New York: Charles Scribner's Sons, 1969.

CHARLES NORDHOFF, *The Communistic Societies of the U.S.,* New York: Dover Publications, Inc., 1966.

J. H. NOYES, *History of American Socialism,* New York: Dover Publications, Inc., 1966.

The history of Robert Owen and the movement associated with his name has produced a considerable literature. Within two years of his death in 1858 a book-length biography of Owen appeared, and the 1860s produced two more studies published in London and Philadelphia. From then on biographies and studies of Owenism have appeared with steady regularity on both sides of the Atlantic. In Britain, thanks to the indefatigable efforts of George Jacob Holyoake, Owen and Owenism were at first linked with the consumers' cooperative movement, and were later taken up by the Fabians. Subsequently, Owen was accorded a niche in the standard histories of British labor and socialism, and the usual treatment of Owenism in recent years has been as a phase in the history of the British working-class movement—a link in the continuous chain which is traced from 1789 to the Wilson government. In America the emphasis has been different. Here Owenism has been treated as part of the communitarian tradition by historians from John Humphrey Noyes to Professor Arthur Eugene Bestor. The standard accounts present it as an episode in the quest for Utopia or an aspect of "freedom's ferment." New Harmony has also exercised a continuing fascination for essayists, novelists, and writers of semi-serious history.

So far no attempt has been made to comprehend the whole of the Owenite record, putting the British and the American material together, and searching for an interpretation of Owenism in relation to the two different societies. If we set aside the various partial interpretations (that is Owenism as an aspect of this or that social or intellectual development in one particular country), the central feature of Owenism is the dual nature of its role in two such different societies as early industrial Britain and agricultural, frontier America. That contemporaries should have considered Owenite ideas and institutions relevant in these two very different contexts is the starting point for new questions and new approaches. Instead of asking what Owenism contributed to the making of the English working class, or how it related to American frontier conditions and westward expansion, we have to examine the points of contact, or similarity, in British and American social experience which made Owenism acceptable in certain situations. The research area is sufficiently small and well-defined to serve almost as a microcosm of Anglo-American society, so that through a comparative—or, more accurately, a relational—approach, questions of a wider significance than the specifics of social reform may be raised. In fact, in this context Owenism becomes a contemporary comment on Anglo-American civilization in the early nineteenth century.

The inter-relationship of the British and American Owenite movements is demonstrated most obviously by their separate chronologies. Owen's first Essay on the Formation of the Human Character, setting forth his *New View of Society,* appeared in London in 1813; and in the summer of 1817 he launched his first great propaganda campaign. From then until 1824 Owen's schemes were continually before the English public, but did not attract much attention elsewhere. In the fall of 1824, however, Owen shifted the scene of his operations to the New World, and early in 1825 launched his first community at New Harmony, Indiana. His Scottish followers at the same time began the first British Owenite community at Orbiston in Lanarkshire. Developments on both sides of the Atlantic were regarded as parts of the same movement, and news of the communities and proposed communities was exchanged regularly. About ten Owenite communities were founded in North America in the 1820s but none lasted more than two or three years; and by 1829 the first phase of Owenism in America came to an end. In Britain attempts to organize stable communities in the 1820s were similarly frustrated, but out of these efforts emerged a new type of Owenite institution—the cooperative trading association. From 1828 cooperative stores increased rapidly and by 1830 the *Cooperator* claimed that 300 existed in the United Kingdom. Upon his return from America in 1829 Owen discovered a considerable working-class interest in his ideas, and from then until 1834 Owenism captured the imagination of many proletarian leaders. First through the National Equitable Labour Exchange (which was an institutionalization of the Ricardian socialist labor theory of value) and then through the Grand National Consolidated Trades Union (an attempt to build a national trades union organization), Owen for a time emerged as the leader of the laboring poor. But these institutions collapsed in 1834 and Owenism in Britain entered a new phase, signalled by the appearance of the journal, the *New Moral World*. The Owenite movement of the 1834–45 period was characterized by renewed efforts to found communities, and by building local branches throughout the kingdom. Five communities were launched, and Halls of Science were opened in the larger towns. In America there was no comparable movement to build a local branch organization, but in the general communitarian revival of the 1840s three Owenite communities were started and Owenite influence was strong in at least two others. As an organized movement Owenism was dead in both countries after 1848, but an Owenite legacy was carried by old disciples into later movements, among them secularism, consumers' cooperation, associationism, and spiritualism.

Throughout its thirty-year history, the Owenite movement has thus to be traced in both Britain and America. A certain unity, especially in the 1820s, was imposed by the domination of Robert Owen himself, and also by the strong fraternal interest which English Owenites had in American communitarian experiments in general. Despite their emphasis on the primacy of social environment, Owenites largely ignored the differences between American and British society and tended to think of a common pattern of social development for both countries. The principles of Owenism were considered universally valid, irrespective of time and place. In fact, however, Owenite concepts and institutions did differ in the two countries. Some elements in the British Owenite tradition were entirely lacking or appeared in greatly diluted form in the American movement; conversely, Owenism in America carried overtones which were not present in Britain. These differences had a reacting and reinforcing effect on what appeared to be a common core of beliefs and institutional experiences. It will be the object of the remainder of this article to relate some Owenite institutions and roles to different contexts, to uncover some roots of Owenite ideology, and to examine the changes, if any, which Owenism underwent in its transplantation from the Old World to the New. Because of limitations of space the analysis will be confined to three aspects of Owenism: philanthropy, communitarianism, and millennialism.

The phrenologists agreed that Owen's bump of benevolence was unusually large. Visitors to New Lanark, impressed by the mills and disarmed by Owen's charm, praised his practical benevolence and enlightened philanthropy. To a whole generation after 1815 he was "Mr. Owen, the Philanthropist," or "the benevolent Mr. Owen." His name was everywhere linked with successful, paternalistic schemes for improving the lot of the poor, and in this role he at first gained the support of the Duke of Kent and influential members of the landed interest and the business world. Philanthropy was a basic motif in the pattern of Owenism.

Owen's plan for the reorganization of society—and by extension for the salvation of the world—originated as a scheme for relief of the unemployed. His philanthropic endeavours had first been directed to improving working and living conditions at New Lanark, then to educational reform and to the restriction of child labor in factories. The "distress" which followed the peace of 1815 turned his attention to problems of the unemployed, and in this context he first elaborated his plan for self-supporting communities of about 1,200 persons, with accommodation arranged in a parallelogram of buildings, and provision for all the educational and social needs of the inhabitants. By 1820 these arrangements had matured into a communitarian plan for the thorough organization of society, embedded in a theory of cooperative socialism and prophetic utterance. But in the first instance Owenism developed within the dimensions of the Poor Laws as inherited from the late eighteenth century and aggravated by the impact of the Napoleonic Wars. It was no accident that the first Owenite organization in 1822 was named the British and Foreign Philanthropic Society for the Permanent Relief of the Labouring Classes, nor that philanthropists were conspicuous among Owen's early followers.

In Britain the Owenite philanthropists included Scottish squires such as Archibald James Hamilton, Irish landlords such as William Thompson, and London businessmen such as John Minter Morgan.[1] They were attracted to Owenism as a solution to the problem of poor relief, and after they had widened their horizons they still regarded it as an exercise in gentlemanly philanthropy. Their ideas of community were for the most part set in an agricultural mold and they strongly resented the values of industrialism.

In America Owenite philanthropy assumed a somewhat different hue. The Poor Law problem in its English form did not exist in the United States,

---

[1] Archibald James Hamilton (1793–1834), the son of the laird of Dalziel and Orbiston, was a lieutenant in the Scots Greys at Waterloo. He became an ardent follower of Owen and was associated with Abram Combe in the Orbiston community experiment, for which he provided the land.

William Thompson (1775–1833), an Irish landowner, identified himself completely with the Owenite Movement, and developed the fullest exposition of Ricardian-Owenite socialism. As a young man he was influenced by the French Revolution and was later a friend of Jeremy Bentham. In addition to his Benthamite and Owenist interests he was also a champion of women's rights.

John Minter Morgan (1782–1854) inherited "an ample fortune" from his father, a wholesale stationer of London, and spent his life pursuing philanthropic interests. As early as 1819 he published a defense of Owen's views, and his *Revolt of the Bees* (London, 1826) was one of the most widely read of the popularizations of Owenism. He was a member of the Church of England, and sought to reconcile his Christian beliefs with Owenite community projects.

nor was squirearchical paternalism appreciated except in parts of the South. American philanthropy stemmed from other roots, usually either evangelical or radical, and this was reflected in the type of philanthropic support which American Owenism attracted. Thus on the one hand was Jeremiah Thompson, a wealthy Quaker merchant and shipowner of New York, who supported both New Harmony and Nashoba; on the other was William Maclure, philanthropic radical and deist. What there was not room for in the American environment was Owen's type of paternalism. As Maclure sagely observed: "the materials in this country are not the same as the cotton spinners at New Lanark, nor does the advice of a patron go so far." The careers and interests of Owen and Maclure were very similar, and their ultimate disagreement after an initially enthusiastic collaboration can be explained as well by differences in the role of philanthropist in Britain and America as by differences in personality or educational policy.

In Britain and America the philanthropists formed an influential group in the Owenite movement. By virtue of their wealth, education, and articulateness they occupied positions of leadership in the communities and other Owenite institutions. They were for the most part able men and of some status in society at large. The type of work they were engaged in— practical philanthropy—was widely approved among the affluent classes from dukes to merchants. Why, then, did Owenite philanthropists gain such meagre support and Owenite institutions wither so quickly, as compared with other philanthropic causes which crusaded successfully in the early nineteenth century? Sunday schools, anti-slavery, and temperance—all aiming at far-reaching social reconstruction under philanthropic leadership —established organizations much more stable and widespread than Owenism. The difference arises in part because Owenism was more than philanthropy, which was not an encompassing framework but only one strand interwoven with others such as community, millennialism, and anti-capitalism. More significantly, Owenite philanthropy was predominantly secular. It was antagonistic toward the religion of evangelical Christianity and the faith of political economy. Consequently it found no favor with the dominant school of philanthropy as represented by William Wilberforce in England or the Tappan brothers in the United States. Owenite philanthropy was part of an earlier tradition, rooted in the humanistic values of the Enlightenment. Utility or the pursuit of happiness was its starting point, not the saving grace of Christ Jesus. The use of millennial language or professions of Christianity by individual Owenites did not change the general secular image of Owenism. In an age of intensive evangelical religion the Owenites stood condemned as infidels, and their philanthropy was therefore discountenanced.

It was not, however, as a scheme of philanthropy but as a plan for social reform that Owenism attracted its widest support. Owen and his followers have gone down in history as the main English school of Utopian socialists, predecessors—together with their Saint-Simonian and Fourierist contemporaries—of Marx and Engels. But the Owenites rejected the term Utopian, and their socialism cannot be analyzed by the canons considered appropriate after the rise of modern socialism in the 1880s. Owenite socialism was, in the words of the *Cooperative Magazine* in 1827, "the true social or cooperative and communional system," a blend of communitarian theory, anti-capitalist economics, and a science of society. These three elements made up the main part of the doctrines of Owenism and together gave it distinctive characteristics as a philosophy of social reform. They also show the similarities and differences between American and British Owenism.

When Owenites spoke of their "communional system" they had several ideas in mind. In the first place they were referring to a general concept of community which they felt was essential for satisfactory human relationships in any society. The absence of such community was diagnosed by Owen as the chief ill of British society in the period 1814–1819: society was fragmented and turned against itself. In his efforts to restore harmony to society Owen became a socialist and was led to condemn all institutions which "individualized" man. Second, for many Owenites the communional system meant the holding of property in common and the abolition of individual ownership. Owen's position on this issue was not completely consistent, nor did he maintain the same views at different periods of his career. His followers similarly advocated varying degrees of communism, some wanting complete equality and community of goods, others content with a less absolute scheme. Third, there was an active belief in communitarianism as a method of social reform. Society was to be radically transformed by means of experimental communities, and this was regarded as a valid alternative to revolution or legislation as methods of effecting social change. In Britain and America there were traditions of community upon which the Owenites could draw in support of these three aspects of their communional system.

In Britain the communitarian element of Owenism had several roots. Men who were interested in community for different reasons found grounds for sympathy with the Owenite movement. When Owenites talked in terms of communitarianism they were using language which was fairly widely understood. A paternalist rural tradition provided a favorable seeding ground for Owenite community ideas as a solution to agricultural disstress and problems of improved husbandry. The Tory belief in an Old England which was a genuine community accounts for the presence of members of the squirearchy among Owenite apologists. Another aspect of community, stemming not from the Tories but from middle-class industrialists, was also associated with Owenism: the idea of community as an instrument of industrial relations. Early factory owners were faced with acute problems of labor shortage and labor discipline, and community provided a solution to some of these difficulties. Owen claimed that the germ of his communitarianism was in his experiences at New Lanark, the model factory village which his father-in-law, David Dale, had created to overcome problems of this sort. A third view of community was provided by an indigenous working-class culture of collectivism. In the later eighteenth century a network of friendly societies, burial clubs, and trade societies attested the strength of this "ethos of mutality." Methodism reinforced it with the language of brotherhood and the essentially neighborhood institution of the chapel. The sense of the loss of community was expressed by contemporaries from Thomas Carlyle to Karl Marx in such forms as the Gospel of Mammonism or the concept of alienation. Owenites saw their task as the restoration of community values in a world which they viewed as artificial and atomized. Harmony was the keynote of the New Moral World, in sharp contrast with the discord of existing society. Neither the Owenites nor their contemporaries were able to define the problem of community in psychological terms, but they realized that the implications of industrialism could not be confined to physical changes. Owenism took account of the uniqueness of industrial society and sought to explain what industrialism was doing to the lives of ordinary people by reference to the concept of community.

In America there were other soils in which communitarianism could grow, notably religious sectarianism, and from this tradition the Owenites profited in several ways. Many of the millennial sects were also communitarian, and with two of them—the Shakers and the Rappites—Owen and his followers were particularly familiar. Owen was interested in the Shakers long before he came to America; and a few days after his first arrival here in November 1824 he visited the Shaker community at Niskeyuna, New York, and was much impressed. He had known of the Rappites at least since 1815. In 1820 he corresponded with Fr. Rapp about his community experiments, and in 1825 bought the settlement of Harmony, Indiana, from the Rappites for his own communitarian experiment of New Harmony. Owenism in America was thus physically and intellectually the inheritor of an established communitarian tradition, a secular version of sectarian communism.

There was a time when American communitarianism was explained in terms of the frontier, and Owenism, with its center in a pioneer settlement on the banks of the Wabash, fitted neatly into this pattern. But Arthur Bestor has argued, convincingly, that the frontier theory by itself is inadequate as an explanation. Communitarianism did not originate on the frontier, nor were frontier conditions particularly favorable to its development. The relationship between the growth of communitarianism and the rapid advance of the frontier in the first half of the nineteenth century is to be found in the more general concept of the West as it appeared to contemporaries. Communitarianism was a method of effecting social change by means of experimental communities and as such was in harmony with certain basic assumptions which Americans made about the West. In a period of rapid growth and unbounded confidence in the future, it was possible to believe that small experiments, if successful, could vitally affect the new society which was emerging—and it was urgent to seize this opportunity before it was too late. Older and more stable societies did not present this opportunity, but the West could be shaped by the conscious efforts of the present generation. Just as in Britain there was a widespread feeling among reformers until the 1830s that the changes wrought by industrial capitalism were not permanent, and that it was therefore not too late to build society on alternative principles, so in America there was an even stronger conviction that society in the West was in a state of flux, and that it was possible to fashion new institutions which would ensure a better world for the future. Owenite communitarianism was acceptable because it shared these assumptions about the nature of social change. And conversely Owenism lost its rationale when it became clear that industrial capitalism in Britain and the institutions of individualism in Amerca were so strongly established that they could not be radically affected by small-scale experiments.

To Owenites, as to other social reformers, America seemed to be the ideal place for community experiments. Not only was land cheap and plentiful, but the intellectual climate seemed to be more favorable to social experimentation. For British radicals the American Republic was an idea as much as a particular country—an idea to which they felt they belonged by sentiment and conviction. Owenites had little difficulty in discovering in the New World ideas and attitudes which were highly compatible with their new view of society. The origin of many aspects of Owenism lies in those elements of Enlightenment thought which were also influential in the early years of the Republic, so that a common base for sympathy and understanding was provided. Take, for example, the case of agrarianism. In the late eighteenth and early nineteenth centuries radical movements were frequently agrarian, reflecting a concern with land and property reform in pre-industrial societies. The Spencean Philanthropists were the main exponents of this philosophy in Britain, and the similarity between Spenceanism and Owenism struck contemporaries. This agrarian bias in Owenism (which at first seems hard to reconcile with the image of Owen as one of the great success stories of the Industrial Revolution) harmonized well with the parallel development of the agrarian myth in America. Within Owenism there was a strong strain of pastoralism, derived largely from eighteenth-century sources, and forming a common bond with other agrarians in America and Great Britain.

The community elements in Owenism thus had several different roots and references. Community in Britain and America was a recognizable concept, sufficiently familiar to be acceptable as a possible solution to a number of different social and economic problems—rural distress, labor shortage, feelings of alienation. Concepts of community in the two countries were similar in those aspects which stemmed from Enlightenment thought or from the problems of early industrialism. But there were differences when community ideas had other origins: for instance, religious sectarianism contained a much stronger bent toward community in the New World than in the old, and the paternalistic community feeling of the English squirearchy was not indigenous in America. Owenism was able to draw upon these different traditions impartially—hence the heterogeneous nature of the Owenite body. As in the case of millennialism, the English and American Owenites played a mutually reinforcing role as communitarians. The Americans accepted Owen's (largely British) ideas of villages of cooperation, and the British Owenites waxed enthusiastic over American sectarian communities, especially the Shakers. Perhaps because of the greater strength of the communitarian tradition in America Owenism was faced with stronger competition than in Britain. Thus in the communitarian revival of the 1840s Owenism in the New World was eclipsed by Fourierism, whereas in Great Britain Owenism remained the dominant communitarian doctrine, despite the attempted introduction of Fourierism and Saint-Simonism. That Owenism should have had a similar following in two such different societies as Britain and America is partly explicable by the nature of its communitarian element. Ignoring political action and minimizng economc problems, communitarians concentrated on social and psychological questions, which provided a sufficient bond between reformers who, on both sides of the Atlantic, were in revolt against the dominant orthodoxies of their respective societies. For Americans, Owenism offered communitarianism without the trappings of religious sectarianism; in Great Britain, Owenite concepts of community provided a remedy for some of the tensions, social and personal, arising from early industrialism.

The third aspect of the Owenite movement which may be used to illustrate the Anglo-American interrelationship is millennialism. In the summer of 1817 Owen proclaimed the commencement of the millennium, and from then on the millennial note was present in most of his writings and also in some of his followers'. It would be tedious to catalogue Owen's successive millennial announcements. His editorial in the first number of the *New Moral World* (November 1, 1834) was representative of innumerable statements both before and later:

> The rubicon between the Old Immoral and the New Moral Worlds is finally passed. . . . This . . . is the great Advent of the world, the second coming of Christ,—for Truth and Christ are one and the same. The first coming of Christ was a partial development of Truth to the few. . . . The second coming of Christ will make Truth known to many. . . . The time is therefore arrived when the foretold millennium is about to commence . . .

Enthusiastic followers at New Harmony and later at Harmony Hall adopted a new chronology, dating their letters from the beginning of the new dispensation. At Harmony Hall (in Hampshire) the letters "C.M." (Commencement of the Millennium) were carved on the outside of the building. The social missionaries frequently played upon the millennial theme. In the *New Moral World* and other Owenite journals, many aspects of the culture of millennialism appeared. Contributors discussed biblical prophecy, the restoration of the Jews in relation to socialism, and animal magnetism as a herald of the millennium. Versifiers sent in millennial poems. Owenite converts wrote letters saying how much they longed for the day of salvation.

In extent and variety these millennial elements in Owenism conformed to certain recognizable variants within the general pattern of eighteenth and nineteenth century millennialism. Generally Owenites were inclined to be post- rather than pre-millennialists, though at times their precise position was confused. Owen was basically a typical eighteenth-century post-millennialist, believing that the millennium was simply a more perfect state of society, which could with equal propriety be called "the Rational State of Human Existence," or "The Brotherhood of the Human Race." But at times he spoke of a second advent and sudden cataclysm which implied a pre-millennialist position at variance with his previous meliorist statements. The interpretation of the millennium most favoured by Owenites, including Owen himself, was inherited from those eighteenth-century millennialists who had secularized the idea of the millennium into a theory of evolutionary progress, by disguising Providence as natural law, and making reason and revelation embrace each other. The New Jerusalem became a state of universal happiness, the millennium a gradual progress toward human betterment. Such millennialists formed, in Ernest Tuveson's words, "a bridge between the chiliasm of the seventeenth century and the liberal political progressivism of the nineteenth." The Owenites helped to extend this bridge, and to carry farther, in popular (often crude) form, the secularization of the millennium.

Just why the Owenite movement should have adopted the form and rhetoric of a millenarian sect has perplexed and embarrassed most British writers. The existence of a continuing tradition of millennialism in America has long been recognized, and it is possible to document a two-way process of exchange between American Shakers, Swedenborgians, and universalists on the one hand and Owenite communitarians on the other. But an examination of evangelical religion in Britain and America suggests further clues. Owenism originated and flourished entirely within the grand era of evangelical ascendancy, c. 1800–1860. The central importance of evangelicalism, especially revivalism, in shaping the American mind in the nineteenth century has frequently been noted. But in Great Britain also, where a traditional religious establishment was more strongly entrenched, the same forces were at work for the spread of evangelical Christianity. The central doctrines of evangelicalism—among them perfectionism, disinterested benevolence, and millennialism—carried definite social implications and frequently committed their adherents to sympathy for various aspects of social reform. One aspect of the evangelical heritage was particularly attractive to social reformers: in the biblical doctrine of the millennium they found a conceptual basis and a rhetoric for their ideas of utopia. The Owenites, like all social reformers, were faced with a problem of communication; how to ensure that their views could be made comprehensible to people who were still thinking along orthodox lines. The sect became the model for effecting the new moral world. Owenism did not, as previous historians have suggested, "degenerate" into a "mere" sect after 1835, the implication being presumably that in its earlier stages it might have been something different, such as a political party or a mass movement of the working class. In fact Owenism developed as a millennial sect, not through failure to achieve some other institutional form, but through the logic of its need to communicate.

The function of Owenism as a sect in relation to the needs of individuals was not markedly different from other millenarian groups. As the settler at New Harmony imbibed from Owen the vision of a New Moral World, he was not far removed in basic aspiration from the Mormon convert who listened to the promises of an early millennium in the City of Zion from Joseph Smith. The Owenite working man who sang his social hymns in the Manchester Hall of Science was striving for much the same goals as his neighbor who sang Wesley's hymns in the Primitive Methodist chapel or listened to the prophet in the Southcottians' meeting place at Ashton. Within the sect he found a congenial home, where the values and goals were different from those of the wider society which he had rejected. The injustices and enormities which outraged him in early capitalist society were replaced by the dream of an earthly millennium.

The existence of so many millennial sects contemporary with Owenism, their recruitment from among different classes, and in two such different societies as America and Britain, suggests that either the role of the sect was very fundamental or it played several different roles. Presentations of millennialism as the "religion of the oppressed" or the "chiliasm of despair" are adequate only for certain groups of millenarians: but Owenites were drawn from wealthy philanthropists, farmers, lower-middle class tradesmen, and working men. Correlation between periods of depression and the strength of millennial sentiment are at best inconclusive. In America religious revivalism, from which millennialism usually emerged, was fostered more by moderate economic recession than by an extreme depression of the 1837 order. However, a severe economic depression could persuade men that only millenarianism was a sufficiently radical remedy for present ills. For Great Britain the correspondence between the growth of millennial sects and the cycle of booms and slumps is similarly ambivalent. Only the total impact of economic change and the consequent upheaval in social relationships provide an adequate context in which all the manifestations of millennialism can be understood. Both Britain and America between 1790 and 1850 were societies undergoing unprecedented changes, the one being transformed into the world's first industrial civilization, the other expanding to conquer a fabulous continent of unbelievably rich resources.

The millennialist sectarian was one who rejected what was being done in this process, rejected the values and institutions of society—all that for the Owenite was meant by the "old immoral world." Early industrial society in Great Britain and the young expansionist republic in America created social realities which were divorced from the social and religious values which they professed. The millenarian refused to accept the incompatibility, as he saw it, between Christian professions and laissez-faire capitalist society, either industrial or agrarian. Owenism was an expression of this conflict and an attempt to resolve it. In the development of this role Owenism became the millennial sect of Rational Religionists.

What then emerges from this brief examination of three of the main constituents of the Owenite movement? It was suggested earlier that Owenism was essentially a comment on early nineteenth century Anglo-American society. In particular it was a comment on the process of social change, a response to new opportunities arising out of profound developments in a rapidly emerging industrial Great Britain and vigorously expanding United States. Owenites rejected these opportunities which they condemned as individualistic and divisive. Instead they clung to social values and attitudes rooted in an older, more stable order. They proposed, as an alternative to present society, a system of cooperative socialism as a basis for the new moral world. But the Owenite movement was not basically backward-looking. Rather it offered an alternative series of categories within which the social foundations of modern England and America could be viewed at a time when effective choice still seemed feasible.

Day-to-Day Resistance
to Slavery

RAYMOND A. BAUER
ALICE H. BAUER

Written in the early nineteen forties, this essay seriously challenged the view
of the slave as "Sambo"—a generation before historians debated its utility.
The Bauers describe the various methods of day-to-day resistance commonly
practiced by southern slaves. Those involving slow work practices and
malingering demanded the utmost in solidarity in the fields and again
suggest the coherent norms and values slave culture developed over time.
Forms of individual resistance, such as self-mutilation, infanticide, and
even suicide were more desperate acts. In both cases, but in different ways,
these slaves challenged the master's control over their lives.

Raymond A. and Alice H. Bauer, "Day-to-Day Resistance to Slavery," *Journal of Negro
History*, 27 (1942), 388–419. Copyright © by The Association for the Study of Negro
Life and History, Inc. Reprinted and footnotes omitted by permission of the publisher.

The tradition that has grown up about Negro slavery is that the slaves were docile, well adapted to slavery, and reasonably content with their lot. A standard work on the Negro problem in the United States says:

> "The Negroes brought into the New World situation and presently re-duced to a perpetual servitude became very rapidly accommodated to the environment and status. The explanation of the comparative ease with which this was brought about doubtless lies in the peculiar racial traits of the Negro peoples themselves. They are strong and robust in physique and so everywhere sought after as laborers. In disposition they are cheerful, kindly and sociable: in character they are characteristically extrovert, so readily obedient and easily contented. More than most other social groups they are patiently tolerant under abuse and oppression and little inclined to struggle against difficulties. These facts of racial temperament and dis-position make the Negroes more amenable to the condition of slavery than perhaps any other racial group."

This concept is gradually being changed as the study of slave revolts, and of the social tension caused by the constant threat of revolt progresses. In answer to the question, " 'Are the masters afraid of insurrection?' (a slave) says, 'They live in constant fear upon this subject. The least unusual noise at night alarms them greatly. They cry out, 'What is that?' 'Are the boys all in'?'"

The purpose of this paper is to study a less spectacular aspect of slavery—the day to day resistance to slavery, since it is felt that such a study will throw some further light on the nature of the Negro's reaction to slavery. Our investigation has made it apparent that the Negroes not only were very discontented, but that they developed effective protest tech-niques in the form of indirect retaliation for their enslavement. Since this conclusion differs sharply from commonly accepted belief, it would perhaps be of value if a brief preliminary statement were made of how belief so at variance with the available documentary materials could gain such ac-ceptance.

The picture of the docile, contented Negro slave grew out of two lines of argument used in ante-bellum times. The pro-slavery faction contended that the slaves came of an inferior race, and that they were happy and con-tented in their subordinate position, and that the dancing and singing Negro exemplified their assumption. Abolitionists, on the other hand, tended to depict the Negro slave as a passive instrument, a good and faithful worker exploited and beaten by a cruel master. As one reads the controversial literature on the slavery question, it soon becomes apparent that both sides presented the Negro as a docile creature; one side because it wished to prove that he was contented, the other because it wished to prove that he was grossly mistreated. Both conceptions have persisted to the present time. Writers who romanticize the "Old South" idealize the condition of the slaves, and make of them happy, willing servitors, while those who are concerned with furthering the interests of the Negroes are careful to avoid mention of any aggressive tendencies which might be used as a pretext for further suppressing the Negroes.

Many travelers in the South have accepted the overt behavior of the slaves at its face value. The "yas suh, Cap'n," the smiling, bowing, and scraping of the Negroes have been taken as tokens of contentment. Redpath's conversations with slaves indicated how deep seated this behavior was. This point of view, however, neglects the fact that the whites have always insisted on certain forms of behavior as a token of acceptance of inferior status by the Negro. The following quotation from Dollard is pertinent:

> "An informant already cited has referred to the Negro as a 'Dr. Jekyll and Mr. Hyde.' He was making an observation that is well understood among Negroes—that he has a kind of dual personality, two rôles, one that he is forced to play with white people and one the 'real Negro' as he appears in his dealings with his own people. What the white southern people see who 'know their Negroes' is the rôle that they have forced the Negro to accept, his caste rôle."

The conceptual framework within which this paper is written is that the Negro slaves were forced into certain outward forms of compliance to slavery; that, except for the few who were able to escape to the North, the Negroes had to accept the institution of slavery and make their adjustments to that institution. The patterns of adjustment which we have found operative are: slowing up of work, destruction of property, malingering and self-mutilation.

The sources of our material are: (1) general works on slavery, labor, and the Negro; (2) the journals and the travel accounts of southerners and of visitors to the slave territory; and (3) the biographies and autobiographies of slaves. Most of the secondary sources take some cognizance of the fact that slaves slowed up their work, feigned illness, and the like, but this behavior is regarded as a curiosity. There has been no attempt by those writers who set down such facts to understand their social and economic significance. The journals and travel-books vary greatly in the amount of information they contain. This, of course, is due to the authors' variations in interest and acuteness. Olmsted's *Seaboard Slave States,* for instance, abounds in anecdotes, and in expressions of opinion as to the extent of loafing and malingering. Susan Smedes' *Memorials of a Southern Planter,* on the other hand, contains just one foot-noted reference to any such behavior. Life stories of ex-slaves emphasize running away, forms of punishment, and other aspects of slavery that would make interesting reading. Yet while references to slowing up work, or feigning illness, are thus few in number, where they are made they are stated in such a way that they leave no doubt that there was a persistent pattern of such behavior.

> "Slaveholders ever underate the intelligence with which they have to grapple. I really understood the old man's mutterings, attitudes and gestures, about as well as he did himself. But slaveholders never encourage that kind of communication, with the slaves, by which they might learn to measure the depths of his knowledge. Ignorance is a high virtue in a human chattel; and as the master studies to keep the slave ignorant, the slave is cunning enough to make the master think he succeeds. The slave fully appreciates the saying, 'where ignorance is bliss 'tis folly to be wise'."

We have felt it wise to quote extensively. Much of the meaning of incidents and interpretations lies in the phrasing of the author—in sensing his own emphasis on what he says. Methodologically, in attempting to analyze an existing stereotype, as we are trying to do here, it would seem wisest to present the picture as it appeared to contemporaries, and thus as given in their own words.

II

The Negroes were well aware that the work they did benefited only the master. "The slaves work and the planter gets the benefit of it." "The conversation among the slaves was that they worked hard and got no benefit, that the masters got it all." It is thus not surprising that one finds many recurring comments that a slave did not do half a good day's work in a day. A northerner whom Lyell met in the South said:

> "Half the population of the south is employed in seeing that the other half do their work, and they who do work, accomplish half what they might do under a better system."

An English visitor, with a very strong pro-slavery bias corroborates this:

> "The amount of work expected of the field hand will not be more than one half of what would be demanded of a white man; and even that will not be properly done unless he be constantly overlooked."

Statements of other writers are to the same effect:

> "It is a common remark of those persons acquainted with slave-labour, that their proportion is as one to two. This is not too great an estimate in favour of the free-labourer; and the circumstances of their situation produce a still greater disparity."

"A capitalist was having a building erected in Petersburg, and his slaves were employed in carrying up the brick and mortar for the masons on their heads: a Northerner, standing near, remarked to him that they moved so indolently that it seemed as if they were trying to see how long they could be in mounting the ladder without actually stopping. The builder started to reprove them, but after moving a step turned back and said: 'It would only make them move more slowly still when I am not looking at them, if I should hurry now. *And what motive have they to do better?* It's no concern of theirs how long the masons wait. I am sure if I was in their place, I shouldn't move as fast as they do.' "

A well-informed capitalist and slave-holder remarked,

"In working niggers, we always calculate that they will not labor at all except to avoid punishment, and they will never do more than just enough to save themselves from being punished, and no amount of punishment will prevent their working carelessly or indifferently. It always seems on the plantations as if they took pains to break all the tools and spoil all the cattle that they possibly can, even when they know they'll be directly punished for it."

Just how much of this was due to indifference and how much due to deliberate slowing up is hard to determine. Both factors most probably entered. A worker who had to devote himself to a dull task from which he can hope to gain nothing by exercising initiative soon slips into such a frame of mind that he does nothing more than go through the motions. His chief concern is to escape from the realities of his task and put it in the back of his mind as much as possible.

There is, indeed, a strong possibility that this behavior was a form of indirect aggression. While such an hypothesis cannot be demonstrated on the basis of the available contemporary data, it is supported by Dollard's interpretation of similar behavior which he found in Southern towns.

"If the reader has ever seen Stepin Fetchit in the movies, he can picture this type of character. Fetchit always plays the part of a well-accommodated lower-class Negro, whining, vacillating, shambling, stupid, and moved by very simple cravings. There is probably an element of resistance to white society in the shambling, sullenly slow pace of the Negro; it is the gesture of a man who is forced to work for ends not his own and who expresses his reluctance to perform under these circumstances."

Certainly description after description emphasizes the mechanical plodding of the slave workers:

"John Lamar wrote, 'My man Ned the carpenter is idle or nearly so at the plantation. He is fixing gates and, like the idle groom in Pickwick, trying to fool himself into the belief that he is doing something—He is an eye servant.' "

"Those I saw at work appeared to me to move very slowly and awkwardly, as did those engaged in the stables. These also were very stupid and dilatory in executing any orders given them, so that Mr. C. would frequently take the duty off their hands into his own, rather than wait for them, or make them correct their blunders; they were much, in these respects, what our farmers call *dumb Paddees*—that is, Irishmen who do not readily understand the English language, and who are still weak and stiff from the effects of the emigrating voyage. At the entrance gate was a porter's lodge, and, as I approached I saw a black face peeping at me from it, but both when I entered and left, I was obliged to dismount and open the gate myself.

"Altogether, it struck me—slaves coming here as they naturally did in comparison with free laborers, as commonly employed on my own and my neighbors' farms, in exactly similar duties—that they must have been difficult to direct efficiently, and that it must be irksome and trying to one's patience, to have to superintend their labor."

To what extent this reluctant labor was the rule may be appreciated when it is pointed out that a southern doctor classified it under the name *Dysaethesia Aethiopica* as a mental disease peculiar to Negroes. Olmsted quotes this Dr. Cartwright as follows:

" 'From the careless movements of the individual affected with this complaint, they are apt to do much mischief, which appears as if intentional, but it is mostly owing to the stupidity of mind and insensibility of the nerves induced by the disease. Thus, they break, waste, and destroy everything they handle—abuse horses and cattle—tear, burn, or rend their own clothing, and, paying no attention to the rights of property, steal others to replace what they have destroyed. They wander about at night, and keep in a half nodding state by day. They slight their work—cut up corn, cotton and tobacco, when hoeing it, as if for pure mischief. They raise disturbances with their overseers, and among their fellow servants, without cause or motive, and seem to be insensible to pain when subjected to punishment.

" '. . . The term "rascality" given to this disease by overseers, is founded on an erroneous hypothesis, and leads to an incorrect empirical treatment, which seldom or never cures it.' "

There are only two possible interpretations of the doctor's statement. Either the slaves were so extraordinarily lazy that they gave the appearance of being mentally diseased, or the doctor was describing cases of hebephrenic schizophrenia. Either situation is startling. The phenomenon was obviously widespread, and if it was actually a mental disease it certainly would indicate that Negroes did not become "easily adjusted to slavery." Whatever the case, it is certain that the slaves consciously saved their energy. Olmsted, who always had his eye open for such incidents, reported:

"The overseer rode among them, on a horse, carrying in his hand a raw-hide whip, constantly directing and encouraging them; but, as my companion and I, both, several times noticed, as often as he visited one line of the operations, the hands at the other end would discontinue their labor, until he turned to ride toward them again."

The few statements on this point we have by ex-slaves seem to indicate that the slaves as a group made a general policy of not letting the master get the upper hand.

"I had become large and strong; and had begun to take pride in the fact that I could do as much hard work as some of the older men. There is much rivalry among slaves, at times, as to which can do the most work, and masters generally seek to promote such rivalry. But some of us were too wise to race with each other very long. Such racing, we had the sagacity to see, was not likely to pay. We had times out for measuring each other's strength, but we knew too much to keep up the competition so long as to produce an extraordinary day's work. We knew that if, by extraordinary exertion, a large quantity of work was done in one day, the fact, becoming known to the master, might lead him to require the same amount every day. This thought was enough to bring us to a dead halt whenever so much excited for the race."

Writer after writer, describing incidents in which slaves were compelled to assist in punishing other slaves states that they did so with the greatest of reluctance.

"The hands stood still;—they knew Randall—and they knew him also take a powerful man, and were afraid to grapple with him. As soon as Cook had ordered the men to seize him, Randall turned to them, and said—'Boys, you all know me; you know that I can handle any three of you, and the man that lays hands on me shall die. This white man can't whip me himself, and therefore he has called you to help him.' The overseer was unable to prevail upon them to seize and secure Randall, and finally ordered them all to go to their work together."

In some cases it was noted that the slave resisting punishment took pains not to treat his fellows with any more than the absolute minimum of violence.

With such demonstrations of solidarity among the slaves it is not surprising to find a slave telling of how he and his fellows "captured" the institution of the driver. The slave Solomon Northrup was such a driver. His task was to whip the other slaves in order to make them work.

" 'Practice makes perfect,' truly; and during eight years' experience as a driver I learned to handle the whip with marvelous dexterity and precision, throwing the lash within a hair's breadth of the back, the ear, the nose without, however, touching either of them. If Epps was observed at a distance, or we had reason to apprehend he was sneaking somewhere in the vicinity, I would commence plying the lash vigorously, when, according to arrangement, they would squirm and screech as if in agony, although not one of them had in fact been grazed. Patsey would take occasion, if he made his appearance presently, to mumble in his hearing some complaints that Platt was whipping them the whole time, and Uncle Abram, with an appearance of honesty peculiar to himself would declare roundly I had just whipped them worse than General Jackson whipped the enemy at New Orleans."

Williams, another slave whose task was to drive his fellows, said:

"He was at these periods terribly severe to his hands, and would order me to use up the cracker of my whip every day upon the poor creatures who were toiling in the field; and in order to satisfy him, I used to tear it off when returning home at night. He would then praise me for a good fellow and invite me to drink with him."

The amount of slowing up of labor by the slaves must, in the aggregate, have caused a tremendous financial loss to plantation owners. The only way we have of estimating it quantitatively is through comparison of the work done in different plantations and under different systems of labor. The statement is frequently made that production on a plantation varied more than 100% from time to time. Comparison in the output of slaves in different parts of the South also showed variations of over 100%. Most significant is the improvement in output obtained under the task, whereby the slaves were given a specific task to fulfill for their day's work, any time left over being their own. Olmsted gives us our best information on this point:

"These tasks certainly would not be considered excessively hard by a northern laborer; and, in point of fact, the more industrious and active hands finished them often by two o'clock. I saw one or two leaving the field soon after one o'clock, several about two; and between three and four, I met a dozen women and several men coming home to their cabins, having finished their day's work.

"Under this 'Organization of Labor' most of the slaves work rapidly and well. In nearly all ordinary work, custom has settled the extent of the task, and it is difficult to increase it. The driver who marks it out, has to remain on the ground until it is finished, and has no interest in over-measuring it; and if it should be systematically increased very much, there is danger of a general stampede to the swamp, a danger the slave can always hold before his master's cupidity."

"It is the custom of tobacco manufacturers to hire slaves and free negroes at a certain rate of wages each year. A task of 45 pounds per day is given them to work up, and all they choose to do more than this, they are paid for—payment being made once a fortnight; and invariably this over-wages is used by the slaves for himself, and is usually spent in drinking, licentiousness, and gambling. The man was grumbling that he had saved but $20 to spend at the holidays. One of the manufacturers offered to show me by his books, that nearly all gained by over-work $5 a month, many $20 and some as much as $28.

"He (the speaker) was executor of an estate in which, among other negroes, there was one very smart man, who, he knew perfectly well, ought to be earning for the estate $150 a year, and who could if he chose, yet whose wages for a year being let out by the day or job, had amounted to but $18, while he had paid for medical attendance upon him $45."

The executor of the estate finally arranged for this man to work out his freedom, which he readily accomplished.

A quantitative estimate can be made from another situation which Olmsted observed. Rain during a previous day had made certain parts of the work more difficult than others. The slaves were therefore put on day work, since it would not be possible to lay out equitable tasks.

"Ordinarily it is done by tasks—a certain number of the small divisions of the field being given to each hand to burn in a day; but owing to a more than usual amount of rain having fallen lately, and some other causes, making the work harder in some places than in others, the women were now working by the day, under the direction of a 'driver,' a negro man, who walked about among them, taking care they had left nothing unburned. Mr. X inspected the ground they had gone over, to see whether the driver had done his duty. It had been sufficiently well burned, but not more than a quarter as much ground had been gone over, he said, as was usually burned in tasked work,—and he thought they had been very lazy, and reprimanded them for it."

Most revealing of all is this statement:

" 'Well, now, old man,' said I, 'you go and cut me two cords today!' 'Oh, massa! two cords! Nobody could do dat. Oh! massa, dat is too hard! Neber heard o' nobody's cuttin' more 'n a cord o' wood in a day, round heah. No nigger couldn't do it.' 'Well, old man, you have two cords of wood cut to-night or to-morrow morning you shall get two hundred lashes—that's all there is about it. So look sharp.' And he did it and ever since no negro ever cut less than two cords a day for me, though my neighbors never get but one cord. It was just so with a great many other things—mauling rails—I always have two hundred rails mauled in a day; just twice what it is the custom of the country to expect of a negro, and just twice as many as my negroes had been made to do before I managed them myself."

"These estimates, let it be recollected in conclusion, are all deliberately and carefully made by gentlemen of liberal education, who have had unusual facilities of observing both at the North and the South."

The slaves were well aware of their economic value, and used it to good advantage. The skilled laborers among the slaves knew their worth, and frequently rebelled against unsatisfactory work situations. Slaves who were hired out would run away from the masters who had hired them, and then either return home, or remain in hiding until they felt like returning to work.

"The slave, if he is indisposed to work, and especially if he is not treated well, or does not like the master who has hired him, will sham sickness—even make himself sick or lame—that he need not work. But a more serious loss frequently arises, when the slave, thinking he is worked too hard, or being angered by punishment or unkind treatment, 'getting the sulks,' takes to 'the swamp,' and comes back when he has a mind to. Often this will not be till the year is up for which he is engaged, when he will return to his owner, who, glad to find his property safe, and that it has not died in the swamp, or gone to Canada, forgets to punish him, and immediately sends him for another year to a new master.

" 'But, meanwhile, how does the negro support life in the swamp?' I asked.

" 'Oh, he gets sheep and pigs and calves, and fowls and turkey; sometimes they will kill a small cow. We have often seen the fires, where they were cooking them, through the woods in the swamp yonder. If it is cold, he will crawl under a fodder stack, or go into the cabins with some of the other negroes, and in the same way, you see, he can get all the corn, or almost anything else he wants.

" 'He steals them from his master?'

" 'From anyone: frequently from me. I have had many a sheep taken by them.'

" 'It is a common thing, then?'

" 'Certainly it is, very common, and the loss is sometimes exceedingly provoking. One of my neighbors here was going to build, and hired two mechanics for a year. Just as he was ready to put his house up, the two men, taking offense at something, both ran away, and did not come back at all, till their year was out, and then their owner immediately hired them out again to another man.' "

One plantation observer wrote to the plantation owner concerning a carpenter he had hired out to one G. Moore:

"Not long before Jim run away G More (sic.) wanted him to make some gates and I sent him theirselves (sic.) and he run away from him and cum home and then he left me withow (sic.) a cause."

Even the threat of a whipping did not deter such slaves from running off for a time when they were displeased. The quotation from Olmsted below is typical of a constantly recurring pattern of statements:

"The manager told me that the people often ran away after they have been whipped or something else had happened to make them angry. They hide in the swamp and come into the cabins at night to get food. They seldom remain away more than a fortnight and when they come in they are whipped."

Some of the resistance took on the aspects of organized strikes:

"Occasionally, however, a squad would strike in a body as a protest against severities. An episode of this sort was recounted in a letter of a Georgia overseer to his absent employer: 'Sir: I write you a few lines in order to let you know that six of your hands has left the plantation—every man but Jack. They displeased me with their work and I give some of them a few lashes, Tom with the rest. On Wednesday morning they were missing. I think they are lying out until they can see you or your Uncle Jack.' The slaves could not negotiate directly at such a time, but while they lay in the woods they might make overtures to the overseer through slaves on a neighboring plantation as to terms upon which they would return to work, or they might await their master's posthaste arrival and appeal to him for a redress of grievances. Humble as their demeanor might be, their power of renewing the pressure by repeating their act could not be ignored."

John Holmes, an escaped slave, told how he ran off and hid in the swamp after an overseer attempted to whip him.

"At last they told all the neighbors if I would come home, they wouldn't whip me. I was a great hand to work and made a great deal of money for our folks."

The same overseer had further trouble with the slaves.

"She (a slave) was better with her fists, and beat him, but he was better at wrestling and threw her down. He then called the men to help him, but all hid from him in the brush where we were working. . . . Then (later) the calculation was to whip us every one, because we did not help the overseer. . . . That night every one of us went away into the woods. . . . We went back, but after a while (the overseer) came back too, and stayed the year out. He whipped the women but he did not whip the men, of fear they would run away."

III

The indifference of the slaves to the welfare of the masters extended itself to a complete contempt for property values. The slaves were so careless with tools that they were equipped with special tools, and more clumsy than ordinary ones:

"*The 'nigger hoe'* was first introduced into Virginia as a substitute for the plow, in breaking up the soil. The law fixes its weight at four pounds, —as heavy as the woodman's axe. It is still used, not only in Virginia, but in Georgia and the Carolinas. The planters tell us, as the reason for its use, that the negroes would break a Yankee hoe in pieces on the first root, or stone that might be in their way. An instructive commentary on the difference between free and slave labor."

"The absence of motive, and the consequent want of mental energy to give vigor to the arm of the slave is the source of another great drawback upon the usefulness of his labour. His implements or tools are at least one-third (in some instances more than twofold) heavier and stronger than the northern man's to counteract his want of skill and interest in his work. A Negro hoe or scythe would be a curiosity to a New England farmer."

Not only tools but live-stock suffered from the mistreatment by the slaves. Olmsted found not only the "nigger hoe" but even discovered that mules were substituted for horses because horses could not stand up under the treatment of the slaves.

. . . . "I am shown tools that no man in his senses, with us, would allow a laborer, to whom he was paying wages, to be encumbered with; and the excessive weight and clumsiness of which, I would judge, would make work at least ten per cent greater than those ordinarily used with us. And I am assured that, in the careless and clumsy way they must be used by the slaves, anything lighter or less crude could not be furnished them with good economy, and that such tools as we constantly give our laborers and find profit in giving them, would not last out a day in a Virginia corn-field—much lighter and more free from stones though it be than ours.

"So, too, when I ask why mules are so universally substituted for horses on the farm, the first reason given, and confessedly the most conclusive one, is, that horses cannot bear the treatment they always must get from negroes; horses are always soon foundered or crippled by them but mules will bear cudgeling, and lose a meal or two now and then, and not be materially injured, and they do not take cold or get sick if neglected or overworked. But I do not need to go further than to the window of the room in which I am writing, to see, at almost any time, treatment of cattle that would insure the immediate discharge of the driven, by almost any farmer owning them in the North."

Redpath verifies Olmsted's statement—by telling how he saw slaves treat stock. It is important to note that Redpath was a strong abolitionist and most sympathetic toward the slaves.

"He rode the near horse, and held a heavy cowhide in his hand, with which from time to time he lashed the leaders, as barbarous drivers lash oxen when at work. Whenever we came to a hill, especially if it was very steep, he dismounted, lashed the horses with all his strength, varying his performances by picking up stones, none of them smaller than half a brick, and throwing them with all his force, at the horses' legs. He seldom missed.

"The wagon was laden with two tons of plaster in sacks.
"This is a fair specimen of the style in which Negroes treat stock."

The indifference to live-stock is well illustrated by an incident which Olmsted recounts:

"I came, one afternoon, upon a herd of uncommonly fine cattle as they were being turned out of a field by a negro woman. She had given herself the trouble to let down but two of the seven bars of the fence, and they were obliged to leap over a barrier at least four feet high. Last of all came, very unwillingly, a handsome heifer, heavy with calf; the woman urged her with a cudgel and she jumped, but lodging on her belly, as I came up she lay bent, and, as it seemed, helplessly hung upon the top bar. . . . The woman struck her severely and with a painful effort she boggled over."

In the Sea Islands off the coast of Georgia, Kemble reported that the slaves started immense fires, destroying large sections of woods through careless or maliciousness.

"The 'field hands' make fires to cook their midday food wherever they happen to be working, and sometimes through their careless neglect, but sometimes, too, undoubtedly on purpose, the woods are set fire to by these means. One benefit they consider . . . is the destruction of the dreaded rattlesnakes."

The slaves on Lewis' West Indies plantation let cattle get into one of his best cane-pieces because they neglected to guard them, being more interested in a dance which was going on. They were fully aware that the cattle were ruining the sugar cane, but kept right on singing and dancing. Lewis was able to get only a handful of house servants to drive the cattle out of the cane, and that not until the cane-piece was ruined.

One tobacco planter complained that his slaves would cut the young plants indiscriminately unless they were watched. When it became late in the season and there was need of haste to avoid frost they would work only the thickest leaving the sparser ones untouched. Another planter said that he could cultivate only the poorer grades of tobacco because the slaves would not give necessary attention to the finer sort of plants. An English visitor said:

"The kitchens and out-offices are always at the distance of several yards from the principal dwelling. This is done as well to guard against the house-Negroes through carelessness setting the houses on fire, for they generally sit over it half the night, as to keep out their noise." (sic.)

The full import of these practices strikes home fully only when they are read in the words of the original observers. Olmsted's comments, and the ease with which he found incidents to illustrate them, are most valuable. So important is his testimony that we must once more quote him at some length.

"Incidents, trifling in themselves, constantly betray to a stranger the bad economy of using enslaved servants. The catastrophe of one such occurred since I began to write this letter. I ordered a fire to be made in my room, as I was going out this morning. On my return, I found a grand fire—the room door having been closed and locked upon it 'out of order.' Just now, while I was writing, down tumbled upon the floor, and rolled away close to the valance of the bed, half a hod-full of ignited coal, which had been so piled upon the diminutive grate, and left without a fender or any guard, that this result was almost inevitable. If I had not returned at the time I did, the house would have been fired."

"On the rice plantation which I have particularly described, the slaves were, I judge, treated with at least as much discretion and judicious consideration of economy, consistently with humane regard to their health, comfort, and morals, as on any other in all the Slave States; yet I could not avoid observing—and I certainly took no pains to do so, nor were any special facilities offered me for it—repeated instances of that waste and misapplication of labor which it can never be possible to guard against, when the agents of industry are slaves. Many such evidences of waste it would not be easy to specify; and others, which remain in my memory after some weeks, do not adequately account for the general impression that all I saw gave me; but there were, for instance, under my observation gates left open and bars left down, against standing orders; rails removed from fences by the negroes (as was conjectured, to kindle their fires with), mules lamed, and implements broken, by careless usage; a flat boat, carelessly secured, going adrift on the river; men ordered to cart rails for a new fence depositing them so that a double expense of labor would be required to lay them, more than would have needed if they had been placed, as they might have almost as easily been, by a slight exercise of forethought . . . making statements which their owner was obliged to receive as sufficient excuse, though, he told me, he felt assured they were false—all going to show habitual carelessness, indolence, and mere eye-service."

But not only did the Negro slaves refuse to work, and not only did they destroy property, but they even made it impossible for planters to introduce new work techniques by feigning clumsiness. They prevented the introduction of the plow in this way on many plantations. Olmsted here cites many instances. Lewis, quoted in *Plantation Documents,* found the same thing to be true in Jamaica.

"It appears to me that nothing could afford so much relief to the negroes, under the existing system of Jamaica, as the substituting of labor of animals for that of slaves in agriculture wherever such a measure is practicable. On leaving the island, I impressed this wish of mine upon the mind of my agents with all my power; but the only result has been the creating a very considerable expense in the purchase of ploughs, oxen and farming implements; the awkwardness and still more the obstinacy of the few negroes, whose services were indispensable, was not to be overcome: they broke plough after plough, and ruined beast after beast, till the attempt was abandoned in despair."

IV

Malingering was a well-known phenomenon throughout the slave states. The purpose of feigning illness was generally to avoid work, although occasionally a slave who was being sold would feign a disability either to avoid being sold to an undesirable master, or to lower his purchase price so as to obtain revenge on a former master. The women occasionally pretended to be pregnant, because pregnant women were given lighter work assignments and were allowed extra rations of food.

In a situation such as this in which physical disability was an advantage, one would expect much malingering. One might also expect to find functional mental disorders, hysterical disorders which would get one out of work. There is some evidence that many had such functional disorders.

"There are many complaints described in Dr. Cartwright's treatise, to which the Negroes, in slavery, seem to be peculiarly subject.

" 'Negro-consumption, a disease almost unknown to medical men of the Northern States and of Europe, is also sometimes fearfully prevalent among the slaves. 'It is of importance,' says the Doctor, to know the pathognomic signs in its early stages, not only in regard to its treatment but to detect impositions, as negroes, afflicted with this complaint are often for sale; the acceleration of the pulse, on exercise, incapacitates them for labor, as they quickly give out, and have to leave their work. This induces their owners to sell them, although they may not know the cause of their inability to labor. Many of the negroes brought South, for sale, are in the incipient stages of this disease; they are found to be inefficient laborers, and sold in consequence thereof. The effect of superstition—a firm belief that he is poisoned or conjured—upon the patient's mind, already is a morbid state (dyaesthesia), and his health affected from hard usage, overtasking or exposure, want of wholesome food, good clothing, warm, comfortable lodging, with the distressing idea (sometimes) that he is an object of hatred or dislike, both to his master or fellow-servant, and has no one to befriend him, tends directly to generate that erythism of mind which is the essential cause of negro consumption' " . . . 'Remedies should be assisted by removing the *original cause* of the dissatisfaction or trouble of mind, and by using every means to make the patient comfortable, satisfied and happy.' "

Of course it is impossible to determine the extent of these disorders. Assuming that Dr. Cartwright's assumption was correct, very few observers

would be qualified to make an adequate diagnosis, and a very small proportion of these would be inclined to accept his interpretation. After all,
functional disorders are in many cases almost impossible to tell from real
disorders or from feigning, and since the behavior which Cartwright describes could very easily be interpreted on another, and easier, level by a
less acute observer.

Of the extent to which illness was feigned there can, however, be little
doubt. Some of the feigning was quite obvious, and one might wonder why
such flagrant abuses were tolerated. The important thing to remember is
that a slave was an important economic investment. Most slave owners
sooner or later found out that it was more profitable to give the slave the
benefit of the doubt. A sick slave driven to work might very well die.

> "But the same gentleman admitted that he had sometimes been mistaken
> and had made men go to work when they afterwards proved to be really
> ill; therefore, when one of his people told him he was not able to work, he
> usually thought, 'very likely he'll be all the better for a day's rest, whether
> he's really ill or not,' and would let him off without being very particular
> in his examination. Lately he had been getting a new overseer, and when
> he was engaging him he told him that this was his way. The observer re-
> plied, 'It's my way too, now; it didn't used to be, but I had a lesson. There
> was a nigger one day at Mr. ———'s who was sulky and complaining; he
> said he couldn't work. I looked at his tongue, and it was right clean, and
> I thought it was nothing but damned sulkiness so I paddled him, and made
> him go to work; but, two days after, he was under ground. He was a good
> eight hundred dollar nigger, and it was a lesson to me about taming pos-
> sums, that I ain't going to forget in a hurry.' "

So one might find situations like this:

> "At one, which was evidently the 'sick house' or hospital, there were sev-
> eral negroes, of both sexes, wrapped in blankets, and reclining on the door
> steps or on the ground, basking in sunshine. Some of them looked ill, but
> all were chatting and laughing as I rode up to make inquiry."

The situation turned in on itself. The masters were always suspicious
of the sick slaves, so that slaves who were moderately sick accentuated
their symptoms in order to make out a convincing case.

> "It is said to be nearly as difficult to form a satisfactory diagnosis of
> negroes' disorders, as it is of infants', because their imagination of symp-
> toms is so vivid, and because not the smallest reliance is to be placed on
> their accounts of what they have felt or done. If a man is really ill, he
> fears lest he should be thought to be simulating, and therefore exaggerates
> all his pains, and locates them in whatever he supposes to be the most vital
> parts of his system.
>
> "Frequently the invalid slaves will neglect or refuse to use the remedies

prescribed for their recovery. They will conceal pills, for instance, under their tongue, and declare they have swallowed them, when, from their producing no effect, it will be afterwards evident that they have not. This general custom I heard ascribed to habit acquired when they were not very disagreeably ill and were loth to be made quite well enough to have to go to work again."

Fortunately in this field we have some quantitative estimates which enable us to appreciate fully the extent of these practices. Sydnor has digested the records of sickness on various plantations. From the Wheeles plantation records he found that of 1,429 working days 179 were lost on account of sickness, a ratio of almost one to seven. On the Bowles' plantation, in one year 159½ days were missed on account of sickness but only five days were on Sundays. This is a recurrent pattern, everybody sick on Saturday, and scarcely anybody sick on Sunday. On the Leigh plantation, where thirty persons were working there were 398 days of sickness. In examining this record Sydnor discovered that the rate of sickness was greatest at the times of the year when there was the most work to be done. Olmsted says that he never visited a plantation on which twenty Negroes were employed where he did not find one or more not at work on some trivial pretext.

Lewis' anecdote is typical:

"On Saturday morning there were no fewer than forty-five persons (not including children) in the hospital; which makes nearly a fifth of my whole gang. Of these the medical people assured me that not above seven had anything whatever the matter with them. . . . And sure enough on Sunday morning they all walked away from the hospital to amuse themselves, except about seven or eight."

Sometimes the feigning did not work, as is shown by two incidents that Olmsted relates:

A Mr. X asked if there were any sick people.

" 'Nobody, oney dat boy Sam, sar.'

" 'What Sam is that?'

" 'Dat little Sam, sar; Tom's Sue's Sam, sar.'

" 'What's the matter with him?'

" 'Don' spec der's nothing much de matter wid him nof, sar. He came in Sa'dy, complaining he had de stomach-ache, an' I give him some ile, sar, 'spec he mus' be well dis time, but he din go out dis mornin'.'

" 'Well, I see to him.'

"Mr. X went to Tom's Sue's cabin, looked at the boy and concluded that he was well, though he lay abed, and pretended to cry with pain, ordered him to go out to work."

A planter asked the nurse if anyone else was sick.

" 'Oney dat woman Caroline.'

" 'What do you think is the matter with her?'

" 'Well, I don't think there is anything de matter wid her, masser; I mus answer you for true, I don't tink anything de matter wid her, oney she's a little sore from dat whipping she got.' "

The manager found the woman groaning on a dirty bed and after examining her, scolded her and sent her to work.

The prevalence of malingering may be better appreciated when one realizes that despite the fact that Olmsted refers to it throughout four volumes of his works, in one place he has five whole pages of anecdotes concerning it.

Pretending to be pregnant was a type of escape in a class by itself, since the fraud must inevitably have been discovered. This in itself may give us some insight into the Negroes' attitude toward the relative advantages of escaping work and of escaping punishment. Just as the slave who ran off into the woods for a temporary relief from work, the pseudo-pregnant woman must have realized in advance that she would inevitably be punished.

"I will tell you of a most comical account Mr. ———— has given me of the prolonged and still protracted pseudo-pregnancy of a woman called Markie, who for many more months than are generally required for the process of continuing the human species, pretended to be what the Germans pathetically and poetically call 'in good hope' and continued to reap increased rations as the reward of her expectation, till she finally had to disappoint the estate and receive a flogging."

One woman sought to escape from the consequences of her fraud. The results were quite tragic:

"A young slave woman, Becky by name, had given pregnancy as the reason for a continued slackness in her work. Her master became skeptical and gave notice that she was to be examined and might expect the whip in case her excuse were not substantiated. Two days afterward a Negro midwife announced that Becky's baby had been born; but at the same time a neighboring planter began search for a child nine months old which was missing from his quarter. This child was found in Becky's cabin, with its two teeth pulled and the tip of its navel cut off. It died; and Becky was convicted only of manslaughter."

An outstanding example of malingering is given by Smedes, a writer who insisted so emphatically on the devotion of the slaves to their masters.

"The cook's husband, who for years had looked on himself as nearly blind, and therefore unable to do more than work about her, and put her wood on the fire, sometimes cutting a stick or two, made no less than eighteen good crops for himself when the war was over. He was one of the best farmers in the country."

The most effective means of retaliation against an unpopular master which the slave had at his command was by feigning disability on the auction block. How often this was done we do not know, but Phillips accepts it as a recognized pattern.

"Those on the block often times praised their own strength and talents, for it was a matter of pride to fetch high prices. On the other hand if a slave should bear a grudge against his seller, or should hope to be bought only by someone who would expect but light service he might pretend a disability though he had it not."

Coleman offers the same opinion:

"Similar actions were not unknown in slave sales. Frequently on such occasions there is a strong indisposition in such creatures to be sold, and that by stratagem to avoid sale, they may frequently feign sickness, or magnify any particular complaint with which they are affected.

"As was customary at a public auction of slaves, the auctioneer announced that Mr. Anderson, the master, would give a bill of sale for his slave with the usual guarantee—'sound of mind and body and a slave for life.' While there began a lively bidding among the Negro traders, George suddenly assumed a strange appearance—his head was thrown back, his eyes rolled wildly, his body and limbs began to twitch and jerk in an unheard of manner.

" 'What's the matter with your boy, Mr. Anderson?' one of the traders asked the owner, who, astonished and puzzled, drew nearer the block. But Mr. Anderson did not answer the question. George was now foaming at the mouth, and the violent twitching and jerking increased precipitiously.

" 'What's the matter with you, boy?' gruffly demanded the trader. 'O, I 'es fits I has!' exclaimed George, whereupon his body doubled up and rolled off the block.

"Of course the auction was hastily terminated. George was hustled off to jail, and a doctor sent for, but, after a careful examination, the medical man was somewhat mystified as to the slaves's actual condition. He advised the master to leave George in the jailer's custody for a while, promising to look in on him the next morning. Under his master's instruction, the wily slave was put to bed in the debtor's room, where he soon sank, apparently, into a sound sleep.

"Next morning when the jailer brought in breakfast, he found the bed empty. George was gone, and nothing was heard of him again until word came, several weeks later, that he was safe in Canada."

Or, again, we read:

"A young girl, of twenty years or thereabouts, was the next commodity put up. Her right hand was entirely useless—'dead,' as she aptly called it. One finger had been cut off by a doctor, and the auctioneer stated that she herself chopped off the other finger—her forefinger—because it hurt her, and she thought that to cut it off would cure it.

"'Didn't you cut your finger off?' asked a man, 'kase you was mad?'

"She looked at him quietly, but with a glance of contempt, and said:

"'No, you see it was sort o' sore, and I thought it would be better to cut it off than be plagued with it.'

"Several persons around me expressed the opinion that she had done it willfully, to spite her master or mistress, or to keep her from being sold down South."

Another instance is described as follows:

"As I came up, a second-rate plantation hand of the name of Noah, but whom the crier persisted in calling 'Noey,' was being offered, it being an administrator's sale. Noey, on mounting the steps, had assumed a most drooping aspect, hanging his head and affecting the feebleness of old age. He had probably hoped to have avoided sale by a dodge, which is very common in such cases. But the first bid—$1,000—startled him, and he looked eagerly to the quarter whence it proceeded. 'Never mind who he is, he has got the money. Now, gentlemen, just go on; who will say fifty.' And so the crier proceeds with his monotonous calling. 'I ain't worth all that, mass'r; I ain't much count no how,' cried Noey energetically to the first bidder. 'Yes you are, Noey—ah, $1,000, thank you, sir,' replies the crier."

The strength of Negro resistance to slavery becomes apparent in the extent to which the slaves mutilated themselves in their efforts to escape work. A girl on Lewis' plantation who had been injured tied pack thread around her wounds when they started to heal and then rubbed dirt in them. In her anxiety to avoid work she gave herself a very serious infection. But this action was mild compared to that of others.

"General Leslie Coombs, of Lexington, owned a man named Ennis, a house carpenter. He had bargained with a slave-trader to take him and carry him down the river. Ennis was determined not to go. He took a broadaxe and cut one hand off; then contrived to lift the axe, with his arm pressing it to his body, and let it fall upon the other, cutting off the ends of the fingers."

"'But some on 'em would rather be shot then be took, sir,'" he added simply.

"A farmer living near a swamp confirmed this account, and said he knew of three or four being shot on one day."

Planters had much trouble with slaves fresh from Africa, the new slaves committing suicide in great numbers. Ebo landing in the Sea Islands was the site of the mass suicide of Ebo slaves who simply walked in a body into the ocean and drowned themselves. A planter writing on the handling of slaves mentions the difficulty of adjusting the Africans to slavery. He advocates mixing them in with seasoned slaves.

"It too often happens that poor masters, who have no other slaves or are too greedy, require hard labor of these fresh negroes, exhaust them quickly, lose them by sickness and more often by grief. Often they hasten their own death; some wound themselves, others stifle themselves by drawing in the tongue so as to close the breathing passage, other take poison, or flee and perish of misery and hunger."

The one problem of Negro resistance to slavery which is most enticing is that of the attitude of slave mothers toward their children. There are frequent references in the literature to Negro women who boasted about the number of "niggers they hade for the massah," but breeding was probably quite secondary to sex activity. It would be interesting to discover the motives behind this apparent pleasure in presenting babies to the master. Some of the women may have been sincere in their pride. What makes this problem peculiarly important is the presence of much indirect evidence that, the Negro mothers either had no affection for their children, or did not want them to be raised as slaves.

We know quite well that African Negroes are (at least reasonably) able to take care of their children, and that the slave women efficiently tended the children of the plantation mistress. Yet one runs across comment after comment that the Negro mothers were ignorant, and careless, and did not know how to care for their own offspring. Typical of such statements is this:

"The Negro mothers are often so ignorant and indolent, that they cannot be trusted to keep awake and administer medicine to their own children; so that the mistress has often to sit up all night with a sick Negro child."

Guion Johnson states that plantation owners in the Sea Islands offered the mothers rewards to take good care of their children. They were paid for those who survived the first year! This at least would indicate that there was something to be desired in their attitude toward their children.

Occasionally one runs across a reference to a slave mother killing her child, but the statements are almost invariably incomplete. For instance, Catterall has a record of a trial, the details of which are: "The prisoner was indicted for murder of her own child," no more. Or a plantation overseer writes, "Elizabeth's child died last night. She smothered it somehow." There is no indication as to whether or not the smothering was deliberate.

Several cases, where it was certain that parents killed their children to keep them from slavery, have been described. They are important enough to be given in detail.

"Of all the cases of slave rendition, the saddest and probably the most circulated at the time was that of Margaret Garner. Winter was the best time for flight across the Ohio River, for when it was frozen over the difficulties of crossing were fewer. Simeon Garner, with his wife Margaret and two children, fled from slavery in Kentucky during the cold winter of 1856 and, after crossing the frozen stream at night, made their ways to the house of a free Negro in Cincinnati.

"Quickly tracing the fugitive Negroes to their hideout in Cincinnati, the armed pursuers, after some resistance, broke down the door and entered the house. There they found Margaret, the mother, who, preferring death to slavery for her children, had striven to take their lives, and one child lay dead on the floor. The case was immediately brought into court, where despite the efforts made by sympathetic whites, rendition was ordered. On their return to slavery, Margaret in despair attempted to drown herself and child by jumping into the river but even the deliverance of death was denied her, for she was recovered and soon thereafter sold to a trader who took her to the cotton fields of the Far South."

"Not only were slaves known to take the lives of their masters or overseers, but they were now and then charged with the murder of their own children, sometimes to prevent them from growing up in bondage. In Covington a father and mother, shut up in a slave baracoon and doomed to the southern market, 'when there was no eye to pity them and no arm to save,' did by mutual agreement 'send the souls of their children to Heaven rather than have them descend to the hell of slavery,' and then both parents committed suicide."

" 'Take off your shoes, Sylva,' said Mrs. A., 'and let this gentleman see your feet.'

" 'I don't want to,' said Sylva.

" 'But I want you to,' said her mistress.

" 'I don't care if you do,' replied Sylva sullenly.

" 'You must,' said the mistress firmly.

"The fear of punishment impelled her to remove the shoes. Four toes on one foot, and two on the other were wanting! 'There!' said the mistress, 'my husband, who learned the blacksmith's trade for the purpose of teaching it to the slaves, to increase their market value, has, with his own hands, pounded off and wrung off all those toes, when insane with passion. And it was only last week that he thought Sylva was saucy to me, and he gave her thirty lashes with the horse whip. She was so old that I could not bear to see it, and I left the house.

" 'Sylva says,' Mrs. A. continued, 'that she has been the mother of thirteen children, every one of whom she has destroyed with her own hands, in their infancy, rather than have them suffer slavery'!"

V

The patterns of resistance to slavery studied in this paper are: (1) deliberate slowing up of work; (2) destruction of property, and indifferent work; (3) feigning illness and pregnancy; (4) injuring one's self; (5) suicide; (6) a possibility that a significant number of slave mothers killed their children.

The motivation behind these acts was undoubtedly complex. The most obvious of the motives was a desire to avoid work. It has been demonstrated that the slaves were acutely conscious of the fact that they had nothing to gain by hard work except in those instances where they were working under the task system. The destruction of property and the poor quality of the slaves' work was mainly due to their indifference to their tasks. There is enough evidence that they could, and did, work hard and well when sufficiently motivated to refute any contention that the Negro slaves were congenitally poor workers.

Many of the slaves reacted to the institution of slavery in a far more drastic fashion than could be manifested by a mere desire to avoid work. Some of these slaves committed suicide; others killed members of their families, usually their children, in order that they might not grow up as slaves.

Possibly the most significant aspect of these patterns of resistance is the aggression against the white masters they imply. Unfortunately, however, though this aspect may be the most significant, it is the least subject to proof. On the plane of logic, there is every reason to believe that a people held in bondage would devise techniques such as have been described above as an indirect means of retaliation. The statement of Dollard, previously quoted, indicates that such techniques (slowness, inefficiency, etc.) are used at the present time as a means of indirect aggression.

The material presented here suggests the need for a reconsideration of the concept of the Negro's easy adjustment to slavery. He was not a cheerful, efficient worker, as has been assumed. Rather, he was frequently rebellious, and almost always sullen, as any person faced with a disagreeable situation from which he cannot escape will normally be. Nor, can the belief that racial inferiority is responsible for inefficient workmanship on his part be supported. For such deficiencies of his workmanship as he manifested, or, indeed, may still be manifested, are seen to be explainable in terms that are in no sense to be couched in the conventional mold of inherent racial differences.

The New Society and
the Changing Old Society
1843-1876

Industrialization proceeded at a rapid pace during this period. A spectacular spurt of railroad building further developed the national market and simultaneously provided an impetus for the growth of heavy industries. The constant influx of immigrants to America provided the cheap labor force necessary both to build the railroads and to work in the new factories.

The continuing process of cultural adaptation as old met new and both changed began to meet grave obstacles. Some older U.S. residents, usually non-workers, emphatically asserted their "Americanness." The new immigrant workingman was perceived as a threat in both class and ethnic terms, and this new perception of an "ethnic threat" (predominantly anti-Catholic) coincided with the emergence of these ethnic groups in the labor movement and in local politics.

If the upper classes felt isolated and threatened by America's emerging cultural pluralism, it was somewhat different for American workers. The work place became the key meeting place of ethnics and blacks with white "Americans" and one another. A highly ambiguous experience, such contact often caused bitter antagonism, but also allowed for close work relationships to develop between ethnic workers, native white workers, and free blacks in the north. This process held, though in different ways, for poor whites and slaves in the south. Even where antagonism resulted, encounters had taken place that contrasted greatly with the experiences of the upper classes whose contacts often caused them to perceive of blacks and ethnics only in the roles of slaves, servants, and laborers.

The emergence of sectional antagonism that culminated in the Civil War tended to "mask" many of these nascent class, ethnic, and racial conflicts, but they emerged more fully in Reconstruction America. For the slaves, the Civil War brought freedom. Demonstrating anew their cultural resilience, they flocked to the Union army, fought courageously, and when placed on the land showed unusual skills, adapting quickly and successfully to freedom. Deep from within their cultural experience, they not only expected land, but demanded it, and only through the persuasive force of the Freedman's Bureau, the coercive force of the Union Army, and later the bloody actions of the Ku Klux Klan were they deprived of it.

The Great Railroad Conspiracy:
The Social History of a Railroad War

CHARLES HIRSCHFELD

The Great Railroad Conspiracy, a detailed study of the conflict between the
farmers and townfolk of Michigan Centre and the Michigan Central
Railroad Company, disputes the optimistic argument that sees the coming
of the railroad as an event for celebration in the life of small towns. Some
towns, or parts of towns, did celebrate—but not always. In their sense of
justice, in their deep antagonism to the alien corporation, and in their
willingness to resort to violence, the farmers of Jackson County hearken back
to the past and prefigure the future. Although living on the "frontier," they
drew the strength to act against the railroad both from past cultural
experiences and from their new situation. This agrarian antagonism to
business, and especially to the railroads, is usually viewed as beginning in
the 1870s with the Grangers. This essay shows its far deeper roots.

Charles Hirschfeld, The Great Railroad Conspiracy: The Social History of a Railroad
War (East Lansing, Mich.: Michigan State University Press, 1953), pp. 3–26. Reprinted
and footnotes 1–29 omitted by permission of the publisher. Originally published in
Michigan History, 36 (1952).

The following works are suggested for further reading:

HENRY CHRISTMAN, *Tin Horns and Calico,* New York: Henry Holt & Co., 1945.
DAVID ELLIS, *Landlords and Tenants,* Ithaca: Cornell University Press, 1946.
PAUL EVANS, *The Holland Land Company,* Buffalo Historical Society Publications, XXVIII (1924).

The story of the great railroad conspiracy goes back to 1846 when the state of Michigan sold its railroads to private chartered corporations. The state had built and operated two railroads since 1837 as part of a broad program of internal improvements designed at once to build up the interior of Michigan and advance the commercial interests of its cities, particularly Detroit. By 1845 the railroads had not reached Lake Michigan from their eastern terminals as required by law, and further public construction and operation seemed to run into an impasse of financial difficulties and not altogether disinterested prejudice. The Central Railroad, which had reached Kalamazoo from Detroit, was the farther advanced in construction and the more profitable of the two roads. It was this road that attracted the attention of John W. Brooks, a civil engineer who had helped build and operate railroads in New York and New England, and James F. Joy, a transplanted Yankee who had won a position for himself at the Detroit bar. These two young men, ambitious and shrewd, saw the immense moneymaking possibilities in a completed transpeninsular railroad that would tap the expanding western hinterland and link it with the eastern seaboard. Brooks used his eastern connections to interest a group of New York and Boston capitalists, and Joy worked on the Michigan legislature; and in 1846, the Michigan Central Railroad Company received a charter and possession of the railroad from Detroit to Kalamazoo for the sum of two million dollars. At the same time, the other railroad, running through the southern counties from Monroe to Hillsdale, was knocked down to the newly chartered Michigan Southern Railroad Company.

Taking over the Central road in the fall of 1846, Brooks as superintendent of the new company, and Joy, as legal counsel, started immediately to improve their investment and realize their golden vision. Money and men were poured into a concerted drive to reach the lake at New Buffalo. Tracks were laid with sixty-pound T-rails and the latest model engines and rolling stock put into operation. The old line of the road east of Kalamazoo was improved with new grades and bridges and the old worn strap rails were replaced with the heavier T-rails. By April, 1849, the Michigan Central spanned the peninsula, was paying eight and nine percent dividends on net earnings of almost $200,000 a year, and the trains were running at thirty miles an hour.

The drive for efficiency and profits soon brought the company into conflict with the farmers along the line of the road. The right of way was largely unfenced, and the cattle of the farmers through whose land the tracks ran were easy marks for the heavier and speedier trains. What incensed the farmers was not only the killing of great numbers of cows, sheep, and hogs, but the fact that the company refused to pay what they considered fair damages. Much livestock had, indeed, been destroyed when the railroad had been owned by the state, but the Board of Internal Improvements, the state's operating agency, had not dared to antagonize the electors by paying less than their claims. One official of the board had complained in 1845 that the damages paid for cattle maimed and killed had reached extravagant proportions and suggested that in cases where no negligence on the part of the engineers could be proven, the farmers should be made to bear half the loss. This impolitic suggestion had, of course, never been adopted. Superintendent Brooks, however, with no concern for the electorate and responsible only to the directors and stock-holders, was determined to pay as little as he could and make the farmers share the risks. He claimed that the cattle were trespassers; that the negligence and cupidity of the owners were contributory factors; and hinted strongly that the farmers were seeking a ready market at each crossing. Brooks denied any legal liability for damages at all, but offered, as a measure of expedience, to pay half of the appraised value. The aggrieved farmers took this offer as an admission of liability and demanded full damages.

When these were not forthcoming, the issue was fully joined. Excitement flared up all along the line of the road from Ann Arbor to Niles in the spring of 1849. Near Niles, where the state had never operated the railroad and where it was reported that one hundred sixty pieces of livestock had been killed in the twelve-mile stretch between Niles and Dowagiac, the farmers retaliated for the half-pay offer by committing serious depredations, going so far as to derail an engine by opening a switch. One infuriated citizen threatened publicly to tie up traffic entirely. West of Kalamazoo, the farmers, under cover of darkness, greased the tracks on the upgrades with lard and tallow salvaged by their wives from the carcasses, to the great annoyance of the train crews who had to get out and sand the tracks before they could proceed. Further east, near Ann Arbor, the tracks were actually torn up, presumably by those who had had cattle killed.

At Marshall, few evening trains passed without being delayed by turned switches or shot at. The violent outbursts there were broadcast and justified by one of the village's leading citizens, John D. Pierce, in a series of letters to the local Democratic newspaper. Pierce, Michigan's first state superintendent of public instruction, a member of the legislatures of 1847 and 1848, and a clergyman by training, had recently had some sheep of his own killed on the tracks and now took up the cudgels for the farmers in the area. He denounced the destruction of livestock and the company's disclaimer of liability and refusal of fair damages. "The road," he declared in June, 1849, "has been for a long time one gore of blood. No heathen altar ever smoked more continually with the blood of its victims." And the company dared to charge that the owners of cattle were the trespassers. Resort to legal action cost more than the cattle were worth. The railroad's "reckless policy" had created "an embittered state of feeling along the whole line" and was responsible for the fact that the injured persons resorted to violence "because they know no other way." Pierce warned the company of the consequences of its policy, even though he had "little hope that any reason or argument which was not addressed to its cupidity would induce a moneyed corporation to change its course." According to one account, the choleric preacher proved his point. When he championed the cause of a poor widow who had a yoke of oxen killed, and Superintendent Brooks contemptuously sent word back to Marshall to "Tell that parson out there he'd better stick to preaching," Pierce replied that if the company did not pay the woman, he himself would see to it that every mile of track in Calhoun County was torn up. Th parson's triumph was complete and biblical, if momentary, when Brooks paid up in that one case. Pierce concluded as follows:

> Something must be done, the honor of the state,—its good name . . . demand it. The road must be fenced—in the meantime something near the value of the property destroyed must be paid. It is an outrage, and evidences utter recklessness of life and limb of both man and beast that the company should run trains over an unfenced road, where all cattle are by law free commoners, at the rate of thirty miles per hour.

Neither at Niles nor Marshall nor anywhere else in the state was the opposition to the Michigan Central Railroad so intensive and so sustained as in the few miles along the line of the road between Grass Lake and Michigan Centre in the eastern part of Jackson County. It was here that collective protest first brought the offer of half pay from Superintendent Brooks, and here that destructive reprisals continued for almost two years to disrupt the railroad's operations. Precisely why it was so seems difficult to ascertain at this distance in time. Perhaps more cattle were killed in Leoni and Grass Lake townships than elsewhere, although the evidence is not conclusive on this point. Perhaps it was that here the farmers found leaders, veritable tribunes of the people, in two men with a stubborn determination to see that justice was done, Abel F. Fitch of Michigan Centre and Benjamin F. Burnett of Grass Lake. Perhaps it was the deliberate choice by Superintendent Brooks of these two townships as the arena in which to break the back of the opposition to the railroad that brought the most violent reaction in the state.

The losses between Grass Lake and Michigan Centre, while substantial, do not seem to have been unusually heavy. One estimate was that forty head of cattle had been killed near the village of Leoni. According to a later estimate, damages to the amount of $800 had been inflicted on the farmers of the vicinity. The editor of a Jackson paper offered the following explanation of the imbroglio some fifty years after the events: East of Michigan Centre, the railroad track crossed a muskeg or sunken lake, "The Dry Marsh" as it was known in the locality, and the cattle in the area, which had previously skirted the marsh, began to use the tracks as a convenient bridge, with disastrous results to themselves. The railroad, moreover, then brought its own appraisers out from Detroit, and the amount of the damages fixed by a company appraiser who saw the animals after they had been dead for several days was not such as to satisfy the owners.

In any case, by the spring of 1849, the increasing destruction of livestock and the company's refusal to pay the damages claimed aroused the farmers in the vicinity to action. At a number of public meetings—railroad meetings, they were called—they collectively requested Superintendent Brooks to modify his policy, to direct the engineers to run their trains more carefully, and, until the right of way was fenced, to pay full damages. At one of the meetings, Abel F. Fitch, Benjamin F. Burnett, and one James Courier were chosen as a committee to represent the group's views to the railroad's superintendent in Detroit. The three accordingly wrote Brooks a letter informing him of the great excitement among the farmers of the region and suggesting the consequences of further inflammation of the popular mind by a policy that was not "more humane." Brooks, in reply, completely denied the validity of the committee's representations. The company, he countered, was not legally liable at all for damages to property along the right of way; he would, however, pay one half of the appraised value of all cattle killed. Meanwhile, he suggested, the company and one of the injured parties could take a test case to the Supreme Court of the state to decide the question of liability, with all costs and fees up to $50 to be borne by the company. If the court decided that the company were liable, he would thereafter pay in full the damages incurred by the farmers. Brooks, at the same time, professed to see an implied threat in the committee's letter and went on to add that he would hold Fitch, Burnett, and Courier morally if not criminally responsible for any injury done the railroad in any atttempts to coerce it.

Brooks' proposal, which was published in the Jackson newspapers, was never seriously entertained. Abel F. Fitch dismissed it on the steps of the American Hotel in Jackson as a "perfect humbug." The farmers followed his lead and ignored it and then struck back in the readiest way at hand—by placing obstructions on the tracks, stoning the trains, and even shooting at the engines as they passed in the night. As Fitch, now become their spokesman, argued, the people had had their cattle killed and could not get redress any other way. When someone suggested going to court, Fitch denied that the people could get their rights that way, and went on to attack the whole judicial system in a cynical diatribe of a man who knew the political game. He stated bluntly that every man had his price and that a judge could be bought as well as any other man; that he had no more confidence in the judges of the Supreme Court than in those of the lower courts—they knew enough law but could be bought as well as others, though in ordinary cases they were well enough; and that he based his opinions on a certain county judge whom he named. He denounced the railroad company as an aristocracy whose influence and money would prevent justice from being obtained in any court. When it was argued that endangering the lives of innocent passengers was not the way to attain the object in view, Fitch heatedly countered that persons who would support such a company ought to be injured.

Fitch's stand was echoed by William Corwin, a teamster at Michigan Centre, who was a young and irresponsible fellow. One morning at the end of May, Corwin was approached by a neighbor, Abram Henry, who mentioned that he had heard some shots fired as the train passed the night before. He asked Corwin if they were firing at the train last night. Corwin casually replied, "Yes, I suppose so." Henry asked if anyone was killed. Corwin said, "No." When Henry then pointed out that by and by they would kill somebody, Corwin burst out: "Damn 'em, if they don't want to be shot let 'em pay for the cattle they have killed." Henry told him that it was a bad idea, for they would kill innocent people who paid their money for riding over the road. Corwin closed the conversation angrily: "Damn 'em, they need not ride over the road if they don't want to be killed."

Not long after, the violent agitation brought the attorney general of Michigan, George V. N. Lothrop, to the scene. He came to Jackson from Detroit to investigate the trouble and try to allay the unrest. On his arrival, he was met by the committee of three who presented the aggrieved farmers' case substantially as they had done to Brooks. When Lothrop suggested a remedy at law, they replied that a poor man would have no chance in a law suit with the company. Fitch and Burnett argued with some warmth that the railroad was to blame for the excitement and lawlessness; that as long as it would not pay fair value for cattle killed, it might expect trouble on the road; and that the people were justified in taking matters into their own hands, for it was the only means they had of bringing the company to terms. Fitch even threatened to send handbills to New York, Buffalo, and Chicago, warning the public that it was dangerous to pass over the Michigan Central. Lothrop returned to Detroit and presented the committee's views to Superintendent Brooks. He then wrote the committee that Brooks insisted that his proposal was a just and liberal one and an earnest of the company's solicitude. Brooks gave them every assurance that any engineer found wantonly destroying cattle would be discharged. Furthermore, it had always been the practice of the company to pay full value for cattle killed when the owner was too poor to bear the loss. For himself, Lothrop condemned the outrages and promised that the offenders, who were no better than "pirates and wholesale murderers," would be severely punished. He then warned the three spokesmen that unless they themselves exerted an active influence to prevent such conduct, they "must expect to be held, in no slight degree, responsible . . ." And like a good politician, Lothrop closed on the note of the necessity of compromise.

Matters remained, however, at an impasse. The verbal exchanges proved to be only preludes to a violent and embittered battle. As the summer of 1849 advanced and as mutual suspicion and hatred mounted, more cattle were killed and further depredations were committed against the railroad. When Orlando D. Williams, a mason at Leoni, had his cow killed, the company offered him half price for it three or four times. He refused the offers and demanded $25 or nothing. He told his neighbor it would be a dear cow for them. Andrew J. (Jack) Freeland, a successful farmer at Michigan Centre, complained he had a number of sheep killed, five or seven, and the company offered him half price for them, but if they did not pay him full price they would be dear sheep. He slyly said that the cars were getting rather skittish about running through Leoni Township, and "damn 'em, they'd better pay up for cattle if they did not want trouble."

The railroad did not pay up and it got the trouble. That summer and fall passenger and freight trains were frequently stoned, shot at, obstructed, and derailed in the ten-mile stretch between Grass Lake and Jackson. The assailants would hide in the undergrowth along the right of way during the night and throw stones, bricks, and bottles and discharge pistols at the passing trains. Sometimes they would sally forth to lay rails and logs across the track or throw switches. Once the passenger train was stoned a little east of Leoni village and the conductor heard a woman scream and went back into the cars and a lady handed him a stone which had lodged in her lap. A man in the next car was badly hurt by a stone which hit him in the breast. The conductor went on to find stones in every car and many windows broken. One night, an engineer later recalled, his passenger train was stoned three times, twice near Fitch's house, which stood beside the tracks at Michigan Centre, and once west of Leoni. On investigation, he found the mark of a brick five inches long on the tank and a big dent on his boiler. Another night that summer, the same engineer was shot at as he approached Michigan Centre. He saw a flash of guns, some four or five of them, from about thirty or forty feet from the tracks and later found the marks of a ball on one of the engine's feed pipes. This engineer had no taste for these extra hazards of railroading and soon left his job with the Michigan Central for one in another state. Another engineer later admitted that he sometimes cowered behind the driving wheel guards as he rode through the badlands at Michigan Centre.

The attacks were varied by placing rails, old ties, and the discarded strap iron rails across the tracks or jamming them in between the joints of the rails and in the switches. The company had to run a hand car ahead of the trains between Grass Lake and Jackson, but the determined assailants would simply hide alongside the tracks and then, after the hand car had passed, run out and do their mischief. Traffic was greatly slowed up and the train schedules were knocked awry, for each obstruction meant stopping the train and getting out and clearing the tracks. The run from Grass Lake to Jackson, which normally took forty-five minutes, sometimes took as long as an hour and twenty-five minutes. The crawling pace through the disaffected areas was indeed a necessity if the trains were not to be run off with great loss of life and property.

Once that summer, the locomotive *Dexter* was drawing a rack train loaded with timber going west in the late afternoon. The conductor, Harmon Spaulding, was in the cab with the engineer and the fireman. The train slowed down after reaching Leoni but then speeded up in order to make way for the eastbound passenger train expected at that time. About a half mile east of Michigan Centre, as the engine rounded a curve running along the Dry Marsh, Spaulding sighted a stick of timber lying across the track. The engineer reversed the engine and then both he and the fireman jumped for their lives. Spaulding stayed on as the wheels hit the log, cut it in two, and ground to a stop near the crossing at Michigan Centre. A group of men came up to the stalled engine, among whom Spaulding recognized Abel Fitch and Ammi Filley, proprietor of the tavern at the Centre. Fitch asked, "Spaulding, what's the trouble?" Spaulding pointedly told him that "some damned hyenas" had put a timber on the track and tried to run the train off. Someone in the crowd shouted they wished they had run it off. To this, Spaulding replied, "I don't see what you have against me, as I have not been running on the road for some time." Filley here chimed in with the remark that they did not care who they killed and would as lief kill him as any one else. Spaulding then asked Fitch what their object was and the latter replied that there had been cattle killed that had not been paid for. Fitch continued, shouting, "Spaulding, by God, the company can never run this road in safety until they come out and pay us our price for killing cattle and damages done to other property." Spaulding then argued that he couldn't see why the obstruction was put on at that time, unless it was intended to catch the passenger train, as they did not know this timber train was coming along. Somebody answered to the effect that the men who put it there knew their business. Spaulding, his temper rising, warned the men that if it had got to that pass that the company could not do business on the road, he for one was ready to come out and defend the road with arms if necessary. Fitch threw the threat right back and said they might come on if that was the game—he had two double-barreled guns and some loaded pistols ready for business and men enough to use them. At this point, Spaulding judiciously decided that matters had gone far enough for the moment; the temper of the crowd seemed to be ugly and a strategic withdrawal was in order. The train moved on only to find more obstructions ahead, several bars of strap rail and the skin of a dead cow, and it was Spaulding who went ahead on foot to remove them.

Yet another form of vicious bedevilment was to set fire to the piles of company lumber stacked along the right of way for the use of the loco-motives. Late one night in the fall of 1849, three of the more law-abiding citizens of Leoni were returning from Jackson on foot along the tracks. They came upon two woodpiles burning about a mile west of Michigan Centre, and went to work to put the fires out. As the train passed, they stopped it and asked for help, but got only an unceremonious damning from the jittery, distrustful train crew. As day broke, the little group, still hard at work putting out the fires, was accosted by three friends somewhat less concerned with the preservation of the property of the railroad. They were Fitch, Filley, and Erastus Champlin, a farmer at the Centre, who explained that they had been hailed by the train crew back at the Centre and told that the woodpiles were on fire. The newcomers were content to stand there, taunting and reviling the fire fighters. Champlin sneered that the train crew was perfectly right in damning them, they ought to be damned, and damn those who didn't damn them. Fitch, with wry humor, told them that they ought to be burnt up with the wood, then the company woud pay their wives half price for the ashes. When one of the conscientious ones remonstrated that he thought it was his duty to try and save property when it was being destroyed, Fitch answered that he had never put any-thing on the track and would not take anything off if he saw the cars coming with Brooks and the whole company in them and "it knocked them all to hell." The fires presumably were put out, but certainly without the help of the vindictive Michigan Centreites. At another time, Fitch refused a request for help in putting out a blazing culvert, saying, "You will have to go out of this town to get help to put it out."

Not all the mishaps that afflicted the railroad in the summer and fall of 1849 could be attributed, directly or circumstantially, to the lawless citizens of Michigan Centre, Leoni, and Grass Lake. Some were simply accidents due to the rather primitive railroading operations. Several engines and trains were derailed after running into cattle grazing on the track, which must have seemed like divine retribution to Fitch and his friends. The negligence of track crews doubtless accounted for a number of accidents. Nor had attacks on the trains disappeared elsewhere along the line of the road. East and west of Niles and between Ypsilanti and Ann Arbor, occasional depredations continued to make travel on the Michigan Central a hazardous venture.

Superintendent Brooks was soon convinced of the need for strong measures to eliminate the threat to the road's operations. Business during 1849 was none too good in any case, what with the poor crop, an outbreak of cholera in the state, and the continued strong competition of the lake boats that took passengers to Chicago around Michigan via the lakes. The attacks by those whom Brooks could only recognize as marauding felons were driving passengers to travel around the lakes rather than risk life and limb on the Michigan Central.

Brooks' first step was to station company police or watchmen along the tracks in the troubled area. He then offered a reward of $500 for the detection and conviction of the criminals who had obstructed or would obstruct the railroad, and circulated printed handbills to that effect along the line. The reward circulars singled out for special consideration those "sundry evil minded persons, in and about the village of Leoni," but also extended its terms to "similar offenders on any part of the road."

These measures did not prove effective. Not a single offender was caught nor a single attack discovered in time. If anything, the presence of the police only put the "sundry evil minded persons" on their guard and led them to resort to devious maneuver; they were easily able to spot and outwit the special watch. Once in August, Brooks and Joy, who directed the legal action, thought they had cornered their game and were ready to make an example that would forestall further attacks, but found they had only caught a tartar. One of the special police, Elwood Cook, went to the grand jury of Jackson County and made out an information against one James A. Lester, charging him with obstructing the railroad. Attorney General Lothrop came out to Jackson from Detroit and prodded the grand jury into issuing an indictment against Lester. It seemed as though the law were at last ready to step in and strike down the enemies of the railroad.

The law, however, reckoned without the determination of Fitch and Burnett. As soon as Lester was arrested, these two came to his defense. They unearthed evidence and brought witnesses to show that it was Cook who had obstructed the railroad and then laid the crime to Lester in the hope of gaining the $500 reward. Fitch and Burnett presented these findings to the not wholly unsympathetic citizens of the Jackson County Grand Jury, which then found a true bill against Cook for perjury four days after it had indicted Lester. With the tables thus turned, Joy had to come to Cook's defense. Neither case, however, came to trial; both were eventually nolle prossed.

This legal defeat convinced Brooks and Joy that they were using the wrong tactics. They realized that they were not facing a number of lawless individuals but a body of citizens united in hatred of the railroad and belief in the justice of their cause. Public sentiment in Jackson County was largely ranged against the Michigan Central and convictions by local juries would be difficult if not impossible to obtain. Detection of the guilty by ordinary police methods had proven ineffective. Action against relatively unimportant individuals, moreover, would not halt the attacks. The company faced the necessity of resorting to extraordinary methods to gain evidence against its enemies and then, of striking at the head and heart of the opposition, at its leaders, at Fitch, Burnett, and the more active of their followers. Brooks and Joy set their sights accordingly.

Fitch had without doubt emerged as the leader of the road's opponents. His position in the community and his opinions had led to his choice on the committee of three that acted for the citizens assembled in public protest; he had probably been active in organizing the meetings in the first place. Subsequently, his leadership was reinforced by the promptings of his conscience, by a self-imposed trust as advocate of the cause of his friends and neighbors. It was expressed in his activities on behalf of Lester and his public defense of the attacks on the railroad and denunciation of the company's policies. And Superintendent Brooks could only have concluded that Fitch was his nemesis, the gadfly of the opposition, when in the fall of 1849 he received a letter from him complaining of the fact that the trains were not stopping at Michigan Centre to pick up passengers who were giving the usual signal. "Now if this policy," Fitch warned in closing, "comes from you or your legal advisers, as did the insulting half pay proposition for killing cattle, if serious accidents do occur on the road, on your head, and yours alone, must rest the responsibility." Brooks promptly answered the letter with maddening politeness, if none too helpfully, by enclosing a handbill with a schedule of train stops. "If any train has passed your station, which according to it, should stop there," he explained, "I would be quite obliged for any information that will point to a specific train, when I can correct it." With that reply, the incident was closed; it was in itself not of great moment, but served to aggravate ill feeling and convince Brooks that Fitch was the instigator of all the company's many troubles.

Abel F. Fitch was an amalgam of shrewdness and idealism that in

most other men happily serves or is made to serve their own aggrandize-
ment. In his case, the two ingredients clashed and eventually led to his
downfall. He had come to Michigan with his wife from his native Connecticut in 1832 and located on the Clinton Road near Jackson where he
opened a tavern which was soon widely known as the old "Fitch stand."
Turning from whiskey to real estate, he took a profitable part in the speculative orgy of the middle 1830's. He invested some of his gains in the
stock of the Jackson County Bank and was implicated in the collapse of
that wildcat institution and made the target of several indictments for conspiracy in 1838. Like most of the businessmen in that frontier community,
he emerged unscatched and unmoved and went on to become a leading
public figure. When Michigan was admitted as a state in 1837, Fitch,
now living in Michigan Centre, a community he had helped develop to
his own profit, was a delegate to the convention which met to organize
the Democratic Party in Jackson County. He enlarged his public services
by organizing a squadron of cavalry, the Barry Horse Guards, in the state
militia in 1843 and was commissioned its captain. Tenders of political
trust by his neighbors made him Inspector of Elections in Leoni Township
and local representative on the Board of County Canvassers in 1850 and
1851. On April 7, 1851, he was elected Supervisor of Leoni Township on
the Democratic ticket. He lived in style at Michigan Centre, in a spacious
home complete with verandahs and shade trees, on an estate valued at
$8,000 with more than five hundred acres of orchards, pastures, gardens, a
lake, and a deer park, as well as productive fields. Gifted with a happy
family of wife and two adopted children, numerous friends, and a sense of
humor, enjoying his books, pictures and music—he played the clarionet—
this prosperous country squire, the richest man in the township, could have
proudly and thankfully rested on his laurels as he looked back at his full
forty-three years.

    If only he had rested content to be as others in his station—solid
law-abiding citizens, members of respectable churches, and vocal but realistic exponents of the ideals of justice and right. But Fitch possessed something of the Yankee conscience that held him to strict account and would
take no tittle of compromise, that made him a come-outer when silence
would have been safer and deeds could have been dismissed as unnecessary
and ineffective. In religion, he was, according to Burnett who knew him
well, a Universalist, that rather broad humane American sect that was outside the pale of organized churchdom and orthodox doctrine. His belief
in God was strong and real as was his faith in His goodness, though he
spoke lightly of His conventional representatives on earth. Once, defending
the men of Leoni, Fitch jokingly laid the shootings to a local Baptist clergyman, and to a Congregational divine in Jackson whom he called "Priest"
Foster, and told how he had remonstrated with them to no avail, such

hardened evil-doers were they. On the greatest moral question of the day, slavery, Fitch was on the side of freedom. According to one promoter of the Underground Railroad in Michigan, Fitch was its agent in Michigan Centre. When he was elected county supervisor, he was sneeringly classified as a free soil loco by the opposition Whig sheet. And when "Priest" Foster, the Reverend Gustavus L. Foster of the Congregational Church in Jackson, delivered a sermon denouncing the Fugitive Slave Law and counselling disobedience, he must have risen greatly in Fitch's esteem. For when Fitch was arrested and his person was searched, the only incriminating evidence found on him was a reprint of the Reverend Foster's "higher law" sermon. And his subsequent notoriety brought him the dubious acclaim of eastern newspapers as one of Michigan's most prominent abolitionists.

Such was the man who had come forward as the advocate of the people's rights in the eastern part of Jackson County—a pillar of society, a shrewd but amiable country squire, and withal, a man of unorthodox bent, with principles, who did not fear to express and act on them. And when he spoke out against Brooks' policies, he was also moved by disinterested principle. "They done wrong," he later explained, "when they took the poor man's last cow without remuneration." His only crime was that he had the "indipendance to tell them [that] to their faces." There is no evidence that Fitch's own interests were at stake or in any way affected or that he stood to gain anything personally by his actions. "If money making was my object," (and Fitch knew well how to achieve that mercenary end), he wrote his wife, "I could sell myself to them for a great price, they have already made advances, but they have waked up the wrong passenger." Nor is there any evidence, as was later alleged by the press, that Fitch was satisfying an old grudge against the railroad arising from a dispute over payment for a parcel of his land.

Fitch did not, however, abandon all caution. Defending and abetting his followers, he never himself took part in any of the attacks. Publicly and before outsiders, he did not even approve, though he might extenuate the acts of violence that endangered the lives of innocent people. He preferred himself to fight the railroad where his influence could be most effective: in the courts, in the legislature, among his friends in the East whom he asked to discourage travel on the Michigan Central. And when Lothrop, now in the service of the railroad, saw Fitch helping in the legislative fight against the road in Lansing in 1851, the latter was sure that the former attorney general "had rather see the evel (sic) one than to have seen me . . . here."

Fitch's adjutant in the campaign against the Michigan Central was Benjamin F. Burnett, the vocal lawyer from Grass Lake, honorifically known as Judge Burnett. The "Judge" was no more than a village lawyer, probably self-trained, a litigant as often as he was counsel, who had

garnered neither laurels nor lucre in his profession. A man of some education and ability, he had also tried his hand at surveying, but by 1850, his
total assets did not exceed $800. His motives in working and clamoring for
those who came to be known as the "railroad conspirators" are not clear.
He may have been something of a maverick, having unsuccessfully run for
county surveyor in 1848 as a Free Soiler. Ambitious, contentious, and not
always scrupulous of legal and conventional niceties, he may have been
fishing in troubled waters when he adopted the cause of the people. Once
having made his choice, however, he stuck to it through abuse and imprisonment. His later journalistic crusade on behalf of the "conspirators,"
in and out of jail, helped keep the issue "before the people" until a measure
of justice was realized.

The third in the village triumvirate was Ammi Filley, brother-in-law
of Fitch and owner of the tavern at Michigan Centre, next to the tracks,
across the road from Fitch's house. His relation to Fitch, his comparative
wealth, and above all, his control of seemingly unlimited supplies of
whiskey gave him some standing among the farmers of the locality, if it
tarnished his name in the county at large. He had come to Michigan from
Connecticut in 1833, and after unsuccessful business ventures in and
around Jackson and some notoriety as the father of "The Lost Boy,"
William Filley, who disappeared among the Indians, had established himself as the tavern keeper of Michigan Centre. He was not poor: his property
was valued at $4,200 and he employed as many as twelve men on his lands,
from which he sent fish and game to the Detroit market. Angered by the
railroad's policy in some altercation over the building of fences, he nursed
his hurt into vindictiveness and unrestrainedly denounced the road, prodded
his friends and employees to violent attacks, and even personally put his
hand to stoning the trains and obstructing the tracks.

It was Filley's tavern that served as the natural headquarters where
discontent was expressed, allayed, and fortified over the bar or at the card
tabel or the nine-pin alley outside. Here grievances were loudly aired and
anger fanned and the escapades hatched, more often than not under the
influence of the liquor which Filley had ordered his bartenders to dispense
so freely. "They generally drank by platoons," one observer reported of
the almost nightly gatherings at Filley's. And if this popular rendezvous
by the tracks was later denominated a "low country tavern," it certainly
was the poor man's club in Leoni Township.

Here Orlando Williams, the stone mason, bibulously boasted of his
feats, imaginary and real, in getting back at the railroad. Here Bill Corwin, the shiftless teamster and occasional barkeep, who took his pay
in liquid kind, got up his bravado for destructive sorties. Here the Price
boys, Eben and Richard, blacksmiths by trade, joined in the roistering
that sometimes led to drunken brawls and sometimes to alcoholic feats of

derring-do. Here Erastus Champlin, farmer, and his two sons, Lyman and Willard, damned the railroad and swore vengeance. And here, too, came the railroad agents to gather their evidence of crimes committed and planned. Sometimes, too, the boys would journey to the tavern at Leoni village for a "ball" or to some "grocery" or hotel at Jackson where the usual round of quaffing, boasts, threats, and forays would be repeated.

During the long winter of 1849–1850 or, in railroad parlance, after the close of the season, activity and talk abated with the cold weather. Once the lakes were frozen, through traffic fell off greatly if not completely, and the occasions and targets for depredations did not present themselves. But once the thaws came and the trains began to run again, the battle was renewed by both sides with increased vigor.

During the spring, summer, and fall of 1850, resentment over more cattle killed and Superintendent Brooks' half-pay policy seemed to grow and intensify. Resentment was soon translated into threats and threats into violence. The burden of complaint was the old one: the company would never run over the road in safety until it paid up for property destroyed; if they could not get their revenge in one way, they would get it in another; they would let the company know there was "a God in Israel; the company would be glad bye and bye to pay up for cattle or if they did not they would catch hell." Lyman Champlin angrily threatened that if they did not pay for the old gray mare they killed, he would keep the railroad wood and fences on fire. In June, Burnett had a cow killed at Grass Lake and when a neighbor joked him for not commencing suit and getting pay for it, he declared he would have full pay or full satisfaction before he receipted for the critter. Bill Corwin, in the course of a conversation with a neighbor, pulled out of his pocket a printed pamphlet called "The Railroad Dream" and read aloud of a poor man's cow being killed and how he had sued the company and got nothing. "By Jesus," Corwin exclaimed, "is the people going to stand this? No, by Jesus, they'll catch it before long."

Sometimes, tongues loosened by alcohol talked in a kind of desperate confidence of a great coup or some ingenious plan to destroy the road at one blow. Jack Freeland once freely and opened described a plan for placing powder on the rails with a fuse running from it, so timed as to explode when the trains passed. Another time, Ebenezer Farnham, a dentist in Jackson who was as much given to drink as to the practice of his profession and who sympathized with the plight of the Leonians, emerged from a "grocery" in that town, collared a passing friend, pulled him into an alley, and said, "I want to tell you something for I believe you to be a pretty damned good fellow." The friend thought the doctor was pretty well corned as he went on: "The railroad—hell and damnation, the railroad will all be blown up in less than a month. . . ." The happy dentist gloated in drunken glee, "$10,000 all gone to hell in one minute and I've got the tools to do it," and hung on to his listener for dear life. Orlando Williams promised the assembled company at Morrison's grocery in Jackson that he would tear up the track from Michigan Centre to Leoni to make the company pay for cattle killed. At Hadden's grocery in Jackson, Williams confidentially offered a fellow barfly a chance to make $500 by burning the roalroad company's steamers, the *Mayflower* and the *Atlantic,* and bringing them to the water's edge. At Filley's one day, between drinks, Williams boasted that the company would be glad to eat salt out of their hands in a few days and that it should be made to pay double value for cattle killed. Bill Corwin almost matched Williams' big talk about what he was going to do to the company. Once in Jackson, he had swapped horses with Caleb Loud, dealer in "Loud's Celebrated Ointment" for horses, and the two were riding around the sheds by the railroad depot. Loud remarked that a fire there would sweep the whole lower town. Corwin put his hand on Loud's arm and said, "Just remember my word, there will be one here before long." Corwin also felt impelled to seek new recruits in back of Morrison's grocery to tear up the track and burn the depot at Jackson, promising large sums of money.

None of these grandiose plans for destroying the railroad ever materialized. But attacks similar to those of the season of 1849 continued to harass the operation of trains between Grass Lake and Jackson. The summer and fall of 1850 were punctuated with the familiar shootings, stonings, obstructions, and burnings.

More than one evening, as a bunch of the boys were gathered at Filley's, someone would suggest that they go and give them a few stones or "give them hell again tonight," and a group would sally out to stone the trains amidst the startled cries of the passengers. One dark night in August, Filley, Jacob Wolliver, his devil or handyman, and the two Price boys got an ax and went out to throw the cars off. Abut three-quarters of a mile west of Leoni, where the tracks crossed a culvert over a six-foot bank, they broke the chairs that held the rails in place and moved them to one side. They then went off forty or sixty rods and lay down and waited. An eastbound train, pulled by the locomotive *Gazelle* ran off and capsized and the train crews worked many hours getting her back on. Filley later described the incident as good clean sport: how when they went out cooning, the road was the best ground to go on; the *Gazelle* was a big coon they caught the other night but they had lost its tail, "but damn 'em," they will have that soon; it had taken a good many men to get the coon on the track again, and he did not want anything better than an ax and a crow bar to shoot a coon with. Fitch, too, indulged in his characteristic humor when he told how the *Gazelle* had got dry and, having no pump aboard, was forced to go down into the marsh for water.

During the state fair at Ann Arbor in September, 1850, a conductor later recalled, it seemed almost impossible to get through Leoni and Michigan Centre at night without some trouble. This was despite the fact that all train crews had been warned to proceed slowly and with great caution through these places. One night during the fair, this conductor was running a train west and at Grass Lake told the engineer he could run to Michigan Centre at normal speed. Soon a passenger asked him why they were running faster than usual and the conductor explained: "There is no danger; we have the head devils on board, and the gang will not hurt them." And he pointed down the car to where Fitch and Filley were sitting, on their way back from a visit to the fair.

That same month, a group from the Centre had gone to Leoni village to help Ephraim Barrett in his law suit against the railroad company for damages for a cow that had been killed. Barrett had been offered $15 and would have liked to accept that sum, but his neighbors urged him not to. The suit at Leoni was fruitless, and the men returned to Michigan Centre embittered. After their return, Filley and Wolliver went out and stuck a tie into the culvert west of Fitch's house so that it would strike the lamp on the next engine that came along. They also put a mudsill across the track nearby, and then retired from the scene. The freight train was duly halted and Fitch and Filley came up and innocently inquired what the matter was. Receiving no enlightenment from one member of the train crew, which was busy removing the obstructions, they repeated their question to another, and got only abuse in reply. "You damned hounds," the train hand cursed, "every one of you should be hung up." Now riled, Fitch and Filley went around to the rear of the train and put on the brakes. The two then went up the track a way and hugely enjoyed watching the sparks fly from the wheels as the train struggled up a grade.

In October, the engine *Rocket* ran off at Michigan Centre after it had hit an open switch. Although the engine tore up the side track it was not upset, but it took about seven hours to get it back on the tracks. With each successful attack on the road, Filley took great delight in giving the company credit in some imaginary ledger against the unpaid balance for cattle killed—$1 for each stoning and proportionately greater amounts for more substantial losses. Fitch, too, made estimates of losses the company had suffered and reckoned that the cattle killed between Grass Lake and Jackson had already cost the company about $400 per head. These vengeful calculations also included mishaps on the Michigan Central with which the boys from the Centre had nothing to do, although they were later charged with them. Two such accidents must be laid entirely to chance or negligence. In June, 1850, a baggage car carrying United States mail took fire and was destroyed a little east of Jackson. Again, a train was thrown off the track at Leoni because a track crew had removed some of the rail at that point and the engineer had not seen their signal in time to stop.

Fitch, except for the time when he had reversed the brakes on the stalled train, continued to confine his activities to those of public advocate. In Michigan Centre and in Jackson, he made no secret of his unyielding opposition to the railroad's policy and of his opinion that the trouble the road was having was fully deserved; that it was the only means of bringing the company to terms; that the depredations would divert travel from the road and "bring them to their milk." He justified the actions of his friends with an illustration: suppose a man owned a large tract of land near the town and the village cattle troubled him, he could dig pits and get the cattle into them—the land being his own, they could not help themselves— the owners of the cattle, however, had a right to take the law into their own hands and that would be their only remedy. Fitch's analogy is pertinent only if one remembers that cattle in that sparsely settled and unfenced country were regarded at law as free commoners and allowed to run at large.

At times, Fitch not altogether jokingly laid the violence to the railroad police, adding that he would like to catch the spies on his land and "fix 'em out." In the same breath, he admitted that stoning was "mild means" his friends were using and boasted that "the company was nearly used up now and had gone down with only fifteen passengers on one train." When someone accused Fitch himself of stoning the cars as they passed his house, he replied with brazen humor that it was "a damned lie" as he was upstairs looking out of the window at the attack.

To his respectable friends, Fitch talked with more caution and some hypocrisy. That fall, Alonzo Bennett, a merchant of Jackson, warned Fitch that the boys had already gone far enough and that a few words from him or a little labor would stop the depredations. Fitch replied that he knew that what the boys were doing was wrong and that they must look out. But, he went on, he had also told them to get pay for their cattle if they could, and if they could not, they must lay their plans so as not to get caught at it. He concluded piously that if the company would only pay full value, "they would have God almighty on their side and be prosperous." About the same time, when the Jackson *American Citizen* editorially condemned both the company for not paying full value and the residents of Leoni for taking the law into their own hands, Fitch personally assured the editor, Charles V. De Land, of his "perfect sympathy" with those sentiments.

Fitch's advocacy of their cause and the failure of the company to catch any of the offenders gave the Leonians a feeling of confidence. Bound together by their grievances and sense of wrong, they were further united in a community of interest by the unhampered successes of their campaign of retaliation and by the conviction that in Fitch they had a protector and influential intercessor with the powers that be. They knew that Fitch was on their side, that he had friends in high political place, that he had a "long head." They were certain "he would stick by them as long as he had any blood left in his body." Too, they were sure that they themselves would stick by one another and find shelter from the law in their common fraternity. They bragged of standing by one another "to swear any hostile witnesses to hell." As Bill Corwin put it: "They could prove that [a] horse was a blacksmith shop and every hair on him a candle if necessary." They counted on their ability to get witnesses of their own to clear them of any criminal complicity. They felt certain that no jury in Jackson County would ever convict them for any act against the railroad.

All these acts and declarations did not, however, add up to a conspiracy within the legal meaning of the term, as was later charged by the state. There was no organized gang with constituted leadership that deliberately planned attacks on the railroad for a clearly conceived common end. The opposition to the Michigan Central in Jackson County was rather a loose and informal affair, with an open and reckless impulsiveness, entirely lacking in secrecy, compounded of common resentment, illegal intent, alcoholic spontaneity, and criminal acts. It verged on conspiracy but never quite jelled into the necessary consistency of purpose, method, and execution.

This communal hostility to the railroad also had its roots in complaints other than those over the destruction of livestock. The additional sources of friction did not loom so large in the minds of those who frequented Filley's tavern or went out to stone the trains from Fitch's peach orchard. But elsewhere in Jackson County and in the state at large, they created strong resentment against the railroad, which together with the ill will engendered by the killing of cattle, was the basis of a broad anti-railroad movement that sought publicly and legally to regulate and curb the powers of the offending corporation.

Inevitable sources of friction were the condemnation proceedings for lands taken over for the right of way, stations, warehouses and shops, as well as the contract jobs for the construction of fences along the line of the road. Farmers invariably found the company's offers too low and the resultant court proceedings only served as irritants. Fences remained unbuilt or in some cases were even torn down. Even the man of God at Marshall, John D. Pierce, refused to build fence at the company's price of $1.75 per one hundred rails. In the mind of one young farm laborer, the chief subject of discussion at Michigan Centre during the many months he worked there was the company's wage policies. He remembered that there was something said about the railroad being a monopoly, and that a feeling was getting up against them because they hired help very cheap, did not pay wages enough, and had a tendency to render wages low. Once Fitch, elaborating on the complaints against the company, catalogued the whole list of its sins. He reiterated his charge that it was "a damned monopoly." He said he thought "the road was damned poorly managed and that a boy ten years old would manage it better than Superintendent Brooks." He thought the chief engineer in charge of construction would be a better superintendent than Brooks, for *he* thought the company ought to pay for cattle killed. Fitch said the road carried produce from Niles as cheap as it did from Jackson, and that it had fixed the price of men at $500, referring to the amount paid to the widow of a man who had been killed by a train the year before at Galesburg.

It was the charges of unfair freight rates and monopoly practices that were taken up most widely in the state. Jackson County shippers had complained of high rates back in 1846 when the state had owned the railroad. Then, in 1848, some shippers at Kalamazoo had protested to Superintendent Brooks against what they thought was unfair discrimination in the rates for carrying their produce to Detroit: the rates from Niles to Detroit were less than those from Kalamazoo to Detroit, a shorter haul by some fifty miles. Brooks, in a published pamphlet, justified the cheaper long-haul rate by the necessity of meeting water-shipping competition at Niles, which had access to Lake Michigan via the St. Joseph River. The cheaper rates and hence the greater volume of business from Niles, he argued, actually enabled the company to charge lower rates from Kalamazoo than would otherwise have been possible. In 1849, after the railroad had been finished to New Buffalo on the lake, the Whig *American Citizen* of Jackson, with no desire to ignore a popular issue, took up the hue and cry. Its editor fulminated against the "dastardly course" the railroad had pursued in charging the citizens of the interior of the state nearly double the price charged those of other states for half the distance. Brooks evidently was fighting the lake shipping companies for the Chicago and Milwaukee trade with the weapon of cheaper long hauls. But the Jackson editor could only see the "enormous charges" of the "Central railroad monopoly" which in his mind were responsible for the lower prices that local products brought and the bad state of business in general in Jackson County. He denounced the road as a "shameful monopoly" and a "humbug concern," and repeatedly urged the necessity of a connecting line from Jackson to the Michigan Southern Railroad at Adrian to give Jackson shippers another outlet to the east, at Monroe on Lake Erie, and thus break the monopoly of the Michigan Central.

The accumulated grievances snowballed into a strong antimonopoly sentiment. Again and again, in the press, in the legislature, at meetings of citizens, and in Filley's tavern, the railroad was attacked as a corporate monopoly whose greed would not be satisfied until it had gobbled up the wealth of the state and the freedom of the people. Fitch and his friends, as we have seen, did not hide their feelings about the absolute corruption of this absolute economic power; one of the company's spies, in order to gain their confidence, found it advisable to talk "against the Road" and call it a monopoly. An angry citizen wrote a letter to the *American Citizen,* which, echoing the editorial opinion of the paper, rang the changes on the theme and demanded to know how long the people would suffer the railroad to dominate them. At Coldwater and at Napoleon, the citizens met to protest against the monopoly of the Michigan Central Railroad. In the legislature at Lansing, the drift of public opinion was crystallized in the warning that "the Michigan Central Railroad Company may possibly, sooner or later, discover that they did not make the State of Michigan, but that the State of Michigan made the company."

4.2

Poor Whites and Negroes
in the Ante-Bellum South

AVERY CRAVEN

In a tentative manner, Avery Craven here opens up an area that has received
little attention—relations between poor whites and slaves. The similarities
he finds in the material conditions of their lives and the social contact they
maintained suggest much about the south's little known white lower-class
world. Somewhat analogous speech patterns, similarities in religious
practices, and seemingly related musical forms may well have had their
origins in these contacts. The later, but limited, attempts by the Populists and
the early postwar labor movements to build interracial protest movements
may also have stemmed from this antebellum world.

Avery Craven, "Poor Whites and Negroes in the Antebellum South," *Journal of Negro History*, 15 (1930), 14–25. Copyright © by The Association for the Study of Negro Life and History, Inc. Reprinted and footnotes omitted by permission of the publisher.

The following article is suggested for further reading:

JAMES BONNER, "Profiles of a Late Ante-Bellum Community," *American Historical Review*, XLIX (1944), 663–80.

The annals of Negro and "Poor White" in the Ante-Bellum South are brief, but brevity in this case does not imply happiness. Southern society was stratified and these groups were not at the top; its social-economic life was primarily rural-agricultural and those who directly till the soil seldom enjoy unbroken prosperity and social advantages. These elements constituted the manual laborers of a section, and a few labor systems yield leisure and luxury to those who toil. What is equally significant, is that Southern life was rapidly expanding from East to West and from the simple to the more complex, and frontiers whether physical or social lay heavy burdens on humble folks. Negro and white alike bore the brunt of these forces and like their kind elsewhere had neither time nor inclination to record their reactions, while others, more fortunately placed, properly considered them of too little consequence for more than briefest mention.

But scarcity of materials may have advantages. Broad approaches to a field badly cluttered with biased and distorting formulae are thereby necessitated and a more general treatment may afford better perspective. It is refreshing, sometimes, to forget the existence of slavery in the Old South and to view the Negro as a co-dweller with the plain white people in the lower rounds of life. To view them both as the lesser elements in an expanding rural order conditioned by geographic factors that ranged from tidewater swamp to rugged mountain and encompassed in their sweep all that stretches from the open capes of Virginia and Maryland to the wind-blown plains of upland Texas and all that lies between crude frontier hut and white-pillared mansion of English-country-gentleman pattern. It is well also sometimes to remember that the South was so varied in its makeup that no generalization can hold from place to place and from time to time; that its life was so individualized by rural and frontier forces that each relationship was a thing unique in itself; that the human element ever looms large in rural worlds and that the accidents of health, weather and personal qualities rise in proportion. It is a brave man, indeed, who can talk glibly of "the South," "the plantation system," "Southern social classes," or "Southern public opinion"! Yet if we cannot deal definitely with the relations between the Negro and poor white we may perhaps better comprehend the basic facts in this important feature of life in the "South that was."

To begin with, the poor whites of the South were divided into at least two groups. There was one element thrown to the bottom largely by the accidents of geographic environment and physical disability, which has been called by a variety of names such as "Sandhillers," "Piney Folks," or "White Trash"; and there was another group ranging from the white who lived with his family well out of the staple belt and occupied himself with self-sufficing farming to the man with a goodly parcel of slaves who was fast crowding up into the ranks of the accepted planters. These men have been designated as "Yeoman." The relations of these people to the blacks, of course, varied greatly from the thousands who never saw a Negro to the master who had even introduced the overseer into his farming economy.

Furthermore, there was wide variation from place to place and from time to time. In the older sections slavery had become widely diffused and a paternalistic relationship evolved that contrasted sharply with the newer West where the ambitious planter crowded his recently arrived force. And within these variations there were others that came as one passed to the Piedmont or Valley of Virginia or turned to the more simple North Carolina world or the more complex order about Charleston. Louisiana boasted more generous inter-racial attitudes than any other state and age softened the lines in Mississippi and Alabama as well as in the older coastal regions. The Negro that looked back to Virginia as a lost paradise was often only paying tribute to conditions which time brought in most places and the other who complained that his western master was "too pushin'" was only commenting on frontier characteristics. We must ever recognize these variations as potent even where concrete illustration fails us.

The first fact that presents itself to one who would view these classes in the large is the striking similarity in their ways of life,—a likeness so complete that the student must conclude that the fact that one was a slave and the other a free man was often a matter of little consequence. One need not go far to see that the larger fact in Southern life was its ruralness and frontier character and that the larger fact in the lives of these people was that they were its simple laborers and common people.

The many descriptions left by the ante-bellum travellers indicate that the home of the poor white and the cabin of the Negro slave varied little in size or comfort. Both were apt to be of but a single room whose plain walls of logs were broken only by doorways and an open fireplace and adorned only by the family clothing or a chance patent medicine advertisement. The openings between the logs were as often "chinked" in the one case as in the other, windows appeared with about equal frequency, and the use of other materials for buildings or the addition of a second room about as common in white hut as in Negro cabin. Olmsted tells of yeoman homes that were but "shabby . . . half furnished cottages and . . . cabins,—mere hovels, such as none but a poor farmer would house his cattle in at the North," or again of homes that were "only a shelter from rain, the sides not . . . chinked and having no more furniture or pretension to comfort than is commonly provided a criminal in the cell of a prison." On the other hand, he describes no Negro abodes that were worse and many that were better. If he found the more prosperous yeoman in a house comparable to the New England homestead, he found the more fortunate Negro sharing to a large degree the comforts of the "big house" on the larger plantations. Nor did conditions differ greatly from the ridges of Virginia, the turpentine forests of North Carolina, to the Creole sections of Louisiana.

The food of white and black, too, was strikingly similar. The well-known Negro rations of meat, meal, and molasses, supplemented by the vegetable garden and hen house, were matched in the white abode by a like fare. A bit of bacon, some corn bread, the inevitable greens, and the "home made coffee," were the things most commonly set before the traveler who was hardy enough to seek shelter and food at the poor man's house.

Both dressed in homespuns, went barefoot in season and by their near-nakedness furnished subject to the traveller for comment with about equal frequency.

The women of both classes toiled in the fields or carried the burden of other manual labor and the children of both early reached the age of industrial accountability. White women cooked and sewed, spun and wove, hoed field crops, cut brush, dug ore, cut wood, and carried about the same reputation for easy virtue as their sable sisters. Olmsted, himself, records over and over the reluctance of the planter to have the poor white domestic on his place because of her irregular moral code and makes mention without fail of discovered Negro virtue.

And both black and white families suffered heavily from the great forces of expansion that worked in Southern life. Households were forever being broken up and their members scattered to the winds as new fields of opportunity opened. The call for fresh human materials fell alike on lower laboring classes. The Walker family (white) of Rockbridge County, Virginia, sent one son to Kentucky, one to Missouri, one to Tennessee, and one to Alabama; its daughters were found in Iowa, Indiana, and North Carolina. Meetings between different members of the family were infrequent and children and grandchildren wandered ever farther afield. Like forces scattered Negro families, but we have been too much thinking in terms of slavery to understand the more fundamental causes of family diffusion that were no respectors of colour.

Nor can one who is dealing in fundamentals overlook the deep longing for companionship, for amusements, and even for the stimulation of alcoholic beverages, which were common to these groups. Nor should he forget that the religious gathering of both was certain to become an emotional debauchery when pent up feelings met points of stimulation. Furthermore, he should note that intellectual stupor and the occasional individual who showed marked superiority to his neighbors and his environment, were to be expected in either quarter in about equal degree, and that both under the lack of reason for undue exertion and physical disability were almost universally declared to be "the laziest people on the face of the earth." In making explanation he will shoot wide of the mark if he separates these folks so much alike, overlooks the common facts of ruralness, primitiveness, and humanness, and considers each as a unique product of slavery or peculiar social organization.

In studying the relations between Negro and poor white we find three points of contact. The "Hill Folks" proper seldom seem to have had direct relations with the plantation world. The paths of these lower groups seldom crossed and when they did mutual dislike was manifest. The Negro held the shiftless victim of hookworm in contempt; and the white, with only his color and the fact that he did not rise to toil and spin with the sun as points of superiority, returned the favor. Such attitudes extended on to the plantation Negro and the poor whites in the immediate neighborhood where complaints of theft and infringement on personal rights were hurled about indiscriminately. Yet close proximity of those beat upon by like forces, broke barriers, and established contacts. A steady stream of corn whiskey found its way from white stills to Negro throats in spite of every effort at prohibition, and illicit meetings ever disturbed the darkness. Sometimes the Negro slipped away to labor at night in the fields of the less energetic white in return for his liquor; sometimes a system of theft was perfected by which plantation equipment and supplies passed in payments; sometimes the black economized on his own rations that he might secretly exchange his surplus for the means of a spree. Relations were ever maintained that benefitted neither and which led masters to constant effort to "buy out" lesser neighbors in order to bring them to an end. It was the realization of common foundations that produced the poor white's attitude toward Negro freedom. "I'd like it if we could get rid of 'em at yonst," said one of them. "I wouldn't like to hev 'em freed, if they was gwine to hang 'round . . . How would you like to hev a niggar feelin' just as good as a white man? How'd you like to have a niggar steppin' up to your darter?"

A second class of relationships belonged to the yeoman group and the Negro free or slave. Living on the edge of the staple belts or outside of them, the yeoman had little need for labor other than that afforded by large families. It might be increasing, but the number of slaves acquired seldom ran to large figures. In the piedmont sections, in the back country of Georgia, Alabama, Mississippi, in numerous corners of North Carolina, in the valleys and mountains of the West, frontier and markets dictated the farm in place of the plantation and placed white and black, owner and slave, master, hired man, son and servant, together at common tasks. The traveller in these sections often saw the owners "holding the plow" among his slaves, while the hired men worked at their sides. From North-west Georgia in 1850 a settler wrote: "John is busy clearing up some of his creek bottom for corn. If he had half dozen of hands he would make some show . . . but he has only Albert (a slave) and a white man hired. . . ." Olmsted found a white man working under the direction of a Negro in Northern Alabama, and Hundley reported that a man could not "travel a day through . . . the South but he will come up with some sturdy yeoman and his sons working in company of their negroes." Like conditions existed among the women folks. Negro and mistress did the house-work together and took their places together at the spinning wheel or loom. Negroes sat at the family table and slept in family beds. In early Georgia the circuit judges were "set down at the tables serving Negro farm hands as well as themselves and the family of the host." In 1835, J. H. Ingraham at Natchez saw "rough, rude, honest-looking countrymen from the back part of the state" joking with their Negroes "with perfect good will and a mutual contempt for the nicer distinctions of color."

Some masters, more easy going than others, allowed their Negroes to run the farm, declaring that they knew more and cared more for good results than they themselves. Discipline, under such conditions was slack. One master declared he had not "licked a nigger in five years" and Hundley declared that most of them "never received a stripe unless some of their younger masters" were "stout enough to give them a lamming in a regular fisticuffs fight."

When hired white help was added in periods of stress they sometimes accepted the social and economic relations as they found them, but in the older sections there early developed certain codes that had to be respected. Some kinds of work the white man would not do, and if set at such tasks he would quit with a frank declaration that he "was not a nigger." He would drive a wagon but not a carriage: he would curry a mule, but he would not brush a gentleman's coat,—conditions that have changed little with the passing of slavery.

The third point of contact between the Negro and the poor white came in the relations of the overseer with his charges. This man was as a rule of the poor white class,—sometimes on his way up to ownership and some-times simply at the level which his abilities enabled him to reach. To him, among other tasks, was given the direction and care of the plantation laboring force; and his success, at least in theory, was measured as much by the well-being of the slaves as in the size of the crops produced. Sometimes he was under a resident owner; too often he ruled for an absentee. But always he was thrown into closest contact with the Negro out in a rural world that denied him access to other relationships. The results were what might have been expected. His influence varied with his own abilities; and the treatment accorded those in his power ran with the weather, the physical and mental disposition of all parties, and the general state of plantation affairs. There were favorites and those always in disfavor; there were efforts toward making a good showing in crops that often led to abuses; there were times of boistrous laughter and days that were equally glum. Some masters were over indulgent, sacrificing respect by freely mingling at work and play with their charges; some were too severe and flew into passions that did damage to both discipline and the disciplined; but all had to live and toil in the same lonesome rural world which reduced them, regardless of race and position, to the common level of human beings and which developed relations that were strikingly normal. Negro women bore mulatto children; Negro men struck back at insult as against an equal; both fled the plantation under mistreatment, and master heard the complaints of pouting slave and overseer as a parent might have listened to his children.

Here again we have thought too much in terms of slavery and lost more fundamental factors. Olmsted was nearer the truth when, listening to the overseer's formula for handling Negroes, he said; ". . . His conversation on this subject was exactly like what I have heard said, again and again, by northern shipmasters and officers, with regard to seamen. . . ."

Of the free Negro and the poor whites we know little other than that merit seems to have been the test for recognition. The few well-known poor whites who rose to prominence are offset by a few unusual negroes. Henry Evans (Negro) preached to a congregation composed of both races, and at times the whites came in such numbers as to threaten to exclude the blacks. John Chavis, a man of color, preached to and taught some of the most distinguished whites of North Carolina. Jehu Jones accumulated $40,000 in Charleston. Thomy Lafon made a half million in New Orleans. Many Negro planters in Louisiana held lands, slaves and gold well above the average; and all over the South there were small Negro farmers whose labor in harvest time made them welcome neighbors. The professional man found white clients, and the carpenter, mason or smith sometimes found his neighbors petitioning that he be allowed to remain among them because of his services. It is very clear that a mere study of the laws which affected free Negroes does not tell the whole truth in regard to their relations to the whites about them.

What larger effects the Negro had upon the poor whites it is hard to say. Many declared that he demoralized them and was responsible for their well-known shiftlessness. Some have felt that the close relations which necessity imposed between these groups soften the edges of racial contact and humanized the whole of Southern society. Of only one thing we are certain. The presence of the Negro added value to white skins regardless of the social or economic status of their owners. Something was added for both good and ill because of the assumption of superiority ever felt by these lowly folks to their darker fellows. It fixed political attitudes; it determined social codes; and it manifested itself in dogged resistance on many a battlefield. If the Negro received less of Americanization from the poor whites than he did from the greater planters, his contributions to these was not in proportion. The great forces that shaped the destiny of common folks willed it otherwise.

In the larger sweep of Southern affairs the relations of Negro and poor white played a decisive rôle. As has already been suggested, the very fact that they occupied the common ground in the lower reaches of Southern life, made them potential rivals in social, economic and political affairs. Only the institution of slavery, which in so many ways did damage to the poor white saved him from competition from his darker fellow. Freedom for the Negro thrust forward a labor problem, tinged with the more bitter race problem. Under such threats the deep gulf between aristocrat and poor white closed as politician and agitator raised the question of white supremacy. Something like a united response was possible on the basis of a common prejudice against men of colour. On this foundation, terribly weak in the face of realities where the great forces of ruralness and frontier dwelling had worked on black and white alike, the South moved for nationalism. The rapidity with which collapse came in the closing days of that struggle from forces that were as much within as without, only emphasized unnatural alliances and the ready acceptance of realities when uncolored by theoretical spinnings. The rapidity of peaceful adjustment when outside influences were withdrawn emphasized the part of which natural forces long at work had played in fixing the habits and attitudes of the great common masses who made up the South.

Some day, perhaps, we shall understand that great rural world that lay below Mason and Dixon's line and swept out ever into the forest in regular frontier style; we may learn something about why human beings behave as they do and we may be able to allow both the Negro and his poor white brother to be plain humans conditioned by such an environment.

4.3

The Early American Response
to Chinese Immigrants
in California

GUNTHER BARTH

The arrival of the Chinese in America resembled that of other immigrant groups, but their native culture made them distinct. Californians responded to their new Chinese neighbors in various ways—often with hostility, and even occasionally with violence. "Native" Americans attacked all immigrant groups at one time or another, but the presence of the race question in the case of the Chinese, as in the case of the blacks, complicated the question.

The following books are suggested for further reading:

MARY COOLIDGE, *Chinese Immigrants*, New York: The Macmillan Company, 1909.
ALEXANDER SAXTON, *Indispensable Enemy: Labor and the Anti-Chinese Movement in California*, Berkeley: The University of California Press, 1971.

Reprinted, omitting all footnotes, by permission of the publishers from pp. 129–56 of *Bitter Strength: A History of the Chinese in the U.S., 1850–1870*, by Gunther Barth (Cambridge, Mass.: Harvard University Press). Copyright 1964 by the President and Fellows of Harvard College.

Chinatown and work camp precipitated California's reaction to the new-comers, provoking strife and stimulating humanitarian attempts at accul-turation. In isolated mountain regions and in bustling urban centers, Californians reacted to the presence of work camps and Chinatowns with sentiments that ranged from open hostility to overt friendliness.

Both the conflict and the concord stemmed from notions underlying and permeating the structure of California society. The Chinese sojourners were another element, like the Indians, Mexicans, Europeans, and Negroes, to distort the vision of California and they were also another challenge, like all other newcomers to the United States, for the humanitarian con-cepts of American culture. Strife and acculturation were the opposite poles of the reaction toward the Chinese sojourners, the varied manifestations of which crystallized around work camp and Chinatown. Both reactions existed side by side like the set of conflicting notions sustaining American California.

Historical studies of California or of the Chinese in the United States have sketched the general setting of, or the events leading to, the first major encounter between Americans and Chinese. Charles Howard Shinn traced the disorder in the mines to "evil-disposed" non-Anglo-Saxons while Hubert Howe Bancroft pinned the responsibility for the turmoil on "immoral" Anglo-Saxons. Josiah Royce's discourse in Hegelian dialectic reduced the social struggle to moral and racial issues. He accommodated a generation that viewed "immoral" foreigners and "evil" Americans as causes of the unrest; and he provided a framework for subsequent com-mentators who also placed the struggle between Californians and foreigners in a purely negative setting.

Mary Roberts Coolidge, in 1909, traced the development of anti-Chinese politics in California to the discontented classes. She attributed the organized antagonism against the sojourners to the "violent race preju-dices and political ambitions" of Governor John Bigler. Later observers of California's nativism emphasized the lack of a mature legal machinery, the absence of a core of stable citizens in the mining districts, and the want of such social restraints as family and church. Elmer Clarence Sandmeyer traced the motivation of the anti-Chinese movement in California to eco-nomic, moral and religious, and social and political shortcomings. Rodman W. Paul considered the transition from the agitation regarding foreign immigrants in general "to a definite hostility towards one specific race, the Chinese, . . . natural and perhaps inevitable."

Recent studies of nativism in California undermine Royce's assump-tion that rabble or respectable men derelict in their concern for order insti-gated the antiforeign actions. The efforts to stabilize California's society and economy in the years from 1849 to 1852, just before the first major clash between Americans and Chinese, suggest that nativism did not originate among dissolute men but among those possessed by and acting from a zeal for order. Newspaper reports, travelogues, and reminiscences, recording the early encounters between Americans and Chinese, show that positive goals motivated the activities which led to the first major clash. The regimented Chinese miners conflicted with California's stand against slavery and posed an obstacle to the building of the true American state. They endangered Californians' hope for the realization of their dream about the future.

Work camp and Chinatown provide two vantage points from which to survey the emergence of California's hostile reaction. The regimented drudgery of Chinese miners reminded Californians of the slave labor which had troubled them earlier. The growing Chinese quarters struck observers as the breeding grounds of immorality which added to the insecurity and the social disorganization brought on by rapid physical and social mobility. Long before the filth of Chinatown raised the ire of Californians, the working methods of Chinese miners had led to clashes between sojourners and Americans. Long after the work camps in the Mother Lode had been accepted, Chinatown remained a focal point of strife.

A running debate among Americans over the nature of their growing society was always in the background of the encounter, while the Chinese attempts to incorporate work camp and Chinatown into American life generally precipitated the struggle. Although the headmen of the companies succeeded in establishing the work camp in the California countryside, they failed to integrate Chinatown into the settlements. The task demanded a choice between the certainty of unceasing strife over Chinatown's filth and immorality and the sacrifice of its essential function as the safety valve of the control system. The headmen avoided that choice. They attempted to pacify agitated Americans with token support of the struggle against Chinatown, a maneuver which succeeded in protecting its role. However, the strategy made the quarter's physical and moral conditions appear a part of the sojourners' second nature. The scheme fixed Chinatown as the focus of perpetual strife which assumed in the eyes of Californians the character of an inevitable struggle.

Companies of Chinese miners furnished the initial point of discord. They raised the specter of Indians and Pacific immigrants, of Mexicans, Chileans, Peruvians, and Islanders, who, as lowly bondmen, had dug gold under supervision of their masters. Extravagant tales told how the heads of Chinese merchant houses in San Francisco manipulated indentured emigrants to their advantage. These stories resembled the wild rumors which earlier had accompanied the penetration of the gold region by wealthy Sonoran merchants who worked their village peons in the mines, sold their provisions profitably, and hurried back to Mexico to invest their gains in securities, while their Mexican workers were left to drift into the mining towns. Hunting for work and undercutting the price of artisan labor, they foreshadowed the trickle of foot-loose and untrammeled Chinese who accumulated in the settlements.

The sight of toiling Chinese mining companies in the ravines and canyons of the Mother Lode kept alive memories of the short step that had separated the work of Pacific bondmen and masters from that of American slaves and their overlords. In the fall of 1851, the editor of the Mokelumne *Calaveras Chronicle* spotted in the vicinity of Jackson "several Chinese camps, with a population of Celestials estimated at two thousand souls." The determined stand of miners on the Yuba River seemed to have been in vain. They had evicted the Texan party of General Thomas Jefferson Green and his Negro slaves from Rose Bar in July 1849, and had prohibited in their mining laws all combinations of masters and servants. This contest, and similar encounters with monopolists and underlings, became meaningless in the face of the Chinese mining villages that dotted the mountain region. Chinatown and work camp negated the determined stand of the California Constitutional Convention against slavery and the presence of free Negroes. The toil of the Chinese indentured emigrants relegated to the realm of empty rhetoric Representative George B. Tingley's philippic in the first legislature. The speech advocated barring from the state immigrants "with habits of life low and degraded, . . . but one degree above the beasts of the fields."

The free laborers in the mines lacked the technical skill and conceptual insight to tackle the dual task of gold mining and state building. As average Americans, at the middle of the nineteenth century, they were familiar with a variety of trades and occupations. Mining, however, was not one of them. Only slowly and hesitantly did the farmers and clerks utilize in their new existence the full measure of Old and New World mining experience. The rush of these miners to the unworked placers in the foothills of the Sierra Nevada was like the movement of farmers to virgin lands of the frontier. In both cases, individuals sought to carve out a livelihood under their own direction with the work of their own hands.

Accustomed to an agricultural society with slaves or free men as alternative forms of labor, the American miners superimposed standards of a free agrarian society upon their young state. They also formulated their apprehensions of the dangers threatening their dream in agrarian terms. Their arguments resembled the objections of farmers to slavery in agriculture: it rendered work dishonorable, drove free farmers from the choicest lands, which then fell into the hands of slave-owning planters. The individualistic miners dreaded competition with slave laborers or with freedmen, which they insisted would drive out free miners who demanded a higher standard of living.

William Shaw, who came from Australia to San Francisco in September 1848, and in the company of a Chinese and a Malay servant mined on the Stanislaus River, vividly recorded the American reaction to his Oriental company. The miners made the presence of his "black confederates . . . a source of complaint," he noticed, "evidently imagining them to be in a state of slavery or vassalage to us, who pocketed the fruit of their labor." Some time afterward, Shaw keenly observed, "this feeling against the coloured race rose to a pitch of exasperation." At several diggings "capitalists had hired numbers of Chinese, Cooleys, and Kanakas, to work for them." The "gang-system was very obnoxious to the Californians, and several parties of that description were abolished; the obligations and agreements entered into being cancelled and annulled by the fiat of the vox populi."

A mass meeting of miners on the Mokelumne River and its tributaries on July 7, 1849, directed the "foreign taskmasters and . . . men in their employ" to leave the placers. The growing unrest in the mines stirred the *Alta* belatedly into action. "How can the evil of slavery," the paper thundered almost a year later, "be tolerated in the mines by the thousands of white men, of whom the habits and education of their whole lives have imparted an unconquerable hatred of the institution?" To introduce "slave labor into the mines . . . will be certain cause of violence and bloodshed," the editorial writer could predict comfortably after violence and bloodshed had ruled the day.

One attempt to disentangle the problems of immigration and labor from the slavery question came from Senator Thomas Jefferson Green. The former slaveholder's Foreign Miners' Tax of 1850 aimed at exploiting rather than expelling alien laborers from the mines. The measure intended to aid American mining capitalists by blocking foreign investors through a system of indenture and taxation. The ingenious device failed to pacify disillusioned miners or to fill California's bankrupt treasury. A new phase in the development of mining multiplied the difficulties of individualistic American goldseekers. The danger which Delegate Henry A. Tefft had envisioned during the debates of the Constitutional Convention now really existed. The "labor of intelligent and enterprising white men who, from the want of capital, are compelled to do their own work," no longer produced adequate returns. The resulting struggle set into motion several waves of expulsions. A few years later Friedrich Gerstaecker dubbed portions of the strife "The French Revolution." The conflict broke up large combines of foreign laborers, but also rallied the advocates of contract labor and traders to the defense of foreigners. This was the background for the first major encounter between Californians and Chinese in 1852 when the state legislature again took up the debate whether to curtail or utilize foreign laborers.

The expulsion of foreign workers from the mines ruined the prospects of American entrepreneurs, traders, and speculators. The unrest in the mountain districts shattered the precarious unity of sentiment on which the individualistic miners aimed to build a free society. The struggle between American factions extended into the following decades the vociferous debate about the nature of California. In the middle of 1849, artisans, merchants, mule dealers, and teamsters, because of strong Mexican competition in their own enterprises, had shared the independent miners' widespread antagonism against servile laborers. Now they joined the formerly isolated exploiters of bonded labor in demanding the protection of foreign hands in the mines. While the retreat of the foreigners upset the market for food-stuffs, mining equipment, and land, the entrepreneurs in the southern mines realized that, regardless of all predictions, free American miners followed the attraction of the northern placers and failed to replace the companies of foreign laborers in the tedious dry diggings of the south. Entrepreneurs realized that only foreign laborers would work for one dollar a day and yet bring business to merchants and traders. Former exclusionists turned exploiters, and while they still agreed with the individualistic prospectors that the hordes of depraved foreign laborers endangered the Californian dream, they attempted to steer a moderate course in the waves of expulsion and to find a substitute for the lost labor force.

Docile Chinese seemed ideally suited to provide the way out of this dilemma. They complemented rather than competed with American miners. As early as 1848 a correspondent of the *Californian* suggested that "laborers on contract may be brought from China . . . , who will work faithfully for low wages," if white workers proved too expensive for agriculture. On January 7, 1852, in his only annual message to the California Legislature, Governor John McDougal gave the first official endorsement to the use of Chinese newcomers in projects to settle swamps and flooded lands. He described them as "one of the most worthy classes of our newly adopted citizens—to whom the climate and the character of these lands are peculiarly suited." Two years earlier, at the Monterey convention, McDougal had still wanted Negroes completely excluded from the state in order to prevent the introduction of contract labor by Southerners. He had then feared that planters would free their slaves by binding them to a contract to work in the mines. Now his concern for the countryside's disorder paralleled his advocacy of law and order against the rule of the San Francisco Vigilance Committee of 1851 and explained his toleration of Chinese laborers as a means of pacifying the mining districts and solving the entrepreneurs' labor problem.

A few months later another former exclusionist, perhaps also under the strain of official responsibilities, experienced a similar change in views. On March 6, 1852, Senator George B. Tingley introduced into the California Legislature a bill to legalize contracts by which Chinese laborers could sell their services for periods of ten years or less at fixed wages. Unexpectedly, he fired the opening gun in the first major clash between Californians and Chinese. The dispute emerged primarily as a quarrel between groups of Americans who held diverging notions on the social and economic structure of their rising society. The California debate overshadowed the part of the Chinese in the struggle. By 1859 newspaper reviews purporting to deal with Chinese sojourners merely summarized stages of the American controversy.

The subject of these endless arguments, the Chinese, hardly emerged from their passive role as silent bystanders. With the same surface indifference with which they endured regimentation, they also suffered the consequences of the dispute. During the initial encounter the headmen of the Chinese district companies shunned participation in the open debate. Unfamiliar with, or distrustful of, public opinion and the role of the electorate for the protection of their· interests they employed methods of persuasion similar to their customary, or businesslike way of handling other affairs. Only after these attempts had failed did they take public opinion into consideration. They then utilized the Foreign Miners' Tax as a suitable vehicle for their objective: the toleration of Chinese mining companies in the Mother Lode. While groups of Americans continued the dispute and vigorously debated problems touching on the form of their society and economy in defense of their specific interests, the headmen with a few bold maneuvers protected the work of the Chinese mining companies in the foothills of the Sierra Nevada.

The life of Chinese indentured emigrants revolved about three primary objectives: to earn and to save money, to pay off the indenture, and to return home to their families in China for a life of relative ease. The structure of Chinese California and the routine of daily drudgery left no room for humanitarian principles, for tribute to a democratic way of life, or for the inclination to join as a new rivulet the stream of immigration to the United States. The success of Chinese California depended on the possibility of working hundreds of indentured emigrants in easily controlled mining companies. The interests of wealthy merchant-creditors and lowly laborers went hand in hand. They found expression in the schemes of the headmen who worked patiently to convince Californians that the presence of the Chinese benefited the state. The fight over the Tingley bill revealed the Chinese strategy.

The temper of the state foredoomed the Tingley bill to failure. The strong popular opposition to the contract labor law caught the backers of the measure by surprise. A similar assembly bill, introduced by Representative A. R. C. Peachy, had forewarned the countryside. This bill provided for a system of contract labor, under which a Chinese or Pacific Islander would sign away his services for a maximum of five years with California courts supervising the execution of the contract. On the evening of the day in mid-March when Representative Peachy's contract labor bill passed the Assembly, an indignation meeting of the citizens of Sacramento warned "its authors, aiders and supporters in the Legislature that they would be followed to their political graves by the public opprobrium or dissatisfaction." Popular sentiment was overwhelming. The newspapers followed it, and "with a most liberal display of patriotism . . . opened in full cry" against Tingley's bill. Only a few politicians or editors cared to counter the general trend. On April 12, the Senate accepted a motion to postpone consideration of the bill indefinitely by a vote of eighteen to two, its author accounting for half the yea votes. On the same day Senator Paul K. Hubbs introduced a bill "to prevent involuntary servitude."

The strong opposition to the contract labor bills surprised the editorial writer of the *Alta* who had originally anticipated popular indifference to the measure. "If the expressions of opinion which have been made in different portions of the state be an index to the public sentiment," he concluded later, "there can be no doubt that the contract law is generally condemned." In earlier editorials, the *Alta* had given measured approval to the project. Attempts to use Chinese labor in California, the paper stated, had always failed because of "the ease with which all labor contracts could be set aside, the temptations of the mines, and the impossibility of coercion." In the past, labor in California had held the whip hand over capital and discouraged speculative investment. With the number of immigrants now reaching a new height and thereby helping to balance the supply of labor and the demands of capital, the *Alta* cautioned that the "permanent results" of the Tingley bill might not be "of that estimable character which should highly recommend it as a true system for a country like ours."

The *Alta*'s qualified endorsement distinguished its comments from those of the other journals. The San Francisco *Picayune* strongly condemned the "movement . . . to introduce among us a system of modified slavery resembling Mexican peonism." Is "any one so simple," the paper queried, "as to doubt that capitalists will avail themselves of its provisions to import crowds of cheap laborers here to work the mines, . . . to build up a large monopoly, to the injury of men of small means, who do their own work?" The Sacramento *Union* viewed the bill as a possible source for "perpetual riots and difficulties." These frontal assaults silenced such proponents of contract labor as the Stockton *Republican* which suggested the use of Chinese to reclaim tule lands for the cultivation of tea and rice. A year earlier, another Stockton newspaper, concerned about the decline of business in the southern mines, had also valiantly defended the interests of entrepreneurs hit hard by expulsionists, while the citizens of this gateway to the southern mines had been instrumental in the repeal of the first Foreign Miners' Tax.

A vigorous minority report summarized the sentiments of the diggings. Philip A. Roach submitted his views to the Senate nineteen days after the introduction of the Tingley bill. The senator considered free labor the foundation of California's society and the chief hope for its future. His description of the rivalry of white labor with Asians possessing an abnormally low standard of living in American eyes reiterated the fears of delegates at Monterey, who had warned the convention that the economic competition of unpaid slave labor in the gold region would drive out free working miners with a higher living standard. Roach's condemnation of the Foreign Miners' Tax of 1850 as "unjust, unconstitutional, and discriminating" marked his report as an eloquent expression of the independent spirit of the countryside which professed to welcome individual foreigners as free miners but rejected companies of foreign laborers as an attempt to introduce bondage and slavery into California and to give "to capital *the hand and heart of labor.*"

While portions of Roach's report rang true to pioneer declarations against slavery and monopoly, other sections advanced beyond these general arguments and appraised particularly California's labor problem. He recognized the entrepreneurs' plight and accepted the introduction of contract laborers for special projects, such as draining swamps, cultivating rice, raising silk, or planting tea, sugar, cotton, and tobacco, "provided they are excluded from citizenship." Underlying this concession was the optimistic assumption that it would be possible to admit bondmen to special occupations on particular lands without damage to laborers elsewhere. However, Roach did not "want to see Chinese or Kanaka carpenters, masons, or blacksmiths, brought here in swarms under contracts, to compete with our own mechanics, whose labor is as honorable . . . as the pursuits" of "learned professions."

With Chinese contract laborers specifically the report dealt only in passing. Senator Roach warned of the dangers of racial mixture and the threat of pagan beliefs to American institutions. He argued that most nations granted reciprocal equality to Americans. But as "regards the Chinese, we are not permitted to enter within their walls." He took the connivance of Chinese officials in the opium trade as an indication that they would send, "if it be to their advantage, . . . every malefactor in the prisons . . . here as contract laborers." A government, "as skilled in tact as is that of the Celestial Empire, could not fail to perceive the advantage of permitting its criminals to emigrate."

During the following weeks miners' meetings restated these arguments. The repercussions of the debates in the legislature and the press shook the gold region with a series of incidents which expelled Chinese mining companies from the diggings. Miners of other nationalities also suffered from the agitation. Even in 1853 "Mexican bandits," not Chinese serfs, were the target of Californians. The waves of expulsion differed from district to district and group to group. Traders, freighters, and transporters continued to show their interest in the presence of the Chinese. At the height of the agitation, in the middle of April, the *Governor Dana* kept transporting Chinese free of charge from Sacramento to Marysville in company with other passengers to promote the development of Butte County. Yet the same county was the scene of several incidents, among them the row at Atchinson's Bar in which thirty Americans "beautifully whipped" a hundred and fifty Chinese. In September, at the Miners' Convention at Jamestown in Tuolumne County, the delegates from Columbia, Shaw's Flat, and Springfield "voted to retain slave labor in the mines."

Senator Roach's report embodied the basic arguments in the subsequent strife between opponents and defenders of the Chinese. The sojourners undermined the foundations of free society, degraded labor, threatened the tranquillity of the mines, encouraged monopolies, and endangered the California dream. The desire for the rapid development of the state's economy, necessitating a large force of cheap labor, had set off this initial debate about the presence of the Chinese. The specific question of contract labor quickly broadened into the problem of Chinese immigration. Four days after the senate had tabled the contract labor bills, the assembly recorded its opposition to the Chinese in a report of the Committee on Mines and Mining Interests which foresaw the time "when absolute prohibition of entry will be necessary for our own protection." The committee recommended calling the attention of Congress to the problem and instructing "our own Representatives . . . to seek a remedy at the hands of the Federal Government by proper treaty provisions . . . determining here at home to exercise the right of our State sovereignty, and protect ourselves should necessity demand."

The clamor for outright exclusion of the Chinese completed the array of goals which emerged during the first encounter. Over several decades a large variety of measures sought to bring about these ends. Gubernatorial messages, state laws, and decisions of the State Supreme Court hardly approximated the pronounced aims. Popular action only temporarily secured the tranquillity of the countryside. Advocates of human rights, missionaries, and vociferous commercial interests joined the early proponents of contract labor in their defense of the Chinese. The decline in trade with China, which accompanied the demand of exclusionists in 1852, persuaded the Assembly Committee on Mines and Mining Interests as early as March 1853, to reverse its previous opposition to the Chinese. Two years later the receipts from the sale of Foreign Miners' Licenses, purchased almost exclusively by the Chinese, had gained an importance for the state and county treasuries which forced exclusionists to a more moderate position. In April 1855, one attempt to restrict the influx of Chinese by some other means than the Foreign Miners' Tax failed when the California Supreme Court declared unconstitutional a law which set a head tax of fifty dollars on the importation of all persons "who cannot become citizens."

The participants in the debate for nearly two decades continued to rely on the set of arguments which emerged in the first major encounter between Americans and Chinese. New issues entered the dispute in the 1860's. The emancipation of the slaves, the development of particular labor problems in the South and East atfer the Civil War, the Burlingame Treaty, the completion of the Transcontinental Railroad, and California's increased clamor for federal aid in its struggle with the Chinese question projected the old arguments into a nationwide setting. The intricacies of national politics, which until the late 1860's had played no major role in California party politics, then added new dimensions to the dispute. The formation of the People's Protective Union in 1859, the rioting of San Francisco laborers against the Chinese infiltration of specific industries, the activity of the Anti-Coolie Association, and the work of the Chinese Protective Society all were part of the trend.

On the surface the initial encounter was a discussion between groups of Americans over the presence of Chinese in California. The subjects of the debate rarely entered the fray with their own arguments. In most cases the Chinese endured placidly whatever consequences the debate produced. In some instances they successfully encountered force with cunning. Occasionally they resisted attack outright and prevailed. Under duress they generally vacated their old mining claims and searched out new diggings in much the same way as they submitted to the rigid regimentation of their bosses or died at the hands of highwaymen, robbers, rioters, or lawmen.

In general, regular courts and law officers dealt with the crimes of Chinese thieves, robbers, and murderers which had in themselves frequently the potential for mob action. The perpetual strife, however, made the Chinese ready victims of whim, greed, and cruelty. The Orientals' inability to testify in court facilitated the brutish pranks of city hoodlums. The industry of docile Chinese miners sustained avaricious tax collectors who let off Chinese with a payment of two dollars instead of four if they did not insist on a receipt. Vagabonds and robbers plundered the Chinese of their savings. The physical affronts ranged from queue-cutting, reported as early as February 1851, to the Los Angeles riot which took the lives of eighteen or nineteen Chinese in October 1871.

In part these incidents were the work of unruly men in an unstable society who maltreated anybody as long as they felt stronger than their victim. In part they represented the highwaymen's awareness that plundering a Chinese camp required less daring and involved a smaller risk than holding up a stage coach. In part the encounters thrived on the extension of the frontier spirit which found right and virtue on the side of the stronger fists and faster gun. The incident of the wild steer which raged through the streets of San Francisco in October 1860, rushed the crowd, singled out a Chinese, "ran at him full tilt and knocked him down, cutting his head severely," symbolized the course of other clashes. However, from this variety of incidents emerged no Californian who killed Chinese as methodically as did Three-Fingered Jack Manuel Garcia in the saga of Joaquin Murieta.

The fabricator of the Joaquin legend, who designed Garcia's peculiar character trait and delineated its consequences in detail, belonged on his father's side to the only racial group on the California scene which consistently showed an inveterate hatred of all Chinese. The polyglot invaders of the sleeping Bucolia evinced a multitude of reactions to the Chinese newcomers. Only with the passage of the Civil Rights Bill did Negro spokesmen in California turn against the Chinese in their newspaper, the San Francisco *Elevator*. "As there is only one step from the sublime to the ridiculous," the *Alta* commented when the *Elevator* called for the prohibition of Chinese immigration in 1866, "so the slave need not travel far to become a tyrant." But the debate in the *Elevator*'s columns in 1869 showed that among Negroes little agreement existed in regard to such an extreme demand. Negroes and Chinese frequented the same dance halls. The Chinese also found other groups sharing their life. Americans entered their employ, Germans occupied their dormitories, tents, and log cabins, Frenchmen sat at their tables, and Mexicans guided their pack horses through the Sierra. All these nationalities intermarried with the Chinese.

California Indians, however, manifested nothing but hostility. The Maidu, the Diggers in contemporary jargon, volunteered their services to tax collectors and tracked down those Chinese miners who had gone into hiding at the first sight of the officials. The Indians, aware of their weakness before the dominant groups, rigorously rejected the even weaker Orientals, and frequently robbed and killed them. At the great Indian Council in Nevada County in the fall of 1854, King Weimah, the head chief of the Grass Valley Indians, objected to his removal to a reservation as long as the Chinese were permitted to remain free in his country. At the time of the council, however, a set of devices already afforded the Chinese in the gold country some protection. They had emerged as result of the Chinese schemes during the initial debate.

The first statement of the struggle purporting to come from the Chinese side received the plaudit of leading California newspapers. Published on April 30, 1852, in reply to John Bigler's special message to the legislature on April 23, the open letter's opposition to Governor Bigler automatically guaranteed its favorable reception by a set of vituperative editors.

Editorials, letters to the editors, and a merchant memorial to the legislature took up the cause of the Chinese. Several journals jumped readily at a ghost writer's defense of the Chinese as a splendid excuse to harass California's chief executive. John Bigler suffered the misfortune of encountering hostile chroniclers during his lifetime and unsympathetic historians after his death. However, the image of the scheming politician, capitalizing on the individualistic miners' "blind nativism" and innate hostility to foreigners, no longer explains the events.

Newspaper reports kept the rapidly increasing arrival figures of Chinese sojourners constantly before the public during the debate over the contract labor law in the spring of 1852. They made the governor's demand "to check this tide of Asiatic immigration" more a reflection of the "lively interest among our citizens on the subject" and less an attempt to secure his re-election in the state campaign of 1852 on the strength of anti-Chinese pronouncements. His opponents quickly utilized the Chinese answer to his message to heckle and ridicule the governor. Mockery and derision lowered Bigler's status in New York, London, and Hong Kong. At the moment they failed to affect his position in California.

If his followers among squatters and miners read the "Letter of the Chinamen to his Excellency, Gov. Bigler" at all, they may have wondered about argument and style. In composition and reasoning it resembled more a missionary's sermon and a lawyer's brief than a document which could have come from those Chinese miners whom they knew, or the Chinese merchant princes whom they had seen from afar. The Chinese authorship of the letter is doubtful. Tong K. Achick and Hab Wa, whose names appear at the end of the document, most likely furnished only the factual information on which the reply was based. An appeal to the general public through an open letter fell outside Chinese practice. Leaders of the merchant community in San Francisco may have been connected with this public reply to the governor's message, or with a second memorial, signed by Chun Aching and Tong K. Achick and published on June 6, 1852. Their hearts, however, backed Tong K. Achick's mission to Sacramento to restore the Chinese sojourners again to Governor Bigler's favor.

The envoy of the "Chinese Committee," itself more characteristic of the customary Chinese procedure than an open letter to the general public, presented the governor with "shawls of rarest pattern, rolls of silk of the costliest texture, and some . . . seventy handkerchiefs of the choicest description." He submitted a "votive offering . . . to appease the stern divinity that rules the destinies of the Celestials in California," the editorial writer of the *Herald* caustically remarked. The outcome of the mission revealed the chasm which separated the hostility of the countryside from the pleasantry of politicians. Although Tong K. Achick was amicably wined and dined at the governor's mansion, his friends and the Chinese in the mining districts were made aware of the shortcomings of the customary policy.

The intermezzo furnished the *Herald* with opportunities to harass John Bigler about the disposition of the presents. Subsequent to the mission, Colonel James E. Zabriskie, a Sacramento lawyer, sued Tong K. Achick and Sam Wo & Co. for a fee of five hundred dollars for acting as go-between for the Chinese and the governor. The trial threw light on the manipulations which accompanied the first Chinese memorial. The remonstrance was signed by Hab Wa and Tong K. Achick, but edited by Colonel Zabriskie, and scrutinized by William E. Cornwall, the governor's private secretary. The executive mansion nevertheless turned down the letter because of its immoderate language. In a reply to the *Herald* the Colonel rejected the implication of several newspapers that he "wrote the letters addressed by the Chinese to the Governor." He disclaimed his authorship in terms which made it quite certain that none of the letters had actually been written by Chinese. The publication of the letters in pamphlet form, for distribution in the mines, misled some people at the time and students of the subject in a more recent day into taking the products as genuine Chinese arguments, "reasonable in tone and admirably stated." Only later did the heads of the Chinese companies use open letters to remonstrate with the governor, the legislature, and the people of California, Congress, and the President of the United States.

The testimony of the heads of the Chinese Four Houses before a sympathetic Committee on Mining and Mining Interests in 1853 revealed the nature of the leading Chinese merchants' concern about the wave of expulsion in the mining districts more accurately than the lofty humanitarian sentiments embodied in open letters affixed with Chinese signatures. The restoration of what Governor Bigler had called the tranquillity of the mines was their chief objective. To achieve that end the Chinese spokesmen felt it necessary to bring "the people in the mining counties . . . to believe that the presence of the Chinese among them was a benefit to the country." They dwelt, therefore, only briefly on the growing tendency of the mining counties to ban Chinese from testifying in court, which Chief Justice Hugh C. Murray belatedly sanctioned in 1854 with his opinion that Chinese testimony, like the testimony of Negroes and Indians, was inadmissible as evidence for or against a white man.

The heads of the Four Houses instead took pains to suggest to the committee an increase of the Foreign Miners' Tax if necessary. They recommended collecting the fee as part of the counties' revenue "to create . . . friends among the tax paying citizens . . . or those who would at least be willing to tolerate their people." The Four Houses offered to provide the county tax collector with an interpreter who would "use the authority of the superintendents of the several houses to make the Chinese

. . . pay . . . his taxes." Anxious about the discipline in their mining companies, they worried about the effect on the rate of wages in the event the legislature passed a law requiring those defaulting their miners' tax to perform public labor. Just "as soon and as fast as it can be done without causing great losses," the headmen promised to arrange a more equal distribution of Chinese miners and to re-establish the population balance in the restless counties of the gold region.

With the quick restoration of normal working conditions in the Mother Lode as their principal goal, the headmen assured the committee they would "exert much influence" to "prevent too large an emigration from China" to California. "After our representation last spring," they emphasized, "the emigration ceased almost entirely for many months, and now has only partially revived." Several newspapers at the time had recorded the dispatch of these messages to China but had given no clue to the arguments of those letters which suddenly halted the influx of Chinese. The Hong Kong *China Mail,* publishing Governor Bigler's statement and letters from Chinese in San Francisco to their countrymen, reported that Chinese California's leading men posted a placard in Hong Kong. The handbill stated that Americans had lost their earlier respect for the Chinese because of the increased number of newcomers during the last two years, "many of whom were in filthy state, and on that account were mocked by foreigners and [made] their countrymen ashamed of them."

The strategy of the heads of the Four Houses, outlined in 1853 during the hearings of the Committee of Mines and Mining Interests in San Francisco, succeeded in its broad objectives. The revenue from the Foreign Miners' Tax, paid almost exclusively by Chinese, provided much of the needed regular income for a great number of mining counties, supporting the headmen's assumption that the payment of the tax would ensure Chinese mining companies a measure of toleration which the labor companies of Latins and Europeans had failed to gain. Their position as taxpayers guaranteed Chinese miners a modicum of protection of life and property, and ensured their continued access to the diggings. That the money from the Orientals was welcome, indeed counted upon, is attested to by the alarm with which the mining counties viewed the railroad construction camps in the 1860's. These camps, and the advance of the mines into the Rocky Mountains threatened to draw off Chinese, and thus deplete revenues. Even the collectors of the Foreign Miners' Tax at times "accommodated their demands to the ability" of the companies. The realistic appraisal of the countryside's temper by the headmen preserved the work camp as an institution while abstract arguments about justice, humanity, and the dignity of labor continued to agitate the opponents and defenders of the bondmen.

With the gradual acceptance of the work camp, Chinatown was left as the focal point of strife. Californians initially observed the growth of Chinatown with pride for it came into view almost naturally as part of the bustling port or the rapidly developing supply centers in the interior. The exotic quarter added another gem to California's crown. Favorable comments about Chinese industry and frugality continued to accompany adverse reaction to the development of a distinct Chinese settlement in the heart of San Francisco. The Grand Jury Report for the December term, 1853, regretted finding "a disposition on the part of some inconsiderate persons to annoy, persecute and maltreat inoffensive and industrious Chinamen." The actions of city officials and the complaints of residents directed attention to a series of distinct grievances around which the strife between American communities and Chinatown revolved.

These charges originally encompassed the whole range of tensions which rose from the accelerated growth of San Francisco. They ranged from the laments of bachelors about Chinese washermen to the Recorder's complaints about the problem of administering oaths to feuding Orientals. They covered the Chief Engineer's difficulties with sanitation and fire fighting, and the irritation of residents at hordes of Chinese bathing naked in the back of company houses, "rendering it impossible for the female portion of the families adjacent thereto to have ingress to or egress from their houses, or to remain at their windows." The years reduced the accusations to two basic indictments: the living habits of the Chinese endangered San Francisco's physical health, the vices threatened the moral character of the city. These charges stimulated waves of reform which sought to tackle some of the problems leading to a concentration of filth and prostitution, with crowded residents and gambling visitors, in Chinatown.

The arrival of shiploads of dying Chinese newcomers, another fire endangering the city's growth, reports about the spread of a cholera epidemic around the world and of leprosy in the Chinese quarter, reform groups threatening the tranquillity of municipal corruption, or attempts to erase San Francisco's immorality by purifying Chinatown—these and other calamities, real and imagined, brought on newspaper exposés, investigations, official reports, and court trials. A constant deterioration of the city's affairs seemed to accompany each local catastrophe. High-sounding measures and radical solutions aimed primarily at pacifying the suddenly aroused collective conscience of the city. The re-education of the sojourners to San Francisco standards of living or the relocation of Chinatown in the sand hills surrounding the sprawling town were gigantic undertakings which rapidly exhausted the momentum of each short-lived burst of indignation. Every attempt to alter Chinatown merely impressed deeper on the quarter the stamp of the "rankest outgrowth of human degradation . . . upon this continent," as the report of the Special Committee of the Board of

Supervisors labeled Chinatown in the 1880's. During two decades of strife Californians came to accept the conditions of Chinatown and regard them as inseparable from the nature of its inhabitants.

A set of incidents in the 1850's illustrated the emergence of Chinatown as a constant source of strife. The "fearful mortality" which decimated the Chinese emigrants on the *Libertad* and the *Challenge* during their passage in the summer of 1854, filled San Francisco with alarm at the possible threat to the city's health. The arrival of the ships and the quarantine of ailing survivors on Goat Island (Yerba Buena Island) in the Bay suddenly concentrated public attention on the modes and conditions of living in the Chinese Quarter. The disaster among the newcomers had been preceded by newspaper references to the filth and stench in Chinatown. Reports of the spread of the cholera "with alarming rapidity all over the Western continent" heightened San Francisco's anxiety about "these offensive dens" furnishing "material for a sweeping epidemic." The agitation also increased the old concern over the fire hazard which the wooden Chinese houses and their primitive cooking facilities represented. Petitions and letters to the editors of the local journals kept before the public eye a memorial by Dr. William Rabe to the Board of Assistant Aldermen "in relation to the Chinese and their filthy quarters." It initiated the second stage of the strife.

The memorial inspired members of the Common Council to a flight of oratory which "left as much light on the question as before." The Board of Assistant Aldermen asked its Committee on Health and Police together with the memorialist to investigate the problem. Within a week the group produced a report which described the "different localities owned by the various Chinese companies" as "the filthiest places that could be imagined." The investigators found houses "with hundreds of Chinamen . . . crowded to excess," who cooked on the floor, without stoves or chimneys, "in a manner similar to our savage Indians." Emphasizing that "these people come here only as hirelings to five . . . companies . . . to die when they cannot serve their taskmasters any more . . . , that the women . . . are the most degraded prostitutes, and that the . . . sole enjoyment of the male population is gambling . . . ," and knowing the sojourners "to be foreign slaves to foreign masters, governed by force and religious dread, and kept in terror by a secret society called the 'Triad'," the Committee stamped the Chinese an "unmitigated and wholesale nuisance." Inflamed by the evidence, the investigators recommended a memorial to the legislature and the "immediate expulsion of the whole Chinese race from the city, or at least their removal outside the more inhabited line of streets." However, doubting the Council's legal authority to enact such sweeping measures, they advocated a series of ordinances which required "that the fire laws be vigilantly enforced; that the police and health regulations be rigidly adhered to; and that the Chinese companies be requested . . . to take their immigrants and sick countrymen beyond the limits of the city."

A meeting of a "large number of the most respectable Chinese residents" initiated the third stage of the struggle. A-hing, a San Francisco merchant, presided, representatives of the "five great companies" graced the assembly, Charles Carvalho interpreted, and William Howard, the publisher of the *Golden Hills' News,* acted as secretary, furnishing the Common Council with a report which would have been a credit to any town meeting on the eastern seaboard. The Chinese defense embodied ready promises to alleviate the shortcomings, gave evidence of good intentions blocked by selfish Chinese or white men, and attempted to direct the reform spirit to the gigantic tasks of prostitution and gambling which promised to slow down the movement effectively. The meeting resolved that the five companies erect a hospital outside the city limits within one month, that "all Chinamen . . . take immediate steps to have their premises cleared," that "the different buildings kept as boarding houses by the companies . . . be cleaned and renovated, and that any excess of boarders injurious to health be immediately removed," and that all fireplaces and kitchens be fireproofed. The group asked for the appointment of an inspector by the City Council to enforce these steps so that "the innocent may not suffer with the guilty," and informed the Council that a great number of Chinese houses had paid and still paid one dollar per week "to one Cross, whom they believe to be a policeman, . . . to clean their . . . quarters," and one more dollar "weekly for protection." The meeting "respectfully requested" the Council "to suppress the Chinese houses of ill-fame, and gambling houses," which the group "considered a great grievance to the Chinese residents."

Disputes of the City Council and the Chinese Committee filled the final phase of this encounter. They centered around the working of the ordinance and the realization of the promises made at the height of the agitation. The measures brought only minor relief from the problem. The weeks "when there was some little excitement . . . on the subject of cholera and . . . the filthy condition" of "these dens of corruption" had passed. Nothing remained for the editorial writer of the *Alta* but to regret that "decided action could not have been . . . put in force." New disturbances agitated the city. On October 7, 1854, Alderman Henry Meiggs escaped in the bark *America* after the discovery of his extensive forgeries which upset the community. Established interests soon prevailed in favor of the old conditions. Real estate owners and sublessors, profiting heavily from Chinese rentals, were a formidable obstacle to all attempts to relocate Chinatown. Variations of this pattern characterized the struggle over Chinatown's filth for decades to come.

Meanwhile there was a running battle over prostitution. At times the crusade bore aspects of a carnival as when the fire companies of several towns directed their hoses at Chinese brothels "to sweep them clean." A multitude of conflicting interests distorted the dividing line separating the struggling parties. District companies fought tongs over the control of the traffic in Chinese females while San Francisco lawyers battled municipal officials over the rights of procurers and prostitutes. Accounts of murders and kidnapings, street fights and assassinations, escapes and suicides, extortions, and trials peopled with perjurers and false witnesses spiced the endless stream of monotonous reports about the arrests of Chinese prostitutes. Charged with tapping upon the window glass to attract prospective customers, the women regularly failed to appear in court and forfeited their bail of five dollars. By the summer of 1859 the constant struggle had driven the Chinese women "from their former abodes on the public streets and compelled them to reside in alleys and by-streets, away from the public gaze," only to initiate the new phase of Chinese prostitution with highbinders, special policemen, blackmailers, immigration officials, ward politicians, mission workers, and bagnios of slave girls.

Chinatown remained for decades the major center of strife between Californians and Chinese. As a result of a changing economy, other fields of employment took over the function which the mining camp had originally fulfilled. Railroad construction, agriculture, and cigar making absorbed companies of Chinese laborers. Others became house servants, shoemakers, and textile workers. With the shifts in the areas of employment, Chinatown gained significance beyond its role as safety valve of the control system. Attracted by new fields of work, increasing numbers of Chinese swarmed into its teeming quarters and added to its old problems. Compressed within narrow confines, filth and immorality persisted, endangering the health and virtue of the growing state, and they soon came to be regarded by Americans as part of the sojourners' second nature. While precise grievances had caused the original clashes, Californians now viewed their struggle as an inevitable and perpetual conflict. Yet by extending American culture to the Chinese, they also responded compassionately to the suffering humanity in their midst.

4.4

The War and the Worker

DAVID MONTGOMERY

David Montgomery surveys the role of northern workers in the Civil War years. He shows that the blanket assertions of racism often hurled at the northern masses represent an insufficient analysis. A study of the New York City anti-draft riots and of the radical Republicans' connections with labor reform in Massachusetts presents clear evidence of the complexity of race relations during the Civil War. Montgomery also focuses suggestively on the role of Germans and Irish in working-class movements. The thrust of Montgomery's essay is to study the worker in his various roles—at the workplace, in ethnic societies, in politics, in the community. Only through this type of study will the ambiguities and ambivalences of working-class attitudes to race and class emerge and be clarified.

The following books are suggested for further reading:

ROBERT ERNST, *Immigrant Life in New York,* Port Washington, New York: Ira J. Friedman Division, Kennikat Press, Inc., 1965.

OSCAR HANDLIN, *Boston's Immigrants,* New York: Atheneum Publishers, 1968.

EARL NIEHAUS, *The Irish in New Orleans,* Baton Rouge: Louisiana State University Press, 1965.

On the evening of November 2, 1865, thousands of workingmen from the Boston area were gathered in Faneuil Hall to hear speeches by local trade-union leaders, Wendell Phillips, and Congressman Benjamin F. Butler. At the close of the rally the plump, heavily bearded machinist Ira Steward stepped to the podium to read a lengthy series of resolutions which concluded:

> RESOLVED, that with grateful hearts we praise our Heavenly Father that He has permitted his angel of peace once more to wave her silver wand over our recently distracted land. That we rejoice that the rebel aristocracy of the South has been crushed, that we rejoice that beneath the glorious shadow of our victorious flag men of every clime, lineage and color are recognized as free. But while we will bear with patient endurance the burden of the public debt, we yet want it to be known that the workingmen of America will in future claim a more equal share in the wealth their industry creates in peace and a more equal participation in the privileges and blessings of those free institutions, defended by their manhood on many a bloody field of battle. . . .

The fledgling labor-reform movement for which Steward spoke was the child of civil war. The political debates of that conflict provided the basic elements of the workingmen's ideology, the alignments of political and social groups effectuated by the war created the framework within which their movement unfolded, and the economic pressures the great struggle engendered spurred them into action. For most wage earners the war had been a nightmare that had given them little reason to endorse the revolutionary measures of the Republicans. The burden of taxation fell heavily on them, greenbacks were associated with severe inflation, and conscription not only gave the state a claim upon their very lives but discriminatorily provided the wealthy citizen with an escape through commutation for cash. Emancipation, though long advocated by a minor-

ity of workers, appeared to most as a threat to unleash from the plantations hordes of Negro laborers who would depress industrial wage levels.
But the fact that toilers disliked the war measures does not prove the
contention of some historians that the Peace Democrats were able to
rouse "the mass opposition of the working classes" against the war effort.

It is certainly true that in any war there is a constant ebb and flow
of the will to fight, and this is especially true of a civil war in which,
to a much greater extent than an international war, the questions of
whether or not to continue the carnage and even of which side to support
are always live issues. Lincoln's administration had to win battles and
votes simultaneously, and often the election campaigns were more important to the ultimate outcome of the struggle than the military encounters. Varied as the views of Northern workers may have been, however,
toward Lincoln, slavery, the draft, and the various military leaders, one
fact remains clear: they were ardently devoted to the cause of preserving
the Union intact. In fact, the same could be said of the industrial laborers,
at least, of New Orleans, Louisville, Covington, and St. Louis in the
slave states. This devotion was rooted in the intense nationalism of the
working classes—their commitment to the world's only political democracy.

The secession crisis roused this devotion. "Come, then," called Daniel
Weaver to his fellow coal miners in January 1861, "and rally around the
standard of union—the union of States and the unity of miners. . . ."
Simultaneously, the mechanics of Louisville, Kentucky, under the leadership of Robert Gilchrist (later an officer of the National Labor Union)
and the molder William Horan, requested fellow trade unionists to convene on Washington's Birthday in Philadelphia to consider steps to preserve the Union. Denouncing both the "traitors in Washington" and the
militant antislavery men, they endorsed the proposed Crittenden Compromise. Significantly, this meeting, the decade's first national assembly
of labor leaders, was held in response to political, not economic, problems, and its resolutions expressed the belief that workingmen would
make better legislators in the crisis than would "party politicians." To
promote the election of workmen to office it established the Committee
of Thirty-Four. The leaders of the movement included such Douglas
Democrats as Gilchrist, Horan, and William H. Sylvis, and such Republicans as Uriah S. Stephens. Finally, it is noteworthy that both the
most famous president of the future National Labor Union (Sylvis) and
the founder-to-be of the Knights of Labor (Stephens) played prominent
roles in this effort.

Rebel bombardment of Fort Sumter transformed the workers' nationalism from a call for compromise to a call for arms. Symbolically,
twelve-year-old Terence V. Powderly, son of a stanch Democrat of Car-
bondale, Pennsylvania, attached an American flag sewn by his mother

to a sapling he had cut and nailed the crude banner to the side of his house. Two of his brothers enlisted early enough to serve at Antietam. The nearby town of Port Carbon sent 518 men to war, one fourth of its population, including the miners of the Petersburg crater in 1864. Across the state, in the hamlet of Cherry Tree, sawmill operator Robert Hughes discovered that the April enlistments had robbed him of all of his twenty-two hands save one old man.

Military enthusiasm wrought havoc on the little trade unions of the time. A Philadelphia union closed its books with the words: "It having been resolved to enlist with Uncle Sam for the war, this union stands adjourned until either the Union is safe or we are whipped." William Sylvis, then secretary of the Philadelphia ironmolders, raised a company which soon disbanded because the men disliked the colonel placed over them; he later enlisted in the Pennsylvania militia. Coal miners of central Illinois made up several companies, drastically depleting union rolls, and elected their paid lecturer, Martin Boyle, a captain. In some small Western towns like St. Paul, Minneapolis, and St. Anthony, enlistments closed down all existing trade unions. The hardiest of the national organizations, the National Typographical Union, doubly stricken by military recruitment of one third of the members of its key New York local and the loss of its large Southern membership, held no convention at all in 1861, and the next year its president, future Congressman John M. Farquhar, joined the army himself.

In all, 37 per cent of the males of military age in the loyal states were or had been in the federal armed forces by May 1865. State militia calls aside, 2,653,062 men had entered the national army. Benjamin A. Gould concluded that of every 1,000 U.S. soldiers, 421 belonged to the working classes (mechanics and laborers), 487 to agriculture, 16 to the professions, 35 to commerce, and the remaining 41 to miscellaneous other or unidentified occupations. Skilled mechanics made up an especially large number of Union volunteers. Only the professional classes (who flocked to the colors in 1861 and 1862) provided more soldiers in proportion to their numbers than did the workingmen.

Foreign-born workmen matched the enthusiasm of the natives. Ten regiments of Germans were raised in New York State alone, one of them exclusively members of the *Turnverein* and another (the "Frémont" Regiment) commanded by the Prussian Marxist Rudolph Rosa. In fact, the *Turnverein,* a combination athletic and mutual insurance society that was the largest secular German organization in the nation, practically turned itself into a recruiting agency. Three fourths of its members enlisted in the army, providing the battalion in Washington that boasted of being the first volunteer group mustered in the national crisis, three companies of the First Missouri Regiment, and almost the whole Seventeenth Missouri. German manpower, organizations, and ideas were transplanted to the fields of battle. The Forty-third Illinois Regiment was constituted almost exclusively of German youth from Belleville, a center of trade unionism and free thought labeled by Wilhelm Kaufmann *"ein kleines deutsches Athen in Amerika."* The Thirty-second Indiana was frequently assembled by its commander, brevet Major General August Willich, for lectures on Marxism, which he delivered in German.

The Irish were not to be outdone by Germans. Despite their traditional loyalty to the Democratic party and hatred of Negroes, James Burn found Irish workmen in the New York–Philadelphia region ardently loyal to the Union. They supplied more than 144,000 soldiers, a larger proportion of their number of military age than the natives in service. New York's famous Sixty-ninth Regiment and Irish Brigade, and the Ninth Massachusetts were Irish units which fought from Bull Run to Appomattox, their standard-bearers carrying the green flag beside the Stars and Stripes. Indeed, the Irish pennant of the Sixty-ninth was sewn in Tipperary and shipped to New York, where General George McClellan ceremoniously presented it to Colonel James Cavanaugh of the regiment. For the Irish, after all, America was *their* country, the land where, quipped John O'Leary, they fear neither law nor landlord, but "fancy themselves growing smart almost with the air they breathe, and feel as if they had become free by that declaration of independence which is forever floating about the moral atmosphere." On the Old Sod, they believed, the only Confederate sympathizers were Englishmen and Orangemen.

In the opening months of 1864 the tenacity of this nationalism was put to the acid test. At the very moment General Grant was preparing to mount his May offensive on all fronts, the enlistment terms of his indispensable, battle-hardened three-year volunteers of 1861 began to expire. The War Department estimated that as early as December 31, 1863, 455 out of 956 volunteer infantry regiments and 81 out of 158 volunteer batteries would simply go out of existence. Many more of the three-year men were scattered as cadre among the raw recruits. Under the terms of the conscription law these veterans could not be drafted. There was no way the government could compel them to stay in the army; yet without them there could be no effective offensive.

The three-year men were offered a $400 bounty, a thirty-day furlough, and a special chevron designating them "veteran volunteers," but these inducements alone could hardly have enticed men who had known three years of death to return for more. In this critical hour 136,000 of the veterans re-enlisted. The weakest returns were in the Army of the Potomac, where General Meade found that almost one half the veterans had gone home, leaving him with 26,000 re-enlistments. Even this force, however, was enough to supply the core of experienced cadre for the advancing army. Down in Georgia whole regiments of Sherman's veterans signed up *en masse*. As those soldiers advanced toward Atlanta in the following months, James Russell Lowell exulted: "I believe the people are more firm than ever."

This loyalty was sorely taxed. The cost of the war rose daily, and the Union party's war measures confronted the working classes with issues far more complex than secession. The will to defeat the Rebels was nearly unanimous, but not so the readiness to bear mounting taxes and inflation, much less to welcome conscription and emancipation of the Negroes. The cost of living rose abruptly, Wesley Mitchell's index based on 100 for 1860 standing at 156 by 1864 and 168 in 1865. Wages inevitably lagged in their upward race with prices, the wage index being 130 for 1864 and 150 for 1865. But even the wage index reveals little, because the income of craftsmen whose skills were in short supply kept abreast of the cost of living rather well in 1864, while those of the unskilled and the women workers fell woefully behind. Pathetically, some seamstresses of Cincinnati appealed to President Lincoln to be paid directly for their work rather than through merchants. "We are unable to sustain life for the prices offered by contractors, who fatten on their contracts by grinding immense profits out of the labor of their operatives," the women wrote. "We are in no way actuated by a spirit of faction, but desirous of aiding the best government on earth, and at the same time securing justice to the humble laborer."

Skilled and semi-skilled tradesmen, on the other hand, incessantly demanded higher "prices" for their work and put down tools without hesitation when they were refused. Some of their strikes were led by unions, others, perhaps many more, involved no unions at all. James Burn, the English hatter, remarked that at his trade in New York he found "a constant struggle between the men and their employers about prices. I have seen as many as four shop-calls [work stoppages] in the course of a day on as many different kinds of work." When the workers, led by "a set of headstrong young men," did "turn out . . . should any man with a proper sense of right and wrong attempt to defend the employer . . . he would surely be branded as a traitor, as well as being made the butt of ridicule by every fool in the shop who chooses to raise a laugh at his expense. . . ."

A similar picture was drawn by an office clerk in the McCormick reaper plant in Chicago in April 1864: "Our molders are going on their fourth strike for an advance of wages since last fall. They now want 25 per cent more!!! Manufacturers will have to shut up shop if things go much farther in this line. . . . We wish we could help it but we are powerless." Determined employers could resort to long and costly lockouts, such as those of the piano makers and unionized daily newspapers of New York. In both these instances the employers could not pass increased costs on to the government or an expanding market; yet even the publishers balked only when their typographers (already paid far above those of nonunion competitors) demanded their second raise of the year. In at least one instance common laborers were able to duplicate the success of the tradesmen. New York's longshoremen staged a series of strikes in the spring of 1863, culminating in the massive June walkout of every worker in and around the docks, which converted an attempted wage cut into a substantial wage increase.

Harassed employers turned to the government for help in resisting the wartime demands of their workers. Ascribing labor's effectiveness in advancing wages to a "labor shortage" they enlisted United States consuls in Europe to step up the flow of immigrants and asked army officers at Southern forts to send "contrabands." Since neither of these steps was adequate to cope with the power of skilled workmen, the manufacturers sought more direct state aid through antistrike legislation and military suppression of strikes. All these measures in turn stimulated the political awareness of the working classes.

A series of strikes in the coal fields around LaSalle, Illinois, in 1863 prompted the legislature of that state to pass an act making it a criminal offense to interfere with another person's going to work, to combine to deprive the owner of property of its lawful use, or to enter a coal mine with the intention of inducing others to leave it. Known as the LaSalle Black Laws, this legislation was the product of bipartisan action. The Democrats who then controlled the Illinois legislature had just passed resolutions condemning the Emancipation Proclamation and were maneuvering to remove control of the state militia from the hands of Republican Governor Yates. The day after the antistrike act was signed by Yates the legislature was adjourned for want of a quorum because Republican members absented themselves to prevent the passage of Democratic peace resolutions.

Similar legislation was proposed in Massachusetts and Minnesota, and in Ohio a bill to prohibit anyone's preventing another person from going to work became law. But the greatest controversy arose over a measure introduced in March 1864, in the New York Senate by Frederick R. Hastings, which exempted from conspiracy prosecution all associations of workmen or employers to establish wages, hours, or rules, but provided fine and imprisonment for the use of any coercive means by these groups. Thus, to interfere with employees' going to work, to force anyone to join a union, or to fine anyone for breaking the rules of the body would be an indictable offense. The bill was quickly identified by the public with Senator Charles J. Folger, chairman of the Senate Judiciary

Committee, to which it was referred, and a leading contender for the Republican gubernatorial nomination that year. The fledgling Workingmen's Union (New York City's central body of English-language trade unions) mobilized massive demonstrations against the bill. The sustained campaign against this proposal, led by William Harding, president of the Workingmen's Union and of the Coachmakers' International Union, inspired the establishment of both a central body of German-language unions in the city (the *Arbeiter-Bund*) and a state Workingmen's Assembly, which quickly became a formidable lobby in Albany. So furious was the storm roused by the workers that Senator Hastings himself saw to it that his bill died in committee and the Republican party passed over Folger to select Reuben Fenton as its standard-bearer for the governorship.

More successful—and more sensational—than these legislative efforts was the use of the army to break strikes. In March 1864, the operatives of the R. P. Parrott Works in Cold Springs, New York, laid down their tools to support their demand for wage increases. Citing its need for the famous Parrott guns, the army sent two companies of troops to the town, proclaimed martial law, and jailed four strike leaders in Fort Lafayette, where they remained seven weeks without trial. Yielding before this show of force, the workers resumed operations at the old wages. At the same time the Machinists' and Blacksmiths' Union and the Tailors' Union went on strike in St. Louis. A month after the strike began, General William S. Rosecrans issued orders prohibiting refusal to work, meetings, and picketing. Perhaps because St. Louis was a major hub of the riverboat operations, indispensable to all military endeavors in the Western theater of war, the petition of the workers for a revision of the order was spurned. In May, General Stephen G. Burbridge took similar action to break a strike of machinists in Louisville.

As the year 1865 opened, employers in many industries, anticipating a fall of demand and prices with the impending end of the war, undertook vigorous efforts to reduce wages. The simultaneous demands of workers for wage increases and their employers for cuts provoked a rash of bitter strikes. In the coal fields around Blossburg in northern Pennsylvania a struggle occurred which manifested all the tendencies of the period in bold relief. In 1863 these miners had affiliated themselves with the American Miners' Association, through which they won raises ranging from 35¢ to $1.10 a ton. Worse yet, from the standpoint of the employers, the union embraced every miner, mechanic, mule driver, and laborer in and around the pits, enforced a closed shop, and regulated hours and output per man. The colliers determined to rid themselves of this "tyranny." In December 1864 the Fall Brook Coal Company and two other firms posted notice that henceforth they would establish all prices unilaterally, that company houses should thereafter "be occupied only by well disposed people, who, without exception, will be required to enter into a special agreement specifying the conditions upon which he or they will occupy," and that the companies would "put down" any resistance to their decrees and decide without interference from a union who was to be hired or fired. When the union members refused to work on such terms, the colliers directed all work to be suspended until the conditions were agreed to and all company houses to be evacuated. In May a sudden raid on company towns by three hundred soldiers, plus a sheriff's posse of equal numbers, took the strikers by surprise. Their leaders were arrested, and miners and families totaling some four thousand persons were evicted and dumped with their household goods in the town of Blossburg. Work was then resumed with wages cut in half and an ironclad oath not to join a union imposed on all rehired miners. The state legislature legalized the action of the operators after the fact by passing the so-called Tioga County Law, which permitted mining companies to evict striking miners from company houses at any time. "Shame!" cried Jonathan Fincher, president of the Philadelphia Trades Assembly. "Eternal shame on the men who can be guilty of such an outrage on honest labor!"

WORKERS AND COPPERHEADS

Labor's involvement in politics and legislation entailed more than simply the effort to free trade unions from statutory or military interference. Spokesmen of the working classes could not avoid orienting their movement in relation to the major political alignments of the day. All major factions, furthermore, assiduously courted the votes of the workingmen. Three important results stand out. First, in every election the votes of the workers were well divided between the parties. Second, despite intense efforts by the Peace Democrats to woo urban workmen, few of the latter— and none of their organizations or leaders—"went Coppery." Third, in several important respects the most aware and active spokesmen of the working classes found themselves drawn into close-functioning relations with the Radicals.

The wartime grievances of the working classes mounted at the very time the enactment of the revolutionary Republican measures threw important sections of the Democratic party into open opposition to the war. The fact that protests from labor and from the Copperheads swelled simultaneously gave the impression in some areas that the workmen were swinging into the camp of the Peace Democrats; and the latter, of course, sought to bring just such a development to pass. The Copperheads, furthermore, enjoyed a formidable advantage: the major grievances which sparked labor protest were all related to the growing power and centralization of government, and opposition to that tendency was the very essence of old-line democracy. Military suppression of strikes, greenback inflation, the specter (for it was never more than that) of liberated Negroes flocking North, and the ubiquitous draft—what could have been better grist for the Coppery mill? Their campaign against the war reached a fever pitch in the spring of 1863. In New York City it was spearheaded by Mozart Hall, the Democratic society of ex-Mayor Fernando Wood, who had been quite a hero to foreign-born laborers during the fifties. As Lee's troops marched north into Pennsylvania and the Lincoln administration prepared to issue the first federal draft call, Wood's organization mounted a series of protest meetings, culminating in a massive Peace Convention at Cooper Institute on June 3 and a Fourth of July rally against conscription. From the rostrum Copperhead orators pounded home the themes that the government's war effort was undermining the Constitution, that conscription claimed the lives of the poor in a rich man's war, and that emancipated Negroes were flooding the North.

Simultaneously, rising rents and higher food prices triggered such a wave of trade organizing and strikes that *Fincher's Trades Review* headlined a June column on New York events "The Upheaving Masses in Motion!" Early that month the entire Manhattan waterfront suspended work in sympathy with the newly unionized longshoremen, and by June 18 the latter triumphantly announced both a 60 per cent raise in daily wages and exclusion of all nonunion members from the docks. Ominously, the aroused workers echoed some Copperhead themes. Among the scab longshoremen violently driven from work by the union were all the Negroes employed on the docks. Even the ardently loyal Jonathan Fincher of Philadelphia, leader of the Machinists' Union and dean of the labor press, begged the national government to prevent an influx of freedmen to the North and, while endorsing the draft act itself, denounced the $300 commutation provision as an "unpardonable crime." On the other hand, his paper warned the New York workers to devote more attention to perfecting their unions and not to be intoxicated by mass rallies and outside speakers. "Already we see the shadowy fingers of politicians, place hunters and capitalists laying hold of the movement for their own selfish ends," the veteran Philadelphia unionist wrote. He concluded with the warning: "Weed out the unworthy ones among you."

Too late! On the morning of Saturday, July 11, the great wheel began to spin in the Enrollment Office in midtown New York. By evening 1,236 names had been drawn and posted. The task of selecting the remainder of the 2,000-man quota was postponed to the following Monday. New Yorkers passed a hot Sunday reading and discussing the names of the elect. On Monday morning longshoremen, railroad trackmen, iron workers, blacksmiths, and others put down their tools to parade in protest against the draft. Members of Fire Engine Company Number 33 (the "Black Joke" Company) learned that among the names drawn from the wheel were some of their own. Such fire companies ranked with the saloons and police force as one of the three pedestals on which the city's Democratic organization rested. The Black Joke men therefore had little difficulty rousing a crowd of supporters and sacking the Enrollment Office itself. This attack ignited rioting in many parts of the city. Near the burning office a Virginian named Andrews, a familiar figure at earlier Mozart Hall rallies, exhorted the crowd to frustrate conscription physically. Some of his audience then stormed an armory on Second Avenue and in the ensuing chaos burned the building with hundreds of their comrades trapped inside, where they were gathering arms.

The rioting thus begun on Monday raged through the city until Thursday night, and a few outbursts were reported even Friday morning as police undertook a city-wide search for loot and participants involved in the earlier debacle. An estimated twelve to fifteen hundred people lost their lives in those four days. To detail the carnage of that week is unnecessary here. The patterns of destruction do deserve attention, however, because the rioters' choice of targets upon which to unleash their spleen reveals some basic social attitudes of the city poor. The reaction of the organized workmen, furthermore, indicates their own conception of their position in society.

The draft act itself was more than simply the first quarry of the turmoil, quickly forgotten in the quest of loot, as some Republican accounts alleged. True, by Monday afternoon the process of conscription had been brought to a complete halt. But on Friday when Archbishop John Hughes addressed a huge crowd urging them to peace, he was continuously interrupted with cries of "Stop the draft." The archbishop's audience was composed of people who were not, or at least no longer, rioting; yet they took up the chant of those who were still battling police many blocks away. Jonathan Fincher, who hurled anathemas at the rioters, attributed the first wrong to the authors of the draft act. Exempt men with families, he demanded, and repeal the $300 commutation privilege. Similarly, Tammany aldermen in the City Council, although they spurned the antidraft agitation, hastily enacted a hefty appropriation of municipal funds to provide the commutation fee for poor men—only to see the measure vetoed by Mayor George Opdyke.

On the other hand, conscription was by no means the only prey of the crowd. As the women of the slums poured into the streets urging on the men and all the declassed criminal and vagrant population of the sprawling port city joined the mob, it quickly directed its attention primarily to Negroes. Any black man, woman, or child who chanced within the reach of the rioters was put to death, often through hideous tortures. Similar wrath was vented upon captured police officers, though seldom on soldiers. A relatively small band did march on a hospital sheltering wounded soldiers, but it was easily dispersed by armed civilians. Homes of the wealthy were subjected to sack unless they were heavily guarded. In such cases, hatred of the rich was well complemented by the urge to loot. The crowd also singled out for vengeance some symbols of industrialism—in particular, railroad tracks and the city's newly purchased street-sweeping machines. A Protestant mission in the dismal Five Points area was destroyed on the first day of the riots. One detachment even descended on Columbia College. It would seem, however, that anti-intellectualism was not as strong a motive in the crowd as was hatred of Negroes, police, labor-saving machines, and Protestants, for a single priest on the steps of the college convinced the rioters to spare that seat of learning.

By Wednesday morning President Thomas C. Acton of the Police Board was certain the tide had turned against the rioters. Through that day and the next his police, now reinforced by five battle-hardened regiments of the Army of the Potomac, confined the rioters to the worst slum areas. Clearing streets with howitzers loaded with grapeshot and chains used at point-blank range, the forces of order then invaded the heartland of their enemy. At this point reports reaching police headquarters mentioned a desperate, revolutionary quality emerging among the rioters, many of whom exhibited fierce heroism defending their barricades. To complete the new picture, on Wednesday night crowds raided and closed houses of prostitution, in the standard tradition of revolutionary mobs. In the dying embers of a race riot were grotesque reflections of Paris's Bloody June Days.

It was also clear by Wednesday that the workingmen whose activities were channeled through organized social institutions were becoming an important segment of forces opposed to the riot. The fire companies, for example, though one of their number had sparked the whole turmoil, were braving rioters' missiles as well as raging flames as they worked tirelessly to keep down conflagrations. After Monday most factories and shipyards resumed operation, despite attacks on their employees by the crowd. Among the troops who assaulted the rioters as ruthlessly as they recently had Lee's forces at Gettysburg was New York's own all-Irish Sixty-ninth Regiment. Civilian volunteers bolstered the predominantly Irish professional police, among them a patrol of a thousand German members of the *Turnverein*. Trade unions of the city took great pains to dissociate themselves from the rioters, and the organized hatters, typographers, carpenters, and cabinetmakers founded the Democratic-Republican Workingmen's Association of New York to propagandize for the Union cause. President Patrick Keady of the New York Practical House Painters' Association gloried in the discovery that no arrested rioters were painters and requested members of his union to use their influence "to prevent recurrence of such disgraceful scenes as were then enacted . . . [by] thieving rascals . . . who have never done a day's work in their lives. . . ."

In a word, workingmen's organizations of all kinds, hostile though they were to the discriminatory impact of the draft on the poor, rallied to the banner of the government—in fact, to the established social structure—in the face of the draft riots. Blaming the outbursts on unemployed foreign-born in the port cities, "professional thieves," heartless speculators, and designing partisan politicians, Fincher editorialized: "The people have too much at stake to tolerate action beyond the pale of the law. Every mob has been put down. . . . No improvement can be made by popular outbursts upon the great superstructure created by the wisdom of our fathers. . . ."

In short, the burdens placed on the working classes by the war roused them to economic and political protest actions. These actions did not signal the accession of labor to the old-line Democrats, but rather the vitalization of an entirely new political force—the labor-reform movement. Nowhere was the distinction more clear than in the workingmen's reaction to the efforts of Benjamin E. Green to convince them through speeches, pamphlets, and newspapers that the Southern planter was their natural ally against the common enemy, the Yankee capitalist. The abolition of slavery, argued Green, had left white and black labor "two poor *divorced* widows" who could be rescued only by resurrecting their stricken husband and protector, the slaveholder. Andrew Cameron denounced Green as an impostor and declared: "The ghost of negro superiority which haunts the peace of Mr. Green has no terrors for us." Green in turn concluded that trade unions offered the workers "a poor and vain reliance" and that "egotism, selfishness, was their only motive."

Workingmen could not and did not yearn with the Copperheads for the dying past. Rather, while bidding slavery and rebellion farewell, labor reformers raised the next question on the agenda. The *Daily Evening Voice* of the Boston Trades Assembly editorialized that the "oligarchy at the South" was "from the very nature of things, antagonist to free labor," but it added that the emerging "question of the day" was: "Have the laboring men of the country any rights which capital is bound to respect?"

WORKERS AND RADICALS

As labor reformers formulated an ideology and a course of action for their nascent movement, they found themselves drawn toward alliances with the Radicals at several significant points, despite the devotion of the latter to the manufacturers with whom the trade unions were in conflict and despite labor's qualms over the great war measures. . . .

The unique politics of Massachusetts were fashioned by the early growth of great textile corporations and the intellectual heritage of the state. The former, by installing commercial wealth directly in a commanding position in the state's manufacturing, created a phalanx of Conservative strength against which the more radical intellectuals and small manufacturers had to contend. Simultaneously, the textile corporations placed in the very heart of the state's labor force a large body of unskilled or semiskilled operatives, largely women, who were chronically unsuccessful in attempts to wring concessions from their employers by means of trade unions. Consequently, as early as the 1830's and 1840's these operatives looked primarily to the legislature for relief.

Thus, parallel to the trade unions of the craftsmen there developed a quite distinct movement of textile operatives aimed mainly at the reduction of working hours by legislative action. To influence the legislature they utilized frequent massive conventions and great petition campaigns. Such efforts readily attracted middle-class intellectuals, who often dominated the conventions, and ambitious politicians who championed the cause of the working girls against the "soulless corporations." As an overseer, probably from the Atlantic Mills, explained this phenomenon, the few young men in the mills (he should have excepted the mule spinners) aspired to become foremen, a goal which was usually reached only by "good conduct and obedience to the will of their employer." The rest of the help consisted of women. "Hence the element that asserts its right and insists upon it, is not there," the foreman concluded, "and it is only by outside pressure brought to bear upon the subordinate help, oftentimes by demagogues, that the thing [shorter hours] can be agitated, or anything accomplished in this direction." Thus, although the operatives, "with scarcely an exception," desired a ten-hour day, the overseers looked upon their efforts "with distrust, as designed more to advance the interest of some political aspirant than to benefit the operative or laboring classes." The prototype of this political spokesman was Benjamin F. Butler.

Finally, in the decades preceding the Civil War the native American workman of Massachusetts had imbibed deeply of the intellectual's culture of transcendentalism, abolitionism, and millennialist reform. Thomas Wentworth Higginson recalled that among the Transcendentalists in the early 1840's were both "the more refined votaries, who were indeed the most cultivated people of that time and place," and "a less educated contingent, known popularly as 'Come-Outers.' " These workmen, consumed with "the Second Advent delusion just then flourishing," were, said Higginson, the very heart of the antislavery movement, "which was not, like our modern civil service reform, strongest in the educated class, but was predominantly a people's movement . . . far stronger for a time in the factories and shoe-shops than in the pulpits or colleges." The Free Soil party in Massachusetts institutionalized the bond between the reformist professional or businessman and the native-born workman. Skilled workers in industrial towns like Worcester and shoe towns like Lynn and Abington provided the main base of support for that party. Henry Wilson, the "cobbler of Natick," so typified the political leader who emerged in these towns that Higginson could assert: "Radicalism went with the smell of leather. . . ."

Simultaneously, the great migration of Irish filled the bottom rungs of labor with immigrants and the textile mills with Irish women. The newcomers quickly allied themselves with the Democrats, but a fusion of the Free Soil and Democratic tickets in 1850 blended the causes of antislavery, trade unionism, and factory legislation. Benjamin Butler, Nathaniel Banks, Henry Wilson, George Boutwell, William S. Robinson, and Charles Sumner emerged as leaders of a coalition aimed at redistricting the state to diminish the conservative influence of Boston, making the ballot secret, and establishing by legislation a ten-hour day. But the coalition was soon shattered. From one side the Pierce administration, aided by the Boston Democrats, who feared a loss of influence under the proposed constitution, brought pressure on the Democrats to break ranks. From the other, nativism waxed increasingly strong among the Free Soilers until many found themselves in the Know-Nothing movement as allies of the very conservative Whigs they had formerly been fighting.

The mid-1850's were thus the time of Know-Nothing dominance. During this period the state's labor movement was thoroughly destroyed by the pitting of native trade unionist against immigrant factory hand and the divorcing of both from middle-class reformers. Democrat Butler and Know-Nothings Banks and Wilson became political enemies. To be sure, the reformist momentum from the coalition period was sufficient to give even the Know-Nothing-dominated legislature an impressive record of minor accomplishments, and the ultimate effect of the period was, in the words of labor reformer Edward H. Rogers, the "maturing of opinion among the leading workmen in the direction of the Republican Party." But the movement for shorter hours was immediately sidetracked in favor of investigations of nunneries, blocking a charter for Holy Cross College, and imposing literacy and residence requirements on the suffrage.

Most serious of all, this period isolated the Catholic Irish from Protestant society and all its reform currents. Abused, hounded, attacked by their neighbors in the name of saving the land from "Catholic bigotry," the Irish (especially in the factory towns outside Boston) withdrew as far as possible from the community around them and dealt with it only through the mediation of the priest and the Hunker Democrat. Thus the Catholic Boston *Pilot* concluded: "Co-operation for any length of time in important matters between *true* Catholics and *real* Protestants is morally impossible." The Baltimore Plenary Council of the hierarchy offered a special caution to Catholics attracted to trade unions. Though there was no ban on societies aimed only at "mutual help," warned the council, the faithful should beware "lest workers, who join these societies, be induced by the deceitful wiles of evil men to give less work than is due from them, against the laws of justice, or in any way injure the rights of those to whom they are subject."

No mass labor movement was possible in Massachusetts until this chasm of ethnic suspicion was bridged. The war provided the setting for this task, but the men who opened the way for Protestant and Catholic workingmen again to find a common cause were the Radical Republicans and the Fenians.

The operative center of Radicalism in the state was the "Bird Club," a group of ten to twenty political, intellectual, and business leaders who met each Saturday afternoon for dinner under the auspices of Frank W. Bird, a successful paper manufacturer of East Walpole. The Bird Club included such figures as Sumner, Wilson, John A. Andrew, Charles Francis Adams, Henry L. Pierce, Franklin B. Sanborn, Samuel G. Howe, Frank P. Stearns, and Elizur Wright. William S. Robinson, author of the "Warrington" columns in the Springfield *Republican,* was its favorite mouthpiece. At the close of the war, Butler was admitted to the charmed circle very briefly, prior to becoming its most prominent enemy. These men led the "Straight" Republicans, who opposed Bank's fusion with the Know-Nothings in the fifties, emerged (in Sanborn's phrase) as an "unrecognized cabinet" during Governor Andrew's administration, dominated the state during the 1860's and went *en bloc* to the Liberal Republican movement in 1872.

The Bird Club came to power with the election of John Andrew as governor in 1860. "The 'Straights' had it all their own way . . ." crowed Warrington, "a complete and glorious victory over Banks and the Know-Nothings, old Boston conservatism, and everything bad." More moderate than his closest political associates, the new governor quickly made his administration acceptable, even admired, in Boston commercial circles, while he relentlessly insisted on the major Radical demands: emancipation, arming of Negroes, civil rights. Astutely, he appointed prominent Democrats to military commands, among them Butler himself. Not only did Andrew insist that the legislature charter Holy Cross College, he dramatically attended commencement at the Catholic institution just as he did at Harvard. And when Patrick Guiney became the state's first prominent Irish Catholic Republican, the governor quickly appointed him an assistant district attorney, over the vehement protests of his party's nativists. Labor reformers were delighted to see W. S. Robinson, among the most prominent champions of factory legislation in Coalition days, given a sinecure as clerk of the House and elected secretary of the Republican State Committee, and his ally Alexander H. Bullock made Speaker of the House. During his three terms, Andrew soothed the antagonisms of the previous decade in the name of national unity and mobilized Conservative, Radical, and labor-reform forces in the state into an apparently harmonious phalanx, far more formidable than the Coalition had been.

The meaning of the change for the workers is apparent in the career of Edwin H. Rogers, a ship joiner in the Charlestown navy yards. This Medford-born artisan had taken part in the trade unionism, Know-Nothingism, and Republicanism which swept through the native workmen of the Boston area in the 1850's. He entered the navy yard during the war, when employment in the yards increased from a low of 245 men in June 1860 to 3,339 in February 1862. Rogers found grievances mounting among the workmen during 1863 and 1864 over both the administration of the draft and problems at work. The log of the yard records three work stoppages during 1863 and one instance (July 15) when the authorities "kept a force under arms to quell an expected riot." Wages were actually reduced after the initial surge of war production—a ship carpenter, for example, receiving $5.00 per day in April 1863, $4.00 in December 1864, and $3.50 (on "new work") in early 1865.

At the request of some of the yard workmen, Rogers ran for the state legislature in 1864 and was elected. In effect, he appeared in the capitol as spokesman for some 4,000 shipyard workers. To his delight, Rogers found the legislature to which he had been elected "largely comprised of men who had been engaged for twenty years in urging the various phases of Reform, all the way from the most intense Abolitionism, up through Free Soil, and the Republicanism, to the triumph in which we all unanimously joined, of voting for the national constitutional step which finally abolished slavery." Because there were but six "Copperheads" in the lower house, Rogers considered the soil ideal for the planting of labor reforms.

Meantime, Boston's labor leaders had determined that reduction of the hours of labor was the foremost reform on their agenda. In September 1863 the Machinists' and Blacksmith's International Union in convention in Boston adopted a resolution proposed by Ira Steward pledging it to campaign "until *over-work,* AS A SYSTEM, is prohibited. . . ." When

Steward and two fellow machinists approached the Boston Trades Assembly for help in this effort, the latter responded by establishing its own committee of three, appropriating $400 to match that already put up by the Machinists and Blacksmiths, and resolving that "a reduction of the number of hours for a day's work, be the cardinal point to which our movement ought to be directed. . . ."

Labor's new agitation fell on soil well prepared by the developments of the preceding decade and a half. Boston's delegates to the Radical German Convention of 1863, with Karl Heinzen as their spokesman, urged that assembly vigorously, if unsuccessfully, to demand a legal limit of eight hours to the working day. Prominent abolitionists endorsed the cause in the following three years, among them William F. Channing, Josiah Abbott, Rufus Wyman, and Ezra Heywood. From New York, Gerrit Smith sent Ira Steward a check annually to help his work. William Lloyd Garrison also sent a contribution and wrote in 1866 that he supported the labor reformers on "the same principle which has led me to abhor and oppose the unequalled oppression of the black laborers of the South." In short, the widely accepted notion that among the antislavery men of the Bay State Wendell Phillips alone was sympathetic to labor's cause is pure myth. For most of these doughty warriors the emancipation of the slaves meant simply that they took time off for one lusty cheer (or fervent prayer of thanks) before plunging back into the work of improving the world. Their spirit was typified by Abby Kelley Foster, whose farm was confiscated when she was quite elderly because she refused to pay taxes to a government which would not let her vote. This lady wrote her daughter in 1870: "Your father went to a County temperance meeting in Webster yesterday and this evening is to be at a debate on the labor question in town. We are all on the go. . . ."

The agitation bore fruit in March 1865 when John W. Mahan, a Boston lawyer who had served as a captain under Patrick Guiney in the Ninth Massachusetts, moved in the state House that the legislature establish a committee to investigate the hours of labor and the propriety of legislation on the subject. When the proposal passed, Speaker Bullock called Edward Rogers to his chamber and asked him to select the members of the committee. Senator Martin Griffin chaired the group, and Rogers and Mahan were among the members, as was Charles McLean, a millwright turned legislator who was to represent the State Labor Union of Massachusetts at the National Labor Congress of 1870.

In May the committee issued its report. Not only did all the workingmen interviewed want an eight-hour day, it declared, but such a change would not hurt industry. In fact, the shorter day would increase both the quantity and quality of production, thus benefiting the community as a whole. The issue, furthermore, involved a moral question higher than this economic one, namely, "the protection, preservation and advancement of man." Stating that "evidence presented almost challenged belief" and revealed the growth of "cringing servility and supineness . . . want of confidence and growing ignorance" among the working classes, who once had been characterized by "manly and sturdy independence," the report concluded: "The state is composed of *men,* and the interest, progress, and advancement of man is the foundation upon which the state rests."

The committee did not recommend any legislation. It merely proposed that the governor appoint a commission of five unpaid members to make a thorough study of hours of labor and conditions in industry and submit its findings to the next legislature. But the ideological significance of the report is immense. The foremost demand of labor reform had been given a clear sanction in terms of the nationalist and utilitarian formulas of the Radicals themselves. The eight-hour day was endorsed for the community good and to be advanced by state action for that end. Reducing hours of labor would hurt no one, help everyone. Thus there would be no need for one class to fight another over the subject. The state could act for the common weal.

For labor reformers the legislative report had an added significance. It provided them for the first time with an official document with which to support their case, and the fact that the report was unanimous lifted their spirits still higher. Ira Steward mailed a copy to Jonathan Fincher, inscribed with his own joyful couplet:

> Let all now cheer, who never cheered before,
> And those who always cheer, now cheer the more.

Thus by 1865 the Bay State's labor movement had emerged stronger than ever and once again made a common front with middle-class reformers. This relationship, as seen from the standpoint of the workingmen, was underscored by the prospectus of Boston's excellent labor paper, the *Daily Evening Voice.* The journal proclaimed its political position "RADICAL BUT INDEPENDENT" and explained: "It advocates the cause of the working classes, believing that the claims made in their behalf are not only consistent with, but conducive and essential to, the GENERAL WELFARE." The "independence, intelligence, and moral development of the masses," it continued, "are the only sure foundation of our Republican System of Government." For this reason, the prospectus concluded, the *Voice* was "friendly" to all causes tending toward these ends, especially "EQUAL SUFFRAGE," and it "recognizes no distinctions or preferences founded on RACE OR COLOR."

Simultaneous with these dramatic developments among basically Protestant Radicals and labor reformers was a remarkable intellectual awakening among the Irish Catholics. A labor movement as effective as that produced by Massachusetts in the 1860's and 1870's could never have been created by the Protestant workers alone—and it was not. By the late sixties increasing numbers of Catholics were emerging from behind the psyohological walls of the ghetto to joln, at tímês êvên to lead, labor organizations. The new and significant Irish figure in America was not the Ribbonman or Molly Maguire, for his mentality was simply anti-Protestant. His dividing line between friend and foe was ethnic, not political or class. Thus the most eloquent of Fenian writers remarked that "it was easier both in 1848 and in the Fenian times to make a rebel of an Orangeman than of a Ribbonman." The new figure was exemplified by William McLaughlin, leader of the huge shoemakers' union in 1869; his successor, Thomas Ryan; John Siney, guiding light of the anthracite miners' union; or Hugh Mc-Laughlin of Chicago, president of the iron puddlers' national organization after 1871. These men were leaders not of ethnic organizations but of workers' organizations. By the 1880's the majority of American labor unions would be headed by Catholics of Irish descent, but in the sixties this role was new for them. Furthermore, the new role of trade unionist subjected the traditional role of Catholic-Democrat to severe stress.

The battering ram that first breached the walls of ethnic isolation, however, was not labor reform, but the Irish nationalist movement. The confluence of the struggles for preservation of the American Union and for separation of Ireland from Britain roused the ardor of America's immigrants from Eiren as had (and could) no other issue, bringing them into conflict with their Church and party leaders here, and making them henceforth contributors, rather than obstacles, to the Radical and labor-reform trends of the decade.

The Fenian Brotherhood, founded in 1857, had four characteristics that set it apart from earlier, or later, separatist movements in Ireland. First, it was a secret society whose aim was, by use of armed force, to "make Ireland an independent Democratic Republic," in the words of the Fenian oath. Thus it rejected not only the parliamentary methods employed earlier by Daniel O'Connell's "Repealers" but also any home rule solution, which would have meant retaining either a tie to England or a monarchy.

In this respect they were similar to the Young Irelanders, who led the uprising of 1848. In fact, their leader, James Stephens, and many prominent Fenians on the American side of the ocean were erstwhile Young Irelanders, such as John O'Mahony and John Savage. But, secondly, they differed from the insurrectionists of '48 in that, while the latter were almost exclusively middle class, student, or gentry in background, the great strength of the Fenians was among industrial workers. The movement was purely nationalist in ideology and objectives, with scarcely a trace of awareness of "labor issues," but its recruits were workingmen and soldiers, and its strength was urban. Thus in the revolutionary history of Ireland it stands as a halfway house between the Liberals of 1848 and the Socialists of 1916. Third, the Fenians operated from bases on both sides of the Atlantic. The brotherhood was founded in America, but its founders sent emissaries to James Stephens asking him to take command in the Old Country. During the Civil War, an Irish Republican government was established in New York. America's Irish, operating from their sheltered sanctuary, were to supply the men, money, and materials to free the mother country.

Finally, the Fenians belonged to the same Western intellectual current of nineteenth-century nationalism as the Radical Republicans. Fenianism and Ribbonism, John O'Leary explained, had nothing in common but illegality. "Ribbonism is purely agrarian and religious . . . while Fenianism is purely national, i.e., anti-English." In fact, the fatal weakness of the Fenians (before their "New Departure" of the late 1870's) was that they were totally oblivious to the agrarian question in Ireland, expecting an armed and enlightened vanguard to carry the revolution alone—Blanqui style. But the crucial point is that since Ireland, like America, was a nation with several ethnic heritages, the Fenian doctrine of nationalism was necessarily akin to that of Elisha Mulford. It embraced men of all historical or ethnic backgrounds within the physical boundaries of the island as part of the nation. Thus Fenians boasted of their Protestant leaders in Belfast, or their Mormon organizer in Dublin. Symbolic of the whole movement was the fiery young Patrick "Pagan" O'Laoghari, who dubbed Christianity the curse of Ireland as it set brother against brother, and adopted for himself a pre-Christian "Irish" faith.

Inevitably, such a movement came into conflict with the clergy. "Hell is not hot enough nor eternity long enough to punish the Fenians," Bishop David Moriarity of Kerry is alleged to have cried, while the charge that James Stephens had enrolled in the French *Carbonari* echoed from pulpits all over the island. The congress of the brotherhood held in Chicago in 1863 responded to these attacks by resolving to "protest against, repudiate and resist all interference with the legitimate exercise of our civic and social privileges as freemen under the American constitution on the part of those who may claim to represent or to receive instructions from any foreign potentate or foreign official whatsoever," for to submit would render them "unworthy" of American citizenship. The Church saw red! Not only did this resolution express the basic error from which, said Pius IX, all others were derived (liberty of conscience), but its language resembled that of a Know-Nothing. The next year Archbishops Martin J. Spaulding of Philadelphia and J. B. Purcell of Cincinnati, and Bishops James Wood of Philadelphia and Duggan of Chicago all warned their flocks to avoid the Fenians. And in 1870 came the official denunciation from the Inquisition in Rome.

The most rapid growth of Fenian circles in America took place quite naturally inside the Union army. Colonel John O'Mahony, the American "Head Centre" of the organization, and Brigadier General Thomas Smith, head of the circles inside the army, pursued a policy of close collaboration with Lincoln's administration, which in turn encouraged Fenians to recruit among the soldiers as a counterweight to Democratic influence. Every Irish soldier was seen by O'Mahony as a trained recruit for the coming struggle in Ireland itself. Although the Fenian dream of 200,000 war veterans led by Philip E. Sheridan disembarking under arms in Cork was never to come to pass, by early 1866 there were in Ireland 150 former American army officers, ready to fight. James Stephens's military staff there consisted of five former captains and colonels of the United States Army, the most famous of whom were Colonel William G. Halpin, commander of a Kentucky regiment, and Colonel Richard O'Sullivan Burke of Meagher's Brigade.

Some Irish nationalists went so far as to become Republicans. Although both General Thomas F. Meagher and Colonel Patrick Guiney were Republicans and nationalists, neither was a member of the brotherhood. On the other hand, ardently Republican Colonel Richard O'Sullivan Burke headed a Fenian circle in the army, and S. B. Conover, who had served as a surgeon in the army, later became a carpetbagger United States senator from Florida and offered his Fenian colleagues the use of his state for prisoner rescue operations. The *Irish Republic,* put out in Chicago by Michael Scanlan and Reverend David Bell (a former Presbyterian minister from Ireland), was pro-Republican. Among Fenians who had never left the Old Sod, sympathy to the Republicans was practically unanimous, and all the exiles who crossed the Atlantic in the late 1860's and early 1870's promptly identified themselves with Grant's party. In 1867, Scanlan utilized such new arrivals as the nucleus for an Irish Republican Club in New York, presided over by Thomas J. Masterson, who was also prominent in the shoemakers' union and was later secretary of the Workingmen's Union of the city.

But party affiliation is not the crucial consideration here. Most American Fenians voted Democratic, and all welcomed the journalistic support given them by John Mitchel, a former Young Irelander who had become intensely pro-slavery and pro-secession in America. At least two veterans of the Confederate army served the Fenians in Ireland: Ohio-born John McCafferty and Irish-born Thomas F. Bourke, who at the outbreak of war was a resident of New Orleans. The important point is that during and immediately following the war, Irish soldiers and workmen in the United States flocked into the brotherhood. In Lawrence, Massachusetts, $5,200 and a hundred stands of arms were raised for the cause. Patrick Collins, organizing for the Fenians in the industrial towns of the state where the Irish population had been tightly repressed and withdrawn since the fifties, helped established seventy-five circles by June 1865.

The massive surge of men and money into the organization created both pressure for quick action and intense factional competition for leadership of the movement. Head Centre O'Mahony found himself challenged in 1865 by a faction led by William B. Roberts, a wealthy New York drygoods merchant, which drew considerable support from the more committed Democrats in the movement, who feared the partisan drift of the men around O'Mahony. It was the Roberts (or "Senate") faction that sponsored the plan to invade Canada and hold it hostage for the liberation of Ireland. While Stephens and his staff in Ireland protested in anguish against this diversion of funds and energy, two attacks on Canada were mounted, one on June 1, 1866, by the Roberts group, and the second six days later by supporters of the Head Centre, who dared not be left out of the action. Both were handily routed by the Canadian militia, and their participants interned by either Canadian or American authorities.

The comic-opera character of the Canadian fiasco tempts the historian to regard it, in Oscar Handlin's terms, as "a distraction for a time." It was certainly disastrous to the revolutionary schemes. British police raids in September 1865 had already crippled the conspiracy in Ireland. Their effectiveness made Stephens disregard the advice of his staff of Americans to strike in the Old Country early in 1866, and his failure to act in turn opened the way for advocates of the Canadian plan to come to the front, then for his own replacement in 1867 by Colonel Thomas J. Kelly, a veteran of Missionary Ridge. Kelly's effort to resuscitate the revolt in the Emerald Isle by bringing eight thousand Springfield rifles and a handful of experienced military men of several countries from New York aboard the *Erin's Hope* was frustrated by a watchful British coast guard. The futility of all this expenditure of lives and energy plunged the Fenians into hopeless factional bickering. On the other hand, Gustave-Paul Cluseret, a French participant in the uprising, significantly saw the Fenians' assault on Canada as the "last act of the War of Secession."

Certainly, for the Irish-American, the dual struggle against secession and against England left an important legacy. First, it offered the Republicans a marvelous opportunity to solicit Irish votes. The task of enforcing the neutrality laws against the invaders of Canada fell upon the Johnson administration. Despite the fact that General George G. Meade, who was sent to seal the border, carried out his task with a minimum of zeal, the commander of the Fenians in Buffalo blamed his defeat on "the extreme vigilance of the Government of the United States."

In the election campaign of 1866, Democrats often advocated Irish independence from the stump, but they had been boxed into the position of advising caution and apologizing for the actions of the President. Republican leaders, on the other hand, lionized the nationalists who had been imprisoned in Canada, and led by N. P. Banks and Robert Schenck, called upon the administration to recognize a lawful state of war between Ireland and England. In September the Fenian Congress responded by adopting resolutions of praise for the congressional Radicals and openly aiding their election campaign. Governor Oglesby of Illinois and even former Know-Nothing Schuyler Colfax were provided with speaking platforms at Fenian picnics. In New York the Fenian organ *Irish American* opposed the National Union candidate for governor, John A. Dix, and helped swing Irish votes to Republican Reuben Fenton. So alert did New York's Democrats become to the perils of this issue that their paper *Irish Citizen* in 1868 busily scotched rumors of new Fenian attacks on Canada, advised Irish voters that neither party would actually aid the independence of their homeland, and urged them to vote Democratic "on American grounds."

Secondly, the labor-reform press threw its support behind the Fenians. The *Daily Evening Voice* of Boston linked Ireland with America's Manifest Destiny, stating that "Americans fully endorse" the independence of Ireland and that the country was full of "combustible Irishmen" and "acquisitive Yankees" who might, if provoked (for instance, by the execution of captured Fenians), come to consider Canada a desirable "speculation in real estate." Labor's nomination of Irish nationalist Patrick Guiney for Congress that fall symbolically sealed the new alliance. Simultaneously, the International Workingmen's Association both in London and in New York made Irish independence a major demand. The subjugation of Ireland, explained Karl Marx, was the bulwark of England's landed aristocracy, the foremost source of cheap labor for England's *bourgeoisie,* and the root of national hostilities not only within the English working class but also between workers in England and those in the United States. Since England was the only country in the world where industry had matured sufficiently to make it ripe for socialism, he continued, "to hasten the social revolution in England is the most important object of the International Workingmen's Association. The sole means of hastening it is to make Ireland independent." In conclusion, he advised two organizers for the I.W.A. in New York: "*A coalition of the German workers with the Irish* (as well as with those English and American workers who are ready to do so) is the most important job you could start at the present time."

4.5

The General Strike:
Southern Blacks in the Civil War

W. E. B. DU BOIS

Slaves possessed a culture that they had established over time. Their acumen during the Civil War should cause us no surprise. Having initially waited to judge the North's intent, the slaves flocked to the Union Army everywhere it went in the South. This process insured their freedom and was vastly safer than revolting against their masters. This "general strike" had important effects on the war, especially when the "strikers" were actively used to fight. The quickness with which the blacks took advantage of the war to press their emancipation, and the skill with which they began to make the transition to free agriculture in Mississippi and on the Sea Islands all gives further evidence of the success they had had in establishing forms of community under the oppression of slavery.

W. E. B. Du Bois, *Black Reconstruction in America*, © 1935 (New York: Russell & Russell, Publishers, 1956), pp. 55–83. Reprinted and footnotes omitted by permission of the publisher.

The following books are suggested for further reading:

BENJAMIN QUARLES, *The Negro in the Civil War,* Boston: Little, Brown and Company, 1953.
WILLIE LEE ROSE, *Rehearsal for Reconstruction,* New York: Vintage Books, Random House, Inc., 1964.

How the Civil War meant emancipation and how the black worker won the war by a general strike which transferred his labor from the Confederate planter to the Northern invader, in whose army lines workers began to be organized as a new labor force.

When Edwin Ruffin, white-haired and mad, fired the first gun at Fort Sumter, he freed the slaves. It was the last thing he meant to do but that was because he was so typically a Southern oligarch. He did not know the real world about him. He was provincial and lived apart on his plantation with his servants, his books and his thoughts. Outside of agriculture, he jumped at conclusions instead of testing them by careful research. He knew, for instance, that the North would not fight. He knew that Negroes would never revolt.

And so war came. War is murder, force, anarchy and debt. Its end is evil, despite all incidental good. Neither North nor South had before 1861 the slightest intention of going to war. The thought was in many respects ridiculous. They were not prepared for war. The national army was small, poorly equipped and without experience. There was no file from which someone might draw plans of subjugation.

When Northern armies entered the South they became armies of emancipation. It was the last thing they planned to be. The North did not propose to attack property. It did not propose to free slaves. This was to be a white man's war to preserve the Union, and the Union must be preserved.

Nothing that concerned the amelioration of the Negro touched the heart of the mass of Americans nor could the common run of men realize the political and economic cost of Negro slavery. When, therefore, the Southern radicals, backed by political oligarchy and economic dictatorship in the most extreme form in which the world had seen it for five hundred years, precipitated secession, that part of the North that opposed the plan had to hunt for a rallying slogan to unite the majority in the North and in the West, and if possible, bring the Border States into an opposing phalanx.

Freedom for slaves furnished no such slogan. Not one-tenth of the Northern white population would have fought for any such purpose. Free soil was a much stronger motive, but it had no cogency in this contest because the Free Soilers did not dream of asking free soil in the South, since that involved the competition of slaves, or what seemed worse than that, of free Negroes. On the other hand, the tremendous economic ideal of keeping this great market for goods, the United States, together with all its possibilities of agriculture, manufacture, trade and profit, appealed to both the West and the North; and what was then much more significant, it appealed to the Border States.

> "To the flag we are pledged, all its foes we abhor,
> And we ain't for the nigger, but we are for the war."

The Border States wanted the cotton belt in the Union so that they could sell it their surplus slaves; but they also wanted to be in the same union with the North and West, where the profit of trade was large and increasing. The duty then of saving the Union became the great rallying cry of a war which for a long time made the Border States hesitate and confine secession to the far South. And yet they all knew that the only thing that really threatened the Union was slavery and the only remedy was Abolition.

If, now, the far South had had trained and astute leadership, a compromise could have been made which, so far as slavery was concerned, would have held the abnormal political power of the South intact, made the slave system impregnable for generations, and even given slavery practical rights throughout the nation.

Both North and South ignored in differing degrees the interests of the laboring classes. The North expected patriotism and union to make white labor fight; the South expected all white men to defend the slaveholders' property. Both North and South expected at most a sharp, quick fight and victory; more probably the South expected to secede peaceably, and then outside the Union, to impose terms which would include national recognition of slavery, new slave territory and new cheap slaves. The North expected that after a threat and demonstration to appease its "honor," the South would return with the right of slave property recognized and protected but geographically limited.

Both sections ignored the Negro. To the Northern masses the Negro was a curiosity, a sub-human minstrel, willingly and naturally a slave, and treated as well as he deserved to be. He had not sense enough to revolt and help Northern armies, even if Northern armies were trying to emancipate him, which they were not. The North shrank at the very thought of encouraging servile insurrection against the whites. Above all it did not propose to interfere with property. Negroes on the whole were considered cowards and inferior beings whose very presence in America was unfortunate. The abolitionists, it was true, expected action on the part of the Negro, but how much, they could not say. Only John Brown knew just how revolt had come and would come and he was dead.

Thus the Negro himself was not seriously considered by the majority of men, North or South. And yet from the very beginning, the Negro occupied the center of the stage because of very simple physical reasons: the war was in the South and in the South were 3,953,740 black slaves and 261,918 free Negroes. What was to be the relation of this mass of workers to the war? What did the war mean to the Negroes, and what did the Negroes mean to the war? There are two theories, both rather over-elaborated: the one that the Negro did nothing but faithfully serve his master until emancipation was thrust upon him; the other that the Negro immediately, just as quickly as the presence of Northern soldiers made it possible, left serfdom and took his stand with the army of freedom.

It must be borne in mind that nine-tenths of the four million black slaves could neither read nor write, and that the overwhelming majority of them were isolated on country plantations. Any mass movement under such circumstances must materialize slowly and painfully. What the Negro did was to wait, look and listen and try to see where his interest lay. There was no use in seeking refuge in an army which was not an army of freedom; and there was no sense in revolting against armed masters who were conquering the world. As soon, however, as it became clear that the Union armies would not or could not return fugitive slaves, and that the masters with all their fume and fury were uncertain of victory, the slave entered upon a general strike against slavery by the same methods that he had used during the period of the fugitive slave. He ran away to the first place of safety and offered his services to the Federal Army. So that in this way it was really true that he served his former master and served the emancipating army; and it was also true that this withdrawal and bestowal of his labor decided the war.

The South counted on Negroes as laborers to raise food and money crops for civilians and for the army, and even in a crisis, to be used for military purposes. Slave revolt was an ever-present risk, but there was no reason to think that a short war with the North would greatly increase this danger. Publicly, the South repudiated the thought of its slaves even wanting to be rescued. The New Orleans *Crescent* showed "the absurdity of the assertion of a general stampede of our Negroes." The London *Dispatch* was convinced that Negroes did not want to be free. "As for the slaves themselves, crushed with the wrongs of Dred Scott and Uncle Tom—most provoking—they cannot be brought to 'burn with revenge.' They are spies for their masters. They obstinately refuse to run away to liberty, outrage and starvation. They work in the fields as usual when the planter and overseer are away and only the white women are left at home."

Early in the war, the South had made careful calculation of the military value of slaves. The Alabama *Advertiser* in 1861 discussed the slaves as a "Military Element in the South." It said that

> The total white population of the eleven states now comprising the Confederacy is 5,000,000, and, therefore, to fill up the ranks of the proposed army, 600,000, about ten per cent of the entire white population, will be required. In any other country than our own such a draft could not be met, but the Southern states can furnish that number of men, and still not leave the material interest of the country in a suffering condition.

The editor, with fatuous faith, did not for a moment contemplate any mass movement against this program on the part of the slaves.

> Those who are incapacitated for bearing arms can oversee the plantations, and the Negroes can go on undisturbed in their usual labors. In the North, the case is different; the men who join the army of subjugation are the laborers, the producers and the factory operatives. Nearly every man from that section, especially those from the rural districts, leaves some branch of industry to suffer during his absence. The institution of slavery in the South alone enables her to place in the field a force much larger in proportion to her white population than the North, or indeed any country which is dependent entirely on free labor. The institution is a tower of strength to the South, particularly at the present crisis, and our enemies will be likely to find that the 'Moral Cancer' about which their orators are so fond of prating, is really one of the most effective weapons employed against the Union by the South.

Soon the South of necessity was moving out beyond this plan. It was no longer simply a question of using the Negroes at home on the plantation to raise food. They could be of even more immediate use, as military labor, to throw up breastworks, transport and prepare food and act as servants in camp. In the Charleston *Courier* of November 22, able-bodied hands were asked to be sent by their masters to work upon the defenses. "They would be fed and properly cared for."

In 1862, in Charleston, after a proclamation of martial law, the governor and counsel authorized the procuring of Negro slaves either by the planter's consent or by impressment "to work on the fortifications and defenses of Charleston harbor."

In Mississippi in 1862, permission was granted the Governor to impress slaves to work in New Iberia for salt, which was becoming the Confederacy's most pressing necessity. In Texas, a thousand Negroes were offered by planters for work on the public defenses.

By 1864, the matter had passed beyond the demand for slaves as military laborers and had come to the place where the South was seriously considering and openly demanding the use of Negroes as soldiers. Distinctly and inevitably, the rigor of the slave system in the South softened as war proceeded. Slavery showed in many if not all respects its best side. The harshness and the cruelty, in part, had to disappear, since there were left on the plantations mainly women and children, with only a few men, and there was a certain feeling and apprehension in the air on the part of the whites which led them to capitalize all the friendship and kindness which had existed between them and the slaves. No race could have responded to this so quickly and thoroughly as the Negroes. They felt pity and responsibility and also a certain new undercurrent of independence. Negroes were still being sold rather ostentatiously in Charleston and New Orleans, but the long lines of Virginia Negroes were not marching to the Southwest. In a certain sense, after the first few months everybody knew that slavery was done with; that no matter who won, the condition of the slave could never be the same after this disaster of war. And it was, perhaps, these considerations, more than anything else, that held the poised arm of the black man; for no one knew better than the South what a Negro crazed with cruelty and oppression and beaten back to the last stand could do to his oppressor.

The Southerners, therefore, were careful. Those who had been kind to their slaves assured them of the bad character of the Yankee and of their own good intentions.

Thus while the Negroes knew there were Abolitionists in the North they did not know their growth, their power or their intentions and they did hear on every side that the South was overwhelmingly victorious on the battlefield. On the other hand, some of the Negroes sensed what was beginning to happen. The Negroes of the cities, the Negroes who were being hired out, the Negroes of intelligence who could read and write, all began carefully to watch the unfolding of the situation. At the first gun of Sumter, the black mass began not to move but to heave with nervous tension and watchful waiting. Even before war was declared, a movement began across the border. Just before the war large numbers of fugitives slaves and free Negroes rushed into the North. It was estimated that two thousand left North Carolina alone because of rumors of war.

When W. T. Sherman occupied Port Royal in October, 1861, he had no idea that he was beginning emancipation at one of its strategic points. On the contrary, he was very polite and said that he had no idea of interfering with slaves. In the same way, Major General Dix, on seizing two counties of Virginia, was careful to order that slavery was not to be interfered with or slaves to be received into the line. Burnside went further, and as he brought his Rhode Island regiment through Baltimore in June, he courteously returned two Negroes who tried to run away with him. They were "supposed to be slaves," although they may have been free Negroes. On the 4th of July, Colonel Pryor of Ohio delivered an address to the people of Virginia in which he repudiated the accusation that the Northern army were Abolitionists.

> I desire to assure you that the relation of master and servant as recognized in your state shall be respected. Your authority over that species of property shall not in the least be interfered with. To this end, I assure you that those under my command have peremptory orders to take up and hold any Negroes found running about the camp without passes from their masters.

Halleck in Missouri in 1862 refused to let fugitive slaves enter his lines. Burnside, Buell, Hooker, Thomas Williams and McClellan himself, all warned their soldiers against receiving slaves and most of them permitted masters to come and remove slaves found within the lines.

The constant charge of Southern newspapers, Southern politicians and their Northern sympathizers, that the war was an abolition war, met with constant and indignant denial. Loyal newspapers, orators and preachers, with few exceptions, while advocating stringent measures for putting down the Rebellion, carefully disclaimed any intention of disturbing the "peculiar institution" of the South. The Secretary of State informed foreign governments, through our ministers abroad, that this was not our purpose. President Lincoln, in his earlier messages, substantially reiterated the statement. Leading generals, on entering Southern territory, issued proclamations to the same effect. One even promised to put down any slave insurrection "with an iron hand," while others took vigorous measures to send back the fugitives who sought refuge within their lines.

> In the early years of the war, if accounts do not err, during the entire period McClellan commanded the Army of the Potomac, "John Brown's Body" was a forbidden air among the regimental bands. The Hutchinsons were driven from Union camps for singing abolition songs, and in so far as the Northern army interested itself at all in the slavery question, it was by the use of force to return to their Southern masters fugitives seeking shelter in the Union lines. While the information they possessed, especially respecting the roads and means of communication, should have been of inestimable service to the Federals, they were not to be employed as laborers or armed as soldiers. The North avoided the appearance of a desire to raise the Negroes from the plane of chattels to the rank of human beings.

Here was no bid for the cooperation of either slaves or free Negroes. In the North, Negroes were not allowed to enlist and often refused with indignation.

Thus the weakness of the South temporarily became her strength. Her servile population, repulsed by Northern pro-slavery sentiment, remained at home engaged in agriculture, thus releasing her entire white population for active service in the field; while, on the other hand, the military resources of the North were necessarily diminished by the demands of labor.

It was as Frederick Douglass said in Boston in 1865, that the Civil War was begun

in the interests of slavery on both sides. The South was fighting to take slavery out of the Union, and the North fighting to keep it in the Union; the South fighting to get it beyond the limits of the United States Constitution, and the North fighting for the old guarantees;—both despising the Negro, both insulting the Negro.

It was, therefore, at first by no means clear to most of the four million Negroes in slavery what this war might mean to them. They crouched consciously and moved silently, listening, hoping and hesitating. The watchfulness of the South was redoubled. They spread propaganda: the Yankees were not only not thinking of setting them free, but if they did anything, they would sell them into worse slavery in the West Indies. They would drive them from even the scant comfort of the plantations into the highways and purlieus. Moreover, if they tried to emancipate the slaves, they would fail because they could not do this without conquest of the South. The South was unconquerable.

The South was not slow to spread propaganda and point to the wretched condition of fugitive Negroes in order to keep the loyalty of its indispensable labor force. The Charleston *Daily Courier* said February 18, 1863:

A company of volunteers having left Fayette County for the field of action, Mr. Nance sent two Negro boys along to aid the company. Their imaginations became dazzled with the visions of Elysian fields in Yankeedom and they went to find them. But Paradise was nowhere there, and they again sighed for home. The Yanks, however, detained them and cut off their ears close to their heads. These Negroes finally made their escape and are now at home with Mr. Nance in Pickens. They are violent haters of Yankees and their adventures and experiences are a terror to Negroes of the region, who learned a lesson from their brethren whose ears are left in Lincolndom!

The Charleston *Mercury,* May 8, 1862, said:

The Yankees are fortifying Fernandina (Florida) and have a large number of Negroes engaged on their works. Whenever the Negroes have an opportunity, they escape from their oppressors. They report that they are worked hard, get little rest and food and no pay.

The Savannah *Daily News* reports in 1862 that many stolen Negroes had been recaptured:

> The Yankees had married a number of the women and were taking them home with them. I have seen some who refused to go and others who had been forced off at other times who had returned.

It was a lovely dress parade of Alphonse and Gaston until the Negro spoiled it and in a perfectly logical way. So long as the Union stood still and talked, the Negro kept quiet and worked. The moment the Union army moved into slave territory, the Negro joined it. Despite all argument and calculation and in the face of refusals and commands, wherever the Union armies marched, appeared the fugitive slaves. It made no difference what the obstacles were, or the attitudes of the commanders. It was "like thrusting a walking stick into an anthill," says one writer. And yet the army chiefs at first tried to regard it as an exceptional and temporary matter, a thing which they could control, when as a matter of fact it was the meat and kernel of the war.

Thus as the war went on and the invading armies came on, the way suddenly cleared for the onlooking Negro, for his spokesmen in the North, and for his silent listeners in the South. Each step, thereafter, came with curious, logical and inevitable fate. First there were the fugitive slaves. Slaves had always been running away to the North, and when the North grew hostile, on to Canada. It was the safety valve that kept down the chance of insurrection in the South to the lowest point. Suddenly, now, the chance to run away not only increased, but after preliminary repulse and hesitation, there was actual encouragement.

Not that the government planned or foresaw this eventuality; on the contrary, having repeatedly declared the object of the war as the preservation of the Union and that it did not propose to fight for slaves or touch slavery, it faced a stampede of fugitive slaves.

Every step the Northern armies took then meant fugitive slaves. They crossed the Potomac, and the slaves of northern Virginia began to pour into the army and into Washington. They captured Fortress Monroe, and slaves from Virginia and even North Carolina poured into the army. They captured Port Royal, and the masters ran away, leaving droves of black fugitives in the hands of the Northern army. They moved down the Mississippi Valley, and if the slaves did not rush to the army, the army marched to the slaves. They captured New Orleans, and captured a great black city and a state of slaves.

What was to be done? They tried to send the slaves back, and even used the soldiers for recapturing them. This was all well enough as long as the war was a dress parade. But when it became real war, and slaves were captured or received, they could be used as much-needed laborers and servants by the Northern army.

This but emphasized and made clearer a truth which ought to have been recognized from the very beginning: The Southern worker, black and white, held the key to war; and of the two groups, the black worker raising food and raw materials held an even more strategic place than the white. This was so clear a fact that both sides should have known it. Fremont in Missouri took the logical action of freeing slaves of the enemy round about him by proclamation, and President Lincoln just as promptly repudiated what he had done. Even before that, General Butler in Virginia, commander of the Union forces at Fortress Monroe, met three slaves walking into his camp from the Confederate fortifications where they had been at work. Butler immediately declared these men "contraband of war" and put them to work in his own camp. More slaves followed, accompanied by their wives and children. The situation here was not quite so logical. Nevertheless, Butler kept the fugitives and freed them and let them do what work they could; and his action was approved by the Secretary of War.

> On May twenty-sixth, only two days after the one slave appeared before Butler, eight Negroes appeared; on the next day, forty-seven, of all ages and both sexes. Each day they continued to come by twenties, thirties and forties until by July 30th the number had reached nine hundred. In a very short while the number ran up into the thousands. The renowned Fortress took the name of the "freedom fort" to which the blacks came by means of a "mysterious spiritual telegraph."

In December, 1861, the Secretary of the Treasury, Simon Cameron, had written, printed and put into the mails his first report as Secretary of War without consultation with the President. Possibly he knew that his recommendations would not be approved, but "he recommended the general arming of Negroes, declaring that the Federals had as clear a right to employ slaves taken from the enemy as to use captured gunpowder." This report was recalled by the President by telegraph and the statements of the Secretary were modified. The incident aroused some unpleasantness in the cabinet.

The published report finally said:

> Persons held by rebels, under such laws, to service as slaves, may, however, be justly liberated from their constraint, and made more valuable in various employments, through voluntary and compensated service, than if confiscated as subjects of property.

Transforming itself suddenly from a problem of abandoned plantations and slaves captured while being used by the enemy for military purposes, the movement became a general strike against the slave system on the part of all who could find opportunity. The trickling streams of fugitives swelled to a flood. Once begun, the general strike of black and white went madly and relentlessly on like some great saga.

> Imagine, if you will, a slave population, springing from antecedent barbarism, rising up and leaving its ancient bondage, forsaking its local traditions and all the associations and attractions of the old plantation life, coming garbed in rags or in silks, with feet shod or bleeding, individually or in families and larger groups,—an army of slaves and fugitives, pushing its way irresistibly toward an army of fighting men, perpetually on the defensive and perpetually ready to attack. The arrival among us of these hordes was like the oncoming of cities. There was no plan in this exodus, no Moses to lead it. Unlettered reason or the mere inarticulate decision of instinct brought them to us. Often the slaves met prejudices against their color more bitter than any they had left behind. But their own interests were identical, they felt, with the objects of our armies; a blind terror stung them, an equally blind hope allured them, and to us they come.
>
> Even before the close of 1862, many thousands of blacks of all ages, ragged, with no possessions, except the bundles which they carried, had assembled at Norfolk, Hampton, Alexandria and Washington. Others, landless, homeless, helpless, in families and in multitudes, including a considerable number of wretched white people, flocked North from Tennessee, Kentucky, Arkansas and Missouri. All these were relieved in part by army rations, irregularly issued, and by volunteer societies of the North, which gained their money from churches and individuals in this country and abroad. In the spring of 1863, there were swarming crowds of Negroes and white refugees along the line of defense made between the armies of the North and South and reaching from Maryland to Virginia, along the coast from Norfolk to New Orleans. Soldiers and missionaries told of their virtues and vices, their joy and extreme suffering. The North was moved to an extraordinary degree, and endless bodies of workers and missionaries were organized and collected funds for materials.
>
> Rude barracks were erected at different points for the temporary shelter of the freedmen; but as soon as possible the colonies thus formed were broken up and the people encouraged to make individual contracts for labor upon neighboring plantations. In connection with the colonies, farms were cultivated which aided to meet the expenses. Hospitals were established at various points for the sick, of whom there were great numbers. The separation of families by the war, and illegitimate birth in consequence of slavery, left a great number of children practically in a state of orphanage.

This was the beginning of the swarming of the slaves, of the quiet but unswerving determination of increasing numbers no longer to work on Confederate plantations, and to seek the freedom of the Northern armies. Wherever the army marched and in spite of all obstacles came the rising tide of slaves seeking freedom. For a long time, their treatment was left largely to the discretion of the department managers; some welcomed them, some drove them away, some organized them for work. Gradually, the fugitives became organized and formed a great labor force for the army. Several thousand were employed as laborers, servants, and spies.

A special war correspondent of the New York *Tribune* writes:

> 'God bless the Negroes,' say I, with earnest lips. During our entire captivity, and after our escape, they were ever our firm, brave, unflinching friends. We never made an appeal to them they did not answer. They never hesitated to do us a service at the risk even of life, and under the most trying circumstances revealed a devotion and a spirit of self-sacrifice that was heroic. The magic word 'Yankee' opened all their hearts, and elicited the loftiest virtues. They were ignorant, oppressed, enslaved; but they always cherished a simple and a beautiful faith in the cause of the Union and its ultimate triumph, and never abandoned or turned aside from a man who sought food or shelter on his way to Freedom.

This whole move was not dramatic or hysterical, rather it was like the great unbroken swell of the ocean before it dashes on the reefs. The Negroes showed no disposition to strike the one terrible blow which brought black men freedom in Haiti and which in all history has been used by all slaves and justified. There were some plans for insurrection made by Union officers:

> The plan is to induce the blacks to make a simultaneous movement of rising, on the night of the 1st of August next, over the entire States in rebellion, to arm themselves with any and every kind of weapon that may come to hand, and commence operations by burning all the railroad and country bridges, and tear up railroad tracks, and to destroy telegraph lines, etc., and then take to the woods, swamps, or the mountains, where they may emerge as occasion may offer for provisions and for further depredations. No blood is to be shed except in self-defense. The corn will be ripe about the 1st of August and with this and hogs running in the woods, and by foraging upon the plantations by night, they can subsist. This is the plan in substance, and if we can obtain a concerted movement at the time named it will doubtless be successful.

Such plans came to naught for the simple reason that there was an easier way involving freedom with less risk.

The South preened itself on the absence of slave violence. Governor Walker of Florida said in his inaugural in 1865: "Where, in all the records of the past, does history present such an instance of steadfast devotion, unwavering attachment and constancy as was exhibited by the slaves of the South throughout the fearful contest that has just ended? The country invaded, homes desolated, the master absent in the army or forced to seek safety in flight and leave the mistress and her helpless infants unprotected, with every incitement to insubordination and instigation, to rapine and murder, no instance of insurrection, and scarcely one of voluntary desertion has been recorded."

The changes upon this theme have been rung by Southern orators many times since. The statement, of course, is not quite true. Hundreds of thousands of slaves were very evidently leaving their masters' homes and plantations. They did not wreak vengeance on unprotected women. They found an easier, more effective and more decent way to freedom. Men go wild and fight for freedom with bestial ferocity when they must—where there is no other way; but human nature does not deliberately choose blood—at least not black human nature. On the other hand, for every slave that escaped to the Union army, there were ten left on the untouched and inaccessible plantations.

Another step was logical and inevitable. The men who handled a spade for the Northern armies, the men who fed them, and as spies brought in information, could also handle a gun and shoot. Without legal authority and in spite of it, suddenly the Negro became a soldier. Later his services as soldier were not only permitted but were demanded to replace the tired and rebellious white men of the North. But as a soldier, the Negro must be free.

The North started out with the idea of fighting the war without touching slavery. They faced the fact, after severe fighting, that Negroes seemed a valuable asset as laborers, and they therefore declared them "contraband of war." It was but a step from that to attract and induce Negro labor to help the Northern armies. Slaves were urged and invited into the Northern armies; they became military laborers and spies; not simply military laborers, but laborers on the plantations, where the crops went to help the Federal army or were sold North. Thus wherever Northern armies appeared, Negro laborers came, and the North found itself actually freeing slaves before it had the slightest intention of doing so, indeed when it had every intention not to.

The experience of the army with the refugees and the rise of the departments of Negro affairs were a most interesting, but unfortunately little studied, phase of Reconstruction. Yet it contained in a sense the key to the understanding of the whole situation. At first, the rush of the Negroes from the plantations came as a surprise and was variously interpreted. The easiest thing to say was that Negroes were tired of work and wanted to live at the expense of the government; wanted to travel and see things and places. But in contradiction to this was the extent of the movement and the terrible suffering of the refugees. If they were seeking peace and quiet, they were much better off on the plantations than trailing in the footsteps of the army or squatting miserably in the camps. They were mistreated by the soldiers; ridiculed; driven away, and yet they came. They increased with every campaign, and as a final gesture, they marched with Sherman from Atlanta to the sea, and met the refugees and abandoned human property on the Sea Islands and the Carolina Coast.

This was not merely the desire to stop work. It was a strike on a wide basis against the conditions of work. It was a general strike that involved directly in the end perhaps a half million people. They wanted to stop the economy of the plantation system, and to do that they left the plantations. At first, the commanders were disposed to drive them away, or to give them quasi-freedom and let them do as they pleased with the nothing that they possessed. This did not work. Then the commanders organized relief and afterward, work. This came to the attention of the country first in Pierce's "Ten Thousand Clients." Pierce of Boston had worked with the refugees in Virginia under Butler, provided them with food and places to live, and given them jobs and land to cultivate. He was successful. He came from there, and, in conjunction with the Treasury Department, began the work on a vaster scale at Port Royal. Here he found the key to the situation. The Negroes were willing to work and did work, but they wanted land to work, and they wanted to see and own the results of their toil. It was here and in the West and the South that a new vista opened. Here was a chance to establish an agrarian democracy in the South: peasant holders of small properties, eager to work and raise crops, amenable to suggestion and general direction. All they needed was honesty in treatment, and education. Wherever these conditions were fulfilled, the result was little less than phenomenal. This was testified to by Pierce in the Carolinas, by Butler's agents in North Carolina, by the experiment of the Sea Islands, by Grant's department of Negro affairs under Eaton, and by Banks' direction of labor in Louisiana. It is astonishing how this army of striking labor furnished in time 200,000 Federal soldiers whose evident ability to fight decided the war.

General Butler went from Virginia to New Orleans to take charge of the city newly captured in April, 1862. Here was a whole city half-filled with blacks and mulattoes, some of them wealthy free Negroes and soldiers who came over from the Confederate side and joined the Federals.

Perhaps the greatest and most systematic organizing of fugitives took place in New Orleans. At first, Butler had issued orders that no slaves would be received in New Orleans. Many planters were unable to make slaves work or to support them, and sent them back of the Federal lines, planning to reclaim them after the war was over. Butler emancipated these slaves in spite of the fact that he knew this was against Lincoln's policy. As the flood kept coming, he seized abandoned sugar plantations and began to work them with Negro labor for the benefit of the government.

By permission of the War Department, and under the authority of the Confiscation Act, Butler organized colonies of fugitives, and regulated employment. His brother, Colonel Butler, and others worked plantations, hiring the Negro labor. The Negroes stood at Butler's right hand during the trying time of his administration, and particularly the well-to-do free Negro group were his strongest allies. He was entertained at their tables and brought down on himself the wrath and contempt, not simply of the South, but even of the North. He received the black regiment, and kept their black officers, who never forgot him. Whatever else he might have been before the war, or proved to be afterwards, "the colored people of Louisiana under the proper sense of the good you have done to the African race in the United States, beg leave to express to you their gratitude."

From 1862 to 1865, many different systems of caring for the escaped slaves and their families in this area were tried. Butler and his successor, Banks, each sought to provide for the thousands of destitute freedmen with medicine, rations and clothing. When General Banks took command, there was suffering, disease and death among the 150,000 Negroes. On January 30, 1863, he issued a general order making labor on public works and elsewhere compulsory for Negroes who had no means of support.

Just as soon, however, as Banks tried to drive the freedmen back to the plantations and have them work under a half-military slave régime, the plan failed. It failed, not because the Negroes did not want to work, but because they were striking against these particular conditions of work. When, because of wide protest, he began to look into the matter, he saw a clear way. He selected Negroes to go out and look into conditions and to report on what was needed, and they made a faithful survey. He set up a little state with its department of education, with its landholding and organized work, and after experiment it ran itself. More and more here and up the Mississippi Valley, under other commanders and agents, experiments extended and were successful.

Further up the Mississippi, a different system was begun under General Grant. Grant's army in the West occupied Grand Junction, Mississippi, by November, 1862. The usual irregular host of slaves then swarmed in from the surrounding country. They begged for protection against recapture, and they, of course, needed food, clothing and shelter. They could not now be reënslaved through army aid, yet no provision had been made by anybody for their sustenance. A few were employed as teamsters, servants, cooks and scouts, yet it seemed as though the vast majority must be left to freeze and starve, for when the storms came with the winter months, the weather was of great severity.

Grant determined that Negroes should perform many of the camp duties ordinarily done by soldiers; that they should serve as fatigue men in the departments of the surgeon general, quartermaster, and commissary, and that they should help in building roads and earthworks. The workmen worked in the camp kitchens and as nurses in the hospitals. Grant said, "It was at this point where the first idea of the Freedmen's Bureau took its origin."

Grant selected as head of his Department of Negro Affairs, John Eaton, chaplain of the Twenty-Seventh Ohio Volunteers, who was soon promoted to the colonelcy of a colored regiment, and later for many years was a Commissioner of the United States Bureau of Education. He was then constituted Chief of Negro Affairs for the entire district under Grant's jurisdiction.

> I hope I may never be called on again to witness the horrible scenes I saw in those first days of the history of the freedmen in the Mississippi Valley. Assistants were hard to get, especially the kind that would do any good in our camps. A detailed soldier in each camp of a thousand people was the best that could be done. His duties were so onerous that he ended by doing nothing. . . . In reviewing the condition of the people at that time, I am not surprised at the marvelous stories told by visitors who caught an occasional glimpse of the misery and wretchedness in these camps. . . . Our efforts to do anything for these people, as they herded together in masses, when founded on any expectation that they would help themselves, often failed; they had become so completely broken down in spirit, through suffering, that it was almost impossible to arouse them.
>
> Their condition was appalling. There were men, women and children in every stage of disease or decrepitude, often nearly naked, with flesh torn by the terrible experiences of their escapes. Sometimes they were intelligent and eager to help themselves; often they were bewildered or stupid or possessed by the wildest notions of what liberty might mean— expecting to exchange labor, and obedience to the will of another, for idleness and freedom from restraint. Such ignorance and perverted notions produced a veritable moral chaos. Cringing deceit, theft, licentiousness— all the vices which slavery inevitably fosters—were hideous companions of nakedness, famine, and disease. A few had profited by the misfortunes of the master and were jubilant in their unwonted ease and luxury, but these stood in lurid contrast to the grimmer aspects of the tragedy—the women in travail, the helplessness of childhood and of old age, the horrors of sickness and of frequent death. Small wonder that men paused in bewilderment and panic, foreseeing the demoralization and infection of the Union soldier and the downfall of the Union cause.

There were new and strange problems of social contact. The white soldiers, for the most part, were opposed to serving Negroes in any manner, and were, even unwilling to guard the camps where they were segregated or protect them against violence. "To undertake any form of work for the contrabands, at that time, was to be forsaken by one's friends and to pass under a cloud."

There was, however, a clear economic basis upon which the whole work of relief and order and subsistence could be placed. All around Grand Junction were large crops of ungathered corn and cotton. These were harvested and sold North and the recipts were placed to the credit of the government. The army of fugitives were soon willing to go to work; men, women and children. Wood was needed by the river steamers and woodcutters were set at work. Eaton fixed the wages for this industry and kept accounts with the workers. He saw to it that all of them had sufficient food and clothing, and rough shelter was built for them. Citizens round about who had not abandoned their plantations were allowed to hire labor on the same terms as the government was using it. Very soon freedmen became self-sustaining and gave little trouble. They began to build themselves comfortable cabins, and the government constructed hospitals for the sick. In the case of the sick and dependent, a tax was laid on the wages of workers. At first it was thought the laborers would object, but, on the contrary, they were perfectly willing and the imposition of the tax compelled the government to see that wages were promptly paid. The freedmen freely acknowledged that they ought to assist in helping bear the burden of the poor, and were flattered by having the government ask their help. It was the reaction of a new labor group, who, for the first time in their lives, were receiving money in payment for their work. Five thousand dollars was raised by this tax for hospitals, and with this money tools and property were bought. By wholesale purchase, clothes, household goods and other articles were secured by the freedmen at a cost of one-third of what they might have paid the stores. There was a rigid system of accounts and monthly reports through army officials.

In 1864, July 5, Eaton reports:

> These freedmen are now disposed of as follows: In military service as soldiers, laundresses, cooks, officers' servants, and laborers in the various staff departments, 41,150; in cities on plantations and in freedmen's villages and cared for, 72,500. Of these 62,300 are entirely self-supporting—the same as any industrial class anywhere else—as planters, mechanics, barbers, hackmen, draymen, etc., conducting enterprises on their own responsibility or working as hired laborers. The remaining 10,200 receive subsistence from the government. 3,000 of them are members of families whose heads are carrying on plantations and have under cultivation 4,000 acres of cotton. They are to pay the government for their sustenance from the first income of the crop. The other 7,200 include the paupers—that is to say, all Negroes over and under the self-supporting age, the crippled and sick in hospital, of the 113,650 and those engaged in their care. Instead of being unproductive, this class has now under cultivation 500 acres of corn, 790 acres of vegetables and 1,500 acres of cotton, besides working at wood-chopping and other industries. There are reported in the aggregate over 100,000 acres of cotton under cultivation. Of these about 7,000 acres are leased and cultivated by blacks. Some Negroes are managing as high as 300 or 400 acres.

The experiment at Davis Bend, Mississippi, was of especial interest. The place was occupied in November and December, 1864, and private interests were displaced and an interesting socialistic effort made with all the property under the control of the government. The Bend was divided into districts with Negro sheriffs and judges who were allowed to exercise authority under the general control of the military officers. Petty theft and idleness were soon reduced to a minimum and "the community distinctly demonstrated the capacity of the Negro to take care of himself and exercise under honest and competent direction the functions of self-government."

When General Butler returned from Louisiana and resumed command in Virginia and North Carolina, he established there a Department of Negro Affairs, with the territory divided into districts under superintendents and assistants. Negroes were encouraged to buy land, build cabins and form settlements, and a system of education was established. In North Carolina, under Chaplain Horace James, the poor, both black and white, were helped; the refugees were grouped in small villages and their work systematized, and enlisted men taught in the schools, followed by women teachers from the North. Outside of New Bern, North Carolina, about two thousand freedmen were settled and 800 houses erected. The department at Port Royal continued. The Negroes showed their capacity to organize labor and even to save and employ a little capital. The government built 21 houses for the people on Edisto Island. The carpenters were Negroes under a Negro foreman. There was another village of improved houses near Hilton Head.

> Next as to the development of manhood: this has been shown in the first place in the prevalent disposition to acquire land. It did not appear upon our first introduction to these people, and they did not seem to understand us when we used to tell them that we wanted them to own land. But it is now an active desire. At the recent tax sales, six out of forty-seven plantations sold were bought by them, comprising two thousand five hundred and ninety-five acres, sold for twenty-one hundred and forty-five dollars. In other cases, the Negroes had authorized the superintendent to bid for them, but the land was reserved by the United States. One of the purchases was that made by Harry, noted above. The other five were made by the Negroes on the plantations, combining the funds they had saved from the sale of their pigs, chickens and eggs, and from the payments made to them for work,—they then dividing off the tract peaceably among themselves. On one of these, where Kit, before mentioned, is the leading spirit, there are twenty-three fieldhands. They have planted and are cultivating sixty-three acres of cotton, fifty of corn, six of potatoes, with as many more to be planted, four and a half of cowpeas, three of peanuts, and one and a half of rice. These facts are most significant.

Under General Saxton in South Carolina, the Negroes began to buy land which was sold for non-payment of taxes. Saxton established regulations for the cultivation of several abandoned Sea Islands and appointed local superintendents.

> By the payment of moderate wages, and just and fair dealing with them, I produced for the government over a half million dollars' worth of cot-

ton, besides a large amount of food beyond the needs of the laborers. These island lands were cultivated in this way for two years, 1862 and 1863, under my supervision, and during that time I had about 15,000 colored freedmen of all ages in my charge. About 9,000 of these were engaged on productive labor which relieved the government of the support of all except newly-arrived refugees from the enemy's lines and the old and infirm who had no relations to depend upon. The increase of industry and thrift of the freedmen was illustrated by their conduct in South Carolina before the organization of the Freedmen's Bureau by the decreasing government expenditure for their support. The expense in the department of the South in 1863 was $41,544, but the monthly expense of that year was steadily reduced, until in December it was less than $1,000.

Into this fairly successful land and labor control was precipitated a vast and unexpected flood of refugees from previously untouched strongholds of slavery. Sherman made his march to the sea from Atlanta, cutting the cotton kingdom in two as Grant had invaded it along the Mississippi.

The first intimation given me that many of the freedmen would be brought hither from Savannah came in the form of a request from the General that I would "call at once to plan the reception of seven hundred who would be at the wharf in an hour." This was Christmas day, and at 4 P.M., we had seven hundred—mainly women, old men and children before us. A canvas since made shows that half of them had traveled from Macon, Atlanta and even Chattanooga. They were all utterly destitute of blankets, stockings or shoes; and among the seven hundred there were not fifty articles in the shape of pots or kettles, or other utensils for cooking, no axes, very few coverings for many heads, and children wrapped in the only article not worn in some form by the parents.

Frantic appeals went out for the mass of Negro refugees who followed him.

A few days after Sherman entered Savannah, Secretary of War Stanton came in person from Washington. He examined the condition of the liberated Negroes found in that city. He assembled twenty of those who were deemed their leaders. Among them were barbers, pilots and sailors, some ministers, and others who had been overseers on cotton and rice plantations. Mr. Stanton and General Sherman gave them a hearing.

As a result of this investigation into the perplexing problems as to what to do with the growing masses of unemployed Negroes and their families, General Sherman issued his epoch-making Sea Island Circular, January 18, 1865. In this paper, the islands from Charleston south, the abandoned rice fields along the rivers for thirty miles back from the sea and the country bordering the St. John's River, Florida, were reserved for the settlement of the Negroes made free by the acts of war and the proclamation of the President.

General Rufus Saxton was appointed Inspector of Settlements and

Plantations and was required to make proper allotments and give possessory titles and defend them until Congress should confirm his actions. It was a bold move. Thousands of Negro families were distributed under this circular, and the freed people regarded themselves for more than six months as in permanent possession of these abandoned lands. Taxes on the freedmen furnished most of the funds to run these first experiments. On all plantations, whether owned or leased, where freedmen were employed, a tax of one cent per pound on cotton and a proportional amount on all other products was to be collected as a contribution in support of the helpless among the freed people. A similar tax, varying with the value of the property, was levied by the government upon all leased plantations in lieu of rent.

Saxton testified:

> General Sherman's Special Field Order No. 15 ordered their colonization on forty-acre tracts, and in accordance with which it is estimated some forty thousand were provided with homes. Public meetings were held, and every exertion used by those whose duty it was to execute this order to encourage emigration to the Sea Islands, and the faith of the government was solemnly pledged to maintain them in possession. The greatest success attended the experiment, and although the planting season was very far advanced before the transportation to carry the colonists to the Sea Islands could be obtained, and the people were destitute of animals and had but few agricultural implements and the greatest difficulty in procuring seeds, yet they went out, worked with energy and diligence to clear up the ground run to waste by three years' neglect; and thousands of acres were planted and provisions enough were raised for those who were located in season to plant, besides a large amount of sea island cotton for market. The seizure of some 549,000 acres of abandoned land, in accordance with the act of Congress and orders from the head of the bureau for the freedman and refugees, still further strengthened these ignorant people in the conviction that they were to have the lands of their late masters; and, with the other reasons before stated, caused a great unwillingness on the part of the freedmen to make any contracts whatever. But this refusal arises from no desire on their part to avoid labor, but from the causes above stated. . . .
>
> To test the question of their forethought and prove that some of the race at least thought of the future, I established in October, 1864, a savings bank for the freedmen of Beaufort district and vicinity. More than $240,000 had been deposited in this bank by freedmen since its establishment. I consider that the industrial problem has been satisfactorily solved at Port Royal, and that, in common with other races, the Negro has industry, prudence, forethought, and ability to calculate results. Many of them have managed plantations for themselves, and show an industry and sagacity that will compare favorably in their results—making due allowances—with those of white men.

Eventually, General Saxton settled nearly 30,000 Negroes on the Sea Islands and adjacent plantations and 17,000 were self-supporting within a year. While 12,000 or 13,000 were still receiving rations, it was distinctly understood that they and their farms would be held responsible for the payment. In other such cases, the government had found that such a debt was a "safe and short one."

Negroes worked fewer hours and had more time for self-expression. Exports were less than during slavery. At that time the Negroes were mere machines run with as little loss as possible to the single end of making money for their masters. Now, as it was in the West Indies, emancipation had enlarged the Negro's purchasing power, but instead of producing solely for export, he was producing to consume. His standard of living was rising.

Along with this work of the army, the Treasury Department of the United States Government was bestirring itself. The Secretary of the Treasury, Salmon P. Chase, early in 1862, had his attention called to the accumulation of cotton on the abandoned Sea Islands and plantations, and was sure there was an opportunity to raise more. He, therefore, began the organization of freedmen for cotton raising, and his successor, William Pitt Fessenden, inaugurated more extensive plans for the freedmen in all parts of the South, appointing agents and organizing freedmen's home colonies.

On June 7, 1862, Congress held portions of the states in rebellion responsible for a direct tax upon the lands of the nation, and in addition Congress passed an act authorizing the Secretary of the Treasury to appoint special agents to take charge of captured and abandoned property. Military officers turned over to the Treasury Department such property, and the plantations around Port Royal and Beaufort were disposed of at tax sales. Some were purchased by Negroes, but the greater number went to Northerners. In the same way in North Carolina, some turpentine farms were let to Negroes, who managed them, or to whites who employed Negroes. In 1863, September 11, the whole Southern region was divided by the Treasury Department into five special agencies, each with a supervising agent for the supervision of abandoned property and labor.

Early in 1863, General Lorenzo Thomas, the adjutant general of the army, was organizing colored troops along the Mississippi River. After consulting various treasury agents and department commanders, including General Grant, and having also the approval of Mr. Lincoln, he issued from Milliken's Bend, Louisiana, April 15th, a lengthy series of instruction covering the territory bordering the Mississippi and including all the inhabitants.

He appointed three commissioners, Messrs. Field, Shickle and Livermore, to lease plantations and care for the employees. He sought to encourage private enterprises instead of government colonies; but he fixed the wages of able-bodied men over fifteen years of age at $7 per month, for able-bodied women $5 per month, for children twelve to fifteen years, half price. He laid a tax for revenue of $2 per 400 pounds of cotton, and five cents per bushel on corn and potatoes.

This plan naturally did not work well, for the lessees of plantations proved to be for the most part adventurers and speculators. Of course such men took advantage of the ignorant people. The commissioners themselves seem to have done more for the lessees than for the laborers; and, in fact, the wages were from the beginning so fixed as to benefit and enrich the employer. Two dollars per month was charged against each of the employed, ostensibly for medical attendance, but to most plantations thus leased no physician or medicine ever came, and there were other attendant cruelties which avarice contrived.

On fifteen plantations leased by the Negroes themselves in this region there was notable success, and also a few other instances in which humanity and good sense reigned; the contracts were generally carried out. Here the Negroes were contented and grateful, and were able to lay by small gains. This plantation arrangement along the Mississippi under the commissioners as well as the management of numerous infirmary camps passed, about the close of 1863, from the War to the Treasury Department. A new commission or agency with Mr. W. P. Mellon of the treasury at the head established more careful and complete regulations than those of General Thomas. This time it was done decidedly in the interest of the laborers.

July 2, 1864, an Act of Congress authorized the treasury agents to seize and lease for one year all captured and abandoned estates and to provide for the welfare of former slaves. Property was declared abandoned when the lawful owner was opposed to paying the revenue. The Secretary of the Treasury, Fessenden, therefore issued a new series of regulations relating to freedmen and abandoned property. The rebellious States were divided into seven districts, with a general agent and special agents. Certain tracts of land in each district were set apart for the exclusive use and working of the freedmen. These reservations were called Freedmen Labor Colonies, and were under the direction of the superintendents. Schools were established, both in the Home Colonies and in the labor colonies. This new system went into operation the winter of 1864–1865, and worked well along the Atlantic Coast and Mississippi Valley. In the Department of the Gulf, however, there was discord between the treasury agents and the military authorities, and among the treasury officials themselves. The treasury agents, in many cases, became corrupt, but these regulations remained in force until the Freedmen's Bureau was organized in 1865.

By 1865, there was strong testimony as to the efficiency of the Negro worker. "The question of the freedmen being self-supporting no longer agitated the minds of careful observers."

Carl Schurz felt warranted in 1865 in asserting:

Many freedmen—not single individuals, but whole "plantation gangs"—are working well; others are not. The difference in their efficiency coincides in a great measure with a certain difference in the conditions under which they live. The conclusion lies near, that if the conditions under which they work well become general, their efficiency as free laborers will become general also, aside from individual exceptions. Certain it is, that by far the larger portion of the work done in the South is done by freedmen!

Whitelaw Reid said in 1865:

Whoever has read what I have written about the cotton fields of St. Helena will need no assurance that another cardinal sin of the slave, his laziness—"inborn and ineradicable," as we were always told by his masters —is likewise disappearing under the stimulus of freedom and necessity. Dishonesty and indolence, then, were the creation of slavery, not the necessary and constitutional faults of the Negro character.

Returning from St. Helena in 1865, Doctor Richard Fuller was asked what he thought of the experiment of free labor, as exhibited among his former slaves, and how it contrasted with the old order of things. "I never saw St. Helena look so well," was his instant reply; "never saw as much land there under cultivation—never saw the same general evidences of prosperity, and never saw Negroes themselves appearing so well or so contented." Others noticed, however, that the islands about Beaufort were in a better condition than those nearer the encampments of the United States soldiers. Wherever poultry could be profitably peddled in the camps, cotton had not been grown, nor had the Negroes developed, so readily, into industrious and orderly communities.

Similar testimony came from the Mississippi Valley and the West, and from Border States like Virginia and North Carolina.

To the aid of the government, and even before the government took definite organized hold, came religious and benevolent organizations. The first was the American Missionary Association, which grew out of the organization for the defense of the Negroes who rebelled and captured the slave ship *Amistad* and brought it into Connecticut in 1837. When this association heard from Butler and Pierce, it responded promptly and had several representatives at Hampton and South Carolina before the end of the year 1861. They extended their work in 1862–1863, establishing missions down the Atlantic Coast, and in Missouri, and along the Mississippi. By 1864, they had reached the Negroes in nearly all the Southern States. The reports of Pierce, Dupont and Shermon aroused the whole North. Churches and missionary societies responded. The Friends contributed. The work of the Northern benevolent societies began to be felt, and money, clothing and, finally, men and women as helpers and teachers came to the various centers.

The scope of our work was greatly enlarged by the arrival of white refugees—a movement which later assumed very large proportions. As time went on Cairo (Illinois) became the center of our activities in this direction. It was the most northerly of any of our camps, and served as the portal through which thousands of poor whites and Negroes were sent into the loyal states as fast as opportunities offered for providing them with homes and employment. Many of these became permanent residents; some were sent home by Union soldiers to carry on the work in the shop or on the farm which the war had interrupted. It became necessary to have a superintendent at Cairo and facilities for organizing the bands of refugees who were sent North by the army. There was an increasing demand for work.

New organizations arose, and an educational commission was organized in Boston, suggested by the reports of Pierce, and worked chiefly in South Carolina. Afterward, it became the New England Freedmen's Aid Society and worked in all the Southern States. February 22, 1862, the National Freedmen's Relief Association was formed in New York City. During the first year, it worked on the Atlantic Coast, and then broadened to the whole South. The Port Royal Relief Committee of Philadelphia, later known as the Pennsylvania Freedmen's Relief Association, the National Freedmen's Relief Association of the District of Columbia, the Contraband Relief Association of Cincinnati, afterward called the Western Freedmen's Commission, the Women's Aid Association of Philadelphia and the Friends' Associations, all arose and worked. The number increased and extended into the Northwest. The Christian Commission, organized for the benefit of soldiers, turned its attention to Negroes. In England, at Manchester and London, were Freedmen's Aid Societies which raised funds; and funds were received from France and Ireland.

Naturally, there was much rivalry and duplication of work. A union of effort was suggested in 1862 by the Secretary of the Treasury and accomplished March 22, 1865, when the American Freedmen's Union Commission was incorporated, with branches in the chief cities. Among its officers were Chief Justice Chase and William Lloyd Garrison. In 1861, two large voluntary organizations to reduce suffering and mortality among the freedmen were formed. The Western Sanitary Commission at St. Louis, and the United States Sanitary Commission at Washington, with branches in leading cities then began to relieve the distress of the freedmen. Hospitals were improved, supplies distributed, and Yeatman's plan for labor devised. Destitute white refugees were helped to a large extent. But even then, all of these efforts reached but a small portion of the mass of people freed from slavery.

Late in 1863, President Yeatman of the Western Sanitary Commission visited the freedmen in the Mississippi Valley. He saw the abuses of the leasing system and suggested a plan for organizing free labor and leasing plantations. It provided for a bureau established by the government to take charge of leasing land, to secure justice and freedom to the freedmen; hospital farms and homes for the young and aged were to be established; schools with compulsory attendance were to be opened. Yeatman accompanied Mellon, the agent of the department, to Vicksburg in order to inaugurate the plan and carry it into effect. His plan was adopted by Mellon, and was, on the whole, the most satisfactory.

Thus, confusion and lack of system were the natural result of the general strike. Yet, the Negroes had accomplished their first aim in those parts of the South dominated by the Federal army. They had largely escaped from the plantation discipline, were receiving wages as free laborers, and had protection from violence and justice in some sort of court.

About 20,000 of them were in the District of Columbia; 100,000 in Virginia; 50,000 in North Carolina; 50,000 in South Carolina, and as many more each in Georgia and Louisiana. The Valley of the Mississippi was filled with settlers under the Treasury Department and the army. Here were nearly 500,000 former slaves. But there were 3,500,000 more. These Negroes needed only the assurance that they would be freed and the opportunity of joining the Northern army. In larger and larger numbers, they filtered into the armies of the North. And in just the proportion that the Northern armies became in earnest, and proposed actually to force the South to stay in the Union, and not to make simply a demonstration, in just such proportion the Negroes became valuable as laborers, and doubly valuable as withdrawing labor from the South. After the first foolish year when the South woke up to the fact that there was going to be a real, long war, and the North realized just what war meant in blood and money, the whole relation of the North to the Negro and the Negro to the North changed.

The position of the Negro was strategic. His was the only appeal which would bring sympathy from Europe, despite strong economic bonds with the South, and prevent recognition of a Southern nation built on slavery. The free Negroes in the North, together with the Abolitionists, were clamoring. To them a war against the South simply had to be a war against slavery. Gradually, Abolitionists no longer need fear the mob. Disgruntled leaders of church and state began to talk of freedom. Slowly but surely an economic dispute and a political test of strength took on the aspects of a great moral crusade.

The Negro became in the first year contraband of war; that is, property belonging to the enemy and valuable to the invader. And in addition to that, he became, as the South quickly saw, the key to Southern resistance. Either these four million laborers remained quietly at work to raise food for the fighters, or the fighter starved. Simultaneously, when the dream of the North for man-power produced riots, the only additional troops that the North could depend on were 200,000 Negroes, for without them, as Lincoln said, the North could not have won the war.

But this slow, stubborn mutiny of the Negro slave was not merely a matter of 200,000 black soldiers and perhaps 300,000 other black laborers, servants, spies and helpers. Back of this half million stood 3½ million more. Without their labor the South would starve. With arms in their hands, Negroes would form a fighting force which could replace every single Northern white soldier fighting listlessly and against his will with a black man fighting for freedom.

This action of the slaves was followed by the disaffection of the poor whites. So long as the planters' war seemed successful, "there was little active opposition by the poorer whites; but the conscription and other burdens to support a slaveowners' war became very severe; the whites not interested in that cause became recalcitrant, some went into active opposition; and at last it was more desertion and disunion than anything else that brought about the final overthrow."

Phillips says that white mechanics in 1861 demanded that the permanent Confederate Constitution exclude Negroes from employment "except agricultural domestic service, so as to reserve the trades for white artisans." Beyond this, of course, was a more subtle reason that, as the years went on, very carefully developed and encouraged for a time the racial aspect of slavery. Before the war, there had been intermingling of white and black blood and some white planters openly recognized their colored sons, daughters and cousins and took them under their special protection. As slavery hardened, the racial basis was emphasized; but it was not until war time that it became the fashion to pat the disfranchised poor white man on the back and tell him after all he was white and that he and the planters had a common object in keeping the white man superior. This virus increased bitterness and relentless hatred, and after the war it became a chief ingredient in the division of the working class in the Southern States.

At the same time during the war even the race argument did not keep the Southern fighters from noticing with anger that the big slaveholders were escaping military service; that it was a "rich man's war and the poor man's fight." The exemption of owners of twenty Negroes from military service especially rankled; and the wholesale withdrawal of the slaveholding class from actual fighting which this rule made possible, gave rise to intense and growing dissatisfaction.

It was necessary during these critical times to insist more than usual that slavery was a fine thing for the poor white. Except for slavery it was said:

"The poor would occupy the position in society that the slaves do—as the poor in the North and in Europe do," for there must be a menial class in society and in "every civilized country on the globe, besides the Confederate states, the poor are the inferiors and menials of the rich." Slavery was a general blessing to the non-slaveholding poor than to the owners of slaves, and since it gave the poor a start in society that it would take them generations to work out, they should thank God for it and fight and die for it as they would for their "own liberty and the dearest birthright of freedmen."

But the poor whites were losing faith. They saw that poverty was fighting the war, not wealth.

> Those who could stay out of the army under color of the law were likely to be advocates of a more numerous and powerful army. . . . Not so with many of those who were not favored with position and wealth. They grudgingly took up arms and condemned the law which had snatched them from their homes. . . . The only difference was the circumstance of position and wealth, and perhaps these were just the things that had caused heartburnings in more peaceful times.
>
> The sentiments of thousands in the upland countries, who had little interest in the war and who were not accustomed to rigid centralized control, was probably well expressed in the following epistle addressed to President Davis by a conscript. . . .
>
> . . . "It is with intense and multifariously proud satisfaction that he [the conscript] gazes for the last time upon our holy flag—that symbol and sign of an adored trinity, cotton, niggers and chivalry."

This attitude of the poor whites had in it as much fear and jealousy of Negroes as disaffection with slave barons. Economic rivalry with blacks became a new and living threat as the blacks became laborers and soldiers in a conquering Northern army. If the Negro was to be free where would the poor white be? Why should he fight against the blacks and his victorious friends? The poor white not only began to desert and run away; but thousands followed the Negro into the Northern camps.

Meantime, with perplexed and laggard steps, the United States Government followed the footsteps of the black slave. It made no difference how much Abraham Lincoln might protest that this was not a war against slavery, or ask General McDowell "if it would not be well to allow the armies to bring back those fugitive slaves which have crossed the Potomac with our troops" (a communication which was marked "secret"). It was in vain that Lincoln rushed entreaties and then commands to Frémont in Missouri, not to emancipate the slaves of rebels, and then had to hasten similar orders to Hunter in South Carolina. The slave, despite every effort, was becoming the center of war. Lincoln, with his uncanny insight, began to see it. He began to talk about compensation for emancipated slaves, and Congress, following almost too quickly, passed the Confiscation Act in August, 1861, freeing slaves which were actually used in war by the enemy. Lincoln then suggested that provision be made for colonization of such slaves. He simply could not envisage free Negroes in the United States. What would become of them? What would they do? Meantime, the slave kept looming. New Orleans was captured and the whole black population of Louisiana began streaming toward it. When Vicksburg fell, the center of perhaps the vastest Negro population in North America was tapped. They rushed into the Union lines. Still Lincoln held off and watched symptoms. Greeley's "Prayer of Twenty Millions" received the curt answer, less than a year before Emancipation, that the war was not to abolish slavery, and if Lincoln could hold the country together and keep slavery, he would do it.

But he could not, and he had no sooner said this than he began to realize that he could not. In June, 1862, slavery was abolished in the territories. Compensation with possible colonization was planned for the District of Columbia. Representatives and Senators from the Border States were brought together to talk about extending this plan to their states, but they hesitated.

In August, Lincoln faced the truth, front forward; and that truth was not simply that Negroes ought to be free; it was that thousands of them were already free, and that either the power which slaves put into the hands of the South was to be taken from it, or the North could not win the war. Either the Negro was to be allowed to fight, or the draft itself would not bring enough white men into the army to keep up the war.

More than that, unless the North faced the world with the moral strength of declaring openly that they were fighting for the emancipation of slaves, they would probably find that the world would recognize the South as a separate nation; that ports would be opened; that trade would begin, and that despite all the military advantage of the North, the war would be lost.

In August, 1862, Lincoln discussed Emancipation as a military measure; in September, he issued his preliminary proclamation; on January 1, 1863, he declared that the slaves of all persons in rebellion were "henceforward and forever free."

The guns at Sumter, the marching armies, the fugitive slaves, the fugitives as "contrabands," spies, servants and laborers; the Negro as soldier, as citizen, as voter—these steps came from 1861 to 1868 with regular beat that was almost rhythmic. It was the price of the disaster of war, and it was a price that few Americans at first dreamed of paying or wanted to pay. The North was not Abolitionist. It was overwhelmingly in favor of Negro slavery, so long as this did not interfere with Northern money-making. But, on the other hand, there was a minority of the North who hated slavery with perfect hatred; who wanted no union with slaveholders; who fought for freedom and treated Negroes as men. As the Abolition-democracy gained in prestige and in power, they appeared as prophets, and led by statesmen, they began to guide the nation out of the morass into which it had fallen. They and their black friends and the new freedmen became gradually the leaders of a Reconstruction of Democracy in the United States, while marching millions sang the noblest war-song of the ages to the tune of "John Brown's Body":

> Mine eyes have seen the glory of the coming of the Lord,
> He is trampling out the vintage where the grapes of wrath are stored,
> He hath loosed the fateful lightning of his terrible swift sword,
> His Truth is marching on!

Toward a New Economics
in the South

JOEL WILLIAMSON

Joel Williamson here carries Dubois's "General Strike" into the 1865–1866 period in South Carolina. The blacks who had gained land during the war refused to surrender it, and often only the coercive force of the Union Army dispossessed them. Other ex-slaves who had not gained land refused to enter into contractual relations with their ex-masters in the expectation of receiving land from the federal government as promised. In this situation, the Freedman's Bureau acted to break the impasse by forcing blacks back to work by any means necessary including the Union Army. The Bureau also acted to protect the ex-slaves' freedom from hostile former masters. Williamson points out that in the winter of 1866 the federal authorities began to reeducate white and black southerners. There is a clear impression that they spent most of their time "reeducating" the blacks who had developed expectations of freedom that the north was now unwilling to meet.

Joel Williamson, *After Slavery* (Chapel Hill, N.C.: University of North Carolina Press, 1965), pp. 64–95. Reprinted and footnotes omitted by permission of the publisher.

Slavery was dead, and the vacuum in relations between labor, capital, and management created by its demise required filling. In nonagricultural pursuits, wage labor was rapidly and easily substituted. In agriculture, however, a highly complex and—for the South—novel pattern gradually evolved. Only in its broadest outlines was the new order prescribed by the victorious North. The infinite detail emerged in a largely free interaction between white employers and Negro employees. In this process, the Negro laborer revealed himself not only as capable of surviving in a competitive society, but also of improving his own material circumstances and of contributing to the total prosperity of his community.

As the war drew to a close, the victors clearly were determined that slavery would be replaced by a system of free labor. Just how the transition was to be effected, and precisely what the new system was to be, Washington had not yet decided. During the spring and summer of 1865, in the absence of specific instructions, economic policy in South Carolina was determined in the field by officials faced with the necessity of contriving means to meet the obvious exigencies of the civilian population around them.

At first, and to some extent throughout Reconstruction, military forces in the state were a source of official policy. By July, 1865, the Department of South Carolina had been created with headquarters at Hilton Head and some seven to eight thousand troops blanketed the state. The commanding general was then Q. A. Gillmore, a graduate of West Point with high soldierly qualities and no apparent political ambitions.

During the summer and early fall of 1865, another agency of the national government became progressively more important in the state: the Bureau of Refugees, Freedmen and Abandoned Lands. Rufus B. Saxton, the assistant commissioner of the Bureau for South Carolina, recruited a staff of specialists and subassistant commissioners primarily from the ranks of the regiments assigned to occupation duty. In addition, a considerable number were enlisted from among the numerous educational and religious missionaries who had arrived before and after the capitulation. Until Saxton was relieved early in 1866, the Bureau in South Carolina was merely a continuation and elaboration in personnel, form, and policy of the organization which had dealt with problems involving the Negro population since 1862.

The problem facing military authorities in South Carolina in the summer of 1865 was the necessity of supplying the immediate needs of large numbers of freedmen for food, clothing, shelter, and medical care. The same problem on a smaller scale had been met by the joint efforts of the army and the benevolent societies in the Sea Islands during the war. The army regularly undertook to feed refugees recently arrived from the mainland until they could support themselves. Before March, 1863, the missionaries in the islands had distributed 91,834 garments, 5,895 yards of cloth, and $3,000 worth of agricultural implements to the freedmen. Also, the missionary force included physicians, as well as teachers and superintendents. As the war drew to a close, the issue of army rations to freedmen and, indeed, to impoverished whites, increased to enormous proportions. The Bureau, empowered to issue food, clothing, and fuel to destitute freedmen and refugees, systematized and continued the practice. The dislocations caused by the war, the transition from slave to free labor, and the poor crops in 1865, 1866, and 1867 perpetuated the need for issues of rations well into 1868. The immensity of the problem is suggested by the facts that in the year following September 1, 1866, the Bureau issued 810,309 rations to freedmen in the state; and in July, 1867, over 15,000 Negroes were supported entirely by government issues.

Charity is hardly the term to describe the actions of Northerners in South Carolina. Both the benevolent societies and the government issued food, clothing, and fuel as gifts only to orphans, the aged, and infirm. All others received such assistance as loans, to be repaid in one form or another. For example, in the spring of 1865, a Northern teacher on Edisto Island quickly disabused the local Negroes of the idea that a barrel of used clothing recently arrived from the North was to be given away. She called in one of their leaders, Uncle Jack, to explain to the others "that they must pay for it with vegetables, eggs, chickens, or whatever they can bring in exchange." Similarly, first as military governor and later as inspector of plantations, Saxton insisted that rations furnished to refugees and settlers be repaid. Further, Bureau policy was to issue rations only in those cases where they were desperately needed and to cease issues as soon as possible. The meagerness of charity in the relief program was completely in harmony with the views of its sponsors. "Indeed, the most dangerous process through which the negro goes when he becomes a freedman is that of receiving the gratuities of benevolence in the shape of food and clothing," wrote a veteran missionary late in 1865. "If you wish to make them impudent, fault-finding and lazy, give them clothing and food freely." Two years later, Laura Towne, who gave her life and much of her personal fortune to the education of the Negroes in the islands, concluded that it was better to "let the people suffer" than to demoralize them by general gifts of food.

Even the Negroes themselves subscribed to the code of charity advanced by their benefactors. Many freedmen in real need refused to apply for rations. After his term as subassistant commissioner for the mountain districts, John W. De Forest asserted: "As far as I could compare the two races, able-bodied Negroes were much less apt to apply for rations than able-bodied 'low-downers' [poor whites]." Those who did accept government aid usually understood that the issues were to be repaid and, by

Saxton's testimony in April, 1865, some 17,000 of his first charges had already done so. In the early postwar years, hard times made repayment difficult. In addition, during the political agitation of 1867 and 1868, the successful candidate for the congressional seat of the Charleston district, an ex-Confederate Army captain named Christopher Columbus Bowen, made considerable political capital for himself by advising the Negroes, as a lawyer, that they could not be legally bound to repay the rations advanced. Nevertheless, the common reaction of the Negroes to government assistance was one of gratitude, and, politically speaking, it could not be said that the Negro bit the hand that fed him.

The key policy of military authorities in South Carolina in the late spring and summer of 1865 was, above all, to return the freedmen to their accustomed labors. Quite properly, officials viewed this as the real solution to the problem of relief. Under official pressure, most Negro agriculturists either located themselves on the Sherman grants, contracted with landowners to work for the remainder of the year for a share of the crop, or remained under such terms on the plantations where they were.

The occupation forces implemented this policy by various means. Positively, the military enjoyed the loyalty of the freedmen themselves, and the very presence of the blue uniforms and the promulgation of official desires through the soldiers usually won ready compliance from the Negroes. The occupation authorities and, in its turn, the Freedmen's Bureau, had the facilities to transport freedmen to places where labor was in demand and to provide them with rations until they became self-sustaining. Negatively, the government was able to wrest compliance from many of the most recalcitrant freedmen simply by ceasing to provide them with rations.

Many freedmen settled upon Sherman grants and remained entirely under governmental control. However, a large majority of Negroes were forced to take employment on the lands of planters and, in many cases, under their late masters. Congress, in the law that created the Freedmen's Bureau, did not prescribe regulations to govern this situation. To instruct both planters and laborers in the ways of free labor and to protect the freedmen during the period of adjustment, local officials relied upon the method that Saxton had perfected in the islands during the war. This so-called "contract system" had emerged as the *direct result* of Saxton's failure to secure the sale of confiscated plantations exclusively to Negro laborers. Most of these lands passed under the gavel into the hands of speculators. Suspicious of these entrepreneurs and stimulated by complaints of ill-treatment voiced by their Negro workers, Saxton, in April, 1864, invoked his military powers to require each employer to draft a contract covering the farming year. The contract detailed precisely the work to be required of the Negroes and the wages and goods in lieu of wages that the freedmen

would receive in return. Saxton also ordered his agents to visit each plantation upon which private parties employed Negroes, to read the contract to
the laborers, to adjust any differences then and there, and to note carefully
on the contract itself the assent of each worker. Any laborer refusing to
agree to each and all provisions was to leave the plantation immediately.

During the late spring and summer of 1865, the officers of the occupation assiduously applied this method throughout the state. The large
number of manuscript contracts extant dated during the summer of 1865
suggests that the program was carried out with remarkable thoroughness.
Typical of these contracts was one signed by the manager and marked by
the 131 freedmen on one of the Alexander Hamilton Boykin plantations
in Kershaw District on July 6, 1865, in the presence of Lt. S. J. Brooks
of the Twenty-fifth Ohio Regiment of Volunteers. By its terms, the laborers
were guaranteed not only their liberty by their late master, but also a third
of the crop at the end of the year—certainly a savory first taste of freedom.

Neither the relief, resettlement, nor the contract policies of the occupation were perfectly administered, and even had they been each contained
intrinsic weaknesses. Nevertheless, in those critical months immediately
following the war while Washington was still undecided as to how free the
Negro was to be, these programs established a modus vivendi for the
former slaves of South Carolina that sacrificed none of their hard-won
freedom. At the same time, the victors were fashioning and improving the
tools that they were to use to fix upon the South a relatively high standard
of economic freedom for the Negro.

Before the war, the white population, North as well as South, had
serious doubts whether or not the mass of slaves—if emancipated—could
survive as free laborers. The Port "experiment," which was in reality a
bundle of experiments, had been designed in part as a test which would
prove that a large mass of the least "civilized" slaves in the South could
be re-educated to support themselves in a free economy. The results of the
experiment in 1862 were inconclusive. In the following year, the Philbrick
group set out to make the test under carefully controlled conditions. "Negro
labor has got to be employed," explained Philbrick on the eve of launching
his venture, "because it is profitable; and it has got to come into the market
like everything else, subject to the supply and demand which may arise for
all kinds of enterprises in which it chances to be employed." In brief: "We
want first to prove that it is profitable, and then it will take care of itself."
Needless to say, it was profitable; a fact that Philbrick took great care to
publicize throughout the North at the end of the year. By the close of the
war, few informed Northerners had any doubts of the Negro's ability to
survive a free economy.

Southern opinion on the subject was by no means so unanimous. The

Northern idea that necessity would compel the Negroes to labor only drew from the average Southerner the retort that "You can't do that way with niggers." Some white Carolinians were convinced that nothing less stringent than slavery would keep the Negroes at labor; virtually all believed that some system of compulsion would be necessary. "We are in a transition to something better or worse," wrote one thoughtful Charlestonian early in the summer of 1865, "and I fear the latter very much, unless some system of labour is organized by which the negroes are compelled to work."

In spite of their misgivings, most white Southerners frankly recognized the end of slavery, and many entered readily and in good faith into the "experiment" in free labor. "The institution of Slavery is I think with a few exceptions considered a thing past," wrote a low-country planter in August, 1865, "and the convention to meet in September next will pass an act to prohibit it for the future." Some ex-slaveholders welcomed the end of the peculiar institution. A. L. Taveau, once a rice planter and a lesser light among the proslavery literati, before the war had believed "like a great many others" that slavery "was necessary to our welfare if not our existence," and that "these people were content, happy, and attached to their masters." The behavior of the Negroes during the war in deserting their masters "in the moment of his need," flocking "in herds to an Enemy whom they knew *not,*" and leaving "their, perhaps, really good Master whom they *did* know from infancy," led him, however, to conclude that "the Negro for forty years" had "been looking for the Man of Universal Freedom," and that he, Taveau, would not restore slavery if he could. A few recent slaveholders regarded free Negro labor as an opportunity for unprecedented prosperity. "We will be better off, & be able to plant more successfully than we have ever yet," predicted a Cooper River grower in July, 1865, anticipating with unfeigned glee the prospect of himself being free of "old idle lazy negroes . . ." The same planter appeared to be not only willing, but eager to contract with some of his late bondsmen, signing an agreement for 1866 in September, 1865, and for 1867 in November, 1866.

At the opposite extreme, however, there was a highly influential minority composed of former slaveholders who believed that the institution of slavery might, after all, be preserved and the Negro thus compelled to continue his labors. Warming under the increasing favor shown by the new President, Andrew Johnson, toward the "natural ruling element" in the South, these men were much encouraged in their proslavery stand. In April, even before the final capitulation of the Confederacy, lowcountry politicians journeyed to Washington and conversed with the President. They were pleased to learn that his manner was not at all hostile as the northern press had led them to expect. On the contrary, Johnson received them with gracious cordiality, and when they departed Southern gentlemen understood that their restoration to civil power would not long be delayed. While Johnson's provisional governor, Benjamin F. Perry, prepared South Carolina for readmission to the Union via a convention of the people scheduled for September, this postwar proslavery party gained strength. In July, an old resident of Colleton District estimated its power at the grass-roots level in his community. There was a conflict, he observed, between "the rich land owners formerly slave owners," many of whom still held "to the idea that slavery may yet be saved to them," and "the great jealousy of the poor" who "seem determined that it should not, even tho they butcher the whole race." "I ought not to say that such a spirit is general," he cautioned, "but it does exist, to what extent is not easily ascertained." Even though their Presidential pardons committed them to recognize the abolition of slavery, some delegates-elect to the coming convention began to agitate for its preservation. Secession Governor Francis W. Pickens, one of the delegates who had accepted both his pardon and abolition in good faith, was alarmed by the resurgence of proslavery sentiment in his native district of Edgefield. "I found our people influenced by men taking the ground that slavery was not & could not be abolished, & swearing they would never submit to it &c," he warned Perry early in September. Across the state in Chester, James Hemphill, a well-informed and highly astute political observer (as well as a delegate to the convention), saw disaster in the new proslavery movement. Recently returned from Washington where he had found "a strong party . . . pressing negro suffrage," Hemphill feared that the Negro party might "prove too powerful for President Johnson and his friends, particularly if there is any disposition here to hold on to the peculiar institution, as some are inclined."

Actually, the Convention of 1865 made quick work of the slavery issue. Perry pointed the way by declaring to the Convention that abolition was the price of readmission to the Union. A few delegates tried to eschew the question; a few others tried to word the provision to show elaborately that they acceded to emancipation only under duress. The large majority, however, voted for this simple statement: "The slaves in South Carolina having been emancipated by the action of the United States authorities, neither slavery nor involuntary servitude . . . shall ever be re-established in this State." Only eight delegates, led by A. P. Aldrich of Barnwell, stood against the provision.

Having recognized the demise of slavery, the Convention turned to deal with the problem of regulating social, economic, and legal relations between Negroes and whites. It empowered the governor to appoint two commissioners to advise the next legislature on what changes in the laws were necessary to make them conform to the new constitution, and "especially to prepare and submit a Code for the regulation of labor, and the

protection and government of the Colored Population of the State . . ."
Shortly thereafter, Perry appointed David L. Wardlaw and Armisted Burt,
both of Abbeville, commissioners for this task. Apparently, Burt assumed
responsibility for drafting the social and economic provisions of the Code,
while Wardlaw dealt with the machinery of enforcement.

It was ironic that the so-called "Black Code" in South Carolina,
one of those measures that the Radicals exhibited so conspicuously in
displaying an unrepentent South still unwilling to do justice to the Negro,
was actually designed as a system for the protection of the Negro. To
some extent, the Code was a concession to outside pressures, an initial
payment on the price of readmission into the councils of the nation. "The
President wishes to see that protection has been afforded or guaranteed to
the freemen before the military authorities are removed," wrote Perry
to Burt in mid-October, urging the latter to rush his draft of the Code
to completion. "Congress will require it before our Representatives are
allowed to take their seats in the Body," he added. Yet, in every important way, the Code was purely a southern document. "Protection for
the Negro" in Washington, or Boston, or Topeka meant protection in his
natural and, occasionally, in his civil and political rights. In Abbeville,
Greenville, and, indeed, in South Carolina as a whole, protection for the
Negro meant protection from himself, from his own inherent inadequacies.
The Code, from the point of view of the "best" of the Carolina whites,
was designed to provide, primarily, this latter form of protection. The
problem was not simply one of semantics, but of fundamentally different
racial philosophies. Whatever their racial likes or dislikes, most Northerners seemingly thought that the Negro was potentially a man like any other
man except for the color of his skin. Perry stated one version of the
southern view a year later: "If all the children in New York City were
turned loose to provide for themselves, how many would live prosper
and do well. The negroes are as improvident as children, and require the
guardian protection of some one almost as much as they do." Anyone
who sought to enlarge the freedom of the Negro was liable to criticism
as an enemy of the Negro, much as one who sought to place a child
beyond the protection of its parents. Those who sought to treat the child
more strictly might also be its enemies; but, as everyone knew, laxity,
not severity, was the common error of the fond parent and more to be
guarded against.

Paternalism, that best side of slavery, thus persisted in the Code
and secured widespread endorsement. Armisted Burt personified the paternal tradition. "Tell all the Servants 'Howdy' for me, and write me
about them," ran a typically thoughtful addendum to a letter to his wife
in 1866. In the minds of such men, there was no doubt that theirs was
the wise, humane solution to the problem of race relations. Even after

the Code had failed, Burt predicted that the Negroes "will soon find that the Southern people are their best friends." Yet, paternalism did not mean that its adherents would yield one iota of their dominance. Burt, himself, in the state Democratic Convention in Columbia in August, 1868, voiced this sentiment when he urged his friends to fight for possession "of this country which was discovered by the white man, settled by the white man, made illustrious by the white man, and must continue to be the white man's Country. [Applause.]"

Under such circumstances, it was hardly surprising that the Code presented to a special session of the legislature early in November prescribed in elaborate detail for the social, economic, and legal subordination of the Negro. In accordance with Perry's suggestions, Burt included provisions allowing employers to impose upon their employees "a deduction of wages" as a punishment for idleness and "neglect of duty &c"; requiring husbands "to work for the support of their families & not be allowed to leave them under any circumstances"; and ordering each family of Negroes "to support the old and helpless members." In the economic sphere, Negro laborers of all classes were, in essence, forced to fix themselves to a "master." Desertion without good cause would result in the deserter's being ruled a vagrant and bound to serve a term with a master assigned by a jury of three freeholders. On the other hand, the conditions of labor were carefully stipulated, and laborers wrongfully discharged were entitled to collect wages for the entire contract period. As provided in the new Constitution (1865), district courts were established to function much as the public guardians of the Negroes.

The Code, in the form of four separate laws, was enacted late in November, 1865, during the regular session of the legislature. It was not passed easily and with little discussion as historians have previously maintained, however; the legislature seethed with dissension on this issue.

The sharpest criticism came from those who did not think the Code was severe enough. This element represented planters and leaders of the heavily Negro populated districts and the persisting proslavery party. Typical of the thinking of this group was that of one lowcountry planter who, in August, had envisioned the necessity of a Spartan-like system in which the whole white community would be mobilized to control the Negroes: "As for making the negroes work under the present state of affairs it seems to me a waste of time and energy. . . . No sheriff & Posse or Patrol, under civil rule will suit our wants. We must have mounted Infantry that the freedmen know distinctly that they succeed the Yankees to enforce whatever regulations we can make." Edmund Rhett, once a "fire-eater" of the first rank and still an enthusiast for slavery, wrote to Burt in October while the Code was still unfinished, urging stringent regulations. Every citizen of the state, he lectured Burt, must have recognized that abolition "is unwise, injurious, and dangerous to our whole system, pecuniary and social." But, since it had been effected by force of arms, "it should to the utmost extent practicable be limited, controlled, and surrounded with such safe guards, as will make the change as slight as possible both to the white man and to the negro, the planter and the workman, the capitalist and the laborer." In other words, "the general interest both of the white man and of the negroes requires that he should be kept as near to the condition of slavery as possible, and as far from the condition of the white man as is practicable. . . . We must face the question," he concluded, "negroes must be made to work, or else cotton and rice must cease to be raised for export." To attain these ends, Rhett proposed a four-part program: Negroes and "their posterity" would be prohibited from acquiring *"Real Estate."* Each Negro would be required to have a fixed domicile, and those who deserted their places without the express approval of the authorities would be "taken up and put to hard labor upon public works in chain gangs." A laborer who violated his contract would be "held both as a vagrant and a criminal" and bound to his masters. Finally, "considering the prejudices prevalent against whipping," employers would be given the disciplinary powers normally possessed by garrison commanders over enlisted soldiers. Such sentiments were well represented in the legislature. James Hemphill, sitting in the senate just before the Code was brought onto the floors of both houses, observed that "every individual member almost can find some ground of objection," and that "many think it too indulgent of the negro . . ."

An attempt to mitigate the harshness of the Code before it passed the legislature came from those more perceptive politicians who were correctly reading the signals from the North. Even Rhett, who thought it entirely possible to enact the laws he recommended, suggested that "this is no time to do it," because "it will only strengthen the Black Republican Party, and render the admission of the State difficult." After the reunion, however, "I believe there will be little difficulty," he indicated, because "the administration will support us." Rhett was something less than sincere in his public expressions; yet, in exchange for the return of political power to themselves, the mitigation party candidly sought to satisfy the demands of the North on behalf of the Negro. During September and October, when their confidence in success was at a peak, this was the core of their strategy, and the approach was not without support among important elements of the white population. "Unless you want to bring the north down on us," James Chesnut had warned the state senator from Kershaw District as he departed for Columbia, "repeal all laws enacted for negroes and leave the emancipated negro and the white man on the same footing before the law." . . .

The Code excited bitter animosity among the Negro population in South Carolina and in the North at large. In Charleston, the Negro community met in Zion Church to denounce the Code and to ask Congress for relief from such measures. In the North, the Code became one of the stepping stones by which the Radicals ascended to overwhelming power in Congress.

Under the very able leadership of the newly elected governor, James L. Orr, the mitigation party recovered rapidly from its defeat on the issue of the Code. In mid-December, Orr vetoed an attempt by the legislature to rewrite the patrol laws so as to use that instrument of the slave period to enforce the provisions of the Code. In a stinging message accompanying his veto, Orr lectured the legislature on the obvious fact that since "the necessity [slavery] has ceased," the patrol laws "should be ignored." In the following month, Orr arranged with the newly appointed commanding general of the department in which South Carolina was included to have the Code set aside by military fiat and "all laws" made "applicable alike to all inhabitants." This adjustment was facilitated by the close personal friendship between the new commander, Major General Daniel E. Sickles, and Orr, an intimacy dating from the high times of the National Democracy in the 1850's when both had been congressmen. Sickles, although unwilling to yield any of his authority, seemed disposed to allow white South Carolinians to adjust somewhat gradually to the demands of the new society.

Under the highly astute guidance of Governor Orr, an interesting and significant movement developed among the white leadership to conciliate Northern sentiment and win readmission. Orr himself sought information from other Southern governors concerning methods their states had used to deal with their Negro populations. "It will be necessary to convene the legislature of this State at an early day to modify our legislation of December last so as to conform to the 'civil rights Act,' and the requirements of the Freedmens Bureau," he explained to the governor of the Old North State, "and I am very anxious to lay before the legislature when it assembles the legislation of our contiguous sister States." The replies probably raised the eyebrows of even the conciliationists. Georgia and North Carolina sent copies of their comparatively lenient Codes; the Republican governor of Virginia rather acidly answered that "The freedmen in Virginia, I believe, enjoy all the Civil Rights of white persons . . ." Soon, several native white journalists and many lawyers joined in denouncing South Carolina's Code as cumbersome and unjust, urging greater flexibility in meeting the demands of the North. The Charleston *Courier,* for instance, by September 1, 1866, was damning the Code as "impractical." In mid-August, Orr was ready to call a special session of the legislature to adjust the laws to treat Negroes and whites equally. Informing Sickles of his intentions, Orr was told that when this was done the civil courts would be allowed to resume jurisdiction over cases concerning Negroes, a power which they had been denied since the occupation.

Although the current of conciliation ran swiftly at the higher levels of leadership, it did not, apparently, run deep. In January, 1866, an elderly planter in Union District heavily discounted the optimism of the conciliationists. "I can see none of that silver lining to the cloud which cheers the eye of Senator Perry and Gov Orr & other political hucksters," he wrote to a friend. "The nigger wont work—he (the institution) will be a free nigger as free niggers always have been—they will worry us until we will be forced to run them off to Yankee land for sympathy, and then will come colonization and the white man's Government." Even the very rational Senator Hemphill objected to the special session, arguing that Orr "might let the Code rock along until the regular session of the Legislature, when the Members would have more leisure, and be in better plight for work." In its special session in September, after a protracted debate in which expediency rather than a real change in sentiment seemed to be the ruling spirit, the legislature did go far toward granting economic and legal equality to Negroes. Nevertheless, it left a ragged residue of social restrictions concerning inter-racial marriages, domestic relations, and vagrancy unchanged. Shortly afterward, with an admonition that all laws were to apply equally to all citizens, Sickles restored full judicial powers to the civil courts outside of the Sea Islands.

The legislature acted with obvious reluctance; yet, even as it acted, the North was raising the price of reunion. Within a few weeks after it revised the Code, the legislature, in its regular session and with Orr's approval, flatly and nearly unanimously rejected the Fourteenth Amendment. With this action, the line was drawn; South Carolina would of its own volition and without a *quid pro quo* make no further concession to Negro equality. The initiative passed again to the North. If Johnson failed in his fight with the Radicals, then South Carolina would go down with him.

The policy of conciliation did not suffice to return normal power to the white leadership in South Carolina. Yet the alliance between Southerners and the national executive resulted directly in the reversal of the land redistribution program inaugurated under Sherman's orders and in changes in personnel in key offices which long worked to the disadvantage of the Negro population.

As described in the preceding chapter, during the late summer of 1865, Saxton was seizing abandoned plantations and settling Negroes upon them as rapidly as possible. Johnson was fully aware of this situation and of the damage it imposed upon his allies in South Carolina, but it was not until mid-August that he moved to oppose it openly, and not until mid-

September that he pointedly ordered Howard to issue instructions which, if strictly enforced, would virtually have nullified the land program. By these orders all lands then held by the government were to be restored if they had not been abandoned "voluntarily" in support of the rebellion or if the rebel owner had been pardoned, a requirement the President himself could easily satisfy. Johnson also decided with his attorney-general that all lands not actually sold, even if condemned by the courts, would be returned to their former owners. In the meantime, on September 3, Saxton had been ordered by the state's military commander to seize no more abandoned property. Without land, the redistribution program was obviously doomed.

Although it is striking that South Carolina landowners made no move until after Johnson had acted in their favor, they then moved rapidly to take advantage of this gap in the federal front. Owners of plantations in the lowcountry took care to establish that the lands from which they were absent were not abandoned. Many returned to their county seats and others appointed friends, neighbors, or, in some cases, former slaves, as agents in charge of their estates. Owners of plantations already confiscated pressed vigorously for immediate restoration by petitioning, retaining lawyers, or asking friends to represent their interests to the authorities. In Washington, William Henry Trescot, ubiquitous as South Carolina's diplomat in the capital and the man who had negotiated for the surrender of federal property to the state during the secession crisis, was made the agent of the state for the purpose of securing both pardons and restoration. By October 15, Trescot had reported to his employers that all confiscated lands, less those condemned for taxes in the Port Royal area during the war, had been ordered restored by the President.

Yet, the game was not to be so easily won. Saxton and Howard moved slowly and with great reluctance in executing the President's wishes. His order of mid-September was not published in South Carolina until September 28, and even then it contained a proviso that land cultivated by loyal refugees or freedmen would not be restored until the crops were harvested or suitable compensation rendered, concessions which the owners were unwilling to make. In October, a highly choleric Johnson personally, orally, and explicitly ordered Howard himself to go to South Carolina to effect a settlement "mutually satisfactory" to the freedmen and the owners. Doubtless as Johnson intended, Howard interpreted this to mean that complete restoration was mandatory. On October 19, Howard, assisted by Saxton, convened a large meeting of settlers on Edisto Island and with heavy heart informed the dismayed Negroes that their lands were to be returned to the planters. Nevertheless, in the machinery for restoration which he established on the same date, Howard created still another instrument for delay. A three-man board, consisting of an owner, a settler, and a Bureau agent, was named for each island. Before reclaiming his lands, the owner had to obligate himself to give the settlers all of the crops in progress, to permit them to retain their homes as long as they would contract with him, to renew leases indefinitely, and to allow the Bureau school to continue in operation. As agent in charge of this program, Howard appointed Captain Alexander P. Ketchum, an officer in the 128th United States Colored Troops assigned to Bureau duty and a man highly sympathetic with the settlers.

After Howard's departure, Saxton and Ketchum made no concessions to the demands of the owners. In November, 1865, John Berkeley Grimball complained that his friend William Aiken had been "persistent at Gen Saxton's office with no result," and that many planters whose lands had been possessed by the settlers were beginning to expect the government to buy the land at its own price and give the Negroes permanent titles. Another owner thought that "The Yankees have instilled into the negroes [*sic*] minds the belief that the Island country which they helped to conquer belongs to them, & they throw every obstacle in the way of the planters revisiting their plantations." The last allegation was not entirely true. Nevertheless, early in February, 1866, Ketchum was still firm in his refusal to endorse any application for restoration.

Highly effective opposition also came from the settlers themselves, who strenuously, bitterly, and even violently resisted dispossession. Many settlers were ex-soldiers who found it difficult to understand how the government could now ask them to give up their homes and take employment under the same men it had urged them to fight only a few months before. One committee of settlers expressed their feelings on this matter movingly, if ungrammatically: ". . . man that have stud upon the feal of battle & have shot there master & sons now Going to ask ether one for bread or for shelter or Confortable for his wife & children sunch a thin the u st should not aught Expect a man . . ." All through the islands, settlers refused to concede any degree of recognition to the claims of the planters by contracting to work for them. A Northern teacher on Wadmalaw found the settlers determined not to "hire with a Rebel." In many places, the Negroes organized militarily to hold their land and to prevent recent owners from even visiting the islands. "Mr. Seabrook, owner of Fenwick Isle," J. B. Grimball reported in mid-November, "told me yesterday that the Negroes on that Island were armed and have announced their purpose to allow no white man on it, and Edisto Isle is said to be much in the same state." Two weeks later another planter delayed bringing his family into the lowcountry because "the Negroes are getting on their high horse & say they intend to fight for the land, particularly on Edisto."

In several instances, the persistence of the owners drove the settlers to the very brink of violence. In one case, Bureau Superintendent Swails brought two recent Rebel owners to a plantation on Wadmalaw Island. There, he was challenged by one of the settlers as to his authority for doing so in the face of Sherman's order excluding from the area all whites not in the government's service. Swails drew his revolver and declared that to be his authority. Soon there was a musket shot and Negro men swarmed down from all directions. Swails then produced a paper from Saxton, but the Negroes advised the party to leave anyway. Followed by the Negroes, the party fled to the island's village, Rockville, where another superintendent assigned to the island talked them out of violence. One of the settlers who had surrounded the party subsequently told a Northern teacher that he had been wounded nine times while he was in the army and would be wounded nine times again before he would submit to a Rebel. "Oh, he says," quoted the teacher, "it was shaking the pistol in the mans face that has made us come here, such things kill us, if they had treated us as men we would not have harmed them—." "Ah," said another settler, "if dey com wid him [Swails], we'll not harm em, but if dey land here alone, we hab musket dat neber lie."

In Washington, the owners were hardly more successful. In the first draft of a bill to extend the life of the Freedmen's Bureau, Howard secured the inclusion of a provision certifying the Sherman grants. Nevertheless, when passed in its final form on February 19, 1866, the bill validated the titles for three years only. In addition, the possibility of a general restoration was conceded by a stipulation declaring that any settlers dispossessed by restoration would be given an opportunity to buy or rent government lands elsewhere, presumably on the plantations confiscated for taxes. Johnson's veto of the bill again left the issue unsettled. On the last day of February, 1866, Trescot complained to Governor Orr that Howard had previously promised to issue a comprehensive order for restoring the Sherman lands, but that he then claimed not to have the power to do so. Trescot was currently pressing the President for action and, sensing where the real difficulty lay, simultaneously winning friends in Congress. "I hired one or two of the radical members of the Committee," he reported, referring to the Committee of Ways and Means which was then considering the question of the tax lands, and had also secured from "general Garfield of Indiana, who is a radical," a promise to introduce a motion for the appointment of a subcommittee to study the restoration question.

The impasse in Washington persisted through the winter and spring of 1866, but vital changes occurred in South Carolina that resulted in the practical dispossession of the Sherman settlers. Early in 1866, the relatively impartial commander of the occupation forces in South Carolina was relieved by the highly political Major General Daniel Sickles. Sickles would soon join the Radicals, but in the winter of 1866, he was still watching for a prevailing political wind and was not averse to promoting favor in both camps. Also, early in February, Rufus B. Saxton was relieved as the Bureau's assistant commissioner in South Carolina on the pretext that the army was being demobilized and major generals of volunteers were no longer needed. Probably, Saxton was dismissed at Johnson's insistence. Saxton was replaced by Robert K. Scott, also a major general of volunteers and a soldier of no fortune. In his forties at the end of the war, he had led a varied and adventurous life. As a young man, he had gone from Pennsylvania to the California gold fields. Afterward, he filibustered in Mexico and South America, and, finally, returned to settle in Napoleon, Ohio. There, he was moderately successful as a physician, merchant, and realtor. During the war, he raised a regiment and ultimately commanded a brigade. Before the end of the war, however, he was captured and brought to Charleston as a prisoner. After his liberation, he was breveted a major general. Politically, Scott was an undoubted Radical, but his radicalism was less blatant than Saxton's, and he was markedly less sympathetic to the Negroes. Within a month after Saxton's relief, Alexander Ketchum, the man whom Howard had chosen to handle the restoration problem on the Islands, was also discharged, allegedly because the Negro regiment upon which his commission rested was being disbanded.

During the winter of 1866, Sickles simply used his administrative power to do what Johnson and the owners had been unable to do by judicial and legal means. First, he refused to recognize any claim for which the settler did not have a warrant properly issued and signed by Saxton himself precisely as Sherman had stipulated in his orders. Since Saxton had urged the freedmen to settle first and leave the details until later, only about five thousand such warrants had been distributed. Further, many of these five thousand title holders had settled on lands other than those described in their warrants. The refusal of the military to recognize any papers which were in any degree erroneous resulted, finally, in only 1,565 titles (representing some 63,000 acres), being validated. By the same order that disallowed the Negro Code, Sickles also directed freedmen everywhere in the state to contract for the coming year or to leave their places. In February, squads of soldiers went through the plantations forcing those settlers without valid claims either to contract with the owner or leave. Needless to say, the Negroes concerned were greatly distressed by this display of steel by an army in which many of them had fought. One northern teacher on John's Island found that attendance in her school was diminishing because "the people [were] so upset about contracting & having to leave—" Scott protested this use of force but was quickly squelched by the imperious Sickles. Bowing to the inevitable, Scott attempted to relocate scattered settlers on the plantations where valid titles were most numerous; but, again, his efforts proved futile. He then concentrated on securing equitable contracts for the dispossessed and pressing the freedmen to labor faithfully. In this, he was largely successful and, by late spring, was enjoying the plaudits of the planters for his work.

The Bureau bill which Congress passed over the President's veto on July 16, 1866, belatedly provided that holders of valid titles to Sherman lands were to be given leases on twenty-acre plots on tax lands in the Port Royal area with options to buy within six years. Early in 1867, Scott relocated those settlers who chose to move. The exchange was a poor bargain for the dispossessed, however, because virtually all the tax lands still held by the government had been sadly depleted by speculating lessees. By the end of the year, 1,980 Negro families, including those who had purchased tax lands during and immediately after the war, were settled on some 19,000 acres in the vicinity of Beaufort. The average plot was hardly large enough to furnish its owners a bare subsistence.

In November, 1868, the Bureau still held abandoned lands in South Carolina amounting to about seventy-five thousand acres. The owners of this land were not pressing the government for restoration; indeed, by 1868, restoration could be effected simply upon the application of the owner. Presumably, this acreage could have been divided into farms and allotted to freedmen. Yet, at the end of the year, the Bureau ordered this property either restored or summarily dropped, much as if its possession was an embarrassment to the government. That Congress did not settle Negroes upon these lands suggests that, ultimately, even the Radical majority in Congress deliberately chose not to offer any further special assistance to Negroes aspiring to become landowners. Perhaps, after all, both Congress and the North at large agreed with the editor of the *Nation* who stated in May, 1867, that land had to be earned rather than given as some Radical leaders desired.

The tax lands were affected by the same currents that moved the history of the Sherman grants. Immediately after the war, the rebel owners of these plantations began to petition for the return of their estates. They found, however, that much of the land had already been sold. Moreover, a large part of the remainder was to be sold exclusively to freedmen on December 6, 1865. The previous owners then entered a prolonged struggle to regain their lands through legal and political action. By the end of 1866, most of the land was sold, having been set aside in ten- and twenty-acre plots first for discharged Negro soldiers, and, subsequently, opened to all freedmen at $1.50 an acre. Badly used "school farms" found few buyers on the open market at $10.00 an acre. Lands retained by the government were rented to freedmen at the nominal rate of $1.00 an acre per year. In 1871, Congress directed that all unsold lands be returned to their former owners upon payment of the taxes due and a ten-dollar penalty. No doubt, much of this was restored. In 1874, Myrtle Bank on Hilton

Head was repossessed by its ante-bellum owner under this law. Thus, an estate worth perhaps $10,000 was regained for the payment of back taxes and penalties to the amount of $318.18. Those plantations which had already been sold were still subject to litigation, and many suits were instituted for their return. Eventually, however, the courts reinstated only those owners who had been minors during the war.

In the winter of 1866, national authorities of all political complexions set out in earnest to re-educate Southerners of both races in the "natural laws" of economics as defined by the North. Officials viewed the problem as twofold. On one hand, employers had to be taught to treat their Negro employees humanely and to pay them a wage sufficient for subsistence. On the other hand, Negroes had to be instructed in the necessity of constant and assiduous labor. Through their power to supervise the negotiation and execution of contracts between freedmen and their employers, the authorities sought to achieve these objectives.

Whites learned their lessons rather rapidly. At first, many employers contracted with Negroes without really being convinced that such was possible. One Cooper River planter admitted early in 1866 that Scott "seemed desirous of doing his duty both to employer and employees in the spirit of justice to both as far as he was competent." Yet, he lamented, "There lies the difficulty. The fairest minded of all these officials seems not to be able [to] comprehend the difference between the 'Nigger' freedman and the white northern laborer." Authorities occasionally threatened to use force against employers. During the winter of 1866, the planters of Barnwell and Edgefield districts organized to keep wages of freedmen depressed to a level that threatened the very subsistence of their workers. Thereupon, Sickles announced his intention of removing the entire Negro population from these districts to areas where their labor was in demand and to maintain them by a special tax on the evacuated districts until they became self-supporting. Such a policy was beneficial to the freedmen, but exasperating to the whites. "Is not it shocking & inhuman," exclaimed Francis W. Pickens of Edgefield, who, incidentally, had just signed a very generous contract with his own 143 freedmen. More often, officers of the occupation resorted to stern admonitions. Typical of these was a circular issued by Scott in January, 1868, in which he deplored the low wages which some planters were offering and advised the freedmen to contract only with planters of proved integrity. The planters, for their part, were advised to offer "liberal and fair contracts," and to pay money wages at the end of the season at a rate which they could afford and still profit, and upon which the laborer could support himself and his family.

Some employers remained skeptical; most rapidly came to see large advantages for themselves in free labor. A few even grew enthusiastic after trying the system for several months. "The Freedmen are not sick these days," exulted a Chester District planter in August, 1866. "The Dr. has not been sent for this year, a remarkable thing for this Plantation that is A Happy change wrought by Emancipation. Another great relief to me is the absence of that old & familiar demand of, 'A piece of meat if you please.' " That this idea had wide appeal among ex-masters was evident in the popularity of a parody on Poe which concluded: "But my victuals to the 'fly trap' of that nigger by my door, Shall be lifted, Nevermore!"

Though they had previously regarded Northerners as interlopers and subsequently condemned military and Bureau officers as advanced agents of political oppression, soon after Sickles and Scott assumed offices in South Carolina many whites came to regard the soldiers and the Bureau rather favorably. In mid-January, Ralph Elliott, in Charleston maneuvering to resume planting operations, gleefully anticipated Saxton's removal. After the event occurred, he happily reported to his sister that Bureau rations were available for employees and, "as Sickles says the nigger must work," Northern capital was again to be had. Back on the land in Beaufort District in the second week in February, Elliott pronounced the military "now very helpful." Armisted Burt, co-author of the Black Code, in Charleston on the date Saxton was relieved, observed that the Yankees intended to have the Negroes either contract or put to hard labor on public works. "I have no doubt the Yankees will manage them," gloated the man whose system for managing Negro labor had been nullified.

The mass of Negroes learned their economic lessons more slowly than the whites, but it was not for lack of instruction. The message of the North to the freedmen of South Carolina was always the same, whether uttered by Chase, Garrison, Gillmore, or Sickles, by Saxton, Scott, Howard, or the lowliest of Bureau officers, or by Northern teachers, preachers, or businessmen. The theme constantly sounded was that only by unrelenting, hard labor could the Negro survive. Nevertheless, the coming of the new year, 1866, saw many freedmen unwilling to enter into labor contracts. "I have seen all the planters from Combahee, Ashepoo, Pon Pon et cet," a Beaufort area planter wrote to his mother from Charleston on January 13, 1866, "not one has yet been able to make the negroes contract . . ."

A variety of reasons motivated this behavior. Many freedmen were, of course, displeased with the specific terms of contract offered by employers. Still, less explicit, more pervasive attitudes lay behind their refusal. One of these was suggested by a Chester District planter who found that "some & perhaps all of my people are determined to work under no white man & as I consider myself as belonging to that class I can't expect them to stay." T. B. Ferguson, the manager of a Cooper River plantation, heard the same sentiments couched in stronger terms when he called his laboring force together early in January, 1866, and asked them (in the presence of a noncommissioned Union Army officer) if they would contract and get to work. They would not work, they replied, "for any rebel son-of-a-bitch." Some of their number then addressed the crowd and elicited general approval of the statement that "the Yankees had placed them there and there they would stay if they had to fight for it."

The strongest and most enduring reason why Negroes refused to contract during the three-year period of military occupation was their hope for a land division and the common impression among them that any negotiations with their late masters might jeopardize their chances for success. This obstacle was most formidable during the fall of 1865 and the following winter. A Northern correspondent, after traveling through the lowcountry and the middle districts in October, November, and December, 1865, noted that freedmen everywhere were hoping for a division of the land and were not disposed to contract. On one plantation in Marion District, he observed that the Negroes would not contract even for a half of the crop, preferring to wait on the settlement of the land issue. "They tell what they'll do at Columby," said one, "and they tell another thing over to headquarters, and I goes for waitin' anyhow." The white community quickly recognized a relationship between land division and a reluctance to contract and urged restoration of confiscated lands as the only solution. "The freedmen on the coast will not contract at all because they expect to get lands and those in the interior contract only reluctantly," Governor Orr wrote to the President early in 1866, pointing out that experience had proved that "complete restoration will restore complete harmony."

During and after 1866, both the Bureau and the military worked hard to convince the Negroes that there was to be no general division of the land under the auspices of the government. Nevertheless, even in areas which never experienced tax sales or Sherman grants, the hopes of the freedmen died hard, and often violently. In Columbia in October, 1865, Grace B. Elmore noted in her diary that her brother had just arrived from Fairfield District where a plot had been discovered among the plantation Negroes "to rise and kill all the whites and take their land." Similarly, in January, 1866, a Charlestonian wrote to a friend that money was scarce because of "the unsettled state of affairs here for the negroes almost unanimously refuse to leave these plantations of which they have possession." This was not only true of the Sherman grants, for, as he noted, "Burr Pringle's negroes on Santee refused to contract with him & being told they have to leave the plantations have burnt down his house & have entrenched themselves on the place."

As the 1867 agricultural season approached, another wave of unrest swept through the Negro population. In December, 1866, about three hundred armed Negroes met on a plantation about nine miles south of Kingstree. By the report of white witnesses, they organized themselves into six military companies and paraded back and forth. Speeches were made and one Negro declared that "the D——d rebels have had their way long enough, now they would have theirs." Any Negro who refused to join the conspiracy was to be killed, and one white resident in the area reported, "It was rumored that they said they would have land at all hazard."

Again, early in 1868, while the all-Republican Constitutional Convention was sitting in Charleston, observers noted "a gradually growing sentiment on the part of the freed people throughout the State" not to contract until they saw that "something was decided in their favor by the sitting of the Convention." Scott responded by requesting an official pronouncement on the subject from the Convention itself. That body answered with a resolution stating unequivocally that it had no lands at its disposal; "that no act of confiscation has been passed by the Congress of the United States, and it is the belief of this Convention that there never will be, and the only manner by which any land can be obtained by the landless will be to purchase it." Subsequent developments in the Convention suggested that the delegates were not entirely candid in this pronouncement, but apparently it did have the effect Scott desired.

It was inconceivable that the government would long allow the Negroes to remain unproductive. Even under Gillmore and Saxton authorities had always urged laborers to agree to reasonable contracts with employers. General Saxton himself attended a mass meeting of freedmen and employers in Sumter in December, 1865, to construct a model contract for agricultural laborers. In the following month, the garrison commander in Camden held a similar meeting in which the government's desires were explained. Under Sickles and Scott, the same program was pressed even more vigorously.

The means employed by authorities to overcome the reluctance of freedmen to contract were various and not entirely coercive as Southern whites preferred to believe. The Bureau did much, positively, to induce Negroes to contract by providing transportation for freedmen to the plantations where they were to labor and by advancing them rations until their crops were harvested. In addition, the Bureau operated a mass employment office. A planter in the vicinity of Pocotaligo, after searching in vain for a laboring force, wrote to his wife early in February, 1866, that "Major Delaney (the negro) says he can furnish 200 hands or more & I will know the fact this evening as Willie will be here." On the next day, Willie returned and reported that Scott had indeed promised to send two hundred Negroes by a steamer and would advance the provisions necessary for making the crop. Finally, as described earlier, the government was not unmindful of the obligation of the planters to pay their employees a fair wage.

When freedmen evinced a persistent reluctance to contract, persuasion was an obvious first resort of federal agents. In March, 1866, a Combahee planter spent a day and a half explaining to his former slaves the advantages of contracting but found they would not agree to work on Saturdays. In desperation, he obtained a letter from the Bureau officer in the area advising the Negroes to contract to work the full six-day week, to which the freedmen then agreed. The best persuasive efforts of the Bureau's agents did not always avail, however. In 1868, when a lowcountry planter leased a plantation, the Negroes told him they "dont want to see him on the place." He exhibited his proposed contract bearing Scott's personal endorsement. Still the Negroes refused, saying they would not work every day as prescribed by the contract, but only a day and a half or two days in the week.

In the face of such intransigence, some agents simply by-passed the opposition of the freedmen. For instance, a planter in Chester District, "greatly harrassed with the Freedmen," had "endeavored to get them to sign a contract & have offered the 4th of the corn &c. the cust᾽ᾱary amt they are perfectly indignant, & will have their Rights or *nothing.* He expected, however, to take the proposed contract to the Bureau ᾱ ᾽nt in the village "& he has promised to sign for them." In cases of uny᾽ ᾽ding resistance, officials often resorted to varying degrees of coercion to ᾱ ᾽ce freedmen to contract. Ceasing to pass out Bureau rations to those ᾱ ᾽t engaged to an employer was an obvious and highly effective device which Scott applied in some extreme cases soon after taking office. In January, 1868, Scott applied this method throughout the state.

When all else failed, authorities left no doubt in the minds of the freedmen that they would use force to eject them from plantations where they refused either to leave or to contract for the coming year. In 1866, for instance, a number of Negro laborers were marched off the premises of W. M. Burney's Cooper River plantation when they persisted in their refusal to contract. In January, 1867, Scott, noting that many Negroes had not contracted (especially on the Sea Islands and along the Santee River) published his intention to remove all who refused to conclude agreements and to afford those removed none of the means of relief at his command. Shortly afterward, a group of erstwhile settlers on a plantation near Savannah declined to renew their contract with the planter, alleging him to be unfair. They also refused to move, apparently acting upon the advice of a Negro lawyer residing in the vicinity. The Bureau first showed its teeth when a Bureau agent appeared on the plantation with five soldiers. The Negroes remained adamant. The agent retired and returned with fifty soldiers. The Negroes then "crowded together in solid phalanx and swore more furiously than before that they would die where they stood before they would surrender their claims to the land." Insults led to leveled guns on both sides. One of the Negroes wearing a sword and belt shouted, "fall in guards," and a company of Negroes fell into ranks. The agent restrained his soldiers with difficulty and finally managed to withdraw his force. The Negroes could not, however, stand against the army.

Having induced employers and employees to contract, the authorities of the occupation also assumed responsibility for seeing that the contracts were fulfilled, again influencing the freedmen with devices which they had used to win their assent to contracts. The great mass of freedmen honored their agreements more or less willingly. Where they did not do so, exhortation was a common resort of the Bureau man. For instance, in the summer of 1868, a Bureau officer in St. John's Parish, Berkeley District, wrote a sharp note to Moses, Peter, Neal, and Nancy on Shelbourne plantation. He had previously told them that their contract required them to work for the planter only two days in each week. He subsequently found that the planter loaned them four mules to work their own crops on their off days and that the freedmen had never labored more than two days for themselves anyway, "since you take Thursday of every week to fast, instead of working your crop, or laboring for rations, as you should have done." "Now you cannot prosper," he lectured, "unless you work, both white & Black, together without quarreling . . ."

In serious cases, the authorities were quick to threaten the use of force to prevent the freedmen from falling into idleness. On St. John's Island, in May, 1866, an elderly Negro woman began to preach that she had had a revelation from heaven forbidding labor on Fridays and Saturdays. The idea gained wide acceptance as "God's truth," and on some plantations work stopped altogether on these days. Scott sent an emissary to tell the Negroes he would drive them all from the island if they did not go back to work and the affair was quickly concluded. Apparently, this disturbance was merely one manifestation of a widespread restlessness among the freedmen in the lowcountry. "Negroes working badly & half task," wrote one lowcountry planter in the late summer of 1866. In the crisis, Scott issued what Armisted Burt considered to be "pretty stringent orders" holding the Negroes to their contracts. Those who neglected their labor were to be arrested and "made to work on the public roads . . ." Frequently, officers in the occupation forces authorized the use of physical punishment upon the freedmen whom they believed to be delinquent in honoring their contracts. In the upcountry district of Laurens, it was said that the garrison commander asked that shirkers be reported to him. One planter complained against two freedmen for malingering and the commander sent out two soldiers who tied the Negroes up by the thumbs. "The negroes begged to be flogged instead," a native white asserted.

In many cases where some form of crop sharing was included in the freedman's wages, Bureau or military officers actually presided over the division. However, as the size of the occupation forces diminished during and after 1866, it became impossible for an officer to supervise the division on every plantation. Moreover, official attention was fully absorbed at the end of each season in settling those cases where a dispute had already arisen. Where an agent (or, as frequently happened, a referee appointed by him) did intervene, the typical solution was to "split the difference." This tendency and the availability of the agent as a mediator, however, apparently caused employers and employees to settle most disputes among themselves or through local magistrates.

Thus, early in the Reconstruction Period, the North disallowed the attempt by white South Carolinians to replace slavery with a controlled system of labor. The North also denied the Negroes any special consideration in the form of rations and lands. Instead, the "contract system," derived from wartime experience in the Sea Islands, was used to re-educate South Carolinians of both races in the ways of liberal economics as they were then understood in the North. The success of the program is indicated by the fact that intervention by the federal authorities in relationships between individual employers and employees, intensive in 1865 and 1866, became progressively less important in 1867 and 1868, and ceased entirely by 1869 when such affairs were surrendered entirely to the officers of the state.